D1083689

A Companion to Irish Literature

Volume Two

Blackwell Companions to Literature and Culture

This series offers comprehensive, newly written surveys of key periods and movements and certain major authors, in English literary culture and history. Extensive volumes provide new perspectives and positions on contexts and on canonical and post-canonical texts, orientating the beginning student in new fields of study and providing the experienced undergraduate and new graduate with current and new directions, as pioneered and developed by leading scholars in the field.

Published Recently

A COMPANION TO

*I*RISH
*L*ITERATURE

Volume Two

EDITED BY

JULIA M. WRIGHT

WILEY-BLACKWELL

A John Wiley & Sons, Ltd., Publication

This edition first published 2010

© 2010 Blackwell Publishing Ltd except for editorial material and organization

© 2010 Julia M. Wright

Blackwell Publishing was acquired by John Wiley & Sons in February 2007. Blackwell's publishing program has been merged with Wiley's global Scientific, Technical, and Medical business to form Wiley-Blackwell.

Registered Office

John Wiley & Sons Ltd, The Atrium, Southern Gate, Chichester, West Sussex, PO19 8SQ, United Kingdom

Editorial Offices

350 Main Street, Malden, MA 02148-5020, USA

9600 Garsington Road, Oxford, OX4 2DQ, UK

The Atrium, Southern Gate, Chichester, West Sussex, PO19 8SQ, UK

For details of our global editorial offices, for customer services, and for information about how to apply for permission to reuse the copyright material in this book please see our website at www.wiley.com/wiley-blackwell.

The right of Julia M. Wright to be identified as the author of the editorial material in this work has been asserted in accordance with the UK Copyright, Designs and Patents Act 1988.

Library of Congress Cataloging-in-Publication Data

A companion to Irish literature / edited by Julia M. Wright.
     p. cm. – (Blackwell companions to literature and culture)
  Includes bibliographical references and index.
  ISBN 978-1-4051-8809-8 (hardcover : alk. paper)
 1. English literature–Irish authors–History and criticism.   2. Epic literature, Irish–History and criticism.   3. Irish literature–History and criticism.   4. Northern Ireland–In literature. 5. Ireland–In literature. I. Wright, Julia M.
  PR8711.C66 2010
  820.9'9417–dc22

2010011933

A catalogue record for this book is available from the British Library.

Set in 11 on 13 pt Garamond 3 by Toppan Best-set Premedia Limited
Printed and bound in Singapore by Fabulous Printers Pte Ltd

1   2010

Contents

Introduction

Julia M. Wright

This *Companion to Irish Literature* is designed to offer a range of theoretical approaches to the full history of Irish literature, and to provide a guide to a wide, but not encyclopedic, range of key issues and authors within that rich tradition. The essays sketch a literary-historical trajectory from the Middle Ages to the present and are divided according to literary period, but they can also be grouped for genre study (for instance, to consider Irish drama from the early modern period forward to the present or Irish poetry over a thousand years), or to investigate Irish-language literature from the medieval period to the present, or to consider the cultural history of gender, including the literary representation of masculinity from the Middle Ages forward. In both volumes, there are essays that deal with translation, religion, nationhood, gender and sexuality, and literary form, as well as myriad other shared concerns. The selection of topics and authors proceeded not on the basis of a canon in which authors constitute fixed literary coordinates, but a motile literary history in which authors are part of an always reflexive and constantly developing understanding of the past; the coverage of authors here is thus topical rather than exhaustive. Hence, both volumes include essays that focus on authors whose importance is newly emerging, others who were more important a few decades ago than now, and others who have been canonical since their work was first circulated. Other essays take a broader sweep of the cultural terrain than an author-centered focus allows and they, along with the author-specific chapters, bring dozens more significant authors into these pages. Together, these two volumes provide a diverse and flexible framework for the study of nearly fifteen hundred years of Irish literature – a companion for a literary journey.

A Companion to Irish Literature, edited by Julia M. Wright
© 2010 Blackwell Publishing Ltd

International Celebrities and Irish Canons

A tourism site enthuses, "Ireland has many a literary celebrity, old and new!" (Tourism Ireland 2008). Swift, R.B. Sheridan, Morgan, and Moore, among others discussed in Volume I of this *Companion*, gained literary celebrity but without sparking much interest in their compatriots' literary work. From the turn of the century forward, however, Irish literature as such has enjoyed considerable status on the world stage – being an "Irish" writer has had a certain cachet, a kind of "cultural capital," that it did not before modernism (Nolan 2007:351). The centrality of Joyce and Yeats to international modernism has made them, and their insistently Irish subject matter, required undergraduate reading for decades, and they are widely included in general teaching anthologies and well represented in bookstores. Their canonical status has arguably contributed to modernizing Ireland's international face: Ireland could no longer be so easily represented as abjectly "primitive" – a view taken to racist depths in the nineteenth century (Curtis 1971; see also Deane 1986; Gibbons 1991) – if it could be a crucial site of modernist innovation for an international readership. Many authors discussed in this volume (and others who are not) have earned considerable sales and ongoing popular and academic recognition internationally, from literary prizes to book-club reading lists. Four have won the Nobel Prize in literature: W.B. Yeats (1923), G.B. Shaw (1925), Samuel Beckett (1969), and Seamus Heaney (1995). The same number have won Booker prizes (now the Man Booker Prize): Iris Murdoch (1978), Roddy Doyle (1993), John Banville (2005), and Anne Enright (2007). A list of international theatrical releases in which Irish authors have writing credit would run into dozens of titles, including such recent films as *P.S. I Love You* (2007), based on a novel by Cecilia Ahern, and *Public Enemies* (2009), co-written by Ronan Bennett. Thus, while many of the essays in Volume I had the task, in part, of introducing writers who are rarely anthologized, sometimes mistaken for "English," and/or known only to specialists on that literary period, most of the essays in this volume focus on authors who, as the saying goes, need no introduction.

The perception of their works' significance is, however, dynamic and historically contingent. Beckett, Joyce, and Yeats were at the heart of the modernist canon long before "Irish studies" became an academic force, institutionalized in scholarly associations, university programs, and journals (in North America, most of these were founded in the 1960s and later), and scholarship on these central modernists was thus grounded in New Criticism's concern with close reading, form, and ambiguity. In more recent decades, Beckett studies has built on this foundational New Critical interest through poststructuralist thought, while the apolitical turn of New Criticism and early modernism studies has been reversed in Yeats and Joyce scholarship through postcolonial theory (see, for instance, Uhlmann 1999; Attridge and Howes 2000), particularly in the wake of Edward Said's groundbreaking 1988 essay, "Yeats and Decolonization." Feminist theory, at the same time, has sharpened work on Irish women authors from the eighteenth century forward, and these feminist approaches are now being developed further through explorations of the wider cultural terrain in which Irish women wrote, including the ways in which religion and class can be more significant political allegiances than gender (see, for instance, Nolan 2007), as a number of essays in this volume demonstrate. Queer studies and other theoretical approaches to identity have further enriched the critical terrain, and ecocriticism is beginning to make its mark in Irish studies (see Dennis Denisoff's essay in Volume I and Maureen O'Connor's in Volume II). These theoretical movements have shifted the canon as well as scholarly understanding of the wider literary history of the twentieth century. Still, Yeats remains central to current academic views of Irish modernism, and he is cited in more essays in this volume than any other author. But the general reading public and academic readers outside of Irish studies are more likely to know Joyce than any other twentieth-century Irish author. Joyce's celebrity is registered in popular culture, including international Bloomsday celebrations and treatments of "The Dead" from John Huston's last film, *The Dead* (1987), to the closing scene of a recent episode of the police procedural *Criminal Minds* (Mundy 2009). Hence there is a large body of work on Joyce and popular culture, largely founded on interest in Joyce's own use of popular culture (Herr 1986; Kershner 1996; Wicke 2004), but less on other modernists in that context, with such notable exceptions as Elizabeth Butler Cullingford's work on Yeats (Cullingford 2001). There is, however, a steadily growing list of important Irish writers, and a steadily changing canon as new writers dislodge older ones, even though some remain fixed at the center of the academic canon.

Celebrity and canonicity are significant forces in the study of twentieth-century Irish literature, as well as objects of scholarly enquiry themselves. Readers of major authors' works are the beneficiaries of the interest (and marketability) such celebrity elicits because it facilitates the publication of diaries, interviews, and other papers – many of the essays in this volume are enriched by such resources. All of this writing about writing by the authors themselves has a significant impact on the nature of criticism on this body of work, and reinforces the centrality of authors in a culture of celebrity – their own pronouncements on their work and on literature become a force to be reckoned with, a kind of authorial control over interpretation that undercuts more poststructuralist views of literary discourse in which the author is decentered or exposed as an organizational concept (Foucault 1984). One of the benefits of situating these twentieth-century authors in relation to the wider history of Irish literature, as is done in this two-volume *Companion*, is to take us beyond the immediacy of the author's historical moment and interpretation of his or her work in relation to it. A longer historical view reveals a more Barthesian intertextuality in which there are myriad threads of concern and allusion that bind the twentieth century to the past, and not just in the long-discussed Revivalist concern with Irish myth and pre-colonial sagas.

The politics of representing the peasantry, for instance, is evident not only in the infamous *Playboy* riots (see Saddlemyer's essay here), but also in the shifting literary fortunes of writers who wrote realist fiction about rural Ireland; it is traceable back to the work of Edgeworth, Carleton, and others in the nineteenth century who are discussed in Volume 1. Writing in Irish continues to be subject to the difficulties, and possibilities, of translation, and other concerns continue from the previous volume. Julia O'Faolain, to take one example, is part of a larger trajectory of Irish women's fiction that extends in this volume from Somerville and Ross forward to Elizabeth Bowen in the early decades of Independence, and to Emma Donoghue in our present, but also reaches back to Frances Sheridan, Edgeworth, Morgan, and others discussed in Volume I. One of the striking features of Volume II is the heavy lines of influence and acknowledgment which criss-cross the essays here. Yeats is mentioned most frequently, but in this he is followed closely by Joyce, Heaney, and Beckett, with O'Casey, O'Faoláin, Lady Gregory, and others also making a number of appearances. But Edmund Spenser, too, is repeatedly cited in this second volume. For the twentieth-century writers discussed here, Spenser is less the author of the notorious *View* – as he was for many writers in preceding centuries – than a poet, particularly of the *Epithalamion* and the less objectionable books of the *Faerie Queene*. Other authors and texts discussed in the first volume echo through this one – from Swift's ongoing influence on satiric writing to the resonance of Finn for writers from the Revival to Edna O'Brien, and from Synge's use of Keating to Ní Chuilleanáin's evocation of courtly love poetry.

Perhaps the strongest literary tie between the two volumes of this *Companion*, however, is realism. Emerging as a literary mode in the early nineteenth century, simultaneously with cultural nationalism as a political mode of representation, realism is deeply yoked to claims about the "real" Ireland. Realism is an intrinsically deceptive mode, an approximation of "reality" that at once relies heavily on literary convention, including in the selection of detail, and yet also makes truth claims. Toril Moi responds to a feminist complaint that fiction never depicts women shaving their legs by adding that "toe-nail clipping" and other grooming practices are also "neglected as fictional themes," but that this "complaint rests on the highly questionable notion that art can and should reflect life accurately and inclusively in every detail": "Resolutely empiricist in its approach, this view fails to consider the proposition that the real is not only something we construct, but a controversial construct at that" (Moi 1985:45). In this volume, this "construct" is nowhere more overtly controversial than in claims to present the "real" Ireland. Many of the chapters here examine challenges to the straitjacket of realism through the even more traditional modes of parody and satire, as well as postmodernism's attention to the instability of language (and meaning). These challenges often seek to resist and/or complicate realism's truth claims, whether those claims address the representation of a particular historical moment (such as the Easter Rising) or examine universalizing myths of "true" Irishness, including "mother Ireland" and other gendered types.

History and the Problem of Periodization

Dividing the twentieth century into literary periods is an ongoing problem in many national literatures, arguably because we are still too close to it. The Romantic period was carved out of literary history a century after it ended, and we do not yet have that much distance even from modernism. There are, moreover, overlapping paradigms: the Victorian era, the long nineteenth century, the (Celtic/Gaelic) Revival, the Irish Literary Renaissance, and modernism constitute a series of cross-connected cultural movements; (late) modernism and the postmodern rely on an organization of literature that stresses literary form; post-war (Rising, Civil, World War I, or World War II), the Troubles, and, more recently, the Good Friday Agreement, mark periods which ground literature in its political-historical moment. There are cross-national constructs as well – international modernism most significantly, but also 1960s counter-culture, globalization, Irish-American and other diasporic literatures, different "waves" of feminism, and so on. Moreover, access to education and print (as well as other media) has diversified the reading and writing publics to a degree not seen in previous centuries. David Pierce's *Irish Writing in the Twentieth Century: A Reader* (2000) handles the problem by going decade by decade – starting with the 1890s – and organizing works by date of publication rather than by author. This mode of organization is supported by criticism which refers to writers by decade (such as the "Thirties Poets" of Irish and British literary studies), and by other decentering anthologies which are also strictly arranged chronologically (such as McGann 1993). Most recent anthologies of twentieth-century Irish literature, however, eschew period divisions, usually by taking a smaller slice of the twentieth-century pie in focusing on genre or region or a specific part of the period (see, for instance, Muldoon 1986; Craig 2006; Harrington 2008).

The problem is further complicated by differences of dating even for the more well-established cultural movements. The Gaelic Revival is usually taken to begin with the work of Standish O'Grady and Douglas Hyde (and soon afterwards Yeats and Lady Gregory), roughly 1880–1920, and associated in particular with the activities of the Gaelic League as well as a broader interest in the recuperation of the Irish language and Irish-language material. But Seamus Deane has argued for a longer "Celtic Revival" that runs 1780–1880 (Deane 1986) and others have pushed the terminus of the movement later into the twentieth century (for instance, Sheehy 1980). The Irish Renaissance (or Irish Literary Renaissance or Irish Literary Revival) is sometimes used interchangeably with the Gaelic Revival but refers less to the Gaelic researchers than the leading lights of Irish modernism, writing in English and gaining international acclaim, many (but not all) building on the Gaelic Revival and centered in Dublin (for a suggestive exploration of Revivalism's complications, see, for instance, Hutton 2003). Using "Revival" without an adjective (Literary or Gaelic) allows a conceptual merging of the two movements for the 1880–1920 period. Modernism, as a term which refers to an international movement, is notoriously difficult to assign precise dates: 1890–1930 is common, but 1890–1940 or simply the first half of the twentieth century are not unusual. Moreover, as a movement associated with both innovation in form and a break with the past, it strains against the recovery work of the Revival, though modernist nostalgia is a better fit with Revival aims. And, of course, authors' bodies of work do not fall neatly into these paradigms or datings.

Bram Stoker and Oscar Wilde, addressed in Volume I, were contemporary with Yeats and Synge, and shared literary as well as social connections. Periodization only gets messier after modernism. There is no definitive "postmodern" era (and if there were it would need to run at least from the 1940s to the present), and the modern and postmodern are so conceptually entangled with each other that that are sometimes difficult to distinguish – Beckett, to take just one example, is widely discussed as a leading modernist and as a founding postmodernist. "Contemporary" is increasingly unwieldy, working well in the 1970s and 1980s when it could be used to refer to two or three decades of writing after modernism, but with each passing decade it expands almost exponentially and now leaves us with the somewhat untenable implication that 1960s literature is "contemporary" with that of the digitized, globalized twenty-first century.

Periodization is not simply a problem of how to organize – or even just provisionally compartmentalize – a diverse array of literary materials, but also a question of the relationship between literary history and political history. The Renaissance/Revival, by its most-used dating of 1880–1920, begins during the Land War (1879–82) and continues through the various Home Rule bills of 1886, 1893, and 1914, part of a century-long fight against the 1800 Act of Union which had abolished the Irish parliament and replaced it with a block of Irish seats in the British parliament. The suspension of progress on Home Rule for the duration of World War I fueled the militant nationalism that led to the Easter Rising of 1916 and the declaration of an Irish Republic. Reaction against the violent suppression of that Rising – including the execution of a number of its leaders – contributed to an election result in 1918 in which Sinn Féin won 73 of 105 Irish seats. That majority led, in turn, to the Declaration of Independence and establishment of an Irish parliament by those Sinn Féin MPs in 1919. The British government did not accept the Declaration, and the Irish War of Independence was fought from 1919 to 1921, ended by the Anglo-Irish Treaty (1921), one of the legislative moves which allowed the eventual partition of Ireland into Northern Ireland and the south (first termed the Irish Free State [1922–37], then Éire [1937–49], and then the Republic of Ireland). Thus, the intense period of nationalist activity from the Land War to Independence almost precisely matches the usual dates for the "Revival" – the Gaelic Revival's idealization of rural people and recovery of pre-colonial literature and myth (as well as the indigenous language) are to an extent the cultural complements of these nationalist movements. Moreover, the Revival comes to an end in the early "Troubles," in the conflict between different political factions in the Civil War (1922–23), a difficult period that arguably made it hard to imagine a cultural-nationalist vision of an inherent Irishness and coherent Irish culture – in the midst of this difficult era, Joyce published *Ulysses*, often seen as a foundational modernist text.

Sociopolitical action in Ireland in this period is not limited to debate and armed conflict over the state(s) and mechanisms through which Ireland would be governed. The Revival is also contemporary with first-wave feminism, and the impact of women writers in this era was widespread, extending far beyond the vital and much-discussed work of Lady Gregory. The New Woman movement and later the struggle for women's suffrage were significant in Ireland as in Britain (see Meaney 2002), and to some degree forged an Irish–British solidarity among women that transcended nationalist concerns. Emily Lawless responded to the New Woman movement in *Grania* (1892), for example, while Eva Gore-Booth – author of such Revival texts as *The Triumph of Maeve* (1905), and sister of Countess Markievicz, an officer in the Irish Citizen Army and later MP – was a member of the women's suffrage movement in England along with her partner Esther Roper (see Donoghue 1997; Edwards 2008). At the same time, while the Revival-modernist canon has traditionally centered on Dublin, a "Northern Revival" was underway as well, and that other Revival's significance is emerging from re-examinations of the literary record (see Kirkland 2003; McNulty 2004), including the substantial authorial and editorial work of Alice Milligan and Anna Johnston (who used the pseudonym Ethna Carbery). Attention to women writers in this period, in other words, is not only uncovering the significance of feminist politics in this nationalist period but also other centers of literary activity.

The 1930s and 1940s would see the rise of Éamon de Valera, founder of the influential political party Fianna Fáil and leader of the Irish government, under various titles, for most of the 1937–73 period. This is also the era in which remaining political ties to Britain were severed, particularly through the 1937 Constitution and the Republic of Ireland Act (1948). As many of the essays in this volume show, the new order in the south required a rethinking of class, sectarian divisions, and the cultural-nationalist project. Partition, and intensifying sectarian divisions, contributed to rising tensions in the north. The early 1970s were thus tumultuous at best, not always for the same reasons, on both sides of the border. In the 1966–72 period, such diverse groups as the Northern Ireland Civil Rights Association, the Ulster Volunteer Force, and the Provisional IRA were founded in the north, with protest marches becoming riots, and growing factional violence leading to injuries and deaths on all sides (including bystanders) – the "Troubles." For many, the iconic event of the Troubles is Bloody Sunday in January 1972, when fourteen civil rights marchers were shot and killed by the British army. In the south, political alliances shifted. The Republic joined what would later become the European Union in 1973, and the Anglo-Irish Agreement of 1985 gave the Republic a place at the table in discussions with Britain about Northern Ireland affairs. Starting in the early 1970s, the Republic recognized rights and increased opportunities for women and marginalized groups. Notable events in the Republic include the partial legalization of contraception (1974), the election of Ireland's first woman president (1990), and the decriminalization of homosexuality (1993). While much of the modernist period was concerned with identifying and promoting a distinctively Irish culture in response to a centuries-old colonial context in which Irish culture was abjected, erased, or ignored, the impact of globalization (including the growing influence of US consumer culture and closer ties to Europe), became significant by the 1970s. American culture is an issue for many of the writers in Part Ten, whether in poets' echoings of Robert Frost, Sylvia Plath, and Wallace

Stevens, in Paul Muldoon's interest in Native American culture and history as well as American popular culture, or in Brian Friel's and Neil Jordan's examinations of US influence in Ireland. The 1990s were also marked by an economic growth spurt associated with the moniker "Celtic Tiger," a period of substantial growth which not only transformed the Irish economy but also reversed a centuries-old trend in migration: Ireland became a place to which to emigrate rather than a place to leave. In the north, the Troubles met their match in various grassroots and high-level movements for peace, culminating in the Good Friday Agreement (1998).

This volume is divided into four parts to organize the diverse array of material here with an eye both to history and to literary issues. Part Seven considers the range of literary production in the 1880–1930 period, placing writers often identified with "Victorian" literature alongside those central to the "Revival" and "modernist" movements, but also seeks to survey major genres. Part Eight focuses on the 1930s and 1940s, but centrally attends to innovations in genre and debates about mode during both the emergence of the postmodern from late modernism and the political sea-changes of the period. Part Nine focuses on the struggle with realism in relation to social change in the 1960s and after, and particularly responses to second-wave feminism and the ongoing divisions of class and religion. Part Ten defines "contemporary" loosely as beginning in 1980. The founding of the influential Field Day project in 1980 offers both a political and a literary milestone, and allows us to think of the "contemporary" as responding to, and moving forward from, the transformations and crises of the 1970s. The post-1980 era is also a remarkable period of literary production – as is evident from such recent books as *Irish Literature since 1990: Diverse Voices* (Brewster and Parker 2009), covering less than two decades of writing – and so Part Ten is the largest section here, sampling authors of different languages, regions, genres, and generations.

Eleven Decades, Four Parts

Part Seven deals with the most canonical of Irish literary periods – Revivalism and modernism – and its ongoing affiliation with the literature of the nineteenth century. As with other literary periods, there are many more authors of significance than can be substantively addressed here, but the price of selectiveness is perhaps higher for modernism and the Revival than other literary movements because the canonicity of the period itself heightens the importance of its authors; in addition to the long-central figures of Yeats, Joyce, Lady Gregory, and Synge, important authors include such figures as AE (George Russell), Ethna Carbery, Eva Gore-Booth, Alfred Percival Graves, Douglas Hyde, Alice Milligan, Patrick Pearse, Dora Sigerson, and Katharine Tynan, among others. In his opening essay on cultural nationalism, Michael Mays begins with the incompatibilities of Irish modernism – of modernism's philosophical differences with nationalism, of modernism's characteristic discomfort with itself, and, symptomatically, of the biographical and literary differences between the two exemplary figures of Irish modernism, Yeats and Joyce. Mays then traces the emergence of cultural nationalism both in Europe and in Ireland, situating the work of Pearse, AE, Yeats, Joyce, and others – and their disputes – in relation to its pressures to sanction particular ideas of Ireland and of Irish identity. The next two essays address authors who bridge the divide between modernism and the Victorian era (though we could easily add Yeats and Synge to this group as well, allying the first with nineteenth-century antiquarianism and the second with *fin-de-siècle* Aestheticism). As Christopher Innes demonstrates, Shaw is not only between periods but also between islands. He is often left on the margins of Irish literary history despite his strong connections to Irish literary culture, including to the Abbey Theatre and the leading figures associated with it (such as Lady Gregory and Yeats). Yet he stands as one of the last of a long line of Irish dramatists who moved to London – and as the first of many writers addressed in this volume who challenged dominant ideas of "Irishness." In the final part of his essay, Innes addresses Shaw's significance on the London stage, particularly in relation to another Irish expatriate playwright, James Fagan, in the wider context of the rich exchanges between the theatrical worlds of London and Dublin. In the next essay, Vera Kreilkamp discusses the writing team of Somerville and Ross and their many contributions to the Big House novel, a tradition rooted in the gothic. As Kreilkamp shows (and other essays in this *Companion* reinforce), the Big House tradition is crucial to Irish literary history for over a century. Somerville and Ross's novels are focused on the Ascendancy as the growing middle class and shifting nationalist politics eroded the Ascendancy's power, symbolized by the rural Big House. Kreilkamp offers an extensive discussion of the writing pair's alliances with and differences from Revival politics and literature, their novels overlapping with the modernism of Yeats and Synge, while their potential to contribute to an emerging feminist literature is checked by their focus on issues of class – their lives remain their most radical contribution to the reimagining of women's roles and options in the early twentieth century.

The final essays in Part Seven deal with three of the key figures of Irish modernism, each representing one of the three major genres: the poet Yeats, the novelist Joyce, and the dramatist Synge. All three worked in other genres, of course: in their essays here, Gregory Castle addresses Yeats' dramatic work, Michael Patrick Gillespie considers Joyce's poetry, and Ann Saddlemyer examines Synge's famous account of the Aran Islands. But the weight of these essays is on the genres for which these three writers are best known, making this section of Part Seven a survey of modernist genres as well as a selection of major modernists. Castle organizes his essay on Yeats according to three stages of his literary career, beginning with his early Revivalist work in folklore and drama as well as verse, focusing on the trope of "tactical misrecognition" – of the past, of the nation, of places, of the peasantry – in relation to the complicated temporality of his writing, and closing with the poet's ambivalent relationship to the Free State and postcoloniality. Yeats thus synecdochally images the complex shifts in nationalism from the Revival, aiming to reconstruct a lost Gaelic past, to the inscription over it of a new, modern order in the Free State, including the displacement of the Protestant Ascendancy (a subject also addressed, for instance, in chapters here on Somerville and Ross, Bowen, and Trevor). In the next essay, Saddlemyer goes beyond Synge's recruitment into the Yeats–Gregory Revival to situate him as well in a wider European, almost cosmopolitan context: he lived in Paris, translated French and Italian literature, learned the Breton language, acknowledged the influence of Rabelais and Villon, and, like Oscar Wilde at nearly the same time, echoes Walter Pater, a leading English thinker for late nineteenth-century Aestheticism (a movement with well-established European and cosmopolitan investments). She also traces the influence of his early training in music on the structure of his work and the rhythms of his language. In the last essay in Part Seven, Gillespie considers the significance of Joyce, a subject which Danine Farquharson will also address near the end of this volume. While Yeats and Synge have roots in the Revival and other nineteenth-century trends, Joyce stands apart as a modernist with more complicated and subtle ties to Revivalism, and so constitutes a fitting end to this section on the transition from the nineteenth century to modernism, especially given the modernist exemplarity of his first novel, *Portrait of the Artist as a Young Man*, addressed here by Gillespie. There is much here to connect Joyce and Synge in particular. Both studied in Paris, lived abroad (though Joyce more extensively), and yet wrote compellingly and in detail about specific Irish locations – for Synge, the Aran islands, and for Joyce, Dublin, as Gillespie details, the setting for all three of Joyce's major novels and, of course, *Dubliners*.

In Part Eight, essays consider late modernism and the first generation of writers who responded to Independence. A number of the essays in this section pair authors to sketch a larger set of debates than a single-author focus would allow – debates about the future direction of the country, the place of the Irish language, the role of the Anglo-Irish Ascendancy, and the importance of the figure of the "writer." As Sandra Wynands shows in her essay on Beckett and O'Casey, the problem of representation is closely allied to the problem of subjectivity and both are implicated in the political questions of post-Independence Ireland. Juxtaposing the social realism (and cultural nationalism) of O'Casey with Beckett's deep suspicion of representation, especially in language, Wynands traces the philosophical implications of Beckett's formal challenges both to dramatic conventions and to ideological premises about language and subjectivity, and our ability to shape the world that they reinforce. In Elizabeth Bowen's fiction, as Eluned Summers-Bremner discusses, this representational problem shifts to domestic settings in which the figurative animation of things disrupts narrative conventions and again decenters subjectivity on terms that echo the position of the Anglo-Irish ruling class (and their houses) in post-Independence Ireland – a crucial reimagining of the Big House tradition of Irish women's fiction from Edgeworth to Somerville and Ross. Writing from the 1920s through to the 1960s, Bowen registers the defamiliarizing impact of political transformations on the understanding of home, of land, and of class. Roughly spanning the same period, the short fiction of Frank O'Connor and Seán O'Faoláin, the subject of Paul Delaney's essay, registers another kind of outdatedness, of tales that eschewed modernism's revisions to literary form in a focus on rural Ireland, a space associated with the pre- (even anti-) modern in the tales of Edgeworth and Carleton (see Volume I). At the same time, as Delaney demonstrates, their fiction both arises from the authors' close engagement with the military and cultural dimensions of early Independence nationalism and registers their disappointment with the result of those struggles – and both argued in their theoretical work for the amenability of the short-story form to the depiction of ambiguity and marginality. The next chapter, by Alan Gillis, turns from drama and fiction to verse – that of Louis MacNeice and Patrick Kavanagh. Like O'Casey and Beckett, they were divided by class and by perspective: MacNeice (like Beckett) takes an international sweep while Kavanagh (like O'Casey) remains largely within Ireland's shores and the limits of realism; Kavanagh likewise comes out of the rural tradition (though critical of his "peasant poet" status), while MacNeice generally remains rooted in urban contexts and the fascination with aesthetics traceable through Oscar Wilde and his modernist contemporaries, echoing the performativity of Beckett's writing and the animation of Bowen's. The final essay in this section, by Joseph Brooker, leads us through the multiple authorial performances of Flann O'Brien (Brian O'Nolan) in which the limits of realism, and even representation itself, are pushed still further, in a comic tangle of meta- and frame fictions, authorial personae, and a regard for Irish-language culture that yet refuses to follow it to cultural nationalism. This investment in the aesthetic and the literary is visible in his major novels, *At Swim-Two-Birds* and *The Third Policeman*, his spoofing of peasant memoirs in *An Béal Bocht*, and his deep engagement with a wider print culture, as his *Irish Times* pieces demonstrate.

While these writers generally focused on the national sea-changes of the first half of the century and allied literary play with an active suspicion of nationalist determinations of identity, the next generation returned, though not neatly or naively, to realism. They did so partly in order to press at the idea of the nation that emerged in the decades after Independence, and partly in response to the larger challenges to received notions that defined the 1960s for Europe and North America in particular. Such challenges, and reaction against them, were part of the context for the Troubles that would shock 1970s Ireland and, for some of these writers, find their counterpart in the Troubles of half a century earlier. Part Nine thus focuses on five novelists who are overtly engaged not only with realism but also with the problems of history. In the first essay in this section, on William Trevor, Gregory A. Schirmer locates the novelist's work in the context of the post-Independence marginalization of Protestant Ireland, putting him in a tradition that includes Bowen in particular but also Yeats and Somerville and Ross, among others, but now with the Ascendancy firmly in the past rather than declining, as it is for Bowen and earlier writers. This sense of history shapes Trevor's work, grounding the Troubles in earlier sectarian conflicts and making historical alienation a key factor in the novels' "psychological realism." The next essay, by Maureen O'Connor, explores the wide body of work by Edna O'Brien. O'Brien's novels have had a varied critical reception alongside steady recognition from the wider public; they were sometimes controversial to the point of being censored, like those of other writers such as McGahern, and often tied up with O'Brien's celebrity persona.

O'Brien's engagement with feminist issues led to reading of her work as "wearily autobiographical," as O'Connor puts it in her essay, but O'Brien's novels include complex and often ironic handling of the material, including her reimagining of early Irish tales. Silvia Diez Fabre's essay considers Jennifer Johnston's fiction, a body of work that, like Trevor's, links the personal and the national past in accounts of the present. While Trevor's Protestant characters are largely from the middle class, however, Johnston returns us to the literary trope of the Big House, a figure revised by Johnston in suggestive ways. Diez Fabre, focusing on three of Johnston's novels, argues for Johnston's efforts to put different national- and subject-positions in conversation, though not optimistically — the conversation rarely leads to any lasting social harmony. While Johnston and Trevor use history to make sense of their characters, Julia O'Faolain, as Christine St Peter argues, also uses her characters to make sense of history. O'Faolain addresses a remarkable range of historical frames in and beyond Ireland. She also mixes her realism with a postmodern play with stereotypes, taking aim, like many post-1968 feminist writers (especially the poets discussed in the next section), at the symbolically redolent figures of virgin, mother, and whore. The final essay in Part Nine, by Eamon Maher, discusses the work of John McGahern, a novelist whose corpus, like that of other authors covered in this section, spans a multi-decade period in which much changed in Ireland. His second novel in 1965 was banned for dealing explicitly with sex and sexual abuse, and *The Dark* also got McGahern fired from his teaching job, but he continued to publish into the twenty-first century. McGahern, as Maher argues, takes a pointedly personal and local approach to realist fiction, eschewing political questions while yet addressing significant social concerns as well as more universal challenges, such as grief.

Part Ten surveys a wide selection of writers from the last three decades, arranged by date of birth, and demonstrates the diversity of writing in contemporary Ireland. Poetry (including song), drama, and fiction are now supplemented by film and television, for instance, and a number of the writers discussed here have also worked as screenwriters — most famously, Neil Jordan, but also, for instance, John McGahern, Roddy Doyle, Martin McDonagh, and Emma Donoghue. At the same time, translation and Irish-language material continue to be significant, as do such older traditions as the *aisling*. The first essays in Part Ten address work by writers from the North, beginning with Brian Friel, who founded Field Day with Stephen Rea in 1980. In his essay, F.C. McGrath traces the phases of Friel's long career in terms of nationalist developments and transformations in Ireland, and particularly Friel's critical stance towards contemporary politics, beginning with his critique of the earthy realism used to support a limiting nationalism, followed by a series of plays that explore the hybridity of Irish language and culture. The next essay, by Eugene O'Brien, considers Seamus Heaney's significant body of work, and particularly Heaney's complex negotiation with the remote Irish past and the troubled present, partly enacted through a dense allusiveness to both literary precursors and community contemporaries. Focusing on key sequences of poems, starting with the bog poems, O'Brien traces Heaney's formal and ideological interest in writing "slant." In the next essay, Richard Rankin Russell addresses the work of three poets, Michael Longley, Derek Mahon, and Medbh McGuckian, all from Belfast. As Russell demonstrates, their poetry is richly complex both formally and thematically, and densely citational.

The next essays in Part Ten deal with four very different writers from the Republic, the feminist poets Eiléan Ní Chuilleanáin and Eavan Boland, novelist John Banville, and screenwriter Neil Jordan. All, however, deal with the burdens of history and the divisions on which it proceeded – North from South, male from female – as well as the literary inheritances through which that history can be explored. In her essay on Ní Chuilleanáin's poetry, Guinn Batten examines the rich significations of vision – witnessing, the oppressive gaze, reflection (and doubling) – and, at the same time, obliquity, ineffability, and ambiguity. Batten also traces Ní Chuilleanáin's interest in a wide array of individuals from history: in literary history, these figures range from Spenser to influential women writers such as Maria Edgeworth and Speranza Wilde; in religious history, Mary Magdalene emerges as an especially important figure, a woman who both preaches but is insistently embodied. The next essay, by Heather Clark, explores Eavan Boland's critique of the conventional connections between woman and nation, particularly in revising images of maternity, as well as the larger controversy about the polemical dimension of Boland's poetry and her approach to it. In particular, Clark argues, Boland has been controversial for her focus on the "self," an inward gaze that seeks to unsettle the objectification of women but has been viewed as a new reductive generalization based on Boland's own perspective, revealing the ways in which revising stereotypes of women is difficult to disentangle from the assumption that a general idea of "woman" is possible. These stereotypes, as Elke D'hoker discusses, appear in John Banville's work to symbolize the dilemmas of the male narrators; his "virgins" and "whores," as well as his use of the gaze, are broadly Western rather than specifically Irish in derivation, however, and are tied to general ideas of "body" and "mind" rather than "mother Ireland." Banville's postmodern novels are rarely set in Ireland, but they exhibit debts to writers such as Beckett and many predominant features of Irish fiction, particularly in being concerned with historical subjects and using parody to address a suspicion of realism (recalling Flann O'Brien in particular), and in his use of elements unique to Irish literature, such as the Big House. In his essay on the films of Neil Jordan, Brian McIlroy demonstrates Jordan's engagement both with political history, in such films as *Michael Collins*, and with literary history, especially in his use of the gothic tradition traced in Part Five of Volume I of this *Companion*, notably in, for instance, his films addressing sexuality, such as *The Crying Game*. Indeed, one segues into the other, as Jordan's revision of Hollywood convention and bending of historical accuracy in *Michael Collins* are extended in the gothic, a mode in which norms can be transgressed and so questions of sexuality and gender can be more fully explored – and, in both historical and fantasy modes, nationality is contested ground for Jordan. On gender, Banville is the odd one out here by reinstating the gender paradigms that his three near-contemporaries all critique, raising interesting questions about the masculinist emphasis of the postmodern novel as a Western literary phenomenon.

The next essay, by David Wheatley, considers another post-Troubles poet from the North, Paul Muldoon, arguably the poet most closely allied with the postmodern. Dense with references to American history and literature, Irish literary history (back to the *immram* and *aisling* and forward to Paul Durcan), and contemporary popular culture (especially Bob Dylan), and formally complex, Muldoon's poetry wrestles with the colonial politics of the past and the present as well as myriad other topics from the sublime to the apparently ridiculous through the interstices between brico-lage and intertextuality. Nuala Ní Dhomhnaill also makes extensive use of wordplay, bricolage, and complex formal structure, but comes out of the important Irish-language poetry movement, *INNTI*, centered in Cork in the 1970s, though her work also responds in some measure to US culture. In his essay on Ní Dhomhnaill, Frank Sewell focuses on her first collection, *An Dealg Droighin*, and the various influences on her work, from American poet John Berryman to Irish myth. Like Boland, Ní Dhomhnaill plays with the gaze and with stereotypes of women to challenge patriar-chal conventions. However, influence, as Danine Farquharson shows in her essay here on Roddy Doyle, is not always simple and positive. Farquharson argues that Doyle's extensive concern with father–son relationships ties his work to the Revival, and con-nects that patrilineal angst to Bloom's "anxiety of influence" (once again raising the masculinist emphasis of postmodern fiction and of the traditional Revival canon), particularly in his debts to Joyce and O'Casey. Farquharson situates Doyle's reluctance to acknowledge any debt to Joyce in terms of the demands of the global literary marketplace. Doyle is very much a realist writer of place (of Dublin), though with postmodern elements of style, and so recalls the rural realists of earlier in the century who were also concerned with pressing social issues – in Doyle's case, as Farquharson shows, this is centrally the impact of the "Celtic Tiger," including the subsequent rise in immigration and so the diversification of Dublin. The final two essays, on Emma Donoghue and Martin McDonagh, deal with two of Ireland's more recent authors. Each began their literary career in the mid-1990s and together they demon-strate the new bilateral flows of migration in Ireland: Donoghue, born in Dublin, now lives in London, Ontario, Canada; McDonagh, born in London, England, to expatriate Irish parents, launched his first plays in Galway. Donoghue, recalling the work of Muldoon in some respects, revises dominant history to recover a more inclusive history (like a number of earlier women writers from Lady Morgan forward to Boland), par-ticularly in addressing the elision of lesbian identity and the sociocultural disciplining of women's sexualities. Jennifer M. Jeffers explores this recovery work of Donoghue's, particularly in terms of her novels' attention to lesbian figures in the past and to the complexities of queer experience in contemporary Ireland. As Jeffers shows, Donoghue does this in part by addressing the historicity of "injurious terms" – in a sense, turning postmodern language against the masculinist emphasis of postmodern fiction. The final essay, by Patrick Lonergan, offers a fitting end to the volume in that it addresses McDonagh's controversial self-presentation, his plays' mixing of the conventional representation of rural Ireland with a disturbing tone and pop-culture allusions that refuse such sentimentality, and the ways in which authorial celebrity (or notoriety) can shape reception. Like other writers discussed in Part Ten, McDonagh also challenges conventional histories and the nostalgic realism that idealizes the rural, but adds to this an exploration of the packaging of Ireland – by tourism, by Hollywood, by other cultural industries – for international audiences, even as he is charged (as were Somerville and Ross a century earlier) with problematically representing the Irish for a global audience.

Many of the essays in this volume demonstrate that, from pre- to post-Rising Ireland, the idea of Ireland, and the politics of its representation, are not only central to much Irish literature of this period but also intertwined with debates about gender, globalization, and the nature of literature itself. At the same time, traditional forms and figures specific to Irish literature, from the *aisling* and the *immram* to the Big House novel and the gothic, from Finn to Mother Ireland, continue to play a significant part in the reimagining of Ireland, while globalization is registered in the growing range of international literary influences on Irish writers.

References and Further Reading

Attridge, D. and M. Howes (Eds). (2000). *Semicolonial Joyce*. Cambridge: Cambridge University Press.

Barthes, R. (1989). "The Death of the Author" (1984). In R. Howard (Trans.). *The Rustle of Language* (pp. 49–55). Berkeley: University of California Press.

Bennett, R., M. Mann, and A. Biderman. (2009). *Public Enemies*. M. Mann (Dir.). Universal Pictures.

Brewster, S. and M. Parker. (2009). *Irish Literature since 1990: Diverse Voices*. Manchester: Manchester University Press.

Castle, G. (2001). *Modernism and the Celtic Revival*. Cambridge: Cambridge University Press.

Craig, P. (Ed.). (2006). *The Ulster Anthology*. Belfast: Blackstaff Press.

Cullingford, E.B. (2001). *Ireland's Others: Gender and Ethnicity in Irish Literature and Popular Culture*. Notre Dame: University of Notre Dame Press/Field Day.

Curtis, L.P. (1971). *Apes and Angels: The Irishman in Victorian Caricature*. Washington, DC: Smithsonian Institution Press.

Deane, S. (1986). *A Short History of Irish Literature*. Notre Dame: University of Notre Dame Press.

Deane, S. (1997). *Strange Country: Modernity and Nationhood in Irish Writing Since 1790*. Oxford: Oxford University Press.

Donoghue, E. (1997). " 'How could I fear and hold thee by the hand?': The Poetry of Eva Gore-Booth." In E. Walshe (Ed.). *Sex, Nation, and Dissent in Irish Writing* (pp. 16–42). New York: St Martin's.

Edwards, H. (2008). "The Irish New Woman and Emily Lawless's *Grania: The Story of an Island*: A Congenial Geography." *English Literature in Transition, 1880–1920*, 51.4, 421–38.

Foster, R.F. (1989). *Modern Ireland, 1600–1972* (1988). New York: Penguin.

Foucault, M. (1984). "What Is an Author?" In P. Rabinow (Ed.). *The Foucault Reader* (pp. 101–19). New York: Pantheon.

Gibbons, L. (1991). "Race Against Time: Racial Discourse and Irish History." *Oxford Literary Review*, 12, 95–117.

Harrington, J.P. (Ed.). (2008). *Modern and Contemporary Irish Drama*. New York: W.W. Norton.

Herr, C. (1986). *Joyce's Anatomy of Culture*. Urbana: University of Illinois Press.

Howes, M. (1996). *Yeats's Nations: Gender, Class, and Irishness*. Cambridge: Cambridge University Press.

Hutton, C. (2003). "Joyce and the Institutions of Revivalism." *Irish University Review*, 33.1, 117–32.

Kershner, R.B. (1996). *Joyce and Popular Culture*. Gainesville: University Press of Florida.

Kirkland, R. (2003). "Dialogue of Despair: Nationalist Cultural Discourse and the Revival in the North of Ireland, 1900–1920." *Irish University Review*, 33.1, 63–78.

Kristeva, J. (1986). "Word, Dialogue, and the Novel" (1966). In T. Moi (Ed.). *The Kristeva Reader* (pp. 35–61). New York: Columbia University Press.

LaGravenese, R. and S. Rogers. (2007). *P.S. I Love You*. R. LaGravenese (Dir.). Based on a novel by C. Ahern. Warner Brothers.

McGann, J. (1993). *New Oxford Book of Romantic Period Verse*. Oxford: Oxford University Press.

McNulty, E. (2004). "From *The Wild Irish Girl* to *A Royal Democrat*: Remembering the Future in the 1890s." *Canadian Journal of Irish Studies*, 30.1, 32–40.

Meaney, G. (2002). "Identity and Opposition: Women's Writing, 1890–1960." In A. Bourke et al. (Eds). *Field Day Anthology of Irish Writing* (vol. V, pp. 1069–73). Cork: Cork University Press.

Moi, T. (1985). *Sexual/Textual Politics: Feminist Literary Theory*. New York: Methuen.

Muldoon, P. (Ed.). (1986). *The Faber Book of Contemporary Irish Poetry*. London: Faber & Faber.

Mundy, C. (2009). "Demonology." *Criminal Minds*. CBS, 2005– .

Nolan, E. (2007). "Postcolonial Literary Studies, Nationalism, and Feminist Critique in Contemporary Ireland." *Éire-Ireland*, 42, 336–61.

Pierce, D. (Ed.). (2000). *Irish Writing in the Twentieth Century: A Reader*. Cork: Cork University Press.

Potts, D. (2000). "Irish Poetry and the Modernist Canon: A Reappraisal of Katharine Tynan." In K. Kirkpatrick (Ed.). *Border Crossings: Irish Women Writers and National Identities* (pp. 79–99). Tuscaloosa: University of Alabama Press.

Said, E.W. (1988). "Yeats and Decolonization." In S. Deane (Ed.). *Nationalism, Colonialism, and Literature* (pp. 69–95). Minneapolis: University of Minnesota Press.

Sheehy, J. (1980). *The Rediscovery of Ireland's Past: The Celtic Revival, 1830–1930*. London: Thames & Hudson.

Tourism Ireland. (2008). "Marian Keyes." http://www.discoverireland.com/gb/about-ireland/experience-ireland/marian-keyes/.

Uhlmann, A. (1999). *Beckett and Poststructuralism*. Cambridge: Cambridge University Press.

Weekes, A.O. (1990). *Irish Women Writers: An Uncharted Tradition*. Lexington: University of Kentucky Press.

Wicke, J. (2004). "Joyce and Consumer Culture." In D. Attridge (Ed.). *The Cambridge Companion to James Joyce* (pp. 234–53). 2nd edn. Cambridge: Cambridge University Press.

Part Seven

Transitions: Victorian, Revival, Modern

30

Cultural Nationalism and Irish Modernism

Michael Mays

"I am no Nationalist," W.B. Yeats wrote in 1937, near the end of an essay purporting to provide an overview of his nearly life-long body of work (Yeats 1961:526). We will return to the vexing question of Yeats' nationalism in a moment, but from the evidence of his own testimony in the same essay, Yeats was no modernist, either, if by that term we mean one who embraced rather than resisted the rising tide of modernity that crested across a vast swath of the globe during the course of his long life (1865–1939). "When I stand upon O'Connell Bridge in the half-light and notice that discordant architecture," he remonstrates,

> all those electric signs, where modern heterogeneity has taken physical form, a vague hatred comes up out of my own dark and I am certain that wherever in Europe there are minds strong enough to lead others the same vague hatred rises; in four or five or in less generations this hatred will have issued in violence and imposed some kind of rule of kindred. I cannot know the nature of that rule, for its opposite fills the light; all I can do to bring it nearer is to intensify my hatred. (Yeats 1961:526)

For many critics, the antimodernism of Yeats (and Pound, Eliot, Lewis, and others) has been a hallmark of modernism, one of its most characteristic if less attractive features. Yet even the most random list of writers commonly denominated as modernist – Marinetti, Mann, Woolf, Stein, Kafka – makes a mockery of any principle of categorization based primarily on political or ideological orientation. Nor need we roam so far afield to complicate the matter. In Yeats and his countryman James Joyce – arguably the greatest poet and the greatest prose writer writing in English in the twentieth century – we find two starkly different figures, contrary in temperament, in outlook, and in their dispositions toward modern life. Despite their marked

A Companion to Irish Literature, edited by Julia M. Wright
© 2010 Blackwell Publishing Ltd

differences in so many other respects, however, both remained – albeit in Joyce's case at some distance – acutely engaged with and invested in Irish cultural and political life, just as Ireland remained for each the fertile subject and ground of their work.

Joyce's ambivalence – towards Irish nationalism, the Catholic Church, the Irish Revival, history, and Ireland generally – is well known. But in tracing the historical and cultural lineage of the Irish people in a lecture delivered in Trieste in 1907, he enthusiastically noted the remarkable fact that such a remote island had for so long been a center of scholarship, "a true focus of sanctity and intellect, spreading throughout the continent a culture and a vitalizing energy." Nor – in a nod to the successes of the cultural-nationalist revival at home – were the glories of that past merely contemporary fabrications. "Even a superficial consideration," he proclaimed, would demonstrate that the Irish nation's insistence upon cultural autonomy was "not so much the demand of a young nation that wants to make good in the European concert as the demands of a very old nation to renew under new forms the glories of a past civilization" (Joyce 1959:157). From the author of *Dubliners*, this is a strikingly charitable, even magnanimous, view of the Irish past. More surprising still is his description of England's role in Ireland's demise, worthy of the hyper-nationalistic Citizen himself: Ireland is poor, he writes, because England wrecked native industry; because it allowed the native population to die through neglect during the Famine; and because its present-day administrators grew rich doing nothing. To be sure, Joyce's lecture reflects the deep-seated ambivalence for which he is famous, and the Irish themselves garner an equal share of the blame for their abysmal condition. Yet on the whole, the lecture offers an even-handed, clear-sighted, and prescient view of the Irish question in the first decade of the last century. Exile may have had its limitations, but it also enabled for Joyce the development of a far more complex and generous relationship to Ireland than that of Stephen Dedalus in *A Portrait of the Artist as a Young Man*.

If he remained in closer physical proximity to, and was much more directly involved with, Irish nationalist politics than Joyce, Yeats nevertheless experienced plenty of ambivalence himself. "I am no Nationalist, except" – he added – "in Ireland for passing reasons." Despite the crucial qualification, it is a provocative claim coming from someone who placed himself over the course of his long career squarely in the midst of Ireland's national struggle for independence. As co-founder of the Irish National Theatre, in his vigorous letter-writing campaigns, in his efforts on behalf of a multitude of cultural enterprises and, eventually, as a senator in the Free State government – to detail only a few of the activities in which he was energetically engaged – Yeats figured prominently in many of the period's most heated controversies. Yet his comment registers an ambivalence that is not merely the product of bitter old age but reflects, rather, the unique position he occupied with regard to Irish nationalism from his early years on. That ambivalence is in part the product of Yeats' own diverse identities: a cosmopolitan, internationally renowned and Nobel-winning man of letters, who maintained close ties with the rural west of Ireland; a familiar figure in both London and Dublin; a Protestant who remained a nationalist his entire life. Even more, however, ambivalence or dialecticism represents a conscious intellectual choice. At once affiliated with and critical of Irish nationalism, as poet, playwright, journalist, and theater director Yeats effectively positioned himself within but also against its wide-ranging force-field. And it was this unusual combination of centrality and distance that structured nearly all of Yeats' engagements with the controversies of his time.

National affiliation, however conflicted or ambivalent, seems to contradict many of the most cherished myths modernism propounded about itself, including especially its internationalist bias and its emphasis on stylistic innovation: the exhortation to "make it new" is in every respect antithetical to the nation's appeal to the past and to the authority of its own traditions. The evident – and seemingly irreconcilable – incongruities differentiating nationalism and modernism have perplexed critics, who have generally opted to treat modernist writers and their work in an either/or manner: in the case of Yeats and Joyce, either as modernists or as Irish, but rarely as both at the same time. Yet modernism's insistence upon its own unfettered freedom is a measure of the degree to which it was already inscribed within the national paradigm it sought to transcend. However strong one's cosmopolitan impulses, by the end of the nineteenth century and the beginning of the twentieth it had become nearly impossible to think of oneself in any other terms than the national. Even if that relationship manifested itself negatively – as it often did for Joyce – the nation remained the touchstone, what one venerated or, sometimes, cursed. Love and hate; pride and shame: these are the counterparts of national ambivalence. Thus, if one could not avoid what Althusser would call the nation's "hail," neither was one destined to be a nationalist in the strict sense of the term.

"A healthy nation," George Bernard Shaw once wrote, "is as unconscious of its nationality as a healthy man of his bones." But, he cautioned, "if you break a nation's nationality it will think of nothing else but getting it set again. It will listen to no reformer, to no philosopher, to no preacher, until the demand of the Nationalist is granted. It will attend to no business, however vital, except the business of unification and liberation" (Shaw 1907:xxxvi). National affiliation, even love of country, signifies one thing; nationalism – and in particular the anticolonial nationalism that prevailed in Ireland and throughout much of the rest of the world from the 1840s on – denotes, as Shaw suggests, something far more active, a strenuous advocacy that goes well beyond national regard. One essential difference between national feeling and nationalism has to do with the way the latter systematically came to subordinate all other values to those of the nation. But in contrasting the nineteenth-century Irish poet William Allingham (1824–89) with Thomas Davis (1814–45), poet and a leader of the Young Ireland movement, Yeats makes another useful distinction. Together they represent, he writes, "two different kinds of love of Ireland." In Allingham, Yeats found "the entire emotion for the place one grew up in which I felt as a child." In contrast, Davis "was concerned with ideas of Ireland, with conscious patriotism. His Ireland was artificial, an idea built up in a couple of generations" (Yeats 1955:319). On one hand, we are right to be suspicious about Yeats' too-easy evocation of a "natural" and an "artificial" love of country. Yet in referring to Davis' "conscious patriotism" Yeats identifies the characteristically programmatic nature of nationalism and its project of creating new nations on old foundations.

When he wrote this in 1909, in the wake of a series of bruising battles with the mainstream of Irish nationalism over Synge's *Playboy of the Western World*, Yeats was understandably wary – and probably a little weary, too – of "ideas of Ireland." The political demise and death of Charles Stewart Parnell, the great Irish parliamentarian and leader of the Home Rule movement in the 1880s, Yeats claimed elsewhere, had opened the door for the cultural revival that flourished in the years leading up to the 1916 Easter Rebellion. The reality, of course, was more complex. Most importantly, for our purposes, Irish cultural nationalism did not simply begin with the creation of the Gaelic Athletic Association, the Gaelic League, or the publication of Standish O'Grady's *History of Ireland*, but had been ongoing since the antiquarianism of the later eighteenth century, through the United Irishmen, to Young Ireland and on. Nor was cultural revivalism an exclusively Irish phenomenon during the period. On the contrary, drawing back just a little from the particularities of time and place enables us to reframe the period of the Irish Revival, and its dynamic energies, within the tremendous, sweeping scope of an emergent modernity. Nationalism and modernism represent two distinctly different responses to these historical phenomena. To be sure, nationalism's influence was more comprehensive and far more successful than modernism's; indeed, in its elitism and exclusive focus on the arts, modernism made a virtue of its limited appeal. Yet it was essential nonetheless. The young Yeats, who had been an admirer of Davis, had many "ideas of Ireland" of his own. Nevertheless, he was right in claiming to be "no Nationalist": even when most committed to the nationalist cause Yeats always maintained some degree of distance and autonomy. If he often found himself at odds with, and increasingly marginalized from, the mainstream of Irish nationalist politics, that marginalization was largely a matter of aesthetic and ideological temperament, which is to say, of choice. For Yeats, as for Joyce, the same qualities that make them such compelling and exemplary modernists – their skepticism, their dialecticism, their commitment to freedom from orthodoxy – made sustained conformity to cause, nationalist or otherwise, unthinkable.

*   *   *

From tribes and city-states to kingdoms and religious and economic empires, human beings have been forming communities – sometimes consensually, sometimes through the imposition of brute force – since earliest recorded history. Yet unlike those venerated forms of community, and despite its repeated, even obsessive, recourse to historical foundations, "the nation" is a recent creation, the product of a distinctly modern cultural and political ideology, "nationalism." Stemming from the Enlightenment thought of Herder, Burke, and Fichte, and from Mazzini and the German Romantics, who first gave shape to a concept of the nation as an essentially spiritual entity, nationalism was a vital – if not necessarily inevitable – response to the profound social, political, and economic upheavals wrought in Europe by industrial and technological modernization. A mechanism of adjustment and compensation, nationalism provided a sense of stability and continuity in a world in which the traditional social, political, and economic orders were undergoing profound crises (Nairn 1981; Hroch 1996). The French and Industrial revolutions – synecdoches for the range of transformations taking place at the end of the eighteenth and throughout the nineteenth centuries – both reflected and intensified the unsettling experience of modernization. At once exhilarating and terrifying, those revolutions changed everything. Or nearly so. As Ernest Renan argued, one thing, at least, had not changed: "We have driven metaphysical and theological abstractions out of politics. What then remains?" he asks. "Man, with his desires and his needs" (Renan 1990:20). Revolution precipitated many forms of crisis, not least, as Renan suggests, where traditional belief systems were concerned. Anglo-European secularization, long under way, had nurtured Enlightenment thinking; the Enlightenment emphasis on new scientific modes of thought in turn accelerated that process, further eroding traditional forms of religious legitimacy. If secularization undermined spiritual authority, however, it had little to offer those "desires and needs" that religious belief had, at least in part, addressed. By providing the solid foundation of an identity at once capacious and limited, nationalism answered the need felt by many in an anxious time of crisis "to find firm ground under their feet, to pull a piece of eternity down into their lives" (Mosse 1993:23).

Yet if its ideological origins are rooted in European Romanticism, nationalism in its mature form developed not in the great European centers of empire, but rather on the colonial periphery, as a necessarily idealist and compensatory response to the real and potential forms of domination posed by the imperial administrative states. "Every modern nation," Etienne Balibar has observed, "is a product of colonization: it has always been to some degree colonized or colonizing, and sometimes both at the same time" (Balibar and Wallerstein 1991:89). Rebutting the traditional view of the nation as a static and timeless form, Balibar's remark serves as a reminder of the dynamic and dialectical forces from which nationalism arose. Having developed gradually over the course of several centuries, the early modern states of Europe – England, France, Spain – served as formal prototypes of the new nation-state. Even with their great wealth and power, their well-organized bureaucratic administrations, and their relative political stability, the transition from traditional to modern forms of life proved arduous and uneven. But in the colonial territories, and those areas of Europe not already integrated into the medieval or early modern state, where ethnic or linguistic groups lacked both the structural solidity and the resources of the developed states, the situation was all the more daunting and urgent.

Threatened with the culture-leveling forces of modernity on the one hand, and with political domination by the imperial powers on the other, the proto-national movements defensively sought to assert and justify their own claims to cultural and political autonomy in a number of characteristic ways: through shoring up a common culture rooted in a shared language, land, or set of traditions; through demands for political self-determination; and through appeals to the restoration or creation of a historically based but disenfranchised community modeled on the "advanced" administrative states. With few other tools to work with, national movements forged their oppositional, inter-class identities based on principles of historically rooted cultural difference. And it was these – often shaky and ethereal – historical claims that led to the difficult but remarkably successful transformation of anticolonial resistance to postcolonial nation-building. Recognizing the utility and appeal of this new commodity – national identity – the imperial powers themselves were quick to appropriate it for their own purposes. And it was only after this isomorphic transformation of national movements into nationalism that the established states themselves, changed completely in substance if not in form, became "nations" in the proper sense of the term.

Conventional wisdom – taking its lead mainly from nationalist ideology – holds that the primary purpose of nationalism is the creation of a political state embodying and reflecting the common values of the historical nation. "Culture," or "cultural nationalism," in this view, is subsidiary to the "larger" political goal, merely a means to that end. In Ireland as elsewhere, however – as the challenges that perpetually beset new states amply demonstrate, not only initially but long after independence – political self-determination is primarily a means for ensuring cultural autonomy and not, as we are accustomed to thinking, an end in itself.

Moreover, nationalism has always been in the first instance cultural, and not merely because cultural forms – language, customs, stories, and so forth – were the most useful, and often the only, resources the nationalist had available. To be sure, the political project of establishing the nation-state required elaborate forms of cultural integration and consolidation. Likewise, the imagined or invented nation has become something of a hackneyed critical concept, yet for many good reasons: the nation-as-construct argument drew attention to the nation as the contested site, not of passively received fixed memories, but of ideologically determined and conflicting representations of the past. But its success not only on the colonial periphery, but in the vastly different circumstances of the metropolitan center, registers the degree to which nationalism became the nearly universal ground of modern identity. That identity is less something we think about than what we think through. Embedded in the conviction that the nation is "the essential human unit in which man's nature is realized," our nature and purpose, Isaiah Berlin contends, are derived from its nature and purpose (Berlin 1980:342). In integrating and subordinating the demands of the politician, the philosopher, and the preacher, the salient point about nationalism, as Shaw so astutely perceived, is the way in which it engenders a unique national identity corresponding to one and only one nation-state. In constituting the nation as the place where we always have been, and can only ever be, at home, the "culture" of nationalism is – with apologies for the tautology – national culture. And in this important respect, all nationalism is cultural.

*   *   *

"Every Irishman forms some vague ideal of his country, born from his reading of history, or from contemporary politics, or from an imaginative intuition," George

Russell, the poet better known as AE, declared in 1899. "This Ireland in the mind it is, not the actual Ireland, which kindles his enthusiasm. For this he works and makes sacrifices" (Eglinton 1899:83). Russell was responding to the journalist John Eglinton's claim that Irish literature should be "cosmopolitan" and that it should look forward rather than back. For Eglinton, the ancient Irish legends such as those rediscovered and made popular by Standish O'Grady's *History of Ireland* "obstinately refuse to be taken out of their old environment and transplanted into the world of modern sympathies" (Eglinton 1899:10). The anti-democratic, anti-modern, and staunchly Anglo-Irish O'Grady had looked to the grandeur of a heroic past as a means of re-energizing a comatose and increasingly irrelevant Ascendancy culture. But the historical past, Eglinton argued, could provide no guidance in negotiating the complexities of the modern present. "Sooner or later," he wrote elsewhere, "Ireland will have to make up its mind that it is no longer the old Gaelic nation of the 5th or 12th or even of the 18th century, but one which has been in the making ever since these islands were drawn into the community of nations by the Normans" (quoted in Lyons 1979:65–66). Yeats disagreed: "Our Irish romantic tradition ... should make Ireland, as Ireland and all other lands were in ancient times, a holy land to her own people" (Eglinton 1899:20). So did AE: "To reveal Ireland in clear and beautiful light, to create the Ireland in the heart, is the province of national literature" (Eglinton 1899:83).

Nationalism, Renan observed, "presupposes" a past, imagining the nation as temporally continuous, a bridge linking a present-day "we" both to our ancestors in the past and to our heirs in the future. Mediating past and future through its responses to contemporary circumstance, national identity exists under the sign of peril: perpetually at risk of the cultural catastrophe – engendered from beyond or within its borders, or through historical calamity – that will sever that fragile bond for good. Always to one degree or another in a state of crisis, national identities must, therefore, be regularly revised and modified, reconstituted and renewed: the more dire the perceived crisis, the more urgent the need for renewal. Agreement among the revivalists about the need to create an Ireland of the heart and mind turned out to be much easier to reach than agreement about what constituted the thing itself. In the meantime, however, that need for ideals was symptomatic of a pervasive, debilitating, and dire problem about which no one disagreed: that modern English materialism had corrupted the Irish people and by its very nature presented an imminent and mortal threat to the Irish nation's centuries-long existence. As John Hutchinson notes, "The aim of cultural nationalists is the moral regeneration of the historic community": until the contaminant of anglicization was purged, there could be no hope for cultural renewal (Hutchinson 1987:16). The case was made most prominently by Douglas Hyde (1860–1949) in his inaugural lecture as president of the National Literary Society in 1892. In "The Necessity for De-Anglicising Ireland," Hyde argued that the Irish people had put themselves in the untenable position of seeking a distinct national political identity while carelessly throwing off the best claim they had for that separate identity: their language and culture. The Irish race, he claimed, was stuck in a halfway house, hating the English and yet continuing to imitate their fashions and customs. If they took the next step and became good Englishmen, so much the better; but "it is a fact and we must face it as a fact, that although they adopt English habits and copy England in every way, the great bulk of Irishmen and Irishwomen ... are ... filled with a dull, ever-abiding animosity against her." Refusing to become the one, it was imperative they become the other and "build up an Irish nation on Irish lines" (Hyde 1894:120).

Hyde would become, the next year, the first president of the newly formed Gaelic League, whose purpose was to restore a dignified sense of national identity rooted in the revival of Irish as a living language. The Gaelic League would find many ardent and influential supporters over the next two vibrant decades, including Patrick Pearse (1879–1916), the leader of the 1916 Easter Rebellion, and D.P. Moran (1869–1936), journalist, editor, and proponent of "Irish Ireland." Like Hyde, Moran thought the Irish the victims of their own colonial confusion, neither English nor fully and uniquely Irish, and he admired the Gaelic League for framing what he thought to be the basic but crucial first questions – what is Irish nationality, and how is it to be realized? Sharing the view that the only true foundation of the nation was its ancient past, Moran also emphasized the importance of a national self-reliance firmly grounded in native culture:

> Ireland will be nothing until she is a nation, and as a nation is a civilisation, she will never accomplish anything worthy of herself until she falls back upon her own language and traditions, and, recovering there her old pride, self-respect, and initiative, develops and marches forward thence. (Moran 1901:39)

Political "nationality," he argued, was a spurious invention of the Protestant Ascendancy meant to justify anglicization and contrasting with a genuine and distinctive Irish cultural civilization. Every popular leader since Grattan's parliament in 1782 – from O'Connell to Parnell and beyond – had embraced the invented tradition at the expense of the legitimate one. But, echoing a recurrent theme, there remained for Moran some nub of Irish being – some inner instinct commanding "Thou shalt be Irish: thou shalt not be English" – upon which the nation could be revived.

"In modern Ireland," F.S.L. Lyons contends in his pioneering study of Irish cultural politics in the post-Parnell period, "culture has been a divisive rather than a reconciling influence" (Lyons 1979:27). Looking back on the period through the historical lenses of the Northern Irish conflict, the Irish Civil War, the Anglo-Irish War, the 1916 Rising, and the mobilization of Ulster Unionists in 1912 – to go no further back in time – it would be impossible to argue otherwise. Nor would one wish to quarrel with Lyons' more general claim, all too apparent from our own historical vantage point, that the challenge of the Irish question in its modern form derives from the competing and often antagonistic claims of at least four different cultures: English, native (predominantly Catholic and Gaelic), Anglo-Irish, and Unionist. Yet despite substantial differences in tone and temperament among the diverse figures of the Revival period, Anglophobia, as R.F. Foster (1993) has noted, was the unifying theme bringing together advocates who shared little or nothing else in common. The implications of those differences would manifest themselves soon enough, but at least initially they were far less important than a shared antipathy toward all things English. In this respect, the idealized images of Ireland, different as they were, confirmed the shared sense of an Irish Difference that justified political self-determination. But again, political independence was less an end in itself than the bulwark that would safeguard a unique and autonomous identity. The language, censorship, neutrality, and sectarianism: these were controversial battlegrounds over an always unstable and contested notion of Irish identity in the years just before and after Independence. But they were also barriers erected to buttress that identity and to insulate it from the contaminating forces of modernity.

In its ability to integrate effectively the conflicting political, economic, and cultural interests of a severely stratified society, Anglophobia served the earlier, anticolonial phase of Irish nationalism well. Nation-building, on the other hand, required a far more complex – and contentious – set of negotiations. Playing out across a remarkable range of public sites – in newspaper columns and meeting halls, in salons and the stalls of the Abbey Theatre, and within the prodigious numbers of clubs, societies, organizations, and associations formed for the promotion of every imaginable thing Irish – those arguments would harden into rigid fixed positions as the new state, insecure in its identity and unstable in its infancy, sought to establish a solid footing in the years following its creation in 1922.

Plagued both by a stagnant economy and a bitterly divisive civil war, the architects of the nation were confronted with a modernization they were ill equipped to manage. In Ireland, as elsewhere throughout the 1920s and 1930s, the new postwar styles and fashions, including jazz dancing, revealing bathing suits, the cropped hair of the sexually liberated flapper, and the literature and film which brought the news of, and more often than not celebrated, these new developments, were, to many, devastating signs of a degenerate world (Brown 1985). Yet if more firmly established European nations struggled to come to terms with a modernity that seemed to be careening out of control, in Ireland – where national self-definition took shape, as we have seen, against a quintessentially modern, industrial, and materialist Englishness – that project was all the more pressing. Through an array of public policies, institutions, bodies, commissions, and councils, the government made every effort to suppress ostensibly corrupting influences emanating from abroad. The dilemma of a new Irish state intent upon establishing a nation worthy of the long imagined and fought-over ideal explains much about the success of the leading statesman of the period, Éamon de Valera, and the conservatism, the self-protectionism, and the insularity which he both advocated and, famously, claimed to embody. Ironically, however, the image of a pristine rural and spiritual land untainted by outside influences merely masked the extent to which modernity's forces had already penetrated the native landscape. It may have been paradoxical, then, but not at all surprising, that it was the ultra-modern radio, with its airwaves impervious to borders of any kind, that de Valera used so successfully in disseminating his traditionalist vision of Gaelic Ireland.

If the difficulties facing the Free State government were extensive, however, its problems paled in comparison with those afflicting the two communities on the northern side of the newly established border. Those distinct and antagonistic ethnic communities had been deeply and profoundly divided for more than two centuries over such basic concerns as religion, education, history, economics, and culture. In the face of such competing and utterly irreconcilable ethno-nationalist claims, a climate of fear, exacerbated by isolation, prevailed on both sides. Yet despite its virtually absolute control over the province, those anxieties proved even greater for the majority Protestant Unionist community than for the Catholic nationalist minority. That trepidation was less remarkable than it appeared since the Union was the only safeguard protecting what was felt to be the sacred Ulster Protestant "homeland," and thus was seen as essential for the preservation of that community's singular culture. A peculiar and oxymoronic "national" identity, Unionism represents a recalcitrant political nationalism almost wholly in the service of cultural protectionism.

* * *

"The nation" has been a site of contradiction and conflict: considering the complex, uneven, and unpredictable forces from which it arose and which it in turn brought to life, it could hardly have been otherwise. For while colonialism made manifest modernity's emerging political order, it also cast into sharp relief actual and substantive economic, linguistic, and cultural differences, not only between countries but also within them. Nationalism's success in mediating the diverse interests and varied allegiances within the nation itself – that is, in reconciling the many formidable obstacles hindering the transition from anticolonial opposition to postcolonial nation-building – was due in no small part to the sophisticated rhetorical strategies nationalism utilized in its project of national restoration.

That project of recovery is predicated upon a disjunctive estrangement: rooted in absence, in loss, national memory "restores" a nonexistent unity out of the disparate and historically decontextualized images of a vaguely familiar past. "I stand on one side of a great rift," Thomas Kinsella wrote in his 1966 essay "The Irish Writer," "and can feel the discontinuity within myself." Lamenting what he perceived to be a sundered Irish identity, Kinsella located the source of that schism in a cultural dispossession: "It is a matter of people and place as well as writing – of coming, so to speak, from a broken and uprooted family, of being drawn to those who share my origins and finding that we cannot share our lives" (Kinsella 1970:59). Discontinuity and dispossession, the sense of a great chasm separating past and present, an organic Irish culture from its fractured, fragmented current state: this theme was prevalent in Irish writing – literary, historical, political, sociological – throughout the nineteenth and twentieth centuries. From Wolfe Tone and Robert Emmet to Patrick Pearse, Éamon de Valera, and Kinsella himself, that "rift" is both *caused by* England's colonial domination in Ireland and *cause for* an urgent program of repair. Hyde's representation of the disjunctive moment is exemplary: "The Ireland of today," Hyde proclaimed in 1892, "is the descendant of the Ireland of the seventh century" (Hyde 1894:126). Its continuity having remained intact, despite wave after wave of alien intrusion, Irish nationality now found itself imperiled by an anglicization that had been making "silent inroads" for nearly a century. Its language lost through neglect, its people slavishly aping English ways, and its country on the very verge of achieving Home Rule, the Irish, Hyde proclaimed, had done to themselves what centuries of conquest had failed to achieve:

> But, alas, *quantum mutatus ab illo!* What the battleaxe of the Dane, the sword of the Norman, the wile of the Saxon were unable to perform, we have accomplished ourselves. We have at last broken the continuity of Irish life, and just at the moment when the Celtic race is presumably about to largely recover possession of its own country, it finds itself deprived and stript of its Celtic characteristics, cut off from the past, yet scarcely in touch with the present. ... It has lost all that [the past generations] had – language, traditions, music, genius, and ideas. Just when we should be starting to build up anew the Irish race and the Gaelic nation ... we find ourselves despoiled of the bricks of nationality. The old bricks that lasted eighteen hundred years are destroyed; we must now set to, to bake new ones, if we can, on other ground and of other clay. (Hyde 1894:128)

The crisis Hyde describes – the imminent loss of the language, and with it the entire foundation of Irish culture – is calamitous. But calamity, paradoxically, offers hope and opportunity as well.

Irish national memory has been, in Eavan Boland's memorable phrase, an "archive of loss." Yet the songs, ballads and images, stories and collective memories that make up the fabric of Irish nationalism's "archive of defeat," Boland adds, simultaneously comprise "a diagram of victory." Considering the "seductive" prospect of doing away with the idea of nation and nationality altogether, Boland muses, "[W]hy did I not walk away? Simply because I was not free to. For all my quarrels with the concept ... I needed to find and repossess that idea at some level of repose" (Boland 1989:19). Constrained by an identity that is, for better or worse, in the first instance national, we cannot wish that identity away. Yet to whatever extent it is disabling, every experience of loss, as Boland's comments suggest, represents an opportunity for "repossession": loss, defeat, dispossession; recovery, victory, repossession. Far from the unique machinations of an isolated historical site, these are the complementary and dialectical components in nationalism's systematic project of nation-building. Emphasizing the rhetorical function of loss in no way diminishes the actual historical and cultural discontinuities – the genuine losses – of Ireland's long and often tragic history. Indeed, without the tangible experience of loss its rhetorical function would be meaningless.

Still, as Joyce recognized clearly, discontinuity is the unhappy condition of all life, but also, therefore – ironically – the very condition that makes "renewal" infinitely renewable. "There can be no reconciliation," Stephen Dedalus says in *Ulysses*, inverting the axiomatic relationship between loss and recovery, "if there has not been a sundering" (Joyce 1986:160). Joyce was enamored enough of the idea to have the slightly drunken Stephen repeat it twice while expounding his theory of Shakespeare in "Scylla and Charybdis." And it is in just this sense that the continuity of the nation is always necessarily retrospective and imposed: a selective stitching together, out of the residual images of the past, of a cohesive, sense-making narrative of the present. Hence Shaw's figure of the nationalist is much less paradoxical than it first appears. As with the man who becomes aware of his bone only once it is broken, so the nation becomes conscious of itself *as* a nation only when its nationality manifests itself as in some way compromised. For Shaw, writing at the height of nationalism's influence, the continuity of the healthy nation was more or less a given, transparent and timeless. In the waning days of that influence, however, it is much easier to see the extent to which nation-breaking – far from Shaw's unhappy accident of history – is an intrinsic function of nationalism's every act of nation-making: the point of departure for a distinctively national identity juxtaposed against and pieced together out of the variegated remnants of the past.

"The only thing that actually de-sutures," Slavoj Žižek has observed, reflecting on the nation's conflicted formation within modernity, "is suture itself" (Žižek 1991:20). The project of "recovering" the nation, of "restoring" one's cultural origins, as Žižek suggests, is conditioned upon the figure of the "rift." And thus, the disparity between the time after and the time before the rift is the enabling condition for the appearance of nationalism as a project, the project of lining up one's practices with one's genealogy: "I might be the author of my poems," Boland muses; "I was not the author of my past. However crude the diagram, the idea of a nation remained the rough graphic of an ordeal. In some subterranean way I felt myself to be part of that ordeal; its fragmentations extended into mine" (Boland 1989:19). Riven by rupture and loss, nationalism weaves together its archives of defeat and its diagrams of victory, linking the time before with the time yet to come.

The project of national restoration, of forging the bonds that unify a people and embed its identity, has always entailed the production of national narratives (Bhabha 1990; Nora 1996). The content or mode of those narratives may change, and certain events and figures will be emphasized or downplayed depending on historical circumstance and narrative need, but their purpose is always the same: to sanction, and to sanctify, the nation which is simultaneously the object of the nationalist's veneration and the subject of a cohesive historical continuum. It would be difficult to invent a better example of this process – in Ireland or anywhere else for that matter – than the one actually provided for us by Patrick Pearse, the Gaelic Leaguer-turned-leader of the Easter 1916 Uprising. Intent upon legitimating his own place in a genealogy of Irish cultural revolutionary nationalism, Pearse sought to align Tone's United Irishmen rebellion and Davis' Young Ireland movement with the armed insurrection he hoped soon to lead. In point of fact, however, the idealism of Davis' romantic nationalism signaled a departure from, rather than a continuation of, Tone's more pragmatic republicanism (Lloyd 1987). Tone's demand for independence had been based not, as Pearse would have it, on a timeless historical condition, but rather on contemporary circumstances, including, among other things, the continuing unresponsiveness of the British administration, Ascendancy bad faith, and the rise of a mercantile middle class in the north-east of Ireland that wanted more control over its own fate. For Pearse, reading 1798 through the lens of nineteenth-century romantic nationalism, such immediate considerations, in a subtle but crucial shift of focus, were no longer seen as discrete causes for breaking with England, but were conceived instead as pieces in the totality of an unceasing colonial oppression. The "meaning" of Tone, so to speak – his role in the history of modern Irish nationalism – had to be retrospectively reshaped and made to conform to Pearse's own contemporary ideal. Whether because of, or despite, its characteristic historical misprisions, it proved highly effective. Through his paradigmatic reading of these two seminal Irish national figures, along with the words and actions that reading inspired, in his own time and in years to come, Pearse did more to enshrine the "gospel" of romantic nationalism in Ireland than anyone since Davis himself.

Long before Pearse, and dating back almost to the moment of the United Irishmen Uprising itself, Tone occupied an exalted position in the pantheon of Irish revolutionary nationalism. Yet as Oliver McDonagh has argued, it was Pearse who was responsible, much more than any other, for elevating Tone to the status of "Founding Father" and for "rendering him at once the St. Paul and the St. Augustine of Irish revolution" (McDonagh 1983:88). Many of the reasons for Pearse's identification with Tone are readily apparent: for one, Tone's life of heroic exploit lent itself to just the sort of mythologizing that Pearse valorized, while the drama of his mysterious death suited Pearse's taste for martyrdom. Equally important, however, Tone functions in Pearse's essay "Ghosts" as the vital link in the latter's seamless national narrative linking the past generations of Irish revolutionaries to Pearse himself. Christ and Cuchulain were archetypes. Tone, by virtue of his relative contemporaneity, served more as an exalted predecessor, a latter-day Irish Christ to Pearse's Paul:

> That God spoke to Ireland through Tone and through those who, after Tone, have taken up his testimony, that Tone's teaching and theirs is true and great and that no other teaching as to Ireland has any truth and worthiness at all, is a thing upon which I stake all my mortal and my immortal hopes. And I ask the men and women of my generation to stake their mortal and immortal hopes with me. (Pearse 1952:293)

Tone's United Irishmen Uprising of 1798 provided an effective historical precedent for Pearse's own Volunteer force. But it was Pearse's narrative – and the tragic drama of the Easter Rising that provided its denouement – that promised national renewal. Messianic and future-oriented, Pearse, the prototypical nationalist, could only look forward by looking back. Destined to sift through the (often incriminating) evidence of an estranged past, the successful national narrative integrates into its totalizing account what relics it can, and ignores the rest. What else could it do with those inchoate fragments of the past that defy contemporary understanding? Lifted out of their historical moment, past events and actions – such as those that gave rise to the United Irishmen – are made meaningful according to the needs of the present moment, and to the narratives in which the continuous unfolding of the nation is plotted, syllogistically, as preordained, sacred, and enduring.

* * *

If Pearse's efforts to provide a historical narrative aligning some version of the past with the needs of the present are typical of nationalism, so, too, is the priority he placed on fidelity to the nation above all else. His conservative, patriarchal vision of a Gaelic, Catholic Ireland would be enshrined in the 1937 Constitution. And his Catholic-nationalist theology of faith and service in the ministry of what he called "patriotism" represents an extreme but typical strain of twentieth-century Irish nationalism. For Pearse, nationalism was at once "a faith and service": a faith consecrated by and measured against a service which was the condition of the authentically national. "It is not sufficient to say 'I believe'," Pearse contends, "unless one can also say 'I serve'" (Pearse 1952:65). Determined to evade not only the nationalist demands the Revival had fostered but all cultural and familial ties that bind, Joyce's alter ego Stephen Dedalus is equally forceful and direct in his repudiation of Pearse's terms of service: "I will not serve," he announces in characteristically high-minded fashion to his friend and foil, Cranly. Striving to create an art free of all external constraint – "selfbounded and selfcontained" – Stephen imagines the artist's relationship to his work as utterly unencumbered: the artist, "like the God of creation, remains within or behind or beyond or above his handiwork, invisible, refined out of existence, indifferent, paring his fingernails" (Joyce 1968:215).

Yet the youthful Stephen's dream of unfettered freedom is impossibly naive, as his friends regularly remind him: about those fingernails, Lynch quips, "trying to refine them also out of existence." However admirable his desire and heroic his efforts, the independence Stephen seeks is – as Lynch's retort ironically underscores – illusory, the hopeless product of wishful thinking. More ensnared in the nets he seeks to fly past, more the product of his culture than he can admit, he opts for an equally unviable Manichean negation. "It is a curious thing," Cranly remarks, "how your mind is supersaturated with the religion in which you say you disbelieve" (Joyce 1968:240). Stephen, of course, was not Joyce, or at least not the mature Joyce who would come to write *Portrait*, *Ulysses*, and *Finnegans Wake*. For Stephen, as for all of us, cultural inheritance is inescapable; it makes us who and what we are. But not simply so. For the older Joyce, the process of coming to maturity requires absorbing, filtering, and finally transforming those values and forms of identity conferred on us by tradition – always more or less successfully.

Moreover, if the identity-grounding allure of the past is inescapable, that past is incapable of providing identity with the stable foundations it seems to promise. Pearse's paradigmatic narrative of the nation was fashioned out of a fantasy of originary recovery. In Joyce's later work, and especially in *Finnegans Wake*, that recovery is both perpetually promised and perpetually denied, simultaneously hopeful and hopeless. Incited by need and desire, the abstracted sigla of the *Wake* are constantly buffeted in their restless and relentless pursuit of identity – the undiscoverable firm ground upon which they might become fully realized "characters." Aligning memory and history – however forcibly – nationalism insists that the foreign past be made familiar. Disavowing the solidity of that alignment, *Finnegans Wake* presents a panoramic cacophony of history and memory, in which Joyce's sigla have only the mysterious vestiges of an alien past from which they must ever attempt to recover the identities which seem to have been lost or stolen from them.

For Yeats too, as for Joyce, Pearsean "service" was anathema to art; writing in the pay of any cause was no art at all, but merely dogma. To be sure, Yeats played an instrumental part in countless causes throughout his life. And he wrote, regularly and often with great zeal, on their behalf. Yet even in those moments of his most strenuous commitment, Yeats insisted upon the freedom and autonomy of the imagination. Defending the National Theatre's production of Synge's *The Shadow of the Glen* in 1903, Yeats reminded the critics in the nationalist press of his own important contributions to the cultural revival, including his influential play *Cathleen ni Houlihan*. At times, Yeats argued, imagination and cause are one, and then, "so much the better." But writing driven by cause is mere journalism – writing made serviceable and ideologically compliant. Literature is journalism's Other: it retains its autonomy; it "must take the responsibility of its power, and keep all its freedom" (Yeats 1962:117).

Embedded in Irish life and geography, Joyce and Yeats – strange bedfellows, indeed – at once affirm historical contingency while refusing to be bound by it. Subject to the cultural, political, and historical conditions of their time, but not in service to them, these quintessentially modernist writers inhabit a literary space that is by their own definition autonomous and unserviceable. That autonomy denotes, of course, a commitment to form and to stylistic innovation. But it also represents, significantly, a series of refusals: the refusal to conform to the demands of orthodoxy; the refusal to be conscripted to causes not its own; and the refusal to be governed by externally imposed or extra-literary rules of order. The political views of far too many modernist writers have failed the test of time: hence claiming for modernism an essential, if qualified, autonomy it previously claimed for itself may well seem strikingly naive. Yet however unfashionable an enterprise, in our own critical moment of relentless historicization we should endeavor to differentiate the ethos of modernist writing from the politics of individual modernist writers. In championing an art free of crude propaganda yet richly engaged with the complexities of modern life, Yeats and Joyce offer models of intellectual independence free of condition, free of cause.

REFERENCES AND FURTHER READING

Adams, H. (1991). "Yeats and Antithetical Nationalism." In V. Newey and A. Thompson (Eds). *Literature and Nationalism* (pp. 163–81). Liverpool: Liverpool University Press.

Anderson, B. (1991). *Imagined Communities: Reflections on the Origin and Spread of Nationalism*. London: Verso.

Balibar, E. and I. Wallerstein. (1991). *Race, Nation, Class: Ambiguous Identities*. London: Verso.

Berlin, I. (1980). *Against the Current: Essays in the History of Ideas*. H. Hardy (Ed.). New York: Viking.

Bhabha, H. (Ed.). (1990). *Nations and Narration*. New York: Routledge.

Boland, E. (1989). *A Kind of Scar: The Woman Poet in a National Tradition*. Dublin: Attic Press.

Boyce, D.G. (1982). *Nationalism in Ireland*. London: Croom Helm.

Brown, M. (1972). *The Politics of Irish Literature*. Seattle: University of Washington.

Brown, T. (1985). *Ireland: A Social and Cultural History, 1922 to the Present*. Ithaca: Cornell University Press.

Deane, S. (1985). *Celtic Revivals: Essays in Modern Irish Literature 1880–1980*. London: Faber & Faber.

Eglinton, J. (Ed.). (1899). *Literary Ideals in Ireland*. London: Unwin.

Foster, R.F. (1993). *Paddy and Mr. Punch: Connections in Irish and English History*. London: Allen Lane.

Gellner, E. (1983). *Nations and Nationalism*. Ithaca: Cornell University Press.

Gibbons, L. (1996). *Transformations in Irish Culture*. Notre Dame: University of Notre Dame Press.

Gregory, A. (Ed.). (1901). *Ideals in Ireland*. London: Unicorn.

Hobsbawm, E. (1990). *Nations and Nationalism since 1780: Programme, Myth, Reality*. Cambridge: Cambridge University Press.

Hroch, M. (1996). "From National Movement to the Fully-Formed Nation: The Nation-Building Process in Europe." In G. Balakrishnan (Ed.). *Mapping the Nation* (pp. 78–97). London: Verso.

Hutchinson, J. (1987). *The Dynamics of Cultural Nationalism: The Gaelic Revival and the Creation of the Irish Nation State*. London: Allen & Unwin.

Hyde, D. (1894) "The Necessity for De-Anglicising Ireland." In C.G. Duffy (Ed.). *The Revival of Irish Literature* (pp. 115–61). London: Unwin.

Joyce, J. (1959). *James Joyce: The Critical Writings*. E. Mason and R. Ellmann (Eds). New York: Viking.

Joyce, J. (1968). *A Portrait of the Artist as a Young Man*. New York: Viking.

Joyce, J. (1986). *Ulysses*. New York: Random House.

Kiberd, D. (1996). *Inventing Ireland: The Literature of the Modern Nation*. Cambridge, MA: Harvard University Press.

Kinsella, T. (1970). "The Irish Writer." In *Davis, Mangan, Ferguson? Tradition and the Irish Writer*. Dublin: Dolmen Press.

Lloyd, D. (1987). *Nationalism and Minor Literature: James Clarence Mangan and the Emergence of Irish Cultural Nationalism*. Berkeley: University of California Press.

Lloyd, D. (1993). *Anomalous States: Irish Writing and the Post-Colonial Moment*. Durham: Duke University Press.

Lyons, F.S.L. (1979). *Culture and Anarchy in Ireland, 1890–1939*. Oxford: Oxford University Press.

Mays, M. (2007). *Nation States: The Cultures of Irish Nationalism*. Lanham, MD: Lexington Books.

McDonagh, O. (1983). *States of Mind: A Study of Anglo-Irish Conflict, 1780–1980*. London: Allen & Unwin.

Moran, D.P. (1901). "The Battle of Two Civilizations." In A. Gregory (Ed.). *Ideals in Ireland* (pp. 25–41). London: Unwin.

Mosse, G. (1993). *Confronting the Nation: Jewish and Western Nationalism*. Hanover, NH: Brandeis University Press.

Nairn, T. (1981). *The Break-up of Britain: Crisis and Neo-Nationalism*. London: Verso Books.

Nora, P. (Ed.). (1996). *Realms of Memory: Rethinking the French Past*, vol. I: *Conflicts and Divisions*. L.D. Kritzman (Ed.), A. Goldhammer (Trans.). New York: Columbia University Press. First published in French 1992.

Pearse, P. (1952). *Political Writings and Speeches*. Dublin: Talbot Press.

Renan, E. (1990). "What Is a Nation?" M. Thom (Trans.). In H. Bhabha (Ed.). *Nation and Narration* (pp. 8–22). New York: Routledge.

Shaw, G.B. (1907). *John Bull's Other Island*. New York: Brentano's.

Yeats, W.B. (1955). *Autobiographies*. London: Macmillan.

Yeats, W.B. (1961). *Essays and Introductions*. London: Macmillan.

Yeats, W.B. (1962). *Explorations*. London: Macmillan.

Žižek, Slavoj. (1991). *For They Know Not What They Do: Enjoyment as a Political Factor*. London: Verso.

31

Defining Irishness: Bernard Shaw and the Irish Connection on the English Stage

Christopher Innes

Together with Samuel Beckett, Bernard Shaw is by far the most eminent modern dramatist born and raised in Ireland – both were Nobel Prize winners (1925, 1969). Yet Shaw is also generally omitted from most discussions of Irish drama, or at best banished to a footnote. Even so, he is representative of Irish drama in several ways. His career illuminates the historical relationship between theater in Ireland and in England. He interprets the cause of Ireland (with his own idiosyncratic perspective) to the English public – even though, like several other twentieth-century Irish drama-tists, his plays about Ireland were initially denied a production in Ireland. Apart from his younger contemporary, James Fagan, Shaw also counts as the last major Irish playwright to move to London and write the majority of his dramatic work for English audiences – although there has of course been one far more recent converse case, where a London dramatist with Irish roots, Martin McDonagh, wrote a series of plays accepted in Ireland as part of the Irish tradition (see CHAPTER 57, MARTIN MCDONAGH AND THE ETHICS OF IRISH STORYTELLING). Shaw's long career thus marks a significant turning point in Irish theater. He was also a champion of both the Abbey Theatre in Dublin – reminding us that it was from England that the crucial support came in founding the Abbey, from Annie Horniman, pioneer of the British Repertory Theatre Movement – and of a playwright such as Sean O'Casey when O'Casey was banished from the Abbey.

For a start, Shaw was one in the long line of playwrights – and indeed actors as well as managers – from Dublin who migrated to the larger audiences of London. Historically this was always a one-way movement, beginning perhaps with Roger Boyle (the first earl of Orrery) in the seventeenth century. Naturally, since Boyle began writing heroic tragedy in response to a direct suggestion by Charles II, his first play, *The Generall*, might have been tried out in Dublin, at a private performance in 1662,

A Companion to Irish Literature, edited by Julia M. Wright
© 2010 Blackwell Publishing Ltd

but from the start it was destined for London. (In a letter, Charles II wrote to Boyle that he had "read your first play, which I like very well and doe intend to bring it upon the Stage, as Soone as my Company have their new Stage in order" [Braverman 1993:37].) Similarly, barely a generation later, the English stage was almost literally invaded from its colony across the water, playwrights with Irish connections populating the whole genre of comedy through the eighteenth century: Farquhar and Goldsmith crossing from Dublin, where Sheridan had been born, while even Congreve, the major English contributor, had been educated at Trinity College Dublin. However, it should be noted that it was not simply the lure of brighter lights that led these Irish playwrights to abandon Dublin: Farquhar was forced out by having wounded a fellow actor on the stage; Goldsmith took up residence in London as a physician, and only later turned to writing; Sheridan came over with his parents, who settled in Bath, and was educated in England. They were followed in the nineteenth century by John O'Keeffe, Dion Boucicault, Oscar Wilde, and of course Shaw himself. All feature in *The Cambridge History of British Theatre*, while they are only too often omitted from histories of Irish theater – although this blind spot was remedied by Christopher Morash's 2002 *History of Irish Theatre, 1600–2000*. Arguably the whole sensibility of Restoration comedy was Irish, even though, with the single exception of Sir Lucius O'Trigger in Sheridan's *The Rivals* (1775), almost none of the characters or the settings had any hint of Ireland. Sir Lucius – hot-tempered and intemperate, impecunious and scheming, impetuously violent but sentimental and given to claims of good fellowship – established the cliché outline of the stage Irishman, and the only piece of Restoration comedy set in Ireland was in direct response to the public appreciation of Sir Lucius, since Sheridan wrote a one-act comic opera, *St. Patrick's Day; or, The Scheming Lieutenant*, for a benefit performance given for the actor playing Sir Lucius, Lawrence Clinch, in May 1775. So while the playwrights maintained Irish connections – *St. Patrick's Day* was performed in Dublin; Farquhar was given a commission in earl of Orrery's regiment to stave off penury, and wrote *The Recruiting Officer* (1706) based on his experiences – few of the references in their plays are Irish (on many of the above writers, see the essays in Volume I).

Such a historical overview underlines the significance of the founding of the Irish Literary Theatre by Yeats, Lady Gregory, and Edward Martyn in 1897, six years after Shaw's influential essay on *The Quintessence of Ibsenism* had been published, when Shaw had already written eight plays for the London stage. Setting out to create a Celtic and Irish school of drama, through the example of their own plays, Yeats, Martyn, and Lady Gregory effectively created a demand for plays on Irish themes, which made it possible for dramatists like Synge to remain in Dublin. At the same time, Irish dramatists – such as Sheridan or Shaw – writing for the English or, in the case of Boucicault, American theater, initiated important themes in Irish drama.

On the one hand Boyle's early tragedy, *The Generall*, contains a strong autobiographical – and thus Irish – relevance. As Baron Broghill, Boyle had supported Cromwell militarily, and helped to rule Ireland for the Commonwealth, only after Cromwell's death turning to Charles II (for which he was rewarded by being named earl of Orrery). Despite its neoclassical character names and idealized settings, his play exactly mirrored the situation of the Protestant Ascendancy, with its eponymous hero (Clorimum) choosing to serve a usurper and regicide for the good of the state, but finally turning to rescue the legitimate heir and reinstate him on the throne. All too typically of this style of tragedy, love – not money, personal aggrandizement, or power – is presented as the prime motivation; but the connection with politics was underlined by Charles II lending his own coronation robes (to clothe the restored prince) for the 1664 production. Following Boyle's play, the general who goes through a double betrayal became a recurring figure in Irish drama, while Boyle's own plays continued to address highly topical themes in romantic disguise – as with *Mustapha* (1665), which castigated Charles II's notorious promiscuity through the picture of a Muslim ruler undone by his harem.

More directly, in terms of Irish relevance, Sheridan's parodistic characterization of Lucius O'Trigger established the figure of the "stage Irishman," while Boucicault's hugely popular Irish melodramas – *The Colleen Bawn* (1860), *Arrah-na-Pogue* (1864), and *The Shaughraun* (1874) (see CHAPTER 28, DION BOUCICAULT) – set the scene for the Dublin Queen's Royal Theatre melodramas of Irish rebellion, political martyrdom, and heroic sacrifice, such as J.W. Whitbread's *Lord Edward, or '98* (1894) and *Wolfe Tone* (1901), and P.J. Bourke's *For Ireland's Liberty* (1914) and *For the Land She Loved* (1915 – advertised in *The Hibernian* with the slogan "Who fears to speak of '98?" (*Hibernian*, November 13, 1915, 8; reproduced in Herr 1991:312). Bourke indeed was responsible for making the first Irish film, *Ireland a Nation*, which was shown only once, on January 8, 1917, and banned the next day. These melodramas may be now forgotten, but at the time they were far more political and far more popular than the plays of the Irish Literary Theatre. And Shaw was closely involved in the Irish Literary Theatre; corresponding with Yeats, visiting Lady Gregory, and perhaps most directly through his influence on Edward Martyn.

Martyn had become a strong supporter of Ibsen, possibly through attending Shaw's lectures on *The Quintessence of Ibsenism* (a book he certainly knew) as well as from seeing the first productions of *A Doll's House* (with Janet Achurch in 1898) and *Hedda Gabler* (with Elizabeth Robins in 1891) – in both of which Shaw was deeply involved. For the time, Ibsen was not only the apostle of naturalism, but also the poet of nationalism and liberation, as the voice of the new Norwegian nation who even helped to forge a language independent of the previous colonial power (Denmark) – all of which were aims shared by the Irish Literary Theatre. In contrast to Yeats' poetic myth and Lady Gregory's peasant folk-comedies, Martyn specifically followed Ibsen with his play *The Heather Field*, performed in 1900 as part of the Irish Literary Theatre's opening season. This psychological tragedy depicts, with unrelenting realism, the disintegrating marriage and financial collapse of a landowner in the west of Ireland, which is mirrored in his unsuccessful battle to root the heather out of his field. (And, Martyn being the first president of Sinn Féin, his play contains very clear political referents, with the landowner Corden Tyrell representing the Protestant Ascendancy, while the heather that outlasts him symbolizes the triumph of the native Irish spirit.)

Beyond this indirect influence Shaw also intervened very overtly in English–Irish politics, with two plays set mainly in Ireland: the short *O'Flaherty, V.C.* and *John Bull's Other Island*. Surprisingly few of his other plays contain Irish characters. The most obvious example, Sir Patrick Cullen in *The Doctor's Dilemma*, who is presented as one of the more sympathetic medical men, is a relatively minor figure, although there is also a very specific Irish setting for one section of his massive Pentateuch, *Back to Methuselah*. This is the pier in *The Tragedy of an Elderly Gentleman*, where the characters land when they arrive at the blessed island of near-immortal "long-livers." It is modeled on the pier at Lady Gregory's country house in Ireland, where Shaw and his wife stayed in the summer of 1920 while he was working on the script.

Like most of the Irish playwrights who went across to England for other reasons than being drawn specifically to London as a theatrical center, Shaw made the transition from Dublin as an autodidact. He forged a name for himself as a political lecturer and leading light of the Fabian Society (which would become the kernel of the British Labour Party), and as a music critic – his reviews still being recognized as among the best of musical criticism – before turning to the theater. Even then he began as a drama critic and a novelist. As a result, in sharp contrast to all the previous Irish playwrights who had come to London, Shaw's dramaturgical approach was political. Living and writing in England for his whole working life, while always aware of his Irish heritage, gave Shaw a unique perspective for his plays; and this independent perspective gave his critique additional point. Undoubtedly his Irish background fueled Shaw's attack on imperialism, possibly most obviously in *Caesar and Cleopatra* – which has an ironic imperialist reversal in Caesar's colonial secretary Britannus – but it also underlies several other works, from *Captain Brassbound's Conversion* and *The Devil's Disciple* to *The Simpleton of the Unexpected Isles*. However, *O'Flaherty, V.C.* and *John Bull's Other Island* had a far more significant impact, with the context of their performance or, in the case of *O'Flaherty, V.C.*, non-performance, giving them almost unique political status.

Like the writings of several other twentieth-century Irish dramatists, Shaw's plays about Ireland were initially denied a production there. (The riots against Synge's *Playboy of the Western World* come to mind, as do the fraught relationship between O'Casey and the Abbey, or the exile of Beckett – along with James Joyce.) Although, according to Shaw, it was written in 1904 at the request of Yeats, *John Bull's Other Island* was rejected and put on instead in London, then later again refused by the Abbey in 1909 – and it was only finally staged by the Abbey in September 1916. In his 1906 preface to the play, Shaw puts the initial refusal down to his play being "a very uncompromising presentment of the real old Ireland" which thus made it "uncongenial to the whole spirit of the neo-Gaelic movement, which is bent on creating a new Ireland after its own ideal" (Shaw 1984:7). However, one of the real reasons was probably Shaw's sporting with national and class stereotypes, in particular the "stage Irishman," represented in the play by Tim Haffigan. When he first appears Haffigan is full of clichéd expressions such as "top o' the morning" or "Begorra," and projecting stereotypical views of the Irish such as "Dhrink is the curse o me unhappy country. I take it meself because Ive a wake heart and a poor digestion, but in principle I'm a teetoatler" (while insisting on larger measure of whiskey), or "I confess to good nature: its an Irish wakeness, I'd share me last shillin with a friend" (when begging for extra money) (71–74). And Haffigan, who is also described in derogatory terms as "*a stunted, shortnecked man … with a small bullet head, a red nose, and furtive eyes*" who "*might be a tenth-rate schoolmaster ruined by drink*," has an accent specifically labeled "*a rollicking stage brogue*" (71). At the same time, when he is challenged, his speech lapses into "*a common would-be genteel accent with a … strain of Glasgow in it*" and we learn that Haffigan "never was in Ireland in his life" (76, 78). As Larry Doyle, a civil engineer who is also Irish but whose accent is entirely English, remarks, talking to his stereotypical English partner Broadbent, "all this top-o'-the-morning and broth-of-a-boy and more-power-to-your-elbow business is got up in England to fool you" into letting "him drink and sponge and brag as long as he flatters your sense of moral superiority by playing the fool and degrading himself and his country" (78).

Along the same lines, on the surface the depiction of Ireland is hardly flattering. The village of Roscullen, with no hotel but seventeen pubs, is peopled by eccentrics such as Keegan, fantastically conversing with an insect. A young man is depicted as showing "*an instinctively acquired air of helplessness and silliness … Englishmen think him half-witted*," while Haffigan's uncle is introduced as having "*a surliness that is meant to be aggressive*" (92, 109). But again we are shown that this is only a surface deception – except that here it is the colonial context that determines the adoption of such "typical" mannerisms. So the youth turns out to be an acute observer, and his apparent simple-mindedness has been adopted because of a "*constant dread of hostile dominance, which he habitually tries to disarm … by pretending to be a much greater fool than he really is*" and indeed being thought half-witted by the English imperialists "*is exactly what he intends them to think*" (92). As for Haffigan's uncle, we learn that he and his brother had cleared stony land to grow potatoes, only to have "the landlord put a rent of £5 a year on them, and turned them out when they couldn't pay," and his surliness "*is in effect pathetic*," expressing only the harshness of his existence (111, 109). By contrast, Roscullen itself may look idyllic, with its unspoilt surroundings and ancient round tower but, to the characters who know the place but have enough outside experience to see it objectively, the village is the epitome of wasted potential – and indeed an icon of Ireland itself. Larry Doyle: "The dullness! The hopelessness! The ignorance! The bigotry! … that hell of littleness and monotony!" (80, 84). Or Keegan:

> … Which would you say this country was: hell or purgatory?
> *The Grasshopper.*   X
> *The Man.*   Hell! Faith, I'm afraid you're right.
>
> (91)

This would be enough to raise the hackles of the Abbey audience. However, Shaw does not depict it as a natural state of affairs. A change in the political context would offer hope for a new future:

Keegan.   Could you have told me this morning where hell is? Yet you know now that
        it is here. Do not despair of finding heaven: it may be no further off.
Larry. [*ironically*]   On this holy ground, as you call it, eh?
Keegan. [*with fierce intensity*]   Yes, perhaps even on this holy ground which such Irishmen
        as you have turned into a Land of Derision.

                                                                                    (161)

Larry Doyle is a one-time Fenian ("now an older and possibly foolisher man" [118])
and a socialist; and his prescription exactly echoes part of Shaw's preface to the play:
that Ireland has to establish a minimum wage, because using the common people's
"poverty to undersell England in the markets of the world" (119) leads to mutually
ruinous industrial competition in which England is forced to take over Ireland in self-
defense (a typically Shavian rationale for colonialism). But in this play Shaw gives
himself two mouthpieces: not only Doyle, the civil engineer (playing perhaps on
Shaw's attempts at "social engineering" on the political level through pamphleteering
for the Fabian Society), but also Keegan, the mad priest, whose stylistic approach is
an exact description of Shaw's own: Keegan says, "My way of joking is to tell the truth.
It's the funniest joke in the world" (95). And like Shaw himself, Keegan has been to
"great cities [where] I saw wonders I have never seen in Ireland. But when I came back
to Ireland I found all the wonders there waiting for me. You see they had been there
all the time, but my eyes had never been opened to them. I did not know what my
own house was like, because I had never been outside it" (95). The same objectivity
applies to Doyle, but Doyle has sold out both his Fenian roots and his socialist principles, as Broadbent's business partner – possibly echoing a sense in Shaw himself that
by establishing himself in England he has also in a sense sold Ireland out.
    Indeed (as a stand-in for John Bull) Broadbent represents English imperialist – and
even postcolonialist – capitalism, and is used in the play to expose the way Ireland is
economically exploited. Broadbent's syndicate has been buying up all of Roscullen:
"Doolen's [pub] is a tied house, and the brewers are in the syndicate. As to Haffigan's
farm and Doran's mill and [Larry's father's] place and half a dozen others, they will
be mortgaged to me before a month is out" (156). And in a remarkably telling forecast
of current sub-prime mortgage scandals, their method is to loan far more than the
land is worth – Larry is quite willing to do this to his own father – knowing
the locals will not be able to pay the interest, aiming to foreclose the moment they
default. This is sound business because (as Broadbent assures the incredulous Keegan)
the capital, knowledge, and organization of the syndicate can make ten times as much
out of the properties as their original owners. In return for dispossessing everyone,
Broadbent promises a luxury golfing hotel and "public institutions: a library, a poly-
technic (undenominational, of course), a gymnasium, a cricket club, perhaps an art
school. I shall make a Garden City of Roscullen" (158). When Keegan accuses them
of planning deliberate bankruptcy of their own syndicate, in order to "get rid of its
original shareholders very efficiently" so they can acquire the new properties they have
built "for a few shillings in the pound," the stage directions note, *"Broadbent and Larry*

look quickly at one another; for this, unless the priest is an old financial hand, must be inspiration." Keegan goes on to excoriate this vision of material prosperity, foretelling:

> you will drive Haffigan to America very efficiently; you will find a use for Barney Doran's
> foul mouth and bullying temper by employing him to slave-drive your laborers very
> efficiently; and [*low and bitter*] when at last this poor desolate countryside becomes a
> busy mint in which we shall all slave to make money for you, with our Polytechnic to
> teach us how to do it efficiently, and ... then no doubt your English and American
> shareholders will spend all the money we make for them ... in gluttony and gambling
> [at the hotel]; and you will devote what they save to fresh land development schemes.
> (160)

While acknowledging (indeed applauding) the truth of this dystopian vision, Broadbent is also a Liberal – a reader of P.B. Shelley and John Ruskin, with a portrait of Gladstone on his wall, who firmly believes himself to be "a lover of freedom, like every true Englishman" (72). Earlier he had reacted with fury, threatening to shoot a landlord – for having done precisely what he himself is proposing to do – and he believes in Home Rule for Ireland (which in 1904 had seemed not only the most freedom England could be expected to grant, but also a real possibility). In the 1906 "Preface for Politicians," Shaw argues strongly for Home Rule as "a Natural Right" – but the play undercuts this version of Irish freedom. The parliamentary seat of Roscullen is up for grabs; Broadbent wins the locals' vote by promising to fight for Home Rule, but his aim of course is to make his land development scheme still more profitable, while his business has convinced him "that frontiers are hindrances and flags confounded nuisances" and that the job of civil engineers is "to join countries, not to separate them" (33, 84). He also gets the girl – winning her from Doyle, with whom she has been in love ever since he left for England eighteen years before. Nora is not only an inversion of Ibsen's heroine (after whom she is named) but also clearly represents Ireland: attractive and "*ethereal*" to Broadbent, "*To Larry Doyle, helpless, useless, almost sexless ... an incarnation of everything in Ireland that drove him out of it*" (94). Before we meet Nora, Doyle attacks the sentimental image of Ireland: "you've got to call the unfortunate island Kathleen ni Houlihan and pretend she's a little old woman. It saves thinking. It saves working. It saves everything except imagination" (81). And this ironic attack on Yeats' and Lady Gregory's nationalistic 1902 play (where Ireland is figured as an old woman who is transformed by patriotic sacrifice into a young girl with "the walk of a queen") reminds us that this sort of duality is an echo of Kathleen ni Houlihan, so that Broadbent's wedding to Nora becomes a truly grotesque ending. While the play is a call to English politicians for Irish independence, the marriage is a warning of continuing postcolonial exploitation, and the fate of Nora a demand that the Irish abandon romantic nationalist rhetoric for economic action.

In the 1906 preface to *John Bull's Other Island* – specifically addressed "for Politicians" – Shaw explicitly discusses the evils of imperialism, citing the Denshawai atrocity (a typically draconian colonialist military response to civil disobedience in Egypt in

1906) as an argument for Home Rule, and *O'Flaherty V.C.* follows this up with a comic view of the military in Ireland. Written in the middle of World War I, the play can be seen as a continuation (along other lines) of Shaw's notoriously provocative pamphlet *Common Sense About the War*, which had arouse public outrage following its November 1914 publication – and in which Shaw specifically underlined his Irish identity, claiming only an outsider could comment objectively on the conflict.

This one-act farce deals with a hot political issue of the times: the Irish who joined up to fight against Germany for England, instead of fighting against England for Irish independence. Later subtitled "A Recruiting Pamphlet" (although its original subtitle was innocuous: "An Interlude"), its proposed staging at the Abbey in November 1915 would have coincided with an actual recruiting campaign being run by the newly organized Department of Recruiting for Ireland, which had opened just a month earlier. Indeed the same copy of the Dublin *Freeman's Journal* (the organ of the Irish Parliamentary Party, led by John Redmond) where the Abbey announcement of *O'Flaherty V.C.* appeared, also carried a piece on the need for Irish recruits, and the front page of the following day's issue was covered with an advertisement calling for "50,000 Irishmen to join their brave comrades in Irish regiments" (Holloway: October 30, 1915:1). The actual campaign was a relative failure, enlisting only 6,050 men (1,535 from Belfast and only 957 from Dublin – numbers that would hardly cover a month's casualties, which the *Freeman's Journal* had estimated as "wastage" of 1,100 men a week, a figure that would be soon dwarfed by the Somme battles).

The recruiting drive had involved a real Irish holder of the Victoria Cross, Lieutenant Michael O'Leary, and it is no accident that, in reporting that *O'Flaherty V.C.* had been censored, the *Freeman's Journal* deliberately mistitled Shaw's play *Michael O'Flaherty V.C.* and even *O'Leary V.C.* to inflame controversy (Arrington 2008:98). While Shaw later found it necessary to make a public statement in the *Irish Independent*, claiming that "the gratuitous identification of O'Flaherty with O'Leary is extremely annoying to me" (Holloway: November 20, 1915), there is certainly an echo of his name in the title, and the description of the way O'Flaherty exaggerates in his recruiting speeches – "that story about your fighting the Kaiser and the twelve giants of the Prussian guard singlehanded would be better for a little toning down" (Shaw 1965b:820) – would clearly have been read as a satiric comment on O'Leary. Moreover, in a letter to Lady Gregory in September 1915, while he was working on the script, Shaw claimed, "The picture of the Irish character will make the Playboy seem a patriotic rhapsody by comparison. ... The idea is that O'Flaherty's experience in the trenches has induced in him a terrible realism and an unbearable candor. He sees Ireland as it is ... and he goes back to the dreaded trenches joyfully for the sake of peace and quietness" (Shaw 1985:309).

The reference to the riots over Synge's *Playboy of the Western World* shows that Shaw fully intended his play to be provocative, and his anti-hero demolishes the "patriotism" of both the English – whom the eponymous hero describes as running about "like frightened chickens, uttering all manner of nonsense" under its influence – and the Irish, whose patriotic fervor is represented by O'Flaherty's mother, "only a silly ignorant old countrywoman ... with all your fine talk about Ireland" (Shaw 1965b:823, 827). Shaw has O'Flaherty say,

> what good has it ever done here in Ireland? It's kept me ignorant, because it filled up my mother's mind, and she thought it ought to fill up mine too. It's kept Ireland poor, because instead of trying to better ourselves we thought we was the fine fellows of patriots when we were speaking evil of Englishmen that was as poor as ourselves. (821)

Neither the authorities in Dublin Castle nor the nationalists, who less than six months later would be leading the Easter Uprising, would have supported the message, which was that "no war is right," and that "Youll never have a quiet world til you knock the patriotism out of the human race" (822, 823). If this wasn't enough, heroism itself is discredited. The only reason O'Flaherty has stood up so bravely to the Germans and killed so many is that he "was afeard that, if I didn't, theyd kill me"; the award of the Victoria Cross is presented as accidental, because "there's hundreds of men as brave as me that never had the luck to get anything for their bravery but a curse from the sergeant, and the blame for the faults of them that ought to have been their betters," while his only reason for fighting for the British instead of the Germans is purely mercenary: they offer a bigger "separation allowance" (821, 822, 825). Even this motivation is mocked since the army deducts over half his mother's allowance to pay for his food at the front.

At first glance, such sentiments, in the context of 1915, would seem sufficient to get the play banned; and the popular legend of the time was reflected in the *New York Times* report, when the play was first performed in America in 1922. The review of the Irish Players New York premiere states, "This Shavian hit, written during the war, was promptly put down by a relentless British censor, but in the last six months it has been given one or two special performances in London" (June 22, 1920:15). However, in fact the authorities were willing to let *O'Flaherty V.C.* be performed, while preferring the opening to be postponed until the recruiting drive was over. And it was the Abbey management (in the figure of one of the Trustees, W.F. Bailey, as well as Yeats, who wrote to Bailey that it should be postponed indefinitely) who were responsible for suppressing the play. The Abbey's reluctance to challenge the Castle authorities has been put down to the insolvency of the company due to wartime conditions (Arrington 2008:87–88). But the record shows that this did not in fact prevent the Abbey from defying the government, since the play that replaced the scheduled triple bill of *O'Flaherty V.C.*, Synge's *The Shadow of the Glen*, and *Duty* by Seamus O'Brien on the Abbey stage was a revival of *For the Land She Loved*, Bourke's melodrama, which had been labeled "a piece of sedition" by the authorities when it opened at the Queen's Royal Theatre just seven months earlier (de Búrca 1983:4). Indeed the advertising slogan, "Who fears to speak of '98?," was created for this Abbey Theatre production.

Ironically, since it demonstrates that the military had little problem with Shaw's play, the first performance of *O'Flaherty V.C.* was by British soldiers at the Front.

Robert Loraine, who had played Tanner (Shaw's alter ego) in *Man and Superman* and who became a military hero in the Royal Flying Corps during World War I, produced the play at "The Theatre Royal" for the troops stationed in Belgium, in February 1917 – with Shaw, on an official visit to the Western Front, attending the dress rehearsal. The play could be given a patriotic twist, as Shaw did, when he claimed (in the preface to the published edition) that it was in fact "a recruiting poster in disguise" (Shaw 1965a:ii, 475–76), arguing that his protagonist's example of going to war to escape from the women in his life and the boredom of home was a more attractive reason for enlisting than the official propaganda. But this is, in fact, an attack on Irish nationalism. And indeed, when the Abbey finally did perform the play in 1920–21 – the production referred to by the *New York Times* (above) – it was only in England with the touring company. *O'Flaherty V.C.* was still felt to be too much of a challenge to nationalist sensitivities, even more than a year after the end of the Great War (which Shaw's O'Flaherty had derided as "a big war; but that's not the same thing" [Shaw 1965b:821]). As Yeats' biographer remarks, "the world had changed. Even then they risked it only in London" (Foster 2003:29).

It is a measure of the political effectiveness of this short farce that it was only performed on the Abbey stage in November 1927 when, as a review in the *Irish Statesman* noted, after waiting "twelve years to salute the Dublin public," O'Flaherty's "uniform had faded a bit and his decorations grown a little tarnished" (Holloway: November 26, 1927:281). Since of course copies of the text had been sent to politicians and civil servants during the process of suppressing the original Abbey production, it could be said that this was a case where censorship itself made a banned work more politically effective. Among the recipients of the text was Sir Horace Plunkett, one of the most eminent Anglo-Irish politicians, who became a friend of Shaw's and was to play a leading role in the Anglo-Irish Treaty in October 1921 – which motivated the re-mounting of *John Bull's Other Island* precisely at that time, in the hope of influencing the outcome of the negotiations.

In addition to these dramatic forays into Irish politics, over the first decades of the twentieth century Shaw effectively headed an Irish theatrical mafia in the London theater, centered around James Fagan: actor, director, playwright, and a major London impresario of the period. Like Shaw, Fagan was Irish, even serendipitously sharing the same middle name although born in Belfast instead of Dublin, and almost twenty years younger than Shaw. Unlike Shaw, Fagan took a law degree at Trinity College Dublin before starting a career as an actor, debuting with F.R. Benson's company in 1895. But the two were very close. Like Shaw, Fagan supported O'Casey in his problems with the Abbey Theatre, in addition to producing the British premiere of *Juno and the Paycock* in 1924 as well as the London premiere of *The Plough and the Stars* in 1926. Fagan's productions were highly successful, and marked the establishment of O'Casey on the London stage.

Both Shaw and Fagan also championed the challenge to social morality represented by Eugène Brieux, with Shaw writing a provocative introduction to an English collection of three Brieux plays translated by Fagan – one of which, *Damaged Goods*, marked Fagan's debut as a producer in 1917 – while Fagan himself translated at least one other play by Brieux, *False Gods*, which was published in a collection together with *Woman on her Own* translated by Shaw's wife, Charlotte Payne-Townshend. Fagan's first original play, *The Rebel*, premiered in 1899, is the only one of his fifteen plays in which Fagan addressed Irish topics or history – about the same percentage as in Shaw's work. A fairly standard combination of romance and melodrama, and fueled by Irish sentiment, *The Rebel* was highly popular in Dublin. Meanwhile, on Broadway the role of "Hellcat" Ryan attracted a star of the time, Edward Aiken (who specialized in Irish romantic parts and went on to appear in *The Bold Sojer Boy* and a revival of Boucicault's 1865 *Arrah-na-Pogue*), while the songs from the play became popular favorites, among them Andrew Mack's serenade "Oh my love!" and "Eyes of Blue" as well as a hymn to freedom and Ireland, "Tara, you shall hear the harp once more," and in 1915 *The Rebel* was turned into a film starring Alan Doone. Like Shaw too, all the rest of Fagan's plays were aimed at the English or (particularly in Fagan's case) American market.

There were close personal as well as professional connections between Fagan and Shaw. So, for instance, in 1905 Fagan wrote and staged a one-act skit, *Shakespeare versus Shaw*. Picking up on, and quoting from, the preface to Shaw's *Caesar and Cleopatra*, it presents a trial for libel brought by the long-dead Shakespeare against Shaw for his assertion that he was "Better than Shakespeare." Fagan's short play marks the very first time Shaw figured in his own right as a dramatist on the stage, as well as the first dramatization of what was to become a popular theme: the Shaw vs. Shakespeare combat. (Over the past century there have been over eighty-four plays and at least two musicals featuring Shaw as a character, including several which represent him in conflict with Shakespeare; see Dietrich 1992.) As the advertisement for the piece makes clear, Shaw was already a famous enough figure to be instantly recognizable when performed as a character on the stage – indeed he was on the same level as the most important theater manager of the Edwardian age, Herbert Beerbohm Tree:

> *Mr. Cyril Maude will represent the poet who was "not for an age, but for all time," and Mr. Edmund Maurice will do the same for the philosophic jester or jesting philosopher who would probably prefer to write himself inversely as "not for all time, but for his age" ... while Miss Annie Hughes, and Miss Irene Vanbrugh, Mr. George Alexander, and Mr. Lewis Waller will appear as themselves, and Mr. Tree will be represented by another actor who will imitate him.* (Fagan 1970:105)

In the play itself, George Alexander appears as two identical people: his public personality as an actor and his "lost ... identity" (117) as a real person, but the subtext to this humor is the challenge by an Irish iconoclast to a cultural icon definitely representing Britain. All these actors are witnesses for the prosecution, with Beerbohm Tree declaring that "Shakespeare to me is a religion" and calling Shaw's claim to be better than Shakespeare, "a very serious joke." The jury is composed entirely of modern dramatists, with the foreman of the jury being J.M. Barrie, who, as one direction indicates, "tr{ies} to make himself popular in the role of a stage Irishman" (126), in an obvious reference to Shaw's 1904 hit, John Bull's Other Island, running at the time at the Royal Court. Hence the outcome of the trial is doubly ironic: "in the case of two such miserable dramatists ... It is a choice of evils" (130). Shaw is found guilty, and – in a reprise of the 1877 Whistler v. Ruskin trial – Shakespeare is awarded damages of one farthing. Shaw's Man and Superman (in rehearsal at the time Fagan's skit was performed) was also echoed: as one witness points out, "there is a character closely resembling Mr. Shaw himself, who ... In the second act ... is discovered in hell" – and so, on claiming that he can't pay, Shaw is dragged down to hell by Shakespeare, who proclaims that it will be Shaw's "punishment for all eternity to listen to my plays performed by the swollen ghosts of actor-managers" (118–19, 130). Forcing Shaw to his knees, Shakespeare leans on his head instead of the pile of books, announcing, "that is thy proper attitude, base Shaw, to me" (130–31).

Given that this "crushing" of the Irish upstart was written and presented by a fellow Irishman, the attack is very much tongue-in-cheek. Both Shaw and Fagan were members of the Dramatists' Club, which met twice a month for lunch at its London premises, and when during World War I Shaw was expelled for his provocative pamphlet Commonsense about the War, Fagan was one of a group who supported Shaw. Then the revival of Pygmalion by Beerbohm Tree's daughter Viola Tree, at the Aldwych in February 1920, was transferred to the Duke of York's Theatre under Fagan's management. So when, three years after the end of hostilities, Shaw felt it would be possible to have his "war play" Heartbreak House produced in England, he turned to Fagan, who had earlier taken over the Royal Court Theatre, where so many of Shaw's earlier plays had been staged. In addition to Fagan's wife, Mary Grey, as Hesione, an Irish actress, Ellen O'Malley (who had performed Nora in the first production of John Bull's Other Island), played the main female character, Ellie Dunn – a casting Shaw strongly supported against the united criticism of reviewers, stating that he "took the greatest care ... that she should be in the sharpest contrast to all the heartbreakers ... The contrast is forced almost to discordance by having Ellie played by a very Irish actress" and commenting, "Only an Irish critic will understand" (Shaw 1985:744, 743).

The London Heartbreak House production may have been a failure, running for only sixty-three performances (half the number of the Theatre Guild production in New York), and leaving Fagan so much in debt that he was forced to abandon the Royal Court. Shaw may have criticized Fagan for having too little faith in the play, and encouraging the actors to "gabble" through their parts, thus making it impossible for them to present the characters (Shaw 1985:750). Fagan owed Shaw over £7,000 in royalty payments after the production, which Shaw, in a letter to Fagan's solicitors, effectively waived, writing generously that only if other creditors foreclosed would he put in a claim: "otherwise he may dismiss it from his mind until his next period of prosperity" (Shaw 1985:776). When he took over the Oxford Playhouse as its first director in 1923, Fagan's opening production was in fact a Shaw play – Heartbreak House. Shaw attended rehearsals and the closing performance, and the cast included a very young Tyrone Guthrie, a descendant of the Irish actor William Tyrone Power, who is known as having rehabilitated the derogatory image of the "stage Irishman" through the way he presented Irish-themed plays, such as Catherine Gore's *King O'Neil* in 1835, his own 1837 *St. Patrick's Eve*, or Eugene Macarthy's *Charles O'Malley* in 1838 (Cave 1991). This time, *Heartbreak House* was so successful that at the end of the final performance Shaw addressed the audience with a variation on the speech he had given at the opening of *Arms and the Man* almost exactly thirty years before, claiming that from the audience's "empty-headed laughter" he appeared "to have written a bedroom farce" instead of "a semi-tragic play after the manner of Chekhov" (Denham 1958:112).

Under Fagan the Oxford Playhouse became very much a Shaw theater. For his opening production in 1924 he chose *Captain Brassbound's Conversion*, followed by *Candida*, while, in addition to *Heartbreak House*, 1926 also saw a revival of *Arms and the Man*. *Heartbreak House* was staged yet again a year later, forming part of an Oxford Playhouse five-week season at the Theatre Royal in Glasgow in 1927, a year when Fagan also staged *The Philanderer* (with Shaw attending some rehearsals) and *Androcles and the Lion*; and in 1928 he also staged *You Never can Tell*. Altogether, even though productions of his own London plays and Broadway transfers took up a great deal of his time, during the five years he was associated with the Oxford Playhouse, Fagan's Shaw productions rivaled those of the Birmingham Repertory, which Barry Jackson had turned into Shaw's English stage home. In short, Fagan's significance in Shaw's career underlines the central Irish presence in English theater.

Quite apart from Shaw, Fagan promoted Irish drama and Irish actors throughout his time in London. For instance, he introduced Lennox Robinson to the London stage (as well as to Broadway), producing his best-known comedy, *The Whiteheaded Boy* – first performed by the Abbey in 1916, and still frequently revived today – which had a highly successful run at the Ambassadors' Theatre in Fagan's production through 1921. When in 1921 the Abbey Theatre, which had been losing money for some time, was forced to close (along with the other Dublin theaters) because of the curfew imposed on Dublin in response to the War of Independence then raging in Ireland, it was to Fagan and Shaw that it turned. The Abbey actress Sara Allgood, who had performed in the 1920 presentation of *O'Flaherty V.C.* at the Stage Society, went to persuade Shaw to give a talk for an Abbey fundraising matinee at the Ambassadors in March of that year. He refused, offering instead to write a newspaper piece advertising this performance of three short plays by Synge and Lady Gregory, leading Lady Gregory to lament, "A letter for me from G.B.S. refusing a lecture for our Theatre fund. He says he is overworked and I'm afraid it is true, but I wish some of his work could be given to Ireland" (Laurence and Grene 1993:157). This was in response to a letter in which Shaw had declared, "I have given up the Dublin [political] people as hopeless. I might as well talk to the cockles on Sandymount Strand. They are not a bit in earnest about the national question, and never have been. It is something to talk about: that is all" (Laurence and Grene 1993:156–57). In his metaphor about talking to the cockles, Shaw is identifying himself with the character of Keegan in

John Bull's Other Island, although of course grasshoppers are far more capable of responding than a bivalve mollusk (close cousin to the clam – the epitome of silence); and his disparagement of Irish politics is perhaps an anticipation of the civil war which was to break out in Ireland barely a year later.

But in May Shaw did, after all, give a fundraising lecture (following Yeats, Lady Gregory, and St John Ervine) in a series organized and hosted by Fagan at his Chelsea home, even if he chose to talk solely about theater instead of politics. Just two weeks later, in June, Fagan lent the Court Theatre to the Irish Players for another performance of *Rising of the Moon*, *Workhouse Ward*, and *Riders to the Sea*, at which Shaw and his wife were present, along with a who's who of the London social and political world, including Lady Randolph Churchill, and Mrs Asquith – where Fagan took the opportunity to auction off a painting by Augustus John, which represented three of the Irish players and had been specially painted for the Abbey Fund. In addition, in order to keep the Abbey acting company intact, Lennox Robinson, who had taken over the Abbey after Yeats' withdrawal, persuaded Fagan to cast several of the Abbey actors in his London and New York productions of *The Whiteheaded Boy*. The fundraisers were a very temporary fill-in, but Fagan set up a company called the Irish Players, and there were at least five Abbey actors in the cast of his revival of *John Bull's Other Island* at the Royal Court in September 1921, including Fred O'Donovan (the first Blanco Posnet in the 1909 premiere of Shaw's one-act play, performed first by the Abbey because it had been censored in England). When the Abbey reopened on August 2, it was with *The Shewing-up of Blanco Posnet* (together with two other short plays, Lady Gregory's *Rising of the Moon* and *Meadowsweet* by Seumas O'Kelly); a week later, on August 8, they ran *John Bull's Other Island* in repertory.

As this shows, throughout the opening decades of the twentieth century there were continual interchanges, both of plays and performers, between London and Dublin in an enriching two-way traffic. These were facilitated by people like Fagan, and encouraged by Shaw, who saw both theaters as being engaged in the same struggle. So, in his Abbey fundraising talk (as reported in *The Irish Times*), "Taking for his subject 'On the Spur of the Moment', Mr. Shaw said that he was an Irishman, and as he stood looking at the distinguished audience, hurrying to the rescue of the Abbey Theatre, his mind went back to a series of desperate enterprises in support of English theaters. They had the same object – to try and get the drama out of the commercial rut" (Hogan and Burnham 1992:28). In addition there was a thriving circle of Irish culture in London, largely centered on Fagan and Shaw. This can be seen not only in the lecture series hosted by Fagan, but also on a more informal level. So, for instance, Sara Allgood spent an afternoon in 1913 singing Irish songs with Mrs Patrick Campbell and Shaw's sister Lucy, at her house.

Shaw's only full-length play devoted specifically to Ireland achieved a particular relevance at a crucial political point in Anglo-Irish relations. At least two of the British negotiators for the Anglo-Irish Treaty, which was finally signed in December 1921 – Winston Churchill and the prime minister of the day, Lloyd George – saw the Irish Players' September production of *John Bull's Other Island*, as did the influential Plunkett; and the play undoubtedly had a direct political effect, even more so than in its original 1904 performances, due to the tense situation of the time. The treaty led to the establishment of the Irish Free State, as well as (through the option allowed to the North) the partition of Ireland. The exposure of exploitative British economic imperialism in the play, together with the theme of independence, raised important issues at a significant juncture – despite, as Shaw wrote in an Author's Note for a 1926 performance of *John Bull's Other Island* at the Regent Theatre, London, the fact that the text had not been updated, even though when it was written in 1904,

> The Irish Free State was unborn and undreamt of, and … Liberals like Mr. Thomas Broadbent, still smarting from their recent unpopularity as pro-Boers, were ardent advocates of Home Rule for Ireland, the emancipation of Macedonia from the Turkish yoke, and, generally, an implacable resistance to oppression everywhere except at home. … But in the main, human nature, though it has changed its catchwords a little, is very much what it was then. There are still Roscullens in Ireland and still Broadbents in England. (Shaw 1984:167)

REFERENCES AND FURTHER READING

Arrington, L. (2008). "The Censorship of *O'Flaherty V.C.*" *SHAW*, 28, 85–106.

Braverman, R.L. (1993). *Plot and Counterplots: Sexual Politics and the Body Politic in English Literature, 1660–1730*. Cambridge: Cambridge University Press.

Cave, R. (1991). "Staging the Irishman." In J.S. Bratton (Ed.). *Acts of Supremacy: The British Empire and the stage, 1790–1930* (pp. 62–128). Manchester: Manchester University Press.

de Búrca, S. (1983). *The Queen's Royal Theatre 1829–1969*. Dublin: de Búrca.

Denham, R. (1958). *Stars in My Hair*. London: Werner Laurie.

Dietrich, R. (1992). "Shaw as Dramatic Icon." *SHAW*, 12, 12–146.

Fagan, B. (1970). "Shakespear v. Shaw." L.H. Hugo (Ed.). *The Shaw Review*, 13, 105–31.

Foster, R.F. (1997, 2003). *W.B. Yeats: A Life*. 2 vols. Oxford: Oxford University Press.

Gregory, Lady A. (1978). *Journals*. Vol. I. D. Murphy (Ed.). Gerrards Cross: Colin Smythe.

Herr, C. (Ed.). (1991). *For the Land They Loved: Irish Political Melodramas, 1890–1925*. New York: Syracuse University Press.

Hogan, R. and R. Burnham. (1992). *Years of O'Casey, 1921–1926: A Documentary History*. Newark: University of Delaware Press.

Holloway, J. Notebook of newspaper clippings, MS 4426, NLI, Dublin.

Laurence, D.H. and N. Grene (Eds.). (1993). *Shaw, Lady Gregory, and the Abbey*. Gerrards Cross: Colin Smythe.

Morash, C. (2002). *A History of Irish Theatre, 1601–2000*. Cambridge: Cambridge University Press.

Shaw, B. (1965a). *The Complete Prefaces of Bernard Shaw*. London: Paul Hamlyn.

Shaw, B. (1965b). *O'Flaherty V.C. The Complete Plays of Bernard Shaw* (pp. 819–28). London: Paul Hamlyn.

Shaw, B. (1984). *John Bull's Other Island*. D.H. Laurence (Ed.). London: Penguin.

Shaw, B. (1985). *Collected Letters*, vol. III: *1911–1925*. D.H. Laurence (Ed.). London: Reinhardt.

The Novels of Somerville and Ross

Vera Kreilkamp

Two well-born Irish cousins, both daughters of Ascendancy Big Houses, began writing fiction together after a decade of traumatic political change for the entrenched rural gentry society they took as their subject. Edith Somerville (1858–1949) and Violet Martin (1862–1915) met as young women in January 1886, the very month that William Gladstone announced his conversion to Home Rule and shortly after Britain's 1885 general election had returned Home Rule candidates to most Irish parliamentary seats. The agrarian outrages of the recent Irish Land War – boycotts, the withholding of rents, cattle maiming, and attacks on landlords and their hunts – were now a searing memory or ongoing reality for a landowning class that had suffered economic losses since the mid-century Famine. By the 1880s assumptions about loyal relations between landlords and tenants that had long shaped the imaginations of Big House proprietors were decisively undermined. Edith Somerville's recollections of these years suggest how anxieties about nationalist and British betrayals had become part of the fabric of the landed gentry's experience. She also reveals her family's resolve that her brothers' opportunities were not to be sacrificed; the daughters' futures are unmentioned.

> There was no change made in the destined professions for the sons; it was on themselves that my father and mother economised; and with effort, and forethought, and sheer self-denial, somehow they "made good," and pulled through those bad years of the early 'eighties, when rents were unpaid, and crops failed, and Parnell and his wolf-pack were out for blood, and the English Government flung them, bit by bit, the property of the only men in Ireland who, faithful to the pitch of folly, had supported it since the days of the Union. (Somerville and Ross 1918:91)

Edith Somerville, as the eldest child of Drishane House, County Cork, and Violet Martin, the youngest of Ross House, County Galway, published sixteen volumes under the male-sounding authorship of OE Somerville and Martin Ross. As dependent unmarried daughters, they lived in their family homes as adults until, with the death of Violet Martin's mother in 1906, Violet moved permanently to Drishane for the remaining nine years of her life. Although her death in 1915 signaled the apparent end of the literary partnership, Edith Somerville continued to write fiction and essays for three decades. All but one of these sixteen additional volumes appeared under the name of an enduring literary collaboration in which the deceased and living partners appeared to communicate through spiritualism. The novels Somerville wrote after 1915 have been largely neglected by critics, who focus almost entirely on the jointly written works. The scope of this chapter will differ in that it seeks to unite Somerville's fiction after her collaborator's death with the critical history of a Somerville and Ross oeuvre. The dual authorship of the fiction, especially complicated by a deceased Violet Martin's apparent hovering presence over Somerville's writing, suggests, as Julie Anne Stevens points out, the complexities of assigning any "single ideological purpose" or unity of voice to this steadfastly collaborative work (Stevens 2007:2).

In overviews of Irish fiction, Somerville and Ross's *The Real Charlotte* is regarded as a major achievement: "one of the few truly totalizing works of Irish fiction ... with all the synoptic assurance of a *Middlemarch*" according to Terry Eagleton, or for Julian Moynahan "a serious contender for title of the best Irish novel before Joyce" (Eagleton 1995:215; Moynahan 1995:183). But despite comparisons with the most canonized of English-language novels, without Google's online texts or, alternatively, the holdings of a large research library, most Somerville and Ross fiction remains inaccessible. Over the past decade, the MLA International Bibliography has listed no more than one or two articles per year devoted to these authors. A welcome change in this pattern of neglect began with Declan Kiberd's inclusion of a chapter on *The Real Charlotte* in *Inventing Ireland* (1996) and another on the long out-of-print *The Silver Fox* in *Irish Classics* (2001). The first new critical monograph on the fiction in a quarter of a century appeared in 2007 when Stevens published *The Irish Scene in Somerville and Ross*. But for writers whose major novel has been compared in import to those of George Eliot or James Joyce, the recent record of interest remains meager indeed. So I begin by posing a problem about reception, both past and present, of a major body of Irish fiction that the following discussion attempts to unravel.

Big House Territory

Somerville and Ross novels are generally viewed as belonging to the genre of Anglo-Irish Big House fiction, appreciated for their reimagining of the central conventions of an older Ascendancy form – and for establishing its viability in the twentieth century for novelists such as Elizabeth Bowen, Molly Keane, Jennifer Johnston, and William Trevor. An Irish nationalist criticism, which operated informally decades before Edward Said's *Orientalism* launched an international postcolonial movement in 1978, viewed this traditional genre as peripheral to the national literary narrative. Until late in the twentieth century, therefore, the Big House tradition received little sustained analysis. The term "Big House" in Ireland signals a country estate, which if smaller than comparable gentry homes in England, still towered over the cabins of tenants whose rents supported the lifestyles of their often improvident and heavily mortgaged landlords. Nineteenth-century novels about the always-threatened house, beginning with Maria Edgeworth's *Castle Rackrent* (1800) and including fiction by Charles Maturin, Charles Lever, and Sheridan Le Fanu, were to create a major Irish genre and a source of several conventions from which Somerville and Ross drew: a gothic focus on Ascendancy guilt, the motif of the decaying house as symbol of social decline, the figures of the improvident and increasingly eccentric or guilt-ridden landlord, the middle-class aspirant scheming for ownership of the Big House (Kreilkamp 1998:20–25).

With the exception of their second joint publication, *Naboth's Vineyard* (1891), Somerville and Ross novels are set on the Anglo-Irish country estate and in nearby Irish villages under the sway of the Big House. The fiction confidently addresses class differences between Protestant landlords, Catholic tenants, and middle-class shopkeepers and farmers – a focus that did much to undermine the authors' reputation in Ireland even before Independence. In an 1895 review of *The Real Charlotte*, nationalist politician and journalist T.P. O'Connor attacked the two authors as *shoneens* for writing for British audiences and mercilessly exposing the purported squalor of Irish life. Reading the fiction in the twenty-first century can be a liberating experience. Under the influence of historical revisionism and gender and feminist criticism, the force of a nationalist focus on Irish culture has so abated that the political pressures shaping the earlier reception of Big House fiction have even come to represent the very vulgarity of insensibility that Daniel Corkery accused the authors of in 1931 (Corkery 1966:10–11). Perhaps the sharpest retort to Corkery's notorious questioning of the "Irishness" of virtually all literature written by an "alien Ascendancy," with Somerville and Ross's *The Big House of Inver* as a particular target of hostility, came with Conor Cruise O'Brien's reminder that the "aristocratic pride" and "blue-blooded contempt for the lowborn" that grated in Somerville and Ross's fiction was central to most Irish Gaelic literature as well (O'Brien 1965:112).

Still, given the critical neglect of the full body of Somerville and Ross's work, its class assumptions may well operate as a gnawing pressure against full acceptance, much as Elizabeth Bowen's equally pronounced elitism – or for that matter, Virginia Woolf's snobberies in regard to English society – had once generated unease. But whereas Woolf – and increasingly Bowen – now belong invulnerably to the pantheon of great modernists on grounds of style, Somerville and Ross's fiction exists in a strange in-betweenness, neither fully Victorian nor fully modernist in theme, but with powerful affinities to both movements. Through its focus on crisis, discontinuity, alienation, and rapid traumatic change – and its accompanying nostalgia for what has been lost – the Big House genre plays a role in what Luke Gibbons characterizes as Ireland's premature "shock of modernity" (Gibbons 1996:6).

As writers self-consciously joining an established tradition, Somerville and Ross began their collaboration with *An Irish Cousin* (1889), a full-blown Protestant gothic text exploiting a range of dark motifs: a deranged and demonized landlord, a setting in a disordered house, a growing class obsession with racial pollution and cultural decline. Their first novel thus reflects the ambitions of two young collaborators who enter the literary marketplace by experimenting with an array of conventions that serve to undermine the authority of their own social class. *An Irish Cousin*'s atmosphere and plot elements reflects the direct influence of Sheridan Le Fanu's *Uncle Silas* (1864), a novel about the schemes of a decadent landlord to murder his young orphaned niece, the legitimate heir of the estate he oversees and mismanages (see CHAPTER 22, JOSEPH SHERIDAN LE FANU). This sensational gothic source for the novice writers' first collaborative work tellingly challenges corrupt Big House patterns of inheritance. Although the novel initially draws on the genres of the national tale, drawing-room comedy, and a darkly inflected and carefully observed social realism, it shapes its plot around native and Anglo-Irish eccentricity and the quasi-feudal relationships between two unequal social groups. It concludes with a plot of sensational gothic revelations exposing the landlord's greed and criminal culpability – as if to justify the young authors' self-deprecating description of their first joint endeavor as a mere commodity, a "penny thriller" or "the Shocker" (Lewis 2005:119). According to Somerville, *An Irish Cousin* began to come alive when she and her partner glimpsed the white face of an isolated Somerville relative from the window of a decrepit Big House. That ghostly woman's face provided the young writers with a vision of the forbidden secrets of their own "old stock": incest, miscegenation, madness, and the exercise of a droit de seigneur by succeeding generations of Big House males (Somerville and Ross 1918:130–31). Such a gothicized vision of Ascendancy abasement recurs in the major novels: in *The Real Charlotte*, for example, we witness Julia Duffy, a product of Catholic/Protestant misalliance, peering from the window: "a thin dirty face, a hooked nose, and unkempt black hair, before the vision was withdrawn" (Somerville and Ross 1977:39).

Somerville and Ross's fears of the consequences of rapid social change shape the plotting and thematic emphases of *Naboth's Vineyard* (1891), their second collaborative project and their only novel focusing solely on rural village society. Here nationalist politics appear as the foreground rather than, more typically for the writers, the background of plot events. As in a number of subsequent works, they turn their harshest eye on a Catholic middle-class stratum, the source of a nationalist ideology threatening their own background. But since many novels – among them *The Real Charlotte*, *The Big House of Inver*, and *French Leave* – explore threats to the Big House from a rising Protestant middle class, their apprehensions about the survival of traditional social divisions are as strongly based on anxieties about class as about ethnicity. Their genealogically obsessed fiction envisions Ireland's rising bourgeoisie, both Catholic and Protestant, as parvenus interested in misalliances with Big House families, or alternatively, as money-grubbing paudeens – not only Donovan the scheming gombeen man in *Naboth's Vineyard*, but also Charlotte Mullen and Lambert in *The Real Charlotte*, Dr Mangan in *Mount Music*, and the debauched, sheebeen-keeping Connors or the ambitious agent Johnny Weldon in *The Big House of Inver*. (Significantly, however, only the threatening Catholics on this list, Donovan, Mangan, and Maggie Connor, must be abruptly killed off.)

Set in 1883 in the immediate aftermath of the most violent years of the Land War, *Naboth's Vineyard*'s melodramatic plot of land-grabbing and class warfare within rural society, as well as its dependence on stock characters, had garnered little favorable attention. The neglect of the novel by post-Independence critics is predictable: it indicts Land War politics as motivated by greed rather than principle and as characterized by cowardly and self-serving violence against the innocent. In *Naboth's Vineyard* sub-human and melodramatic figures resemble literary versions of the *Punch* cartoons that Somerville studied as a young girl in her grandfather's library (Lewis 2005:2). Viewing the native Irish through a bald physiognomic lens redolent of those caricatures, the novel, according to more than one reader, is shaped by suppositions about Irish Catholic inferiority, as written with the "assumption ... that vulgarity and stupidity are qualities proper to the poor" (Cronin 1972:29). Characters are compared to a range of animals, from pigs to wolves; faces are potato-like or brutal, fingers are coarse, a servant girl is "elephantine," the gombeen man's eyes are hooded, a farmhand's face resembles that of a trapped animal.

But *Naboth's Vineyard*'s proto-modern attention to the violent consequences of societal breakdown under the Land League, and its dark depiction of Irish village life, might be best assessed in the context of the authors' previous novel about the disordered house and criminal culpability of the landlord. *An Irish Cousin* had deployed gothic conventions to expose not the horrors of middle-class greed in rural Ireland, but disarray in the highest stratum of that same society. Together these neglected early novels suggest the range, even the amplitude, of two apprentice writers' initial response to the Irish social disorder they witnessed, as well as their eagerness to deploy existing fictional conventions, including melodramatic plots and stock types, to convey such crisis. In the only existing sustained critical examination of the novel, Stevens reads *Naboth's Vineyard* in the tradition of Zola, as a "grotesquely realistic view" of the costs of rapid social change fueling class warfare (Stevens 2007:16). She emphasizes Somerville and Ross's early refusal to participate in a picturesque cover-up of brutal conflicts in the Irish countryside disseminated by decades of Celtic Revivalists.

In *Naboth's Vineyard* a hated absentee landlord is present only in the hostile remarks of local men who gleefully refuse to help control a fire in his woods. But in their third novel, *The Real Charlotte*, Somerville and Ross move from portraying such hostile political passions toward the landowning class to ruefully eyeing an Ascendancy house fading into ineffectual torpor. Although the novel's middle-class protagonist claws her way up to respectability by rapaciously acquiring property from those descending the social ladder, Charlotte Mullen's ambitions to marry her young cousin to the Big House heir are decisively thwarted. Rather than anatomizing criminal culpability on the gentry estate, Somerville and Ross develop another emerging convention; they characterize the effeteness and depletion of will that will increasingly mark Ascendancy progeny in twentieth-century fiction, suggesting how a depleted Big House society fails to reproduce itself. Thus Charlotte's cousin, a vital but impoverished young

Dublin ingénue whose unschooled energy might have revitalized an aristocratic house and its descendants, is doomed instead to disastrous romantic choices and a catastrophic death. Francie Fitzgerald's fate is engendered not just by her romantic fantasies and recklessness, but by her suitor Christopher Dysart's effete decency and self-conscious intellectual circumspection – by the pervasive failure of sexual and social energy characterizing the diffident Big House male.

Still writing as Somerville and Ross after her collaborator's death, Edith Somerville continued publishing novels set on the country estate, among them *Mount Music* (1920), *An Enthusiast* (1921) and, most successfully, *The Big House of Inver* (1925); each exposes the resolutely philistine life of the landed gentry, even as W.B. Yeats was elegizing the beleaguered Big House as an endangered source of national vitality and high culture. *The Big House of Inver* conflates Ascendancy defeat with a violence and moral shoddiness already inherent in its purported eighteenth-century aesthetic flowering. The history of the Prendeville family flaunts an acquisitive colonial presence in Ireland. The civilization that it brings to the west of Ireland is characterized by extraordinary physical beauty – of houses, paintings, horses, and young men – but also by insolent pride, hedonism, and a shiftless improvidence victimizing women. Somerville published *The Big House of Inver* during a revolutionary decade that witnessed the burning of more than 200 Big Houses as alien presences in the Irish landscape. The novel concludes with the fiery destruction of an eighteenth-century Georgian mansion, setting up a literary trope for future post-Independence novels, most famously Bowen's *The Last September* (1929) only four years later (see CHAPTER 37, ELIZABETH BOWEN: A HOME IN WRITING).

Revivalist Territory

Despite their steadfast fictional portrayal of a doomed and self-destructive Ascendancy society, after the composition of *The Real Charlotte* the collaborators begin to explore the territory of a Revivalist form of literary modernism. Although Unionist in their political sympathies, Edith Somerville and Violet Martin shared traits with their more politically liberal Revivalist contemporaries; they too were Protestant in background, suspicious of England, and, more in the case of Somerville than Martin, deeply involved in spiritualist movements. Their mastery of the various forms of English spoken in Ireland was unequalled, and they sought in their writing not to create the literary language Synge brought to the Abbey, but to reproduce, in their words, "a tongue, pliant and subtle, expressing with every breath the mind of its makers" (Somerville and Ross 1920b:184). Like Yeats, although typically through a comic lens, Somerville and Ross also invoke possibilities of alliance – a quasi-feudal relationship – between Anglo-Irish landowners and a rural peasantry, a class of farmers and country people whom they knew well and frequently incorporated into their fiction. In 1919, the first year of hostilities of the War of Independence, when Irish tenants were attacking Protestant garrisons in west Cork near Drishane, Somerville and Ross's narrative voice nevertheless invokes the "sympathy and understanding between the uppermost and the lowest of Irish social life, which is not extended, by either side to the intervening one" (Somerville and Ross 1920a:88). In *An Enthusiast* (1921), written in the worst years of the Anglo-Irish War when Sinn Féin raids and brutal British reprisals were tearing apart the countryside, the novel's idealistic young protagonist advocates not rebellion, but the agricultural reform advocated by Horace Plunkett's cooperative movements, which were being incorporated into an array of Revivalist activities (Mathews 2003:5–6). Dan Palliser's instinctual relationship with his "loveable and laughable" servant is viewed as implying "a deeply felt and ancient friendship, such a form of friendship as has existed for many long centuries, and gives a perfectly unconscious contradiction to the many theories of class-hatred" (Somerville and Ross 1985:18, 19). Yet the young landlord's belief that the peasantry will never abandon the "old stock" dooms him, for he dies during the crossfire of an IRA raid on his house. Neither in history (Horace Plunkett's Big House was destroyed in 1923 during the Civil War) nor in Somerville and Ross's darkly prescient fiction do the ideals of the reforming landlord fare well in a revolutionary state.

In their commitment to the hierarchies of the past – politically expressed both in Violet Martin's lifelong political Unionism and Somerville's later evolution to a more liberal support of Home Rule and agricultural cooperative moments as an alternative to Sinn Féin – both women opposed the increasingly aggressive flexing of political muscle by a nationalist Catholic bourgeoisie. But if Somerville and Ross voice a resistance to modernity redolent of Yeats' conservative strain of literary modernism, they never fully embraced Revivalist solutions. Their conservatism must be carefully balanced against their ongoing fictional exposure of the Ascendancy's responsibility for its own decline. And unlike prominent Revivalists who reimagined a native Catholic peasantry in order to establish bonds between a beleaguered Protestant class and a native Gaelic aristocratic tradition, Somerville and Ross resisted versions of the heroic peasant. They never sentimentalized a country people they knew far more intimately in language and habits than did urban Revivalist contemporaries such as Yeats or Synge. Somerville and Ross's rural people, unlike Yeats' Connemara fisherman, "a man who is but a dream" (Yeats 1996:149), or Synge's heroic suffering mothers in *The Aran Islands* or *Riders to the Sea*, are, rather, characterized through mimetically rendered speech patterns and darkly naturalistic details of appearance and settings characteristic of realistic fiction. Tenants and servants are emotionally labile and superstitious – but as class-bound and conservative as their eccentric landlords. In *Mount Music*, a Big House servant objects to her master's attendance at the Catholic chapel, sensing that his religious affiliation and his attendance are shameful, as if he had taken to sitting with the maids in the servant hall. Such minor characters are unapologetically presented through the lens of class difference, and always from the perspective of the Big House; they are uneducated, usually dirty and, in their speech and habits, certainly less "civilized" than their gentry landlords. But they manage, through their sly civility, to thwart and undermine the wishes of their social superiors;

seemingly in touch with an ineffable source of folk knowledge, they accrue powers of prediction.

The natural courtesy and trust this fiction occasionally posits between master and servant typically expresses itself through a comic realism. In *Mount Music*, the dairy-maid Mary Twomey transmits essential local gossip affecting the fate of a Big House heir being enticed into marriage with a local Catholic girl. But despite some unflattering characterization – Mary stands four feet high, is strikingly plain, and resists modern hygienic improvements to her person or in her barn – the narrator also asserts that she has a soul as great as that of a "warrior or fighting queen in the brave days of old" (Somerville and Ross 1920a:88). The mistress converses with "sympathy and understanding" with her servant, having an implicit confidence in Mary's "good breeding" – a breeding evident in their mutual engrossment in outdoor affairs (they are both country women), but even more by their certainty of a shared "chivalrous point of view" (Somerville and Ross 1920a:88). Such attention to the relationship between mistress and retainer establishes a bond between an illiterate, slovenly, and stubbornly conservative dairymaid and a somewhat officious Big House lady. The scene illustrates Somerville and Ross's tricky balancing of seemingly oxymoronic elements – a Revivalist imagining of the shared aristocracy between landlord and peasantry set against a comic realism emerging from the authors' intimate familiarity with the stable yard and kitchen.

Irish servants and tenants have access not just to local gossip, but also to long folk memories and to a mythic, even ineffable knowledge of the countryside that landlords, English visitors, or emerging middle-class rural capitalists such as Charlotte Mullen ignore at their peril. In *The Real Charlotte* a squalid and impoverished native country people are described though the same discourse of degeneracy as that deployed in *Naboth's Vineyard*. Charlotte's ferocious housekeeper, the vulturine Norry the Boat, permanently has "dust and turf-ashes hung in her grizzled eyebrows," while a kitchen visitor, Nance the Fool, is reduced to "a bundle of rags with a cough in it" squatting on the floor (Somerville and Ross 1977:18, 109). But characters envisioned through such a lens of degeneracy, in particular Norry the Boat and the mixed-breed old women Julia Duffy, voice dark truths in their role as indigenous folk historians.

In *The Silver Fox* (1898), a novel exploring the clash between a traditional way of life and the forces of modernity, Slaney Morris' respect before what outsiders term the primitive "superstition" of the country people distinguishes her from English visitors to Ireland. Whereas the English engineer Glasgow's brash certainty in reason and economic calculation shapes his plan to construct a railroad across a rural bog, the country people invoke fairy mythology in their warnings against change. Anglo-Irish Slaney, not the disdainful engineer, comprehends the rural folk and their fears – fears made manifest with the appearance of a ghostly silver fox when Glasgow begins blasting a fairy rath. He seeks to obliterate what the tenants describe as the bottomless bog of Tully, their folk explanation for a scientific truth: the bog lies over running water and indeed cannot be filled. The young Anglo-Irish woman fruitlessly warns the brash English interloper against his disdain for Irish superstition:

Slaney had seen and heard – between the sunset and the dawn – things not easily
accounted for; she herself accepted them without fear; but she knew – as any one who
knows well a half-civilized people must know – how often a superstition is justified of
its works. (Somerville and Ross 1900:53–54)

Declan Kiberd argues that in such passages, despite harsher judgments of the
Ascendancy elsewhere, Somerville and Ross invoke a possible bonding between
the Big House and the cabin. In Anglo-Irish Slaney, Kiberd suggests the authors
celebrate "a richly responsive sensibility" that is capable of forging alliances "with the
instinctual integrity of the Irish poor" (Kiberd 2001:377).

The ferociously hostile characterization of the English in *The Silver Fox* again positions Somerville and Ross's fiction within a Revivalist modernism: the redefinition of
the colonial overlord as crassly and boorishly materialistic, culturally inept, and far
less "civilized" than the Anglo-Irish or Irish who are in touch with tradition rather
than an unmoored commercial modernity. The oeuvre persistently targets English
visitors to Ireland; the motif most obviously reflects a contemporary Ascendancy sense
of betrayal and abandonment by Britain (Gladstone's face adorned the bottom of many
a Big House chamberpot), but also recalls a pervasive anti-English theme in earlier
Anglo-Irish Big House fiction by Edgeworth and Lever. Examples abound. In *The
Real Charlotte*, Miss Hope-Drummund, a clueless English visitor who is angling for
the resistant Anglo-Irish heir, becomes a source of humor, as does the English-born
Lady Dysart, the Big House mistress who enthusiastically plants flats of chickweed
rather than asters in her garden. *The Silver Fox* characterizes not only the engineer
Glasgow, but also the landlord's new English wife Lady Susan, as vulgar egoists,
lacking the refined consciousness of the Anglo-Irish protagonist. In *Dan Russel the
Fox*, Fanshawe, a rich, large, and simple young Englishman "with a slow-moving,
logical mind," is comically manipulated into marriage by one of a large, witty family
of Irish "buccaneers" (Somerville and Ross 1911:210–11). The narrator of *The Big
House of Inver* pointedly notes that the nouveau riche English Sir Harold Bulgrave,
who buys up the exquisite eighteenth-century Georgian mansion, has also purchased
his coat of arms on the London marketplace.

Somerville and Ross's targeting of English vulgarity or cultural ineptness in Ireland,
also evident in the Resident Magistrate collections originally written for a British
sporting magazine, undermines O'Connor's easy labeling of the collaborators as
shoneens, writing for British audiences at the expense of the Irish. Somerville's 1923
response to her brother's assertion that she was more English then Irish suggests her
firm sense of nationality and identity in a post-Independence era when fearful Big
House owners were fleeing their ancestral homes: "My family has eaten Irish food and
shared Irish life for nearly three hundred years, and if that doesn't make me Irish I
might as well say I was Scotch, or Norman, or Pre-Diluvian" (quoted in Lewis
1985:164–65). The fiction makes her point as clearly. *Mount Music*'s narrative tone
toward improvident Big House proprietors retreating to England conveys Somerville's
exact contempt for those who desert their country; the Anglo-Irish Talbot-Lowrys are

"too agitated by their coming journey to have a spare thought for sentiment; too much beset by the fear of what they might lose, their keys, their sandwiches, their dressing-boxes, to shed a tear for what they are losing, and had lost" (Somerville and Ross 1920a:313).

Gender Territory

Gifford Lewis' recent biography of Edith Somerville frames her and Violet Martin's lives within the suffragist battles concurrent with their 1889–1915 writing partnership. The biographer describes both women as "eloquent in their revolt against a patriarchy which made use of them, but yet kept them powerless," noting that they were converted to active participation in feminist causes after attending a 1908 Hyde Park rally in London (Lewis 2005:3, 6). Given Somerville and Martin's involvement in suffrage activities (they became president and vice president of their local branch of the Irish Women's Franchise League in 1909), Lewis's inclination to view them through a feminist lens is appealing. But Somerville and Ross's fiction is as centrally caught up with issues of social class as with gender. Untangling the two pressures suggests the complexity of a body of fiction evincing both a contemporary awareness of gender inequity and a more traditional insistence on the probity of class divisions so central to the Big House society the two writers supported. One might even argue, against the feminist grain, that Somerville and Ross's deepest loyalties reached backwards to the social values of an Irish Protestant Big House society that they nevertheless anatomized so critically in their fiction, and that their strongest aversion was to a breakdown of distinctions leading to class and ethnic misalliances. For feminist criticism their novels embody tensions similar to those suggested by the work of Emily Lawless, another politically conservative novelist writing from the Big House in the same period. Gerardine Meaney writes that Lawless' *Grania* (1892) reveals "how nineteenth-century habits of imperialist perception could haunt progressive, feminist thinking" (Meaney 2002:977). Such a haunting characterizes Somerville and Ross's fiction as well.

That Somerville and Ross's novels have attracted less attention from feminist critics than we might expect may well reflect the strength of these competing pressures in the fiction. Ann Owen Weekes focuses on the arbitrariness of gender roles in *The Real Charlotte* – Charlotte's beloved tomcat is named Susan and a Big House theatrical performance involves significant cross-dressing – to argue for the novel's subversive attacks on patriarchal class and gender systems. At a time of rapidly changing gender patterns in British and European societies, Somerville and Ross envision Irish women's lives as constrained by social codes that deny their fictional characters the freedom that both authors struggled to achieve. Readers have often placed Somerville and Ross, who write about moral and social distinctions in village settings, in the tradition of Jane Austen or Charlotte Brontë. Kiberd, for example, argues that "one of the profounder achievements" of the collaboration was a dramatization of the "mortified

female consciousness" – and of the intense loneliness of women within a society of
the less gifted, intelligent, and sentient (Kiberd 2001:362). Kiberd's reading of the
fiction in relation to Austen's might be pushed further: its isolation and entrapment
of the Ascendancy woman – occurring a century after Austen's marriage novels and
in a period when the contemporary "new woman" began to assert her demands – arguably depicts an even bleaker social world for Irish women than that found in early
nineteenth-century English village society.

The autobiographically inspired *French Leave* (1928) suggests how feminist inclina-
tions are checked by anxieties about class expectations and the pressures of patriarchal
control. In its early scenes, the novel focuses, always in a comic mode, on the heroine's
struggles with the family patriarch; it begins with that rhetorical striving for feminist
"eloquence" that Lewis would see as characterizing Somerville and Martin's lives.
Depicting the efforts of a young Ascendancy daughter to study art in Paris in
the 1880s, *French Leave* reflects Somerville's own youthful maneuvers against family
opposition to achieve that same goal. The narrative voice in *French Leave* lashes out
against a father's attempts to thwart the young protagonist's ambitions:

> Patricia was not the only girl who in those far back days was dashing herself against the
> bars of her cage, but she was certain – as I suppose, are most sufferers from prejudice
> and injustice, especially those sufferers who are young – that in no cage were the bars
> so strong and so close together as that which enclosed her, of which her father kept the
> key. (Somerville and Ross 1987:46–47)

Somerville and Martin knew this cage well; they supported an Anglo-Irish society that
denied unmarried women like themselves personal autonomy, economic independence,
or the right to inherit the family homes they spent their adulthood propping up. Or,
as Weekes puts it, they "depict a society whose hideous injustices, both personal and
political, they recognize ... but nevertheless cherish" (Weekes 1990:79). Moreover, in
imaginatively accepting and reflecting the class assumptions (indeed, the snobberies)
of their social world, they denied their more subversive fictional characters freedoms
that they sought. The two writers became successful novelists and journalists, with a
professional interest in the business of publishing – and for Somerville later in her life,
in the business of raising horses, breeding cattle, and farming at Drishane. Their professional careers supported not only their own lives, but also their ancestral homes
owned by absent brothers, houses that they tirelessly managed. After their 1886
meeting, they chose a mutually protective relationship with each other rather than
marriage. In *Irish Memories*, published after her collaborator's death in 1915, Somerville
writes of her joyful and life-altering encounter with Martin as a transformative moment
that proved to be the "hinge of [her] life" and the beginning of a new era (Somerville
and Ross 1918:122): "For most boys and girls the varying, yet invariable, flirta-
tions, and emotional episodes of youth, are resolved and composed by marriage. To
Martin and to me was opened another way, and the flowering of both our lives was
when we met each other" (122, 125). Despite the uniformly bleak depictions of the

marital state in their novels, Somerville and Ross's fiction offers few possibilities of homosocial companionship outside of marriage, the "way" that the two writers had themselves chosen – or, given the gender imbalance or lack of marriageable men in late nineteenth- and early twentieth-century Ireland, had productively settled on. In *French Leave* Patricia's lively female friendships in the Paris scenes offer a rare instance of supportive relationships between women, but only as a temporary bohemian substitute for the mandated marriage plot of her life.

Nor do the novels offer any examples of women who overcome the "prejudices and injustices" against which Patricia protests – figures who successfully unlock the cage and escape their socially prescribed roles. Much of the fiction depicts, rather, failed rebellions; on rare occasions, as in *French Leave*, a subversively inclined young woman attains happiness (or at least the expectation of it) only though her final acquiescence to a marriage long anticipated by her troglodyte of a father. Patricia rejects the advances of an inappropriately middle-class Irishman, who is now a talented art student in Paris, and retreats into the family fold. A century after Austen, Somerville and Ross envision a Big House society still operating within early nineteenth-century social patterns: the rare glimpses of fulfillment available to women are imagined only through socially sanctioned patterns of matrimony. The two novels attempting happy endings on the pattern of Austen's marriage plots depict prospective husbands, in each case cousins incestuously emerging from claustrophobic Anglo-Irish family clans, who are less intelligent, imaginative, and morally complex than their wives. Patricia's handsome cousin Jimmy in *French Leave*, like Christian Talbot's Larry Coppinger in *Mount Music*, provides neither the wit nor the shared moral intelligence that Austen's Darcy and Knightley bestow (in addition to their considerable wealth) on Elizabeth Bennet and Emma Woodhouse – or the physically maimed Rochester on Jane Eyre. Writing about a patriarchy that exploited them, Somerville and Ross create a fictional oeuvre filled with reprehensible or, at best, inadequate males. And a body of fiction written by women who found happiness outside conventional gender arrangements offers no such options to its female characters.

Typically in Somerville and Ross's novels, intelligent, desiring, or rebellious women are thwarted, returned back into the fold of social convention or, in a few works, expelled from society. Katharine Rowan, the young aspiring writer and protagonist of the hunting novel *Dan Russel the Fox* (1911), is an independent orphan, strikingly free of family constraints. Both Somerville and Martin saw their education sacrificed to that of their male siblings; their efforts to write novels were viewed as distracting them from their primary social responsibilities in the drawing-room and on the tennis court. The description of Katharine's freedom suggests significant authorial envy by two women enmeshed in the affections and constrictions of large, patriarchal Anglo-Irish families.

> Katharine was an orphan and an only child, circumstances for which pity is convention-
> ally due; yet they are not without their advantages. ... she was now, at the age of
> twenty-six, that rare and enviable creature, an independent young woman, enjoying to

its ultimate half-crown the income that would have been her eldest brother's, had he existed. Her trustees passed on to her, beautifully and inevitably, her dividends, the straps of her trunks bounded her responsibilities; she was free to come and go as she listed. (Somerville and Ross 1911:65)

As with visitors in early national tales, Ireland is transformative for the young woman. Rapidly becoming obsessed with hunting, she falls for an inarticulate Irishman, relapsing from a position of relative if contemptible middle-class respectability to the role of kennel boy, stable helper, and chief whip; John Michael becomes the companion of her hunting days and the subject of her "dream" and "delirium" (246). His dark good looks and complete lack of social presence comically excite the cosmopolitan visitor:

> weighed down by shyness palpable enough to touch a heart of stone. ... he eyed Katharine from under his curling black eyelashes like a thing at bay. She felt that if so much as a twig cracked he would melt into the upright piano, even as Daphne was merged in the laurel. (85)

The English visitor's growing passion for this inarticulate, Laurentian young man is inseparable from an ecstatic enthusiasm for the Irish hunt — behavior that her official admirer Ulick Adare, an effete Anglo-Irish writer residing in London, characterizes as a form of savagery. His judgment, if undermined by the eroticizing of the hunting scenes, nevertheless, remains thematically operative throughout the novel. As in *The Silver Fox*, Somerville and Ross's other major hunting novel, *Dan Russel the Fox* acknowledges the class arrogance of the hunt and its socially disruptive role in an agrarian countryside as one of the riders "dash[es] through a farmyard, with hens and geese in shrieking flight round him, cur-dogs barking hysterically, and, somewhere in the background, a mother slamming a half-door upon a flock of children" (112). Writing about *The Silver Fox*, where hunters, "self engrossed ... brutal and desecrating" (Somerville and Ross 1900:165), intrude upon the wake of a young drowned countryman, Kiberd observes how the hunt functions on two levels: as a metaphor not only for "desire," but also for "antagonisms" over the land between landlord and tenant (Kiberd 2001:367). Even as they invoke their lifelong passion for hunting in their fiction, Somerville and Ross can attend to the sport's darker social implications, the consequences of which they were well aware. In 1881–82, after the Land League organized campaigns against landlords by poisoning coverts and attacking hunting parties with pitchforks, the sport was cancelled throughout most of the island.

Dan Russel the Fox's many hunting scenes, like those in the Resident Magistrate stories, convey an eroticized loss of control as huntsmen call to the hounds "in a rapture of love," and Katharine sheds her former self (Somerville and Ross 1911:119). Moreover, descriptions of the hunt invoke gender role reversal — significant in the writing of two devoted females who chose a relationship with each other over marriage, were passionate horsewomen (Somerville became Ireland's first woman Master of the Hunt in 1903), and took on the male role of competent farm manager. Riding through the countryside Katharine feels she deals "with primeval things, danger, and speed, and the face of nature, and the chase, which is near the heart of nature … *as a man among men*" (128; my italics). Ulick, however, maintains a "misanthropic silence" at being forced to play the role of "the attentive Desdemona to the adventure-ful Othello of a breezy and booted female" (127). In releasing the male in her, hunting offers Katharine an identity that her intellectual and cosmopolitan society has denied her; in Ireland she hunts like a man, while her disgruntled anglicized admirer finds himself reduced to the passive female role.

But, as in other Somerville and Ross novels, the subversive woman who moves beyond her class's prescriptive gender roles, particularly one described as "breezy and booted," faces chastening. Katharine's English companion quotes Hannah More to her: "'Never make a friend out of your own class'," warning the young woman of the "agony" of social shame in pursuing a "fox-hunting yokel … whose solitary means of expression is to blow a horn!" (187, 301). Following the precepts of Austen rather than the authors' closer contemporary, D.H. Lawrence, Katharine rejects the role of a Lady Chatterley with her gamekeeper. Unwilling to abandon her class background, she finally acknowledges the barrier of John Michael's class identity: "No matter how she hid it from herself, the consciousness of his class was always there; it was as if he were a child, with some slight lameness or disfigurement that she would shelter with a fierce tenderness" (262). Predictably she abandons John Michael and Ireland, and we last see her where the novel began, in the Alps, paler and thinner, with a loss of her former assertive vigor. An aborted and socially transgressive breaching of class boundaries has depleted, not invigorated, the upper-class woman. More ominously, as with Francie Fitzgerald in *The Real Charlotte*, or the unhappily married Harriet Donovan of *Naboth's Vineyard*, Somerville and Ross depict the fate of subversively inclined or unsocialized women who stretch their social bonds too tautly. Both reck-lessly desiring women enter into disastrous marriages and contemplate adultery; both are summarily punished – Francie abruptly killed off, Harriet sentenced to a living death in a convent.

The Real Charlotte, however, offers a dazzling display of unbridled female compe-tence. Attending to Charlotte Mullen's triumphant subversion of an array of Irish Victorian gender codes encourages a productive resistance to more traditional readings of Charlotte simply as malevolent villain, "a splendidly realized and entirely convinc-ing figure of evil" (Cronin 1972:40). Although the novel's narrative voice mercilessly insists on Charlotte's flabby pallor and squat, thick figure, with her features and her body representing the antithesis of the womanly woman, her butch self-presentation is also liberating. Recognizing the hopelessness of her appearance, Charlotte sheds the burdens of feminine vanity and turns her energies to the business of building her financial and social position rather than of adorning her person or her dirty home. Ferociously intelligent, she reads English newspapers and reviews and is rumored to have advanced French literary works in the bookshelves she has constructed with her own hands. Her ferreting intellect, her cultural sophistication in a provincial village, as well as her formidable energy and ambition, distinguish her from other women, particularly her two major rivals, helplessly complacent Lucy Lambert or recklessly impulsive Francie Fitzgerald.

The rural village responds with awe and considerable fear to Charlotte, for her "big, pale face had an intellectuality and power about it that would have made her conspicuous in a gathering more distinguished" (Somerville and Ross 1977:160). Unburdened by the pressures of a patriarchal family, this 40-year-old mannish woman operates, seemingly, as a free agent. And, unlike the men in the Lismoyle, with whom she freely mingles, drinking and joking and joining their political conversations, Charlotte understands and profits from the new Land Acts in her role as a slumlord on Ferry Row, and finally as a landlady of a gentry farm. Nicole Pepinster Greene observes, moreover, that Charlotte's ability to switch from one linguistic code to another – from Irish, to Hiberno-Irish, to standard English, or even French – offers her opportunities to manipulate every social stratum in the community (Greene 2000:131–34).

Yet more traditional readings of Charlotte also have their place. In *The Real Charlotte*, autonomy, competence, economic independence – the traits that Somerville and Ross expressed even as they operated within the constraints of family and community – are available only to a moral and physical monster, an unbridled and subversive figure who breaches gender, social, and ethical codes. A land-grabber and rackrenter, Charlotte exploits her tenants on Ferry Row, shamelessly reads private correspondence, causes Lucy Lambert's death, schemes to destroy Lambert's marriage to Francie, and plots to banish Julia Duffy in order to make a grab at the old woman's home to elevate her own status. And, as with other women in Somerville and Ross's fiction who, to a far lesser degree, subvert gender codes, Charlotte is denied what she most desires. Her vindictive jealousy, impelling her to boast of her role in Lambert's professional ruination minutes before learning of his wife's death, cuts off the emotional future to which she has devoted her life.

In their creation of a strikingly mannish and independent woman, and in their insistent reminders of Charlotte's physical deficiencies, Somerville and Ross offer female abjectness as the motivation of Charlotte's formidable drive for power. A strangely confessional intrusion acknowledges and begs for pity for the vulnerabilities of the powerful monster the narrator has created:

> It is hard to ask pity for Charlotte, whose many evil qualities have without pity been set down, but the seal of ignoble tragedy had been set on her life; she had not asked for love, but it had come to her, twisted to burlesque by the malign hand of fate. There is pathos as well as humiliation in the thought that such a thing as a soul can be stunted by the trivialities of personal appearance, and it is a fact not beyond the reach of sympathy that each time Charlotte stood before her glass her ugliness spoke to her of failure, and goaded her to revenge. (Somerville and Ross 1977:276–77)

In their productive careers Edith Somerville and Violet Martin, like their memorable fictional character, transcended the narrow female role models prescribed for them. Working within a conservative network of family, community, and gender codes, they nevertheless achieved professional success and considerable economic independence. The bleakness of their greatest novel, however, where traits of female autonomy and energy are yoked to the shocking moral transgression of a monstrously mannish woman, suggests their darkest reading of the dying patriarchal community they steadfastly embraced. The narrative voice's tentatively phrased call for pity for Charlotte and her "ignoble tragedy," in its invocation of female humiliation, might be expanded to embrace a community of Irish women.

References and Further Reading

Bowen, E. (1929). *The Last September*. London: Cape.

Collis, M. (1968). *Somerville and Ross: A Biography*. London: Faber & Faber.

Corkery, D. (1966). *Synge and Anglo-Irish Literature*. Cork: Mercier Press.

Cronin, J. (1972). *Somerville and Ross*. Lewisburg, PA: Bucknell University Press.

Eagleton, T. (1995). *Heathcliff and the Great Hunger*. London: Verso.

Gibbons, L. (1996). *Transformations in Irish Culture*. Cork: Cork University Press.

Greene, N.P. (2000). "Dialect and Social Identity in *The Real Charlotte*." *New Hibernia Review*, 4.1, 122–37.

Kiberd, D. (1996). *Inventing Ireland*. Cambridge, MA: Harvard University Press.

Kiberd, D. (2001). *Irish Classics*. Cambridge, MA: Harvard University Press.

Kreilkamp, V. (1998). *The Anglo-Irish Novel and the Big House*. Syracuse: Syracuse University Press.

Lewis, G. (1985). *Somerville and Ross: The World of the Irish R.M.* New York: Viking.

Lewis, G. (2005). *Edith Somerville: A Biography*. Dublin: Four Courts Press.

Mathews, P.J. (2003). *Revival: The Abbey Theatre, Sinn Féin, the Gaelic League and the Co-operative Movement*. Notre Dame: University of Notre Dame Press.

Meaney, G. (2002). "Identity and Opposition: Women's Writing, 1890–1960." In A. Bourke et al. (Eds). *The Field Day Anthology of Irish Writing* (vol. V, pp.976–80). New York: New York University Press.

Moynahan, J. (1995). *Anglo-Irish: The Literary Imagination in a Hyphenated Culture*. Princeton: Princeton University Press.

O'Brien, C.C. (1965). *Writers and Politics*. New York: Pantheon Books.

O'Connor, T.P. (1895). "A Book of the Week: The *Shoneens*." *Weekly Sun*, 5 (19 January), 1–2.

Somerville, OE and M. Ross. (1891). *Naboth's Vineyard*. London: Spencer Blackett.

Somerville, OE and M. Ross. (1900). *The Silver Fox* (1898). London: Longmans, Green & Co.

Somerville, OE and M. Ross. (1903). *An Irish Cousin* (1889). London: Longmans, Green & Co.

Somerville, OE and M. Ross. (1908). *Further Experiences of an Irish R.M.* London: Longmans, Green & Co.

Somerville, OE and M. Ross. (1911). *Dan Russel the Fox*. London: Methuen & Co.

Somerville, OE and M. Ross. (1915). *In Mr Knox's Country*. London: Longmans, Green & Co.

Somerville, OE and M. Ross. (1918). *Irish Memories*. New York: Longmans, Green & Co.

Somerville, OE and M. Ross. (1920a). *Mount Music*. New York: Longmans, Green & Co.

Somerville, OE and M. Ross. (1920b). "The Anglo-Irish Language" (1910). In *Stray-Aways* (pp. 184–92). London: Longmans, Green & Co.

Somerville, OE and M. Ross. (1977). *The Real Charlotte* (1894). London: Quartet Books.

Somerville, OE and M. Ross. (1978). *The Big House of Inver* (1925). London: Quartet Books.

Somerville, OE and M. Ross. (1985). *An Enthusiast* (1921). London: Sphere Books.

Somerville, OE and M. Ross. (1987). *French Leave* (1928). London: Sphere Books.

Stevens, J.A. (2007). *The Irish Scene in Somerville and Ross*. Dublin: Irish Academic Press.

Robinson, H. (1980). *Somerville and Ross: A Critical Appreciation*. Dublin: Gill & Macmillan.

Weekes, A.O. (1990). *Irish Women Writers: An Uncharted Tradition*. Lexington: University Press of Kentucky.

Yeats, W.B. (1996). *The Collected Poems of W.B. Yeats*. R.J. Finneran (Ed.). New York: Scribner.

33

W.B. Yeats and the Dialectics of Misrecognition

Gregory Castle

Revivalism and Misrecognition

One of the most challenging tasks confronting those who wish to read Yeats is to decide which Yeats to read. The editors of the *Norton Anthology of English Literature* make the case for multiplicity: "one key to Yeats's greatness is that there are many different Yeatses: a hard-nosed skeptic and an esoteric idealist, a nativist and a cosmopolitan, an Irish nationalist and an ironic antinationalist, a Romantic brooding on loss and unrequited desire and a modernist mocking idealism, nostalgia, and contemporary society" (Greenblatt et al. 2006:2022). I submit that there is really only one Yeats, who re-creates himself continuously through a career of self-correction or self-conquest. His development as a poet, dramatist, memoirist, and essayist was determined to a significant degree by a dialectical logic of misrecognition – or "reading for error" – in which future potential is tied to a pedagogical orientation to temporality, particularly to the past, both recent and remote. Throughout his career, Yeats mobilized a quintessentially Revivalist attitude toward time and temporality in order to structure his own attitude toward the past, toward his own memories, and toward the very language that offers him, through the micro-structure of verb tenses, the artistic means to convey temporal affect (a *feel* for time: nostalgia, anticipation, regret, desire, the uncanny). The Revivalism to which Yeats contributed in so many genres persists in no small measure because the first period of his career (1888–1910) became, in some important ways, the memory of later periods (the middle, 1910–28, and the late, 1928–39). That is to say, rather than speak of Yeats breaking with Revivalism after the death of his friend, the playwright John M. Synge, or after 1916, we ought perhaps to speak of Revivalism transforming under the pressure of the poet's knowledge of the role of misrecognition and of his growing sense of identity with

A Companion to Irish Literature, edited by Julia M. Wright
© 2010 Blackwell Publishing Ltd

Anglo-Ireland, which suggests that Revivalism is not inherently or even primarily dedicated to recovering a pristine, pre-colonial Gaelo-Catholic past.

In the Hegelian philosophical tradition, recognition is a fundamental concept in the dialectical processes of consciousness. With Jacques Lacan and Slavoj Žižek, *mis*-recognition is emphasized as perhaps even more fundamental, for it is the mechanism by which we constitute our imaginary ego ideal. Our sense of ourselves, our past and our possible futures, hinges on an inaugural misrecognition in the mirror phase of our early development, when the child misrecognizes herself as an autonomous being. This is the advent of what Lacan calls the Imaginary Order, and from this point the subject moves toward the truth of the "self." Thus we can say, with Žižek, that "the Truth arises from misrecognition," which means that misrecognition is "an immanent condition of the final advent of the truth" (Žižek 1989:57, 64). For Lacan the truth of the "self" is bound up with unconscious desire that can only be known through mediation by the Symbolic Order. In a similar way, the philosophical and historical truth of which Žižek speaks is an impossible one, for the future in which it arises can only be posited. Nor is there a single leap of recognition, but rather a number of intermediate stages of error and false prophecy, naive or *strategic* mis-recognitions that give way to more cunning or "knowing" instances of *tactical* misrecognition. I use the terms *tactic* and *strategy* as they are employed by Michel de Certeau in his theory of subversive "everyday" practice. For Certeau's project, a *strategy* is a "calculus of force-relationships" in which institutional power becomes "isolated from an 'environment'" and acquires a "mastery of time through the foundation of an autonomous place" (Certeau 1984:xix, 36). A *tactic*, by contrast, is an "improper" move in the strategic spheres of power; it resists both "a spatial or institutional localization" and "the constraining order of the place or of language" (Certeau 1984:xix, 30). Tactics "pin their hopes ... on a clever *utilization of time*" (Certeau 1984:39) by temporalizing or reterritorializing the spatial autonomy of *strategy*.

For Yeats, as for so many other Irish Revivalists, the two poles of the dialectic of misrecognition are characterized by nostalgia ("the backward glance"), connected to the institutional or strategic conception of the past as spatialized and strategic, autonomous, cut off from the living present, and retrospective reappraisal ("the corrective gaze"), a tactical orientation toward nostalgia that reterritorializes the past, overthrowing its autonomy in a "tensed temporality" (the tensions of time articulated in the verb tenses of memory and anticipation), an imbrication or "nesting" of verb tenses that in effect abolishes the difference between memory and anticipation. For this reason, the stage of naive, backward glancing, the strategic revival or reacquisition of the autonomous past, is *necessary*, for only through misrecognition can we arrive at the truth of our own relationship to the past, which is always deferred, put off until later. And while in Yeats' early work, the corrective gaze is untimely and uncertain, bound up with a much stronger impulse toward nostalgia and the backward glance, we see even here a nascent corrective relation to the past.

Revivalist pedagogy contests the strategic "emplacement" of the past as absolutely prior, as an origin (ἀρχή, *archē*) that determines all subsequent temporality. Its history

lessons go against the imperialist grain by rectifying historical error in new representations. Despite its deep affiliations with nationalist movements, however, Revivalist
discourse does not ossify into what Homi Bhabha calls a "national pedagogy" – one
confident in the "pre-given or constituted historical origin [of the "nation's people"]
in the past" (Bhabha 1994:145). Revivalists of all stripes used and reused disciplined
forms of "looking back" to teach the history of Ireland, its coming of age before
modernity, and to critique imperialist histories that subordinated Irish experience to
master-narratives of freedom and progress or that simply declared it "outside of time."
Yeats' project was by contrast a timely one, driven by the dialectics of misrecognition.
He acknowledges as much at the end of his career when, in "Circus Animals' Desertion"
(1939), he tells us that dialectics is the starting point for transcendence: "I must
lie down where all the ladders start / In the foul rag and bone shop of the heart"
(39–40).

Misrecognition is like that rag and bone shop, the necessary ground for futurity.

The Early Period: 1888–1910

In his early, explicitly Revivalist, phase (1888–1910), Yeats focused primarily on the
Gaelo-Catholic folk tradition, particularly on the otherworldly elements of folk tales,
legends, and mythology. Indeed, in his earliest poems, of the late 1880s and early
1890s, temporality is given a spatial dimension, a pervasive sense of *elsewhere* – Tir
na nÓg, "the waters and the wild" ("The Stolen Child," 10), the "woven shade" ("Who
Goes with Fergus?" 2). Alongside the world of "heavy mortal hopes," there extends
indefinitely the "little space for the rose breath" ("To the Rose upon the Rood of
Time," 14). This otherworldly temporality is like the play of days upon water in "Lake
Isle of Innisfree": "I will arise and go now, for always night and day / I hear lake water
lapping with low sounds by the shore" (9–10). The Isle of Innisfree is both an
enchanted place and a metonym for an innocent and pristine past. At this stage, Yeats
is not unlike the old fisherman "who paced in the eve by the nets on the pebbly shore,
/ *When I was a boy with never a crack in my heart*" ("The Meditation of the Old
Fisherman," 11–12). This temporal organization of a remembered space posits an
ideal, and this process can be judged in one of two ways: as a naive wish or as a cunning
mask. *False* recognition or *mis*recognition.

In folklore and legend, the worldly is stitched to the otherworldly as the folktale
subject moves into the timeless ethnographic present (Fabian 1982:80–86). Yeats
gives numerous examples of this in *Celtic Twilight* (first published in 1893), for which
a nostalgic backward glance might well serve as a colophon. Unlike *Fairy and Folk
Tales* (1888), a conventional anthology of previously published material, *The Celtic
Twilight* is a generic anomaly, as Edward Hirsch (1991) describes it, which contains
tales purportedly told to the poet by the rural Irish. For Yeats, traditional Irish materials were "embodiments of the universal and archetypal, they offered not only a way
of transcending parochialism but also a source of positive values absent in modern

life, a way of reapproaching the unfallen world" (Marcus 1987:xv–xvi; see also Castle 2001:60–68). In these tales, as in the early poetry, Yeats appears to long for these values and, as the many references to ghosts, spirits, and other supernatural beings indicate, to envision a future in which the "topsy-turvydoms of faery glamour" (Yeats 1969:8) would be as present to him as they are to his "native informants." As early as 1893, then, he was reconstructing the "mythology" to which "we gave ourselves up in old times" (Yeats 1969:80), trying to breach the autonomy of the past, the "dim kingdom" accessible only by mystical or visionary means. The folkloric fictions that followed in 1897, *The Secret Rose* and *Stories of Red Hanrahan*, continued this project, drawing on Christian and hermetic mysticism to launch an "imaginative conquest of Irish history" (Martin 1972:97–98).

These folkloric texts portray an Irish character very different from the fanciful and sentimental, turbulent and irrational Celt described by Ernest Renan and Matthew Arnold, the most influential popular Celticists of the nineteenth century. Arnold's sense of the Irish as politically impotent and susceptible to "natural magic," related in *On the Study of Celtic Literature* (1867), provoked Yeats to respond in "The Celtic Element in Literature" (1897); however, his claim that he wished to "restate a little" (IV:129) their arguments belies the corrective that he introduces through a skillful interpretation of their naive misrecognitions. For he created (in Certeau's sense) more *useful* idealizations, which served the pedagogical function of rectifying their naive but authoritative misrepresentations. At the same time, he respectfully opposed Douglas Hyde's program of "de-anglicization," calling for a "national literature which shall be none the less Irish in spirit from being English in language" (Yeats 1986:338). Far from excluding the folk traditions, a national literature must be founded on them: "we are young nation," he writes in "Nationality and Literature" (1893), "with unexhausted material lying within us in our still unexpressed national character, about us in our scenery ... and behind us in our multitude of legends" (Yeats 1970:273).

The same logic of misrecognition that allowed Yeats to reaffirm the role of the past in an Irish national literature can be found in the love poems in *The Wind Among the Reeds* (1899). Elizabeth Butler Cullingford has argued that these poems borrow from traditions of courtly desire (Cullingford 1993:25), and this is certainly evident in poems like "He wishes for the Clothes of Heaven," in which misrecognition unfolds in the oscillations of a tensed temporality that limns the occulted significance of the beloved who "Drown[s] love's lonely hour in deep twilight of rest" ("He bids his Beloved be at Peace," 11). These poems frequently take the form of "love elegies" that involve the "aggressive absenting of the beloved" (Ramazani 1990:18). Throughout *Wind Among the Reeds*, the poet's desire is commandeered by a logic of misrecognition, in which loss is absolute, the beloved consigned to an autonomous past: "the loveliness / That has gone from the world" ("He remembers Forgotten Beauty," 2–3). In some cases, however, the poet seeks to breach this autonomy, to look forward to a time when misrecognition and falsehood will be rectified, even by the "children's children" of those who have told lies about his beloved ("He thinks of Those who have spoken Evil of his Beloved," 6).

These love poems are permeated by a temporality of fairy enchantment, "dream-heavy hour[s]" ("He remembers Forgotten Beauty," 16) that suggest that the poet's beloved, like the idealized peasant, can exist only in a meditation upon time. The early drama emphasizes this temporal enchantment by entwining it with the "homogeneous empty time" of world history (Benjamin 1968:261). *The Countess Cathleen* (1892) situates the Irish peasantry in the autonomous past of myth and legend, "a remote time" that nevertheless evokes the Famine of a much more recent epoch. The popular nationalist play, *Cathleen ni Houlihan* (1902), co-written with Lady Augusta Gregory, recasts the Uprising of 1798 as a parable of misrecognition. The figure of the old woman, Cathleen ni Houlihan, personifies the divergency, the going astray, of the recognitions she encourages: "When the people see me quiet, they think old age has come on me and that all the stir has gone of out of me" (II:88). But as young Patrick Gillane discovers, a final recognition lies at the heart of true patriotism, for the beleaguered and iconic old woman, the Shan Van Vocht, is *really* "a young girl, and she had the walk of a queen" (II:93). These plays often involved a misrecognition of the actual socio-economic conditions of the Irish peasantry (Hirsch 1991; Fleming 1995), but it was precisely Yeats' idealizations that served in a tactical way to overcome the far more insidious image of the "stage Irishman," who "carries a shillelagh, is loyal to the point of naïveté, never far from a fight or a song, and, most importantly, twists language into unexpected shapes with his 'bulls,' or illogical logic" (Morash 2002:46).

Yeats' work with the Irish Literary Theatre, and later the Irish National Theatre, which he faithfully documented in the theatre's journal *Beltaine* (succeeded by *Samhain* and *Arrow*), more than anything else in the early period offered a measure of his commitment to cultural nationalism. In what are arguably his most achieved dramatic works, those based on the exploits of the Iron Age hero Cuchulain, Yeats explores the dimensions of a heroism defined as much by error, misrecognition, and ambivalence as by superior courage, strength and fortitude. Most of these plays – *On Baile's Strand*, *The Green Helmet*, *The Only Jealousy of Emer*, *The Death of Cuchulain* – are based on accounts well known to readers of the Ulster cycle of Irish legends, a version of which Lady Gregory published under the title *Cuchulain of Muirthemne* (1902).

Cuchulain is in some ways an allegory of a future-oriented logic of misrecognition. When, in *The Green Helmet* (1910), he offers his own life in payment of a debt incurred by his companions, he tells his wife, Emer, "when my story is done / My fame shall spring up and laugh, and set you high above all" (II:254). His companions have failed to recognize the challenge issued by the Red Man (a head for a head), which turns out to be a test that Cuchulain passes when he offers himself as a sacrifice, a tactical misrecognition that Yeats engineers in order to stress that the hero's bravery is a message for a time to come. The Red Man, while placing the prized helmet on Cuchulain's head and praising his heart, hand, and "laughing lip," says, "these things I make prosper, till a day come that I know, / When heart and mind shall darken that the weak my end the strong, / And the long-remembering harpers have matter for their song" (II:255). Cuchulain is less the icon of past glories than the champion of the future, *when he will be remembered* by the harpers who will immortalize him. Fame, for the warrior, is a guarantee of a final recognition, of being well known in coming times.

At the Hawk's Well (1917), one of the *Four Plays for Dancers* (1921), marks the turn to a more stylized representation of the Cuchulain story. In these plays, Yeats makes tactical use of Japanese Noh drama, to which Ezra Pound introduced him while the two writers were working together at Stone Cottage in England (1913–16). Noh is a highly stylized, vigorously non-mimetic dramatic form that incorporates ritualistic acting, chanting, song, sparse instrumentation, and impressionistic costuming, set design, and masks. In Noh plays, the autonomy of the past is ironically guaranteed by revenants who demand retribution for past acts. *At the Hawk's Well*, based on the Noh play *Yoro*, departs from this tradition by focusing on Cuchulain's desire for immortality. Having misrecognized the guardian of the well (a "Woman of the Sídhe" who takes the form of a hawk), Cuchulain incurs her wrath, and the play concludes with him heading into a battle that will guarantee his fame. In *Fighting the Waves* (1930), a revision of an earlier play, *The Only Jealousy of Emer*, the ghost of Cuchulain comes to Emer, not to make retribution but to secure this futurity. Emer's "lamentations" have "dragged him hither," and she discovers that she must sacrifice her dream of a domestic life or lose her husband to a future in the sea god Manannan's house, where "he will be as the gods who remember nothing" (II:460–61).

The struggle between memory and forgetting is evident as early as 1904, when, in the title poem of *In the Seven Woods*, Yeats writes of having forgotten a recent excavation of Tara, the seat of ancient Irish kings: "I have forgot awhile / Tara uprooted" ("In the Seven Woods," 5–6). The space of the forgetful present, like Manannan's house, is for Yeats devoid of humanity, of speech and signs – "the Quiet / Wanders laughing and eating her wild heart" (10–11) – and this pleases him. It is an otherworldly space of forgetting but it is also the anticipation of a mark, of a bull's eye – the final recognition signified by "that Great Archer," with his "cloudy quiver," "Who but awaits His hour to shoot" (12–14), an apt image of the ambivalence and hesitancy of misrecognition. The same mood of quiet waiting, tempered with lovelorn melancholy, is found in "Adam's Curse," a frankly pedagogical poem that focuses on lessons "they do not talk about at school": the labor of beauty and of the poet's attempt "to articulate sweet sounds together" (19, 10). The labor of overcoming misrecognition may account for the weariness in the penultimate section, the sense of worn-out time, of "time's waters" washing the moon, breaking "in days and years" (32–33). This breaking, this rhythmic, wave-like rising and falling, links the process of temporality with a movement of vast liquid space. The unity of the process is sustained mainly in the spatial effect, the "oceanic" image of vastness and vast configurations and systems of change. The concluding section brings a determined poem, one strongly oriented toward the pedagogical, to the impasse of ambivalence.

We see this ambivalence – forgetfulness, temporal ironies, displacements, inconsistencies, and so on – throughout *In the Seven Woods* and the volume that followed, *The Green Helmet*, volumes that record a shift in Yeats' focus from Gaelo-Catholic folkways to the Anglo-Protestant Ascendancy, frequently figured in the image of Maud Gonne as Helen of Troy, most famously in "No Second Troy." In "A Woman Homer Sung," Yeats slyly links the mythic subject, through the medium of an oscillating, tensed temporality, to a contemporary beloved. He dreams of the past, thrusting his thoughts toward the future, for *"coming time* may say / 'He shadowed in a glass / What a thing her body *was'"* (12–14; my emphasis). He recognizes that his own "shadowy" conceptions will be rectified, and the future assured, precisely by virtue of his own tactical misrecognitions of his beloved in the past. In the meantime, his beloved's "sweet" pride can be known only by a backward glance that skims a "heroic dream" of "life and letters" (20–21). The recursive loop of these early love poems recaptures the past in a temporality that points ahead and installs futurity, not a pure or primeval past, as the goal of Revivalist desire.

The Middle Period: 1910–1928

In the run up to World War I, Yeats reshaped Gregory's Seven Woods and her Georgian manor according to the same logic of misrecognition that structured his experiences with Maud Gonne and the "fairy-faith" of the rural Irish. In "Upon a House shaken by the Land Agitation" (1910), Yeats misrecognizes Coole Park, failing to see its strategic place in a larger socio-economic context, not yet able to move beyond an equally strategic idealized habitat for "lidless eyes" and "eagle thoughts" (4–5). At this time the poet's turn to Coole Park and the Anglo-Irishry was complicated by his attitude toward an emergent Gaelo-Catholic middle class, which could not carry the weight of his idealizations. "In dreams begins responsibility," the poet writes in an epigraph to *Responsibilities* (1916), and it is clear in this volume that he has taken a new measure of his own duty as an artist. At the core of *Responsibilities* are the *Poems Written in Discouragement* (1913) in which Yeats confronts Paudeen, an urbanized peasant who "play[s] at pitch and toss" ("To a Wealthy Man," 31), because that is the limit of his access to culture: games to be played on terra firma. By contrast, the patron, whose access to culture is linked to access to transcendence, needs to "Look up in the sun's eye and give / What the exultant heart calls good" so that futurity will *breed* the best and provide the "right twigs for an eagle's nest," high above the fray (33–34, 36).

"September 1913" extends this argument and recalibrates the logic of misrecognition in a way that reinforces the de-idealization of the peasant and the compensatory idealization of Anglo-Irishry. In the poem's refrain, the characteristic backward glance would appear to have frozen its object into the statuary of elegy: "Romantic Ireland's dead and gone / It's with O'Leary in the grave" (7–8). This makes perfect sense, since the elegy is the quintessential mode for celebrating the autonomy of the past. Yeats realizes that one cannot "turn the years again" and bring back "those exiles *as they were*" (25–26; my emphasis), for their truth lies precisely in their having been exiled. Were we able to bring back Edward Fitzgerald, Robert Emmet, or Wolfe Tone, their reckless heroism ("that delirium of the brave") would be rejected as the madness brought on by "Some woman's yellow hair" (22, 28). In the same stroke, Yeats consigns "Romantic Ireland" to an utterly bereft, autonomous past, "dead and gone," and creates a poetic memorial (see also "Easter 1916") that serves the pedagogical function of tutoring the Irish about their own political myopia. This is not the naive nostalgia of the poet who yearns for the past, but the tactical corrective gaze, extravagantly cloaked in the rhetoric of nostalgia, that seeks to move beyond naivety.

Responsibilities represents the difficulties of this stage and suggests that, for tactical misrecognition to do its work, Yeats would need to turn a corrective gaze upon what he has consigned to the past so that he might postulate a new future for himself, his poetry, and Ireland. This is to some extent accomplished in "The Fisherman," published in *The Wild Swans at Coole* (1919), in which the Gaelo-Catholic peasant is eulogized by the poet in the manner of one who witnesses the passing of an effigy. He confesses that he had constructed an idealized image of the peasant, through a kind of ethnographic redemption (Castle 2001:87–91), in reaction to the degradation of "great Art beaten down": "Suddenly I began, / In scorn of this audience / Imagining a man … A man who does not exist, / A man who is but a dream" (26–28, 35–36). Helen Vendler has noted that this "satirical poem" is primarily devoted to "a slashing attack on the contemporary urban crowd, among whom Yeats sees none but the craven and the insolent, drunken knaves and common wits" (Vendler 2007:189). As in "Paudeen" and "September 1913," there is a sense of inadequacy, for the fisherman is "an incomplete symbol for a positive nationalist culture" (Vendler 2007:191). An "incomplete symbol" of this kind can function adequately *only* as an allegory in which the fisherman dramatizes the poet's naive misrecognition of the rural Irish. His "bold prophecy" (Vendler 2007:191) – "I shall have written him one / Poem maybe as cold / And passionate as the dawn" (38–40) – is cast in the future perfect, the space of a final recognition, which is shrouded in ambivalence ("maybe"), as is appropriate for a futurity that is constituted by what *will have happened*.

Surrounding this landmark of rectification are powerful elegiac misrecognitions of the Anglo-Irishry. In the great "group elegy" "In Memory of Major Robert Gregory," the backward glance is not that of a "collectivity [that] mourns for an individual" (Ramazani 1990:32) but rather that of an individual who requires, for his own futurity, the autonomy of a band of dead friends. Though firmly in the past, each ghostly avatar (Lionel Johnson, Synge, George Pollexfen, Robert Gregory) presents a *tableau vivant*, a dialectical image of elegiac longing, by which the poet secures himself for the future: he "gathers strength by dramatizing his triumphant relationship with the dead" (Ramazani 1990:43). The past and present perfect tenses enable an imbrication, a temporal recursiveness, by which the autonomous past is invested with futurity:

> We *dreamed* that a great painter *had been born*
>
> .   .   .   .
>
> And *yet he had* the intensity

> *To have published* all to be a world's delight
>
> .   .   .   .
>
> I *had thought* …
>
>   to *have brought* to mind
>
> All those that manhood tried
>
>   (65, 71–72, 89–91; my emphasis)

The tactical corrective limned by these perfect tenses, in this and other poems in the collection, posit the no-longer-possible past only in order to pave the way for the probable future. As in "The Wild Swans at Coole," the poet glances backward – even while he imagines those "nine-and-fifty swans," which will "delight men's eyes when I awake some day / To find they have flown away" (6, 29–30).

Misrecognition takes on a decidedly corrective dimension in poems such as "A Prayer for my Daughter," in *Michael Robartes and the Dancer* (1921), which ironically employs elegy to prophesy a de-idealized future for the infant Anne Yeats. The poet seeks, through mythic misrecognitions of Maud Gonne, to guarantee for his daughter a future in which she is "self-delighting, / Self-appeasing, self-affrighting" (67–68). A tensed temporality of present and future perfect forms – "May she be," "Helen being chosen," "I'd have her chiefly learned" (17, 25, 33) – introduces misrecognition (in this case, of Gonne) in order to posit a final, unifying recognition in the future: "O, may she live like some green laurel" or, again, in "a house / Where all's accustomed, ceremonious" (47, 73–74). A similar pattern is discerned in Yeats' meditation on the world-historical event of the Easter Rising, which repeats, in significant ways, the ambivalent dynamic of "September 1913," in which a patently backward glance is put under the pressure of a corrective gaze. "Easter 1916" expresses the poet's sense of ambivalence about the Rising, specifically whether the poets, writers, and teachers who took part were sacrificed for any good reason. The question – "Was it needless death after all?" (67) – is thrown into futurity, and like all such questions can only be answered later, for only then can we tell if what is now *misrecognized* as needless can be claimed as a final recognition, the unity that is truth. But, the poet asks, what if this "needless death," were only an "excess of love," a bewilderment (72–73). The same question is posed in an occult register in "The Second Coming" (1921), in which the larger picture of historical bewilderment suggests not needlessness but an unknown and terrifying future purpose: "what rough beast, its hour come round at last, / Slouches towards Bethlehem to be born?" (21–22)?

By the early 1920s Yeats was testing the sufficiency of time by occult means. Though his involvement in mysticism and the occult went back at least to the early 1890s and the Order of the Golden Dawn, his first extended contribution to these traditions was *Per Amica Silentia Lunae* (1917), a curious work, which he described as "an explanation of the religious convictions and philosophical speculations that I hope govern my life" (quoted in Foster 2003: 75). Dedicated to Iseult Gonne, Maud's daughter, it is an attempt to explain his belief in the dialectical or agonistic quality of poetry that emerges from our misrecognitions: "We make out of the quarrel with others, rhetoric, but of the quarrel with ourselves, poetry" (V:8). This mystico-autobiographical work ontologizes the "war of spiritual with natural order" (Yeats 1897:vii) and makes it a *fact* of being: "There are two realities, the terrestrial and the condition of fire" (V:25). Such antinomies preoccupied Yeats, intensifying after his marriage to Georgie Hyde-Lees, herself an adept in spiritualism and quite willing to conduct occult experiments, such as the automatic writing sessions that were the foundation for *A Vision* (Harper 2006). This latter text, first published in 1925, is an attempt to render systematic (i.e., strategic) the seeming anarchism of the writing produced by Georgie. It was a strange collaboration, and an even stranger text, that Yeats made somewhat more accessible in the 1937 revised edition. But he also ironized it by, among other things, including "A Packet for Ezra Pound," which puts his whole mystical project into a strange dialogue with continental modernism.

It is tempting to draw lines of affiliation between *A Vision* and the mystification of *Bildung* – an "age-long memoried self" (III:216) – that we see in the autobiographies of the 1920s, later published in *Autobiographies* (1955). In these texts, particularly in *Trembling of the Veil* (1922), Yeats describes a process he called *dreaming back*, in which we live our lives "backward for a certain number of years, treading paths that we have trodden," aiming for a "crowning achievement," the plunge forward into a unity of being (III:283–84). These memoirs are disciplined forms of backward glancing that at times thematize the corrective gaze that the poet turns upon the pleasurable fictions of himself: "My memories had magnified / So many times childish delight" ("Towards Break of Day," 10–11). The memoirs counsel the aesthetic transformation of the self into Mask and Image and explore the poet's personality (*Bildung*) as the "suffering of desire." A hermetic aestheticism posits not simply a transformation of language by human creativity but the "re-creation of the man through … art" (III:217). But it is not until *Dramatis Personae* (1935) that Yeats focuses, with Swiftian precision, on a key period of the Revival era (1896–1902), and sketches an exquisite misrecognition of that epoch, a summing up and a memorial: self-conscious, artful, untrue, but with the ring of truth that one hears in that other great modernist memoir of misrecognition, Walter Benjamin's *Berlin Chronicle* (1932).

The Late Period: 1928–1939

By 1928 Yeats was internationally known, having won the Nobel Prize in 1923 and served in the Irish Free State Senate for two terms. His acquisition of an eleventh-century Norman tower in County Galway, not far from Coole Park, brilliantly conveys the way the past points the way to the future, for the tower is part of a modest dynastic ambition. "I, the poet William Yeats," he declares, "restored this tower for my wife George; / And may these characters remain / When all is ruin once again" ("To be Carved on a Stone at Thoor Ballylee" [1921], 1, 4–6). In this, one of his earliest epitaphic verses, Yeats plans ahead to send his message, helpless in its bottle, beyond the time when the tower will be a "ruin once again." In the late period, futurity increasingly springs from the poet's sense of his own mortality, which he expresses in memorial verse that is less elegiac than *self-elegiac*, to use Ramazani's term. "Sailing to Byzantium," which opens *The Tower* (1928), is a poem about old age, about the living soul coupled to an aging body, couched in a stark generational difference: the young succumb to terrestrial time – "Whatever is begotten, born and dies" – while old men long for "Monuments of unageing intellect" (6, 8). It is a frank revelation, in the present perfect, of a desire for transcendence: "I *have sailed* the seas and come / To the holy city of Byzantium" (15–16; my emphasis). Yeats misrecognizes Byzantium in advance, tactically and cunningly, in order to articulate the desire for a transcendence that it is not entirely freed from terra firma. In "The Tower," he gives himself a choice between "abstract things" and the unmediated world of "battered kettle[s]" (15–16), and settles on an uneasy accommodation between them. The tower itself is a strategic vantage point, panoptical and pseudo-transcendent, on the "battlements" of which the poet surveys the past in the service of the present. In the long roster of his creations in part II, Yeats calls to mind an imaginary dramatis personae, including Mary Hynes and Red Hanrahan. He reintroduces Hanrahan as a creation of *his* thought ("I thought it all out twenty years ago," 64) and an assertion of *his* right to represent, and in these gestures he lays claim to the very principle of misrecognition, for Hanrahan "Reckoned up every unforeknown, unseeing / Plunge" into the "labyrinth of another's being" (109–10, 112). The corrective gaze by definition negotiates labyrinths: gaze turned upon a prior gaze, correction upon correction, the logic of misrecognition moving toward greater clarity of vision. The poem's conclusion is performative in the purest sense: a last will and testament, a legal disposition toward the past for the sake of the future, those "upstanding men / That climb the streams" (122–23). The poet bequeaths his pride in a swan song, a transfer of power and imagination, in which time is abolished in a "Translunar Paradise" (156). He "makes his peace" with memory and time, which encourage his illusions of the timeless, "Mirror-resembling dream" (164–65).

Many of the anxieties that we see in the late poems, particularly in *The Tower*, stem from Yeats' consciousness of being an Anglo-Irishman in a Catholic Free State. Postcolonial theory in Yeats studies has grappled with this anomalous state (Lloyd 1993; Fleming 2001), one that makes it difficult to place him in a "subaltern" position within a neo-Hegelian system of dialectical struggle (see Memmi 1967). Nevertheless, I think Marjorie Howes is right to situate Yeats within a constellation of processes and problems that he shared with postcolonial writers all over the world. "What Yeats and postcolonial studies share," she argues, "is a troubled political conception of culture in which an enormous faith in culture's transformative and emancipatory power confronts a series of issues that are both foundational and damaging to that faith" (Howes 2006:55). This cultural faith is in part driven by a radical nationalist pedagogy that focuses specifically on the unique social and historical conditions of postcolonial Ireland. In fact some critics, such as Edward Said (1990), regard Yeats as a "poet of decolonization." Nevertheless, it is difficult to square the postcolonial Yeats with the "unregenerate Ascendancy elitist." "To respectable nationalist

Ireland," Foster writes, "Yeats's idiosyncratic style of slightly bohemian grandeur seemed archaic, affected, and un-Irish" (Foster 2003:297, 257).

In the historical sequences in *The Tower*, Yeats' attitude toward the Free State is mediated by themes of dynastic stability and proper inheritance. The poet turns to a temporality of generations that links his own presence-in-the-world to the presence of those who have come before and those yet to come. The language of begetting – "images that yet / Fresh images beget" ("Byzantium," 38–39) – is the language of the "Ancestral Houses" that he celebrates at the opening of "Meditations in Time of Civil War" (1928), the great houses with "long galleries, lined / With famous portraits of our ancestors" ("Ancestral Houses," 36–37). His own misrecognitions, bound up with questions concerning the relation between ethics and aesthetics, are cunning and calculated, designed not only to call into question his own imaginary investments in Coole Park (a project he will continue in *The Winding Stair*) but also to posit still another misrecognition, the terrible beauty of fantasy: "We had fed the heart on fantasies, / The heart's grown brutal from the fare" ("The Stare's Nest by My Window," 16–17). "Nineteen Hundred and Nineteen" (1928) more explicitly laments the "ingenious lovely things" (1) that have disappeared, and metes out blame to all, especially those who mock greatness and who are unable to see the true nature of this historical violence, of "weasels fighting in a hole" (32). It is fitting that both sequences close with apocalyptic imagery, temporal non sequiturs, discontinuous and impressionistic visions of "last days," which serve as the rhetorical equivalent of final recognition. The refusal of teleology in these poems, which is emphasized by their anachronistic placement in the volume ("Meditations" preceding "Nineteen Hundred and Nineteen"), is of a piece with the questions that end "Leda and the Swan," Yeats' great miniature on the subject of world history. What, he asks, are the implications of the "broken wall, the burning roof and tower" (10) that serve as metonyms for the "sudden" forces of history? What is the role of the individual in historical processes? Is the human subject left in the place of Leda, who may or may not have "put on [the Swan's] knowledge with his power" (13)? These questions point to a lost cultural assurance and therefore harmonize with the implied questions in the great Anglo-Irish elegies.

The Winding Stair (1933) sustains this elegiac note, beginning with the lyrical and subtly explosive "In Memory of Eva Gore-Booth and Con Markiewicz." This lean, almost impersonal elegy imagines a double misrecognition. The poet seems to look back upon a golden time of "kimonos" and "gazelles" and to mourn the loss of both sisters to political causes: like Maud Gonne, they have misrecognized the value of their own beauty. The poet's misrecognition of *their* misrecognitions is tactical in part because it is driven by a perceived need for aesthetic redemption: the poet *must* misrecognize the object of his elegiac desire, *must* use the tropes of misprision and naivety in an attempt to sustain his faith in transcendence. "The innocent and the beautiful / Have no enemy but time" (24–25), because in time, in the temporality of action and reflection, all innocence and beauty are subject to the mechanisms of nostalgia and the desire for some "vague Utopia" (11). In either case, time is the only experience that threatens the purity and pristinity of hope. "A Prayer for my Daughter" had asked, "How but in custom and in ceremony / Are innocence and beauty born?" (77–78). Now the poet stands amid the ruins and shadows of "ancestral houses," appealing with a fitting irony to the very forces of destruction that have ridden into this aristocratic world on the "filthy modern tide" ("The Statues," 29). Therefore, the appeal to apocalypse, to the destruction of time, is on reserve: "Bid me strike a match and blow" ("In Memory," 32).

Ironically, the Anglo-Irish Big House and its dominant mood of "pride established in humility" ("Coole Park, 1929," 16) permitted a more "knowing" position, in large measure because the corrective gaze the poet is able to cast over his memories and works makes possible the kind of cunning misrecognitions that were unavailable at earlier stages of his career. The dark, nearly gothic "Coole Park and Ballylee, 1931" employs a symbolic natural world to figure a dynastic temporality as old as the hills: "ancestral trees / Or gardens rich in memory glorified / Marriages, alliances and families" (34–36). It conveys the sentiments of a minority in fear of its social and historical annihilation, which accounts for the iteration of disconsolate phrases: the "last inheritor," "the last romantics" (30, 41). This, too, is a persistent trend in Anglo-Protestant discourse, but Yeats' version of it is keyed to his concern for a social class set adrift, "Like some poor Arab tribesman and his tent" or, better, a swan drifting "upon a darkening flood" (40, 48). It is this tragic *dis*placement rather than traumatic violence that undermined the political and cultural will of the Anglo-Protestant Ascendancy.

In *The Winding Stair*, the poet begins decisively to comprehend the extent to which his strategic misrecognitions (mythologies, systems, codes that structure entry into heavens and utopias) had failed to free him from the necessity to recapture the autonomous past, which is, he now discovers, the route to a kind of cultural melancholy. The elegies in this volume thus represent an advance on those in *The Wild Swans at Coole*, for they are moving out of melancholy into a mourning that "holds the match" to idealizations. However, the desire for destruction is balanced, in "Vacillation," by a desire to find unity in antinomy, to create a dialectical image for a "sudden blaze" of blessedness (41). Vacillation is thus a form of "profane illumination" (Benjamin 1986:190) that unveils and embraces the contradiction at the heart of antinomies, which is brilliantly conveyed by the image of a *singular* tree "half all glittering flame and half all green" ("Vacillation," 12). As in "The Tower" and "Under Ben Bulben," the poet imagines his heirs, "Proud, open-eyed and laughing to the tomb" (32–34), because they see death less as a barrier to the future than as its guarantee. Unlike the historical sequences, this one ends on a meditative note in which the poet invokes the Catholic mystic Von Hügel and St Teresa of Avila, who occupy a past that requires an absolute separateness parallel to a heaven in which autonomy is achieved through becoming "eternalised" (83). Homer's "unchristened heart" provides the poet with access to the living past of legend, while Von Hügel can offer nothing more than the embalmed and autonomous past, which religion seeks to reacquire miraculously, as when "a modern saint ... scooped out Pharaoh's mummy" (83–84).

The general mood of "tragic gaiety" in *New Poems* (1938) and the final grouping usually referred to as *Last Poems* (1939) is adumbrated with brutal classical economy in "Meru," the last of twelve "supernatural songs" in *Parnell's Funeral and Other Poems* (1935). The poet writes that "Civilization is hooped together, brought / Under a rule, under the semblance of peace / By manifold illusion" (1–3). Hooped together, semblance, illusion: these are tropes of misrecognition that survive the annihilation of the poet's "glory and his monuments" (14). In "Lapis Lazuli," the poet offers the solace of aesthetics, for the rebuilding of a ruined culture constitutes the primary motive force of art: "all things fall and are built again / And those that build them again are gay" (35–36). Tragic gaiety, even in the midst of violence, paves the way toward the (only possible) future. It is a kind of rectitude, a courageous and practical pedagogy, that will halt dialectics long enough to craft an image, to teach "The lineaments of a plummet-measured face" ("The Statues," 32). The gaiety of Hamlet or Lear is that state of mind that transforms the "dread" experienced in the present into something "aimed at, found and lost" ("Lapis Lazuli," 18). The futurity to which tragedy appears to point – "Heaven blazing into the head" (19) – is an earthly ideal, a mode of transcendence that is predicated on the standpoint of loss and violence: a futurity, in short, that depends on the tactical misrecognition of violence as something other than the annihilation of the self, of art, of "old civilizations." This is why "modernity is always quoting primeval history" (Benjamin 1986:157) – that is to say, why modernity requires its absolute other, but can arrive at it, can discover a prehistory for itself, only by quoting it. Amid the destruction of civilizations that have been painstakingly developed, there stands the rebuilder, the one whose creative gaiety builds up again what has been lost. Tragic gaiety, then, is a profoundly historical perspective, requiring "utopian strength … a promise which does not fetishize what it promises" (Benjamin 1968:179). From a perspective half-way up the mountainside, the violence below can be transformed into art, the trauma of living, of crisis and movement, immortalized in stone: "Every accidental crack or dent / Seems a water-course or an avalanche" ("Lapis Lazuli," 44–45). The enigmatic figures with "ancient, glittering eyes" (56), who halt at the point of transference, the "little half-way house" of error and fantasy, remind the poet of the extent to which transcendence is a misrecognition of earthly conditions.

A similar moment of transference animates "Under Ben Bulben," that great testamentary poem, in which the relation between the present and the past unfolds within an abstract contemporaneity. "Buried men" are not left behind, cut off from the future, but rather "thrust … / Back in the human mind again" (23–24). The violence of nationalist revolt ("fighting mad"), which comes after "all words are said," is a unifying experience; it completes a "partial mind" (27–28, 30). The "great forefathers" are not locked in the confines of an autonomous past, but are there *in the present*, they are not to be "shirked" (38–39). For it is these figures from the past, stripped of nostalgia, who "Bring the soul of man to God" and who guarantee a kind of racial rectitude by "fill[ing] the cradles right" (40–41). They are called upon to *guarantee the future*, and this calling obliterates the autonomy of the past and indicates how it might live again. It is, after all, the purpose of art, and of our awareness of the living past, to aim for a "purpose set / Before the secret-working mind: / Profane perfection of mankind" (51–52). It is this purpose, this obligation to rebuild culture, that underwrites the poet's judgment of the "Base-born products of base beds" (72).

Yeats' long-standing interest in the Anglo-Protestant Ascendancy is here couched frankly in terms of a valuable and vital social formation, an eternal, highborn race. His verse structures the temporality of misrecognition in subtle indications of priority; the de-idealized, wayward figures of late modernity – "the sort now growing up," with their "unremembering hearts and heads" ("Under Ben Bulben," 70, 72) – are rejected in favor of a unity of culture: "Sing the peasantry, *and then* / Hard-riding country gentlemen" (74–75, my emphasis; see also III:214–15). In this context, the temporal priority given to the peasant paradoxically effects its re-idealization in the context of the newly idealized Anglo-Irishry. In the concluding section, the poet consigns himself to a burial ground in which his own death, his own past, is not so much commemorated – "No marble, no conventional phrase" (89) – as memorialized in a dialectical image. The horseman who passes casts a corrective gaze (a "cold eye") upon the past ("life") and the future ("death") (92–93): for in death, the poet guarantees the "coming days." Though working critically through the problem of temporality and misrecognition, Yeats nevertheless installs a new ideal, a more knowing one to be sure, a new starting point, a "half-way house," where dialectics pause on their journey to truth.

In one of his last works, *Purgatory* (1938), Yeats translates his concern for Anglo-Ireland in terms of racial corruption and self-murder. In some ways, *Purgatory* comes closer than any of his other plays to conveying the ancestral terror at the heart of Noh drama. The Big House at the center of the play is the living emblem of social class caught in the grip of a tragedy of its own making. The sense that the Anglo-Irish *kindred* is always in crisis and that inheritance and reproduction are repetitions of an original sin is powerfully dramatized in terms of "mixed" marriage and intergenerational violence: "My father and my son on the same jack-knife!" (II:543). But the kindred relations depicted in the play are not those of a classical Oedipal variety. "In *Purgatory*," writes Howes, "kindred relations are those of violence, discontinuity and death. … conventional relations between fathers and sons – affection, Oedipal rivalry – are purely incidental to their Yeatsian kindred relation" (Howes 1997:184). Like *On the Boiler* (1938) and other prose works in this period, *Purgatory* expresses the poet's interest in eugenics (Childs 2001), and in this context the themes of ancestry and bloodlines are given a gothic, nearly sublime dimension. Throughout his career, Yeats put images and ideas into a creative process of correction and review; perhaps we can say the same of these late works, in which adherence to belief gives way to a kind of performative or alienated assent. On this view, ideas and images are not *believed in*; indeed, they are not a matter of belief at all, but of rhetorical or aesthetic contingency, of being *ready to hand* (like automatic writing) for the poet's tactical reuse. The danger is to mistake this reuse – central to the process of misrecognition – for a stable and enduring belief, when it is something more fragile and unpredictable: a way of reading and writing about the past that requires the tactical mobilization of error and misprision.

The taunting gaze of misrecognition, first expressed in "The Stolen Child" – in which the *Sídhe* lure children to an enchanted space, "Where the wave of moonlight glosses / The dim gray sands with light" (13–14) – is rendered in works like *Purgatory* as a tragic necessity that takes on the character of a murderous irruption, a brutal contingency. At the end of his career, the dialectics of his own enlightenment (*Bildung*) permit him to recognize the value of misrecognition: "Those masterful images because complete / Grew in pure mind, but out of what began?" (33–34). The answer to his question – "a mound of refuse or the sweepings of a street" (35) – points towards the past ("old kettles, old bottles") and the future where rectification transforms "old rags" into heavenly raiment, the unity of "pure mind," whose dialectical image is a half-way point.

REFERENCES AND FURTHER READING

Unless otherwise noted, all references to Yeats are to the twelve-volume *Collected Works* (1989) edited by R.J. Finneran and G.M. Harper. Citations of poetry are from Volume I, and give the line number(s) cited; dates given for the poems are those listed in this volume. All other citations of Yeats' works are to volume and page number of the edition.

Benjamin, W. (1968). *Illuminations*. H. Arendt (Ed.), H. Zohn (Trans.). New York: Harcourt, Brace & World.

Benjamin, W. (1986). *Reflections: Essays, Aphorisms, Autobiographical Writing*. P. Demetz (Ed.). E. Jephcott (Trans.). New York: Schocken.

Bhabha, H. (1994). *The Location of Culture*. London: Routledge.

Castle, G. (2001). *Modernism and the Celtic Revival*. Cambridge: Cambridge University Press.

Certeau, M. de. (1984). *The Practice of Everyday Life*. S. Rendall (Trans.). Berkeley: University of California Press.

Childs, D.J. (2001). *Modernism and Eugenics: Woolf, Eliot, Yeats, and the Culture of Degeneration*. Cambridge: Cambridge University Press.

Cullingford, E. (1993). *Gender and History in Yeats's Love Poetry*. Cambridge: Cambridge University Press.

Doggett, R. (2006). *Deep-Rooted Things: Empire and Nation in the Poetry and Drama of William Butler Yeats*. Notre Dame: University of Notre Dame Press.

Fabian, J. (1982). *Time and Other: How Anthropology Makes its Object*. New York: Columbia University Press.

Fleming, D. (1995). *"A Man Who Does Not Exist": The Irish Peasant in the Work of W.B. Yeats and J.M. Synge*. Ann Arbor: University of Michigan Press.

Fleming, D. (Ed.). (2001). *W.B. Yeats and Postcolonialism*. West Cornwall, CT: Locust Hill Press.

Foster, R.F. (1997, 2003) *W.B. Yeats: A Life*. 2 vols. Oxford: Oxford University Press.

Greenblatt, S. et al. (Eds). (2006). *The Norton Anthology of English Literature*. 8th edn. Vol. II. New York: Norton.

Harper, M.M. (2006). *Wisdom of Two: The Spiritual and Literary Collaboration of George and W.B. Yeats*. Oxford: Oxford University Press.

Hirsch, E. (1991). "The Imaginary Irish Peasant." *PMLA*, 106, 1116–33.

Howes, M. (1997). *Yeats's Nations: Gender, Class, and Irishness*. Cambridge: Cambridge University Press.

Howes, M. (2006). "Postcolonial Yeats: Culture, Enlightenment, and the Public Sphere." *Field Day Review*, 2, 55–73.

Lloyd, D. (1993). *Anomalous States: Irish Writing and the Post-Colonial Moment*. Dublin: Lilliput Press.

Marcus, P.L. (1987). *Yeats and the Beginning of the Irish Renaissance*. 2nd edn. Syracuse: Syracuse University Press.

Martin, A. (1972). "*The Secret Rose* and Yeats's Dialogue with History." *Ariel*, 3.3, 91–103.

Memmi, A. (1967). *The Colonizer and the Colonized*. H. Greenfeld (Trans.). Boston: Beacon.

Morash, C. (2002). *History of Irish Theater*. Cambridge: Cambridge University Press.

Ramazani, J. (1990). *Yeats and the Poetry of Death: Elegy, Self-Elegy, and the Sublime*. New Haven: Yale University Press.

Said, E. (1990). "Yeats and Decolonization." In *Nationalism, Colonialism and Literature* (pp. 69–95). Minneapolis: University of Minnesota Press.

Vendler, H. (2007). *Our Secret Discipline: Yeats and Lyric Form*. Cambridge, MA: Harvard University Press.

Yeats, W.B. (1897). *The Secret Rose*. London: Lawrence & Bullen.

Yeats, W.B. (1969). *Mythologies*. New York: Collier-Macmillan.

Yeats, W.B. (1970). *Uncollected Prose*. Vol. I. J.P. Frayne (Ed.). New York: Columbia University Press.

Yeats, W.B. (1986). *The Collected Letters of W.B. Yeats*, vol. I: *1865–1895*. J. Kelly and E. Domville (Eds). Oxford: Clarendon Press.

Yeats, W.B. (1989). *The Collected Works of W.B. Yeats*. R.J. Finneran and G.M. Harper (Gen. Eds). 12 vols. New York: Macmillan.

Žižek, S. (1989). *The Sublime Object of Ideology*. London: Verso.

34

John Millington Synge – Playwright and Poet

Ann Saddlemyer

To theater historians the name of John Millington Synge is synonymous with riots at Dublin's Abbey Theatre over the first production of *The Playboy of the Western World* in January 1907. He is also remembered for a few striking comments on the playwright's role: "All art is a collaboration"; "On the stage one must have reality, and one must have joy"; "In a good play every speech should be as fully flavoured as a nut or apple"; "In Ireland, for a few years more, we have a popular imagination that is fiery and magnificent, and tender" (Synge 1995:96–97); "The drama, like the symphony, does not teach or prove anything" (Synge 1995:28). Yet Synge's career as a dramatist was surprisingly short. His first completed plays were written during the summer of 1902 and his sixth and last, never polished to his satisfaction, appeared in 1910, the year after his death. During that brief span he also published essays and reviews, a book on his visits to the Aran Islands, reworked without success an early autobiographical play, and completed a volume of poems and translations. His preface to this last, written just months before he died, can be viewed as a summary of his theories on language and, indeed, of life as expressed through all his work:

> it is the timber of poetry that wears most surely, and there is no timber that has not strong roots among the clay and worms. Even if we grant that exalted poetry can be kept successful by itself, the strong things of life are needed in poetry also, to show that what is exalted, or tender, is not made by feeble blood. It may almost be said that before verse can be human again it must learn to be brutal. (Synge 1982a:xxxvi)

This passage reflects Synge's study of the French symbolists, especially the theories of Mallarmé and Verlaine, who were concerned with *timbre*, the tonal color and sound of the words and their structure. As a writer who had been trained as a musician,

A Companion to Irish Literature, edited by Julia M. Wright
© 2010 Blackwell Publishing Ltd

Synge was determined that his plays and poetry be rich not only in choice of subject but in mood and expression.

Edmund John Millington Synge was born in Dublin on April 16, 1871 into a family of strict evangelical persuasion. Because of ill health he received most of his tutoring at home, anxiously watched over by his mother, who had been widowed when he was barely a year old. When he was 18 he followed family tradition by enrolling in Trinity College Dublin, and in the same year he also began his studies in the Royal Irish Academy of Music. Apart from an early Wordsworthian hymn to nature published in the college journal, the only thing remarkable about the three years at Trinity is his first place in the examinations in Hebrew and Irish, whereas at the Academy he was awarded a scholarship and medal in counterpoint. In 1893 he traveled to Germany to study violin and piano, but very soon realized that he was not temperamentally suited to a career as a professional musician. And so, much to the disapproval of his family but like many other Irish writers and artists seeking fulfillment, Synge moved on to Paris, where he enrolled in language courses at the Sorbonne (concentrating on Petrarch and French literature) and then spent a short time in Rome and Florence to further his study of Italian. Having flirted fleetingly with the idea of serving as an interpreter on ocean liners, he decided to earn a living as a journalist, optimistically as a leader writer on Irish literature for French newspapers. Paris became his base for seven years, interrupted by summers with his mother in various rented houses in County Wicklow. Meanwhile, he exchanged language lessons and even joined a weekly debating society, scrupulously entering in his diary the number of times he spoke.

It was in Paris, on December 21, 1896, through a network of Irish exiles, that Synge encountered William Butler Yeats, who was fired with enthusiasm both for the creation of an Irish literary theater and for the Aran Islands off the west coast of Ireland, which he had recently visited. Although Yeats first thought Synge could help the movement as a scholar and popularizer, it is quite possible that this new acquaintanceship inspired Synge's next course at the Sorbonne, a study of Irish and Homeric civilizations. More importantly, it eventually led to his first trip to Aran two years later, at which time he met Yeats' colleague Lady Gregory. However, he still remained European in his outlook, and ten months after his return from the west of Ireland he made a journey to Brittany to further his study of the Breton language. Despite four more visits to Aran, his last in 1902, he continued to spend his winters in Paris, achieving some modest success publishing essays, and writing book reviews for Irish newspapers and journals.

Significantly, once he turned from the study and practice of music to that of literature, Synge's early attempts at self-expression were in the languages he was studying at the time – first in German (the draft of a play), later in French (essays of various kinds). Yet even then he was in search of an individual style, which he described in his notebook as the "portrait of one's own personality, of the colour of one's own thought" – "strengthening" his writing by *making personal*" (Saddlemyer 1965:211–12). The essays drawing on his experiences on the Aran Islands, his later visits to the

Blasket Islands and his frequent walks through County Wicklow reflect this subjectivity and sensitivity to the colors and moods he encountered. And although he was cautiously becoming involved in Yeats' and Lady Gregory's plans for a new literary movement in their own country, he did not relinquish his interest in European literature. Some time during the late 1890s he had shown two impressionistic pieces to a friend, *Vita Vecchia* and *Étude morbide*; after completing *The Playboy of the Western World* in 1907 he returned to these early works and began to revise them. When leaving his papers for Yeats to go through after his death on March 24, 1909, he included this ambivalent instruction: "the other early stuff I wrote, I have kept as a sort of curiosity but I am anxious that it should not get into print. ... I do *not* want my good things destroyed, or my bad things printed rashly" (Synge 1984:155). Clearly he needed to preserve that "early stuff," or at least have it read and acknowledged.

The title of the first of these early works, *Vita Vecchia* (The Old – or rather, Later – Life), is modeled on – and a response to – *La Vita Nuova* (The New – or Early – Life), the earliest known work by Dante. In *Vita Vecchia* (also entitled "The Vale of Shadow"), Synge follows in miniature Dante's pattern of prose interspersed with poems; like the *Vita Nuova*, his *Vita Vecchia* is a mixture of biography and allegory, reciting a series of dream-visions. Dante was recording his first glimpse as a 9-year-old boy of Beatrice, the idealized figure who haunted his dreams, his life, and *The Divine Comedy*. *Vita Vecchia* is made up of poems connected by prose passages that veer between straightforward narrative with recognizable incidents from Synge's experiences in France, Italy, and Ireland, and dream-like visions of unattainable women. But again and again this unfinished composition returns to a celebration of the "wonderful glory" of the Irish countryside, descriptions of the Wicklow hills he worshiped in his childhood, and his distress at the briefness of the cycles of the natural world, themes that would remain with him for the rest of his life (Synge 1982b:16–24).

Also unpublished and rejected by Yeats was Synge's next "Imaginary Portrait," *Étude morbide*, again written during the late 1890s in Paris and bearing just as clearly not only the marks of his current studies but also of his musical training. If *Vita Vecchia* reflected his admiration for Dante and the Italian language, *Étude morbide* was influenced by his study of contemporary French writers, in particular Huysmans, Mallarmé, Baudelaire, Maeterlinck, and Villiers de l'Isle-Adam. It also records his eclectic readings – Spinoza, Herbert Spencer, the Stoics, the mystics, and Thomas à Kempis, whom he contemplated translating and from whom he quotes in an unpublished dialogue between the saint and Rabelais (Synge 1982c:183–86).

Even the title – *Étude* – is reminiscent of the artistic movements of the time: the form, a short musical composition emphasizing a particular technical skill and usually for a solo instrument, would have been familiar to Synge as a music student. Designed as a series of diary entries, *Étude morbide* is closely related in subject matter and temperament to *Vita Vecchia*, and, like it, is a work of personal as well as literary exploration rather than a factual autobiographical record: the hero is a violinist involved with more than one woman, who records his dreams and anguish at failing as an artist, and seeks solace in nature. However, indicative that Synge still considered himself European in temperament and interest, this time it is not the Wicklow hills that provide comfort to the overwrought narrator, but a journey to Finisterre, the north-western part of Brittany which Synge had visited in 1899 after his first trip to Aran (Synge 1982b:25–36).

In his death-bed instructions to Yeats, Synge insisted that this early "morbid thing about a mad fiddler in Paris, which I hate" not be published (Synge 1984:155). But again, he preserved *Étude morbide* among his papers, perhaps because it is so closely related to his first completed play, *When the Moon Has Set*, the script he submitted to Yeats and Lady Gregory as early as 1901 and continued to revise for many years. The manuscripts of *Vita Vecchia* express both the narrator's determination to "Crusade against the crude force of Christianity" and the idea which becomes the essential plot of *When the Moon Has Set*: "At this time I began a long poem in blank verse about a nun who was set free from her bondage … and met and married a person, who represented myself" (Synge 1982b:19n). The play is more overtly autobiographical than *Étude morbide*, emphasizing Synge's anguish over the rejection by his first love Cherrie Matheson because of religious differences, and drawing on tales of the inhabitants of Wicklow (for more details on Synge's early life, see McCormack 2000). But the ideas and musical motifs threaded through all the versions of *When the Moon Has Set* and echoed in both the *Vita Vecchia* and *Étude morbide* have their origin in notebook jottings dating from Synge's first year in Paris, 1895.

That he kept all three, along with other early poems marked "Reserved" and "Biographical Matter only not to be printed as literary work" as well as other scattered scenarios and dramatic fragments, indicates how strongly Synge felt about preserving "the colour of one's own thought" or, as he was to put it to Yeats, "as a sort of curiosity" (Synge 1984:155). And again it reflects his aesthetic theory as jotted down in his notebooks: a work of art "must have been possible to only one man at one period and in one place" (Saddlemyer 1965:214). That early voice of his works in Paris was the first tentative step not only towards the expression of his own personality, but also of his determination to create works for the theater that are "literature first – i.e. to be personal, sincere, and beautiful – and drama afterwards" (Synge 1983:81). This meant not only in choice of subject but in style, perhaps showing forth for the first time in the speech of the young servant girl in *When the Moon Has Set*:

> She'll be coming in a minute I'm telling you, and let you be taking your own rest. You're wanting it surely, for we were thinking it's destroyed you'd be driving alone in the night and the great rain, and you not used to anything but the big towns of the world. (Synge 1982c:157)

While still at work on *When the Moon Has Set*, Synge had seen and later written about "une pièce charmante" in Irish, Douglas Hyde's *Casadh an tSugáin* (*The Twisting of the Rope*), performed by a small group of amateurs in Dublin (Synge 1982b:381). More importantly he reviewed Lady Gregory's prose version of the early Irish epic *Cuchulain of Muirthemne*, praising her first extended use of the language which would become known as "Kiltartanese," named after the county near Coole, her home in the west of Ireland:

> The Elizabethan vocabulary has a force and colour that make it the only form of English that is quite suitable for incidents of the epic kind, and in her intercourse with the peasants of the west Lady Gregory has learned to use this vocabulary in a new way, while she carries with her plaintive Gaelic constructions that make her language, in a true sense, a language of Ireland. (Synge 1982b:368)

However, although in Synge's early play the setting and country speech may be Wicklow, unlike Gregory's characters rooted along the Clare/Galway border, the Anglo-Irish artist-hero of *When the Moon Has Set* still longs for Paris.

As late as 1902, while working on the early drafts of his first three plays for the Irish Literary Theatre established by Yeats and Gregory, Synge was still sufficiently influenced by nineteenth-century poetic drama to attempt two plays in blank verse: the first, "A Vernal Play," where shepherds and maidens meet in the glens of Wicklow to admire the beauty of trees, flowers and sunsets (Synge 1982c:189–93); and the second, "Luasnad, Capa and Laine," an equally self-conscious attempt based on a tale in *The History of Ireland* by the seventeenth-century priest and historian Geoffrey Keating (see CHAPTER 5, ANNALISTS AND HISTORIANS IN EARLY MODERN IRELAND, 1450–1700), where all the characters perish in the waves (Synge 1982c:194–205). It is not difficult to detect the influence of the symbolist dramas *Axel* (1890) by Villiers de l'Isle Adam and *The Shadowy Waters* (1900) by Yeats. A third effort, "The Lady O'Connor," its plot taken from a story he was told on Aran, was also started in verse, but by 1904 – while Synge was working on his fourth play, *The Well of the Saints* – had shifted uneasily to prose. In phrasing and characterization "The Lady O'Connor" rotates between clumsy poetic echoes of his first finished plays, *Riders to the Sea* and *The Shadow of the Glen*, while looking forward to the lively lines of *The Playboy of the Western World*. By now Synge had realized that conventional poetic drama was not his strength; but as an axis between his unfruitful early efforts and later accomplishments, the fragmentary manuscripts and scenarios for "The Lady O'Connor" deserve closer examination (Synge 1982c:208–14). At any rate, as he became more involved in the theater movement in Dublin, he did not turn his attention to verse-writing again for at least two years.

Not that he stopped seeking *le mot juste*. That Synge was still caught up in aesthetic impressionism while recording his earliest response to Aran is evident in the dependence in his travel writings on the vocabulary of Walter Pater: the pages are peppered with the words "intense," "curious," "strange," "luminous," "magnificent," "wonderful brilliancy," "inconceivable," even "delicious." His notebooks approved of Pater's insistence on finding "everything in the instant" (Saddlemyer 1965:215); particularly on his first visit to the furthermost west of Ireland he remarks on the "affinity between the moods of these people and the moods of varying rapture and dismay that are frequent in artists, and in certain forms of alienation" (Synge 1982b:74). As he is rowed over to Inishmaan from the larger island, he records the "moment of exquisite satisfaction to find myself moving away from civilization in this rude canvas canoe of a model that has served primitive races since men first went on the sea" (1982b:57). Like the traditional Irish whiskey, "grey poteen, which brings a shock of joy to the blood" (1982b:73), Synge's impressions of the islanders on his first two visits to Aran are charged with a Hopkins-like sensibility: "there is hardly an hour I am with them that I do not feel the shock of some inconceivable idea, and then again the shock of some vague emotion that is familiar to them and to me" (1982b:113). Even his prose swings between almost rhapsodic evocations of his own emotional response ("one of the moods in which we realize with immense distress the short moment we have left us to experience all the wonder and beauty of the world"; 1982b:139) and matter-of-fact descriptions of island life and his remoteness from it when, like the old storyteller Pat Dirane who teaches him Irish, he provides "minute details to show that he was actually present" (1982b:72). Just as sharply, *The Aran Islands* concludes with the bare statement, "The next day I left with the steamer."

This "shock of new material," as he admitted himself, first in Paris and more irrevocably in the west of Ireland, created the style of language and storytelling we now recognize as his alone. Synge's teachers on Aran also confirmed what he had gained from Pater and knew to his cost as a musician, that all art aspires towards the condition of music. When he meets his first guide, old Mourteen, he describes how the storyteller "sat down in the middle of the floor and began to recite old Irish poetry, with an exquisite purity of intonation that brought tears to my eyes though I understood but little of the meaning" (1982b:56). The old woman in whose cottage he lived recited verses from Douglas Hyde's *Love Songs of Connaught* "with exquisite musical intonation, putting a wistfulness and passion into her voice that seemed to give it all the cadences that are sought in the profoundest poetry" (1982b:112). On a later visit he was counseled by an old net-mender on Kilronan pier, "A translation is no translation, he said, unless it will give you the music of a poem along with the words of it" (1982b:149). Sound and feeling must work upon each other, as he was to write in his final preface and illustrate in the musical tone poem *Riders to the Sea* and the contrapuntal/harmonic structure of his later plays.

Synge therefore first deliberately rendered his own response to the world around him, and then became an accomplished, sensitive translator of others. The language in his plays heightens the qualities of the speech he heard on Aran and on the Wicklow roads, while remaining true to the thought behind it. His training as a musician and a keen ear for rhythm and pattern enabled precision, even in sharp contrasts; sometimes he did not have to do anything more than quote selective phrases he heard and jotted down in the notebook he always carried with him. Although in many ways Yeats would carve the memory of his friend into a distorted image, he was perceptive in claiming, "Perhaps no Irish countryman had ever that exact rhythm in his voice, but certainly if Mr Synge had been born a countryman, he would have spoken like that" (Synge 1982c:64). The language he gives his characters is indeed personal and artificial, a deliberate creation, but it suggests a living, vibrant speech. However, even though he knew the company well and frequently wrote with individual players in mind, the actors always found it difficult mastering sentences that were not attuned to their own everyday language and had to be trained, like singers, to catch Synge's carefully contrived phrasing (see Kiberd 1993 for a detailed analysis of the influence of the Irish language on Synge's work).

Synge did not give up his room in Paris until he had completed the manuscript of *The Aran Islands* and submitted two short plays to the small company first established by the brothers William and Frank Fay. (This would soon be superseded by Yeats and Gregory's Irish Literary Theatre, eventually to have its own home in the Abbey Theatre, which the Fays would join as chief actors and directors.) *Riders to the Sea*, the first play he completed in 1902, owes its setting, plot, and even some of its speeches to Synge's experiences on Aran, especially what he learned of the frequent drownings at sea. But it also reflects most strongly his early training as a musician in its construction out of silence a threnody of tragic intensity; each phrase and movement is carefully orchestrated against the constant reminder and rhythms of the sea, as the two young girls try to protect their grieving mother while all encounter the inevitable death of the last remaining son. Almost too painful to bear (fishing villagers in Scotland refused to attend), the play moves steadily from a hesitant sense of impending loss through grief, swelled by the keening neighbors, to old Maurya's triumphant final acceptance: "No man at all can be living for ever, and we must be satisfied" (Synge 1995:12). Much of the imagery and phrasing comes directly from Synge's notebooks, as does his own response to the sea and wind as he walked the cliffs, then transmuted into a structure similar to the progress of the fugue.

For his second short play – and the first to be produced – Synge turned to the Wicklow countryside familiar to him since childhood. *In the Shadow of the Glen* (the first word of the title was soon dropped) is set in a cottage at the far end of Glenmalure, which he knew well from the many months he spent in the area with his mother and her summer visitors. He too had experienced the strange moods of Nora Burke, her loneliness and the influence of the mists which could cause distraction as they crept up from the valley, as it does to the missing hero in the play, the herd Patch Darcy. Synge had heard the story of a husband pretending to be dead from his old Irish teacher on Aran; but if *Riders to the Sea* was the result of his observations of life on the harsh rocks of the west, *The Shadow of the Glen* was drawn out of his feelings and desires as he put them in the mouth of the lyrical Tramp who rescues Nora Burke from a loveless May–December marriage. Once again, the play begins in silence with a woman quietly moving about her kitchen, but this time her companion is a dead body. It is this scene that greets a shocked tramp who seeks shelter from the rain. After she invites the stranger in she makes a brief escape to summon a young herd whom she sees as a likely successor to old Dan Burke. But the "dead man" rises to declare the trick he is playing on his "bad wife," and the suspense turns from mournful to comic. Instead of the traditional ending to the story, Synge adds a coda that lifts the play out of farce into poetry with the Tramp's offer: "We'll be going now, lady of the house – the rain is falling but the air is kind, and maybe it'll be a grand morning by the grace of God" (Synge 1995:25). The play ends with the crusty old farmer inviting the callow young herd to join him in a quiet drink, but ringing in the ears of the audience is Nora's final challenge to them as well as to those on stage:

> "You think it's a grand thing you're after doing with your letting on to be dead, but what is it at all? What way would a woman live in a lonesome place the like of this place, and she not making a talk with the men passing? And what way will yourself live from this day, with none to care you?" (1995:25–26)

Although Synge disparaged Ibsen as old-fashioned, there is much in the spirit of Nora Burke that is reminiscent of the Nora of *A Doll's House*. On its first production the play sparked considerable outrage among prominent Irish nationalists, who insisted that no true Irish woman would be unfaithful to, much less leave, her husband; they may also have been offended by Synge's making a wandering homeless tramp the successful wooer. But Yeats was delighted with the controversy, for it launched their fledgling movement onto a much larger stage.

Both these plays were written during the summer of 1902 in County Wicklow; *The Shadow of the Glen* was produced the following year by W.G. Fay's Irish National Theatre Society, and *Riders to the Sea* a few months later. During that same remarkable period Synge started work on a longer play set in Wicklow, *The Tinker's Wedding*, which over the years underwent many different drafts, finally settled in two acts, and was published in 1907. Production, however, was considered by Yeats and Lady Gregory to be too "dangerous" for a Dublin audience. With this play Synge moved out of shadow into the bright sunshine of comedy. The life of the tinkers complements the loveless world of *The Shadow of the Glen*, providing a glimpse of the life of the nature-loving tramp (Synge made few distinctions between tinkers, tramps, and travelers) and, in the disreputable old tinker woman Mary Byrne, the vigor of an old age unhampered by the restrictions of a "settled" society with its church-going ways. The bare bones of the plot – a quarrel between tinkers who want to be married and the grasping priest who is tricked out of payment – come from a tale told him by an old Wicklow tramp; many of the details he transferred to the play are found in his Wicklow essays, including a vehement denunciation of the police by a drunken, shameless flower-seller. While Mary exults in singing outrageous ballads and insists on her drop of porter at nightfall, the local priest is representative of the conservative orthodox world that has no place for the tinkers and their like. It is the age-old debate between Oisín and St Patrick, where the inhabitants of two separate societies envy and at the same time distrust each other, and where the worlds of both collapse in folly.

Of the two orthodoxies, it is clear from his travel essays that Synge believes that the world-view of the vagrants, tinkers, and travelers is more "natural." It is their awareness of the transience of the seasons that makes old Mary Byrne wise and Sarah Casey restless: the young woman blames her "queer thoughts" on the coming of spring and the change of the moon (the play was originally entitled "Movements of May");

and the "old drinking heathen" sings her own hymn to a morning "when there's a warm sun in it, and a kind air, and you'll hear the cuckoos singing and crying out on the top of the hills." The visions of both priest and tinker have their own wisdom, fueled by the power of the word, but it is Mary who reminds us that nature exacts her penalty in the isolation and sorrow of old age and certain death: "What good are the grand stories I have when it's few would listen to an old woman … ? Maybe the two of them have a good right to be walking out the little short while they'd be young." Yet typically, she continues with her own cry of independence: "what's a little stroke on your head beside sitting lonesome on a fine night, hearing the dogs barking, and the bats squeaking, and you saying over, it's a short while only till you die" (Synge 1995:32–40). *The Tinker's Wedding* ends in farce, which Synge believed has its place in the full spectrum of emotional play. His preface to the drama, when it was finally published, insists that "Of the things which nourish the imagination humour is one of the most needful, and it is dangerous to limit or destroy it" (1995:28). But at the same time he admitted that "it looks mighty shocking in print," and reluctantly acknowledged that *The Tinker's Wedding* "is rather impossible for our audiences, so I fear we shall never be able to put it on" (Synge 1984:89, 127). The play was not produced at the Abbey Theatre until 1971.

Wicklow was also the setting for Synge's next work, *The Well of the Saints*, an even darker comedy. Again, though the play is set further back in time, two blind beggars eventually turn away from the authority of church and society, choosing, instead of the gift of sight, their own illusions in a world of risk rather than the wandering saint's promise of the life of "simple men, who do be working every day, and praying" (Synge 1995:92). Martin and Mary Doul (the surname is Irish for "blind") have spent their lives companionably making wicks by stripping rushes for sale by the roadside, all the time innocently believing in the mocking villagers' tales of their remarkable beauty. A wandering friar arrives offering the gift of sight from water of a holy well, but the blessing turns bitter as the old couple see themselves, and the harsh world about them, as it really is. Mary Doul, who has always been more complacent, quickly creates a new illusion:

> When I seen myself in them pools, I seen my hair would be grey, or white maybe in a short while, and I seen with it that I'd a face would be a great wonder when it'll have soft white hair falling around it, the way when I'm an old woman there won't be the like of me surely in the seven counties of the east. (1995:85)

But for the dreamer Martin, reality is too painful and revealing, despite his efforts to create a new world of wonder; "it's few sees anything but them is blind for a space" (1995:79). When their sight fades again, it is he who rejects the saint's offer of a second chance at living in the real workaday world, and the two beggars, rejected by the villagers who have also been forced to see themselves in a new clear but harsher light, grope their way to a certain death. When *The Well of the Saints* was first produced in February 1905 by what had by then become the Abbey Theatre, Willie Fay fretted that all the characters were bad-tempered. But Synge insisted that "what I write of Irish country life I know to be true and I most emphatically will not change a syllable of it" (Synge 1983:91). While drafting his preface to *The Tinker's Wedding* two years later, he continued to emphasize that "when a work is rich and unique it must be taken freshly and directly from life, and it must be many-sided, so that it has a universal quality" (Synge 1982d:291; for more on Synge's plays, see for instance Grene 1975 and such recent studies as Cusack 2009).

In all Synge's characters anger is very close to the surface, ready to break out in violence at the denial of a dream and betrayal by the hoped-for savior who himself proves to be a sham. But with his next play, *The Playboy of the Western World*, it is the poet-hero who discovers his true self while the Mayoites who praise the daring and bravery of a man who dared to kill his Da are left disillusioned and disappointed. Before our eyes the timid, dirty tramper, Christy Mahon, flourishes under the admiration of Pegeen Mike, the shebeen owner's lively daughter, and the countryfolk who crowd in to hear how he killed his Da with a loy. As the story enlarges in grandeur and detail, Christy truly becomes the hero they want him to be, winning the heart of Pegeen and the sympathy of the lusty Widow Quin, who is also an outsider. But when Old Mahon, very much alive, appears in search of his son and Christy tries to prove himself by killing him again, the Mayoites' dreams are shattered and they turn on the playboy with bitterness and brutality. It is Pegeen who voices their disappointment and the moral of the fable: "I'll say a strange man is a marvel with his mighty talk; but what's a squabble in your back-yard and the blow of a loy, have taught me that there's a great gap between a gallous story and a dirty deed" (Synge 1995:144). The play has both a comic and a tragic ending – Christy, now "master of all fights" over his bullying father, leaves to conquer other worlds, his parting shot: "Ten thousand blessings upon all that's here, for you've turned me a likely gaffer in the end of all, the way I'll go romancing through a romping lifetime from this hour to the dawning of the judgment day." But the curtain falls on a heartbroken Pegeen: "Oh my grief, I've lost him surely. I've lost the only playboy of the western world" (1995:146).

The disturbance on the first night of *Playboy* in January 1907 is well known; it would appear that nationalists came prepared to cause trouble, and saw their opportunity when Willie Fay as Christy uttered the famous words "a drift of chosen females, standing in their shifts itself" (1995:143). (The speech was made even more incendiary by the distracted actor's substitution of "Mayo girls" for "chosen females.") The public were both shocked and bewildered by the play, drawn in by the charm of the poetic dialogue, then in quick reversal appalled by the murderous actions they had been led, along with the onstage audience, to applaud. But Synge vigorously defended the contrapuntal structure he had worked over many drafts to achieve: "the romantic note and a Rabelaisian note are working to a climax through a great part of the play, and … the Rabelaisian note, the 'gross' note if you will, must have its climax no matter who may be shocked" (Synge 1984:47).

Meanwhile a new note had entered his writing. While working on *Playboy* Synge fell deeply in love with the actress who first walked on in *The Well of the Saints* and played one of Maurya's daughters in *Riders to the Sea*, then took over the role of Nora Burke in *The Shadow of the Glen* and, triumphantly, became Pegeen Mike. In almost daily letters and frequent walks in the Wicklow hills, his courtship of young Molly Allgood became more and more intense, turning him back to poetry through his lyrical love letters. In 1906 he sent these lines (not included in the *Collected Works*) commemorating their artistic partnership and his delight in finding love at last:

> To you Bride, Nora, Kathleen, Molly Byrne,
> I of my age have brought the pride and power,
> And seen my hardness in your sweetness turn
> A new delight for our long fame a dower.
> And now you bring to me your young girl's pride,
> And sweeten with your sweetness all my days,
> Telling me dreams where our red lips have cried
> The long low cry that folds all earthly praise.
> And so in all our lot we hold a mart
> Of your young joy and my too gloomy art.

In Synge's early works, including *When the Moon Has Set*, the heroes are musicians; *Riders to the Sea* depends upon a musical structure, though his other early efforts at playwriting are a long way from the simplicity and internal rhythms of *Riders*. But from *The Shadow of the Glen* on, that persona has been replaced by the poet: the tramp who sings so sweetly of the joys of nature (and in whose role Synge wooed Molly); the zesty vulgar rhapsodies of the irrepressible old tinker woman Mary Byrne in *The Tinker's Wedding*; the seductive urgings of blind Martin Doul of *The Well of the Saints*; and, of course, Christy Mahon of *The Playboy of the Western World*, poet *par excellence*, who not only tells his story "lovely" but wins "a fiddle was played by a poet in the years gone by."

In addition, he experimented with free translations from the Italian and French, primarily Petrarch and Villon. Significantly the preface accompanying these poems condemns false poetic diction and material of the very kind he was guilty of writing in the 1890s. By now he had come to understand that essential to what he called "vital verse" were humor and a "poetic feeling for ordinary life," both qualities singularly lacking in such works as *Vita Vecchia*, *Étude morbide*, and *When the Moon Has Set*:

> What is highest in poetry is always reached where the dreamer is leaning out to reality, or where the man of real life is lifted out of it, and in all the poets the greatest have both these elements, that is they are supremely engrossed with life, and yet with the wildness of their fancy they are always passing out of what is simple and plain. (Synge 1982b:348)

When hesitantly submitting his poems to Yeats he explained his own evolving aesthetic, which again emphasized his turn to the "Rabelaisian": "I am most interested now in my grim[m]er verses, and the ballads, (which are from actual life)" (Synge 1984:195) and which he had heard on later trips to the west, especially the Blasket Islands.

Two of those "grimmer" poems – the ballad "Danny" and the notorious "Curse" ("To a sister of an enemy of the author's who disapproved of the Playboy") – were rejected by Yeats' sister Elizabeth, publisher of the Cuala Press, though reinstated by Yeats in the later commercial edition. Synge's own selection included only two love lyrics, but he explicitly condemned the more anaemic art of some of his Irish contemporaries:

> The Passing of the Shee
>
> *After looking at one of A.E.'s pictures.*
>
> Adieu, sweet Angus, Maeve and Fand,
> Ye plumed yet skinny Shee,
> That poets played with hand in hand
> To learn their ecstasy.
>
> We'll search in Red Dan Sally's ditch,
> And drink in Tubber fair,
> Or poach with Red Dan Philly's bitch
> The badger and the hare.

It was to the fifteenth-century poet, thief, and vagabond François Villon that Synge most frequently turned when seeking examples of the strong writing, the "romance of reality" he now thought essential to poetry. Again and again in his early notebooks he uses Villon as a benchmark for "the wonder of [the] world set against the misery of age and death" (Saddlemyer 1965:211), and his most powerful translations are from Villon and Petrarch. Villon's poem "The Beautiful Helmet Maker" becomes Synge's relentless "An Old Woman's Lamentations" with the vivid description "That's what's left over from the beauty of a right woman – a bag of bones, and legs the like of two shrivelled sausages going beneath it" (Synge 1982a:80).

Most of these translations – or rather versions – are written in prose, about the same time he was struggling to find a new voice for what was to become his last play, *Deirdre of the Sorrows*, which includes some of the phrases used in the translations. He wrote to Molly, "My next play must be quite different from the P. Boy. I want to do something quiet and stately and restrained and I want you to act in it" (Synge 1983:250). After seeing produced five folk plays rooted in the Ireland he himself experienced, *Deirdre of the Sorrows* was, he claimed, "an experiment chiefly to change my hand." "[I]t would be amusing to compare it with Yeats' and Russell's [plays] – but I am a little afraid that the 'Saga' people might loosen my grip on reality" (Synge 1984:56):

> when one comes to deal with them they seem very remote; – one does not know what they thought or what they ate or where they went to sleep, so one is apt to fall into rhetoric. In any case I find it "an interesting experiment," full of new difficulties, and I shall be the better, I think, for the change. (1984:121–22)

In addition, the tale of Deirdre and the Sons of Usnach was well known as the most familiar of all legends of the Cuchulain cycle. Not only had the plays of Yeats and George Russell about the two doomed lovers already been produced on the Abbey stage, but it was also a centerpiece in Lady Gregory's *Cuchulain of Muirthemne* which Synge had reviewed approvingly in 1902 (Synge 1982b:367–70). But where the earlier versions had emphasized the prophetic aspect of the tale and "a story will be told forever," he concentrated on the inevitability of strong personalities remaining true to themselves in choosing an early death over the dwindling unhappiness of old age. The play begins in the darkness of twilight, with storm clouds gathering, as the three brothers of Usnach come upon the high King Conochubor's hunting lodge, where the beautiful Deirdre, whom he plans to make his queen, is hidden away. Both Naisi and Deirdre know what is foretold, and both defy the prophecy to seek a free life in the woods. But even the warm passion of their love cannot blot out the inevitable, and the second act, which opens in the bright, clear air of early winter, is full of forebodings, heralded by the protective old nurse Lavarcham and the mad wild Owen. "I've dread going or staying," Deirdre tells Lavarcham:

"It's lonesome this place having happiness like ours till I'm asking each day, will this day match yesterday, and will tomorrow take a good place beside the same day in the year that's gone, and wondering all times is it a game worth playing, living on until you're dried and old, and our joy is gone forever." (Synge 1995:166)

The ending is cold, first with a lovers' quarrel and finally the chill of death, as Deirdre stands over Naisi's grave, triumphant in her loneliness: "I have put away sorrow like a shoe that is worn out and muddy, for it is I have had a life that will be envied by great companies. ... It was the choice of lives we had in the clear woods, and in the grave we're safe surely" (Synge 1995:186). Each character in the play contributes to the spectrum of that choice and various aspects of love, from the maternal care of old Lavarcham to the aging Conchubor's longing for Deirdre's youth and beauty, from the fraternal loyalty of Naisi's two brothers to the mad longings of the spy Owen and the crippling helplessness of the chieftain Fergus, whose oath of protection has been betrayed by an old, barren king. It is fitting that this *Liebestod* ends with the high king's palace going up in flames.

Even though his scenarios and drafts reached version "K," Synge died before he could complete *Deirdre of the Sorrows* to his satisfaction. Act III was probably alright, he told Yeats, but asked that he and Lady Gregory introduce the grotesque character of Owen into the first act and develop his wildness further in the second act. Wisely, his fellow directors chose not to edit the manuscript, although it was Gregory, with the assistance of Molly Allgood, who cobbled together the final version from hundreds of typed pages, and directed the first production with Molly, as Synge intended, playing Deirdre. Although the play as now published does not have the roughness he had worked into *Playboy*, the pain and anger with which the two lovers turn on each other while facing the end reflect once again the rage against death and the inability to live out a dream, a theme running through all of his work. Here, in his last play, Synge once again made his work "personal," capable of being written by only one man in one place at one time; the unapproachable is made familiar, the general becomes individual, and, most of all, the formal is transformed into the colloquial in a free and vital mood.

That composing *Deirdre of the Sorrows* completely changed Synge's style is debatable, for once again we have a broad spectrum of emotion and a conscious effort to provide a full range in speech; Deirdre, the Sons of Usnach, and Conchubor betray only slight dialect, in contrast to the peasant idiom of Owen and Lavarcham. Synge had dismissed historical drama with the words, "I only care for personal lyrical modern poetry and little of that." In recognizing that he too must move on, he understood that poetry – and poetic drama – must change; the language of history can no longer be dressed in fustian. He concluded, "For the present the only possible beauty in drama is peasant drama, for the future we must await the making of life beautiful again before we can have beautiful drama. You cannot gather grapes of chimney pots" (Synge 1982d:394).

But Synge also realized that his unique artificial language could easily fall into bathos or parody: "The Mist that Does be on the Bogs," a parody of *The Shadow of the Glen*, appeared very quickly after the first production, and many later imitations are rightly dismissed as "Synge-Song." When his German translator Max Meyerfeld asked for a simple transliteration of *The Well of the Saints*, Synge replied rather doubtfully,

> I can do a few pages at first, and then any particular passages that you find difficult. I do not think you will find the general language hard to follow when you have done a few pages, as the same idioms are often repeated, and the purely local words are not very numerous. However I perfectly understand that it will be a difficult language to translate. (Synge 1983:115)

James Joyce, who frequently chanted old Maurya's final speech, wisely translated *Riders to the Sea* into standard Italian, trying to follow the original rhythms as closely as possible.

Today Synge's plays are performed in many languages throughout the world and have been adapted by later playwrights. But perhaps, when we consider Synge's achievement as poet and playwright, it is to his colleague Yeats we must turn for the most appropriate acknowledgment: "In the arts he knew no language but his own" (Yeats 1999:378).

References and Further Reading

Bushrui, S.B. (Ed.). (1972). *Sunshine and the Moon's Delight: A Centenary Tribute to John Millington Synge*. Gerrards Cross: Smythe.

Cusack, G. (2009). *The Politics of Identity in Irish Drama: W.B. Yeats, Augusta Gregory and J.M. Synge*. New York: Routledge.

Grene, N. (1975). *Synge: A Critical Study of the Plays*. London: Macmillan.

Grene, N. (Ed.). (2000). *Interpreting Synge: Essays from the Synge Summer School 1991–2000*. Dublin: Lilliput Press.

Harmon, M. (Ed.) (1971) *Synge Centenary Essays*. Dublin: Dolmen.

Hogan, R. and J. Kilroy. (1978). *The Abbey Theatre: The Years of Synge, 1905–1909*. Dublin: Dolmen Press.

Johnson, T.O. (1982). *Synge: The Medieval and the Grotesque*. Gerrards Cross: Colin Smythe.

Kiberd, D. (1993). *Synge and the Irish Language*. 2nd edn. London: Macmillan.

Kilroy, J. (Ed.). (1971). *The "Playboy" Riots*. Dublin: Dolmen.

King, M.C. (Ed.). (1982). *When the Moon Has Set*. In *Long Room* (pp. 24–25). Dublin: Trinity College.

King, M.C. (1985). *The Drama of J.M. Synge*. London: Fourth Estate.

Kopper, E.A. Jr. (Ed.). (1988). *A J.M. Synge Literary Companion*. Westport, CT: Greenwood Press.

McCormack, W.J. (2000). *Fool of the Family: A Life of J.M. Synge*. New York: New York University Press.

Mikhail, E.H. (Ed.). (1977). *J.M. Synge: Interviews and Recollections*. London: Macmillan.

Saddlemyer, A. (1965). "'A Share in the Dignity of the World': J.M. Synge's Aesthetic Theory." In R. Skelton and A. Saddlemyer (Eds). *The World of W.B. Yeats* (pp. 207–19). Seattle: University of Washington Press.

Saddlemyer, A. (1977). "Synge and the Doors of Perception." In A. Carpenter (Ed.). *Place, Personality and the Irish Writer* (pp. 97–120). New York: Barnes & Noble.

Saddlemyer, A. (Ed.). (1982). *Theatre Business: The Correspondence of the First Abbey Theatre Directors*. Gerrards Cross: Colin Smythe.

Skelton, R. (1971). *J.M. Synge and his World*. London: Thames & Hudson.

Synge, J.M. (1982a). *Collected Works: Poems* (1962). R. Skelton (Ed.). Gerrards Cross: Colin Smythe.

Synge, J.M. (1982b). *Collected Works: Prose* (1966). A. Price (Ed.). Gerrards Cross: Colin Smythe.

Synge, J.M. (1982c). *Collected Works: Plays I* (1968). A. Saddlemyer (Ed.). Gerrards Cross: Colin Smythe.

Synge, J.M. (1982d). *Collected Works: Plays II* (1968). A. Saddlemyer (Ed.). Gerrards Cross: Colin Smythe.

Synge, J.M. (1983). *Collected Letters,* vol. I: *1871– 1907*. A. Saddlemyer (Ed.). Oxford: Clarendon Press.

Synge, J.M. (1984). *Collected Letters,* vol. II: *1907– 1909*. A. Saddlemyer (Ed.). Oxford: Clarendon Press.

Synge, J.M. (1995) *The Playboy of the Western World and Other Plays*. A. Saddlemyer (Ed.). Oxford: Oxford University Press.

Yeats, W.B. (1999). *Autobiographies* (1935). W.H. O'Donnell and D.N. Archibald (Eds). New York: Scribner.

35

James Joyce and the Creation
of Modern Irish Literature

Michael Patrick Gillespie

Life

James Joyce was born on February 2, 1882, at 41 Brighton Square in Rathgar, at that
time a suburb south of Dublin. He was the oldest surviving child of John and May
Joyce's large family. Early in his childhood the Joyces enjoyed a comfortable middle-
class lifestyle so prosperous that the young James was able to begin his education at
Clongowes Wood College, the exclusive Jesuit boarding school in County Kildare.
John Joyce's profligacy, his aversion to work, and his attraction to alcohol, however,
drove the family first into austerity and eventually into poverty. After three years at
Clongowes Wood, John Joyce could no longer pay the school fees, and James was
compelled to leave. He and his younger brother Stanislaus had a brief stint in a school
run by the Christian Brothers before they became scholarship boys at the Dublin
Jesuit school, Belvedere College, where he completed his primary and secondary
education (see Bradley 1982). From there he matriculated to University College
Dublin, his third school affiliated with the Society of Jesus.

While much happened in Dublin during Joyce's childhood, including the rise and
fall of Charles Stewart Parnell, to shape his creative consciousness, it would be difficult
to overestimate the impact of his Jesuit training. Joyce valued the experience for his
entire life, and long after he had rejected the authority of the Roman Catholic Church
he continued to speak with pride of the education he had received from the Jesuits
(see Sullivan 1958). Anyone familiar with Joyce's writing and with the pedagogical
philosophy of St Ignatius, the Society's founder, will see that the intellectual curiosity,
the independence of thought, and the vigorous articulation of ideas so important
to the Jesuits stand at the center of all of Joyce's writings. His Jesuit training certainly
influenced his early work (see Noon 1957). While still in Ireland, he wrote several

A Companion to Irish Literature, edited by Julia M. Wright
© 2010 Blackwell Publishing Ltd

plays (now lost), a collection of poems, later published as *Chamber Music*, some occasional verse, book reviews, and essays. Most significantly, during his final years in his
native city, he began work on the short stories that would later make up the *Dubliners*
collection, and on the narrative that would eventually become *A Portrait of the Artist
as a Young Man*.

After graduating from University College Dublin in October 1902 Joyce spent a
brief period in Paris. He went ostensively to pursue a medical degree. In fact he lived
a bohemian existence, immersing himself in the craft of writing, reading eclectically
at the Bibliothèque nationale, and struggling to survive by giving occasional language
lessons and getting sporadic sums from home. In April 1903 he was summoned back
to Dublin because his mother was dying. He remained in the city for a year and a
half.

Despite the impact of Dublin on Joyce's writing – all of his fiction is set there
paralleling the years of his growth to manhood – the conservative, Catholic, colonial
atmosphere of the city was too much for his independent sensibilities. In October
1904 Joyce left Dublin with Nora Barnacle, a young girl from Galway recently come
to the city to work as a chambermaid, determined to go to the continent to become a
writer. To survive he planned teach English at a Berlitz school. He eventually found
a position in Trieste, a port city at that time on the edge of the Austro-Hungarian
empire, where he and Nora could begin a family without the formality of marriage
vows, something they never could have done in Dublin (see McCourt 2000). (During
his adolescence, Joyce had left the Catholic Church, and from that time he fiercely
resisted the discipline that it or any social institution sought to impose. He and Nora
married in 1931 and only then to protect the inheritance rights of their offspring.)

Joyce, Nora, and their children (Giorgio and Lucia, born in 1905 and 1907) lived
a chaotic and penurious existence in Trieste. Although Joyce continued to give language lessons, the family often had to rely upon the financial and emotional support
of Joyce's brother Stanislaus, who had joined them there. Nonetheless, while in that
city, Joyce managed to complete *Dubliners*, discard the naturalistic novel *Stephen Hero*
that he had begun in Dublin, and write *A Portrait of the Artist as a Young Man* in its
place. World War I forced Joyce, who held a British passport, to leave Trieste for
neutral Switzerland. (Stanislaus remained behind in a detention camp.) Joyce and his
family lived in Zurich from 1915 until 1919. During that time he wrote much of
the early draft of *Ulysses*, and formed a lifelong attachment to the city (see Budgen
1960). When the war ended, however, Zurich became too expensive, and the Joyces
returned very briefly to Trieste. There they found that Stanislaus, who had been
released from internment, had developed an independence that made him far less
amenable than previously to taking on the financial obligations of his brother and his
brother's family. After a brief stay in a crowded apartment, Joyce was only too happy
to accept Ezra Pound's suggestion that the family move for a short time to Paris.
What he planned as a temporary displacement lasted over twenty years, a time marked
not only by the completion of *Ulysses* but also by the composition of Joyce's last and
most controversial piece of writing, *Finnegans Wake*.

After the Germans invaded France at the beginning of World War II, the Joyces felt it imperative to leave the capital city. They spent several months in rural France, and then, late in 1940, they were able to enter Switzerland. Joyce's return to his beloved Zurich was short-lived. On January 10, 1941, he became ill and was admitted to a Zurich hospital. Within three days he died, following surgery performed to treat a perforated duodenal ulcer. He is buried in Zurich at Fluntern cemetery (see Jolas 1949; Ellmann 1982).

Writing

According to Richard Ellmann, Joyce's best-known biographer, Joyce began writing at the age of 9 when he composed a poem (now lost), "Et Tu Healy," which castigated those who failed to support the Irish politician Charles Stewart Parnell when Parnell's private life came under public criticism. While growing to maturity in Dublin, Joyce experimented in a number of genres. He wrote several plays, a few early poems, and a series of prose sketches, now all lost. His first surviving work is an essay, "Ibsen's New Drama," published in the esteemed English journal *Fortnightly Review* when he was 18. He followed that with a satirical poem, "The Day of the Rabblement," attacking the Irish Literary Theatre. During his time at University College Dublin and for the few years preceding his final departure from Ireland, Joyce wrote essays, reviews, and lectures that would later be collected, along with occasional pieces done over the course of his life, in *The Critical Writings of James Joyce* (for a full account of Joyce's writings, see Fargnoli and Gillespie 2006).

Between 1901 and 1904 Joyce composed a series of interrelated poems that he would publish in 1907 under the title *Chamber Music*. The poems follow, in cyclical fashion, the emotions and attitudes of an impressionable young man experiencing the ecstasies and frustrations of love and ultimately the dejection of loneliness and betrayal. The poems stand clearly as the preliminary efforts of a writer still searching to find his voice. While they maintain an inner integrity and certainly merit examination, they do not come close to the achievements that Joyce would later attain in his fiction (see Joyce 2001). Joyce's skill as a poet never matched that of his countryman W.B. Yeats (and the prominence that Yeats already enjoyed may have discouraged the young Joyce from pursuing an interest in poetry more vigorously). However, his talent for fiction emerged in short order. In a remarkable three years, between 1904 and 1907, Joyce composed the fifteen short stories that came to make up the *Dubliners* collection.

Some readers have mistakenly viewed the stories in *Dubliners* as apprentice pieces, undertaken to allow Joyce to test and refine the ideas and techniques that would animate his subsequent fiction. In fact, although not every story is of equal merit, when one examines the collection as a whole one finds the same kind of sophisticated stylistic maneuvers and complex contextual examinations that prove so engaging in *A Portrait of the Artist as a Young Man*, *Ulysses*, and even *Finnegans Wake*. Indeed, though not manifest as overtly, careful scrutiny will reveal in *Dubliners* the same modernist and postmodernist traits – the rejection of institutions in favor of the individual, an inclination to see the world as arbitrary, a deferral of closure, and an embrace of ambiguity – that characterize the later writings (see Leonard 1994).

From the project's inception, Joyce saw the stories as a loosely knit whole providing caustic social observations on life in his native city. By and large, the stories examine in detail the foibles, frustrations, and self-deceptions that beset middle- and lower-middle-class Catholic Dubliners around the turn of the nineteenth century. The realistic detail was so striking that printers (at that time vulnerable by English law to lawsuits for whatever they brought into print) feared local shopkeepers would object to being mentioned by name in the work. However, although Joyce chronicled the city setting with meticulous geographic accuracy, his primary aim was to evoke Dublin as the emotional and spiritual locus of a profoundly wounded and deeply frustrated collective consciousness. As he tells Grant Richards, his eventual publisher, in a letter written in May 1906 regarding the composition of his stories, "My intention was to write a chapter of the moral history of my country and I chose Dublin for the scene because that city seemed to me the centre of paralysis" (Joyce 1966:II:134). Joyce organized *Dubliners* with the same attention to detail that he gave to each individual story. He divided the collection into narratives of childhood, adolescence, maturity, and public life, with a final story added as a coda. Each stands on its own, but together they form a powerful impression of the stagnant Irish society that Joyce fled when he left for the continent in 1904 (see Herr 1986).

"The Sisters," "An Encounter," and "Araby" make up the accounts of childhood. Each focuses on a transformative moment in the domestic, public, and emotional life of an unnamed young boy, the first-person narrator of these stories, though none elaborates on what insights, if any, the child derives from these experiences. In "The Sisters" the boy endeavors to come to terms with ambivalent feelings aroused by the death of an old priest who had been his teacher and friend. "An Encounter" details the boy's reaction when he and a friend, on a day when they are skipping school, meet an eccentric old man who appears to be a pedophile. Vague uneasiness rather than specific shock characterize the exchange the boy has with the old man, and it is his sense of vulnerability rather than a response to the man's predilections that dominates the final lines of the story. "Araby" presents the consequences of the boy's infatuation with a young girl in both a straightforward and a sardonic fashion. In all three stories this balance of empathy and irony both distances and affiliates the boy with readers.

In "Eveline," "After the Race," "Two Gallants," and "The Boarding House," the fascination and consequences of sex and sexuality, sometimes manifested overtly and sometimes implicitly, serve as ways of measuring adolescence. This designation may at first seem a misappellation given the ages of the central characters in these stories. However, in every instance Joyce's individuals behave in a fashion that shows that emotionally, spiritually, and even intellectually they are still in the process of coming to maturity. "Eveline" depicts the intolerable position of a young girl trapped in a situation she resents, caring for her father and siblings after her mother dies yet paralyzed by fear when given the opportunity to escape. "After the Race," perhaps the least impressive effort in the collection, examines the world of Jimmy Doyle, the spoiled son of a self-made and very successful businessman. Jimmy is cavorting with friends in a night of drinking and gambling, yet throughout it all he appears as little more than an awkward bystander, willing to pay to witness the exotic behavior of his erstwhile friends. "Two Gallants" takes a harsher view of Dublin night life. Offstage, John Corley, the ne'er-do-well son of a police inspector, charms money and perhaps sex from a servant girl. However, the narrative focuses on Lenehan, his companion, who wanders aimlessly about the city for the few hours it takes Corley to accomplish his task. The spiritual emptiness of Lenehan's life combined with his lack of self-reflexiveness make Jimmy Doyle's antics seem harmless. "The Boarding House" stands as the most painful story in the group, exploring the diverse perspectives brought to bear on an out-of-wedlock pregnancy. Though the formidable Mrs Mooney succeeds in bullying her roomer, Bob Doran, into agreeing to marry her pregnant daughter Polly, the narrative suggests consequences that will blur the delineation between victims and victimizers.

The next four stories, "A Little Cloud," "Counterparts," "Clay," and "A Painful Case," highlight in various ways the sterility of adulthood. Little Chandler, the central character of "A Little Cloud," has steady job, a family, and an orderly domestic life, yet he cannot avoid seeing himself as a failure when compared with his peripatetic journalist friend Ignatius Gallaher. Farrington, the aging alcoholic clerk of "Counterparts," feels surly resentment toward his menial job and bullying boss, yet when he confronts his son after an unsatisfying night drinking he can do nothing more than replicate the slights he has felt over the course of the day. "Clay" looks at the fragile existence of Maria, a middle-aged, cook's assistant at a Magdalene laundry, who through a major act of the will ignores her condition of isolation and vulnerability. "A Painful Case" offers the harshest view in the group. James Duffy is a man of ordinary habits and extra-ordinary self-control. He willfully cuts himself off from all society and vigorously resists any effort to stir his emotions. He closes the story feeling resentment rather than pity over the news of the suicide of an acquaintance, Mrs Sinico, who had befriended him for a time but whom he spurned when he feared she was becoming attached to him.

"Ivy Day in the Committee Room," "A Mother," and "Grace" examine public life by highlighting each of Dublin's central institutions: nationalism, the family, and religion. "Ivy Day" offers a straightforward representation of the sentimentalism surrounding commemorations of Parnell's death. In the process, the narrative neatly conveys, without actively ridiculing, the delusions this attitude creates. "A Mother" delineates in a far less sympathetic fashion the trap of social pretensions and the intolerance society shows to a woman who seeks to assert herself. "Grace" illustrates with caustic effect the superficiality of religion in the lives of ordinary Dublin men.

The final story, "The Dead," stands as a counterpoint to all those preceding it. In representing Gabriel Conroy, Joyce shows a fussy man made vulnerable and ultimately wounded by middle-class pretensions. At the same time, by the end of the story readers come to see Gabriel as a very different person from the similarly supercilious James Duffy. The final introspective lines of "The Dead" leave open the possibility of insight and even redemption as Gabriel contemplates the profundity of the genuine love and devotion Michael Furey displayed for Gretta Conroy long before she married Gabriel. Whether this insight will produce a change in Gabriel remains unresolved, but its mere possibility suggests a hopefulness evident in no other story in the collection (see Norris 2003). (In a September 25, 1906 letter to his brother Stanislaus, Joyce laments being "unnecessarily harsh" in his representations of Dublin, stating, "I have not been just to its beauty" [Joyce 1966:II:164]. When he composed "The Dead" a year later, he did much to redress these slights.)

After the completion of *Dubliners*, Joyce began work in earnest on what would become his first published novel, *A Portrait of the Artist as a Young Man* (1916). In fact, *Portrait* had two avatars. In early 1904 Joyce composed "A Portrait of the Artist," an extended prose meditation amalgamating fictional narrative and philosophical exposition. From there he turned to a naturalist novel, *Stephen Hero*, that proposed to offer an account of the coming to maturity of an artist in painstaking naturalistic detail. Joyce abandoned it in late 1904, and around 1907 he returned to the theme with a radically different stylistic approach.

From the moment of its publication *A Portrait of the Artist as a Young Man* established itself as the paradigmatic modernist novel (see Epstein 1971). In five chapters its narrative traces the successive loosening of the ties of family, Church, and nation on the consciousness of the title character, Stephen Dedalus, and his consequent reconfiguration as an independent being. By the end of the novel Stephen has rejected the authority of each of these institutions to dictate his behavior, and has set himself up as the sole moral arbiter of his universe.

The account of Stephen's maturation unfolds in an experimental style strikingly different from conventional works of the time. The discourse proceeds in a choppy, episodic fashion, leaving self-conscious narrative gaps that the reader must complete. Indeed, the role of the reader in the production of meaning becomes a crucial feature in a novel that combines powerful evocative force with self-conscious artifice. When Stephen proclaims near the end his intention "to forge in the smithy of my soul the uncreated conscience of my race," the punning gesture that begins his statement signals the complexity and indeterminacy of all art.

Joyce, of course, does not wait until the final lines to introduce the concept of fabrication, in all its derivations. From its title onward, turning on the indefinite article, *A Portrait of the Artist as a Young Man* declares its stylistic independence and commitment to indeterminacy. The opening lines underscore this: "Once upon a time and a very good time it was there was a moo-cow coming down the road, and the moo-cow met a nicens little boy named baby tuckoo." The narrative never troubles itself to punctuate the sentence or to identify the speaker – although internal clues suggest it could be the little boy's father telling the story, the little boy repeating his father's story, or the narrative voice recording the interchange – and in the process it signals to the reader that he or she will be called upon time and again to make the choices required to impose a kind of unity on the discourse, even as it tacitly acknowledges the subjectivity and provisionality of those choices (see Gifford 1967).

The novel progresses from descriptions of Stephen at the earliest age of perception, moves through his adolescence, and ends with him as a young adult having completed a university education and about to leave Ireland for Paris. Each episode highlights a distinct phase in Stephen's life. Chapter 1 follows his early schooling at Clongowes Wood College. Chapter 2 recounts the family's financial decline and Stephen's move to Belvedere College and his sexual awakening. Chapter 3 examines Stephen's renewed commitment to Catholicism as a result of a retreat conducted at Belvedere. Chapter 4 foregrounds Stephen's transition from Catholicism to art. And chapter 5 records Stephen's life at University College Dublin and his final break with his family, the Catholic Church, and Irish nationalism.

While each episode offers engaging imaginative moments, the narrative skill with which Joyce moves the discourse forward deserves particular comment. Not only is each chapter a careful thematic progression in Stephen's movement toward self-realization. Each chapter also adopts a vocabulary and a perspective evocative of the age and precocity of Stephen at that point in the narrative. Further, it does so not through the voice of Stephen himself but through the perspective of a detached narrator, oscillating between subjectivity and irony throughout the novel (see Riquelme 1983).

A great many sophisticated examinations of *Portrait* have appeared since the novel was first published. Nonetheless, despite the best efforts of some fine critics, the impulse remains strong in some readers to see Joyce's novel as an autobiographical account of the author's life. This can only needlessly circumscribe the pleasure of reading the work. The impulse to conflate the two lives is easy to understand. Striking parallels obtain between the artist and his creation. Like Stephen, Joyce attended Clongowes Wood College until his father's spendthrift habits forced him to leave and to begin as a scholarship boy at Belvedere. (As noted above, Joyce also had a brief sojourn away from the Jesuits with the Christian Brothers, but he spares his fictional creation that indignity.) Many of the experiences of the young Stephen echo those of Joyce, and the movement away from the Catholic Church and into a life of the imagination must have been quite familiar to the writer even as he depicted it in his fiction. At the same time, significant differences obtain, such as young Joyce's popularity at Clongowes and his less than averse attitude toward school sports. In any case, reading Joyce's fiction as a crib to his life denigrates both. *Portrait* stands as perfectly self-contained and perfectly satisfying imaginative experience. To suggest that one needs to know Joyce's life to comprehend it or that it should be taken as a guide to understanding Joyce's biography subverts the essence of the work (see Gillespie 1989).

Almost immediately after completing *Portrait*, Joyce began writing *Ulysses*. (In fact, he was thinking about some of the themes of the novel as early as his days composing *Dubliners* when he considered writing a story about a Dublin Jew whose wife was unfaithful, tentatively titled "Mr. Hunter.") Before taking up that work, however, I would like to offer a few remarks about a play that he wrote in 1918, *Exiles*.

Although Joyce as a young man had admired Ibsen and apparently made early (no longer extant) efforts to write plays in the same vein, it was not until he had established himself as an author that he turned again to drama. *Exiles* explores what life might be like for a Joyce-like figure who returns from self-imposed banishment to attempt to live again in Ireland. It contrasts Richard Rowan with his lifelong friend Robert Hand, who has remained behind. An intellectual, spiritual, and emotional rivalry plays out between them, but their freighted exchanges merely underscore the insufficiency of their representations.

Just as Joyce's poetry does not live up to the standards set by his fiction, *Exiles*, while workmanlike, cannot match the novels and short stories. A stiffness and predictability circumscribes the main characters. Didacticism rather than exposition creeps into the dialogue, and an uncharacteristic tediousness stifles representations of all of the individuals involved (with the possible exception of a milkman's horse, who never appears on stage). With a modernist gesture the rest of the play ends with ambiguity, but its conclusion reflects the mental exhaustion of the characters rather than an insight into the complexity of their dramatic world (see MacNicolas 1979).

In stark contrast *Ulysses* stands as a creative *tour de force*. It is a book that threatens to ruin literature for anyone who reads it, for no work of fiction can meet the standards it sets. Because he has written *Ulysses*, Joyce imposes himself on every author who follows, for none can escape the influence, exerted either directly or indirectly, of this powerful work (see Goldman 1966). For readers familiar with Joyce's earlier writings, the context of *Ulysses* is both familiar and innovative. The gritty evocation of the rhythm of ordinary life, first introduced in *Dubliners*, punctuates the discourse. Joyce continues and extends the imaginative energy and creative experimentation that distinguish *Portrait* to make *Ulysses* a powerful work of art.

At the same time, sharply unique content and form make *Ulysses* a distinct departure from earlier efforts. It relentlessly examines the most intimate elements of human life. Defecation, urination, masturbation, fornication, menstruation – nothing proves to be off limits, yet in every instance the narrative offers their representation to advance the plot and reinforce rather than undermine the humanity of the characters. (This respect for his characters is a hallmark worth emphasizing. It sets Joyce apart from a number of subsequent writers – such as John Irving, Martin Amis, or T.C. Boyle – who are adept at displaying the gritty elements that highlight the weaknesses of their characters but who have no ability to show the fuller natures that exist beneath the foibles.) Stylistically Joyce also extends the achievements of *Portrait* to make *Ulysses* a graphic demonstration of the imaginative achievements that come naturally from innovative construction. While ellipses, free indirect discourse, and deferral dominate the structure of the former novel, in the latter Joyce extends these features through stream of consciousness, stylistic parody, and narrative dissociations that produce enhanced reader engagement through an exponential increase in potential meanings.

Instability becomes a creative force, and even the most ostensively unambiguous features of the work are mutable. Although *Ulysses* takes place on a single day, June

16, 1904, and seems to move linearly through the discourse, in fact time and again Joyce disrupts the pattern. The narrative opens at 8 a.m. in the Martello tower, Sandycove, and follows Stephen Dedalus over the next three chapters until around 11. Then the discourse jumps back to 8 a.m. at the opposite end of the metropolis, Leopold Bloom's house on Eccles Street. Throughout the day, characters' recollections jump back and forth through their lives. When the discourse reaches the hallucinogenic episodes of the Circe chapter, time has taken on a circularity and an elasticity that belie the concerted effort to insert temporal markers into the narrative.

Form also disrupts linear expectations. As the chapters unfold in their distinctive constructions, readers find themselves moving from one dominant style to another. In the first six, diverse demonstrations of interior monologue initially challenge and ultimately (through growing familiarity) condition one's comprehension of how the action is unfolding. About the time that one begins to feel comfortable with that approach, the mysterious headings that intrude into the discourse of the seventh chapter disrupt one's sense of the logic informing the novel's construction. Such shifts in style, unanticipated and divorced from all the forms preceding them, continue through the remainder of the work in a virtuoso performance showing Joyce's command of a wide range of writing (see Wales 1992).

Finally, the reader's sense of reference remains provisional throughout the work. One finds the most obvious example in the extended hallucinogenic dramatization of the Nighttown episode (see Shechner 1974). However, shifts in voice throughout the work continually call into question the source of specific comments and the legitimacy of particular observations. All this underscores subjectivity, yet rather than frustrating understanding it offers readers an interpretive freedom unheard of in other works.

Despite the thematic and stylistic innovations that I have already noted, the lasting impact of *Ulysses* comes from the narrative's representations of the human experience. With an attention to detail that one sees in such writers as Flaubert and Dostoyevsky and an empathy that surpasses that of any previous artist, Joyce presents the drama of ordinary life. He focuses on three central figures – Stephen Dedalus, Leopold Bloom, and Molly Bloom – and in telling their stories he captures the essence of urban life (see Peake 1977).

As noted above, the narrative begins with three chapters devoted to Stephen Dedalus in a suggestion that it will take up where *A Portrait of the Artist as a Young Man* ended. The discourse finds Stephen back in Ireland and even more dissatisfied than he was before he left. In short order one encounters the themes that will define Stephen's nature over the course of the novel: guilt over his mother's death, frustration at the lack of artistic recognition, a sense of isolation from his family and a concurrent need for some type of father figure, and a general dissatisfaction with the life he is now living. We see diverse manifestations of Stephen's nature: the domestic individual, sharing the Martello tower with Buck Mulligan, the public figure, teaching at Mr Garrett Deasy's school in Dalkey, and the private person, questioning life and art as he walks along Sandymount Strand.

As readers begin to feel a clear sense of how Stephen is being represented and how to comprehend him, the narrative shifts abruptly to begin the day again by focusing on Leopold Bloom for the next three chapters. As with Stephen, in short order the discourse introduces the themes that will define Bloom's nature over the course of the novel: an uxorious love for his wife Molly and the incumbent unease over her impending adultery, a deep concern for his daughter Milly yet a resignation over an inability to control events, and an ongoing sense of sorrow over the suicide of his father and the death shortly after birth of his son Rudy. We see the domestic Bloom, at home in Eccles Street, the private Bloom, as he walks around Dublin in the mid-morning, and the public Bloom as he attends the funeral of Paddy Dignam.

For the next eleven chapters, the narrative oscillates between Stephen and Bloom. In the process it introduces a panoply of minor characters – memorable figures such as Buck Mulligan and Simon Dedalus and enigmatic ones like Denis Breen and the Man in the Macintosh. In every instance these figures enrich the cultural context of the narrative, giving readers a much fuller sense not only of Bloom and Stephen but of the highly articulated and profoundly contradictory world which they inhabit. The day unfolds, on the one hand, as a perfectly ordinary one for each man. Stephen spends the morning teaching, receives his salary, and then carouses with friends and acquaintances into the night. Bloom makes breakfast for Molly, goes to Dignam's funeral, stops at the offices of *The Freeman's Journal* where he too is paid, and then wanders about the city until well into the night, putting off returning home. At the same time it is a unique day for both men. Stephen, discontented with his job and his living arrangements, seems to come to the decision to abandon both. Bloom, resigned to endure what he cannot change, spends a painful day avoiding the harsh truth that his wife is committing adultery. By the time these men leave the narrative at the end of the penultimate chapter, readers have learned a great deal about both but have come to no clear conclusions on the nature of either (see Hayman 1970).

In the final chapter, the discourse gives itself over to the long, rambling, unpunctuated monologue of Molly Bloom. Numerous references to her have appeared over the course of the narrative, but this disquisition stands as the reader's first extended exposure. As she voices her thoughts, her concerns, and her desires, she both confirms and contradicts the diverse impressions that the recollections of her husband and other Dubliners have produced in the reader's mind. In the process, Molly provides not simply a coda to the novel but an emphatic reassertion of the complexity and its accessibility. Stephen, Bloom, and Molly stand as representative of the human condition. They highlight the range of emotions, needs, assumptions, and beliefs that define us all. At the same time, they illustrate in marvelous detail how such similar features lead to highly subjective individuals (see Fargnoli and Gillespie 2006).

Almost immediately following the publication of *Ulysses*, Joyce undertook an even more radical creative experiment, *Finnegans Wake*. It occupied the rest of his creative life, and I will discuss it in detail below. However, over the course of completing *Ulysses* and undertaking *Finnegans Wake*, Joyce also composed additional poetry that should receive some, though not extended, notice. In 1927 he published a collection,

Pomes Penyeach, that includes thirteen poems, twelve and a tilly as Joyce would put it, written between 1913 and 1924. The verses follow personal and autobiographical themes and touch on Joyce's life, and that of his family, in Trieste and Zurich. Though he continued writing limericks and other comic verse, the only other serious attempt at poetry that he made was "Ecce Puer," a work combining the emotions of joy over the birth of his grandson Stephen with the sorrow he felt at the death of his father. Although Joyce's verse pales in comparison to his fiction, an awareness of it remains a useful supplement to our sense of his creative consciousness.

Joyce's forays into verse, however, mark only brief diversions from the creative task that dominated fifteen years of the closing decades of his life, beginning in 1924. He called it his *Work in Progress*, and did not reveal the actual title, *Finnegans Wake*, to anyone but his wife Nora before its publication in 1939. Though the title itself seemed modest, the goal of his final piece was no less than the rearticulation of the protocols of prose fiction. In the process he produced a work that remains unduplicated by other writers and at best only partially understood by its readers (see Campbell and Robinson 1966).

In each of his earlier pieces of fiction, from *Dubliners* through *Ulysses*, Joyce had resisted the hegemony of Cartesian thinking and had sought to counteract its dominant perspective of cause and effect, linear logic as the force animating conceptions of the world surrounding us. In each case, he had pushed the boundary beyond his own and others' previous efforts. Epistemologically, Joyce always faced the inhibitive consequences of readers' assumptions regarding the inherent linearity of language. Iconographically, as long as he wrote in a form that proceeded from left to right in rigid sequence, he could never completely free responses to his books from the tyranny of Cartesianism. With *Finnegans Wake*, Joyce instituted a new form of writing and consequently demanded new habits of reading (see Booker 1995).

Joyce founded the structure of *Finnegans Wake* on circularity. The narrative begins in mid-sentence "riverrun, past Eve and Adam's, from swerve of shore to bend of bay, brings us by a commodius vicus of recirculation back to Howth Castle and Environs," completing a thought initiated 628 pages later in the final line "A way a lone a last a love a long the." This construction catches in both description and modulation the sinuous movement of the river Liffey oscillating back and forth between Dublin Bay and its source in the hills, and it set a paradigm for nonlinearity that would inform all subsequent prose constructions. In this fashion, the discourse of *Finnegans Wake* represents language in its most recognizable and in consequence its most recondite form, words functioning at multiple levels by slipping free of directive representations.

This occurs because *Finnegans Wake* makes overt the complex features of the highly subjective communication process – multiplicity and imprecision – that we all embrace and understand yet which we all sublimate. The demand that we confront this process can, initially at least, be quite jarring for readers, for despite our facility at communicating we steadfastly maintain assumptions that deny the mutable, nonlinear aspects of the process. On even the simplest levels, whenever words come into play they assert a malleability that gives the lie to assumptions of the certitude of meaning. Familiar terms – beauty, goodness, ugliness, evil – seem from a distance to enjoy self-evident meaning, yet when they are held up to close scrutiny the presumed integrity of these terms dissolves like aspirin tablets in a glass of water. The meaning that one person assigns to any of these terms will differ, sometimes slightly sometimes greatly, from that which the next person designates. The consequent understanding that we enjoy in communication has itself an inherent impermanence, something open to constant revision (see Cheng 1995). Joyce understood and reveled in this condition like no other contemporary author. Samuel Beckett certainly had a syntactic understanding of the condition similar to Joyce's, indeed Beckett may well have derived it from Joyce, but for Beckett this insight into the mechanics of speech led to despair over its applicability: words could never be pinned down (see CHAPTER 36, THE WORD OF POLITICS/POLITICS OF THE WORD). For Joyce, however, the same realization produced a sense of joyful liberation: words could never be pinned down.

Joyce reflected his sense of freedom by using language that celebrated the multiplicity inherent in everything that he wrote. In highlighting the instability of words, he made readers aware of the implicit demand for multiple interpretations of every iteration. Punning, portmanteau words, multi-lingual puns, layered allusions, and cultural resonances all work to foreground the rich possibilities inherent in every linguistic expression. "O foenix culprit," a phrase introduced at *FW* 23.16 and then recurring in variant form throughout the work, illustrates a number of these strategies. It plays upon the phrase *felix culpa*, the fortunate fall, which St Augustine uses to characterize the sin in Eden and its consequences which led to Christ's incarnation and humanity's redemption. It also brings to mind the murky charge that the central character, HCE, committed some sort of disgraceful act in Phoenix Park, and so is a wrongdoer associated with the park. It further questions the ability to assign blame – foe-nix/not the culprit. And with the links to the classical phoenix and the Christian concept of resurrection, it invokes images of immortality shared across cultures.

Finnegans Wake, also like Joyce's earlier fiction, takes the representation of fundamental human concerns as its primary goal. In his previous writing, Joyce had pursued a synecdochal approach, inferring from specific interactions a commonality and a uniqueness in all human experience. In the process, he made the exploits of Dubliners at the turn of the nineteenth century both entirely familiar and charmingly distinct for readers around the world. In his final work Joyce moved toward metonymy. Characters immediately call to mind archetypal associations only to reinforce the specificity of their natures. As a result, they move easily between micro and macro levels of representation to underscore the cyclical nature of human experience while simultaneously highlighting its idiosyncrasies.

In its bare outline, *Finnegans Wake* follows a typical Dublin family: Humphrey Chimpden Earwicker, a pubkeeper living near Phoenix Park; Anna Livia Plurabelle, his wife; Shem and Shaun, their twin sons with antagonistic, antipathetic natures; and Issy, their daughter, an implicit sexual threat to the mother and a clear sexual temptation to the men in the family. With all of the obvious social, spiritual, and sexual associations, *Finnegans Wake* alludes to a rise and fall and reinstatement – much as that epic and personal progression depicted in the Irish American folk song, "Finnegan's Wake." The narrative presents the struggle for identity and recognition of the personal level, the local level, the national level, the mythical level, and a range of other categories. Its discourse explores human weaknesses and foibles. It dissects human triumphs and failures. In the process, the work reflects the complexity that each condition layers upon the characters, making everyone less clear-cut but no less significant.

In the end *Finnegans Wake* succeeds as a complex work of art because it never loses sight of the simple human needs at the heart of the most diverse of individuals. Joyce understands happiness, fear, insecurity, complacency, and a range of other factors that shape our natures. He is adept at representing them without judgment or irony. His characters, both in *Finnegans Wake* and over the course of his fiction, certainly behave with a measure of foolishness just as they also retain a substantial portion of dignity. Although he may have left the Catholic Church behind in his adolescence, throughout his life he held to the belief that balanced both the inherently flawed nature of humans and their undeniable perfectibility.

This perspective informed his writing, and it gave him the sense of *Finnegans Wake* as a profoundly comic work. He saw humans in all of their flaws and with all of their potential. From this he derived a sense that the flaws could have no lasting, debilitating effect because we possess the power to diminish their impact, to deflate their significance, by laughing at them. This gesture did not so much assault our dignity as remind us of the possibility of forgiveness and redemption, which is what one would expect from this profoundly Catholic writer (see Boyle 1978).

Joyce's canon gives readers the greatest gift an author can bestow. His works evoke our imaginative engagement. They underscore the distinctiveness of individual experience and the generality of our collective consciousness. And they remind us of the beauty inherent in everyday life.

REFERENCES AND FURTHER READING

Booker, M.K. (1995). *Joyce, Bakhtin, and the Literary Tradition: Toward a Comparative Cultural Poetics.* Ann Arbor: University of Michigan Press.

Bowen, Z. and J.F. Carens (Eds). (1984). *A Companion to Joyce Studies.* Westport, CT: Greenwood Press.

Boyle, R. (1978). *James Joyce's Pauline Vision: A Catholic Exposition.* Carbondale: Southern Illinois University Press.

Bradley, B., SJ. (1982). *James Joyce's Schooldays.* Dublin: Gill & Macmillan.

Budgen, F. (1960). *James Joyce and the Making of Ulysses.* Bloomington: University of Indiana Press.

Campbell, J. and H.M. Robinson. (1966). *A Skeleton Key to* Finnegans Wake (1944). Repr. New York: Viking Press.

Cheng, V.J. (1995). *Joyce, Race, and Empire.* Cambridge: Cambridge University Press.

Deming, R.H. (1977). *A Bibliography of James Joyce Studies.* 2nd edn., revised and enlarged. Boston: G.K. Hall.

Ellmann, R. (1982). *James Joyce* (1959). Rev. edn. New York: Oxford University Press.

Epstein, E.L. (1971). *The Ordeal of Stephen Dedalus: The Conflict of the Generations in James Joyce's* A Portrait of the Artist as a Young Man. Carbondale: Southern Illinois University Press.

Fargnoli, A.N. (Ed). (2003). *James Joyce: A Literary Reference*. New York: Carroll & Graf.

Fargnoli, A.N. and M.P. Gillespie. (2006). *A Companion to James Joyce: A Literary Reference to his Life and Work*. New York: Checkmark Books.

Gifford, D. and R.J. Seidman. (1967). *Notes for Joyce:* Dubliners *and* A Portrait of the Artist as a Young Man. New York: E.P. Dutton.

Gillespie, M.P. (1989). *Reading the Book of Himself: Narrative Strategies in the Works of James Joyce.* Columbus: Ohio State University Press.

Goldman, A. (1966). *The Joyce Paradox*. London: Routledge & Kegan Paul.

Groden, M. (1977). *Ulysses in Progress*. Princeton: Princeton University Press.

Hayman, D. (1970). *Ulysses: The Mechanics of Meaning*. Englewood Cliffs, NJ: Prentice Hall.

Herr, C. (1986). *Joyce's Anatomy of Culture*. Urbana: University of Illinois Press.

Jolas, M. (Ed). (1949). *A James Joyce Yearbook*. Paris: Transition Press.

Joyce, J. (1907). *Chamber Music*. London.

Joyce, J. (1914). *Dubliners*. London: Grant Richards.

Joyce, J. (1916). *A Portrait of the Artist as a Young Man* (serialized 1914–15). New York: B.W. Huebsch.

Joyce, J. (1918). *Exiles: A Play in Three Acts*. London: Grant Richards.

Joyce, J. (1939). *Finnegans Wake*. London: Faber & Faber.

Joyce, J. (1957). *Letters of James Joyce*. Vol. I. S. Gilbert (Ed). London: Faber & Faber.

Joyce, J. (1959). *The Critical Writings of James Joyce*. E. Mason and R. Ellmann (Eds). London: Faber & Faber.

Joyce, J. (1966). *Letters of James Joyce*. Vols. II and III. R. Ellmann (Ed). London: Faber & Faber.

Joyce, J. (2001). *Poems and Shorter Writings*. R. Ellmann and A.W. Litz (Eds). London: Faber & Faber.

Kenner, H. (1956). *Dublin's Joyce*. London: Chatto & Windus.

Lawrence, K. (1981). *The Odyssey of Style in Ulysses*. Princeton: Princeton University Press.

Leonard, G. (1994). *Reading* Dubliners *Again: A Lacanian Perspective*. Syracuse: Syracuse University Press.

Levin, H. (1960). *James Joyce: A Critical Introduction* (1944). London: Faber & Faber.

MacNicholas, J. (1979). *James Joyce's Exiles: A Textual Companion*. New York: Garland.

Magalaner, M. and R.M. Kain. (1956). *Joyce: The Man, the Work, the Reputation*. New York: New York University Press.

McCourt, J. (2000). *Years of Bloom: James Joyce in Trieste 1904–1920*. Dublin: Lilliput Press.

Noon, W.T. (1957). *Joyce and Aquinas*. New Haven: Yale University Press.

Norris, M. (2003). *Suspicious Readings of Joyce's Dubliners*. Philadelphia: University of Pennsylvania Press.

Peake, C. (1977). *James Joyce: The Citizen and the Artist*. Stanford: Stanford University Press.

Rice, T.J. (1982). *James Joyce: A Guide to Research*. New York: Garland.

Riquelme, J.P. (1983). *Teller and Tale in Joyce's Fiction: Oscillating Perspectives*. Baltimore: Johns Hopkins University Press.

Scott, B.K. (1984). *Joyce and Feminism*. Bloomington: Indiana University Press.

Shechner, M. (1974). *Joyce in Nighttown: A Psychoanalytic Inquiry into* Ulysses. Los Angeles: University of California Press.

Sullivan, K. (1958). *Joyce among the Jesuits*. New York: Columbia University Press.

Valente, J. (1995). *James Joyce and the Problem of Justice: Negotiating Sexual and Colonial Difference*. Cambridge: Cambridge University Press.

Wales, K. (1992). *The Language of James Joyce*. New York: St Martin's Press.

Part Eight

Developments in Genre and Representation after 1930

36

The Word of Politics/Politics of the Word: Immanence and Transdescendence in Sean O'Casey and Samuel Beckett

Sandra Wynands

Sean O'Casey and Samuel Beckett never met. Indeed, it seems difficult to imagine the occasion enabling two such fundamentally different people to meet. Both enjoyed their first success as writers relatively late in life, but one had turned his back on a promising career as a professor at Trinity College Dublin, while the other was an autodidact who had fought his way out of the Dublin slums, where he had toiled as an unskilled laborer. One was a political activist for the socialist cause, while the other engaged in no explicit political activity beyond working as a messenger in the French resistance. One was never fully able to free himself from financial constraints, while the other chose a modest existence, giving most of his money away to struggling artist friends. Beckett could not wait to get out of Ireland, preferring France at war to Ireland in peace, while O'Casey embraced Irish culture and language, its national cause, and, especially, its poor, although he also chose to build his literary career in exile in London. Particularly, Beckett wrote in his adopted language, French, and chose to translate himself into English in a second step, while O'Casey was rooted in the idiom of the Irish working class and used its language to heighten awareness of their plight.

A fundamentally different understanding of drama is reflected here and Beckett and O'Casey find themselves on either side of a chasm that divides the dramatic community as such. O'Casey uses drama to communicate the ills of social circumstances and to mobilize his audience to change them – so he hopes. That is, the theater for O'Casey becomes the locus of communication and interaction. Beckett, on the other hand, induces experiences that do not so much move audiences towards one another as make them turn inward, because his theater challenges language as such and with it the very conceptual principles on which a person bases his or her actions in the world.

A Companion to Irish Literature, edited by Julia M. Wright
© 2010 Blackwell Publishing Ltd

To O'Casey, then, Beckett's preoccupations must seem decadent and socially irresponsible, while in Beckett's view O'Casey blithely overlooks the root problem of all the ills he attempts to fight. O'Casey had the following to say about Beckett's *Waiting for Godot*:

> Beckett? I have nothing to do with Beckett. He isn't in me; nor am I in him. I am not waiting for Godot to bring me life; I am out after life myself, even at the age I've reached. What have any of you to do with Godot? There is more to life than Godot can give in the life of the least of us. That Beckett is a clever writer, and that he has written a rotting and remarkable play, there can be no doubt; but his philosophy isn't my philosophy, for within him there is no hazard of hope; no desire for it; nothing in it but a lust for despair, and a crying of woe, not in a wilderness, but in a garden. (quoted in Krause 1976:94–95)

It would be mistaken, however, to assume, as O'Casey seems to do, that Beckett is a decadent, quietist nihilist. Beckett is very concerned about violence and injustice: *Catastrophe* is the most politically outspoken example, but *The Unnamable* and *Not I* share its sense of urgency in a different tonality. The ideological divide separating the two writers is of a different nature than mere political awareness: Beckett is an idealist while O'Casey is a materialist.

O'Casey is convinced that in order to improve the lives of human beings we need to change the circumstances in which they live. Beckett approaches the problem of human liberation from the opposite point of view: he believes the patterns that make violence possible are buried in the way we conceptualize the world through language. We need to change the way we think and our material circumstances will change as a consequence. He condones neither Didi and Gogo's passivity nor their belief that Godot's arrival will be their salvation; that much is implicit in the play's outrageous humor – after all, where is the indomitable spirit of hope to be found if not in humor? Didi and Gogo are didactic examples, not ones to be emulated. As an audience we are to change our thinking in those ways Didi and Gogo prove unable to accomplish and to take our lives into our own hands rather than leave our fortune up to the whims of others, celestial and otherwise. *Godot*, as we shall see, is then not as apolitical as it may appear.

For O'Casey language is a sign of belonging to a community and a cause: he Gaelicized his name from Shawn Casey to Sean O'Casey as soon as he discovered his Gaelic heritage and the cause of Irish independence, which for him always remained tied and subservient to socialist ideals. The vernacular of his plays, which may or may not be authentically Irish, is to bring to life the world of the Dublin tenements, the plight of the Irish slum dwellers, for whom he fought as a union activist and as a writer and among whose ranks he counted himself. Language becomes a marker of identity and of circumstance – of material conditions.

Beckett's relationship to language is fundamentally different. He always comes to language as an outsider, regardless of which language he writes in. He has no language that is properly his own; he prefers, at times, to write in his second language and then to translate himself into his first language, English, whose conventions are not native to him, but as antiquated as a Victorian bathing suit (Beckett 1983a:171). French becomes a distancing device which enables him to approach English through the back door. Beckett's status as self-translator is unique among modern literary figures, yet often neglected. Strictly speaking, the fact that any Beckett text exists in two languages renders it inherently split: nothing is said only once, but always twice, with variations due to the untranslatability of any language's particular idiom and cultural context. Yet because each version appears to be underwritten by Beckett, the author and origin of the text, it is taken as complete in itself, which it vehemently is not. Leslie Hill saliently observes that, despite the doubling it consistently performs, Beckett's work remains single-minded in its pursuit of absolute irreducibility: "the work makes a virtue of its resistance to all forms of external representation, including political ones, and refuses to be co-opted into any cause other than its own irreducible singularity" (Hill 1997:910). Hill posits the possibility, indeed the performance, of non-identical singularity in Beckett's texts – singularity, that is, which cannot be reduced to onto-theological proportions of origin or telos.

He gives a subtle analysis of the functions of the one overtly political statement in Beckett's oeuvre, the "Up the Republic!" in *Malone meurt/Malone Dies*. The expression appears in English in both texts, with different shades of meaning in each, and it simultaneously proclaims and withdraws support for a cause: it proclaims support by its sheer presence in the text and by the overt meaning of its content; it withdraws support because of what the expression accomplishes in Beckett's text. The political discourse to which the expression belongs "operates there solely as an ironic residue of itself" (Hill 1997:913): "that's what I like about me ... that I can say, Up the Republic!, for example, or Sweetheart!, for example, without having to wonder if I should not rather have cut my tongue out, or said something else," Beckett writes, and Hill observes that "Up the Republic!," just like "Sweetheart!," "plays the part of a piece of empty or irrelevant rhetoric" (1997:912). For this reason it has become commonplace to portray Beckett as a thoroughly apolitical writer. Yet, Hill argues, the disconnect between political discourse and political reality is not merely a characteristic of Beckett's personal attitude towards the political, but reflects a mechanism common in political discourse as such: it becomes divorced from the reality it originally described while power-play and scuttling for position take over. Differently put, as language once passionately felt runs its course through official government channels, it becomes emptied of meaning and disconnected from its cause, and more often than not the "counterculture" participates in this process of "gentrification." The language was divorced from its cause long before it underwent the ironic treatment in Beckett's text.

The process is one of reification, which is difficult to avoid within discursive language, and so the idealist Beckett would consider any discursive strategy an avoidance of the root problem, which is representation itself. "Literature," Wallace Stevens pointed out in his "Adagia," "is based not on life but on propositions about life, of which this is one" (Stevens 1957:171). This means that the relationship between literature and the world is not primarily mimetic. Literature does not seek to imitate the world; rather, it illustrates its own *theory* of what it means to be alive in the world. This search for meaning in human existence is crucially hampered by the deficiencies of the human faculties, perceptual and cognitive, and by our resulting inability to see phenomena for what they are. Most artists of the twentieth century recognize this gap between representation and reality. Beckett is not exceptional because his art is non-representational, which it is to a startling extent. Most of his contemporaries also recognized the necessity to emancipate writing from the narrow constraints of representation, a process many other art forms had already completed. Beckett is exceptional in the rigor with which he reflects on language, our mode of thought and the primary "means" by which we make sense of the world – and more still: it is much more than just a means of representation. Beckett's project is to free language from its yeoman position of a means to an end – the end of expression, for instance, of an (artistic or political) idea. His philosophical rigor leads him towards a non-instrumentalist view of language.

Beckett's engagement with the political occurs at the level where political discourse is formed – of language itself – and it draws attention to the inability of political discourse to signify the reality of political struggle without being co-opted by political power structures. The task in investigating Beckett's political engagement, Hill writes, is therefore "not to seek out discursive concepts," which would identify Beckett with one political cause or another, "but to examine textual effects"; such an approach is "not to fall short of the political; it is … to raise the very question of the political as such" (Hill 1997:911).

O'Casey remains caught up in discursive concepts; indeed, he thinks an engagement with them to be the very sign of political activism. He is acutely aware that concepts are subject to corruption, that there is a strong likelihood for concepts to be used for demagogic purposes, as *The Plough and the Stars*, for instance, demonstrates. In it O'Casey shows violent nationalist rhetoric infiltrating the noble cause of political independence, a problem close to his own heart. Significantly, the one spouting nationalist rhetoric and encouraging violence in the name of the national cause remains anonymous and is identified simply as the "Voice of the Man," an amorphous entity removed from the actuality of human relationships. These signs of awareness of the dangers inherent in concept and representation nonetheless remain themselves representational. For the materialist O'Casey this is not a contradiction, and yet art which engages with the political in this representational manner easily turns into an exercise in putting out fire with gasoline, precisely when it attempts to acknowledge representationally, that is in a manner equally bound to the logic of copy and original, the disconnect between a concept's original experiential content and its gutted discursive copy. Beckett avoids this particular pitfall with a performative approach to language, which aims to present rather than represent.

There is a rift between the thing itself and our concept or image of it, or more precisely, in phenomenological terms, we impose our intention on phenomena whose givenness will then fall short of our intention: although we may see only three sides of a cube, for instance, and intuition is thus limited, our pre-existing concept of a cube tells us what kind of an object is at hand. Our intention then fills in the remaining three sides. Likewise, our first-hand experience of Paris, limited as it will necessarily be, will fall short of a concept of Paris to which myth, books, and films have contributed. In every case, our concept of a thing precedes our experience of it and this intention allows us to constitute the phenomenon as meaningful. Yet this need not necessarily be so. The contemporary phenomenologist Jean-Luc Marion argues that the Husserlian poor phenomenon, which functions with an overload of intention over intuition, is, not least, a question of attitude. And this attitude has, throughout the history of the West, been overwhelmingly dualist.

In antiquity and the Middle Ages, Europeans conceived of the world around them as a vertical dualism between the absolute realm of the Good or the Divine and the finite realm of human beings, where the latter participated in the former and was directly proportionate to it. Then, with the advent of modernity, this shifted to a horizontal dualism between subject and object, self and other, *res cogitans* and *res extensa*. Dominantly, the relationship between subject and object is conceived of hierarchically, not least because, phenomenologically speaking, the subject constitutes the world of givens as objects according to the intention it has of them. In Husserl's transcendental reduction, adequation of intention and intuition is posited as an ideal (see his *Logische Untersuchungen*), yet one that can never be realized (Marion 2002:191): phenomenological intuition can never, or only rarely, fulfill and be adequate to the subject's intention. The world is subject to our will and *Vorstellung* (representation) and truth becomes almost inaccessible. We habitually perceive the world as ready to hand, instrumental to the designs we have on it. War, environmental destruction, indifferent bureaucracies, and other types of violence are the result. In order to perceive and represent the world differently, to break with this history and to conduct ourselves non-violently, we must embark on a rigorous process of contesting our own conceptualizations – an endless process, as Beckett knows: "It seems impossible to speak and yet say nothing, you think you have succeeded, but you always overlook something, a little yes, a little no, enough to exterminate a regiment of dragoons," the narrator in *The Unnamable* proclaims in exasperation (Beckett 1994:305).

Part of this process of contestation is to question our own attitude. Marion vividly uses the example of touching a wall as an illustration of two radically different ways of approaching the world. Thus it is possible to touch the wall for information and signification, as is the case when one fumbles in the dark to find the light switch or attempts to ascertain whether the object at hand is indeed the lamp (Marion 2007:394). In a different context one might touch the same or a different surface differently: in order to experience its texture, or, in interaction with another person, "in order to console and soothe, to excite and enjoy, therefore without objective signification, indeed without identifiable or sayable signification. Thus touch does not manifest an object, but a saturated phenomenon" (Marion 2007:395). A "saturated phenomenon" gives itself with an excess of intuition over intention and thus disables us as constituters of phenomena.

Along similar lines, Beckett deconstructs the assumptions we make when we choose to valorize intention over intuition. His art creates a space in absolute openness, so that phenomena may give themselves in excess of our conceptual blueprints and remain absolutely irreducible to onto-theological categories. He investigates the conditions under which such self-showing may occur. Onto-theological metaphysics was itself a creation of the conceptual mind, which considers itself the constituting force behind a meaningful world. Post-metaphysical phenomenology does not contest that a phenomenon becomes meaningful only for a perceiving entity, yet that perceiving entity no longer constitutes the phenomenon as meaningful. We merely receive it in its givenness. Beckett's theatrical art is full of such phenomena. *Not I* is one, for instance, because it moves too fast and is too dense to be absorbed in its entirety from a single vantage point.

The postmodern re-evaluation of subjectivity is an important first step before this reordering of the phenomenological universe can take shape. Thus characters in Beckett's early plays — when his plays still sported characters — are not full-fledged agents and masters of their fate. Hamm and Clov do not live; they merely exist. Likewise, we as readers or viewers attempt to see the play as coherent subjects and producers of meaning. We attempt to reconstruct a story, to extract a plot from the hints dropped throughout *Endgame*: what happened and why? But the play encourages and resists our efforts to build a coherent image in equal measure.

Before long, it becomes clear that it is irrelevant what kind of disaster happened before the commencement of the *Endgame*, or even whether it happened at all. The disaster zone outside might simply be the product of two psychotic minds working in seamless symbiosis. We are to focus rather on the type of interaction between the two characters, which is what the play dramatizes for us. Hamm and Clov are not the authors of a happy collaboration: they corner one another until one, and thus the other, is unable to move. Hamm is a violently overbearing nostalgic, Clov the passive-aggressive indispensable servant who delights in destroying Hamm's clear, romantic visions.

Theodor Adorno famously saw *Endgame* as the Dialectic of Enlightenment in its final stages. In its wake it leaves human beings amputated both mentally and physically, like Nagg and Nell, by unquestioning adherence to an extremely impoverished concept of reason: instrumental reason. Beckett shows us to be former Cartesian Centaurs, as Hugh Kenner put it (Kenner 1968:117), who, having partly substituted their unpredictable and deficient bodies for machines, now find that instrumental reason fails them. Instrumental reason has come back to haunt them, now that they are disabled and unable to function, with their bicycles rusted or gone, alienated from themselves, their bodies, and one another.

Caught in the Dialectic of Enlightenment, Adorno argues, we not only use reason to emancipate ourselves from the threatening vagaries of the natural world but we also allow it to alienate us from ourselves and from our fellow human beings, to reify not only the world around us, which we perceive as subject to our will, but also our fellow creatures. Adorno sees the Holocaust as the ultimate manifestation of this perverted rational practice: the complete dehumanization of fellow human beings and their industrial murder and processing. He concludes that "the catastrophes that inspire *Endgame* have shattered the individual whose substantiality and absoluteness was the common thread in Kierkegaard, Jaspers, and Sartre's version of existentialism. Sartre even affirmed the freedom of victims of the concentration camps to inwardly accept or reject the tortures inflicted on them" (Adorno 1991:249) – the latter an absurd idea, and testimony to the unshakable foundations of a centered subjectivity in which existentialism was rooted and which Beckett exposes as an illusion, even a dangerous one. The persistent critique of rationality in Beckett's work, which we also see in the portrayals of Watt and of Molloy as "dogged systematizers" (Kenner 1968:119) who develop a mathematical pattern so that their shoes or sucking stones may be distributed evenly, goes hand in hand with his critique of subjectivity.

Always acutely aware of different media, Beckett was among the first to make technologies of reproduction the self-conscious center of attention in a play. The process of decentering that was to reach its pinnacle and its turning point in *The Unnamable* can be seen in *Krapp's Last Tape*. Daringly, as in *Rockaby*, the actor on stage remains almost completely silent throughout the play. Instead, we hear previous recorded versions of Krapp elaborate on the narrative of his life, while the current Krapp provides primarily nonverbal commentary ranging from mild disapproval to outright anger. The taped versions of Krapp competing with one another assume the iterative qualities of writing in the Derridean sense. The tape recorder emphasizes the mediated nature of any narrative, which in the play becomes merely a more or less fictional sketch of what might have happened: a version of Krapp's life as constructed by him thirty years ago: a proposition about life implicit in narrative, not the experience of life itself. And this narrative construct elicits only head-shaking bemusement and anger from the present-day Krapp, who has moved on from the young romantic he once was, but who also recognizes the young Krapp on the tape as a (maybe insincere?) narrative invention whose ideals the real Krapp in the end finds himself unable to live up to or disapproves of.

In German there are two words for experience: *Erfahrung* and *Erlebnis*. It is no coincidence, Hans-Georg Gadamer points out, that *Erlebnis*, the newer word, first comes to prominence during the Enlightenment and the rise of the subject (Gadamer 1975:55). The root of *Erlebnis* is related to *leben*, meaning "to live." The sum of a person's *Erlebnisse*, then, is what constitutes the retrospective narrative of a life and the personality formed by that life. Conversely, the sum of these experiences makes a person constitute new experiences in a predetermined way. The root of *Erfahrung*, on the other hand, is *fahren*, "to travel" or "to drive." It is the older word of the two. The inevitable upheaval of traveling, the new experiences a traveler encounters, imply shocks to a subject's cherished stability and integrity. Kevin Hart points out that the English word, experience, contains *peri*, from which modern English derives "peril." *Erfahrung* "keeps in play a notion of experience as a setting at risk, a voyage that may well involve danger" (Hart 1998:9).

The multiple versions of the technologically mediated Krapp indeed seem to imply that Beckett is wary of the immediacy of *Erlebnis*, but not of the immediacy of experience differently conceived, namely as *Erfahrung*. The play does not give us Krapp sharing his most intimate life experience through the immediacy of his speaking voice as a direct manifestation of his subjectivity. Making love in a boat gently rocking from side to side could have been an *Erlebnis*, a unique and originary experience fundamental to and affirmative of Krapp's subjectivity. It could have been an experience to shape the innermost being of Krapp as he sits before the audience that day, thirty years later. Instead of eliding the propositional nature of any play and emphasizing the mimetic, Beckett enhances it through a double distancing device: the "spool" and Krapp's strong reaction of distaste to the sultry romanticism of his earlier incarnation as he shuts the machine down.

Beckett's art increasingly embarks on the perilous journey of an exploration of limits. His journey is hence not primarily, even if it is intensely, inward. But it is not *Erlebnis*. Rather, it is *Erfahrung*. *Erlebnis* denotes an inner experience whose content makes a person who she is. It makes up her *Leben*, her life. *Erlebnis confirms* one's subjectivity. Beckett's work is a confrontation, a process of radical contestation in which that which generates meaning meets its Other, an Outside – that which continuously evades any meaning. It is important to note that Beckett configures the problem as one of transcendence, as a truth veiled. A writer's highest goal, he thinks, can only be "to bore one hole after another in [language], until what lurks behind it – be it something or nothing – begins to seep through." Else literature alone "is to remain behind in the old lazy ways that have been so long ago abandoned by music and painting." In other words, representational painting is passé, and so is representational writing: "Is there any reason why that terrible materiality of the word surface should not be capable of being dissolved?" (Beckett 1983a:172).

The Unnamable is such an exploration of limits. In it the speaking voice vies with numerous others, but to see the novel as another exercise in decentering subjectivity falls short of the radical nature of Beckett's project. The speaking voice is not one subjectivity among many, not even a fragmented one. Rather, the speaking voice systematically strips itself of any semblance of subjectivity. For this reason the German title of *The Unnamable*, *Der Namenlose*, is entirely inadequate. In literal translation *Der Namenlose* means "the one without a name." The title continues to treat the speaking voice as "one," as an indivisible entity as yet unnamed. What is truly unnamable, however, cannot be constituted by any conceptual operation, no matter how inadequate. Beckett's text is, in fact, deconstructive. It methodically questions its own conceptual operations in order not to name. It is an attempt to speak and say nothing, that is, to advance no conceptual propositions at all.

Still *The Unnamable* is redolent with breathless syntactic structures that speak of a chase – the exhausting pursuit of an excessively elusive entity, an unnamable whose perfect expression is impossible, not least because language itself is already co-opted by powers that use it as an instrument of power and control and has first to be wrested free from them: "none will ever know what I am, none will ever hear me say it, I won't say it, I can't say it, I have no language but theirs, no, perhaps I'll say it, even with their language, for me alone, so as not to have lived in vain, and so as to go silent, if that is what confers the right of silence, and it's unlikely" (Beckett 1994:328). Yet even this pursuit is ambivalent. It becomes increasingly clear that it is not a matter of dogged insistence in the hope of chasing down the perfect expression in the end. At least after a certain point of exhaustion Beckett appears to revel in the ambivalence of being locked into a performative aporia of his own creation, an aporia that only appears in the process of writing and whose nature will shortly become clear. Consequently, Beckett reaches a turning point in his career after *The Unnamable*. Here is its last sentence:

> I'll go on, you must say words, as long as there are any, until they find me, until they say me, strange pain, strange sin, you must go on, perhaps it's done already, perhaps they have said me already, perhaps they have carried me to the threshold of my story, before the door that opens on my story, that would surprise me, if it opens, it will be I, it will be the silence where I am, I don't know, I'll never know, in the silence you don't know, you must go on, I can't go on, I'll go on. (Beckett 1994:418)

This passage appears to suggest a different idea of language than the usual referential one. The narrator says that he must find and use words to describe the unnamable only until they find *him*, until *they* say *him*. This view of language is performative: the words say, they are able to make figuratively present. It is no longer we who say things with words as our instruments of representation. For us as thinkers and "users" of language this means that language becomes radically experiential. In late Heidegger (see *Gelassenheit* [1959]), the phenomenological horizon, the conceptual framework before which the subject traditionally constitutes phenomena, becomes synonymous with representational thinking. The horizon is what faces us, what we are in front of, in our *vor-stellen*. It needs to become part of a *Gegend* or *Gegnet* (Heidegger 1959:59). This is a surrounding landscape, or, as it is sometimes inadequately translated, the "encountering region," which surrounds us once we have stopped treating the world as subject to our will. Or to put it another way, we are always in the *Gegnet* (it is not in a transcendent elsewhere) but sometimes we see only the horizon.

Representational language is instrumentalist, but the chase after direct presentation (of the unnamable) is problematic because it posits the existence of a transcendent realm beyond and therefore a similar dualism as is inherent in the instrumentality of representational language. Indeed, if we take seriously the absence of a telos, of perfect expression, say, then the idea of perfection becomes irrelevant and counterproductive, because it dangles before our noses the carrot of a world of transcendent truth, which we are then so intent on chasing down that we have nothing but irreverent disregard for the actual world that surrounds us. If the transcendent world is truth, then the surrounding one must be mere appearance: *Schein* (appearance) rather than *Sein* (reality). But this is an utterly dualistic view. David Loy, a comparative philosopher, points out that this intent to "solve" the problem of transcendence is the very thing which maintains the problem: "We try to 'peel away' the apparent world to get at the real one, but that dualism between them is our problematic delusion, which leaves, as the only remaining candidate for real world, the apparent one – a world whose actual nature has not been noticed because we have been so concerned to transcend it" (Loy 1992:248). In "Three Dialogues" Beckett reveals himself to be wary of the concept of artistic expression precisely for its dualism: ex-pression. A thought or *Vorstellung* precedes its own representation as an object or a work of art. The artwork's "success" (an alien word in the Beckett canon, if ever there was one) is judged by the artist himself according to whether or not it achieves some hypothetical adequacy to the *Vorstellung*. This will not work for Beckett. He is instead learning to "fail better." Art must not be objectified. It would cease to be art and become an object of exchange. Beckett's dream is of art "too proud for the farce of giving and receiving," he says in "Three Dialogues" (Beckett 1983a:148). Art is not part of an economy of exchange, such as representation, where reified objects are up for negotiation. Art is autonomous – detached from its creator and its audience, indeed emptied of both, and it will give itself completely on its own terms.

The problem of reification in language, as O'Casey and other overtly political writers encounter it, is one of transcendence: it is necessary to transcend discursive thought, yet not to an elsewhere imagined to be outside the immanent. Such a move would reintroduce the dualism of representation into the transcendent and reify it. Thus Beckett stays with the aporia of writing. To understand this aporia better we must turn to a writer who spent his most productive years in the shadow of existentialist Paris: Maurice Blanchot, with whom Beckett has much more in common than with the existentialist mainstream with which the Esslin school of Beckett criticism has insisted on identifying him. Blanchot's definition of writing is startlingly similar to Beckett's stated inability to express – no doubt the result of two careers spent pondering the same questions, obsessing about the same issues. Beckett thinks art is "the expression that there is nothing to express, nothing with which to express, nothing from which to express, no power to express, no desire to express, together with the obligation to express" (Beckett 1983a:139), while to Blanchot "the writer finds himself in the increasingly ludicrous condition of having nothing to write, no means with which to write it, and of being constrained by the utter necessity of always writing it. Having nothing to express must be taken in the most literal way" (Blanchot 2001:3). For him, writing is the pursuit of a point which comes into existence only in the process of writing, but which recedes as one draws closer. What approaches in the process of writing is what Blanchot calls the Outside: an empty, absolutely irreducible space emptied of all interiority and detached from writer and reader alike. It is emptied of the intention of the writer or the expression of his innermost feelings and, likewise, of the projections of the reader, "where speaking would neither affirm being nor need negation in order to suspend the work of being that is ordinarily accomplished in every act of expression" (Blanchot 2003:387). To confront the neutral of the Outside is not just another possibility, but the very point where possibility, will, and power cease. To underline his point Blanchot distinguishes between the work and the book. The work (of writing) – as opposed to the book as cultural object, operative in the power-structures of the world – is a never-ending task of slippage, because any conceptualization of its nature would place the work immediately on the side of the book. It becomes clear that, although it is called the Outside, this space is not outside at all, but inside and outside at the same time. Or, strictly speaking, it is neither inside nor outside, because it does not advance any concepts in the first place. It is not transcendence that disappears in the process, but rather the dualism between immanence and transcendence, and a transcendence of the second order emerges, which undoes the dualism of immanence and transcendence.

Such a movement of radical contestation of concepts as it occurs in Beckett and Blanchot one can perhaps best call "transdescendence," to borrow Jean Wahl's useful term. In *Existence humaine et transcendance*, Wahl posited the idea of "hierarchies of transcendence" (Wahl 1944:37), consisting of transdescendence and transascendence. Both aim at an absolutely irreducible space, but while transascendence describes a theological line of questioning that is concerned with the actuality of divine manifestation, the movement of transdescendence is situated in the depths of language and of being and investigates the conditions of such manifestations without ascribing any historical actuality to them. It tries to prepare the ground, as it were, for the self-showing of phenomena, including the ultimate phenomenon of the divine. Modernity has largely been preoccupied with the latter: for us as moderns, the divine remains unknown, while the strategies of our questioning nonetheless remain directed at God and his unknowability.

Later in his practice, in the so-called "closed space novels," *Company, Ill Seen, Ill Said*, and *Worstward Ho*, but also in his dramatic work, Beckett tries to avoid all forward movement – lest it suggest a hidden teleology: the goal of perfect expression. The prose is increasingly approximated to the pictorial quality of his stage images. It is well known that paintings were important to Beckett: the itineraries of his travels were often planned around pictures he wanted to see, and some of his closest friends were painters (Avigdor Arikha, Jack Yeats, and the van Valde brothers, especially Bram). Indeed, paintings achieve the very saturated sense presentation he strove to achieve in his own work. In his homage to Jack Yeats he writes, "In images of such breathless immediacy as these there is no occasion, no time given, no room left, for the lenitive of comment" (Beckett 1983a:149). Paintings give themselves all at once; their reception does not unfold slowly in time, bit by bit, the way the narrative arts do. With the former, reception also takes place in time, but it is entirely up to the viewer to structure that process. One's gaze can jump around in a picture. A novel, on the contrary, can also be reread, and read in pieces, but at some point one ought to have a sense of its progression from the first page to the last. Beckett avoids even the usual patterns of syntax, with parts of speech directed towards gradual completion of a sense unit, and prefers instead paradoxical, verbless sentence fragments devoid of action, creating momentous spaces without history or future: "Another place where none. Whither once whence no return. No. No place but the one. None but the one where none. Whence never once in. Somehow in. Beyondless. Thenceless there. Thitherless there. Thenceless, thitherless there" (Beckett 1983b:92).

At first sight it would appear as if the self-showing of phenomena inherent in the idea of saturation privileged the material world over the world of ideas, but this is not the case. Marion's phenomenology questions the valorization of intention over intuition that had been one of the mainstays of phenomenology ever since Descartes' *cogito, ergo sum* put the ball securely in the subject's court: if ontological certainty (I am) can be arrived at only through categories pertaining to the subject (I know), then the subject must also be the final instance meaningfully to constitute phenomena. The emphasis was on experience, not on the phenomenon. Yet saturation of intuition does not simply turn the tables on this old valorization, now conferring absolute ontological status on the phenomenon. Any phenomenological perspective makes sense only through a perceiving entity, not through the object by itself, so phenomenology is by definition an idealism rather than a materialism, yet that perceiving entity's experience can no longer be reduced to categories of subjectivity, which uses experience (*Erlebnis*) as raw material on the basis of which it confirms its subjectivity. Marion calls this kind of experience "counter-experience." Counter-experience arrives with such an overflow of givenness as to overwhelm the perceiver's ability to make sense of the experience. It challenges subjectivity instead of confirming it. The "I think," which had hitherto proclaimed itself as the absolute center, turns into "I am affected" (Marion 2002:250).

This is the case surprisingly early in Beckett's career – in *Waiting for Godot*, the object of O'Casey's scorn. As Richard Begam points out, for a play in which nothing happens it is concerned with a surprising number of performatives rather than constatives, which it either talks about or enacts: damning/forgiving, praying, begging, comforting, insulting, inviting to sit or to go. What is more, Pozzo's speech about the sunset, banal in content but dramatized to perfection by modulations of voice and gesture, and by onomatopoeia ("pppffff! Finished!"), "is pure theatre" (Begam 2007:151), and so are Didi and Gogo's associative language games, which are entirely self-sufficient and which they enact to pass the time: "Moron! – Vermin! – Abortion! – Morpion! – Sewer-Rat! – Curate! – Cretin! – (*with finality*). Critic!" (Beckett 1956:48). The play represents as little as is possible within a dramatic framework consisting of characters engaged in (admittedly minimalist) activities and instead performs itself: Didi and Gogo are unable to go (or exit the stage) because they *are* the play *Waiting for Godot* – without them the play would stop (Begam 2007:158).

At the formal level the play performs the very sublation of the dualism of representation which it suggests philosophically. Martin Esslin saw that the Absurd derives from the tension between permanence and impermanence (Esslin 1980:24–25): an a priori life purpose such as an afterlife has disappeared from the existentialist universe, and yet we continue to perceive ourselves as more than just the biological, which moves irreversibly towards death. The fundamental anxiety of the non-theological world is our perception of ourselves as atemporal beings caught in the flux of time. But this anxiety is not a given of our existence but a function of our world-view. In other words, one can do otherwise than simply continue heroically in the face of utter pointlessness, which is the only option for Esslin. Didi and Gogo do not see these choices because they configure their problem dualistically, as a dilemma between staying and leaving. If they leave they miss the potential salvation Godot might bring, but staying does not make Godot arrive and life might continue pointlessly until they die. They are locked into the dilemma and thus life will indeed continue pointlessly.

Similarly, we conceive of time and space dualistically. We habitually conceive of objects as self-existing objects *in* space, but this perception is a delusion: objects are as irreversibly spatial as the "rest" of space. Likewise, we perceive ourselves as self-existing entities *in* time is if in a container and thus create the anxiety of being caught in the flux of time against our will. As soon as we perceive ourselves as inherently temporal beings, however, the dualism between permanence and impermanence disappears (see Loy 1988:219–20), and with it the absurd dilemma in which Didi and Gogo are caught. For if there is no "content," there is no container either: the linear progression of time disappears and we are finally free to live in the moment, as Didi and Gogo do at the best of times, when their only horizon is the immediacy of the language games in which they engage. As audience we can delight in their comic routines and the waiting game becomes irrelevant, because we no longer wait for a telos or a goal; indeed, we do not wait – for Godot or for the resolution of the play.

Politics is the art of the possible. It must be pragmatist and cannot concern itself with what it recognizes to be impossible. Idealist fundamentalism is out of place in political activism because it condemns the world of possibilities to inertia. In writing or in literature, however, the subject (as constituted meaningfully by the world of possibility) encounters what Roland Barthes calls "the neutral," which has no meaning as possibility, but contests such meaning and which is "outside" the distinction of possibility and impossibility. Barthes writes that the neutral is "that which outplays ... the paradigm, or rather I call Neutral everything that baffles the paradigm" (Barthes 2005:6). And a paradigm is a binary oppositional structure of the kind that generates meaning in the West. Let us remember the importance of the experience of literature for Beckett. Literature is immediately experiential, like painting, and especially literature is *Erfahrung*, as a type of experience which is a threat to stable subjectivity. If we extend the metaphor of life a little further still, we can say with Blanchot that Beckett's practice of literary contestation occurs in the aporia of death as possibility and impossibility – as possibility because death's uniqueness defines a person as an individual with a world of action and possibility before her, and as impossibility because the same death strips a person of that very world of action and possibility.

Beckett's is a literary apophaticism and Beckett is an unusually self-conscious and accomplished exponent of something that happens in literature generally. If Derrida is right and literature is the adventure of creating an absolutely irreducible discourse (see, for instance, Derrida 1992:47), then its own strategies, and certainly the strategies of literary criticism, have to be apophatic. In this sense, Beckett performs spiritual practice in the most fundamental sense of the word: the "object" of his curiosity, language, is not objectified, dissected. His writing creates both the subject and object of study, if such terminology is still adequate. He creates the irreducible space and does so by making apparent the process of writing itself. Self-referentially, Beckett both produces and describes absolute irreducibility. Primary and secondary discourse interpenetrate. The process of writing becomes literature's "object," or its topic, and writing "produces" a literature that "embodies" this object and in this sense no longer has an object, just as God cannot be the "object" of negative theology. In this way it becomes the apotheosis of the space of literature. At the transcendental level of the literary, in a space of transdescendence, Beckett creates a dark icon of the transcendent divine.

REFERENCES AND FURTHER READING

Adorno, T.W. (1991). "Trying to Understand *Endgame*." In S.W. Nicholson (Trans.). *Notes to Literature* (vol. I, pp. 241–75). New York: Columbia University Press.

Barthes, R. (2005). *The Neutral*. New York: Columbia University Press.

Beckett, S. (1956). *Waiting for Godot*. New York: Grove Press.

Beckett, S. (1964). *Endgame*. London: Faber & Faber.

Beckett, S. (1983a). *Disjecta*. London: Calder.

Beckett, S. (1983b). *Worstward Ho*. In *Nohow On* (pp. 87–116). New York: Grove.

Beckett, S. (1994). *The Trilogy: Molloy, Malone Dies, The Unnamable*. London: Calder.

Begam, R. (2007). "How to do Nothing with Words, or *Waiting for Godot* as Performativity." *Modern Drama* 50.2, 138–67.

Blanchot, M. (2001). *Faux Pas*. C. Mandell (Trans.). Stanford: Stanford University Press.

Blanchot, M. (2003). *The Book to Come*. C. Mandell (Trans.). Stanford: Stanford University Press.

Connor, S. (2007). *Samuel Beckett: Repetition, Theory and Text*. Aurora: Davies.

Derrida, J. (1992). "This Strange Institution Called Literature." In D. Attridge (Ed.). *Acts of Literature* (pp. 33–75). London: Routledge.

Esslin, Martin. (1980). *The Theatre of the Absurd*. Harmondsworth: Penguin.

Gadamer, H.G. (1975). *Truth and Method*. New York: Seabury.

Hart, K. (1998). "The Experience of Poetry." *Boxkite*, 2, 285–304. http://209.85.129.132/search?q=cache:97Y3Qgi1984J:arts.monash.edu.au/cclcs/research/papers/experience-of-poetry.pdf+Kevin+Hart+experience+of+poetry&cd=1&hl=en&ct=clnk&client=firefox-a; accessed May 12, 2009.

Heidegger, M. (1959). *Gelassenheit*. Stuttgart: Klett-Cotta.

Heidegger, M. (1969). *Discourse on Thinking: A Translation of Gelassenheit*. E.H. Freund (Trans.). New York: Harper.

Hill, L. (1997). "'Up the Republic!': Beckett, Writing, Politics." *MLN*, 112.5, 909–28.

Kenner, H. (1968). *Samuel Beckett: A Critical Study*. Berkeley: University of California Press.

Krause, D. (1976). *Sean O'Casey and his World*. London: Thames & Hudson.

Loy, D. (1988). *Nonduality: A Study in Comparative Philosophy*. Amherst: Humanity.

Loy, D. (1992). "The Deconstruction of Buddhism." In H. Coward et al. (Eds). *Derrida and Negative Theology* (pp. 225–53). Albany: State University of New York Press.

Marion, J.-L. (2002). *Being Given: Toward a Phenomenology of Givenness*. J.L. Kosky (Trans.). Stanford: Stanford University Press.

Marion, J.-L. (2007). "The Banality of Saturation." In K. Hart (Ed.). *Counter-Experiences: Reading Jean-Luc Marion* (pp. 383–418). Notre Dame: University of Notre Dame Press.

Stevens, W. (1957). "Adagia." In S.F. Morse (Ed.). *Opus Posthumous* (pp. 157–80). London: Faber & Faber.

Wahl, J. (1944). *Existence humaine et transcendance*. Neuchatel: Éditions de la Baconnière.

Wynands, S. (2007). *Iconic Spaces: The Dark Theology of Samuel Beckett's Drama*. Notre Dame: University of Notre Dame Press.

37

Elizabeth Bowen: A Home in Writing

Eluned Summers-Bremner

Elizabeth Bowen's writing has a peculiarly charged relation to the question of home and belonging. Perhaps more than any other modernist writer, her fiction is peopled by lost souls who carry their lostness into every place, and relationship, they occupy. Childlike adults – naive yet resistant to the conventions that are thought to make for happiness – or children the events of whose lives have made the world seem dangerous and enigmatic, appear with regularity from her first collection of stories, *Encounters*, published in 1923, to her final, experimental novel, *Eva Trout, or Changing Scenes* (1968). Characters in states of anxious stasis are, however, often matched by houses and objects that have sentience – windows "stare" and furniture is said to "know" things – so that a strange material surplus is apt to gather in domestic scenes or those depicting landscape.

What gives Bowen's fiction its dramatic charge is that this material surplus, while almost always imbued with historical resonance, seldom makes historical knowledge available to her characters, with whom we naturally attempt to identify, and thus tends to be registered by the reader as an obstacle to narrative progress. The obstruction is seldom unenjoyable, however, because the situation faced by the fiction's characters is also likely in some degree to have affected readers. The peculiar life into which Bowen startles objects and houses, landscapes and moving vehicles, seems to represent the difficulties her characters have in fitting their desires into a world already full of other people's desires, past and present. The sense of desiring life Bowen grants to things, including houses, thus conveys – and this, to me, is her chief innovation and the source of her claim to be an important modern writer – a sharp sense of the human being itself as an object for which it is difficult to map in advance a specific place in human history.

A Companion to Irish Literature, edited by Julia M. Wright
© 2010 Blackwell Publishing Ltd

The sense in which we are unable to fully grasp our object status or appearance in the eyes of others had an obvious historical reference point for Bowen. As an only child she inherited her family's seat, Bowen's Court in County Cork, in 1930 on her father's death, a situation she memorably described as constituting "something between a *raison d'être* and a predicament" (Bowen 1950a:161). The phrase nicely captures the sense of transplantation from another culture that produced the Anglo-Irish and the sense of finding oneself in a fix, on Irish land, in a large house with largely empty rooms, the historical meaning of which altered rapidly and dramatically in the early years of the twentieth century.

Bowen's writing found early and continuing success. She was made a CBE (Commander of the British Empire) in 1948, was granted an honorary doctorate from Trinity College Dublin in 1949, and was made a Companion of the Royal Society of Literature in 1965. During World War II she wrote a history of her ancestral house, *Bowen's Court*, as well as a memoir, *Seven Winters*, detailing her memories of the family's Dublin residence. In 1923 Bowen married Alan Cameron, a secretary for the department of education. While the couple lived in Northampton, Oxford, and London, she frequently found time to visit Bowen's Court. When Cameron died in 1952, Bowen wrote not only for pleasure but also to finance the upkeep of the house, a task which seemed unending. She lectured in America and wrote for magazines to support this endeavor, but was eventually forced to sell the property in 1960, understanding that the farmer who bought the house intended to live in it. However, he demolished it soon after the sale.

In a 1940 essay, "The Big House," Bowen is candid about the historical imposition that houses like Bowen's Court made on the Irish landscape: "These houses ... were planned for spacious living. ... Unlike the low, warm, ruddy French and English manors, they have made no natural growth from the soil – the idea that begot them was a purely social one" (Bowen 1986a:26). Bowen notes that the most spacious parts of such houses were those made to welcome visitors: "halls ... living-rooms ... staircases," and that there was "a true bigness, a sort of impersonality, in the manner in which the[y] ... were conceived." Decline, however,

> set in almost at once ... big houses that had begun in glory were soon maintained by struggle and sacrifice. ... Husbands and wives struggled, shoulder to shoulder, to keep the estate anything like solvent, or ... to hold creditors off; their children grew up *farouches*, haughty, quite ignorant of the outside world. And in this struggle for life ... the big house people were handicapped, shadowed and ... queered – by their pride, by their indignation at their decline and by their divorce from the countryside in whose heart their struggle was carrying on. (Bowen 1986a:27)

The situation of the early twentieth-century Anglo-Irish is portrayed most memorably in Bowen's second novel, *The Last September* (1929), set during the 1920 Civil War. The book's title and its chapter headings – "The Arrival of Mr and Mrs Montmorency," "The Visit of Miss Norton," and "The Departure of Gerald" – indicate the house's centrality to the novel and also that its fate, from the first, is sealed. Gerald, the British soldier with whom Lois Farquar, the young girl staying at Danielstown, is having a romantic dalliance, "departs" by being shot by Republicans, while the house itself is torched and burns. As protagonist, Danielstown's rooms and fittings are often personified, yet it is also depicted as an alien presence within the landscape. The Naylors, who own Danielstown, are engaged in a furious effort not to notice that guns are being hidden "in the lower plantations" (Bowen 1998a:61), and that their Catholic servants' families harbor fugitives. Lady Naylor expresses her allegiance to the "impersonality" or remoteness with which the Anglo-Irish presence in Ireland was first conceived by claiming never to listen to gossip, it being, in her view, "a very great danger ... to the life of this country" (57). The naivety of this allegiance hastens the Naylors' demise.

When Lois is returning to the house with Hugo Montmorency after visiting a family whose son is on the run, Danielstown's unnatural position within the landscape is conveyed by the manner in which its demesne trees "make a dark formal square like a rug on the green country" (66). Lois, seeing how trees blot out the lawns, wonders that the house's inhabitants

> were not smothered; then wondered still more that they were not afraid. ... The house seemed to be pressing down low in apprehension, hiding its face, as though it had a vision of where it was. It seemed to gather its trees close in fright and amazement at the wide, light, lovely unloving country, the unwilling bosom whereon it was set. (66)

The Anglo-Irish are targets because, while feeling themselves to be more Irish than English, the houses they inhabit are becoming increasingly identified with land grievances. Revolutionary fires render ominous the work of Catholic servants – lighting hearths and cooking meals – on which the house's life depends:

> Down among them, dusk would stream up the paths ahead, lie stagnant over the lawns, would mount in the tank of garden, heightening the walls, dulling the borders like a rain of ashes. Dusk would lie where one looked as though it were in one's eyes, as though the fountain of darkness were in one's own perception. Seen from above, the house in its pit of trees seemed a very reservoir of obscurity; from the doors one must come out stained with it. And the kitchen smoke, lying over the vague trees doubtfully, seemed the very fume of living. (67)

As historical relics, of course, the Naylors are objects, most notably of resentment. But the sense of a "darkness ... in one's own perception" created by the dusk suggests that the Naylors' sense of themselves as belonging in the countryside is achieved at the price of their not seeing the relation between land and people that had existed there before. The mix of Anglo-Irish privilege and rural Catholic labor that brought such houses into being becomes abhorrent in the era of reimagined certainties: a reservoir, indeed, of ancient grievances.

The fact that the social life of the house is fed by the regional presence of the British garrison, which provides young men for dances and tennis parties, is but the latest version of a hybridity the Naylors do not recognize. Both Lois and her cousin Laurence, a student at Oxford, are orphans, and they alone among the characters seem to grasp the precariousness of the household's position. While the house and its furniture demonstrate the strange awareness, common in Bowen, of the fate that awaits its inhabitants – chairs stand around "dejectedly," mirrors "vacant" (34) – nature itself is given force and life, seeming to take on the revolutionary impulse of the region. When Lois, returning from a walk one night, is passed by a lone gunman who does not see her, the avenue seems to herald his arrival: "Laurels breathed coldly and close ... Her fear of the shrubberies tugged at its chain ... fear like the earliest germ of her life that had stirred in [her mother] Laura" (33).

In *Bowen's Court*, Bowen claimed that

> each member of these isolated households is bound up not only in the sensation and business of living but in the exact sensation of living here. The upkeep of the place takes its tax not only of physical energy but of psychic energy people hardly know that they give. Each of these houses, with its intense, centripetal life, is isolated by something very much more lasting than the physical fact of space: the isolation is innate; it is an affair of origin. (Bowen 1942:19–20)

The time of origin is the only time the house has – or had – to call its own. But the reference to "psychic energy people hardly know that they give" indicates that the temporal structure provided by mealtimes and similar rituals – playing tennis, sitting on the steps after dinner – being of outdated import, costs the house's inhabitants more in 1920 than it would have done in the past. Inanimate objects such as rooms and furnishings attain a peculiar power because, having been in place so long, they support, in ways their users no longer notice, traditional ways of behaving. The silence of rooms, on the other hand, seems to model the pressure – strongly endorsed by Myra and Richard Naylor – not to speak of dangerous things.

Thus after seeing the gunman Lois plans to tell of her adventure, which "held ground for a moment as she saw the rug dropped in the hall by Mrs Montmorency sprawl like a body across the polish," but "[t]hen confidence disappeared, in a waver of shadow, among the furniture" (Bowen 1998a:34). Lois and Laurence, the latter linked by name to Lois' dead mother Laura, together embody the Anglo-Irish lack of a future, the fact that there is no one nation or enduring hybrid with which they can safely be aligned.

Bowen herself lost her mother, and also her father, early in life, and she was willing to acknowledge that these losses may have played their part in her fiction. In a conversation with V.S. Pritchett and Graham Greene, she claimed that "[m]y writing ... may be a substitute for something I have been born without – a so-called normal relation to society"; she also indicated that she had "thriven ... on the changes and chances, the dislocations and ... contrasts which have made up so much of my life"

(Bowen et al. 1969:23; 1986b:283). In claiming that "[m]y books *are* my relation to society" (Bowen et al. 1969:23), Bowen indicates that books are not only a means of communication with others but also forms — that is, components within structures — of social belonging. The distinctiveness of her prose, as a result of what Maud Ellmann calls "frictional disjunctions between modes of writing" (Ellmann 2003:4) — mixing social comedy, for instance, with a gothic strain — has the effect of emphasizing the materiality, even the substantiality, of her language. Words, like rough-edged components of a house being built, frequently stand out in their own right, distinct from sense, requiring the reader to maneuver self-consciously around them.

This effect is particularly acute in Bowen's fourth — and until that point most experimental — novel, *To the North* (1932). Machines — a plane, trains, cars, and telephones among them — play a significant role in the narrative, but only in so far as they engage an inchoate energy that drives and paradoxically arrests, rather than motivates, the characters. The novel opens with a train journey taken by Cecilia Summers back to the house she shares with her sister Emmeline, and ends with Emmeline's fatal drive northwards in a car, which, with "taut ungoverned speed" (Bowen 1945a:284), also kills Emmeline's unpleasant boyfriend, Markie. *To the North* documents the break-up of Cecilia's and Emmeline's home as Cecilia decides to marry Julian Tower and Emmeline's relationship with Markie hastens her death. The novel brings to mind one of Bowen's descriptions of writerly process, a description that seems to parallel the work's intrinsic strangeness:

> Plot might seem to be a matter of choice. It is not. The particular plot for the particular novel is something the novelist is driven to. It is what is left after the whittling-away of alternatives. The novelist is confronted ... by the impossibility of saying what is to be said in any other way. (Bowen 1945b:18)

Bowen then claims that the writer "is forced towards his plot" by "what is to be said." This "what is to be said" consists of accumulated "subjective matter ... impressions received, feelings" and so forth, "and something else — *x*. This matter is *extra* matter. It is superfluous to the non-writing life of the writer. ... It is destined to be elsewhere" (Bowen 1945b:18).

In *To the North* "something else — *x*" seems not only to have pursued the author but also to appear within the novel as the strange quality driving the characters unhappily northwards. It insinuates itself between the characters and the reader by means of a particularly opaque, demanding syntax. Here, for instance, is Cecilia, seated next to Julian, thinking about her dead husband Henry:

> From her marriage a kind of vulgarity Julian's tentativeness aroused in her had been absent, and that year when, however little she knew of Henry, he had best known herself, had a shadowy continuity among her impressions. Henry was with her casually, as though he came strolling into the room; there were cues he could never resist, incidents that provoked him to actuality. (Bowen 1945a:44–5)

The prose works to distance the reader from identification with Cecilia through the way the syntax instantiates not only her confusion but also the distance at which she operates from her own feelings, a distance which is in turn felt by us. As her sister Emmeline knows, their own alliance is "largely defensive: Henry's death had been something ravaging, disproportionate; around Oudenarde Road a kind of pale was put up against one kind of emotion: nothing on that scale was to occur again" (171).

In the brave new world Cecilia inhabits, the displacement offered by cars and foreign trips and telephones enables her – mercifully, perhaps – to avoid the question of the cause of her unhappiness. Constant activity seems required to forestall a kind of existential absence, a real uncertainty about how much what one feels can be accessed by oneself, and, then, conveyed to other people. Thus at "twenty past ten on a restlessly sunny morning when she was half dressed … and was tempted to feel she did not exist," Cecilia rings Lady Waters and feels herself "crystallise over the wire" (33). Alone in her house after a lunch party, "[n]obody waited for her at the door of her own bedroom," "[n]othing else paused … momentarily no one cast a shadow" (154–55). This "nothing" is catching, too, leading Emmeline to claim, "Nothing feels part of me, yet I live here too. I feel I leave nothing but steam in the bath." And when Emmeline asks Julian, "is your house ever like that?," he replies, "It may well be: I don't know" (222).

The restless quality that drives the characters is never specified, but seems to force them northwards, into the ether. In the north, air takes on an extra, thickened quality, becoming snow, mist, density. So in this novel in which machines drive or otherwise govern the behavior of the characters they become dense, too, but somehow misty: ephemeral objects to be transported. As people express their desires through move-ment, their desires remain formless, since they are perpetually being transferred to new places. And as this movement is governed by machines, there is a backwash, a residue of dissatisfaction that rolls back over the characters like smoke from a train, difficult to harness and materially troubling. Yet so long as the characters keep moving, the residue never achieves its purpose of retrospectively causing them to reflect on their desires. Thus they grow ever more desperate and frenetic. It would have been "sad" for Cecilia to have returned from Italy "unnoticed," for example; nonetheless, "melancholy invade[s] her" even while she is called to the telephone from her bath (31).

Bowen's own displacement plays its part in her fiction. In *Seven Winters* she observes how a combination of presence and absence inhered in her understanding of who she was and which place she belonged to. Bowen was born in Dublin but celebrated her childhood birthdays at Bowen's Court. The adult Bowen describes her childlike understanding of the fact that she was not born at the ancestral home in these terms: "by having been born where I had been born in a month in which that house did not exist," as an absent house does not exist for a child who cannot see it, "I felt that I had intruded on some no-place" (Bowen 1971:2). The phrase, with its Beckettian overtones, remarks concerns that occur repeatedly in the short fiction. Again and again, houses appear to be "no-places": homes made unhomely by the addition of an extra component of absence such as a ghost or palpable sense of foreboding; a "doubling" of losses or of meaning. And equally often, characters are, or feel themselves to be, intruders: either because a house rejects them, or because they have not found what they sought in the world and have become "hangers-on" or doubles within the social scenes of their own lives.

In "Her Table Spread," for instance, Mr Alban, who is visiting the house of Valeria Cuffe, discovers that he has "disappeared personally" once it is revealed to him by the ladies at dinner that "[t]he destroyer" – a navy ship – "had come today," docked in the harbor (Bowen 1983a:419). However, the first thing we are told about Mr Alban is that "his attitude to women was negative" (419). Thus when, later, he learns "he was less than half the feast" (420), the ladies being distracted by the prospect of more exciting visitors, we find that "the destroyer" has confirmed a pattern already in operation. Mr Alban, with his negative attitude to half of humanity, has "failed to love," but refuses responsibility. It is Mr Alban himself who destroys his prospects, as, in a quite different way, Valeria does hers: "nobody did anything about [his failure]. ... He knew some spring had dried up at the root of his world. He was fixed in the dark rain, by an indifferent shore" (420). Thus while Valeria, one of Bowen's ostensibly grown-up but intensely naive female characters, loses herself in childlike imaginings ("she was a princess," she would marry the ship's Mr Garrett [421–22]), the barren Mr Alban has sought an ersatz life that makes him appear vampiric: "A degree of terror was agreeable to his vanity: by express wish he had occupied haunted rooms" (423).

In "The New House," by contrast, Cicely Pilkington manages to escape a subservient life with her brother once their mother dies and she receives a marriage proposal before brother and sister move and "this new house fastens on to [her]" (Bowen 1983b:57). Her brother Herbert, on the other hand, seeing Cicely as "a ghost-ridden ... woman," does not see that his negative view of his sister effectively doubles the house's power to unman him. The house, like Herbert, is already a pale imitation of a more established presence: "At the root of his malaise was a suspicion that the house was sneering at him; that as he repudiated the small brick villa so the house repudiated him; that Cicely and the house had made a pact against him, shutting him out" (56).

In "Human Habitation," absence is given a disconcerting presence such that recognizable human reality seems to disappear altogether. Two students, Jameson and Jefferies, are on a walking tour of England's Midland canals when a wrong turning sees them following, in the rain, a seemingly endless path that fails to take them where they are headed. So mind-numbing is the men's fatigue that Jefferies comes to think they "had stepped unnoticingly over a threshold into some dead and empty hulk of a world drawn up alongside" (Bowen 1983c:151). On seeing house lights, the men decide to ask directions. They discover a young woman living with her child and aunt, waiting desperately for a long-expected man named Willy. While Jefferies looks into the girl's "distraught eyes with nostalgia for something that they held" (157),

Jameson delivers a teatime lecture about the brave new world that, according to student-imbibed socialism, they are all about to inherit. Jefferies, however, experiences a "sudden shifting of his values" that makes him "dizzy" (157). Leaning back to think,

> he could visualize nothing but the living-room. ... After all, it all came back to this – individual outlook; the emotional factors of environment; houses that were homes; living-rooms; people going out and coming in again; people not coming in; other people waiting for them in rooms that were little guarded squares of light walled in carefully against the hungry darkness, the ultimately all-devouring darkness. After all, here was the stage of every drama. Only very faintly and thinly came the voice of Jameson crying in the wilderness.
>
>   Whatever you might deny your body, there must always be something, a somewhere, that the mind came back to. (157)

While in one sense Jefferies is indeed remarking a pattern in an age-hold human drama – as Penelope waited for Ulysses, so country women wait for their men – the implication is that it is these men's too-ready willingness to believe the world runs according to rational principles that has made them vulnerable to nature in an almost anti-human form. So while Jameson rants about the future, Jefferies hallucinates a "living-room" that is not only built for life but throbs with sinister power (Hildebidle 1989:90). And while Jameson pictures the future as "a great perfect machine ... [that] roars around in ecstasy," claiming that "there's nothing between our something and *that* something, cohesive, irresistible, majestic" (Bowen 1983c:157), Jefferies seems to grasp that such irresistible ecstasy could not be guaranteed to be benign. The "something ... the mind came back to," however illusory, would still be needed as a refuge from the future's unknowable darkness.

Bleak houses and pressurized language combine to make unhomely worlds in the novels that follow *To the North*. And the strange forms of belonging instantiated by Bowen's fictions, as well as a continued concern for orphaned or otherwise vulnerable children and young women, testify to the acute dislocations of her early years. The Dublin house in which she was born was given up when Bowen was 7 following signs of her father's mental illness, diagnosed as "anemia of the brain" (Hopkins 2001:116). Bowen was kept away from him for some time, then both mother and daughter went to live in England, staying first with a cousin in the seaside town of Folkestone in Kent, and then in several rented villas in the area.

Owing to her father's mental difficulties, Bowen herself was not allowed to learn to read until the age of 7, for fear that his condition was hereditary and that over-stimulation might unbalance her (Hopkins 2001:117). It is tempting to see Bowen's distinctive use of language as the product, in part, of forestalled desire, as though her pre-reading self felt a hunger the strength of which meant she could never take the use of words for granted. She herself describes her experience of childhood reading in these terms:

one stripped bare the books of one's childhood to make oneself. ... The child is ... rapacious, mobile and single-minded. ... What do I mean by those books making myself? In the first place, they were power-testing athletics for my imagination. ... It was exhilarating to discover what one could feel. ... Then, by successively "being" a character in every book I read, I doubled the meaning of everything that happened in my otherwise constricted life. Books ... represented life, with a conclusiveness I had no reason to challenge, as an affair of mysteries and attractions, in which each object or place or face was in itself a volume of promises and deceptions, and in which nothing was impossible. (Bowen 1986c:51)

By 1911 Bowen's father had recovered sufficiently to be able to work again, but in that same year her mother was diagnosed with cancer, news that was kept from the child. When her mother died there had been no chance for Bowen to re-establish ties with her father. She developed a stammer which she never lost, and had what she later described as an experience of "total bereavement" (Bowen 1986b:289). The claim to have "doubled the meaning of everything that happened" is rendered poignant when we consider that, since the cause of the separation between Bowen and her father was not explained to her, the same fears must have been replayed in relation to her mother's death (Lassner 1991:43). In an essay on Sheridan Le Fanu's *Uncle Silas*, Bowen claims that "[t]wo things are terrible in childhood: helplessness (being in other people's power) and apprehension – the apprehension that something is being concealed from us because it is too bad to be told" (Bowen 1986c:111; quoted in Foster 2001:163). Both concerns would repeat themselves, often in combination, in her novels and stories.

In *The House in Paris* (1935), these matters are to the fore. The narrative concerns two transient children and three adults whose lives are authored by others, in this case mothers, to unhappy ends. The young Leopold Grant-Moody has come to wait in the house of the sinister Madame Fisher in Paris for his mother, whom he has never seen, to arrive. In the course of waiting Leopold learns, by reading a letter to Madame Fisher from his guardian, of his helplessness over his future in these adults' eyes, as well as the fact that this view of his character has been concealed from him. Added to the indication that Leopold's Jewish father and unmarried mother make him an object of prejudice and pity for his guardians, is the absence of an explanation of why his mother fails to arrive.

The House in Paris thus picks up the theme of secrets and scandal explored, in a much quieter way, in Bowen's second novel, *Friends and Relations* (1931), where two would-be lovers manage to overcome their passion and put familial obligations first. In *The House in Paris*, however, familial obligations themselves are poisonous. 11-year-old Henrietta Mountjoy, who is also passing through Paris en route to her grandmother's house in Mentone, and through whose eyes we are introduced to the Fisher house, notes its unhomely character immediately. She finds it "antagonistic, as though it had been invented to put her out. She felt the house was acting, nothing seemed to be natural; objects did not wait to be seen but came crowding in on her, each with what amounted to its aggressive cry" (Bowen 1998b:24). The crowding and crying of objects reverses the usual relation that obtains between characters and houses, whereby the latter are backdrops – ideally, supportive ones – for action. Similarly, the novel's structure – in which the first and third sections, both named "The Present," depict a single day and enclose a middle section, "The Past" – inverts the usual arrangement whereby the past lies behind or upholds the present. For as Henrietta notes with perspicacity, "she had dropped down a well into something worse than the past in not being yet over" (50). While the first section ends and the third begins with the same phrase, delivered to Leopold by Madame Fisher's daughter Naomi – "Your mother is not coming. She cannot come" (66, 191) – the middle section gives us the backstory of Leopold's mother Karen's absence from Leopold's life. This is a past that is not yet over, not only because it continues to affect Leopold but because the breakdown of the relationship between Leopold's mother, Karen Michaelis, and his father, Max Ebhart, was in large part based on the view that unbelonging is intrinsic to Jewishness and thus endures throughout history. Max was represented, both by Karen's mother and by Naomi Fisher's mother – Naomi having been engaged to marry Max at the point at which the affair between Karen and Max which produced Leopold began – as a being extrinsic to temporal narrative. His only continuity in the French context – his racial heritage – was not to belong.

The past is also not over because, effectively, a murder has been committed that has not been acknowledged as a crime. In service of social and personal ideals, that change should not happen in the Michaelis family (Bowen 1998b:70, 124) and that the control-center commanded by Madame Fisher over the lives of young girls in her care should continue without restraint, Max's love for Karen was exploited. Love's tendency to return us to the time when we were as yet unpeopled spaces marked by others' desires causes Max to voice his fear that his Jewishness and the anxieties it attracts will make life difficult for Karen. Indeed, in the year of the novel's publication the Nazi government passed the Nuremberg laws, which deprived Jews of citizenship in Germany, and led them in greater numbers to countries such as France (Layton 1992:89, quoted in Radford 1999:42). Madame Fisher, who works on Max's uncertainty by manipulating the desire of her daughter Naomi for Max, causes Max to kill himself by cutting his wrists, and he bleeds to death at her fireside.

As in *The Last September*, domestic objects are made to participate in the fantasy of changelessness insisted upon, in *The House in Paris*, by Karen's mother Mrs Michaelis as much as by Madame Fisher, a fantasy that has violence at its heart. When Karen returns from Hythe where she has been with Max and where Leopold has been conceived, "[u]nconscious things … doors, the curtains, guests … lent themselves to this savage battle for peace" (Bowen 1998b:173). People, correspondingly, are rendered silent. Max becomes the object of each mother's desire to assert her view of history and to de-emphasize the change in a person's way of being in the world that love, founded on a commitment to that which can never be fully grasped in another, can author. However, the power of their view of the past is limited by the linguistic repetition that brackets the "Past" section of the novel: "Your mother is not coming; she cannot come." For "The Past" has given us access to Karen's story, and it heralds, in section 3, the arrival of Karen's husband Ray, who offers to take Leopold to Karen.

Leopold's traumatic discovery of the view of himself held by his guardians, combined with the heartbreaking news that his mother is not coming, also causes him to face, for the first time, the fact of his own displaced origin. He learns that he is not, as he had imagined, the missing center of his mother's world. It is Ray's arrival in Karen's stead that enables Leopold to discern that his mother has a life, with this man, apart from Leopold. Thus Karen becomes for the first time for Leopold a person rather than a missing, idealized support. Yet this realization could arguably not have occurred without the presence of another child, Henrietta, who assists, precisely because she is both present and unknown – a stranger – by standing in for the momentary externalization of Leopold's grief. This grief, unconsciously cherished, has formerly sustained Leopold's view of himself at the center of his fantasy of his mother's world, at the price of keeping him from imagining a life of his own. Leopold's

> solitary despair made Henrietta no more than the walls or table. This was not contempt for her presence: no one was there. Being not there disembodied her, so she fearlessly crossed the parquet to stand beside him. … Finally, she leant her body against his, pressing her ribs to his elbow so that his sobs began to go through her too. … After a minute like this, his elbow undoubled itself against her and his left arm went round her with unfeeling tightness, as though he were gripping the bole of a tree. Held close like this to the mantelpiece he leant on, Henrietta let her forehead rest on the marble too: her face bent forward, so that the tears she began shedding fell on the front of her dress. An angel stood up inside her with its hands to its lips, and Henrietta did not attempt to speak. (Bowen 1998b:197)

If *The House in Paris* develops in more sustained fashion the theme of secrecy and scandal of the earlier *Friends and Relations*, *The Death of the Heart* (1938) echoes Bowen's first novel, *The Hotel* (1928), which places a young, intelligent woman in a foreign context, Italy, in order that she might gain insight into her own behavior and the kind of life she wants. The foreign context into which Portia Quayne, the 16-year-old protagonist of *The Death of the Heart*, is thrown, however, is that of a family, specifically, that of Anna and Thomas Quayne into whose care Portia's father, on his deathbed, has commended her for a year. Portia, now an orphan, is the result of an affair her father had with an actress named Irene, and has been visited upon Thomas and Anna because of her father's feeling that she "had grown up exiled not only from her own country," England, "but from *normal, cheerful* family life" (Bowen 1998c:15).

This view is found to be ironic, since Thomas' and Anna's relationship is anything but normal and cheerful. The couple have no children, and it is suggested that Anna has been damaged in some way by an earlier relationship with a war veteran, Robert Pidgeon, who has treated her badly. Portia's only friend and confidante in the Quayne household is the housekeeper Matchett, her closeness to whom only alienates Anna further. As the novel opens Anna is walking in Regent's Park in winter with her novelist friend St Quentin, having just put herself in an even more difficult position by happening upon, and reading, Portia's diary. Anna finds the view of herself in the diary "distorting" (Bowen 1998c:10). Portia's blend of uncommon innocence and budding authorial style (the diary's opening reads, "So I am with them, in London" [11]) makes the view of the Quaynes she presents sufficiently denaturalized to unsettle and sufficiently credulous to shame Anna. Portia, after all, has never known a settled home.

Her lack of a settled upbringing – Portia's childhood has lately been spent staying, with her mother, in off-season tourist hotels – makes it unsurprising that she might seek to create a home for herself in writing. And it is Portia's writing that leads to her awakening into adulthood, or, more accurately, to finding herself in the position of having engaged, through writing, the unpredictable world of others, since writing presupposes a reader even if, initially, writer and reader are the same. And Portia's relation to the Quaynes *is* altered by her writing. Even before she learns, from St Quentin, about Anna's act of betrayal, Portia's stay with Anna's former governess Mrs Heccombe and her family at Seale-on-sea affords a new sense, not only of Thomas and Anna, but of their lives as separate from hers. Thus her diary moves from such insightful barbs as "Then we sat in the drawing-room and they wished I was not there" (115), to the following description, enabled by Portia's growing awareness that, through writing, she can reflect on her own absence from a scene:

> [S]he thought of Windsor Terrace. *I am not there*. She began to go round, in little circles, things that at least her senses had loved – her bed, with the lamp turned on on winter mornings, the rug in Thomas's study, the chest carved with angels out there on the landing, the waxen oilcloth down there in Matchett's room. Only in a house where one has learnt to be lonely does one have this solicitude for *things*. One's relation to them, the daily seeing and touching, begins to become love, and to lay one open to pain. (139)

World War II marks a turning point in Bowen's fiction. She was particularly productive in this period, publishing stories regularly while performing air raid duties and reporting to the British government on the activities and morale of neutral Ireland. *Bowen's Court* and *Seven Winters* were also written during the war. *The Heat of the Day* (1948), perhaps her best known and most acclaimed novel, was based on her wartime experience. It seems that the condition of being bombed had on Bowen a salutary effect, in the sense that it brought into sharper, more practical focus a situation she had experienced already as the inhabitant of an Anglo-Irish Big House expecting the house to be burned. However, while the inhabitant of a Big House is distanced from the surrounding countryside both physically and politically, the resident of blitzed London inhabits a close-knit community united by fear. This fear, however, has usefully expressive outlets in the form of the need to attend to the dead and wounded and to return to one's home to assess damage, all of which provide a temporary reason, at least, to go on living. For Bowen, whose early life had been so unsettled and whose points of identification were with a doomed, outdated class, the war provided exactly the right amounts of instantaneous fear, excitement, courage, and fellow-feeling to generate some riveting, atmospherically haunting fiction.

Bowen's wartime stories demonstrate a new authority over her material. The pressures of wartime enable her to revisit rural Irish scenes by means of characters who are haunted, as she was, by their pasts, and whom the pressures of war cause to regress helplessly to unresolved, emotionally pressing situations. The blowing away of the walls of houses to reveal the remains of intimate scenes meant that Bowen's own tendency to render houses lifelike – uncomfortable, as in *The House in Paris*, or, as in *The Last September*, afraid – achieved a kind of historical endorsement. The sudden exposure of a private, domestic scene makes a house seem to have secrets like a person. And the rapidly altering cityscape of London provided the perfect setting for the author's skill at rendering the uncanny import of an absent presence, as in the following description from *The Heat of the Day*:

> Most of all the dead, from mortuaries, from under cataracts of rubble, made their anonymous presence – not as today's dead but as yesterday's living – felt through London. Uncounted, they continued to move in shoals through the city day, pervading everything to be seen or heard or felt with their torn-off senses, drawing on this tomorrow they had expected – for death cannot be so sudden as all that. Absent from the routine which had been life, they stamped upon that routine their absence – not knowing who the dead were you could not know which might be the staircase somebody for the first time was not mounting this morning, or at which street corner the newsvendor missed a face, or which trains and buses in the homegoing rush were this evening lighter by at least one passenger. (Bowen 1998d:91–92)

It is the uncommon "heat" generated by risk in wartime London that causes Stella Rodney, the heroine of *The Heat of the Day*, to fall for Robert Kelway, who, it emerges, is a fascist spy. Stella and Robert meet, and fall in love, in the aftermath of a bomb explosion, which makes their survival seem fated, and which also means they feel less than the usual need to investigate what might be true of each other beneath the surface. Bowen's language in the novel mimes the situation in which everything, from whether one would survive tomorrow to what one would do after the war, was uncertain. Thus the story opens with an outdoor scene to which "people were being slowly drawn ... by the sensation that they were missing something" (7), but it does not guess at what this something might be. Uncertainty becomes a private theater of war as Stella learns that Robert may be passing British secrets to the Germans. Then, "[n]o act was not part of some calculation; spontaneity was in tatters; from the point of view of nothing more than the heart any action was enemy action now" (142).

The Heat of the Day, like *The House in Paris*, includes a visit to an Anglo-Irish Big House, which, in the later novel, serves as a counterpoint to the continually altering cityscape of London's war. In *A World of Love* (1955), a Big House again takes center stage. While, this time, the house is not threatened by fire, an uncommonly hot June renders its inhabitants more than usually sensitive to the ways in which past actions have limited the changes they are able to effect in the present. Echoes of *The Heat of the Day* are provided by 20-year-old Jane's falling in love – at first sight – with the visitor to the nearby castle she has gone to the airport to collect. However, this event, occurring at the close of the novel – a novel whose elaboration of the painful afterlife generated by Anglo-Irishness can be seen as a work of mourning (Corcoran 2004:72) – turns out to signal Bowen's departure from such concerns once and for all. Just as Jane is brought to the brink of a new life away from Montefort, so Bowen's last two novels are markedly different from anything she had written before.

Both novels return to earlier themes. *The Little Girls* (1963) explores the question of whether the past, and, in particular, the feelings and hopes of childhood, can be preserved. But it is *Eva Trout* (1968) that most strikingly revisits Bowen's earlier fiction by means of its tribute to gothic conventions and its larger-than-life heroine, whose destiny is to be perennially wrongfooted. Eva, both an orphan and an heiress, struggles to find and hold on to the relations in life that others take for granted: friends, mentors, lovers, and, finally, a child, which she abducts, and who rewards this act by shooting her – whether by accident or design – on a railway platform at the story's end. Eva is a child of her century, embracing, as in *To the North*, cars, planes, and other forms of technological displacement. But she is insensitive to the kind of social nuances that in Bowen's earlier fiction provide houses with a sense of unconscious life. The novel's subtitle, "Changing Scenes," is instructive: wherever Eva goes, she crashes through social facades to the same end, her desperate need to find someone to whom she deeply matters.

As the first Bowen novel in which houses lack depth, *Eva Trout* is nonetheless a fitting end to Bowen's oeuvre. In starkly anti-social terms that, oddly, fit the period of the 1960s with its scenes of social disarray and shifts of generational allegiance, the novel dramatizes what it is like to have inherited a legacy that appears to augur a future, but which produces scenes the meaning of which is seldom clear to Eva. As Neil Corcoran remarks of this novel, "the categories of living and of making fictions are confused only at our greatest peril" (Corcoran 2004:144), and we learn from *Eva Trout* that one cannot fabricate, by means of wealth, a missing home or family. Bowen was not Eva, of course, even if her orphaned status made her feel similarly lost at times. Fantasy is ultimately fatal to Eva, but we, Bowen's readers, are fortunate that, for her, the distinction between living and making fictions was not always so obvious. Bowen's legacy to us is work enlivened by the question of the extent to which it is possible to make, or find, a home in writing. It is a question that it may be up to her readers to resolve.

References and Further Reading

Bowen, E. (1942). *Bowen's Court*. Longman, Green & Co.

Bowen, E. (1945a). *To the North* (1932). Harmondsworth: Penguin.

Bowen, E. (1945b). "Notes on Writing a Novel." *Orion*, 2, 18–29.

Bowen, E. (1950a). "The Moores" (1939). In *Collected Impressions* (pp. 160–64). London: Longmans, Green & Co.

Bowen, E. (1950b). "The Big House" (1942). In *Collected Impressions* (pp. 195–200). London: Longmans, Green & Co.

Bowen, E. (1971). *Seven Winters* (1942). Dublin: Cuala Press.

Bowen, E. (1983a). "Her Table Spread." In *The Collected Stories of Elizabeth Bowen* (pp. 418–24). Harmondsworth: Penguin.

Bowen, E. (1983b). "The New House." In *The Collected Stories of Elizabeth Bowen* (pp. 53–58). Harmondsworth: Penguin.

Bowen, E. (1983c). "Human Habitation." In *The Collected Stories of Elizabeth Bowen* (pp. 147–59). Harmondsworth: Penguin.

Bowen, E. (1986a). "The Big House" (1946). In H. Lee (Ed.). *The Mulberry Tree: Writings of Elizabeth Bowen* (pp. 25–30). London: Virago.

Bowen, E. (1986b). "Pictures and Conversations" (1975). In H. Lee (Ed.). *The Mulberry Tree: Writings of Elizabeth Bowen* (pp. 265–83). London: Virago.

Bowen, E. (1986c). "Out of a Book" (1946). In H. Lee (Ed.). *The Mulberry Tree: Writings of Elizabeth Bowen* (pp. 48–53). London: Virago.

Bowen, E. (1986d). "Uncle Silas" (1947). In H. Lee (Ed.). *The Mulberry Tree: Writings of Elizabeth Bowen* (pp. 100–13). London: Virago.

Bowen, E. (1998a). *The Last September* (1929). London: Vintage.

Bowen, E. (1998b). *The House in Paris* (1935). London: Vintage.

Bowen, E. (1998c). *The Death of the Heart* (1938). London: Vintage.

Bowen, E. (1998d). *The Heat of the Day* (1948). London: Vintage.

Bowen, E. (1999). *Eva Trout, or Changing Scenes* (1968). London: Vintage.

Bowen, E., G. Greene, and V.S. Pritchett. (1969). *Why Do I Write? An Exchange of Views Between Elizabeth Bowen, Graham Greene and V.S. Pritchett* (1948). London: Folcroft Press.

Corcoran, N. (2004). *Elizabeth Bowen: The Enforced Return*. Oxford: Clarendon Press.

Ellmann, M. (2003). *Elizabeth Bowen: The Shadow Across the Page*. Edinburgh: Edinburgh University Press.

Foster, R.F. (2001). "Prints on the Scene: Elizabeth Bowen and the Landscape of Childhood." In *The Irish Story: Telling Tales and Making it Up in Ireland* (pp. 148–63). London: Penguin.

Hildebidle, J. (1989). *Five Irish Writers: The Errand of Keeping Alive*. Cambridge, MA: Harvard University Press.

Hopkins, C. (2001). "Elizabeth Bowen." *Review of Contemporary Fiction*, 21.2, 115–51.

Lassner, P. (1991). *Elizabeth Bowen: A Study of the Short Fiction*. New York: Twayne.

Layton, G. (1992). *Germany: The Third Reich, 1933–45*. London: Hodder & Stoughton.

Radford, J. (1999). "Late Modernism and the Politics of History." In M. Joannou (Ed.). *Women Writers of the 1930s: Gender, Politics and History* (pp. 33–45). Edinburgh: Edinburgh University Press.

38

Changing Times: Frank O'Connor and Seán O'Faoláin

Paul Delaney

Frank O'Connor and Seán O'Faoláin enjoy a curiously assured place in the literary canon. Their work has been widely anthologized by publishers, scholars, and fellow writers, and it is long since they earned their reputations as masters of the short-story form. Both published scores of stories in their lifetime, and most comparative studies of short fiction continue to acknowledge their importance to the theory, practice, and development of the genre. Both also wrote perceptive commentaries on the form, and O'Connor's study *The Lonely Voice* (1963) in particular is still considered a seminal text in short-story criticism. In more general terms, few surveys of twentieth-century Irish writing forget to mention either figure, and both are often thought to have contributed to the shape of modern Irish culture – as storytellers, in the first instance, but also as essayists, translators, campaigners, biographers, novelists, critics, and mentors. If both writers' status is secure, however, their value to the canon is more uncertain. For all the lip-service paid to O'Faoláin and his work, his stories have been out of print for decades and he has only intermittently attracted close critical attention. O'Connor, for his part, has suffered from a paucity of detailed criticism and, aside from overarching comments in general surveys, "a respectful forgettingness" seems to have descended on his work, as the novelist Julian Barnes recently remarked (Barnes 2005:vii).

This stance of polite neglect has been a long time in the making. With respect to O'Connor, Thomas Flanagan identified it as far back as 1969 when he predicted, "it will be a while before [O'Connor's] work will be properly appreciated" (Flanagan 1969:150). Flanagan's comments were framed as part of an extended obituary on the late writer (O'Connor died in 1966), and were informed by recent transformations in Irish society. According to Flanagan, these changes were so great that "there may no longer be room or need for a writer like O'Connor" (Flanagan 1969:150). Changes in

A Companion to Irish Literature, edited by Julia M. Wright
© 2010 Blackwell Publishing Ltd

Ireland's economic policy following the first Programme for Economic Expansion in the late 1950s, for instance, proved fundamental, as the protectionist principles of a previous generation were abandoned and Irish markets opened up to foreign investment. These developments were coupled with and in part enabled by rapid transformations in the socio-cultural fabric, as Irish society engaged to an ever greater degree with the forces of liberalism, modernization, and secularization. This loosening up was felt in many spheres of cultural activity and impacted on the ways in which O'Connor's work was interpreted: very quickly his stories seemed to belong to another age as they spoke of a distant world of inverted passions, inhibited personalities, and small-town horizons. With the outbreak of violence in the North, and the emergence of a new generation of poets and playwrights across the island, this apparent obsolescence was compounded. For many, O'Connor's stories appeared indulgent, formulaic, or irrelevant when read against the pressing urgencies of the Troubles. Such criticism, however, only told part of the tale and neatly sidestepped key issues which remained pertinent, including O'Connor's studied engagement with the dynamics of history and the representation of violence – his early story "Guests of the Nation" (1931), with its poignant reflection on the effects of murder in the name of an allegedly just cause, is a striking example of this, as is his harrowing essay "A Boy in Prison" (1934), with its stress on the realities of torture, brutalization, internment, and hunger strike during the Civil War. Notwithstanding the timeliness of such texts, Terence Brown succinctly summed up the situation when he suggested that, as O'Connor "faded into the historical frame" in the late 1960s, his work appeared to "lose its purchase on Irish sensibilities and cease[d] to seem necessary to us" (Brown 2007:41).

A similar fate has befallen O'Connor's friend and associate Seán O'Faoláin. Once a central figure in Irish cultural debates, O'Faoláin has become shorthand for the fight against provincialism and censorship in recent decades. He is principally remembered for his editorship of the literary journal *The Bell* from 1940 to 1946, when he led the struggle against state suppression and cultural isolationist policies, and so provided, in the words of Roy Foster, "the record of an alternative culture" to the governing ideologies of the day, laying waste many of the shibboleths and tired prejudices which were endemic in post-Independence Irish society (Foster 1988:548). Favorite targets of *The Bell* included myopic nationalist movements which were crudely Anglophobic as well as organizations and individuals who propagated a sentimental approach to questions concerning religion, nationality, the Irish language, or the past. O'Faoláin's creative work has often been read solely in the light of these imperatives, and his short fiction has been consigned to this narrowly defined historical context. Clearly locked into the period in which they were written, or more often the period in which they are set (in particular the middle decades of the twentieth century), O'Faoláin's stories – with their focus on nationalist mystification, provincial intolerance, bourgeois mediocrity, and subservience to the Catholic Church – can appear leaden or dated to contemporary eyes. Fittingly, when a special issue of the *Cork Review* was published to mark the occasion of his death, in 1991, the editor defined O'Faoláin's legacy in terms of loss and belatedness. "O'Faoláin has left a mark on Ireland which will take years to measure," Seán Dunne lamented (in a striking if unwitting echo of Flanagan on O'Connor); yet for all his achievements, "his name is seldom included" in popular or academic debates, and "he has not received real credit for what he did" (Dunne 1991:3).

Further reasons might be advanced to account for the absence of both writers from contemporary critical discourse. It is significant, for instance, that both writers' fame is principally associated with a form which is notoriously vulnerable to the vicissitudes of taste and time. Short fiction has a precarious existence in the academic marketplace, and is routinely considered the preserve of emerging writers in the publishing world. Ian Reid, Valerie Shaw, Clare Hanson, and Charles E. May are just a few of the critics who have drawn attention to this problem in other contexts, and in many respects Reid's diagnosis of the "immature state" of short-story theory remains true thirty years after it was first noted (Reid 1977:1). In addition, O'Connor and O'Faoláin each favored a stance and a style which have become virtually unsustainable in recent times. A defining feature of both writers' works is an assurance of tone and subject matter which was already outmoded by the time of their writing, and both were committed to traditional modes of narration which appear jaded or unfashionable in today's world. Both expressed a preference for realist storytelling practices which require, or seem to require, little explication, and in neither writer's oeuvre is there much evidence of the formal experimentation or the existential or linguistic crises which dominated literature in the wake of modernism. Quite simply, one could forget that O'Faoláin and O'Connor were compatriots and contemporaries of Samuel Beckett, Flann O'Brien, and Elizabeth Bowen (all the subjects of other essays in this volume).

If O'Connor and O'Faoláin appear exhausted or out of date, however, this ironically might provide the basis for a reconsideration of their legacy. Both writers, after all, lived through a time of profound change – change which partially accounts for the speed with which they have been remaindered – and both were well placed to record that change in their fiction and non-fiction. Both also contributed to that change in the course of their lives, engaging in core debates – concerning modernization, decolonization, freedom of expression, and the importance of tradition – and penning life-stories which have since been considered representative in the evolution of the modern nation-state. Declan Kiberd, for example, has commented on the ways in which "O'Connor's autobiography in Ireland" (the two volumes *An Only Child* [1961] and *My Father's Son* [1968]) "becomes effectively the autobiography *of* Ireland," while Richard Bonaccorso is part of a chorus which has declared that O'Faoláin's life and memoir, *Vive Moi!* (1965), "seems an essentialization of the modern Irish existence" (Kiberd 2005:vii [original emphasis]; Bonaccorso 1987:101). At the risk of over-simplifying the similarities between the two writers – for there was much that distinguished them, including important differences in temperament, class, opportunity, and political interest – there are many points of correspondence, and much continues to be gained by reading them in tandem.

O'Faoláin was born in Cork at the dawn of the twentieth century; O'Connor was born three years later, in 1903, in a poorer part of the same city. Both spent their formative years growing up in a city, and a country, which seemed uncertain of its cultural and political boundaries. Both were born to parents with loyalties to the Church and the Crown (their mothers were devout Catholics; O'Faoláin's father was a member of the Royal Irish Constabulary; O'Connor's father was a soldier in the Munster Fusiliers), and both were part of the generation which tested these loyalties by falling for the Irish language and the romance of the Gael. Through the influence of the polemicist and short-story writer Daniel Corkery, both became involved in Gaelic League circles (O'Faoláin gaelicizing his name from John Whelan); both retained this passion for Irish in later years, long after they had fallen out with Corkery and the official language movement. Through their involvement in the Gaelic League, O'Faoláin and O'Connor were also co-opted into advanced nationalist circles and served as volunteers during the War of Independence; they subsequently took the republican side during the Civil War. Like many of their peers, both young men were defined by their experiences during this crucial period in modern Irish history; they were also bitterly disappointed by the country that grew out of independence. As both saw it, the radical potential of independence was squandered as the leaders of the revolution sacrificed promises in the name of narrow-mindedness, moral decay, and cautious conservatism. For O'Connor, the Irish Free State that came into existence was a world founded upon abstraction, insularity, and "the death-in-life of the Nationalist Catholic establishment" (O'Connor 1961:189). For O'Faoláin, it was "a dreary Eden" dominated by puritanical codes of conduct and "a new, native, acquisitive, middle class intent only on cashing in on the change of governments" (O'Faoláin 1939:180; 1965:173). Dissatisfaction and disillusionment became the defining notes of O'Faoláin's and O'Connor's work in subsequent years, as they turned – like many contemporary disaffected nationalists – from the society which they had helped to create. If this gained force as the years progressed, it was nonetheless apparent from the outset of their careers.

O'Faoláin's debut volume of short stories, for example, presents a number of characters who are already disenchanted with the struggle for and the meaning of independence. Tellingly entitled *Midsummer Night Madness and Other Stories* (1932), the collection draws obvious analogies with Shakespeare's popular comedy, but does so in a spirit of unrest, as it is set against the backdrop of the charged 1919–23 period. In O'Faoláin's world, the characters do not wake to find that all has been resolved, or that peace and harmony have been restored, by the close of the day. On the contrary, many of the stories are told in retrospect and negotiate with acts of recollection and the working of memory. (This was one of O'Faoláin's greatest preoccupations and provided the focus of several of his later collections, including *I Remember! I Remember!* [1961].) It is frequently suggested that the characters concerned will never free themselves from the consequences of their actions and that they will continue to narrate their stories, and reflect on their activities, long after the events that have been witnessed. In addition, *Midsummer Night Madness* dramatizes the restrictions that are placed on love and intimacy at a time of war. Many of the stories, including the long title story, take place as curfew is declared, and a recurring image which discreetly binds the collection together is that of young lovers being torn apart as the Tans invade Cork's streets. A number of the stories suggest the perversion of love and desire at such a time, as sexual energies are projected onto violent acts and brutal encounters, and on several occasions there is a disquieting eroticization of military activity and political violence – "The Small Lady" is a case in point, as it brings together the themes of abduction, seduction, and murder.

This pattern is repeated through to the final story, "The Patriot," where love threatens to be replaced by, or to mutate into, doctrinaire beliefs and the call to arms. In essence, "The Patriot" draws upon the Shakespearean motif of separated lovers (a gunman on the run, a clichéd girl waiting patiently at home), and fuses this with the dramatic conventions of the love triangle – the gunman, the girl, and the self-styled "patriot." The eponymous patriot presents himself as impossibly selfless and chaste to his fellow insurrectionists – his devotion to the cause is widely praised, and he is popularly thought to be consumed by the political "passion ... to which he had given his life" (O'Faoláin 1980:162). However, there is an implicit suggestion that he is more manipulative and unseemly than he appears. In "The Patriot," the informing principles of the revolution are represented in the most depressed and squalid of lights (the story is suitably set in the closing days of the Civil War), and are transformed into the stuff of drunken clichés and bigoted propagandists. It is telling, therefore, that the story – and with that the volume – should end with a turn from these principles, as the central character (the gunman) turns his back on political abstractions (his patriot-mentor), and at the same time looks towards his lover in the privacy of a darkened room. If peace is unrealized by the book's end (a late scene records the inflamed passions at a political rally in a socially divided island), some hope is nonetheless expressed in its touching, tender conclusion. Hope is also filtered through the juxtaposition of modes and styles in the collection, and in particular through O'Faoláin's deployment of – and oscillation between – grim realism and a more youthful, optimistic romanticism, which is best expressed in the lyrical story "Fugue."

Whatever hope is glimpsed in *Midsummer Night Madness*, is lost in O'Faoláin's second volume, *A Purse of Coppers* (1937). Its opening story, "A Broken World," provides a clear statement of intent and offers a bleak assessment of cultural and intellectual activity in post-Independence Ireland. "A Broken World" is structured in three parts and presents three characters travelling on a train to Dublin – a depressed priest, a moronic farmer, and an aloof intellectual and narrator. The abiding impression is of poverty, which is emotional, ideological, financial, spiritual, and civic; however, although poverty is endemic, it is scarcely articulated. In the judgment of the "silenced," because once radical, priest, this is because the people have become "too respectful" since they had "the last bit of rebel spirit [knocked] out of them" by Church and state (O'Faoláin 1980:170, 165–66). The key words which are repeated time and again are "lonely" and "silent," and it is implied that each of the characters is defined and restricted by social paradigms and cultural expectations. This perhaps explains why each of the characters is figured as a representative type or cliché (none of the three characters is named and each of them is barely realized). It also accounts for the tripartite structure of the story, as each of the characters dominates a section but is effectively framed by or consigned to that section (in each section one of the characters tells or reflects on a story, but departs the train with the conclusion of that story). "A Broken World" concludes with the clearest of intertextual references, to Joyce and "The Dead," as the narrator reaches his destination alone and looks out on a familiar, snow-clad scene. "I could not deny to the wintry moment its own truth," he reflects, "and that under that white shroud, covering the whole of Ireland, life was lying broken and hardly breathing" (O'Faoláin 1980:173). The narrator longs for some inspiring thought or ideal which might galvanize the state and unite its people: "what image of life … would fire and fuse us all," he asks, "what triumph, what engendering love" (O'Faoláin 1980:173). His hopes are quietly frustrated, however, and the story instead closes with an image of an atrophied society incapable of resuscitation.

The despair which is painfully registered in "A Broken World" is repeated across the pages of *A Purse of Coppers*, where talent is repeatedly wasted and characters are defined and placed by the society in which they find themselves. In "The Old Master," for instance, a pretentious clerk is subjected to the pressure of moral zealots and compelled to protest against his own dreams and fantasies; in the process, he becomes the target of local gossips, and is framed, quite literally, by the descriptive cruelties of the narrator – in the opening sentence of the story he is described "geometrically" by the narrator as "a parabola of pomposity in a rectangle of gaslight" (O'Faoláin 1980:174). In "A Meeting," a former revolutionary is robbed of her liveliness and potential, and restricted to a life of domestic servitude in a rural backwater – "Jesus, I'm fed to the bloody eye-teeth with this bloody hole and all in it!" she never quite manages to say (O'Faoláin 1980:277). And in "Admiring the Scenery," the loneliest of men reflects on what might have been, "weeping to himself, the drops creeping through his tightly closed eyes" (O'Faoláin 1980:202).

"Again and again in O'Faoláin's work," Corcoran has remarked, "Ireland is imaged as … a 'broken world,' its characters desiring spontaneity but suffering repression, looking for political or spiritual satisfaction but enduring abjection and disconsolation" (Corcoran 1997:73). O'Faoláin's three novels of the post-Revival period, *A Nest of Simple Folk* (1934), *Bird Alone* (1936), and *Come Back to Erin* (1940), exemplify this thesis, and are aligned with the mood and concerns which define *A Purse of Coppers*. Each of these novels dramatizes the struggles of an imaginative individual in a restrictive location, and each bears witness to the failures and disappointments of life in a depressed, fragmented society. In one of the bitterest of his essays, "The Dilemma of Irish Letters" (1949), O'Faoláin reflected on these deficiencies and argued that they accounted for the failure of the novel as an art form in modern Ireland. Irish society was too "thin" to carry its weight, he commented, recalling Henry James' famous critique of Nathaniel Hawthorne; he also suggested that these deficiencies explained the contemporaneous rise and popularity of the short-story form. "In such an unshaped society there are many subjects for little pieces, that is for the short-story writer," O'Faoláin concluded, but "the novelist or the dramatist loses himself in the general amorphism, unthinkingness, brainlessness, egalitarianism and general unsophistication" (O'Faoláin 1949:375–76).

Dejection and disconsolation provide meta-themes which can be traced across O'Faoláin's oeuvre; however, a softening of focus, and a freeing of potential, can also be discerned in his creative work from the early 1940s on. Although many of the characters in *Teresa and Other Stories* (1947) remain disappointed, this ceases to be all-encompassing, and characters are no longer readily described or placed by social conventions, cultural expectations, or narrative logic. On the contrary, O'Faoláin's work increasingly represents characters who defy the expected paradigms, as they present themselves to themselves, and to everyone around them (including us as readers), as uncertain creatures who delight in – but are sometimes worried by – the loss of absolutes and the ambiguities of their situation. In the story "Lady Lucifer," the idea is posited that people are "nothing but a random balance of opposites" and that it "depends from hour to hour which way the balance swings" (O'Faoláin 1980:434). This theory is advanced to counter the discourse of moral essentialism and cultural pigeonholing, and provides a key to reading the larger collection.

In *Teresa*, characters are repeatedly presented in an ambivalent or inconsistent light, and preconceptions and expectations are routinely denied, deferred, or frustrated. The impulsive young novitiate of the title story is a fine example, as she flamboyantly performs her beliefs and aspires to perfection in the company of an unconventional older nun. Similarly, in the modulated "The Man who Invented Sin," and again in the richly phrased "Unholy Living and Half Dying," recognizable character types are presented but carefully conflated, and the lines which distinguish the devout from the secular, and the sheltered from the worldly wise, are simultaneously drawn and erased by the characters themselves and their narrators. In "The Silence of the Valley," these preconceptions are further undermined as O'Faoláin depicts a scenario which at first sight seems commonplace – traditional Ireland on the verge of extinction, symbolized by the death of an elderly *seanchaí* or local storyteller. This scenario is renegotiated, however, so that the traditional world which is envisaged is neither pure nor romantic (as it is often idealized by Revivalists and cultural nationalists); instead, it is gloriously hybrid, interweaving local beliefs with international concerns, and mapping populist tastes onto respected, inherited practices. The world the *seanchaí* depicts, and the aging society he is a part of, disregards ready-made distinctions in favor of the truly eclectic – the narrative records, for instance, how people used to travel for miles to hear his "views on Hitler and Mussolini and the Prophecies of Saint Columcille, which foretold that the last battle of the last world-war would be fought at Ballylickey Bridge" (O'Faoláin 1980:367). It is also insistently vulgar, as the narrator recalls with relish "some of [his] more earthy stories that were as innocent and sweaty as any Norse or Celtic yarn of the Golden Age: such as the dilemma of the sow eating the eel which slipped out of her as fast as it went into her" (O'Faoláin 1980:367). In "The Silence in the Valley," it is not just traditional paradigms which are joyfully upset by the narrator – all of the characters who inhabit the story are more complex and conflicted than they initially appear. The story focuses on a group of tourists who visit the home of the *seanchaí* in west Cork. Each of the tourists is unnamed and each is presented as a generic type (the priest, the inspector, the American, the Celt, and the Scotswoman); however, none is rigidly framed, as they range beyond the roles that they are allocated to struggle with ambiguities, inconsistencies, and self-doubts. The easily offended Celt, who is the mouthpiece of all kinds of obvious clichés and ideological absurdities, is a case in point, as he "labour[s] to resolve his own contradictions" in the course of the story (O'Faoláin 1980:375). In many respects, the irresolvable struggles that the Celt faces are shared by the other characters in *Teresa*.

Late in his career, O'Faoláin supposed that it was the job of the writer to explore the "contradictions, inconsistencies, and incompatibilities" which define us as human (O'Faoláin 1976:10). O'Faoláin's stories, particularly his mature and later stories, are characterized by such incompatibilities, as they engage with the pressures which compel us "to adapt to change" in a modernizing world (O'Faoláin 1976:10). Rarely is it suggested that these contradictions can be resolved or easily settled, or that adaptation can be achieved painlessly, without a price. Rather, as John Hildebidle has noted, "a conflict of loyalties and intentions … is at the heart of all of O'Faoláin's fiction," and much of the power and suggestiveness of his work resides in the fact that this conflict defies any resolution (Hildebidle 1989:131). Time and again, characters are caught between the attractions of traditional and contemporary modes of identification, and a rich array of contrasts and oppositions provides the structural basis of many of his stories – the relationship between Ireland and Europe is a persistent concern, as is the interplay between penance and delight, repulsion and longing, and social obligations and private desire. "Lovers of the Lake" (*The Finest Stories of Seán O'Faoláin* [1957]) is but an obvious instance of this, as it skillfully describes the relationship of an adulterous couple, Jenny and Bobby, in mid-twentieth-century Ireland. From the outset of this deeply sympathetic story, it is clear that the characters' love for one another is genuine; however, it is also clear that Jenny, in particular, is trapped in a hopeless situation since, as a practicing Catholic, she has no option other than to submit to the prior claims of her marriage. This is the dilemma which provides the central thrust of the story, and it is something which is denied any easy outcome by O'Faoláin as he holds back from offering his characters any neat or simple answers.

The equivocal design of "Lovers of the Lake" is characteristic of O'Faoláin's later work, as he writes to undercut received assumptions and cultural expectations – consider his sensitive exploration of deracination and the loss of traditional skills in "The Sugawn Chair" (*I Remember! I Remember!*), for example, or his reversal of gender roles in "The Faithless Wife" (*Foreign Affairs and Other Stories* [1976]). Significantly, equivocation is also illustrative of his thinking on the art of short fiction more generally. In his critical study *The Short Story* (1948), O'Faoláin claimed that the formal requirements of the genre ensured that it was not only the appropriate medium for Irish prose writers (because of the various shortcomings which he subsequently identified in "The Dilemma of Irish Letters"), but that it was also the form which was best suited to trace states of ambiguity, uncertainty, and irresolution. "Telling by means of suggestion or implication is one of the most important of all the modern short story's shorthand conventions," he comments; "It means that a short-story writer does not directly tell us things so much as let us guess or know them by implying them" (O'Faoláin 1948:150–51). Frank O'Connor further distinguished between the novel and the short story in his influential study *The Lonely Voice*, arguing that isolation and marginality are the fundamental constituents of the latter form. "My own view of the difference between the novel and the story," he remarked, might be summed up in the distinction between "characters regarded as representative figures and characters regarded as outcasts, lonely individuals" (O'Connor 1963:55).

"Always in the short story there is [a] sense of outlawed figures wandering about the fringes of society," it is proposed in *The Lonely Voice*. "As a result, there is in the short story at its most characteristic something we do not often find in the novel – an intense awareness of human loneliness" (O'Connor 1963:19). An awareness of solitude and the peripheral is at the heart of O'Connor's oeuvre, as he looks to the experiences of those "submerged population groups" which exist on the margins of post-Independence Irish society – children, for instance, and depressed dreamers, as well as timid bachelors, forlorn priests, spirited women, small-town anonymities, the socially illegitimate, and the rural poor (O'Connor 1963:18). O'Connor's work is characterized by the desire to articulate the concerns, and crucially the voices, of such people – people who would "emigrate to the ends of the earth" if they were granted the opportunity, he elsewhere claimed, "not because the country was poor, but because it was mediocre" (O'Connor 1961:147). Many of O'Connor's characters are dejected and solitary, and most share the capacity for self-delusion; "loneliness" is the key word which defines their condition. The closing lines of one of his earliest and finest stories, the justly acclaimed "Guests of the Nation," are representative in this respect, particularly in the form in which they were first published in *Guests of the Nation* (1931). (The lines were refined several times in later years, and the story exists in at least four different versions – O'Connor was famous for continuing to revise his stories, even the ones which were well known and widely anthologized.)

"I stood at the door, watching the stars and listening to the shrieking of the birds dying out over the bogs," the narrator, Bonaparte, confides, as he struggles to recall, and bear witness to, his involvement in the murder of two captured English soldiers in County Cork during the War of Independence (O'Connor 1931:17). This struggle is barely detected in the early stages of the story, where Bonaparte conjures up a warm, domestic setting, and describes the genuine friendship which develops between the English prisoners and their Irish guards. The tone of these sections is playfully ironic, and this is evinced in the title of the story (the "guests" are hostages), and also in the names which are given to the characters – the earthy Belcher, the argumentative Hawkins, the palpably unheroic Noble and Bonaparte, and the seemingly mundane Jeremiah Donovan (whose name sounds local and commonplace, but richly combines allusions to the prophet Jeremiah, an iconic nineteenth-century Fenian [Jeremiah O'Donovan Rossa], and the author himself [O'Connor's real name was Michael O'Donovan]). Irony is also registered through the early sequences of the story, as the captive Englishmen go native, play cards with their captors, flirt with the country girls, and attend local dances; at these dances, they learn traditional Irish steps but do not take part, "because our lads at that time did not dance foreign dances on principle" (O'Connor 1931:6). The gentle comedy which dominates the opening sections is illusory, however, and gives way to a reality which is at once brutal and shocking, as the pressures of war impact upon the narrative and the burgeoning Anglo-Irish relationships.

Several clues are given which point towards the fate of the two Englishmen: Belcher is associated with ashes from the outset of the story, and it is said that it is his habit to wander "in and out [of the room] like a ghost, without speaking"; Hawkins, for his part, partakes in a venomous dispute about the existence of the afterlife, the night before he is killed (O'Connor 1931:7). When the hostages are executed, the tone and pace of the story abruptly change, and the narrative turns inward to focus on the psychological consequences of this action. For the most part, the story is told in retrospect (thus the above-mentioned clues can be supplied by the narrator, as he is recalling the story from an unspecified point, sometime after the events narrated). However, when the executions are enacted, the narrative subtly conflates tenses, and momentarily flickers between present and past modes of narration. After Hawkins is shot, Bonaparte is forced to remember how "We all stood very still, watching him settle out in the last agony":

> Then Belcher took out his handkerchief and began to tie it about his own eyes (in our excitement we'd forgotten to do the same for Hawkins), and, seeing it wasn't big enough, turned and asked for the loan of mine. I gave it to him, and he knotted the two together and pointed with his foot at Hawkins.
>   "He's not quite dead," he says. "Better give him another."
>   Sure enough, Hawkins's left knee is beginning to rise. I bend down and put my gun to his head; then recollecting myself, I get up again. Belcher understands what's in my mind.
>   "Give him his first," he says. "I don't mind. Poor bastard, we don't know what's happening to him now." (O'Connor 1931:15–16)

The conflation of past and continual present in this scene, although slight, is telling, and reinforces the idea that the story is a kind of fictional trauma narrative. As a trauma narrative, "Guests of the Nation" is an attempt by the narrator to reconstruct and understand a nightmarish event from his past. Given the ghastly nature of the event, however, it is hardly surprising that it refuses to remain locked in the past, as it haunts Bonaparte's conscience and struggles to gain articulation. Like Hawkins, who is horrifically represented "beginning to rise" from the dead, the story suggests that the memory of this event will be endlessly returned to by the narrator, and that it will continue to resurface in his thoughts and be replayed through the act of narration. (It is fitting, therefore, that O'Connor should have returned to revise this, his most famous story, on so many occasions.) "It is so strange what you feel at times like that," Bonaparte concludes.

Noble [one of Bonaparte's comrades] says he saw everything ten times the size, as though there were nothing in the whole world but that little patch of bog with the two Englishmen stiffening into it, but with me it was as if the patch of bog where the Englishmen were was a million miles away, and even Noble and the old woman, mumbling behind me, and the birds and the bloody stars were all far away, and I was somehow very small and very lost and lonely like a child astray in the snow. And anything that happened to me afterwards, I never felt the same about again. (O'Connor 1931:18)

Many of O'Connor's characters share this experience of isolation, and are made to feel "somehow very small and very lost and lonely" in the course of their stories. Many also experience the loss of illusions and dreams along the way – "imaginative improvisations," they are called in *An Only Child* (O'Connor 1961:178). This loss, although painful, proves fundamental for the growth of individuation in O'Connor's work, and results in some form of self-realization and independence.

Guests of the Nation charts a similar terrain to *Midsummer Night Madness*: it is also set against the military struggles of 1919 to 1923, and a number of the stories are interlinked, with characters stepping across the pages to share in discussions, activities, relationships, and settings (this is also the case in O'Faoláin's volume). In many ways, as Brown has remarked, it is a book of "forsaken enthusiasms," as a sardonic weariness is expressed by the characters who see through political euphemisms and reflect on earlier romantic beliefs (Brown 2007:43). In "Nightpiece with Figures," for instance, a young rebel replies "cynically" to abstract talk about duty and nation, while in "September Dawn," a fellow insurrectionist proclaims – with more than a nod towards Sean O'Casey – that it is his earnest desire "to live for Ireland, not to die for it" (O'Connor 1931:53, 58). Throughout the collection, ideological abstractions are synonymous with the lack of moral principles, and the reality of warfare is sordid and base. In "Machine-Gun Corps in Action," there is nothing to distinguish between Free State and republican soldiers, and a corrupt shopkeeper is happy to sell his gun to the highest bidder; in "Soirée Chez Une Belle Jeune Fille," a republican rendezvous doubles up as a dairy and "also a brothel of sorts, but this [the principal character] did not learn until long after"; and in "The Patriarch," the deflated narrator reveals how "after the first flush of enthusiasm has died away," guerrilla fighting "is a filthy game in which obstinacy and the desire for revenge soon predominate" (O'Connor 1931:130, 159). The fight for independence – in both the public and the private spheres – is inflected with an Oedipal significance in *Guests of the Nation*, and the rebellion of sons (and also daughters) against failed or absent fathers is one of several motifs which bind the collection together. This rebellion is also indicative of the pattern of intergenerational conflict which underlies the structure of the volume more generally. A radical disconnection between the generations is suggested throughout the collection, and this is rendered most explicit in "September Dawn," when an IRA volunteer takes shelter in a relative's house. As the elderly aunt reminisces about Parnell and an earlier world, her conversation is said to become "remote and insubstantial" to the young gunman – "and so they talked," the narrator laments, "each failing to understand the other" (O'Connor 1931:66).

The failure of understanding is carried forward into O'Connor's second volume, *Bones of Contention* (1936), where further glimpses are provided of a world in transition, and communities are depicted contending with the demands of divergent cultural practices and competing value systems. According to O'Connor's biographer, James Matthews, *Bones of Contention* is a consequence of the young writer "fumbling for a style" after *Guests of the Nation* (Matthews 1976:51). Drawing back "from the nation at large to smaller and less colourful groups," O'Connor looked towards those who would subsequently become representative characters in his fiction – outcasts and lonely individuals, like "peasants, drunken musicians and tired old men," rather than the soldiers and lovers who wandered across the pages of the previous collection (Matthews 1976:51). The narrative techniques which are employed in *Bones of Contention* are quite different from those which provide the basis of *Guests of the Nation*: the stories are told in a casual manner, with large sections of the text consisting of reported conversations or speeches, and relatively little space given over to explanations, narratorial reflections, or physical descriptions.

"In the Train" and "The Majesty of the Law" provide two exemplary instances of this. In both texts, O'Connor uses dialogue to effectively tell the story, and in each case very little information is supplied by the external, third-person narrator. What is more, in both stories the narratives enact, and are illustrative of, a clash of values and cultural allegiances in the newly independent state. In both stories, an illegal act is performed which requires investigation (a young woman has murdered her abusive husband in the first story, an elderly man has assaulted his neighbor in the second), and this results in an encounter between the authorities of the Free State (in the guise of the police force) and the inhabitants of remote pockets of rural Ireland. That encounter is relaxed, as the policemen walk freely into the spaces that the poor inhabit (a train carriage, a dilapidated cottage), and are welcomed without suspicion and with hospitality. In both cases, the policemen and the peasants smoke and drink together, they discuss acquaintances and shared interests, and they enjoy "lively bursts of conversation, and long, long silences" ("The Majesty of the Law" [O'Connor 1981:325]). The policemen even manipulate the rules that they purportedly enforce, negotiating their way around the poteen laws for instance. In many respects, they are shown to be at one with the communities that they patrol. Even so, the rural communities refuse to cooperate fully with the abstraction that is the law, as they consider it an intrusive force which does not adequately match the rhythms and patterns of their lives. It is of little relevance that this law is the law of the Free State, and that it is no longer associated with an imperial state apparatus, for in both stories the communities insist on their right to punish transgressors locally, according to traditional codes of conduct and established modes of reparation. Thus it is clear that the neighbor who informs against Old Dan Bride in "The Majesty of the Law" will pay a harsh price for his actions. Similarly, Helena in "In the Train" is sentenced to an anxious future, as she returns to live amongst the people who defended her before the courts – they will get their revenge at home, shunning her for the rest of her days. As an elderly peasant cruelly promises, they will "give her the hunt," for "What right have she in a decent place?" (O'Connor 2005:302).

"The Majesty of the Law" and "In the Train" both suggest, at some level, a failure of understanding and a radical disconnection between different communities – rural and urban, oral and literate, poor and middle-class, traditional and modern – in post-Independence Ireland. Both stories also illustrate O'Connor's overarching belief in the centrality of the themes of marginality and loneliness for the practice of short fiction. In both texts, the characters are positioned on the social periphery; they live on the cusp of their communities, at the very edge of the recently established state. What is more, in both stories the central characters are presented alone. This is dramatically rendered in "In the Train," where Helena sits in an empty train compartment, and only speaks in the final section of the story. This structural device sets her apart from her neighbors, who are crammed into an adjoining carriage, and are permitted to roam through the train and talk across the different sections of the story. Loneliness is also realized throughout the narrative of "The Majesty of the Law," and especially in the memorable, assonantal closing image, where Old Dan is depicted "set[ting] out alone along the road to prison" (O'Connor 1981:327). If both texts exemplify O'Connor's later thesis regarding the parameters of short fiction, however, they nonetheless also demonstrate a fundamental paradox which critics have observed in his work – as loneliness becomes so prevalent that it begins to define the reality of communal life and the representatives of communal life, as well as the "outcasts, lonely individuals" who are delineated in *The Lonely Voice*. In "In the Train," for instance, it is remarkable how many of the characters (apart from Helena) declare their loneliness in the course of the story, characters who are otherwise presented as part of a distinct social network or an identifiable group – the sergeant's wife, for example, as well as the policeman Delancey, the peasant Thade Kendillon, and the barely sketched anonymous drunk ("I'm a lonely man," the latter confesses, after saying goodbye to his friends. "And I'm going back to a lonely habitation" [O'Connor 2005:303]). Commenting on this point, Julian Barnes has asked whether the experience of loneliness actually makes O'Connor's characters "typical, rather than atypical, of the society to which they belong" (Barnes 2005:xii).

Critics have also discerned the paradox that loneliness is often registered in the most sociable forms of narration by O'Connor. Many of O'Connor's stories are insistently oral and strive to represent the rhythms and sounds of the spoken word in print; in some respects, this is the most radical and ambitious feature of his work, even if it risked sounding increasingly obvious or formulaic in his later years. In an interview conducted with the *Paris Review* in 1957, O'Connor elaborated on this element of his stories: "I notice particularly the cadence of [people's] voices," he commented, "the sort of phrases they'll use, and that's what I'm all the time trying to hear in my head, how people word things. ... I'm terribly aware of voices" (O'Connor 1957:8). From *Bones of Contention* through *Crab Apple Jelly* (1944) and *The Common Chord* (1947), to *Domestic Relations* (1951) and the later collections, O'Connor's stories often prioritize an anecdotal or conversational mode and employ the device of a knowing narrator who has complete control over his subject-matter and assumes a level of intimacy with his characters and intended readers. His great tragedy of social misunderstanding and familial division, "The Luceys" (*Crab Apple Jelly*), is but one instance of this, as it opens with the boldly declarative personal statement: "It's extraordinary, the bitterness there can be in a town like ours between two people of the same family" (O'Connor 1981:67). O'Connor's use of anecdotes, and his deployment of familiar narrators ("like ours" speaks volumes), is so extensive that it could be said to hint at the truly social and sociable – rather than the isolated or attenuated – nature of his short fiction. In this respect, it is entirely appropriate that his work has been glossed by Seamus Deane's shrewd observation regarding the shape of Irish writing more generally. "Although much Irish writing is concerned with alienated lives, it is not itself a literature of alienation," Deane has suggested, in an essay on another of O'Connor's great contemporaries, Mary Lavin. "Society and literature retain their intimacy in Ireland to such a degree that our best literature is still, in the widest sense of the term, social" (Deane 1979:244; see also Brown 1985:159). Exploring the ways in which O'Connor's stories, and also O'Faoláin's fiction, continue to remain social, or relevant, is an essential first step in the critical rehabilitation of both writers' legacy in the early twenty-first century.

References and Further Reading

Arndt, M. (2001). *A Critical Study of Seán O'Faoláin's Life and Work*. Lewiston: Edwin Mellon Press.

Barnes, J. (2005). "Introduction." In F. O'Connor. *My Oedipus Complex and Other Stories* (pp. vii–xiii). London: Penguin.

Bonaccorso, R. (1987). *Seán O'Faoláin's Irish Vision*. Albany: State University of New York Press.

Brown, T. (1985). *Ireland: A Social and Cultural History, 1922–1985*. 2nd edn. London: Fontana.

Brown, T. (2007). "Frank O'Connor and a Vanishing Ireland." In H. Lennon (Ed.). *Frank O'Connor: Critical Essays* (pp. 41–52). Dublin: Four Courts Press.

Corcoran, N. (1997). *After Yeats and Joyce: Reading Modern Irish Literature*. Oxford: Oxford University Press.

Deane, S. (1979). "Mary Lavin." In T. Brown and P. Rafroidi (Eds.). *The Irish Short Story* (pp. 237–47). Gerrards Cross: Colin Smythe.

Dunne, S. (Ed.). (1991). *The Cork Review*, special issue on Seán O'Faoláin.

Flanagan, T. (1969). "The Irish Writer." In M. Sheehy (Ed.). *Michael/Frank: Studies on Frank*

O'Connor, with a Bibliography of his Writing (pp. 148–64). Dublin: Gill & Macmillan.

Foster, R.F. (1988). *Modern Ireland 1600–1972*. London: Allen Lane.

Harmon, M. (1966). *Seán O'Faoláin: A Critical Introduction*. Notre Dame: University of Notre Dame Press.

Harmon, M. (1994). *Seán O'Faoláin*. London: Constable.

Hildebidle, J. (1989). *Five Irish Writers: The Errand of Keeping Alive*. Cambridge, MA: Harvard University Press.

Kiberd, D. (2005). "Introduction." In F. O'Connor. *An Only Child and My Father's Son: An Autobiography* (pp. vii–xiii). London: Penguin.

Matthews, J. (1976). *Frank O'Connor*. Lewisburg: Bucknell University Press.

Matthews, J. (1983). *Voices: A Life of Frank O'Connor*. Dublin: Gill & Macmillan.

O'Connor, F. (1931). *Guests of the Nation*. London: Macmillan. Repr. Dublin: Poolbeg, 1979.

O'Connor, F. (1934). "A Boy in Prison." *Life and Letters*, 10.56 (August), 525–35. Repr. in Michael Steinman (Ed.). *A Frank O'Connor*

Reader (pp. 292–304). New York: Syracuse University Press, 1994.

O'Connor, F. (1936). *Bones of Contention and Other Stories*. London: Macmillan.

O'Connor, F. (1944). *Crab Apple Jelly*. London: Macmillan.

O'Connor, F. (1957). "The Art of Fiction" (interview). *The Paris Review*, 19, 1–24.

O'Connor, F. (1961). *An Only Child*. London: Macmillan.

O'Connor, F. (1963). *The Lonely Voice: A Study of the Short Story*. London: Macmillan.

O'Connor, F. (1981). *Collected Stories*. New York: Knopf.

O'Connor, F. (2005). *My Oedipus Complex and Other Stories*. London: Penguin.

O'Faoláin, S. (1932). *Midsummer Night's Madness and Other Stories*. London: J. Cape.

O'Faoláin, S. (1937). *A Purse of Coppers*. London: J. Cape.

O'Faoláin, S. (1939). *De Valera*. Harmondsworth: Penguin.

O'Faoláin, S. (1948). *The Short Story*. London: Collins.

O'Faoláin, S. (1949). "The Dilemma of Irish Letters." *The Month*, 2.6 (December), 366–79.

O'Faoláin, S. (1957). *Finest Stories of Seán O'Faoláin*. Boston: Little, Brown.

O'Faoláin, S. (1965). *Vive Moi! An Autobiography*. London: Rupert Hart-Davis.

O'Faoláin, S. (1976). "A Portrait of the Artist as an Old Man." In M. Harmon (Ed.). *Irish University Review*, 6.1, 10–18 [special issue on Seán O'Faoláin].

O'Faoláin, S. (1980). *The Collected Stories of Seán O'Faoláin*. Vol. I. London: Constable.

Reid, I. (1977). *The Short Story*. London: Methuen.

39
"Ireland is small enough": Louis MacNeice and Patrick Kavanagh

Alan Gillis

Louis MacNeice and Patrick Kavanagh, both from Ulster, were two of the most influential poets of the Irish mid-century. Beyond that they had little in common.

Kavanagh was born in 1904 and was reared in Mucker, a townland in Inniskeen, Monaghan. He was removed from school at the age of 13 to become a cobbler and subsistence farmer. He read poems mostly from school textbooks, unaware of modern literature until 1925, when he discovered the *Irish Statesman*, a journal edited by George Russell. He remained a farmer in Mucker until he published *Ploughman and Other Poems* in 1936, after which he went to London, where he gained a commission to write *The Green Fool*. Buoyed by its initial success, he moved to Dublin in 1939 to become a full-time writer. Although things didn't quite work out he remained based in Dublin, experiencing angst, bad luck, controversy, and poverty until a turnaround in fortunes in his last years. He died in 1967.

MacNeice was born in 1907 in Belfast and was reared in Carrickfergus, on the Antrim coast, where his father was rector of the Anglican church (later becoming a bishop). His mother died when he was 5, and he was mostly looked after by a cook and a governess until sent to boarding school in England at the age of 10, later moving to Marlborough College and Oxford. During the 1930s he worked as a lecturer in classics in Birmingham and then at Bedford College. *Poems* appeared from Faber & Faber in 1935, and MacNeice went on to publish a prodigious quantity of writing. After flirting with a move to America at the outbreak of World War II, he eventually settled in London, where he was a much-traveled scriptwriter and producer for BBC Radio, until his death in 1963.

The pair seem to be mirror opposites. MacNeice was Protestant, while Kavanagh was Catholic; MacNeice was from Northern Ireland, while Kavanagh was from the Republic of Ireland; MacNeice gained an elite education in England, while Kavanagh

A Companion to Irish Literature, edited by Julia M. Wright
© 2010 Blackwell Publishing Ltd

was self-taught in Mucker; MacNeice was urban and urbane, while Kavanagh was rural and gruff; MacNeice lived in London, while Kavanagh lived in Dublin; MacNeice apparently suffered little financial strain or career anxiety, while Kavanagh was impoverished and always out for a job. MacNeice's work is marked by political contexts, by World War II, by international travels. Kavanagh's work is marked by his being stuck in Dublin throughout Ireland's neutrality and subsequent gloomy isolation. One of Kavanagh's most famous poems is "Epic," a sonnet on the value of local happenings: "I have lived in important places, times / When great events were decided" (the great event in question, here, being a skirmish over the ownership of "half a rood of rock"). This, against the claims of international events: "That was the year of the Munich bother" (Kavanagh 2005:154; all citations of Kavanagh's poetry refer to this edition unless otherwise noted). By contrast, one of MacNeice's most famous poems is *Autumn Journal*, a long work triggered precisely by the "Munich bother" of 1938.

Kavanagh's achievement in the face of his upbringing constitutes a remarkable feat and a turning point in the sociology of modern Irish literature. Yet he was scornful of those who romanticized him and thus bypassed his poetry's basis in hard graft and inner steel: the long, learned, technical, and uneven process of nurturing and forging lyric skill. In the same spirit, however, it would be moronic to assume MacNeice had it all on a plate. A good education and so on means nothing without the same hard will and innate talent. Thus, although it would be wrong to ignore their differences, it might also be misguided to overstress them.

They shared crucial affinities. Both were vituperative critics of Irish culture. Both were lifelong enemies of cant, dogma, and inauthenticity. Both had the experience of negotiating with modernism. MacNeice, for a long time, was known as a politically engaged peer of W.H. Auden, while Kavanagh often described himself as an apolitical dandy. Yet Auden was one of Kavanagh's favorite poets and *The Great Hunger* is a radical political poem, while MacNeice is one of our great poets of sensual individualism. Meanwhile, MacNeice was a city poet acknowledged for capturing urban experience, while the "peasant" poet Kavanagh was acknowledged for his poems of rural Monaghan. Yet Kavanagh was also a city street poet, while MacNeice was brilliant on natural landscapes.

Kavanagh is renowned for introducing matter-of-fact realism and vernacular directness to Irish poetry. He learned his trade in a literary environment dominated by "Celtic Twilight" poetry. Overly imitative of early Yeats, this had become a kind of house style for Irish poetry, lumpen with enervated aestheticism, formulaic sonority, and hackneyed mythology. In this context, Kavanagh's trademark frankness appears revolutionary:

> We borrowed the loan of Kerr's big ass
> To go to Dundalk with butter,
> Brought him home the evening before the market
> An exile that night in Mucker.

(173)

However, such an apparently unmediated style was hard-earned. Kavanagh was at pains to insist that his style was not the innate expressiveness of a "peasant." In retrospect, he wrote, "During my early years in Dublin the virtue of being a peasant was much extolled. ... Knowing nothing better I accepted it and flaunted my peasantry." He thus became, he claimed, "the established peasant poet" in Dublin. Yet, he argued, "Far from the poet being a peasant ... he is the last word in sophistication" (Kavanagh 2003:274–75). The Irish Literary Revival, of course, was obsessed with peasants, but writers such as Yeats, Synge, and Lady Gregory were educated, cosmopolitan, Protestant, and landed. Never one to mince his words, Kavanagh later claimed, "I would say now that that so-called Irish Literary Movement which purported to be frightfully Irish and racy of the Celtic soil was a thoroughgoing English-bred lie" (Kavanagh 2003:306).

Nevertheless, the Revival had deepened a tendency to view pastoral modes as *the* quintessential Irish literary domain. There was still an overriding sense that the countryside, rather than urban modernity, constituted the heart of Ireland. And so, given the somewhat outré nature of Yeats as an immediate contemporary, and the staleness of much of the rest of Irish verse, it is unsurprising that Kavanagh might have been hyped as the real deal. But he was sorely aware that no proper poetic expression is wholly natural, and he quickly became suspicious of the idea that verse might be intrinsically representative of national truths. In political terms, pastoral symbolism was being propagandistically co-opted by the state as a means of shrouding the increasingly harsh realities of Irish life. In the face of such prevailing stereotypes, Kavanagh had to find his voice at a time when the nature of his subject matter and chosen mode of writing were nationally at a watershed.

On the face of things, he was ill equipped to deal with such a scenario. He later wrote, "when a country body begins to progress into the world of print he does not write out of his rural innocence – he writes out of Palgrave's *Golden Treasury*" (Kavanagh 2003:106). His major problem was that he had little contemporary poetry available to him. Beyond that, however, it is worth noting that Palgrave's *Golden Treasury*, and other books like it, may well have been fine sourcebooks. Although he was self-schooled, his biographer Antoinette Quinn argues, "Little by little he acquired as complete a knowledge of English poetry as if he had attended an Irish secondary school, possibly even an Irish university, of the period" (Quinn 2003:48). Moreover, he was able to independently value the aura of what verse he had: "Walking alone in the fields or on his solitary walks to and from, he would repeat phrases and lines over and over, savouring the language and the sentiments, so totally at odds with those he heard around him every day" (Quinn 2003:48). Who is to say such a slow digestion of rhythm and cadence is not the best schooling a poet might ask for?

Meanwhile, it is easy to suggest in hindsight that, when Kavanagh discovered modern literature, it was unfortunate that he did so through Russell's *Irish Homestead*. Quinn argues that this journal was Kavanagh's "university, indoctrinating him through its editor's articles and reviews in a particular aesthetic" (Quinn 2003:48). The snag was that Russell promulgated "a poetry at odds with the texture and idiom of contemporary life," filled with "indistinct images, vague diction and other-worldly aspiration" (Quinn 2003:56). Now, it should be stressed that anything might be made to work in a poem: there is no inherently bad style or formula. However, problems arise when the formula is set as a default position and is not explored through the act of its expression. Kavanagh himself would later attack such clichéd writing, including his own early work. Stereotypical strains can be heard, for example, in "Address to an Old Wooden Gate," with its "fairy-columned turf-smoke" and "Time's long silver hand" (5). But even at this stage Kavanagh gave such phrasing a twist: "Time's long silver hand has touched our brows, / And I'm the scorned of women – you of cows" (5). The comedic effect may be inadvertent, but this couplet demonstrates his effort to drag his models into his own field of concern. In any case, some of his juvenilia is memorable: "The hill wind shakes / Sweet song like blossoms on / The calm green lakes" (7). In "Four Birds," an owl is "Night-winged / As a ghost / Or a gangster" (12). Yet Kavanagh had difficulties with derivativeness and generalization. He had a pronounced religious and high-Romantic streak, and he struggled to calibrate the concrete and the conceptual. It was in this regard that Russell's influence was baleful, as exemplified in the climax of "Ploughman": "I find a star-lovely art / In a dark sod. / Joy that is timeless! O heart / That knows God!" (7). Despite the tingle of allure as "star-lovely" descends on "dark sod," by the time this sod has found its way to God the verse has become a smooth iteration of a pre-packaged sentiment. The rhyme pretends to clinch a revelation, yet merely joins the dots, habitual and glib, so that the sense of transcendence is asserted, not achieved. Nothing is in doubt and therefore nothing is at stake.

However, the trope itself – the discovery of infinity in the clay, or divinity in the dirt – was central to Kavanagh's art. It returns, for example, in "To the Man After the Harrow": "The seed is flying far today – / The seed like stars against the black / Eternity of April clay" (35). In contrast to "Ploughman," these lines are not the clinching finale to this poem, but come in the first stanza. The poem ends,

> Forget the men on Brady's hill.
> Forget what Brady's boy may say,
> For destiny will not fulfil
> Unless you let the harrow play.
>
> Forget the worm's opinion too
> Of hooves and pointed harrow-pins,
> For you are driving your horses through
> The mist where Genesis begins.

(35)

To be sure, "destiny will not fulfil / Unless you let the harrow play" sounds hollow, but this is offset by the specificity of the preceding two lines. Who the men on Brady's hill are, or what Brady's boy said, is a mystery. Yet these lines delineate a verisimilar scene and embody a sense of lived experience within it. Meanwhile, the success of the ending seems to derive from the origin of "Genesis begins" in the "pointed harrow-pins." The big vision is launched from solid lexical ground, rooted in a workaday world. By being so particular, the harrow-pins become characterful, redolent of fields and labor. Kavanagh's message is that the transcendent is not found in things, but in the names of things.

"Stony Grey Soil" moves in a different direction to this uplift and expansion, but its affect is achieved through a similar rootedness. The poem builds up an incantatory head of steam, part song and part prayer, cursing and accusing the land: "You per-fumed my clothes with weasel itch, / You fed me on swinish food," "You burgled my bank of youth!" (38). It ends,

> Mullahinsha, Drummeril, Black Shanco –
> Wherever I turn I see
> In the stony grey soil of Monaghan
> Dead loves that were born for me.

(39)

Again the epiphany, although implosive and negative this time, is bound up with the sanctity of the naming. Dead love is born and woven into the sonic fabric of those place-names, and emanates back again from their un-English strangeness with haunt-ing power. They are specific to Monaghan, a poetic nowhere, yet they are everywhere. In an important essay, Seamus Heaney claims, "Kavanagh's place names are there to stake out a personal landscape, they declare one man's experience, they are denuded of tribal or etymological implications" (Heaney 1980:140). But this poem's poignant surge draws the reader into its realm of affect, and must also, therefore, have a com-munal element. This stony grey soil may be Kavanagh's, but it is also Ireland's. Indeed, it belongs to any reader.

There is an element of fury in Kavanagh, a sense of being cheated. His fields are cursed for not being the verdant wonders of pastoral dream, blighted by the banality of the real: "My black hills have never seen the sun" (21). His fields have well-nigh broken his back. His labors have been in vain. He has dedicated himself to a Romantic ideal that was a lie: "To be damned and yet to live" (18). Country neighbors laugh at him for his pretensions, while city readers condescend to his naivety: "They laughed at one I loved"; "They said / That I was bounded by the whitethorn hedges / Of the little farm and did not know the world" (183). He hits out at his readers, himself, rural culture, city culture, lyric poetry, nature itself.

This rancor is key to *The Great Hunger*. As suggested, the ideal of Ireland as a pastoral Eden was ideologically co-opted by the Irish state, and, especially from the mid-1930s onwards, was being contaminated by the increasing divergence between rhetoric and reality. The more poverty-stricken life became, the more hypocritical became the symbolism that was central to Ireland's self-representation. In retrospect Kavanagh's turn to stark realism within a pastoral mode may seem like an obvious maneuver, but it was a paradigm shift for Irish poetry, trampling over lyric civility with a hobnail boot. Influenced by realists such as Sean O'Faoláin and Frank O'Connor (see CHAPTER 38, CHANGING TIMES: FRANK O'CONNOR AND SEÁN O'FAOLÁIN), and marking a major advance in fusing modernist naturalism (that "urban" mode indelibly associated with Joyce) with pastoral lyricism, the poem was a political and aesthetic event. If the "peasant" Kavanagh was meant to be the "real thing," the government would soon wish he'd shut up and tread back to his stony grey fields.

Of course, the poem's subject matter was crucial. Centering on a protagonist, Patrick Maguire, the poem remorselessly conveys the frustration, hardship, boredom, futility, and sexual angst of his isolated existence. But the poem (published in 1942) is also innovative in a way that would have been impossible to predict from the rest of Kavanagh's work at that time. Quinn writes that the poem, "organized as a montage, is extraordinarily flexible, continually altering angle and direction. ... Maguire's life is framed with rapid changes of focus and from a deliberately diverting play of angles" (Quinn 1991:130). As it shifts from scene to scene, it shifts in form and tone; high melodrama is followed by caustic wit:

> O he loved his ploughs
> And he loved his cows
> And his happiest dream
> Was to clean his arse
> With perennial grass
> On the bank of some summer stream.
>
> (67)

The poem's tragic note is thus undercut by a comedic strain, and the poem is marked by a striking mixture of ironic intelligence and raw hurt. Heaney encapsulates its significance:

> It is the nearest Kavanagh ever gets to a grand style, one that seeks not a continuous decorum but a mixture of modes, of high and low, to accommodate his double perspective, the tragic and the emerging comic. ... Kavanagh's technical achievement here is to find an Irish note that is not dependent on backward looks towards the Irish tradition, not an artful retrieval of poetic strategies from another tongue but a ritualistic drawing out of patterns of run and stress in the English language as it is spoken in Ireland. It is as if the "stony grey soil of Monaghan" suddenly became vocal. (Heaney 1980:122–23)

Given Heaney's claims, it's worth looking closer at this "Irish note."

Some of Kavanagh's edge and energy stemmed from an aggravated realization of his early work's uncouth innocence. Echoing the rush of the "sod" to reveal "God" in "Ploughman," Patrick Maguire is castigated because, when meeting a girl, "He rushed beyond the thing / To the unreal" (70). Against this, Kavanagh wrote, "I want by Man, not God, to be inspired. / This year, O maiden of the dream-vague face, / You'll come to me, a thing of Time and Space" (25). Getting "Time and Space" into his verse, as we have seen, was partially achieved through using proper names alongside a context-specific diction. Kavanagh is a laureate of place-names: Donaghmoyne, Glasdrummond, Rocksavage, Shancoduff, Roscommon, Ballaghaderreen, Candlefort, Drumcatton, Seola, Dromore, Corofin, Castleblayney, Rathdrumskean. But his poetry's quality of rootedness was also a matter of rhythm and intonation.

Some critics have overstressed his vernacular idiom. Certainly, his verse did not reflect his day-to-day speech. Quinn writes,

> [H]e used crude farmyard expressions and swear words that were not current in Dublin's polite drawing rooms. ... Kavanagh's talk, which was larded with "fuck" and "fuckin," and with references to bitches, hoors, cunts, bollocks, arses, was coarse even by middle-class male standards. Several none-too-squeamish men have remarked on the grossness of his speech. Ben Kiely, for instance, cites the phrase, "as ignorant as the back of me balls that never saw shite." (Quinn 2003:142)

A diluted version of such earthy speech only really finds an outlet in Kavanagh's novel *Tarry Flynn*, notably through the figure of the mother: "of all the mane men that ever was you're the manest" (Kavanagh 2000:5). But something of this colloquial vigor nevertheless gives Kavanagh's verse its impulsion, and is played off against meter and line with crafted suppleness. His sense of his own voice was bound up with the imagery of clay: "Unless clay is in the mouth the singer's singing is useless" (85). And his own clay-bound poetic, his distinctive "note," is thus a matter of diction, rhythm, and idiomatic speech-effect working in tandem.

Along these lines, Kavanagh transformed the meaning of "rootedness." Being a "peasant" from the country did not make him rooted, but creating an authentic poetic style did. He wrote,

> "He has his roots in the soil" is a well-known phrase and people who say it generally mean that the man was born and reared in a country place. But the real soil in which a man's roots are is the soil of common experience. You can follow the tracks of the writer whose feet are in that soil – Blake, Wordsworth, Milton, Shelley or Yeats – their clay trail is the trail we can follow. ... However high they raised their mystical heads they all had their feet on the clay earth. (Kavanagh 2003:207)

As this suggests, rootedness does not imply a renunciation of the mystical or transcendent (it is interesting that he chose Protestant radicals as his models); it simply means that any epiphany will work only if grounded in clay-bound language. Kavanagh criticizes one writer for not quite being authentic, for rushing to the unreal, by claiming, "What makes his work deceptive is the fact that he is very nearly on the earth. He is ... about an inch from the top of the grass" (Kavanagh 2003:209).

For Kavanagh, reality and timelessness are interrelated, but their relationship is vexed. The naive Maguire wishes for a Blakean form of plenitude everywhere: "In a crumb of bread the whole mystery is" (72). But when his fields fail to deliver, this leads to a heightened sense of negation in which nature seems bereft of any meaning whatsoever:

> From the raged road surface a boy picks up
> A piece of gravel and stares at it – and then
> He flings it across the elm tree on to the railway.
> It means nothing,
> Not a damn thing.

(71)

Part of the crisis in *The Great Hunger* stems from the difficulty in negotiating between these poles: "All or nothing. And it was nothing" (72). Yet the poem, if not Maguire, is also able to look beyond such apocalypticism towards a more contingent mode of apprehending divinity: "God is in the bits and pieces of Everyday – / A kiss here and a laugh again, and sometimes tears, / A pearl necklace round the neck of poverty" (72). And this more provisional grasp of the numinous underwrites the emerging comedic element of *The Great Hunger*, and enriches the best of Kavanagh's other lyrics.

With the abandonment of "all or nothing" absolutism, the commonplace comes to be endowed with wonder, or at least the potential for it. Ordinary fields and workaday objects no longer need be scorned. At times, the transcendent surprises; at other times, it is bequeathed through the poet's authority: "Gods make their own importance" (184). In the best poems, this occurs not through egotistical will but through poetic technique, which Kavanagh referred to as love. Nevertheless, the curse of negation is still vital to Kavanagh's mature comedic vision. Because it is fueled by pastoral idealism, the poet's field of vision had promised paradise. Its actual fallen drabness was therefore felt as a curse of damnation. But now it can be redeemed in verse through love, or technique. Innocence is rediscovered through the portals of experience. Crucial to this poetic is the element of contingency, already noted in "To the Man After the Harrow," as Kavanagh's textured language is voltaged by an open-endedness as to what a poem's imagery might ultimately signify, bestowing a fertile strangeness on normality. He seeks to catch the "newness" in "every stale thing"; "the difference that sets an old phrase burning" (111).

This style found its high point in eighteen poems written in the second half of 1957, which Kavanagh ultimately regarded as his finest work. Having recovered from an operation for lung cancer in 1955, he had spent the first half of 1957 in New York, where he evidently enjoyed, and felt affiliated with, much new American poetry. Kavanagh's so-called "noo pomes" are lithe with improvisatory energy: fusions of spontaneity and incantation, sensuality and epiphany, throwaway slackness and sonnet-tight certitude. With a sense of swoop and surprise, some of them crucially transplant Kavanagh's pastoral vision to the city. His message was that the subject matter did not matter. A hospital could be as Edenic as any hill or field. Indeed, "The Hospital" proclaims, "nothing whatever is by love debarred" (217), echoing "Innocence": "I knew that love's doorway to life / Is the same doorway everywhere" (183). Kavanagh expanded, "Real roots lie in our capacity for love and its abandon. The material itself has no special value; it is what our imagination and our love do to it" (Kavanagh 2003:273).

Despite this utopianism, Kavanagh's relationship with the city was cantankerous. He is famous for dismissing the ideal of nationalism: "A common passport is not a common ground" (185); "Irishness is a form of anti-art" (291). Yet he freely made use of other forms of crude social groupings, often venting prejudice through such generalizations. Meanwhile, for all his insistent independence, he was clearly obsessed with an ideal of the bard as a communal spokesperson. Sometimes, through his desire to be popular, he hit a populist bullseye. From "On Raglan Road" (immortalized by the singer Luke Kelly) to "Spring Day," folk work constitutes a major part of his legacy, and demonstrates a formal range and dexterity he is rarely credited with. But he often strained to show his common touch, and much of his oeuvre lacks the linguistic charge and imaginative force of his best work. Having tried two other socially representative long poems, contemporaneous with *The Great Hunger* ("Why Sorrow?" and "Lough Derg"), the social aspect of his verse broadly degenerated into misfiring satire and sour grapes. He became obsessed with kicking against the pricks: "The most immoral place of all / Is the middle of the road" (140); "Malice is only another name for mediocrity" (Kavanagh 2003:244). And while such preoccupations were probably laudable given the cultural dilapidations of his time, his verse frequently fixates merely on the idea of the Poet, tilting attention away from poetry onto a tired and vacuous cult of personality.

For all that, Kavanagh brought to Irish poetry a hugely enabling can-do spirit. A moribund Dublin culture could be redeemed in the same way that Monaghan's stony grey fields could be. Just as pastoral symbolism had to be shattered and then rebuilt, free from formulas and stereotypes, so Irish writing at large needed to interrogate its stock images and habits. However, just as Kavanagh's innocence could only viably function through experience, his fierce individuality likewise relied upon broader cultural vistas. He famously wrote, "The provincial has no mind of his own; he does not trust what his eyes see until he has heard what the metropolis – towards which his eyes are turned – has to say on any subject"; while, by contrast, the "parochial mentality ... is never in any doubt about the social and artistic validity of his parish" (Kavanagh 2003:237). But this is not quite accurate. On the evidence of Kavanagh's own work, parochial artists feed off the metropolis, but then must learn to assert their individuality in order to make their art authentic. In "Epic" the validity of the parish is asserted through the example of Homer. Thus, behind Kavanagh's rhetoric, metropolitan culture is not rejected, but is instead reconstituted to foreground self-empowerment. In essence, Kavanagh's poetic reasserts the primacy of individuality over communality, yet remains bound to the broader culture.

One lost ballad of Kavanagh's, "The Battle of the Palace Bar," recounted the legend of a mêlée over Louis MacNeice in 1939: a "wild hooey ... over Louis." A fist-fight broke out after Austin Clarke had dismissed the Ulsterman: "Let him go back and labour for Faber and Faber." As Quinn relates, Kavanagh wrote:

> They fought like barbarians, those highbrow grammarians,
> As I have recorded for the future to hear.

And in no other land could a battle so grand
Have been fought over poetry, but in Ireland my dear!

(Quinn 2003:127)

Kavanagh was notoriously dismissive of his peers, but made a striking exception for MacNeice. Quinn recounts a meeting between Kavanagh, towards the end of his life, with a young Eavan Boland: "His conversation was a 'catalogue of dismissals' for, while well disposed to younger poets, he was scornful of those of his own generation. One exception was Louis MacNeice. MacNeice was a king, he told her" (Quinn 2003:437).

Despite this, MacNeice's poetic beginnings could not have been more different from Kavanagh's. MacNeice begins "In quiet in diet in riot in dreams" (MacNeice 2007:19; all citations of MacNeice's poetry refer to this edition unless otherwise noted). His early verse is a harlequinade of sensory bombardment and linguistic self-excitement, mostly prancing, but sometimes dancing: "The corpses blink in the rush of the river, and out of the water their chins they tip / And quaff the gush and lip the draught and crook their heads and crow" (623). It is in thrall to the touch, taste, and smell of things, enrapt by a light-sensitive visual vivacity, orchestrated by sonic fixations. Everything is already aestheticized: "The garden to-night is all Renoir and Keats" (621). The verse becomes snide in its self-delight, and the hedonism heralds its own vacuity: "You are a hole in a strawberry net / And strings divide the you that is me from the me that is you, / And it is all rather a tedium and a sweat" (663).

Histories of 1920s poetry tend to emphasize the influence of Ezra Pound's call for hard-edged objective verse, shorn of adjectival mellifluence. They tend to emphasize a turn towards elliptical perplexity. But MacNeice's juvenilia show scant interest in terse constraint. Instead he welcomes back euphony and prosodic excess. From the beginning he claims the whole of the harmonium of language as his resource. His early writings are already distinguished by the hallmarks of his mature work: dynamic swerving of one line into another, impulsive use of internal rhyming for rhythmic propulsion, rollicking repetitions, syntactic elasticity, and metrical dexterity impelled by anapestic momentum. Moreover, the juvenilia's obsession with the interconnections between the fun of language and the futility of language signals a dialectic between energy and negation, being and non-being, that will run through his larger oeuvre. All MacNeice needed was some content.

As mentioned, he initially made his name as a Thirties poet. Like many labels, the idea of Thirties poetry seems straightforward from a distance, but when inspected more closely the definition becomes hazy. MacNeice himself defined his generation through its repudiation of aesthetic involution, passivity, and "disinterest" (traits which, once rigidified as stylistic norms, had become the more tepid inheritance of modernism), to be driven instead by an awareness that the contemporary climate demanded politicized engagement. MacNeice argued that "it is the poet's job to make sense of the world, to simplify it, to put shape on it" (MacNeice 1938:191). Coming to such a view, MacNeice found his voice when he left Oxford for Birmingham, a job, marriage, and parenthood (and, very swiftly, marital break-up). He found his voice in a historical environment shaped by the yin of rising communism, the yang of reactionary fascism, and the erosion of the liberal middle ground, in the midst of economic depression following the Wall Street crash of 1929. He found his voice when he began confronting his alienation from his native Irish culture. In the early 1930s his voice was forged, as it were, in the furnace of these combusting contexts.

At first glance, it might seem that his awakening social conscience involved a rejection of the surface glamour of his juvenilia. Arguing against putting style before content, he writes, "the poet's first business is *mentioning* things" (MacNeice 1938:5). The problem with putting style before content is that it can lead towards an evasion of life as it is lived: the world before your eyes and in your ears. This can in turn lead towards the solipsism and nausea of the prison-house of the self. It can lead towards riding roughshod over actuality, warping or disregarding things as they are. At its most insidious, it can lead to an identification of individuals as types, and to the mass manipulation synonymous with Hitler, Stalin, and other regimes of the 1930s on their march towards catastrophic horror. In this context, major motifs of Thirties poetry came to involve ideas of poetry as socio-political diagnosis and historical witness. MacNeice's verse ticks all these boxes, yet the simple root of his social conscience stems from this commitment to the world, to "*mentioning* things," as a means of checking self-infatuation and arrogance.

Thus MacNeice finds his voice by letting the pressure and presence of reality press back against his will to form, and his verse is accordingly jam-packed and brimful with detail, stuffed full of stuff: street scenes, consumables, fashions, the inner city and the open fields. His verse gives us "the thrumming of telephone wires" (13), "steam-organs, thigh-rub and cream-soda" (16), a "suburban clatter" in which "the lawn-mower sings" (27). He specializes in lists of things that seem fit to burst out of themselves: "the proud glass of shops / Cubical scent-bottles artificial legs arctic foxes and electric mops" (22). His work is notable for its poems of place: "Birmingham," "Carrickfergus," "The Hebrides," "Dublin," "Cushendun." He specializes in panoramas of exactitude and abundance, which typically zoom from wide-screen vistas to minute particulars, then swoop back out again with surging momentum. All of this comes to a head in his long poem *Autumn Journal*, which Michael Longley claims is "the apotheosis of MacNeice's desire to fit everything in" (Longley 1988:xviii). One of MacNeice's foremost legacies, in such verse, lies in his making a recognizably bourgeois "everyday" the lyric's field of action, rather than its detached subject matter.

While MacNeice certainly valued the concrete over the abstract, he leaves no room for callow anti-intellectualism. The world of "things" involves thinking about them, and his verse counterpoints a music of things with a music of thought, creating a richly interwoven fabric – a dance of object and subject, fact and possibility. Moreover, his fidelity to the actual is both ignited by and orchestrated through his heady stylization. A poem is not a poem if it is a passive record of things; it must be a new creation in itself. Fundamental to his poetics is a split at the core of poetry, as it simultaneously records and creates, or refers and reconstitutes. Thus the flair of his early writing is in no way abandoned. His obsessions with tactility, light, color, and sound-effects remain crucial. We read of "light delicate as the chink of coins" (13); a "lurid sky over stained water / Where hammers clang murderously" (25); "yellow merriment; cackle of ripples; / Lips of the river that pout and whisper round the reeds" (31). As "Ode" would have it:

> Coral azalea and scarlet rhododendron
> Syringa and pink horse-chestnut and laburnum
> Solid as temples, niched with the song of birds,
> Widen the eyes and nostrils, demand homage of words.

(35)

For this "homage of words" to be authentic, verse must reflect the way the world impresses "On the tongue on the eyes on the ears in the palms of one's hands," in order to re-create the primal sensation that "World is crazier and more of it than we think" (24). Fronting up to actuality, MacNeice's verse gives us back a new version of reality, reconfigured in the dreamtime of the poem.

Nevertheless, MacNeice became somewhat cagey about style. In a sense, his early proclivity for hyper-stylization is carried over like a hangover into the Thirties, as his poetry opens its eyes to "a precise dawn / Of sallow and grey bricks, and newsboys crying war" (28), with its head still swimming from the bright lights and after-effects of bourgeois self-indulgence. Sensory abandon becomes nauseous, with "lights irritating and gyrating and rotating in gauze" (3). Rhythmic rhyming becomes tainted with exhaustion, the dissipated "surface vanity" (11) of the advertising jingle: "where we feel / That we know in advance all the jogtrot and the cake-walk jokes, / All the bumfun and the gags of comedians in boaters and toques" (6). Funhouse rhymes and reeling musicality engage with a self-parodic milieu, as MacNeice's trademark propulsion becomes mimetic of the velocity and vapidity of capitalism: "Mrs Carmichael had her fifth, looked at the job with repulsion, / Said to the midwife 'Take it away; I'm through with over-production'" (95).

Yet a crucial aspect of MacNeice is his refusal to detach himself and criticize from some vantage point of presumed innocence. He is frequently in thrall to what he condemns, intoxicated by modernity's "beauty narcotic and deciduous" (5), which gives his verse its pivotal sense of complicity. The poems often address a communal "us" or "we" (who must either sober up or lighten up, depending on the context), rather than a finger-wagging "you" or "they." More paradoxically, there is frequently little to distinguish between the good and the vacuous: "Sharp sun-strop, surface-gloss, and momentary caprice / These are what we cherish" (26). At the core of his poetic is a love of flux and pizzazz: "Let us too make our time elastic and / Inconsequently dance above the dazzling wave" (32). Yet such an ideal seems dangerously close to the flippancy of "I don't care always in the air / Give my hips a shake always on the make / Always on the mend coming around the bend" (77).

Excessive style leads to a closed-off system: a self-containment disenfranchised from reality; vacuity and deadness. But a lack of style leads to circumscribed passivity: a disengagement from reality; banality and deadness. Much of MacNeice's verse negotiates between these poles. Many poems involve a kind of dialectical movement. "Train to Dublin" begins in the torpor of a train carriage, with mechanized monotony and the imprisonment of a predestined journey, but then breaks free to roam with creative plenty:

> I give you the incidental things which pass
> Outward through space exactly as each was.
>
> I give you the disproportion between labour spent
> And joy at random; the laughter of the Galway sea.
>
> (17–18)

By contrast, "Sunday Morning" moves in the opposite direction, as bourgeois freedom swiftly becomes closed off like "a sonnet self-contained in rhyme," and the poem turns to shatter its own illusions: "there is no music or movement which secures / Escape from weekday time. Which deadens and endures" (21). In such ways, MacNeice's verse swings from freedom to negation, negation to freedom. Much of his dialectical tension involves the nature of time. Indeed, MacNeice is obsessed by time. Yet time and style are ultimately aspects of a metaphysical continuum: a realm of ever-threatening petrifaction and death; a realm of intuited freedom and possibility; the realm in which we abide.

What is key to MacNeice is the way in which stylistic tensions are continuous with existential struggles, which, in turn, become continuous with his poetry's sense of politics. Style intrinsically binds individuality with culture and history. Style's fusion with subject matter creates an inherently dramatic field of force: a moral theater of open-ended scrutiny. What he most often attacks is bourgeois self-absorption, the illusion of individual autonomy. He writes, "try and confine your / Self to yourself if you can" (143). Individuals must confront alienation and death. There may be nothing one can do to avert these, yet one cannot ignore them. In a similar manner, society must confront inequality and injustice. Bad style becomes synonymous with ideological failure, while disempowering time become synonymous with impending war. Social reality, metaphysics, and poetic style all contain the seeds of negation within themselves. There can be no transcendence. And yet poetry can nevertheless act as a beacon, to the extent that authentic style involves a simultaneous vigilance and embrace, a combustion of self and otherness, shaping will and shifting content: a pact and balance that must be constantly renewed.

MacNeice wrote, "The faith in the *value* of living is a mystical faith. The pleasure in bathing or dancing, in colour or shape, is a mystical experience. If non-utilitarian activity is abnormal, then all men are abnormal" (MacNeice 1967:16). Ultimately, his verse upholds a buoyant conception of such faith through its vim and resourcefulness. His lines have a singing clarity, affective wit, and memorability that are infectious and affirming. One takes from MacNeice, first and foremost, pleasure in the enduring imprint made by poems such as "Bagpipe Music" and "Meeting Point." One is haunted by the sensation of recurrence, scrutiny, and probity that flows through the repetitions and sonorities of a great many of his lyrics.

Yet his faith in the value of living was tested by Ireland. Particularly in "Valediction" and "Canto XVI" of *Autumn Journal*, MacNeice condemned Ireland as a land of fear and loathing, damned by its culture of hypocrisy and callous violence: "I envy the intransigence of my own / Countrymen who shoot to kill and never / See the victim's face become their own" (137). These poems are prismatic, flowing, impressionistic and flamboyant panoramas. Yet, as Edna Longley points out, they also manage to contain "specific economic, social and political analysis" (Longley 1988:21). "Canto XVI," she argues, indicts the North for "unemployment, inequality, an offshore economy, irresponsible capitalism, injustice and repression," while the "Free State's sins" include "censorship, doctrinaire Gaelicization, environmental vandalism [and] selective sympathy for 'the souls of the killed' after the Civil War" (Longley 1988:21, 24). Yet this diagnostic analysis in the poem is somehow made emotionally searing. Longley claims that, for MacNeice, "Ireland functions as an anti-Utopia, a kind of social and political original sin" (Longley 1986:70). But this wellspring of negation is intensely personalized, a gravitational vortex of compulsive and alienated self-identification: "Curséd be he that curses his mother. I cannot be / Anyone else than what this land engendered me" (8).

In "Valediction" he proclaimed, "Farewell, my country, and in perpetuum" (9). Always self-knowing, each time he dismissed Ireland he instinctively recoiled to counterpoint the act with a reassertion of disturbed affiliation. He was hyper-responsive to Irish landscapes and skylines, which contributed to the fluidly sensuous vivacity of his poetry. His parents were from the west, and he is haunted by its coastlines. The existential-ecological exploration of "Western Landscape," in particular, provides a soaring complement to Kavanagh's poetics of innocence. But fundamentally, his relationship with his homeland reflected his relationship with himself. His exile doubled as a form of integral self-estrangement. His sense of home was infected by what his biographer Jon Stallworthy described as his conviction "at some psychological level that he was responsible for his mother's illness and death" (Stallworthy 1995:37). Meanwhile, he was equally troubled by his father: "My father made the walls resound, / He wore his collar the wrong way round" (200).

For a long time, MacNeice remained driven by his quest for responsible vision, ethical balance, and rational optimism. Arguably, however, by the 1950s his verse had become stale: "This middle stretch / Of life is bad for poets" (349). Yet his oeuvre was then capped by a remarkable late bloom, fueled by a dramatic stylistic swerve. Throughout his career, as if haunted by the fantasia of his early work, hallucinogenic hints had lurked within his lyrics; the loops and swerves of his lines, at times, took on the pallor of motion sickness. Surrealistic qualities had become more pronounced in some of his World War II poems, and this deregulated sensibility fused with the mordancy of poems such as "Autobiography" and "Prayer before Birth" to create the extraordinary effects of his last two collections: *Solstices* and *The Burning Perch*.

Throughout the Thirties, the idea of time as perpetual motion had counteracted the idea of time as a stone-dead wall of finality. In *Autumn Journal*, it had seemed a good thing that "no river is a river that does not flow" (102). But in "Variation on Heraclitus," where "Even the walls are flowing, even the ceiling," the idea of flux has become flummoxing (560). Here, MacNeice's virtuoso rhythms and syntax create a perturbed momentum, tinged with nausea, as if the poem is trying to catch up with its own sense: "none of your slide snide rules can catch what is sliding so fast" (560). In earlier poems, repetitions had been used for dynamic propulsion and rhetorical structure, lifting moments of remembrance out of time. In the late poems, by contrast, repetition creates claustrophobia and paranoiac disjuncture. Having stated that "Reappearance presumes disappearance," "Variation on Heraclitus" concludes, "One cannot live in the same room twice"; and the late poems obsessively manipulate the uncanny duality of sameness and transformation bound up in repetition (560).

Discussing MacNeice's syntax, Edna Longley argues that whereas *Autumn Journal* had been a poem of conjunction, with its huge proliferation of "and ... and ... ands," the late poetry comes to be dominated by asyndeton: the omission of conjunctions. This asyndeton creates effects of compression and fragmentation; and so, while the style of *Autumn Journal* produced a "rationally interconnected sentence," asyndeton "seems allied to some of the jumps of 'dream logic'," and these late poems suggest "there are black holes rather than cosmic links between phenomena" (Longley 1988:127–28). Through this chimerical syntax, meaning and even reality slide through the fissures between the poems' constant departures and returns. In "Soap Suds," a "brand of soap" provokes an involuntary reminiscence of childhood. But memory slips practically become body shifts as MacNeice twists this conventional scenario to create a radical destabilization of identity. Indeed, the poem's disquieting formal innovation seems to bend the very rules of time and space, as reality becomes a bad dream, a mind not in control of itself.

MacNeice had always been sensitive to the phantasmagoria of commodification, but in these late poems the dissolution of solidity becomes rampant and the world of objects appears categorically estranged. In "Flower Show," the flowers turn their sights on the speaker, overturning the normal subject–object flow of engagement, and fervidly overpowering the subjective gaze as normality becomes a nightmare:

> Squidlike, phallic or vulvar, hypnotic, idiotic, oleaginous,
> Fanged or whalebones, wattled or balding, brimstone or cold
> As trout or seaweed, these blooms, ogling or baneful, all
> Keep him in their blind sights; he tries to stare them down
> But they are too many, too unreal.
>
> (582)

MacNeice had long exploited clichés, jingles, and snatches of song to create a familiar hum of communality, which his poems would then manipulate. Now, nursery-rhyme effects and nonsense refrains repeat arrhythmically, almost sinisterly, to create simultaneous recognition and disorientation (especially in the unforgettable "tra-la" of "The Taxis," and "Crawly crawly" of "The Introduction"). Ground-breaking prosodic invention creates a sensation that agency lies with weird impersonal forces, arbitrary and phobic, beyond subjective control. MacNeice's new sound-shapes thus forge original ways of representing the cultural embeddedness of consciousness. His technique also dramatizes how mind and society are framed by psychopathologies related to death and omniscient anxiety. In a Cold War context, MacNeice's trademark historical sense comes to be shaped by non-human evolutionary and cosmological perspectives: "the human / Race recedes and dwindles, the giant / Reptiles cackle in their graves, the mountain / Gorillas exchange their final messages" (602). Indeed, quite where the perspectives come from, in some of the poems, is unsettling. They seem to be framed beyond mortality. In the bad dream of culture and history, the death of individuality is not the end: "It was too late to die" (586); "If you want to die you will have to pay for it" (593).

In *Autumn Journal*, MacNeice had asked, "Why do we like being Irish?," and had answered, "because Ireland is small enough" (139). The implication was that Irish culture creates an illusion of normality and stability by apparently remaining free from globalization and its constant dissolution of tradition. Kavanagh's verse showed one way of dealing with the twentieth century's slow eradication of autonomy (since globalization merely does to the nation what nationalism does to the region: disenfranchising it and making it perplexingly unreal). MacNeice's last poems show another version of the historical moment. In them, the past seems to be ever present like the subconscious let loose in a dream, incessantly and phantasmagorically recycling itself, while the future seems to have already occurred. With this work, he created an authentic vision that leaves one bewitched, bedazzled, bemused, and more than a little alarmed.

REFERENCES AND FURTHER READING

Brown, T. (1975). *Louis MacNeice: Sceptical Vision*. Dublin: Gill & Macmillan.

Gillis, A. (2005). *Irish Poetry of the 1930s*. Oxford: Oxford University Press.

Heaney, S. (1980). *Preoccupations: Selected Prose 1968–1978*. London: Faber & Faber.

Heaney, S. (1988). *The Government of the Tongue*. London: Faber & Faber.

Kavanagh, P. (2000). *Tarry Flynn* (1948). London: Penguin.

Kavanagh, P. (2001). *The Green Fool* (1938). London: Penguin.

Kavanagh, P. (2003). *A Poet's Country: Selected Prose*. A. Quinn (Ed.). Dublin: Lilliput Press.

Kavanagh, P. (2005). *Collected Poems*. A. Quinn (Ed.). London: Penguin.

Longley, E. (1986). *Poetry in the Wars*. Newcastle upon Tyne: Bloodaxe.

Longley, E. (1988). *Louis MacNeice: A Study*. London: Faber & Faber.

Longley, M. (1988). "Introduction." In L. MacNeice. *Selected Poems* (pp. xiii–xxiii). London: Faber & Faber.

MacNeice, L. (1938). *Modern Poetry: A Personal Essay*. Oxford: Oxford University Press.

MacNeice, L. (1967). *The Poetry of W.B. Yeats* (1941). London: Faber & Faber.

MacNeice, L. (1987). *Selected Literary Criticism of Louis MacNeice*. A. Heuser (Ed.). Oxford: Clarendon Press.

MacNeice, L. (2007). *Collected Poems*. P. McDonald (Ed.). London: Faber & Faber.

Marsack, R. (1982). *The Cave of Making: The Poetry of Louis MacNeice*. Oxford: Clarendon Press.

McDonald, P. (1991). *Louis MacNeice: The Poet in his Contexts*. Oxford: Oxford University Press.

Quinn, A. (1991). *Patrick Kavanagh: Born Again Romantic*. Dublin: Gill & Macmillan.

Quinn, A. (2003). *Patrick Kavanagh: A Biography*. Dublin: Gill & Macmillan.

Smith, S. (Ed.). (2008). *Patrick Kavanagh*. Dublin: Irish Academic Press.

Stallworthy, J. (1995). *Louis MacNeice*. London: Faber & Faber.

40

Irish Mimes: Flann O'Brien

Joseph Brooker

Dry Chat

On January 27, 1944, the writer who called himself Flann O'Brien published the following in the *Irish Times*:

> "How rarely," says Mr Sean O'Faolain in the *Irish Times*, "one hears the name, today, of Henry James."
>
> Fair enough. (Though around in my place, Mr O'F., the crowd often speak of him Tuesday evenings, few friends in for a glass of sherry and some dry chat.)
>
> But my memory is as bad as the next. What actually was the name of Henry James? It's on the tip of my tongue. Shanachy or Shaughnessy or some name like that unless I'm very much mistaken. Willie James the brother I knew well. (O'Brien 1999:115)

This slice of writing has been picked almost at random, a vivid little side entrance to the oddly shaped edifice of Flann O'Brien's oeuvre. But I want to demonstrate how dense with interest this writer could be in even his briefest and apparently throwaway pieces – of which there were many. With a little attention the snippet starts to look emblematic, gathering favorite features and telling themes. They include the fact that this is not a piece of literature in the strictest sense, but a newspaper column: the form in which its author was most prolific. We note that he proceeds via engagement with another writer: public dialogue and provocation fuel the writing. Indeed the interlocutor himself wrote in the same newspaper as Flann O'Brien: this is a family tussle, with a writer whom O'Brien repeatedly baited but for whom he occasionally wrote copy.

A Companion to Irish Literature, edited by Julia M. Wright
© 2010 Blackwell Publishing Ltd

The vision of a Jamesian literary set casually gathering in Dublin is fanciful; its author's social life was conducted around the circuit of Dublin's pubs, not sherry-tippling soirées. But the fantasy bears scrutiny for its details. Tuesday evenings at which one speaks of Henry James sound reminiscent of the *mardis* that Stéphane Mallarmé held in Paris in the 1880s, occasionally attended by a figure closer to home: W.B. Yeats, who followed Mallarmé by establishing his own soirées on Mondays in London (Foster 1997:167). The parenthesis thus recalls the history of literary modernism, continental or Irish, and it is typical of Flann O'Brien to make casually knowing reference to that modern tradition while being clear that this is all, in fact, a way of gently needling the pretensions of his interlocutor. But if he is unserious about literary sophistication, his own language retains its subtlety. "Few friends in for a glass of sherry and some dry chat"? Of course it's the sherry that we would expect to be dry; but the writer has quietly shifted the adjective to the chat. It makes sense – the chat could easily be dry too – while slightly displacing the usual phrases. This is a man who finds it hard to leave a familiar form of words alone, without nudging it somewhere different or finding a way to frame and distance it. He does so, though, in the most blithely offhand manner: there is no real pretense of artistry here, just the gently parodic imitation of sophisticated nonchalance.

But the heart of the jest is in the third paragraph. "What actually was the name of Henry James?" – the question makes little sense, already containing its own correct answer. What would it mean for the name of Henry James to be different from "Henry James"? The point is really aimed at Seán O'Faoláin. Again studiously scrutinizing a combination of words, Flann O'Brien is taking the portentous terms of O'Faoláin's studied lament and making them look foolish, by suggesting that they logically imply something much more bizarre than what O'Faoláin meant. When O'Brien is in this mood it is difficult to get anything past him: almost any way in which O'Faoláin had elected to put his case could probably be driven into a muddle by the satirist's relentless literalism. The particular case is especially interesting, though. The best-known literary precedent is Lewis Carroll's *Through the Looking Glass* (1872), in which little Alice enters a fantastic alternative world based on the characters and conventions of a chess board. An aged White Knight offers to sing her a song, noting that "The name of the song is called '*Haddocks' Eyes*'." Alice asks, "Oh, that's the name of the song, is it?" No, the Knight replies, "That's what the name is *called*. The name really *is* '*The Aged Aged Man*'." It transpires also that the song (rather than its name) is called "*Ways and Means*," but "really *is*" "*A-Sitting On A Gate*" (Carroll 1994:187–88).

Carroll's Knight dismembers our sense of the relation of a thing to its name, driving unsuspected wedges between an object's true identity, its name, what it is called, and what the name is called. Something similarly bewildering is blithely at work in the column, where "Henry James," despite all appearances, is not the name of Henry James. To compare Flann O'Brien to Carroll is to emphasize the density of his play with logic, a play that can sometimes begin to unscrew the world as we know it even as he offhandedly pours the imaginary sherry. Carol Taaffe, in her recent study of O'Brien's work, makes much of the connection with Carroll and thus with "nonsense" writing in general (Taaffe 2008:69–77), while acknowledging that nonsense can make disturbing senses of its own.

James' alternative names are Irish: "Shanachy or Shaughnessy or some name like that." This could be a man in the pub, laying claim to half-forgotten knowledge: "Willie James the brother I knew well" is a characteristic formula, a piece of false familiarity with the famous from a writer in a small, crowded literary capital. Another oddity attends all this: the James family really were descended from Irish stock, their grandfather having emigrated from County Cavan to the United States in the late eighteenth century. It is hard to know whether Flann O'Brien knew what an odd grain of truth inhered in his fancy. But there is still a larger irony here. This entire skit about the multiplication and instability of names was written by a writer who played with names more inveterately than most. This column was not even published under the name "Flann O'Brien" but under the alter ego "Myles na gCopaleen," of which more in a moment. What actually was the name of Flann O'Brien? Not Shanachy or Shaughnessy or even na gCopaleen but Brian O'Nolan – a name which itself contained alternatives, whether dispensing with the O or taking on the Irish spelling Ó Nualláin. "Flann O'Brien" was first hit upon late in the 1930s, and appeared on the front of O'Nolan's first novel *At Swim-Two-Birds* (1939). The name, O'Nolan wrote to his publishers in November 1938, "contains an unusual name and one that is quite ordinary. 'Flann' is an old Irish name now rarely heard" (Cronin 1989:88).

There is more to be said about authorial identities, but for a moment let us take a cue from that novel, which regularly stops in its tracks and offers interruptive headings. One of them reads: "*Synopsis, being a summary of what has gone before*, FOR THE BENEFIT OF NEW READERS," followed by a list of characters and their actions in the plot (O'Brien 1967:60–61). For the benefit of readers new to Flann O'Brien, let us try a second opening to our story, in the form of a synopsis.

Being a Summary

Brian O'Nolan (1911–66) was a man from the North of Ireland who made himself an archetypal Dubliner. Through the 1930s, in collaboration with fellow graduates of University College Dublin, he produced comic projects such as the brilliant but short-lived magazine *Blather* (1934–35). Following his father's death in 1937, he supported his family financially by working in Ireland's civil service. Meanwhile, under what would become his best-known pen name, he sought to begin a career as Flann O'Brien, author of experimental fiction. The attempt was brilliant but brief. *At Swim-Two-Birds* was a remarkable debut, and initial praise from Graham Greene and James Joyce has remained in long use on its covers. His second novel, *The Third Policeman*, was an astonishing feat: written rapidly and intuitively, it unfurls one of literature's uncanniest physical and intellectual landscapes. Longmans, *At Swim*'s London publisher, rejected *The Third Policeman*. The author, their report declared, "should become less fantastic and in this new novel he is more so" (Cronin 1989:101). O'Nolan was abruptly confronted with a kind of failure, even if he had in fact just produced his masterpiece. With wounded evasiveness, he reeled off a variety of fanciful tales to tell his Dublin friends and rivals that the manuscript had been lost rather than dismissed. He feared that his career as a novelist was at an end, and indeed he would never again write such substantial and sustained work in the genre. He found an alternative creative outlet. In the summer of 1940 he orchestrated a series of parodic exchanges in the letters pages of the *Irish Times*. The newspaper's editor requested an audience with O'Nolan, and the result was a regular column, starting in October that year, and signed with the new pen name "Myles na gCopaleen." *Cruiskeen Lawn* (Irish for "the full little jug") was initially written in Irish, then wended its way over to a basis in the English language. It endured in the *Irish Times* for a quarter-century, becoming a fixture of national or at least metropolitan life. The column was a sideline to O'Nolan's day job in the civil service, until 1953 when ill health brought him compulsory retirement from the latter.

The 1940s did produce promising sidelines: *An Béal Bocht*, his satire of wide-eyed peasant memoirs, appeared in 1941 with Myles na gCopaleen fancifully named as editor, and O'Nolan made forays into the theater, notably *Faustus Kelly*, a political satire staged at the Abbey Theatre in 1943. But for the most part, extended works were beyond him for two decades. By the 1960s he was increasingly prone to illness and hospitalization. Yet his career held one last twist. In 1960 *At Swim-Two-Birds* was reissued in London. O'Nolan was now dismissive of his debut; but as though inspired by this vote of confidence, he mustered the energy to begin writing fiction again. Two novels, *The Hard Life* (1961) and *The Dalkey Archive* (1964), made him once more a contemporary novelist before his early death.

At this point O'Nolan's literary status was weaker and more uneven than his talents merited. *Cruiskeen Lawn* had made him a household pseudonym in Ireland, but his reputation abroad was patchy. The position altered after his widow Evelyn sent the manuscript of *The Third Policeman* to his London publisher, and the novel appeared at last in 1967. That book and *At Swim-Two-Birds* are now recognized as belonging in the Irish modernist company of Joyce and Beckett – or are treated as proleptic postmodern fictions, forerunners of Nabokov and Borges, Barth and Vonnegut. O'Nolan has meanwhile begun to receive his due in Irish studies, for his work and the country in which he lived can illuminate each other. In 1989 Anthony Cronin, an old acquaintance of O'Nolan's, published a biography which provided a fuller picture of the life and times; it remains unsurpassed, but has gradually been joined by new scholarship exploring the relations between O'Nolan's writing and his world (Curran 1997, 2001; Brooker 2004; Taaffe 2008).

The life of Flann O'Brien is easily enough told. It has many points of interest, but little sudden drama: in an inversion of the willful exile of Joyce and Beckett, he hardly even left Ireland after the 1930s. But all this is more properly the life behind or beneath "Flann O'Brien," not to mention Myles na gCopaleen. If the life lacks adventure, the writing does not lack life. A large part of this writer's career is the forging in language of selves, voices, and worlds quite other than those of the quiet man in the hat in the corner of the Scotch House – though he finds his way into the writing too. A return to the question of names may illuminate this multiplicity.

Impostures

In comic magazines of the 1930s, O'Nolan had already posed as one "Brother Barnabas," or as an employee of the proprietor the O'Blather. 1940 brought Myles na gCopaleen, a name snatched from Dion Boucicault's play *The Colleen Bawn* (1860), itself an adaptation of Gerald Griffin's novel *The Collegians* (1829) (see CHAPTER 28, DION BOUCICAULT). It was apt that O'Nolan's most persistent, prolific authorial identity should derive from two levels of intertextuality. Like his real name, this one's transcription was elastic. With deliberate Gaelic pedantry, he spelled the surname with a small g and capital C. The sliver of yet another name emerged when *Cruiskeen Lawn* went over exclusively to English and Myles began to hope for international recognition: now he was Myles na Gopaleen, with the plainer capital G. To that extent there were at least three major identities in play: Brian O'Nolan, Flann O'Brien, Myles na gCopaleen, and their variants. Yet in an autobiographical piece late in life O'Nolan suggested that a writer, outdoing T.S. Eliot's cats, might need even more than three names:

> [In] 25 years I have written ten books (that is, substantial opera) under four quite irreconcilable pen-names and on subjects absolutely unrelated. Five of those books could be described as works of imagination, one of world social comment, two on scientific subjects, one of literary exploration and conjecture, one in Irish and one a play (which was produced by the Abbey Theatre). (Cronin 1989:225)

It is characteristic of O'Nolan that, as he claims to be telling the unembellished truth about himself, he pulls from his sleeve four books which biographers have been unable to locate. In an intriguing passage in the same text he makes a more programmatic demand:

> [A writer] must have an equable yet versatile temperament, and the compartmentation of his personality for the purpose of literary utterance ensures that the fundamental individual will not be credited with a certain way of thinking, fixed attitudes, irreversible techniques of expression. No author should write under his own name nor under one permanent pen-name; a male writer should include in his impostures a female pen-name, and possibly vice-versa. (Cronin 1989:225)

Pen names, it seems, protect the real self beneath them from being typecast. O'Nolan would sometimes refer to his personae as discrete individuals: when Cronin suggested, in the 1950s, that he publish a novel under the old name "Flann O'Brien," O'Nolan replied "I don't know that fellow any longer" (Cronin 1989:197). But writer and persona might not be so swiftly dissociated. In John Wyse Jackson's formulation, "For the first ten years, say, between 1930 and 1940, he was seeking a voice. During the next ten years or so, he had found it. After about 1950, he had become that voice" (O'Brien 1989:8). The mask of Myles became hard to remove, or to distinguish from any underlying face. But at his best O'Nolan became more himself, and more than himself, in writing. Even late in his life he was still planting new names: his columns for the *Southern Star* (1955–56) were signed John James Doe, and those for the *Nationalist and Leinster Times* (1960–66) attributed to George Knowall. But the suddenest blitz of guises, female impostures and all, was in the letter-column controversies of 1940.

The debates were staged by O'Nolan and a small number of Dublin friends, mainly through the summer of 1940. As we have just seen, they proved pivotal in O'Nolan's life, as they won him a place in the *Irish Times* which made him money rather than costing him on stamps. Otherwise they look like a by-way in his career – and were largely unavailable to a contemporary reading public until Jackson's invaluable edition of early work – but they can also be viewed as exemplary of his comic intelligence and practice.

O'Nolan, then in his late twenties, and friends would ambush a serious contribution to the newspaper with a barrage of epistolary commentary and critique that became ever more preposterous. One synthetic spat took its occasion from a production of Chekhov's *Three Sisters*, another from a book review by Patrick Kavanagh. The correspondents make reference to these given terms, but in a series of lengthy missives which spiral off into erudite digression and patent fantasy (O'Brien 1989:186–226). In pompous, ornate rhetoric, "F. O'Brien" and his correspondents discuss the Boy Scout movement, the state of the Dublin sewers, and the (reimagined) private lives of Joseph Conrad or Henrik Ibsen, tenuously affecting to refer to the original matter in hand while being in fact flagrantly impertinent. One F. MacEwe Obarn (surely Niall Montgomery, a long-standing associate who fancied himself a Joycean) writes a letter in the style of Joyce's *Finnegans Wake*, published the previous year; "Lanna Avia" (another *Wakean* name) writes a letter backwards; a chemically enhanced "Na_2Co_3" signs off "Yours (in solution)." The editor of the *Irish Times*, R.M. Smyllie, picks up the trail and makes his own contribution as "(The) O'Madan," while the mysterious Oscar Love in Blackrock ends each haughty letter with a poem. Evidently not all of these figures were Brian O'Nolan, but he was behind some of Lir O'Connor and his sister Luna, Whit Cassidy, Paul Desmond, "F.L.J.," N.S. Harvey, Judy Clifford, Jno. O'Ruddy, and (Mrs) Hilda Upshott. This writer whose names would have so many variants never took on so many alter egos as here – even while part of the point is that we cannot be certain exactly how many came from his hand.

Jackson calls the phoney epistolary controversy a "new art form" (O'Brien 1989:186), and we should indeed consider the peculiar genre that confronts its reader. It is no unified work, just a chance collection of scraps to be placed in chronological sequence. It has no predetermined order: it is a text whose end its first author cannot foresee. Yet the controversy possesses a shaky continuity: the comic spirit that runs through the whole is a signal asking not only to be received and interpreted correctly, but to be appropriated and redirected by the reader who gets the joke. The fake controversy is built on the vagaries of the public textual space offered by the newspaper: it structurally allows for the unforeseen digression and the uninvited guest.

The epistolary controversies can be viewed as a distraction from more substantial writing. By that very token, they can also be viewed as exemplary moments in the career of a writer who diverted himself into a newspaper column for fully twenty years. The formal features noted above – comedy, fragmentation, the occupation of public space, the openness to contingency – are characteristic of this writer, but find as pure a realization here as anywhere. With their preposterous names and projected voices, the *Irish Times* debates also tease at the conventions of authorship. These are stretched further still in Flann O'Brien's first novel.

Out of Control

After the Luftwaffe bombed a warehouse holding Longmans' copies of *At Swim-Two-Birds*, Brian O'Nolan blamed Hitler for his failure to become a celebrated writer. Yet *At Swim* was never going to be an easy book for public consumption, even if, to its author's delight, it held *Gone with the Wind* off the Dublin bestseller spot for one week. The novel is a metafiction, a crafty exploration of storytelling: it contains multiple narratives, one held inside the other, the relations between them uncertain. The first-person frame is voiced by an unnamed Dublin student who is writing a novel, from which he periodically reads to his friends. The novel concerns an author, Dermot Trellis, who considers himself a moralist and is practicing a form of literary aversion therapy, by writing a novel of behavior so unwholesome that it will deter the public from sin. Trellis' book is not written in the usual way, with characters simply invented and maneuvered by the author. Instead, within the world of the student's novel, characters are more like actors: independent entities who are paid to take part in fiction. As the student explains in a cod-manifesto:

> Each [character] should be allowed a private life, self-determination and a decent standard of living. This would make for self-respect, contentment and better service. ... Characters should be interchangeable as between one book and another. The entire corpus of existing literature should be regarded as a limbo from which discerning authors could draw their characters as required, creating only when they failed to find a suitable existing puppet. The modern novel should be largely a work of reference. (O'Brien 1967:25)

That last line would prove pertinent to much of O'Nolan's writing. Trellis, meanwhile, employs such disparate "puppets" as Dublin cowboys, the legendary hero Finn MacCool (see CHAPTER 2, FINN AND THE FENIAN TRADITION), and the Pooka MacPhellimey, an Irish folk-devil who engages in superbly pedantic dialogue with a

Good Fairy. When he cannot hire a character from another book, he creates one through the scientific technique of "aestho-autogamy," in which characters are born fully grown. The method, the student notes, could solve "many social problems of contemporary interest" and save on the cost of child-rearing; it is also a parody of every novelist's practice (O'Brien 1967:40–41).

Crewed by its impossible ensemble of hired and created characters, *At Swim* tacks between literary modes: the incongruous yarn of the Ringsend rustlers, the ancient feats narrated by Finn MacCool, and the melancholy verse of mad King Sweeny, another figure from Irish legend. (O'Nolan, expert in Irish, produced for the character his own sensitive renditions of the original poetry.) *At Swim* contains many stories, but it is also about storytelling. It cuts frequently back and forth between the "frame" story and the fictional worlds that lie within it; it invents bizarre new rules for the relations between (fictional) author, text, and characters, then abruptly alters them, pulling the rug out from under the reader.

The student's frame story might have made a colorful *Bildungsroman*, but this prospect is blocked as the narrating prose is kept purposefully cold and aloof. The young layabout tells the story with perversely robotic precision: "I perused a number of public notices attached to the wall and then made my way without offence to the back of the College, where there was another ruined College containing an apartment known as the Gentleman's Smokeroom. This room was usually occupied by card-players, hooligans and rough persons" (O'Brien 1967:34). In this manner the style refuses the seductive warmth of the youthful memoir. But it can be stranger still. It regularly interrupts itself with italicized factual digressions. Invited out for a drink, the student warns that he is "no Rockefeller" – "thus utilizing a figure of speech to convey the poverty of my circumstances." The narrative halts and observes, "*Nature of figure of speech:* Synecdoche (or Autonomasia)" (46). It is as though *At Swim* is already a critical edition of itself, studded with scholarly annotations.

But its other layers are what make it such a circus. A central event in the student's manuscript is the birth of Trellis' illegitimate son, Orlick – who arrives, perhaps unsurprisingly in this book, not as a baby but as a "stocky young man" in "dark well-cut clothing," his first words a piece of oratorical eloquence (145–46). The other characters – notably the "plain men" Furriskey, Shanahan, and Lamont – are by now chafing under Trellis' regime, and seek to punish him for their poor treatment. Having drugged Trellis into sleep, they thus persuade Orlick – who has inherited Trellis' literary gifts – to take up the author's pen and seize command of his father's story. What follows is Orlick's manuscript: a radical departure in which we see the author, Trellis, turned into a character in someone else's text. The move relates to everyday metaphors about storytelling: it literalizes the idea that characters can "take on a life of their own" and hence come to redirect the writing process. As Brinsley says of his friend the student, "the plot has him well in hand" (99).

A story can also be tussled over or repeatedly requisitioned. When Orlick puts down his pen for a trip to the bathroom, Shanahan and Furriskey in turn pick it up, and the novel's world is promptly reshaped by their hands and the limits of their prose (181–83). The characters' glee at seeing Trellis mauled by the Pooka and hauled before a judge and jury is not an imaginary compensation for his treatment of them: it is an actual revenge, which is intended to lead to his physical destruction. The traditional idea of the curse – a performative piece of language which could inflict damage on its recipient – is part of the fate of King Sweeny described in *At Swim*: it is also renewed in the novel's sense of narrative as an offensive weapon.

The novel's narrative levels thus implode into one another. The book as a fractured whole combines an impulse toward intricate coherence, and a tendency willfully to tumble into turmoil. If its layers seem to open ingeniously onto one another, its pages also frequently open themselves to any old thing, like the *"Mail from V. Wright"* (37) which suddenly spills racing tips all over the page. The letter really existed: Niall Sheridan gave it to Brian O'Nolan, who promptly incorporated it into his book. As Cronin records, other documents that came O'Nolan's way enjoyed the same fate (Cronin 1989:85). "The modern novel," we recall, "should be largely a work of reference" (O'Brien 1967:25), edited together from other texts whenever possible, and if the student's manuscript is one instance of this principle, *At Swim* itself is another. O'Nolan signed his own typescript not as author but as "Chief Controller" (Taaffe 2008:38). The book can seem anything but controlled – which only emphasizes how radical this writer's conception of authorship could be.

If *At Swim* is structurally intricate, it is also texturally rich. O'Nolan revels in the recording of certain classes of Dublin speech, unerringly heard and lovingly recycled into comedy:

> Do you know what it is, said Furriskey, you can drown me three times before you roast me. Yes, by God and six. Put your finger in a basin of water. What do you feel? Next to nothing. *But put your finger in the fire!* (O'Brien 1967:155)

This is also the novel that conjures Jem Casey, the proletarian poet who penned the verse:

> In time of trouble and lousy strife,
> You have still got a darlint plan,
> You still can turn to a brighter life –
> A PINT OF PLAIN IS YOUR ONLY MAN.
>
> (77)

This doggerel remains Brian O'Nolan's best-known piece of writing; it turned out to be superbly memorable and recitable in an age of advertising slogans and Irish heritage trails. The plain men's appreciation of the "pome" is itself a delight of dialect and rhythm, from a writer who admitted late in life that he had "made something of a fetish of Dublin speech": all the more so because it was usually "botched" by people who "didn't know how to listen" (Cronin 1989:237). O'Nolan, in the ludic tradition of Samuel Beckett or Paul Muldoon, delighted in games, ironies, forms; but his work would also repeatedly return to a base in the local dialects that he alternately cherished and derided.

In Any Event Indescribable

Speech and voices also distinguish Flann O'Brien's second novel, but here they sound not so much overheard and recorded as fantasized and distorted. A "tricky man" met on the road ("He was tricky and smoked a tricky pipe and his hand was quavery. His eyes were tricky also, probably from watching policemen") inveighs against life itself, "for there is a queer small utility in it. You cannot eat it or drink it or smoke it in your pipe, it does not keep the rain out and it is a poor armful in the dark if you strip it and take it to bed with you after a night of porter when you are shivering with the red passion" (O'Brien 1988:45–46). Further along, a fat policeman credits the narrator's claim that his father has gone to "far Amurikey," "the Unified Stations" to be precise: "a great conundrum of a country ... a very wide territory, a place occupied by black men and strangers. I am told they are very fond of shooting-matches in that quarter" (59–60). Our narrator, like *At Swim's*, is nameless, and his prose shares the student's formality; but it is also inveterately estranging in its descriptions of the countryside through which he passes, throwing out one dazzlingly skewed sentence after another:

> We were now going through a country full of fine enduring trees where it was always five o'clock in the afternoon. It was a soft corner of the world, free from inquisitions and disputations and very soothing and sleepening on the mind. There was no animal there that was bigger than a man's thumb and no noise superior to that which the Sergeant was making with his nose, an unusual brand of music like wind in the chimney. (83)

Hugh Kenner has observed that the book's English often seems to carry the ghost of a learned, antiquated Irish (Kenner 1997:67): it feels like a vividly unwieldy translation from an original that in fact never existed.

It is worth emphasizing the novel's extraordinary stylistic qualities, because from a distance they are all too easily overwhelmed by its structure and melodramatic conclusion. *The Third Policeman* looks simpler than *At Swim*. Its narrative remains on a single, first-person plane, its style consistent if idiosyncratic. Yet the book has its own chilling twists. The protagonist and his associate John Divney live in rural Ireland. They murder a rich local man, Old Mathers, and steal his cashbox, which Divney claims to hide in Mathers' house for later retrieval. After three tense years, Divney sends the narrator in to pick up the box. When his hand touches it, something changes: something "indescribably subtle, yet momentous, ineffable" (O'Brien 1988:24). He and the reader do not know it yet, and the moment is soon forgotten amid the novel's queer progress, but the change is a substantial one: he is dead, killed by a mine that the devious Divney had planted for him. This only emerges at the novel's end, when the narrator finally returns home to find Divney, affluent, married, and terrified of the ghostly sight of him. The narrator, we begin to realize, has been walking through an underworld: and he now begins to walk through it again with Divney at his side, on what seems set to be an endless cycle. If *At Swim* was intricately non-linear, *The Third Policeman* finally shuns linear time through the simpler strategy of circularity.

The novel's vision of the afterlife is surreal, disturbing, and stunningly imaginative. Many of the book's oddest paradoxes are introduced by the policemen with whom the narrator tangles, in a police station whose very appearance makes its existence feel unlikely. On first seeing it, the narrator tells us, "I had never seen with my eyes ever in my life before anything so unnatural and appalling and my gaze faltered about the thing uncomprehendingly as if at least one of the customary dimensions was missing, leaving no meaning in the remainder." As he approaches, the building seems to "change its appearance," becoming "uncertain in outline like a thing glimpsed under ruffled water." He sees the front and back simultaneously, geometry wavering and reforming as he walks and the paragraph unfolds, until the whole world seems only to exist "to frame it and give it some magnitude and position so that I could find it with my simple senses and pretend to myself that I understood it" (55–56). The police station exemplifies the novel's world: it is too strange to be credited, yet must be confronted and lived in anyway. Our pretense that we understand can quickly come to deceive us, as the next unlikely character enters and the previous fracture of reality is covered by hasty forgetting.

Repeatedly, O'Nolan deploys the novel's strange idiom to reach the limits of representation – as when the policemen present a series of objects whose "appearance, if even that word is not inadmissible, was not understood by the eye and was in any event indescribable" (140). Elsewhere, Policeman MacCruiskeen shows the narrator his collection of home-made boxes of infinitely decreasing size, on which he continues to work despite their being effectively invisible; we also hear about some inaudible music, a spear so thin it can pass harmlessly through a man's hand, and a mangle capable of stretching light and making it scream. The book's best-known conceit is Sergeant Pluck's Atomic Theory, in which the passage of atoms between adjacent objects means that people and bicycles are gradually turning into one another (85–94).

The Third Policeman unflaggingly invents a new logic, a new physics, which sound internally consistent yet nonsensical. Its dream-like mix of plausibility and impossibility, presented in a picaresque series of alarming encounters, makes it distantly akin to *Alice in Wonderland*, whose echoes in O'Nolan we have already heard. To this scenario it adds yet another level of absurdity – the story of the philosopher de Selby, whose crackpot yet strangely logical theories and experiments are recounted in footnotes. Eventually the footnotes begin to detail not only de Selby's work, but the scholarly debate around it, in an elaborate parody of exegesis. The book's craziness, like de Selby's, is very rational. It is suffused with thought – not the hazy meanderings of a Virginia Woolf, but the obsessive logical struggle of a Beckett. O'Nolan put into one book enough matter for several. The only mystery more puzzling than those investigated by the policemen is why, after one rejection, he hid it away for the rest of his life. Cronin ascribes this to the shame of its initial rejection. But Kenner adds that the book must have unnerved O'Nolan, as it does any sensitive reader. He kept the manuscript in a dresser in the parlor, but may have felt that its mind-bending fantasy should not be unleashed after all, if the real world was to retain any plausibility.

The Badge of Poverty

O'Nolan's generation were heirs to the Irish Revival in culture, as well as to political independence. The independent state made a cult of the Irish-speaking "Gaeltacht" of the rural west, venerated as the heart of a pious nation. The Irish language, long discouraged by British rule, was central to this vision, and was keenly promoted by the state. Proficiency in Irish was a requirement for civil servants like Brian O'Nolan. He had been fluent from childhood and loved the language, but was disdainful of those who used it for social advantage or promoted their Irishness as more authentic than others'. In a letter to Sean O'Casey, he stressed in turn the creative importance of the Irish language and his nausea at the "baby-brained dawnburst brigade" who had made it a dogma and a tool of chauvinistic nationalism (Cronin 1989:131). Taaffe has demonstrated O'Nolan's ongoing ambivalence about language revivalism in the 1940s. He spent many column inches belittling revivalism for its simplicity, and in an unpublished manuscript of 1947 he sternly judges it a failure. The Gaeltacht's symbolic status as the heartland of tradition had made government reluctant to see it modernized: accordingly, in O'Nolan's words, the Irish language had remained "the badge of poverty as well as of nationhood" (Taaffe 2008:120).

He was repeatedly scornful of ethnic assertions of Irishness, encountered in the press or in the Dublin streets: they tainted the language "(which is a fine and elegant thing)" with "eccentricity, scenes in public, shrill extremism, childishness, even lunacy" (Taaffe 2008:124–25). O'Nolan enjoyed striking conservative stances: he was endlessly disdainful, for instance, of literary liberals' laments against Ireland's draconian censorship. But he was also quite consistent in his disdain for jingoism and false racial distinctions. This is of a piece with his rationalism. His surrealist imaginings are apt to take place against a background of reasoning, whether serious or, as in Pluck's Atomic Theory, absurd. O'Nolan's is a comedy of the intellect: he has little time for romance in any sense. This might be counted a limitation. But it helps to ensure O'Nolan's perennially unimpressed attitude to any overheated emotion: patriotic fervor or racial pride seem to him not only dangerous but infantile. In 1943, in another broadside against Irish revivalism, he coldly noted the parallel between its denunciation of "the dirty nigger culture of America" and the treatment of Jews in Europe (Taaffe 2008:115). Elsewhere he wondered why the Irish were so devoted to avowing their own nationhood: "I know of no civilisation to which anything so self-conscious could be indigenous. Why go to the trouble of proving that you are Irish? Who has questioned this notorious fact? If, after all, you are not Irish, who is?" (O'Brien 1999:145).

The single creative work that most directly addressed these questions was *An Béal Bocht*, whose English title, *The Poor Mouth*, suggests the sly performance of poverty. The book is an affectionate parody of the Gaelic memoirs written by such islanders as Séamas Ó Grianna, Peig Sayers, and Tomás Ó Criomhthain, whose texts would long be used in school Irish-language classes. Bonaparte O'Coonassa grows up in the distant, fictional district of Corkadoragha, where driving rain is constant, potatoes are always on the menu, and Gaels share their beds with pigs. *The Poor Mouth* details his violent schooling and bizarre escapades in deadpan style: the narrator's voice is innocent, even foolishly buoyant, as he describes the squalid circumstances of the Gael, whose like, he assures us, will not be there again. Next to its elaborate predecessors the novel looks simple enough, but it has its own cunning. Borrowing types, scenes, and styles from an existing genre, it exemplifies the theory of literature articulated in *At Swim-Two-Birds*, and the effect is to suggest that the Gaels have too often been scripted, made to live up to the moral standards and "literary fate" (O'Brien 1993:67) demanded by nationalist narratives. O'Nolan's Gaels themselves are self-conscious about the fictions they must follow, reminding each other to stick to generic conventions. In one of the funniest moments, Bonaparte describes a visit to the Rosses, where he learns the ways of the locals:

> Some were always in difficulty; others carousing in Scotland. In each cabin there was: i) one man at least, called the "Gambler," a rakish individual, who spent much of his life carousing in Scotland ... ii) a worn, old man who spent the time in the chimney-corner bed and who arose at the time of night-visiting to shove his two hooves into the ashes, clear his throat, redden his pipe and tell stories about the bad times; iii) a comely lassie named Nuala or Babby or Mabel or Rosie for whom men came at the dead of every night with a five-noggin bottle and one of them seeking to espouse her. One knows not why but that is how it was. He who thinks I speak untruly, let him read the good books, or the *guid buiks*. (65)

The reader should not be too surprised when each of the stereotypes is encountered, all the way through to the subsequent description of a local woman: "She had a son named Mickey (his nickname was the *Gambler*) but he was carousing yonder in Scotland" (68).

The metafictionalist O'Nolan can be a bookish writer, but in *The Poor Mouth* he turns his own bookishness against the domination of life by outdated fiction. He saves his severest satire for a Gaelic revivalist festival, whose president announces that "There is nothing in this life so nice and so Gaelic as truly true Gaelic Gaels who speak in true Gaelic Gaelic about the truly Gaelic language" (54–55). O'Nolan wrote this in Irish, in a gesture exemplary of the book's canny immanent criticism.

For Which the City of Dublin is Famous

Two decades on, *The Hard Life* and *The Dalkey Archive* are slighter feats. The former manages some criticism of the Catholic Church, though it did not fulfill O'Nolan's goal of having a book banned by the Censorship Board (Cronin 1989:214). The latter incongruously recycles material from the then unpublished *Third Policeman*, along with an entertaining cameo from James Joyce. O'Nolan here is out to settle scores with the maestro to whom he was sick of being compared, while also inadvertently casting him in his own image (Taaffe 2008:204). Both novels lack the stylistic acumen of the earlier work; given O'Nolan's condition by the 1960s, it is something that they were written at all.

But a far greater work had been taking shape for years, in the columns of the *Irish Times* – which is where we came in, with Myles' irrepressible goading of his contemporary Seán O'Faoláin. *Cruiskeen Lawn* was printed on tomorrow's chip-paper, but it contains some of the world's wittiest prose, along with surrealist satire of the young Irish state and a uniquely pedantic attention to linguistic detail. Myles slips between crisp standard English and multiple Dublin dialects, suddenly sounding like an O'Casey character or a beret-sporting bohemian; again O'Nolan is demonstrating his ear for local speech. In extended dialogues we meet a Dubliner who reports on the unlikely accomplishments of his omniscient relative, "the Brother": "The brother says the seals near Dublin do often come up out of the water at night-time and do be sittin above in the trams" (O'Brien 1977:53). Elsewhere the column is interrupted by the collective voice of the Plain People of Ireland, who allow Myles to mock and indulge an imagined readership. Sudden, outlandish puns take over the text, sometimes to pointed effect. Just after Hiroshima, he begins a sentence: "Talking still of the abombic tomb – I *meant* atomic bomb, but leave it, I am a neutron in such matters" (O'Brien 1999:173). More elaborately, the Catechism of Cliché plays solemn havoc with familiar forms of words, teasing the reader to reconstruct the prefabricated phrase from the elaborate questions that rearrange it:

> *What nourishing confection for which the city of Dublin is famous the world over does it take?*
> The biscuit.
> *With what laudable epidermis is it customary to identify our friend?*
> A decent skin.
> *An imaginary decent skin?*
> No, a real decent skin.
> *What is he as good an Irishman?*
> As ever wore a hat. (O'Brien 1977:211)

Cruiskeen Lawn's newsprint origin makes it easily overlooked by literary canons. But critics have lately made the case for it as a major modern work (Young 1997). As modernist studies become interested in ostensibly ephemeral texts, O'Nolan's extensive work outside the major literary genres can be reassessed without condescension:

it even makes him oddly central, rather than vulgarly irrelevant, to reassessments of the period.

Looking back at the Irish literature of the twentieth century, we can focus our gaze on different levels of literary activity. We may read acknowledged masterpieces, of a number and distinction famously out of proportion to the size of the country and its population: *Ulysses*, *The Tower*, the *Playboy*, Beckett's trilogy – and indeed *At Swim-Two-Birds* and *The Third Policeman*. We can also concentrate on the busy world of letters from which these monuments emerged: the great supporting cast of lesser-known writers, periodicals, newsprint debate, and cultural polemic, all of which provided the contentious soil from which modern Irish literature could grow and which is increasingly given attention in its own right. *Cruiskeen Lawn*, perhaps uniquely, belongs to both categories. It was part of the daily conversation of Dublin, a prolonged cut and thrust between editors, reviewers, bishops, politicians, councillors, liberals, and philistines. It is one place where one can find a willfully distorted cultural history of mid-century Ireland. But it can also be said to add up to something enduring of its own: an accidental Irish masterpiece whose linguistic facility and comic joy at their best rival almost all the others. In one column, Myles na gCopaleen protested that his journalism was "not merely passing trash to stuff a small hole in a businessman's day," but would have to be judged in a longer historical perspective – for surely, should Ireland last long enough, the mid-twentieth century would mathematically become ancient history, and *Cruiskeen Lawn* might eventually be "hailed as one of Ireland's most valuable pre-historic treasures" (O'Brien 1999:54). It is a pointed moment of self-assertion undercut, as his writing so often was, by its latent ludicrousness. He probably thought that much of his writing, especially the columns, would be forgotten. But thanks to its own qualities and to the later labors of editors and scholars, we can now look at the range of Brian O'Nolan's best work, the brilliant early novels and the uniquely episodic, if not epic, saga of *Cruiskeen Lawn*, and believe that it will last as long as that of other great Irish writers: Synge, Joyce, Beckett, and maybe even Shanachy, Shaughnessy, Henry James or whatever his name was.

REFERENCES AND FURTHER READING

Asbee, S. (1991). *Flann O'Brien*. Boston: Twayne.

Brooker, J. (2004). "Estopped by Grand Playsaunce: Flann O'Brien's Post-colonial Lore." *Law and Literature*, 31.1 (March), 15–37.

Brooker, J. (2005). *Flann O'Brien*. Tavistock: Northcote House.

Carroll, L. (1994). *Through the Looking Glass*. Harmondsworth: Penguin.

Clissmann, A. (1975). *Flann O'Brien: A Critical Introduction to his Writings*. Dublin: Gill & Macmillan.

Clune, A. and T. Hurson (Eds). (1997). *Conjuring Complexities: Essays on Flann O'Brien*. Belfast: Institute of Irish Studies.

Costello, P. and P. Van de Kamp. (1987). *Flann O'Brien: An Illustrated Biography*. London: Bloomsbury.

Cronin, A. (1989). *No Laughing Matter: The Life and Times of Flann O'Brien*. London: Grafton.

Curran, S. (1997). "'No-this-is-not-from-the-Bell': Brian O'Nolan's 1943 *Cruiskeen Lawn* Anthology." *Éire-Ireland*, 34.2–3, 78–92.

Curran, S. (2001). "'Could Paddy leave off from copying just for five minutes': Brian O'Nolan and Éire's Beveridge Plan." *Irish University Review*, 31.2 (Autumn/Winter), 353–75.

Foster, R.F. (1997). *W.B. Yeats: A Life,* vol. I: *The Apprentice Mage.* Oxford: Oxford University Press.

Hopper, K. (2009). *Flann O'Brien: A Portrait of the Artist as a Young Post-Modernist.* 2nd edn. Cork: Cork University Press.

Imhof, R. (Ed.). (1985). *Alive Alive O! Flann O'Brien's At Swim-Two-Birds.* Dublin: Wolfhound.

Kenner, H. (1997). "The Fourth Policeman." In A. Clune and T. Hurson (Eds). *Conjuring Complexities: Essays on Flann O'Brien* (pp. 61–71). Belfast: Institute of Irish Studies.

O'Brien, F. (1967). *At Swim-Two-Birds* (1939). Harmondsworth: Penguin.

O'Brien, F. (1977). *The Best of Myles.* London: Picador.

O'Brien, F. (1988). *The Third Policeman* (1967). London: Grafton.

O'Brien, F. (1989). *Myles Before Myles: A Selection of the Earlier Writings of Brian O'Nolan.* J.W. Jackson (Ed.). London: Paladin.

O'Brien, F. (1993). *The Poor Mouth* [*An Béal Bocht*] (1941). London: Flamingo.

O'Brien, F. (1999). *Flann O'Brien at War.* J.W. Jackson (Ed.). London: Duckworth.

O'Keeffe, T. (Ed.). (1973). *Myles: Portraits of Brian O'Nolan.* London: Martin Bryan & O'Keeffe.

Ryan, J. (1987). *Remembering How We Stood: Bohemian Dublin at the Mid-Century.* Dublin: Gill & Macmillan.

Shea, T.F. (1992). *Flann O'Brien's Exorbitant Novels.* Lewisburg: Bucknell University Press.

Taaffe, C. (2008). *Ireland through the Looking-Glass: Flann O'Brien, Myles Na gCopaleen and Irish Cultural Debate.* Cork: Cork University Press.

Young, S. (1997). "Fact/Fiction: *Cruiskeen Lawn,* 1945–66." In A. Clune and T. Hurson (Eds). *Conjuring Complexities: Essays on Flann O'Brien* (pp. 111–18). Belfast: Institute of Irish Studies.

Part Nine

Debating Social Change
after 1960

41

Reading William Trevor and Finding Protestant Ireland

Gregory A. Schirmer

Marginality is at the center of William Trevor's writing, and Protestant Ireland – from elderly descendants of the Anglo-Irish Ascendancy to dusty shopkeepers in provincial towns, lonely farmers, spinster schoolteachers, and clergymen with thinning congregations – has provided him the most telling means of expressing it, offering what he himself called "the perspective that art demands," a point of view that is a part of, but not inside, Irish society (Trevor 1994:177). Looking through that fading lens, Trevor has found a way to dramatize his grim vision of loss, disappointment, shrinking possibility, and alienation, and, more locally, to probe the forces lying behind the sectarian violence in Northern Ireland while measuring the destructive effects of that culture of violence on individuals. Even the laconic, ironic quality of Trevor's style, that cool distance from his characters that he insists on, that love of the passive voice, that tendency to observe human nature with one eyebrow raised, as well as the dark comedy threaded through his work are rooted in the marginalized experience of Protestant Ireland.

Born into a provincial, middle-class Protestant family, and so knowing that outside point of view from the inside, Trevor has made this cultural terrain his own; no other major Irish writer has written so knowledgeably or so thoroughly about Irish Protestants of various stripes. This detailed attention to so marginalized a sector of Irish society has come with a price; although Trevor is widely regarded outside Ireland as one of the most important writers of his day, it is not difficult to encounter discussions inside Ireland about contemporary writing in which names such as John MacGahern, Roddy Doyle, John Banville, Colm Toibín, Edna O'Brien, Dermot Bolger, Anne Enright, Patrick McCabe, Sebastian Barry, Bernard MacLaverty, Jennifer Johnston, and Deirdre Madden would figure, but not Trevor's. The marginalization of Trevor's work inside Ireland may have something to do with his keeping a foot in

A Companion to Irish Literature, edited by Julia M. Wright
© 2010 Blackwell Publishing Ltd

both Irish and English fiction – with the exception of George Moore at the beginning of the twentieth century and Elizabeth Bowen in the middle of it, only Trevor has come to writing Irish fiction after having established himself in the English tradition – but it also can be explained by his consistent focus on a population group that not only exists on the edges of mainstream Irish culture, but also is very much politically out of favor. There is a precedent for the ambiguous status of Trevor's writing inside Ireland in the reception of Bowen, whose Irish fiction is concerned exclusively with Ascendancy culture (see CHAPTER 37, ELIZABETH BOWEN: A HOME IN WRITING), and about whom there are still debates as to whether she should be considered an Irish writer at all.

Writing in 1949 of what it was like to be a Protestant in Ireland in the middle decades of the twentieth century, a period that Trevor often turns to in his fiction, the essayist and translator Arland Ussher describes precisely the world from which Trevor constructs his images of alienation and loss:

> the non-Catholic feels himself far more cut off from his nation than does, let us say, a Roman Catholic in present-day England; he feels rather as a heretical Jew might feel in an Orthodox Jewish community. The life of his country is an intricate pattern of fasts and festivals, pilgrimages and retreats, in which he has no part. He enjoys almost perfect toleration ... but he finds it hard to converse freely or intimately with Catholics, he cannot ... marry or give his children in marriage to them, he tends not to visit at their houses – not so much because he would be unwelcome in them as that he would feel embarrassed by a different outlook and habit of life. This means that in a nation of three millions he must seek for friends and intimates, wives or husbands, among a minority of less than two hundred thousand. ... In these circumstances it would be surprising if the non-Catholic did not feel himself something of a stranger and a "foreign body" in Eire. (Ussher 1949:102–03)

Trevor himself, in his collection of autobiographical writings *Excursions in the Real World*, recalls in similar terms his experience of growing up Protestant in Ireland in the decades immediately following the establishment of the Free State: "I was born into a minority that all my life has seemed in danger of withering away. This was the smalltime Protestant stock, far removed from the well-to-do Ascendancy of the recent past yet without much of a place in de Valera's new Catholic Ireland" (Trevor 1994:xiii).

This experience made itself felt in Trevor's writing relatively late in his career, in part because he began by writing about his adopted rather than his native country. Trevor published four novels set in England before he wrote *Mrs Eckdorf in O'Neill's Hotel* (1969), a novel set in Dublin (but not particularly concerned with Irish issues), and after *Mrs Eckdorf* he published four more English novels before turning to distinctively Irish themes in *Fools of Fortune*, which appeared in 1983, when Trevor was 55. His first collection of short stories, published in 1966, included no Irish stories, and one must wait until *Beyond the Pale*, published two years before *Fools of Fortune*, to find a collection containing as many Irish as English stories. And although it must be said that some of his most accomplished stories – "The Ballroom of Romance,"

"Teresa's Wedding," "The Paradise Lounge," "The Property of Colette Nervi," "Events at Drimaghleen," "The Third Party," "Honeymoon in Tramore," "Kathleen's Field," and "The Dressmaker's Daughter" – have to do with Catholic Ireland, it is his engagement with Protestant Ireland that, over the long haul, has defined his status as an Irish writer. More important, it has enabled him to move beyond the rural versions of Joycean paralysis found in early stories such as "The Ballroom of Romance" and "Teresa's Wedding," and beyond the Dickensian social satire that characterizes much of his early fiction about England, to create a more psychologically complex and nuanced fiction sensitive to the impact of social and political issues on individuals, and expressive of a coherent if discouraging vision of the human condition.

The turning point in that process was the outbreak of sectarian violence on a large scale in Northern Ireland in the early 1970s. In a radio interview in 1981, Trevor described the enormous impact that the violence in the North had on him:

> As an Irishman I feel that what is happening in Ireland now is one of the great horrors of my lifetime, and I find it difficult to comprehend the mentality, whether Irish or British, that pretends that it will somehow all blow over. It will not. There will be more death, more cruelty, more fear, more waste. The nightmare will go on. ... Compassion is thrown to the winds, distortion rules. (MacKenna 1999:110)

Trevor's first fictional response to that nightmare is the story "The Distant Past," which appeared in *Angels at the Ritz* in 1975, three years after Bloody Sunday. This is also Trevor's first piece of writing in which Irish Protestants – in this instance, the Middletons of Caraveagh, an elderly brother and sister living in a decaying Georgian house on the edge of a provincial town sixty miles from the border – are used as a barometer for the destructive psychological effects of the conflict in the North. Although marginalized as Protestants, the Middletons have enjoyed a more or less benign relationship with the largely Catholic population of the town for many years, largely by means of repressing historical memory, but they are completely ostracized once the violence in the North starts, diminishing tourism, and so prosperity, in the town. The story carefully calibrates the alienation that the Middletons experience as the community revitalizes the prejudices and divisions of the past, and concludes with an image that registers, in deliberately shocking terms, how high a price the Middletons must pay for being Protestants:

> Now and again, he thought, he would drive slowly into the town, to buy groceries and meat with the money they had saved, and to face the silence that would sourly thicken as their own two deaths came closer and death increased in another part of their island. She felt him thinking that and she knew he was right. Because of the distant past they would die friendless. It was worse than being murdered in their beds. (Trevor 1992:355–56)

Trevor sees the violence in the North as rooted in part in narrow, sectarian interpretations of Irish history guaranteed to pass hatred and a desire for revenge from one generation to the next. Because Irish Protestants not only played a significant role in Ireland's violent past but also exist in the present in a position of extreme vulnerability, they have proved a particularly effective means of dramatizing both the tendency to read the Irish past in sectarian terms and the disastrous effects, especially in Northern Ireland, of doing so. The protagonist of "Autumn Sunshine," which appeared in *Beyond the Pale* (1981), is a Church of Ireland rector, Canon Moran, whose wife has recently died, and who has only a handful of parishioners. When his daughter Deirdre comes back from England for a visit, she brings along her boyfriend Harold who, although English, has acquired a fiercely, not to say viciously uncompromising, nationalist view of Irish affairs. That Harold, as an Englishman, holds such a view suggests that the politics of extremism can be taken on board by anyone who chooses to read history in a certain way, and while visiting Deirdre's father, Harold becomes obsessed with an incident that occurred near the rectory during the 1798 Uprising, in which twelve Irishmen and Irishwomen, believed to be insurgents, were herded into a barn owned by a farmer named Kinsella and burned to death. Harold's interpretation of this incident is so entirely inflammatory – he even defends the later killing of Kinsella by his farm laborers although Kinsella was nowhere near the barn at the time of the fire, and seems to have had nothing to do with it – and so obviously feeds the seething need to hate someone that lies just beneath the surface of his character, that in his sermon the following Sunday the rector brings up the incident, seeking to interpret it from the point of view of reconciliation rather than sectarian hatred: "He tried to make the point that one horror should not fuel another, that passing time contained its own forgiveness" (Trevor 1992:848). But very often in Trevor's work such attempts at truth-telling make little or no difference; there is only a handful of parishioners (Deirdre and Harold not among them) to listen to the rector's appeal, and, as the rector knows, they "found his sermon odd" (Trevor 1992:848). After Deirdre and Harold leave for England the next day, the rector realizes, as do the Middletons in "The Distant Past," how difficult it is to reverse the destructive flow of history in a country with a past marked by violence, prejudice, and revenge. Canon Moran cannot help but relive the moment in Kinsella's barn, and his involuntary reconstruction of the specific details of that horrific event offers little hope for any eventual reconciliation between Protestant and Catholic, Unionist and nationalist, in the mind of the rector, or on the streets of contemporary Belfast and Derry:

> his mind was full of Harold's afflicted face and his black-rimmed fingernails, and Deirdre's hand in his. And then flames burst from the straw that had been packed around living people in Kinsella's Barn. They burned through the wood of the barn itself, revealing the writhing bodies. (Trevor 1992:850–51)

One of Trevor's most accomplished stories about the violence in the North, "Attracta," also published in *Beyond the Pale*, takes as its protagonist a 61-year-old Protestant woman who teaches school in an Irish provincial town that seems a long way from Northern Ireland. (The town has many of the characteristics of Skibbereen,

County Cork, one of the towns that Trevor lived in while growing up, and nearly as far from Northern Ireland as it is possible to be on the island of Ireland.) Like a number of Trevor's Protestant characters, Attracta has never married, has no children, and, because of her religion, has never been fully accepted into the community. She is connected to the violence in the North partly by feelings of compassion, and partly because of a history that is constructed on the divisions that compassion would, ideally, transcend. She is deeply disturbed by a newspaper account of the story of a young English girl named Penelope Vade, whose husband, a British soldier, was killed while on duty in the North, and whose severed head was posted to her in a biscuit tin. Responding in a spirit of hope and reconciliation, Penelope moved to Belfast to join the Women's Peace Movement, but in the wake of the surrounding publicity, was raped by seven men, presumably extreme nationalists, and in despair killed herself. As he frequently does, Trevor connects the violence of the 1970s and 1980s in the North to the conflict seen by many as a crucial moment in the foundational history of the republic, the Anglo-Irish War. Attracta's parents were shot by mistake in an Irish Republican Army ambush meant for the Black and Tans, and just as Penelope Vade attempted to respond to her husband's death with forgiveness, so the man and woman responsible for the death of Attracta's parents, a local Protestant nationalist named Devereux and a Catholic woman named Geraldine Casey, have tried to make amends by looking after Attracta; indeed Devereux has become something of a father figure to her. But these manifestations of compassion cannot stand up to the toxic pressures of Irish history, or the momentum of violence itself, what Attracta calls "vengeance breeding vengeance" (Trevor 1992:687). When Attracta tries to break the cycle of revenge by telling her students her own story along with that of Penelope Vade, her truth-telling, like that of Canon Moran in "Autumn Sunshine," falls on deaf ears; her students see her as out of touch, in part no doubt because she is Protestant, and, in the end, she loses her job, her one vital connection to the community. The failure of Attracta's efforts to stop the perpetuation of a culture of violence by means of a story that connects past and present also exposes a certain skepticism on Trevor's part about the ability of his own narratives to do the same thing in more or less the same way.

Two other Trevor stories, one published in the mid-1980s and one in the mid-1990s, rely on marginalized Protestant characters to measure the destructive effects of Ireland's long history of occupation and resistance. The character of Fogarty, the Protestant butler working in a Big House during the time of the famine of the late 1840s in the title story of Trevor's 1986 collection *The News from Ireland*, dramatizes the irrational prejudice that nourishes the roots of the violence in the North in the closing decades of the twentieth century. Fogarty exhibits a fierce, destructive loyalty to the Anglo-Irish Protestant Ascendancy, although he does not belong to it, and an equally unforgiving desire to exclude anyone outside that circle. The English governess from whose point of view much of the story is told is a "stranger and visitor to Ireland," Fogarty says, and indeed the entire history of Ireland is populated, in Fogarty's exclusionist version of it, with strangers and visitors: "the Celts, whose ramshackle gipsy empire expired in the same landscape, St Patrick with his holy shamrock, the outrageous Vikings preceding the wily Normans, the adventurers of the Virgin Queen" (Trevor 1992:881). That these deep-seated prejudices are part of the psychological makeup of a Protestant in love with the Ascendancy rather than the very different prejudices that might inspire a nationalist who would see the Ascendancy as the enemy demonstrates how, for Trevor, the difference between Unionist and nationalist is less important than the poisoned ground the two sides share: a view that draws on the past to justify sectarian violence in the present. (For an extensive discussion of this story, see Fitzgerald-Hoyt 2003:96–111.)

"Lost Ground," published in *After Rain* (1996), dispenses with the historical distancing of "The News from Ireland," but the story dramatically documents the damage done to individuals by exclusionist readings of Irish history; extremist positions on both sides of the Unionist/nationalist divide in contemporary Northern Ireland are constructed, the narrator says, on "the endless celebration of a glorious past on one side and the picking over of ancient rights on the other; the reluctance to forgive" (Trevor 1996:155). One of the two sons of the Protestant Leeson family, running a farm in contemporary County Armagh, has moved to Belfast to work as a butcher's assistant, and has been caught up in the Unionist paramilitary movement; the other, Milton, has a bizarre vision of a Catholic saint in his father's orchard, and is inspired to take to the streets, in the tradition of Protestant preaching, to plead for reconciliation between Protestant and Catholic in the North. The barriers to any such reconciliation are evident in the responses, on both sides, to Milton's preaching, which, like Attracta's teaching and Canon Moran's sermon, represents an attempt at truth-telling. The local Catholic priest, to whom Milton turns for information about the saint he believes he has seen, views the experience in markedly sectarian terms – "Why should a saint of his Church appear to a Protestant boy in a neighbourhood that was overwhelmingly Catholic?" (167) – while the Leesons try to keep Milton under lock and key until his brother, whose reputation as a hard-man Unionist paramilitary is being compromised by Milton's activities, arrives at the farmhouse with one of his cronies, on the twelfth of July, and Milton is killed in his bedroom. The frailty of any hope for reconciliation between these historically driven points of view is painfully evident in the discouraging note of repression and acceptance on which the story ends: "The family would not ever talk about the day, but through their pain they would tell themselves that Milton's death was the way things were, the way things had to be" (183).

The two novels that Trevor published in the 1980s, *Fools of Fortune* (1983) and *The Silence in the Garden* (1988), take the condition of the faded Anglo-Irish Protestant Ascendancy in the early decades of the twentieth century as a vehicle for dramatizing the deadly pressure exerted on the present, particularly in the North, by Ireland's divisive and violent history. The shift in Trevor's writing away from the social satire that dominates his fiction of the 1960s and 1970s, and toward the darker, more psychologically informed work of his maturity is particularly evident in reading *Fools of Fortune*, his first novel inspired by the Northern violence, against his first novel set in

Ireland, *Mrs Eckdorf in O'Neill's Hotel*, published fourteen years earlier. By taking as its protagonist an eccentric journalist whose vision of herself as a truth-teller, an agent of compassion, is constantly called into question, *Mrs Eckdorf* raises an issue that much of Trevor's early fiction is devoted to: the fragile force of love and compassion in a world driven by self-interest, greed, and a kind of loneliness that seems endemic to modern society. Mrs Eckdorf's madness at the end of the novel, the causes of which are unclear, undermines the humanistic values that she seems, at her best, to embody. By contrast, the madness of Imelda, at the end of *Fools of Fortune*, is not at all ambiguous in its causes or in its meanings; it is clearly the product of a history of sectarian hatred and revenge repeated over and over. The daughter of the doomed relationship between the Anglo-Irish Willie Quinton and the English Marianne Woodcombe, Imelda has internalized the terrible events of her family's history, including the burning of Kilneagh by the Black and Tans, and her father's brutal murder of Sergeant Rudkin, the man he holds responsible for it. Imelda has not witnessed these events, but has re-created them in her own damaged imagination, drawing on stories she has heard, in other words, on subjective versions of the past. And so her madness dramatizes precisely the process by which a history of violence and revenge is destructively absorbed by each succeeding generation:

> She closed her eyes and in the room above the vegetable shop blood spurted in a torrent, splashing on to the wallpaper that was torn and hung loosely down. The blood was sticky, running over the backs of her hands and splashing on to her hair. It soaked through her clothes, warm when it reached her skin. ...
>
> The screaming of the children began, and the torment of the flames on their flesh. The dogs were laid out dead in the yard, and the body of the man in the teddy-bear dressing-gown lay smouldering on the stairs. The blood kept running on her hands, and was tacky in her hair. (Trevor 1983:218–19)

Trevor is writing here at the top of his form. And if he is writing out of a perspective that Georg Lukács theorizes as "an awareness of human existence as always historically conditioned" (Kreilkamp 1998:15), that historical conditioning, translated into the specific and deadly terms that connect one period of Irish "troubles" to another, is rendered with a psychological realism not evident in Trevor's earlier fiction. Abandoning the multiple centers of consciousness and ironically distanced narrators that he relies on in much of his early work, Trevor constructs *Fools of Fortune* in alternating first-person accounts that register, often shockingly, the psychological damage done to individuals by events grounded in prejudice and revenge. At the same time, it is significant that these intimate, first-person accounts are written by two people who, in different ways, are marginalized inside Irish society. The tenuous social positions of the Anglo-Irish Willie and the English Marianne make them psychologically vulnerable, and contribute decisively to the destruction of any normal relationship between them. It is no accident that shards of Yeats' "The Lake Isle of Innisfree" run with ironic force through the demented mind of Imelda at the end of this novel that documents, among other things, the destruction of the Protestant Ascendancy by the force of a history of hatred and violence in which it is deeply implicated.

The Silence in the Garden contains its own ghostly, ironic reference to Yeats in the name Sarah Pollexfen, a poor relation who is part of the Rolleston family of Carriglas, and in this novel Trevor turns once again to the Anglo-Irish Protestant Ascendancy to explore the ways in which, in the course of Irish history, vengeance breeds vengeance. Trevor's representation of the Anglo-Irish Big House is more invested in this novel than it is in *Fools of Fortune* in specifically colonial and postcolonial issues. (For a generally Marxist discussion of *Fools of Fortune* and *The Silence in the Garden* in the context of the Big House novel, see Kreilkamp 1998:220–33.) The reader is reminded that the Rollestons came to Ireland in the seventeenth century, in the bloody wake of Cromwell, sending the natives "on their way to the stony wilderness of Mayo" (Trevor 1988:41). Carriglas sits on an island cut off from the largely Catholic town across the water, and although a bridge is to be built to the mainland, it will come on to the island on the other side from where the house stands, and it will be named after Cornelius Dowley, a local nationalist hero responsible for the death of the Rolleston family butler. Moreover, Carriglas harbors a dark secret, and unlike the secret that Mrs Eckdorf believes to be part of the history of the hotel in *Mrs Eckdorf at O'Neill's Hotel*, this one is rooted in sectarian prejudice and colonialist assumptions: the Rolleston children once hunted Cornelius Dowley with a rifle, and they did so, according to what Mrs Rolleston tells Sarah, "as of right" because "they were the children of Carriglas" (184). That shameful bit of history, with its consequences during the time of the Troubles – the mistaken murder of the butler, killed by a republican booby trap intended for the Rolleston children, followed by the reprisal killing of Dowley by the Black and Tans – belongs to a history of killing and revenge stretching back to the arrival of the Rollestons in Ireland and, by implication, forward to the violence in contemporary Northern Ireland.

While *Fools of Fortune* confines itself largely to Kilneagh and the people connected to it, *The Silence in the Garden*, set for the most part in 1931, represents in considerable detail the life of the town across the water from Carriglas. To some extent this social breadth works against the chief aims of the novel. Unlike the comic interlude in *Fools of Fortune* in which the former mathematics teacher at Willie's boarding school urinates through a bedroom window on the man responsible for his dismissal, a comic version of the theme of revenge that lies at the heart of the novel, the often comic treatment of the life of the town in *The Silence in the Garden* does not always sit easily with the toxic history of Carriglas. Moreover, especially in comparison with *Fools of Fortune*, *The Silence in the Garden* does not go very far in dramatizing the psychological effects of the perpetuation of sectarian hatred; the novel is written in the third person, relying on multiple centers of consciousness, the narrative point of view of much of Trevor's earlier fiction, and there is no character like the diseased Imelda to register the psychological cost of being victimized by a history of violence and revenge.

With the exception of "Lost Ground," published in 1996, and two stories in *The Hill Bachelors* (2000), *The Silence in the Garden* marks the end of Trevor's writing about the conflict in Northern Ireland. After 1988, his fiction about Irish Protestants increasingly portrays them as figures of alienation, loneliness, and emotional paralysis without the historical or political framework of *Fools of Fortune* and *The Silence in the Garden*. This shift is signaled in Trevor's novella *Nights at the Alexandra*, published a year before *The Silence in the Garden*. The story takes place in a provincial Irish town during World War II, the backdrop of much middle-class Catholic fiction by writers such as Mary Lavin, Frank O'Connor, and Seán O'Faoláin. But Trevor's provincial Ireland, viewed through the experience of marginalized Protestants, is a far grimmer place than the communities found in the work of most Catholic writers taking the provinces as their fictional terrain. Harry, the protagonist of *Nights at the Alexandra*, describes himself at the beginning of the story in terms that reflect both the general theme of loneliness in Trevor's writing – "I am a fifty-eight-year-old provincial. I have no children. I have never married" (Trevor 1987:9) – and Trevor's parallel preoccupation with the position of Protestants in provincial Ireland. Harry is the son, he says, of "a Protestant family of the servant class which had come up in the world, my father now the proprietor of the timberyard where he had once been employed" (Trevor 1987:11), and his status as a Protestant in a Catholic community ensures that he can never find, as can the characters in O'Connor's or O'Faoláin's or Lavin's fiction, solace in the life of that community. At some distance from the town stands Cloverhill, which has all the trappings of a former Ascendancy house, but is now inhabited by a German man and his English wife, the Messengers, who have moved to neutral Ireland because of the war. The story that Harry narrates of his adolescent friendship with the Messengers, especially with Frau Messenger, is one in which the longing for a life beyond the provincial confines of his native place, inspired in part by Frau Messenger's cosmopolitanism and in part by the cinema that Herr Messenger builds for his wife, is inevitably disappointed, and in the end Harry is left alone, unwilling or unable to leave the community from which, as a Protestant, he is permanently alienated.

Trevor's most sustained and accomplished portrait of psychological paralysis and social alienation, *Reading Turgenev* (1991), also contains his most thorough examination of the Protestant middle class in provincial Ireland. Set for the most part in the 1950s, *Reading Turgenev* describes the quietly desperate lives of two Protestant families, the Dallons, who are farmers, and the Quarrys, who are shopkeepers, living at a time when the economic life of Ireland favored Irish Catholics – "All over the county wealth had passed into the hands of a new Catholic middle class, changing the nature of provincial life as it did so" (Trevor 1991:5) – and when Protestants were at least as decimated by emigration as were Catholics:

> Families everywhere were affected by emigration, and the Protestant fraction of the population increasingly looked as if it would never recover. There was no fat on the bones of this shrinking community; there were no reserves of strength. Its very life was eroded by the bleak economy of the times. (14)

This economic desperation serves as a backdrop to the emotional and psychological desperation that lies at the center of *Reading Turgenev*, embodied primarily in the marriage between Mary Louise Dallon and Elmer Quarry. The marriage is without passion, indeed without sexual consummation, suggesting the eventual extinction of the class. (Mary Louise's one sister marries a Catholic, and it is made clear that her children will be brought up Catholic.) The passion that Mary Louise does feel, for her ailing, doomed cousin Robert, is the stuff of fantasy; its only physical manifestation consists of a single kiss that takes place in a graveyard.

Reading Turgenev was published under one cover with a novel called *My House in Umbria*, and although the title of the volume, *Two Lives*, clearly refers to the female protagonists of the two novels, it also suggests the two lives that Mary Louise has open to her – the suffocating routine of a provincial Protestant shopkeeper in a household dominated by her husband's two twisted sisters, or the impossible, and impossibly romantic, relationship with her cousin. Mary Louise's inclination to fantasy as a way of escaping the loneliness and hopelessness of the first of these two lives is figured most dramatically when, after Robert's death – like Frau Messenger in *Nights at the Alexandra*, he dies young – she builds a shrine to him in an attic in the Quarrys' house, and lives there, surrounded by the markers of her fantasy, her dead cousin's books and other mementoes of him, completely cut off from her husband, her family, and her community. Her supposed madness – the Quarrys eventually have her institutionalized – has nothing of the social implications of the apparent insanity of Mrs Eckdorf in *Mrs Eckdorf in O'Neill's Hotel*, nor anything of the historical pressures behind the unbalanced mind of Imelda in *Fools of Fortune*, but Mary Louise, ostracized by birth from one of the community's "two lives," that of local Catholics, and by desperate choice from the other, that of the handful of Protestants in the town, is the most powerful figure of alienation in all of Trevor's writing.

The title *Two Lives* carries another resonance within *Reading Turgenev*, one that raises questions about the value and efficacy of fiction itself, including Trevor's. In the world of social reality, Mary Louise is trapped in a deadening marriage and marginalized culture, but she also lives part-time in the world of fiction, the world of Turgenev's novels, from which Robert reads to her during their few times together. Given the correspondences between Turgenev's writing about provincial Russia in the nineteenth century and Trevor's fictional representations of provincial Ireland in the middle of the twentieth century, and between the ironic, detached styles of both writers, the novel certainly suggests a parallel between reading Turgenev and reading Trevor. With that parallel in mind, one could argue, on the one hand, that Turgenev's fiction provides Mary Louise with an inner freedom that sustains her in the worst of times, and that this kind of imaginative experience is one of the values of reading fiction, be it Turgenev's or Trevor's. And Trevor does take some trouble to dramatize the process by which Mary Louise translates the words of Turgenev into an imagined reality that, like the Messengers' cinema in *Nights at the Alexandra*, points to a world that lies beyond the confines of her marriage and her class:

She was seeing in her mind's eye Pavel Petrovich's study, its green velvet and walnut furniture, its vivid tapestry. Her cousin's voice curtly issued Arkady's orders; distressfully it conveyed to her Mitya's convulsions. "Madame will see you in half an hour," the butler said. Swallows flew high, bees hummed in the lilac. A peasant with a patch on his shoulder trotted a white pony through an evening's shadows. Sprigs of fuchsia decorated the hair of a woman in black. (Trevor 1991:95)

On the other hand, Robert's reading is a poor substitute for love in the flesh – "Inviting her into the world of a novelist had been her cousin's courtship, all he could manage, as much as she could accept" (220) – and these reading sessions fuel fantasies that lead Mary Louise away from any engagement with the real world and toward the shrine in the Quarrys' attic and, eventually, the madhouse.

In *The Story of Lucy Gault* (2002), Trevor self-consciously strips the narrative of the historical and political resonances that inform *Fools of Fortune* and *The Silence in the Garden*. *The Story of Lucy Gault* begins in the same historical period as *Fools of Fortune*, the time of the Black-and-Tan War, and in an Anglo-Irish Big House, Lahardane, that is not unlike the Quinton's Kilneagh. Moreover, three young men associated with the republican movement have come to burn Lahardane to the ground. But in the first two sentences of the novel Trevor disposes of the fire, and therefore of the whole chain of historical consequences that are the driving force of *Fools of Fortune* and that expose the underlying causes of the sectarian violence in Northern Ireland:

> Captain Everard Gault wounded the boy in the right shoulder on the night of June the twenty-first, nineteen twenty-one. Aiming above the trespassers' heads in the darkness, he fired the single shot from an upstairs window and then watched the three figures scuttling off, the wounded one assisted by his companions. (Trevor 2002:3)

The Story of Lucy Gault has little to do with historical determinism, and less with Northern Ireland. (That it was published four years after the Belfast Agreement was signed may have something to do with this.) Rather, the novel is a vision of loneliness and exile, and what drives the lives of its unfortunate characters is chance, those "purblind Doomsters," in the words of Thomas Hardy (Hardy 1982:9), whose pessimistic vision of the human condition as governed by some kind of cosmic roll of the dice informs much of *The Story of Lucy Gault*. The boy, whose name is Horahan, is wounded by accident. The other event central to the novel's plot, Lucy's fall in the woods the morning her family is supposed to leave Lahardane to escape any possible reprisals for the wounding of Horahan, is also a matter of chance, as is the belief of her parents, on finding her summer vest on the strand, that she has drowned by accident that morning. (In fact, the vest had been buried in play by the family dog on an earlier occasion.) The night before he leaves Lahardane, Captain Gault concludes that although political elements cannot be discounted completely in considering his situation, the history of Ireland, as divisive and violent as it is, cannot fully account for what has happened to him and his family: "Chance, not wrath, had this summer ordered the fate of the Gaults" (Trevor 2002:36).

The destructive consequences of the operation of chance are inevitably compounded in *The Story of Lucy Gault* by class. The exile of the Gaults is, in part at least, an outcome of their being Anglo-Irish Protestants at the time of the Black-and-Tan War (and as such revises conventional nationalist narratives about the exile of the native Irish). Moreover, the Gaults' exile is mirrored in Lucy's isolation at Lahardane, where, a virtual orphan, she lives like an Elizabeth Bowen character exiled inside a Big House slowly but surely sinking back into the dust. Lucy rarely ventures beyond the front gates, and she spends much of her time reading Victorian novels, becoming a kind of Miss Havisham figure, completely cut off from the world around her. The doomed love between Lucy and Ralph echoes the futile relationship between Mary Louise and Robert in *Reading Turgenev*, one of a number of allusions in *The Story of Lucy Gault* to earlier Trevor novels. (Ralph's father runs a sawmill like that run by the Quintons in *Fools of Fortune*, and Lucy, like Robert in *Reading Turgenev*, is maimed psychologically and physically, having developed a limp from her fall in the woods. Also, Horohan eventually ends up in a mental institution, and his madness echoes Imelda's in *Fools of Fortune*; like Imelda, he refuses to speak, and he dreams of the burning of Lahardane just as Imelda is haunted by visions of the burning of Kilneagh.) Moreover, like so many of Trevor's Anglo-Irish characters, Lucy is the last of the family line. By the time her father returns, an old man, to Lahardane, following the death of Lucy's mother, the centuries of a Gault presence in Ireland are about to come to an end: "Their people would end when they did, all duty to them finished, all memory of them dead. Only the myths would linger, the stories that were told" (Trevor 2002:195). As its title suggests, *The Story of Lucy Gault* asks to be read as one of those myths or stories, and there is something of the parable or fable about this novel, including a plot that can hardly be called realistic. But it is a parable or fable that imagines not just the end of a specific class and its way of life, but also the condition of alienation and loneliness in the modern world.

In the preface to his collection *Late Lyrics and Earlier* (1922), Hardy says that human suffering can be "kept down to a minimum by loving-kindness," but only "when the mighty necessitating forces ... happen to be in equilibrium, which may or may not be often" (Hardy 1982:558). There are moments in Trevor's work in which he affirms, albeit conditionally, the power of love and compassion to offer some comfort to his victims, and in several of his later stories the possibility of "loving-kindness" is embodied in a kind of nostalgia for the disappearing way of life of certain Irish Protestants whose very marginalization seems to inspire a strengthening of the bonds between human and human. In "Timothy's Birthday," a story from *After Rain* (1996), the isolation and seemingly inevitable extinction of the Anglo-Irish Protestant Ascendancy is rendered in terms more elegiac than ironic, and the story quietly celebrates the values of an older Ireland by setting them against the greed and vulgarity often associated with the materialistic Ireland of the Celtic Tiger. The first part of the story follows in minute and sympathetic detail the preparations that an aged couple, Odo and Charlotte, who are hanging on by their fingernails to their dilapidated Big House, make for the celebration of the birthday of their only son, who lives in Dublin and visits his parents just once a year, on his birthday. It is clear from those preparations, and from the response of the couple when Timothy fails to turn up and sends his gay partner in his place, that the love of forty years, tied up with the house and its history, and inspired in large part by Odo's and Charlotte's marginalized position in the culture, provides them with a source of genuine strength. Unlike the Middletons of "The Distant Past," who are destroyed by the rekindling of old sectarian animosities when the violence in the North erupts, Odo and Charlotte are able to endure not only the absence of their son but also the crudity of his partner, a small-time thief who makes off with a family ornament after Odo and Charlotte feed him: "Their love of each other had survived the vicissitudes and the struggle there had been; not even the bleakness of the day that passed could affect it" (Trevor 1996:52). In "Of the Cloth," from *The Hill Bachelors* (2000), an elderly Protestant clergyman named Grattan Fitzmaurice finds himself more and more isolated in the increasingly secular Ireland of the late 1990s: "He was out of touch, and often felt it: out of touch with the times and what was happening in them, out of touch with two generations of change, with his own country and what it had become" (Trevor 2000:21). But when the young local Catholic priest Father Leahy pays Grattan a visit following the funeral of Grattan's gardener, the first visit ever made by a Catholic priest to the Protestant rectory, the two men experience a moment of human connection that transcends, just for that moment, the sharp divisions between their faiths and backgrounds, and the decline of both their religions in contemporary Ireland: "But the priest had come this evening. ... Small gestures mattered now, and statements in the dark were a way to keep the faith" (Trevor 2002:39). (For the argument that the stories in *Hill Bachelors* represent a somewhat less grim and historically determined view of Ireland than does much of Trevor's earlier writing, see Fitzgerald-Hoyt 2003:173–89.)

Trevor has been writing about Ireland for a very long time now, and at a consistently high level of achievement. It is worth remembering that when his first Irish short story appeared, in *The Ballroom of Romance* in 1972, most of the writers who are considered important contemporary Irish novelists were either just starting out, or not on the map at all: Francis Stuart's *Black List, Section H* had appeared the previous year, Jennifer Johnston's *The Captains and the Kings* the same year, and John Banville's *Birchwood* the next; and it would be some time before writers such as Julia O'Faolain (*No Country for Young Men*, 1980), Bernard MacLaverty (*Cal*, 1983), Roddy Doyle (*The Commitments*, 1987), Deirdre Madden (*Hidden Symptoms*, 1986), Dermot Bolger (*The Journey Home*, 1990), Patrick McCabe (*The Butcher Boy*, 1992), Colm Tóibín (*The Heather Blazing*, 1993), Dermot Healy (*A Goat's Song*, 1994), Anne Enright (*The Wig My Father Wore*, 1995), Mary Morrissey (*Mother of Pearl*, 1995), Seamus Deane (*Reading in the Dark*, 1996), Eugene McCabe (*Death and the Nightingale*, 1998), and Sebastian Barry (*The Whereabouts of Eneas McNulty*, 1998) began pushing Irish fiction in directions unimaginable to authors writing about Ireland in the 1960s and 1970s. Yet for all the extraordinary vitality and variety of contemporary Irish fiction, as it has grown alongside the growth of Trevor's career, it is only Trevor who has documented with such depth and compassion the full range of the Protestant experience in Ireland, only Trevor who has weighed the psychological costs and charted the historical causes of the sectarian violence in Northern Ireland by viewing the Troubles through the long, historical lens of the Protestant presence on the island, and only Trevor who has brought to imaginative life a vision of alienation and loneliness by examining the lives of one of Ireland's most marginalized peoples.

REFERENCES AND FURTHER READING

Cahalan, J.M. (1999). *Double Visions: Women and Men in Modern and Contemporary Irish Fiction.* Syracuse: Syracuse University Press.

Fitzgerald-Hoyt, M. (2003). *William Trevor: Re-imagining Ireland.* Dublin: Liffey Press.

Foster, J.W. (Ed.). (2006). *The Cambridge Companion to the Irish Novel.* Cambridge: Cambridge University Press.

Hardy, T. (1982). *The Complete Poems of Thomas Hardy.* J. Gibson (Ed.). New York: Macmillan.

Imhof, R. (2002). *The Modern Irish Novel: Irish Novelists after 1945.* Dublin: Wolfhound Press.

Kreilkamp, V. (1998). *The Anglo-Irish Novel and the Big House.* Syracuse: Syracuse University Press.

MacKenna, D. (1999). *William Trevor: The Writer and his Work.* Dublin: New Island Books.

Mahoney, C.H. (1998). *Contemporary Irish Literature: Transforming Tradition.* New York: St Martin's.

Morrison, K. (1993). *William Trevor.* New York: Twayne.

Paulson, S.M. (1993). *William Trevor: A Study of his Short Fiction.* New York: Twayne.

Peach, L. (2004). *The Contemporary Irish Novel: Critical Readings.* Basingstoke: Palgrave Macmillan.

Schirmer, G.A. (1990). *William Trevor: A Study of his Fiction.* London: Routledge.

Trevor, W. (1983). *Fools of Fortune.* New York: Viking.

Trevor, W. (1987). *Nights at the Alexandra.* New York: Harper & Row.

Trevor, W. (1988). *The Silence in the Garden.* New York: Viking.

Trevor, W. (1991). *Two Lives: Reading Turgenev and My House in Umbria.* New York: Viking.

Trevor, W. (1992). *The Collected Stories.* New York: Viking.

Trevor, W. (1994). *Excursions in the Real World: Memoirs.* New York: Alfred A. Knopf.

Trevor, W. (1996). *After Rain.* New York: Viking.

Trevor, W. (2000). *The Hill Bachelors.* New York: Viking.

Trevor, W. (2002). *The Story of Lucy Gault.* New York: Viking.

Ussher, A. (1949). *The Face and Mind of Ireland.* New York: Devin Adair.

42

The Mythopoeic Ireland of Edna O'Brien's Fiction

Maureen O'Connor

The Irish, like many people, love a scandal, and if the scandal is perpetrated by someone with dash and style, so much the better. This is one source for the enduring fascination with and even admiration for the late Charles Haughey, former taoiseach, despite the facts of his various proven crimes, including embezzlement, tax evasion, and the acceptance of bribes. That the money was used to bankroll an extravagant lifestyle featuring a private island, a yacht, and a few racehorses has the effect in some minds of rendering Haughey a colorful character, a lovable rogue, and not a criminal. It is interesting to note, then, that in 1960, long before he led his party, while still just a lowly government minister, Charles Haughey stood beside the archbishop of Dublin, John Charles McQuaid, in denouncing as a "smear on Irish womanhood" a different kind of scandal, the publication of the novel *The Country Girls*, by Edna O'Brien. Until recently, it has perhaps been this novel's notoriety, as well the novelist's considerable good looks and sometimes dramatic self-presentation, which has kept O'Brien alive in Irish cultural memory, even though she has published steadily in the fifty years since; not only sixteen novels, but also short fiction, plays for television and stage, poetry, books for children, and biographies as well as other non-fiction works. The twenty-first century has seen a change in Ireland's attitude toward its most successful woman writer, however. Her native country has begun to appreciate an author who is, in the words of James Cahalan, "rivalled in the scope of her international fame perhaps only by Brian Moore, among Irish novelists of either gender" (Cahalan 1988:286). She is a member of Aosdána (an "affiliation" for those who have made an "outstanding contribution to the arts in Ireland," an association set up, as it happens, by Haughey when taoiseach) and the recipient of numerous literary awards, including the European Literature Prize, the Italia Prima Cavour, the Kingsley Amis Award, the *Los Angeles Times* Fiction Award, the American National Arts Gold Medal

A Companion to Irish Literature, edited by Julia M. Wright
© 2010 Blackwell Publishing Ltd

for Lifetime Contribution, the Irish Pen Lifetime Award, and the 2006 Ulysses Medal
from University College Dublin, where she was also appointed adjunct professor of
creative writing. She holds honorary degrees from the University of Limerick, the
National University of Ireland, Galway, and Queen's University Belfast. She is
the first successful Irish woman writer to come from a rural, Roman Catholic background, and the first to grant such women a voice, to create an international place in
literature for them.

Seamus Heaney observed in May 2009, when presenting O'Brien with her latest
accolade, the Bob Hughes Lifetime Achievement in Literary Ireland Award, that "she
has a strong sense of the idiom of Ireland," an idiosyncratic language that yet survives
in a landscape which, throughout her writing, is infused with legend and myth. The
role of the land in O'Brien's work, which engages the cultural, historical, and social
significance of the landscape, is not only central to her fictional narratives but also
informs the dynamic of the fraught and complex history of her reputation and reception in the land she feels possessed and haunted by. In her 1976 memoir, *Mother
Ireland*, O'Brien suggests that "a country encapsulates our childhood and those lanes,
byres, fields, insects, suns, moons and stars are forever re-occurring and tantalizing
me" (O'Brien 1976a:88). The word "country" in this context works in two ways, each
contained in the other: it indicates the rustic, the non-metropolitan, and, by extension, it indicates the country of Ireland, "forever re-occurring" for O'Brien. She is ever
evoking the countryside, even in work ostensibly set in Dublin or London, or even
further afield. Of her deeply felt connection to the landscape of her youth, O'Brien
has said, "I happened to grow up in a country that was and is breathlessly beautiful,
so the feeling for nature, for verdure and for the soil was instilled in me" (quoted in
Roth 2001:104). While London is often the setting for O'Brien's novels, she rarely
sets her work in Dublin. *The Country Girls* concludes its narrative there, and the hospital which is the setting for much of her latest novel, *The Light of Evening* (2006), is
located in the Irish capital, but the city barely registers in that novel. O'Brien has
remained resolutely rural in her evocations of Ireland. Even in her most recent work,
which investigates the experiences of the now elderly Irish émigrés in London, workers
who left Ireland in the postwar boom of the 1950s when the influx of Irish into
England was at a historic high, rural Ireland is a constant, if only as the fetishized
object of nostalgic longing.

Born Josephine Edna O'Brien on December 15, 1930 to Michael and Lena (Cleary)
O'Brien of Tuamgraney, County Clare, she was the youngest of four surviving children. Life in her home town, O'Brien recalls, "was fervid, enclosed and claustrophobic"
(O'Brien 1976a:28). Michael O'Brien had inherited the house in which the family
lived and a good deal of surrounding land, but his addiction to horseflesh and to drink
led to much of the land being sold off. O'Brien's father, like the father of her most
important literary influence, James Joyce, was listed as a bankrupt in *Stubbs Gazette*.
Edna attended the National School in Scariff and then the Convent of Mercy in
Loughrea, County Galway. In 1946 she moved to Dublin, where she worked in a
chemist's shop and attended night classes in pharmacy, during which time she began

to write, inspired by the purchase, for fourpence on the Dublin quays, of *An Introduction to James Joyce* by T.S. Eliot. Like Joyce, O'Brien would go on to be pilloried in Ireland for obscenity, accused of immorality, and banned by the Irish censors (among others). In Dublin she met Ernest Gébler, Irish-born and of German-Czech background, a successful writer whose first novel, *The Plymouth Adventure*, had sold millions of copies in the United States and was made into a film starring Spencer Tracy and Gene Tierney. O'Brien and Gébler married in 1954 and had two sons, Carlo and Sasha. The family relocated to England in late 1958, and the marriage ended in the 1960s. Since 1959 O'Brien has principally resided in London, though she visits Ireland frequently. While still a pharmacology student in the 1940s she began contributing occasional pieces to Dublin periodicals and newspapers including *The Irish Press*, and was encouraged in her writing by Peadar O'Donnell, then editor of *The Bell*.

After moving to London, her short stories began to appear in periodicals such as *The Saturday Evening Post* and *Ladies' Home Journal*. In the course of her job reading manuscripts and writing reports for the Hutchinson publishing house her abilities were recognized, and with the support of Hutchinson in London and Knopf in the United States, along with an advance of £50, she wrote *The Country Girls*, the first of seven of her books that would be banned by the Irish Censorship Board. The book's representations of sexual desire, sexual abuse, and even sexual humor set in the rural west of Ireland, the traditional site in nationalist iconography of the "authentic" and uncorrupted heart of the nation, meant that it was met with outrage and condemnation. At home the reactions were shock, shame, and feelings of betrayal. The scandal of O'Brien having previously eloped with a divorced "foreigner" compounded her family's sense of disgrace. Edna O'Brien was denounced from the pulpit by the parish priest who later conducted a book burning in the chapel yard. Lena O'Brien relayed the humiliating details to her daughter and claimed that several women fainted (Edna suggested that may have been from the smoke). Vicious letters were written anonymously from the village to the author, one local woman claiming to have been possessed by the devil as a result of reading the novel (Carlson 1990:72). In several interviews, O'Brien recalls the discovery, after her mother's death, of a defaced copy of *The Country Girls* – which was dedicated to her mother – in which words and passages were effaced, whole pages torn out. However, even as her family and neighbors felt betrayed and exposed, and the Irish authorities, both secular and religious, vilified the text, reviews in the British press praised the novel as "fresh" and "natural," "unforced," "unselfconscious," "lyrical," and "charming."

Critical attitudes abroad began to change, however, by the time the ironically titled *Girls in their Married Bliss*, the third novel in what became *The Country Girls Trilogy*, appeared in 1964 (the second novel, *The Lonely Girl*, which would be retitled *Girl with Green Eyes*, was published in 1962). The trilogy follows the fate of the two young Irish women through disillusioning love-affairs and unhappy marriages, and the books, appropriately, grow darker, more cynical and satirical, as the protagonists emerge from their adolescent dreaminess and mature, no longer girlishly "fresh" and "charming." O'Brien's next two novels, *August Is a Wicked Month* (1965) and *Casualties of Peace* (1966), are not set in Ireland, but both feature women struggling with changing expectations of sex and marriage, a change often conveyed through the contrast between the rural Irish girlhoods they have left behind and their more "sophisticated" urban lives. Other later "non-Irish" novels, such as *The High Road* (1988) and *Time and Tide* (1992), feature similar protagonists, Irish women poised between two worlds: one comforting and maternal, yet blighted by the mutually reinforcing oppressions of church, state, and family; the other exciting and stimulating, yet finally offering only sexual exploitation promoted as "enlightenment" and "liberation." Superficial readings of these works, encouraged by the titillating fact of their being banned in her home country, secured O'Brien's growing reputation as a writer of racy novels, a reputation which, along with her physical beauty, skill in self-promotion, and her occasional attendance on the "swinging London" scene of the 1960s and 1970s, resulted in the trivialization and critical dismissal of her work as merely commercial, too transparently and wearily autobiographical, and preoccupied solely with "women's" personal concerns; that is, insufficiently socially engaged at a time when gender and social roles were in flux and identity politics were developing. Interviews and reviews increasingly focused on her looks, her voice, her clothes, and her "fey" and "charming" Irishness. O'Brien was proving especially popular with audiences in North America, but her work has always been taken more seriously there than in Britain or Ireland. Eminent supporters, such as John Updike, Alice Munro, Mary Gordon, and Philip Roth praised and appreciated her early work and have continued to champion her.

Irish commentators, in the meantime, were divided in their opinion of this rising international figure at the close of the first decade of her fame. Benedict Kiely defended the "convent girl with her temper riz" against the censors and predicted great things for her (Kiely 1969:159), while Sean McMahon deplored her "retardation" and her "neo-feminist propaganda" (McMahon 1967:79). O'Brien was subsequently seen to abandon the source of her original inspiration, to have become corrupted and debauched, having turned her back on Ireland. However, *A Pagan Place* (1970) and *Night* (1972), as well as a number of short stories that appeared frequently in prestigious periodicals over the years, most frequently *The New Yorker* (most of which were published in story collections), several of her well-received plays, including *A Cheap Bunch of Nice Flowers*, *The Gathering*, *Flesh and Blood*, *Our Father*, and *Family Butchers*, and the stylized memoir/cultural history *Mother Ireland*, are all set in Ireland. However, even when O'Brien effected an ostensible "return" to her native land, in her latest "Irish" trilogy – *The House of Splendid Isolation* (1994), *Down by the River* (1996), and *Wild Decembers* (2000) – she again provoked controversy, especially in Ireland, where commentators dismissed her as out of touch. *The House of Splendid Isolation* features a sometimes sympathetically drawn IRA gunman on the run in the Republic; the plot of *Down by the River* is drawn from the infamous 1992 "X case" of a 14-year-old Irish rape victim who was barred from traveling to London for an abortion; and *Wild Decembers* tells a story of land hunger and murder set in 1970s Ireland. Most controversial of all in her long career has been O'Brien's 2002 novel, *In the Forest*, based on a horrific triple murder committed eight years earlier only a few miles from where O'Brien grew up. Outcry against the book was vehement, and its author was excoriated throughout Ireland. The reaction was as bad as or worse than that aroused by *The Country Girls* over forty years earlier.

As much – usually contentious – cultural debate as her work inspires, with the exception of *Edna O'Brien*, Grace Eckley's slim volume of 1974, little serious scholarly work was done on O'Brien for decades, and she rarely made more than a token appearance in anthologies or bibliographies. Her output has been prodigious, yet only *The Country Girls* has intermittently and grudgingly been entered into the Irish literary canon. This has begun to change, a shift initiated by a 1996 special issue of the *Canadian Journal of Irish Studies* dedicated to O'Brien. In the last ten years, three book-length academic studies of O'Brien have appeared, two collections of essays, and a monograph by Amanda Greenwood, also entitled *Edna O'Brien* (2003), and a number of others are promised by North American, British, and Irish academics; she is also the subject of work under way by scholars in France, Italy, and Finland, countries in which her work in translation has long been considered a serious object of academic consideration. It is still possible, however, as recently as October 2006, to come across a review of *The Light of Evening* complaining that "like the fiddlers who clog up Dublin's cheesier theme pubs you can't help but wish that occasionally O'Brien would change her tune" (Hughes 2006). This review offers an example of the way in which it is often specifically O'Brien's Irishness that provides a platform for the remarkably *ad hominem* justifications for derogation of her work, even though her stated intention, from her first novel, has been to "eschew hypocrisy and stage-Irish rigmarole" (quoted in Carlson 1990:71).

O'Brien has acknowledged and regretted the "allocation" to Irishness, in her own words, "the tendencies to be wild, drunk, superstitious, unreliable, backward" (O'Brien 1976a:23), and has always been particularly sensitive to the dangers for the Irish, and particularly an Irish woman, to be identified with "the land itself" – the west of Ireland, especially – whether via romantic clichés of misty lakes and castles or venerable colonial stereotypes of the country as a blighted wasteland. In the course of *The Country Girls Trilogy*, for example, the character Caithleen comes to embody the equally problematic idealized and reviled versions of the rural Irish landscape. In the first volume Caithleen says, of a much older married man's efforts to seduce her, "I could hear the bulrushes sighing when he said my name that way and I could hear … all the lonesome sounds of Ireland" (O'Brien 1987:162). In *Girl with Green Eyes*, Eugene Gaillard, the man whom Caithleen will marry, says admiringly to her, "You're wild, you must have grown up out in the open." Caithleen's reaction is a tellingly deflating one, expressive of her miserable self-image: she thinks of the "front field at home with pools of muddy water lodged around the base of trees" (1987:320). By the novel's conclusion, after Eugene has begun to reproach her for her lack of discipline, her need to develop self-control and practice better hygiene, he will express contempt for her "country soul." Towards the end of the trilogy's final volume, Caithleen, now Kate, in London, separated from her husband, and recovering from a nervous breakdown, tells an admirer at a party that she is from Ireland, adding, "The west of Ireland": "But [she] did not give any echo of the swamp fields, the dun tree-less bogs, the dead deserted miles of country with a grey ruin on the horizon: the places from which she derived her sense of doom" (1987:494). Instead, she goes on to spin "lies" about a "solitary stone castle," the romantic scene completed by a lone white horse. In the trilogy's *Epilogue*, which O'Brien wrote in 1986, more than two decades after the publication of *Girls in their Married Bliss*, Baba speaks of scattering Kate's ashes (she has committed suicide), "between the bogs and bog lakes and the murmuring waters and every other fucking piece of depressingness that oozes from every hectometre and every furlong of the place and that imbued her with the old Dido predilections" (1987:523). The *Epilogue* appeared as O'Brien was working on *The High Road* (1988), in which the Irish protagonist/narrator recalls being on a lecture tour of America and ironically having to resort to "not a Gael but Spenser" for her descriptions of Ireland, that "battle-haunted, famine-haunted land," but, even then, knowing there was no way to convey

> what it was to walk roads and byroads where nature was savage; a landscape shot at times with a beauty that was dementing, indigo, fuchsia, but for the most part perme-ated with an emptiness redolent of the still greater emptiness, giving a sense of having been stranded, left behind by history and by the world at large, a severed limb of a land full of hurt and rage, a rage that enters and transmutes the way the moss and the damp pass into the tombstones. (O'Brien 1988:19)

O'Brien is rarely credited with either the irony or the historical and political acuity evident in a scene like this. Greenwood deplores the fact that O'Brien's "capacity for self-irony has been recurrently ignored" (Greenwood 2003:2), and finds the explana-tion for the ongoing critical underestimation she suffers in the fact that "[c]ontinuing constructions of O'Brien as 'Celtic,' exotic and sexually 'dangerous' have severely limited her status as writer" (2003:12). Greenwood, along with other scholars, most significantly Rebecca Pelan and Heather Ingman, have effectively and persuasively inveighed against characterizations of O'Brien's output as reducible to politically irrelevant, autobiographical romance, and have done so largely through analyses of the social constructions of gender and sexuality in an Irish socio-political context. While this approach is necessary and of great value, the role of O'Brien's rural, Roman Catholic background and the related history of the Irish landscape as an ironically "unnatural" construct (particularly the west of Ireland, whose topography has been shaped by a history of conflict and suffering) has yet to be considered in discussing the impact of her work, though it has informed her fiction from the start, as the above discussion of the fatal realization of Caithleen Brady's identification with "the country" briefly demonstrates.

Some of the most significant early interventions in the critical reconsideration of O'Brien's body of work noted the novelist's "demythologizing" project, one aimed at examining a particular post-Independence vision of Ireland oppressive to women in its reinforcement of colonial figurations of the nation as helpless, suffering female in need of salvation at the hands of her sons or lovers. Alicia Ostriker has observed that "At first thought, mythology seems an inhospitable terrain for a woman writer. There we find the conquering gods and heroes, the deities of pure thought and spirituality so superior to mother nature" (Ostriker 1985:12).

Certainly the Irish Free State exploited Irish myths to its own masculinist ends, but I would like to suggest that O'Brien also attempts to "*re*-mythologize" Irish experience in her fiction, reaching back to earlier Irish traditions found in archaic narratives which represented, in the words of Frances Devlin-Glass, "an interdependency of power between women and men" (Devlin-Glass 2001:106–07), grounded in a vision of the female body – and the natural world with which it was closely associated – as sacred; in other words, a social order in which women and the natural world were given political and spiritual significance. O'Brien's gritty, unsentimental portrayals of rural Irish life place the ordinary into unexpected relationship with the legendary past, sometimes ironically, but often in poignant and spiritual ways, and frequently all at once. The insistent identification of women with animals in her early fiction begins to attempt a transvaluation of the animal that harks back to Irish legends that valued and respected both animals and women, and treasured rather than denigrated their powers of reproduction and regeneration. This kind of revaluation is an extremely dangerous one. The narrator of *A Pagan Place*, for example, who creates a Druid grove – her pagan place – to escape to, has the terrifying example of the violent policing of her sister's sexuality ever before her. It is significant that her sister is repeatedly described as being an animal in need of restraint and containment.

The ancient power emanating from Irish topography centers around sacred sites such as groves of trees, wells, outcroppings of rock, and those mysterious mounds known as fairy forts, thresholds between the "real world" and Tír na nÓg, land of the dead and land of the *sidhe*, or fairies. David Lloyd maintains that this kind of "myth and folklore are not simply sedimented popular versions of outmoded philosophies, but function, rather, as the names and screens affixed by historians in those openings where there might be a way into alternative logics of time and space" (Lloyd 1999:76). It is the suppressed alternatives to official narratives to which O'Brien's fiction allows access. *Mother Ireland* opens with a description of "The Land Itself" (the title of the first chapter):

> Countries are either mothers or fathers, and engender the emotional bristle secretly reserved for either sire. Ireland has always been a woman, a womb, a cave, a cow, a Rosaleen, a sow, a bride, a harlot, and, of course, the gaunt Hag of Beare. (O'Brien 1976a:1)

Several of these identities clearly refer to Irish myth and legend: Ireland as a woman, whether that is Dark Rosaleen, Kathleen Ní Houlihan, or the Sean Bhean Bhocht (poor old woman), Ireland as a cow – Druimfhionn Donn Dílis (the dear brown cow) – and as the Hag of Beare, the Cailleach Bheara. Of course the Hag of Beare, like the powerful Irish war goddess the Mórrígan, was associated with nature and on occasion specifically with a cow. In the *Táin Bó Cúailnge*, the mythic cycle with cattle in its name – the cattle raid of Cooley – the Mórrígan fools Cúchulainn into healing her of the wounds he has inflicted on her by appearing to him in the form of an old woman with a cow. Cúchulainn blesses her three times – each time she gives him a drink of milk – and thereby cures her of the three wounds she sustained when in three different animal forms, an eel, a wolf, and a red heifer, all embodiments assumed in order to frustrate and foil Cúchulainn, who has earned her enmity by insulting her in an early meeting, when he encountered her as she was driving a heifer from his territory. It is in the form of a heifer that she warns the Brown Bull of Cooley of the forthcoming raid. Mórrígan also takes the form of a crow at various points in the narrative, probably most memorably at Cúchulainn's death.

In addition to its many appearances in *Mother Ireland*, the *Táin Bó Cúailnge* (see CHAPTER 1, TÁIN BÓ CÚAILNGE) is explicitly referenced in a number of O'Brien's novels, including *The House of Splendid Isolation, Down by the River, Night, In the Forest*, and *Wild Decembers*. Other cycle legends that appear in O'Brien's fiction include the "Frenzy of Mad Sweeney," or *Buile Suibhne Geilt*, and the story of the Children of Lir, or *Clann Lir*. O'Brien's interest in and knowledge of Irish legends and folklore is well documented. In 1986 she published *Tales for the Telling: Irish Folk and Fairy Stories*, her own versions of traditional stories that include tales about Finn, leader of the Fianna (see CHAPTER 2, FINN AND THE FENIAN TRADITION). In 1979 she compiled excerpts from a selection of Irish texts in her book *Some Irish Loving: A Selection*, texts which include a number of versions and translations of ancient legends. Her lengthiest introduction – to the book's opening section dedicated to "The Fantastic" – focuses on Cúchulainn stories in particular. The Mórrígan also appears in this introductory essay. The element that these narratives – the Cúchulainn stories, the *Táin*, Mad Sweeney, the Children of Lir – have in common is shape-shifting between the animal and the human.

Devlin-Glass says of the female divinities in the *Táin* that they fail to "binarize" and "hierarchize" the distinctions between human and animal. The Mórrígan in particular is identified, according to Devlin-Glass "with the animal life of the kingdom" (Devlin-Glass 2001:121) and is, according to Rosalind Clark, "the sovereignty goddess least susceptible to being Christianized and patriarchalized" (Clark 1991:200). One of the ways in which O'Brien has critiqued Christianity and patriarchy throughout her career is through a historically and culturally informed re-sacralizing of our embodiment, that which we share with animals. O'Brien makes use of the *Táin* and of Irish myths, such as the Children of Lir, when her characters undergo human–animal metamorphoses, emphasizing, as do the traditions she is drawing on, the vital links between the animal, the human, and the supernatural/spiritual worlds. Ostriker's consideration of the destabilizing possibilities inherent in women's literary use of myth includes the way in which a poet such as Adrienne Rich "identifies with a 'mermaid' and 'mermen' and says that 'We are, I am, you are … the one who find our way back / back to this scene'" (Ostriker 1985:12). The transformative power of the hybrid animal–human figure here captures androgyny, and requires a formal "fluidity" even at the level of syntax, a pronominal deliquescence, that refuses to naturalize structures of difference and dominance.

The juxtaposition of a kind of exalted vision of a mythic legendary past with the realities of what passed for the "spiritual" in mid- and late twentieth-century Irish life provides much of the tension and tragedy in O'Brien's fiction, even as recourse to this past is often necessary for psychological survival. The Catholic Church, especially in its deployment of a myth of a different order, that of the Virgin Mary, emerges again and again as a source of destruction and rapine, in every sense. Ecofeminist Karen J. Warren speaks of a "logic of domination" according to which "superiority justifies subordination" (Warren 1990:129), revealing the interrelated aspects of social domination and the domination of nature. Such a logic establishes and requires the kinds of binaries central to several "patriarchal theological tenets," according to Carol J. Adams: "transcendence and domination of the natural world, fear of the body, projection of evil upon women, world-destroying spiritual views" (Adams 1993:2). Christianity's distrust of the body, its renunciation of the sexual, is intensified in Catholic Ireland. Cheryl Herr asserts that "Ireland has literally eroded, in the sphere of representations that constitute social identity, a comfortable sense of the body" (Herr 1990:6), and Ingman, in a discussion of O'Brien and other Irish women writers, points to "the way in which the Catholic religion developed in Ireland where the patriarchal construct of the Virgin was used to control and define women" (Ingman 2007:116). In *Down by the River*, for instance, the novel based on the X case, the cult of the Virgin is evoked again and again by men and women who do not want the significantly named Mary, a young girl impregnated by her father, to travel to England for an abortion. The first incestuous rape occurs (textually) when father and daughter are fishing. Just before the attack, the father jokingly speaks of "Finn Mac Comhill who ate of the salmon of knowledge. ... We'll be the same" (O'Brien 1998:3). The apparently idyllic pastoral scene quickly becomes nightmarish. The father is only pretending to fish, and generally acting "like he acted with visitors." His behavior is as deviously, yet exiguously, misleading as are his words, his reference to a hero's search for wisdom a clumsy screen for his brutal intentions.

There are too many instances of such moments throughout O'Brien's fiction, in which the legendary past appears to ironically comment on the sordid reality of the present, to enumerate here, but one powerful example of the triumph of the "pagan" occurs in the novel *Night*. This stream-of-consciousness first-person narrative has been described as a kind of revision of Molly Bloom's soliloquy. What no one has seemed to notice are the many playful, ironic, and celebratory parallels with the *Táin*. Mary Hooligan the narrator, refers to Queen Maeve more than once, and the novel is a kind of extended pillow talk with the reader playing the role of Ailill, Maeve's husband with whom the assertive queen enjoys a very competitive relationship. Mary enumerates her riches (which are comically few, shabby, and mostly borrowed, yet she relishes them) and asserts her independence. Like Maeve, Mary revels in the here and now with perhaps insufficient regard for the future, and insists on the indulgence of her immediate needs and desires. She also shares with Maeve a preoccupation with cattle.

Mary is a woman who regularly witnesses human–animal metamorphoses: "I see the animal starting up in people, first it is a paw, then the entire tendon of a leg that goes striped and furry" (O'Brien 1974:25). She refers to herself when she remembers having posed uncomfortably for an art class as "like a polyp [the aquatic invertebrate] without my robes and my decoys" (74), which may at first suggest that she is not entirely free of Christian unease with the body, but it is the objectification of the exercise to which she responds, the disrespect shown for what she is offering, a sniggering, smutty failure to acknowledge the spiritual aspects of the exchange. Similarly, an unhappy sexual experience leaves her and a defensive, unsympathetic lover "no longer like people, but bits of meat, uncooked, flinching" (70). And of course, meat, in the modern western world, is alienated animal flesh. Immersion in the natural and with the animal in particular is in fact a glorious and lyrical celebration in the novel. Significantly, this occurs frequently in long perorations on that beast so important to Irish mythology, the cow. The novel also features many lyrical passages about birds, and bird transformations figure centrally in Irish mythology, such as when the Mórrígan becomes a raven. However, the cow recurs in remembrances and re-creations of home and family:

> We shat in the same places. That is to say the hills and the dales, the lambent meadows of Coose. ... Cows concern me. The world's hide, the world's blameless udder. I would have stayed near to them in the dark, mingled their breath with mine. I still champion them ... I have a feeling that they are disappearing from our lives altogether. I shall miss them, I shall pine. ... Soon their lowing, their hide, their teats, their udders, their saunter, their curling tails, their matted tails, the dry and undry scour of their rumps, their dipping umbilical cords, soon all these will be after images, spectres of thing as that we once saw at morningtide or at eveningtide, or when on our annual vacations. (33–34)

Solidarity with the cow can be an instrument of resistance in other novels, as when in *Casualties of Peace* the character Willa remembers "her first little rebellion" against her abusive husband, letting a "dazed stupefied" cow out if its confinement against his wishes to shit in the new snow: "It made a crazy shape and the liquid trickling out defiled more snow. And how I welcomed it: slime on the unlimited whiteness" (O'Brien 1968:134). This novel also features an imagined transformation into a bird on the part of Willa's friend Patsy:

> If she were a swallow she would soar very high to the loneliest emptiest part of the sky, away from the irritation of fellow birds, nests, eggs, repetitiveness. Away with the clouds. Coming down for food and a little spring wooing. As the semen darted in her she would fly, letting it spill out in a wild jet of betrayal. No aftermath. Freedom, freedom, freedom. Even as a bird she clung to femaledom. No doubt as a bird her songs would be dirges. (44)

These identifications with animals almost too easily associated with the female are released from modern iterations of domesticity and sexual availability and recapitulate their pre-modern symbolic significance.

In *The House of Splendid Isolation* the bird-transformation myth of Sweeny appears explicitly, but this time it is used to describe a male character. McGreevey, the IRA gunman on the run, is compared to "mad Sweeney in the poem" (O'Brien 1995:222) as he moves through the trees, but this is toward the end of the novel when he is about to be captured, when it appears nature has betrayed him. He has undergone several transformations by this point, and the older woman, Josie, with whom he has been living in a quasi-hostage situation, is shot and killed when she is taken for McGreevy, an acknowledgment of the danger of the kind of mutability and androgyny implicit in transformation myths. An earlier passage in the novel, however, provides an example of the way in which, in O'Brien's later fiction, male characters begin to partake of significant moments of paradoxical humanization via zoontology.

In these late novels, men's access to potential redemption via a kind of shapeshifting also comprises a kind of transgendering, or perhaps the transcendence of gender, by participating in that most female of activities, birth. This is true of McGreevy, a character for which O'Brien was widely excoriated. She not only humanized a "terrorist," but allowed him to express idealism as informing his ruthlessness as a killer. McGreevy's humanization is in part achieved through his feminization. Significantly, this is first signaled when he demonstrates the effects of the kind of insistent dehumanization to which women are frequently subject:

> They call him an animal. … Half-asleep; the fields he's crossed and the drains he's fallen into come weaving in over him. He thinks he's eating hay, chewing it like a cow, and then chewing the cud. … Straw streaking across his face and his mind spinning like meat on a spit. (O'Brien 1995:14)

So we have the all-important cow reappearing here – not a bull, but a cow. This descent into the animal is ironically transformed into a demonstration of unheralded "humanity." Just at this moment of disorientation, distress, and self-alienation to the point of mild hallucination, McGreevy, hiding in a barn, hears an animal moaning in pain. Seeing that a cow is in distress with a calf that is too big, he helps her deliver and sees in her suffering a link to the history of masculine contest and strife in which he is yet embroiled in one of the novel's references to the *Táin*:

> He talks to her, says things to her, to silence her moans. … He finds some [rope] and coils it around the jutting hooves … all the while saying these idiotic things. From the gate he uses as leverage the moans follow him, something primeval in them, the moans of cows and cattle of ancient times, for which land and fiefdoms were fought over. (15)

That scenes of birth are the site of such transfiguration is a striking development in O'Brien's career-long interrogation of the custodial institutions of church, family, and state, especially their interest in patrolling women's sexual and reproductive roles. The rapist-father of *Down by the River* experiences a similar moment of near-redemption in helping a horse to give birth, a scene at which his daughter is present, a moment of transformation that gives her hope for a "normal" relationship between them. O'Brien has repeatedly portrayed post-Independence Ireland as obsessed with the control of the land and control of women, and so the conflation of women and animals in her texts can be a fatal one.

Significantly, in O'Brien's novels dating from the mid-1990s she increasingly locates the psychic damage created by violently imposed patriarchal imperatives in her male characters. The latest "unnatural" and "beastly" male character to be given controversially sensitive, even sympathetic, treatment is her most irremediably savage creation, the horrific "Kinderschreck" of *In the Forest*, Michen O'Kane. O'Kane, who murders a young woman, her small son, and a priest, is given his nickname, before any of the killings have even taken place, by a German man living in O'Kane's rural home village to which he has returned from England after a long and troubled absence. This novel, saturated in folklore and fairy tales from many traditions including the Irish, is about poisoned childhood and desecrated nature, and the two phenomena are counter-implicated.

After being shuffled through a series of Irish religious institutions, where he is sexually and physically abused – by older boys and priests and religious brothers – he goes on to prison in England and further brutal institutionalization and dehumanization. He returns to the rural village of his childhood, where no one will claim him and yet where he is allowed to terrorize the community. A reluctance to take responsibility for his lifelong mistreatment has ultimately tragic consequences. O'Kane, who is made alien by the strange and foreign name of Kinderschreck, is not treated as fully human on his return home. As he tells one of his victims, "I get very low and lonely. ... People leave out bread and milk for me the way they would for a dog" (O'Brien 2002a:127). He is called a specter, a poltergeist, a sprite, a devil complete with horns and hooves, a wolfman who sometimes hoots like a donkey. He is, above all, an animal, and refers to himself that way, sometimes piteously, sometimes aggressively. Like the narrator of *A Pagan Place*, O'Kane attempts escape by retreating to the forest. He decides "He would give himself a secret name, Caoilte, the name of the forest" (4), Caoilte being the name of one of the Fianna, another mythic resonance. He does this in memory of his mother, who, in a heartbreaking attempt at whimsy, called him "a true son of the forest" after he stayed out in the woods all night to escape the unbearable sight of his father beating his mother. At his mother's death, O'Kane is haunted by the memory of the jeering reception that met his claims then to be "a true son of the forest," when his classmates called him instead "A mammy's boy, a patsy, a pandy, a sissy, and a ninny." After the murders, when he is in jail for his terrible crimes, another metamorphosis occurs:

> He had birds coming in the window whistling tunes and he whistled back. Then one day six or seven red hens from home came and he talked to them and asked them if they were laying well. He had great times with them. He learned the chookchookchook-chookchookchook that they did after they laid. One morning they didn't come and he cried. Pigs came, but they got stuck, they got wedged between the bars, their pink hairy rumps not able to get out. They taught him grunts, and the screws listened outside the

cell and looked through the spyhole, made bets whether he was or was not a pig. Instead of Fattie they called him Piggy. (236–37)

Once again, through animals, O'Brien locates an almost shocking, somehow chilling, poignancy in what should be an utterly unsympathetic figure. The hens and pigs, emissaries from O'Kane's unfulfilled dreams of domesticity, love, and mother, offer only fleeting comfort; in fact, his identification with them means further abuse, as the prison guards, representatives of patriarchal social control, act like O'Kane's earliest tormentors, schoolyard bullies learning to be "hard" men at the expense of mothers and animals, those designated worthless because most threatening to self-similar male subjectivity. It is significant that a young mother is O'Kane's first victim – mothers don't tend to enjoy much longevity in O'Brien's work – as this is a novel about a larger crime that Amanda Greenwood has called "cultural matricide." She has said of this novel that it "expresses wider-reaching concerns about the degree of nihilism and violence generated by existing social and symbolic orders" (Greenwood 2003:20).

O'Kane, whose own mother was taken from him when he was a very young boy, has a troubled relationship with animals. He is obsessed by them, visited by them in memories, dreams, and fantasies, identifies with them (ambivalently), longs for their company (he particularly misses a pet fox from his childhood), but also hates them for their vulnerability and the abjectness, the victim status, that they share with him. He tortures and kills them as a boy for this reason. The animals he encounters in real life are mostly the roadkill on the new roads, bodies that continue to speak to him. The green spaces he played in as a child are gone; his refuge, the forest, is still there, but reduced, encroached upon by the kind of irresponsible building that has point-lessly expanded rural villages across Ireland in the last ten to fifteen years. The villagers of the novel, including O'Kane, are trapped between an older, nature-based tradition that endures, but only barely, in a landscape that is being rapidly despoiled and a more modern iteration of the values of their former colonial masters through which they see their earlier selves as savages. A deep feeling of shame persists that they are always in danger of disqualification from the ranks of the civilized, and these shames and fears are projected onto the inhuman other, however that is defined. In this dys-functional community – which O'Brien herself says is a reflection of conditions from Clare to the West Bank – natural resources, including children, are ignored, exploited, discarded, with disastrous results. A vision of avenging nature appears in the first pages in the book, when a woman who was part of the search party for O'Kane's victims recalls a dream of "tall trees no longer static but moving like giants, giants on their gigantic and shaggy roots, their green needly paws reaching out to scratch her, engulf her" (O'Brien 2002a:1). The novel ends with a brief chapter from O'Kane's early childhood, a re-creation of his first night in the forest, which, perhaps thanks to the heroic terms in which his mother tried to cast the event, is not remembered as a terrified flight from violence but as a prelapsarian fantasy of unity with the natural world culminating in a comically overdetermined Freudian scene of floating through an ocean of kindly, maternal cows: "They were far taller than he was, their coats were silky, and they had big soft pink diddies" (262).

At the end of the *Táin*, the Bull's final frenzy scars the land. Devlin-Glass sees this as the result of a failure to share power with the goddess. A similar kind of failure makes inevitable the horrors recounted in *In the Forest*. O'Brien has spoken of writing a novel about the ways in which the Celtic Tiger has utterly desacralized the Irish landscape, which recalls her description of the famine in *Mother Ireland*: "the *anima mundi*, the soul of the land, was lying dim and dead" (O'Brien 1976a:60). This time it is the Irish themselves, ourselves, that have brought this destruction about.

REFERENCES AND FURTHER READING

Adams, C.J. (1993). *Ecofeminism and the Sacred*. New York: Continuum.

Cahalan, J. (1988). *The Irish Novel: A Critical History*. Boston: Twayne.

Carlson, J. (1990). *Banned in Ireland*. Athens: University of Georgia Press.

Clark, R. (1991). *The Great Queens: Irish Goddesses from the Morrígan to Cathleen Ní Houlihan*. Gerrards Cross: Rowland & Littlefield.

Colletta, L. and M. O'Connor (Eds). (2006). *Wild Colonial Girl: Essays on Edna O'Brien*. Madison: University of Wisconsin Press.

Devlin-Glass, F. (2001). "The Sovereignty as Co-Lordship: A Contemporary Feminist Rereading of the Female Sacred in the Ulster Cycle." In F. Devlin-Glass and L. McCredden (Eds). *Feminist Poetics of the Sacred: Creative Suspicions* (pp. 106–34). Oxford: Oxford University Press.

Eckley, G. (1974). *Edna O'Brien*. Cranbury: Associated University Presses.

Gebler, C. (2000). *Father and I: A Memoir*. London: Little, Brown.

Gillespie, M.P. (1995). "(S)he Was too Scrupulous Always: Edna O'Brien and the Comic Tradition." In T. O'Connor (Ed.). *The Comic Tradition in Irish Women Writers* (pp. 108–23). Gainesville: University Press of Florida.

Greenwood, A. (2003). *Edna O'Brien*. London: Northcote House.

Guppy, S. (1984). "Interview with Edna O'Brien." *The Paris Review*, 92, 22–50.

Herr, C. (1990). "The Erotics of Irishness." *Critical Inquiry*, 17, 1–34.

Hughes, S. (2006). "Déjà vu in Dublin and New York." *The Observer*, 15 October. http://www.guardian.co.uk/books/2006/oct/15/fiction.features.

Ingman, H. "Edna O'Brien: Stretching the Nation's Boundaries." *Irish Studies Review*, 10.3, 253–65.

Ingman, H. (2007). *Twentieth-Century Fiction by Irish Women: Nation and Gender*. Aldershot: Ashgate.

Kiely, B. (1969). "The Whores on the Half-Doors." In O. Dudley Edwards (Ed.). *Conor Cruise O'Brien Introduces Ireland* (pp. 148–61). London: Deutsch.

Laing, K., S. Mooney, and M. O'Connor (Eds). (2006). *Edna O'Brien: New Critical Perspectives*. Dublin: Carysfort.

Lloyd, D. (1999). *Ireland after History*. Notre Dame: Notre Dame University Press.

McCrum, R. (2002). "Deep Down in the Woods." *The Observer*, April 28. Retrieved from http://books.guardian.co.uk/departments/generalfiction/story/0,,706211,00.html.

McMahon, S. (1967). "A Sex by Themselves: An Interim Report on the Novels of Edna O'Brien." *Éire-Ireland*, 2.1, 79–87.

Moloney, C. and H. Thompson. (2003). *Irish Women Writers Speak Out: Voices from the Field*. Syracuse: Syracuse University Press.

Morgan, E. (2000). "Mapping Out a Landscape of Female Suffering: Edna O'Brien's Demythologizing Novels." *Women's Studies: An Interdisciplinary Journal*, 29.4, 449–76.

Nash, C. (1994). "Remapping the Body/Land: New Cartographies of Identity, Gender, and Landscape in Ireland." In A. Blunt and G. Rose (Eds). *Writing Women and Space: Colonial and*

Postcolonial Geographies (pp. 227–249). London: Guilford.

Nye, R. (1972). "Good Words for the Most Part in the Right Order." *The Times*, October 5, 10.

O'Brien, E. (1967). *August Is a Wicked Month* (1965). Harmondsworth: Penguin.

O'Brien, E. (1968). *Casualties of Peace* (1966). Harmondsworth: Penguin.

O'Brien, E. (1970). *The Love Object*. Harmondsworth: Penguin.

O'Brien, E. (1974). *Night* (1972). Harmondsworth: Penguin.

O'Brien, E. (1976a). *Mother Ireland*. Harmondsworth: Penguin.

O'Brien, E. (1976b). *A Scandalous Woman and Other Stories*. Harmondsworth: Penguin.

O'Brien, E. (1978). *Johnny I Hardly Knew You*. Harmondsworth: Penguin.

O'Brien, E. (1980). *Mrs. Reinhardt and Other Stories*. Harmondsworth: Penguin.

O'Brien, E. (1981). *Some Irish Loving: A Selection*. Harmondsworth: Penguin.

O'Brien, E. (1987). *The Country Girls Trilogy*. New York: Plume.

O'Brien, E. (1988). *The High Road*. New York: Plume.

O'Brien, E. (1992). *Tales for the Telling: Irish Folk and Fairy Stories*. London: Puffin Books.

O'Brien, E. (1995). *The House of Splendid Isolation* (1994). New York: Plume.

O'Brien, E. (1998). *Down by the River* (1996). New York: Plume.

O'Brien, E. (1999). *James Joyce*. New York: Penguin.

O'Brien, E. (2001). *A Pagan Place* (1970). Boston: Houghton Mifflin.

O'Brien, E. (2002a). *In the Forest*. Boston: Houghton Mifflin.

O'Brien, E. (2002b). *Wild Decembers* (2000). New York: Mariner Books.

O'Brien, E. (2006). *The Light of Evening*. London: Weidenfeld & Nicolson.

O'Brien, E. (2009). *Byron in Love*. London: Phoenix.

O'Brien, P. (1987). "The Silly and the Serious: An Assessment of Edna O'Brien." *Massachusetts Review*, 28.3, 474–88.

O'Connor, M. (2010). "'Becoming-Animal' in the Novels of Edna O'Brien." In C.L. Cusick (Ed.). *Out of the Earth: Ecocritical Readings of Irish Texts*. Cork: Cork University Press.

Ostriker, A. (1985). "The Thieves of Language: Women Poets and Revisionist Mythmaking." In D. Wood Middlebrook and M. Yalom (Eds). *Coming to Light: American Women Poets in the Twentieth Century* (pp. 10–36). Ann Arbor: University of Michigan Press.

Pelan, R. (1993). "Edna O'Brien's 'Stage Persona': An 'Act' of Resistance." *Canadian Journal of Irish Studies*, 19.1, 67–78.

Roth, P. (2001). *Shop Talk: A Writer and his Colleagues and their Work*. New York: Houghton Mifflin.

Sage, L. (1992). *Women in the House of Fiction: Post-War Women Novelists*. New York: Macmillan.

St Peter, C. (2000). *Changing Ireland: Strategies in Contemporary Women's Fiction*. New York: St Martin's Press.

Warren, K.J. (1990). "The Promise and Power of Ecofeminism." *Environmental Ethics*, 12.2, 127–48.

Woodward, R. (1989). "Reveling in Heartbreak." *New York Times Book Review*, 42, 50–51.

43

Anglo-Irish Conflict in Jennifer Johnston's Fiction

Silvia Diez Fabre

I am neither a philosopher nor a politician, an academic nor a former of opinion in any way. All I know how to do is tell stories: the same story, some people say, over and over again. That may be true, but for me it has been something else, it has been a reassembling of facts, my facts, and an attempt to give those facts a relevance, to make me relevant, to identify myself: not give myself a label, because we are all diminished by labels, but to shout that I am on the side of the nation, with a small n, while recognising that, for all our fine words, we have not yet achieved the Nation with a large one. (Longley 1991:10)

I quote above an extract from a speech delivered by Jennifer Johnston during the Cultures of Ireland Group Conference held in Dun Laoghaire in 1991, to introduce her personal and literary engagement with Ireland's sense of self. The slow progression of Ireland after Independence as a peaceful community is a primary concern in Johnston's fiction. The novels written in the twentieth century painfully acknowledge the lack of freedom in Ireland and the feelings of moral isolation affecting the people. Johnston gives vivid accounts of individuals who are stagnating in Ireland or trying to escape. Beneath their problems of personal identity lies the problem of their national identity. Johnston's novels hark back to the past, trying to understand the reasons for social disturbance and individual unhappiness from the time of the 1920s Troubles up to the present. In order to capture the full picture of Johnston's Ireland, the situation of the present needs to be interpreted in the light of history, which her novels suggest but never develop.

The lives of the characters in her novels are burdened by their personal past, which works as a reflection of the history of their nation, defining at the same time their identity in a national framework. The novels are mindful of the violence of the 1920s

A Companion to Irish Literature, edited by Julia M. Wright
© 2010 Blackwell Publishing Ltd

Troubles as a struggle for freedom that confronted the people and divided Ireland. There are repeated allusions to the impact of the early twentieth-century cultural revival on shaping the idea of Irish purity and demonizing English influence over the island. This in turn explains the context of nationalist Ireland, loyal to a version of Irishness essentially Catholic and hostile to English roots and to Protestant affiliation. There is also the pull of England as expressed in Unionist feelings and in the Irish experience of exile. All of these elements play a role in the lives of the people, paving the way for the division between Catholics and Protestants, nationalists and Unionists, Irish Ireland and British Ireland. It is as a result of this background that national self-definition has a pervasive effect on the lives of the individuals – whether Protestant or Catholic – who are the protagonists of the stories north and south of the border. It is essential to keep in mind this historical overview, conveyed through cultural allusions in the novels, because, in Johnston's fiction, it forms the basis of the Anglo-Irish conflict and is the cause of social disturbance and individual unhappiness.

Any discussion about this writer would be incomplete without addressing the major themes that various critics have identified in her work. As the personal and the historical are so intertwined, it is difficult to say whether Johnston is more interested in personal situations of loneliness against the background of time and tradition, or in portraits of class defined in time and place. "Rather than look at Johnston's works as historical or naturalistic novels," José Lanters advises us, we should "approach them by means of the suggestive pattern created by the layers of allusions that are to be found in her work" (Lanters 1989:210). Linden Peach concurs with this view, and points out "the fusion of the natural with the mythical" (Peach 2004:101). On the other hand, a great body of critical work has approached Johnston as an Irish woman writer. Her female characters have raised the issue of female selfhood (Hargreaves 1988), and Ann Owens Weekes offers a perceptive gender analysis of the cultural context recreated by Johnston in order to question traditional myths (1990). A Kristevan reading allows Heather Ingman the scope to study gender and nation with greater insight into the politics of gender (Ingman 2005, 2007).

I agree that a straightforward reading of Johnston's fiction fails to grasp the importance of her personal consideration of what it means to be Irish and of the varied strategies she uses for this purpose. Here I will approach her novels about Irish individuals who feel they are outsiders in Ireland as allegorical representations of Anglo-Irish conflict in the nation, focusing on *How Many Miles to Babylon?* (1974), *The Captains and the Kings* (1972), and *The Illusionist* (1995). I have chosen *How Many Miles to Babylon?* and *The Captains and the Kings* from the Johnston novels which recreate the Big House as a symbol of Anglo-Irish conflict because, respectively, they are set in a period of Irish history which shows the situation of the nation before and after Independence. It must be noted that Johnston is often considered to belong to the Big House literary tradition, writing about the decay of the Ascendancy in the twentieth century. The most comprehensive study on the Big House to date points out Johnston's subversion of this literary tradition (Kreilkamp 1998). Johnston has stated that she does not identify with the Ascendancy or with the Big House novel as a writer (Gonzalez 1998). I would suggest that the Big House is used in her novels as a setting which is symbolic of the Anglo-Irish conflict of the nation because of its historical association with the Anglo-Irish. *The Illusionist* (1995), for instance, is a parable-like novel that deals with the conflict in Northern Ireland. Published shortly after the 1993 Joint Declaration of Peace (more commonly known as the Downing Street Declaration), the novel revolves around the problems that a married couple encounter because of their British and Irish identities. The problems of the main characters are centered on the way in which they view their freedom, and on the confrontation which ensues between them, disrupting their family life, and these two aspects are used in the novel to reflect on the question of peace in Northern Ireland.

I will read these novels in the light of the cultural project carried out by revisionists working for social harmony in Ireland, arguing that this cultural movement of national awareness motivates Johnston's literary art and her suggestive narrative. A revisionist interpretation of the cultural confrontation that exists in Irish society promulgates a more flexible national identity based on diversity or "varieties of Irishness" (Foster 1989). As a consequence, a process of dialogue is required to evaluate the cultural roots of Irish problems and to re-evaluate the monolithic concept of the Irish nation, as Johnston's fiction demonstrates. Her stories offer repeated attempts to cross the borders of class, religion, and political allegiance by establishing relationships – of love or friendship – between characters who represent different Irish identities. Thus, a recurring theme in her work is the need for human connection. If people are unable or unwilling to empathize with others, there is no hope for society. Love or friendship are based on mutual dependence, as each person's identity is partially shaped by the shared relationship. The fact that these relationships ultimately fail reflects the difficulty of overcoming the divisions of the past and engaging in a multicultural concept of the nation.

At the same time, through the main characters in these novels, personal identity reflects the failure of the nation to provide a peaceful home for its people. The protagonists experience the loss of maternal or matrimonial love, which in turn makes them incapable of creating a family home. The concept of the Irish nation as a family home is reminiscent of the cultural myth of Mother Ireland, happily married to the ruler of the land and caring for her children. The novels discussed here portray characters who feel isolated in the family home because of their mothers' negative influence on their personal growth. In turn, none of them manages to create a family home or to empathize with an inclusive sense of the nation. Johnston's novels, however, seem to reach the conclusion that the future of the nation demands an imaginative effort on the part of the people. Their main characters compensate for their sense of failure or isolation through their artistic creativity, either through music or literature.

How Many Miles to Babylon? is set in the early twentieth century, some time before the 1920s Troubles which led to Independence. It deals with the life of Alexander Moore, who writes his own story as a member of an Anglo-Irish family. He also explains the circumstances in which he has been condemned to death by a British court martial in World War I. Presented as awaiting death in the midst of this war, which preceded the outbreak of the Irish War of Independence, this character's situation is suggestive of the proximity of the end of colonial Ireland. The first part of the novel is centered on Alexander's Anglo-Irish childhood and youth, and highlights the role played in the family by his English mother. The second part takes place in the British army during World War I: Alexander has been forced to enlist by his mother. The novel moves from the Big House to a context of English domination in order to explore his conflicted sense of identity in the face of his colonial background. This exploration conjures up the myth which was used to justify the English colonization of Ireland: the English race was supposed to be a masculine one, strong-willed and efficient, and consequently a good match for the feminine Irish race, emotional and sentimental. At home Alexander feels more inclined towards his father's mild temperament than his mother's authority. This is the cause of frequent arguments between his parents, since Mrs Moore believes her Irish husband is not giving Alexander a proper education:

> "You never speak with authority," she said as the door closed. "You don't ever sound as if you knew what you were talking about. You have always been an ineffective man."
>
> His hand was trembling as he picked up his glass. He had temporarily laid down his pipe.
>
> "I suppose that's as good a word for me as any."
>
> "Ineffective and old."
>
> I put out a hand and touched his knee. It was a brief gesture, as ineffective as one he might have made himself.
>
> "It's whatever you say. I'll do whatever ..."
>
> He laughed.
>
> "You do what your mother tells you, my boy. That's the way ... Yes." (Johnston 1988:30)

When Alexander eventually goes to war, as his mother wants him to do, he finds out that he is not seen as an English officer:

> "Will I fall the men out, sir?"
>
> He looked at me surprised.
>
> "For a cup of tea or something?"
>
> "No," he said, and turned round towards the fire. He dipped his head towards the mug in his hands. I knew that had Bennett asked the question the answer would have been different. The same with Sergeant Barry. I was useless as far as the men were concerned. I could neither control them nor give them comfort in any way. (132)

Alexander's feminine inefficiency is also implicitly voiced by Major Glendinning: "If nothing else, Moore, if nothing else, I will make a man of you" (121).

The fact that Alexander is both the protagonist and the narrator of the story allows him to reflect on the way his experience, as well as his interpretation of it in the act of writing, have been shaped by the received impressions of the past. These impressions, like the traditional nursery rhyme "How many miles to Babylon?" recalled by Alexander (2, 9, 69–70, 73), have settled gradually and definitively in the collective memory over generations. *How Many Miles to Babylon?* thus examines Ireland's identity in the light of its cultural past, in particular with reference to the imprint of the colonial myth of English superiority versus Irish inferiority, complemented by the Yeatsian ideals of social harmony between an Anglo-Irish aristocracy and an Irish peasantry (Diez Fabre 2007).

The bonds of friendship that develop throughout the novel between Alexander and Jerry, the stable boy on his family's estate, question the imperative that their difference in identity and class should be confrontational, in spite of the opposition that their respective families represent. As Jerry comments, "One's as bad as the other" (16). They decide to keep their personal relationship secret, and share their common passion for horses as "partners" (17), breeding and training them. They see each other as equals, and their exceptional friendship thus anticipates the end of colonial Ireland but also embodies the notion of a free, inclusive nation. In the war, Alexander's closeness to Jerry, a simple Irish soldier, is considered a serious breach of duty for an English officer. The situation reaches a crisis when Jerry is condemned to death for desertion, having abandoned the camp for a few days in order to find out the whereabouts of his father, believed missing in the war. Alexander shoots Jerry in his prison cell and therefore Jerry avoids the humiliation of a public execution, but as a result Alexander himself is condemned to death. Despite his personal conflict between Englishness and Irishness throughout the story, Alexander eventually understands his double Anglo-Irish identity: he does not rebel against his mother, neither does he fail to fulfill his duty as a soldier, though he refuses to behave like an officer towards Jerry. In prison, and remembering Major Glendinning, he pointedly observes, "He will never make a man of me now" (1). Alexander's breach of duty as seen from the outside relies on his decision to preserve his personal relationship with Jerry in terms of equality. *How Many Miles to Babylon?* is based upon the recognition that freedom requires the solidarity of the Irish people, whatever their differences in identity. Yet the fact that Alexander's fate, like Jerry's, is ultimately subject to an English decision casts a shadow on the future of the nation.

The Captains and the Kings is centered on Mr Prendergast's solitary life in his family mansion around the late 1960s. His financial situation does not allow him to keep servants, although he still has an old gardener who started working in Kill House at the time of old Mrs Prendergast. Since his wife's death, he seems to have found his own space alone in the house, "the way he had always wanted to be" (Johnston 1990:13). The main character in this novel is clearly presented as a man enclosed in himself. He attends the Protestant service because he enjoys playing the organ there, but he goes to the church by car: "He felt less vulnerable, as if he were not leaving the house at all" (31). He has hardly kept in contact with his only daughter, living in London, and now that he is a widower it does not appeal to him "to create even the most formal relationship" (45). Through the portrait of Mr Prendergast, *The Captains and the Kings* paints Ireland as a nation of moral decay because of its loss of faith in personal relationships and therefore in human values such as love and friend-ship. Playing the piano is the only passion in his life and he enjoys it in private. Strangely enough, it is the son of the local shop owners who opens up Mr Prendergast's self-enclosed world. The first time they meet their social differentiation and separate identities become evident, for Diarmid Toorish, a boy representative of the "Celts" in Mr Prendergast's view (14), has been sent by his parents to the man in "the big house" to ask him for work (105). Mr Prendergast cannot afford to pay for any more employ-ees than Sean, the gardener. The leading role of the landlord which is suggested here has long been overdue in Irish society, after centuries of absenteeism. Nevertheless, it is outside the frame of conventionally Irish social patterns that Mr Prendergast and Diarmid create an ideal, though secret, relationship, akin to the way a grandfather and a grandson would behave towards each other. Their friendship can only survive at the price of secrecy, for everybody would disapprove of Mr Prendergast mixing with "that Toorish brat" (62). This is the case with Sean, who becomes suspicious of a relationship which is "not natural" for a person who has never cared for anybody (75): "Nose always stuck in a book. ... No time for a soul. Hardly a civil word out of him in the course of a day. 'Mawnin', Sean, Evenin' Sean', in his bloody West British accent" (24).

Diarmid dreams of becoming a soldier. His innocent admiration for the military background of Mr Prendergast – the medals he obtained in World War I and the soldiers he played with as a child – marks the beginning of their friendship in a novel appropriately entitled *The Captains and the Kings*. Through Diarmid, Mr Prendergast discovers affection, a feeling which had been denied him by his English mother, who saw him, sharing similar English views to Mrs Moore's in *How Many Miles to Babylon?*, as an ineffectual son. At the same time, Diarmid feels free from the pressures of his own environment while enjoying the old man's company, since his parents do not allow him any freedom, least of all a career choice. The process of mutual discovery has a double effect. Mr Prendergast confronts his memories or "ghosts," "the pointing fingers of the past" which had traced a life deprived of affection (73): "He had merely been routed, weakling that he was, by a lady in black, whose diamonds flashed with grey splendour each time she moved her hands" (49). Mr Prendergast's inability to come up to the standards of his Anglo-Irish class is not gender-marked in his own home, as is the case with Alexander Moore. It is rather Sean, whose Irishness is rep-resentative of a lower middle class opposed to Mr Prendergast's Anglo-Irish class, who hints that he might not be sexually "natural" (75). Mr Prendergast tries to make up for his life's failure and becomes involved in helping Diarmid by hiding him temporarily in the mansion until a satisfactory solution to the boy's future can be found. The consequence is that he is accused of pedophilia. In the novel, the officers of the law, and implicitly of the purity of the nation, misinterpret the mixing of Irish identities and what the friendship between an old Anglo-Irish man and a young Gaelic Irish boy means. They simply enforce the rules of social and national behavior. It is not surprising then that Mr Prendergast should define his situation as "ludicrous" (110) now that, in his old age, he has seen an opportunity to redeem his destructive isolation. Diarmid's words prove to be right: "They catch you before you can do anything about it and put you in a cage" (56). Despite the tragic end of their story, Diarmid's fascination with the old man's use of words – such as "flamboyant" (43, 46) – is a metaphor in the novel for the child's opportunity to learn a new language of love while playing with Mr Prendergast, and perhaps to be able to understand that the real struggle lies in breaking down the barriers of social and national prejudice. The novel seems to indicate that their friendship was worth a try, as is suggested by Mr Prendergast sitting at the piano, playing Chopin's *Nocturnes*, while he waits for the arrival of the two policemen of the Garda Síochána. As they enter the house he says, "That was as near perfection as I will ever achieve. Ever have ... ever" (123). The protagonist of this novel, a pianist, feels in tune with a great musician from a country, as he once explained to Diarmid, "with a history not unlike our own. Tragic and violent" (18).

The Illusionist (1995) shows Johnston's concern for the evolution of the peace process in Northern Ireland to bring an end to the violence of the 1960s Troubles. The novel offers a cryptic narrative and is subtly indirect while it challenges the assumptions of Ireland's freedom and the illusions of reconciliation between Protestant Unionists and Catholic nationalists brought about by the peace process. In the novel Stella remembers the failure of her married life in England, as a Dubliner exiled in London. Her memories are revived by the recent death of her ex-husband Martyn, killed by an IRA bomb in a London street. The difficult relationship that this Irishwoman looking for freedom in London establishes with Martyn, a British man of unspecified origin and secret life, is evocative of the issue that divide the peace process, namely a nationalist minority hoping for Irish self-determination and a Unionist majority whose sense of identity does not make this hope clear. Their love story is continually overshadowed by a climate of mutual mistrust. When Stella meets Martyn, a freelance illusionist and a man who has no ties with country or family, she believes she has found in this genuine self-made man a good match to help her realize her dream of becoming an independent Irish woman. She has strong family ties herself. Yet with Martyn she feels liberated from the oppressiveness of her conservative home, which embodied the ideals of nationalist Ireland, as Stella's frequent memories of her mother attest:

> I don't mean to be unkind, but at that stage of my life I had to find things out for myself, discover courage, make mistakes. She always found it quite difficult to let me do any of these things. She believed in grammar, not just the grammar of language, but also that of behaviour in both public and private living. She believed in God. She believed that woman's power existed only as far as she could manipulate men. (Johnston 1995:7–8)

On the other hand, Stella tries to come to terms with Martyn's patronizing secretiveness about his origins, or about his work as a businessman, which seems to rely on the efficiency of his secretary Angela. These aspects of Martyn's life, however, account for his daring project to become one of the world's greatest illusionists and make

Stella feel guilty about her suspicious mind. It is possible to draw a parallel here between Stella's feelings about her humble ambitions in contrast to Martyn's, and the minority position of the nationalists in Northern Ireland compared with their Unionist counterparts. Martyn does not like what he sees as Stella's mother-like inquisitiveness: "I have invented myself. ... There is no need for you to pry into how I achieved this trick" (47). He does not think much of her Irish background either, coming from a country renowned for its fairytale "leprechauns" and for "Guinness" (21). However, for a man with no recognizable roots, she represents the family woman who can provide him with a loving home: "You are my family. ... Only you. You are all I have" (35). Martyn's desire to share his inventive life with Stella – though he never says so – is expressed in his desire to get married, while Stella accepts the risk of equal partnership: "Let's do it. ... Let's fall in love" (25). The fact that they want to settle as husband and wife puts their individual aspirations to the test and raises doubts about the steady nature of their home, at the same time challenging their willingness to make allowances for each other's dreams. The story of their marriage revolves around the question that troubles the process of reaching an agreement in Northern Ireland: is it possible to create a home by reconciling the Unionists' desire for stability and peace and the nationalists' hopes for freedom?

It is as a result of Martyn's death that Stella spends a day with her daughter, on a visit from London after the funeral. She tries to understand how the experience of family life has shattered the illusions of love. Stella has abandoned her job, accepting that she should become the domestic wife he wanted her to be. She had felt confined, as her mother had, to the limits of her domestic realm yet she was powerless when subject to Martyn's needs and wishes and to his spoiling of their daughter. Here there is an interesting subversion of the important role that the family woman plays in southern Ireland as a nationalist symbol for the nurturing of the nation. For Stella does not even have the restricted power of her mother. Instead of fighting for the recuperation of her active role in society as a modern woman, Stella initiates a sur-reptitious struggle for freedom that is reflected in her suspicions of and her verbal aggressiveness towards Martyn's independent life as an illusionist. In contrast, Martyn seems to be on the winning side, though he fails to reinvent his role as a husband. He reproduces the contemporary pattern of the busy money-making man who is hardly ever at home while he keeps his public life secret. Martyn needs Stella to be a submissive wife who can make him feel at home when he is working on his illusionist performances, but she becomes more resistant. Stella remembers one day when she refused to drive Martyn to the station: "You could drive yourself. ... You could stay at home and spend the day on the telephone. Or at a last resort, if life is too unbear-able, you could do a Captain Oates" (187). Stella alludes here to Captain Lawrence E.G. Oates who, by leaving his companions during Scott's expedition to the South Pole in 1911, expected to give them a better chance of survival at the expense of his own death. Adopting a different, though similarly gloomy, historical metaphor, Stella gives the name "Guy Fox" to a fox she protects even if it ravages Martyn's white doves (105). This is a clear reference to the Gunpowder Plot, organized by Guy Fawkes with a few Roman Catholics to blow up the Houses of Parliament on November 5, 1605. Elsewhere in the novel, Stella feels afraid she might not keep her new typewriter and defends her rights over it on the grounds that it is not "a lethal weapon" (141).

As a result of Martyn's death Stella understands the family confrontation and remembers herself, trying to enforce her personal freedom in the home. She also remembers both Martyn and their daughter, intending to enforce a quiet, peaceful life to her own cost. Her final escape back to Ireland demonstrates that she is unable to resolve her problem of identity – Irish by birth, British by adoption. Still, Martyn's self-assurance has concealed an equally confused identity: on reading his will, Stella and her daughter discover that he had been leading a parallel life with Angela, his English lover, with whom he had another daughter. Stella acknowledges that "it was the macabre manner of his death that created the whirlpool of memories in [her] head" (163). This helps her to see how, on returning to Ireland, she lost her daughter. Emotionally maimed by the loss of maternal love, her daughter rejects her Irish mother and stands up for her Englishness instead. Stella also comments on the irony of Martyn's death through "the virus of [her] country's illness" (163), symbolizing the end of British Irish illusions for peace and freedom.

Since the story remembered by Stella is interspersed with snatches of conversation with her daughter on the day of Martyn's funeral, the narrator's aim is to prevent the reader from taking sides in the political problem, as it is conveyed by a story based on the elusive magic of words in the hope of mutual understanding: "I am attempting to tell a story. Starting at the tail end is part of my writer's bag of tricks. I suppose I could call myself an illusionist also, except for the fact that he has already bagged that title" (9).

REFERENCES AND FURTHER READING

Casal, T. (2000). "Jennifer Johnston's War Novels." In P.J. Matthews (Ed.). *New Voices in Irish Criticism* (pp. 99–105). Dublin: Four Courts Press.

Casal, T. (2007). "Frightened with My Own Hatred: Telling Violence in Jennifer Johnston's *Fool's Sanctuary* and *The Invisible Worm*." In W. Huber (Ed.). *Ireland: Representation and Responsibility* (pp. 53–66). Trier: Wissenschaftlicher Verlag Trier.

Diez Fabre, S. (2007). "Jennifer Johnston's *How Many Miles to Babylon?* Questioning the Past among Echoes of Literary History." In P. Lynch (Ed.). *Back to the Present: Forward to the Past* (pp. 110–17). Amsterdam: Rodopi.

Foster, R.F. (1989). "Varieties of Irishness." In M. Crozier (Ed.). *Cultural Traditions in Northern Ireland* (pp. 5–24). Belfast: Queen's University Press.

Gonzalez, R. (1998). "Jennifer Johnston interviewed by Rosa Gonzalez." In C.C. Barfoot (Ed.). *Ireland in Writing* (pp. 7–20). Amsterdam: Rodopi.

Hargreaves, T. (1988). "Women's Consciousness and Identity in Four Irish Women Writers." In M. Kenneally (Ed.). *Cultural Contexts and Literary Idioms in Contemporary Irish Literature* (pp. 290–305). Gerrards Cross: Colin Smythe.

Ingman, H. (2005). "Nation and Gender in Jennifer Johnston: A Kristevan Reading." *Irish University Review*, 35, 334–48.

Ingman, H. (2007). *Twentieth-Century Fiction by Irish Women: Nation and Gender*. Aldershot: Ashgate.

Johnston, J. (1988). *How Many Miles to Babylon?* (1974). Harmondsworth: Penguin.

Johnston, J. (1990). *The Captains and the Kings*. (1972). Harmondsworth: Penguin.

Johnston, J. (1995). *The Illusionist*. London: Sinclair-Stevenson.

Kreilkamp, V. (1998). *The Anglo-Irish Novel and the Big House*. Syracuse: Syracuse University Press.

Lanters, J. (1989). "Jennifer Johnston's Divided Ireland." In C.C. Barfoot (Ed.). *The Clash of Ireland: Literary Contrasts and Connections* (pp. 209–22). Amsterdam: Rodopi.

Longley, E. (1991). *Culture in Ireland. Diversity or Division*. Belfast: Institute of Irish Studies, Queen's University.

Lynch, R.S. (2000). "Public Spaces, Private Lives: Irish Identity and Female Selfhood in the Novels of Jennifer Johnston." In K. Kirkpatrick (Ed.). *Border Crossings: Irish Women Writers and National Identities* (pp. 250–68). Tuscaloosa: University of Alabama Press.

Peach, L. (2004). *The Contemporary Irish Novel: Critical Readings*. Basingstoke: Palgrave Macmillan.

Weekes, A.O. (1990). *Irish Women Writers: An Uncharted Tradition*. Lexington: University Press of Kentucky.

44

Living History: The Importance of Julia O'Faolain's Fiction

Christine St Peter

May you live in interesting times, says the Chinese curse, and most ordinary folk would gladly avoid such times were they able. Not least among the dangers is the way all the participants will have their own perspective, ready to dismiss challenges to their version of "truth," even as some group or other will have the power to enforce its own, with violence if necessary. But even if one is only at the periphery of the tumultuous events, or witnessing them across a national border or in a different time, all periods of history are interesting if one has an acute moral sense and a keen eye for injustice, incompetence, or venality. This describes precisely the central dynamic of all seven of Julia O'Faolain's novels: she puts her characters into their particular web of troubled history and sees how they respond. While we also find this in some of the short stories in her four collections, the author has too few pages in a short story to paint the larger canvas. The protagonists of her novels are usually some version of an intelligent outsider, sometimes Irish or Italian visitors to a foreign country, sometimes persons swept into destructive events in their own changing culture, trying to understand the upheavals, and struggling to find their footing in the gale. In 2006 O'Faolain said she is drawn to "certain moral dilemmas and situations [in which] I see hesitant characters destroying themselves and the morally certain – there were so many of those in the Ireland where I grew up – destroying others" (Cooney 2006:114).

Her characters' finely wrought responses to the ways their personal lives play out in their respective historical contexts make for psychologically compelling fiction. But that statement, important as it is, does not do justice to the remarkable reach and complexity of O'Faolain's art. Her fictional world is huge, gathering in several of the major historical currents of France, Italy, North Africa, Ireland, and the United States since the 1950s as well as reimagining the turmoil of sixth-century Gaul, and the world-changing epoch of Pope Pius IX's nineteenth-century Vatican. Few Irish

A Companion to Irish Literature, edited by Julia M. Wright
© 2010 Blackwell Publishing Ltd

authors have attempted fiction on such an epic scale, reaching so often and so variously beyond the borders of Ireland. To be sure, O'Faolain's background is unusually cosmopolitan, rich in the cultural capital gained by living abroad studying foreign cultures and languages, but she has put that knowledge to work with great sophistication. In these ways she figures as one of the most unusual of "Irish" writers and, I would argue, one of the most important of the last half-century.

Although all of O'Faolain's works have at the time of their publication been widely and positively reviewed in top periodicals on both sides of the Atlantic, very few critical studies of her work exist. Of these, almost all focus on her mid-career, Booker-nominated 1980 novel *No Country for Young Men*. The reasons for this interest are understandable: as William Trevor puts it, the novel is "skillfully spun and splendidly readable ... illuminated by a seriousness that is refreshing to encounter; though entertaining and rich in comedy, it eschews the trivial and is actually *about* something" (Trevor 1980:25). About many somethings, in fact, and the pleasure one has in a novel of O'Faolain's is the skill with which she manages to incorporate so many characters and plotlines, creating a rhythm that can be breathtaking in the energy and speed of its storytelling. O'Faolain characteristically deploys a huge cast of characters across an entire novel, but also often does this even within a single chapter. Here is an example from the early pages of *No Country for Young Men*, offered as illustration of her characteristic narrative method.

In chapter 6 we find a number of characters caught in a complex skein of larger political and social contexts that show the impossibility of control in the lives of individuals, even powerful ones. The crossed, or lost, threads create ruptures that will destabilize, confuse, and even kill some participants. The careful reader will read the intelligent, witty dialogue with delight, but, privy to the lurking tragedy, will also watch in dread as the narrative unfolds. Gathered into this single chapter are significant cameos of James Duffy, an American scholar qua innocent abroad in IRA territory in 1979; Grainne O'Malley, daughter of a famous Irish nationalist family, just returned to Dublin from a trial separation from her husband, spent in London volunteering at a home for battered women; her aunt Judith O'Malley, in two manifestations, the first as a young, sex-fearful, diehard Republican in 1921 during the early "Troubles" and the second in her 1979 present as a occasionally mad nun; a chorus-like group of brutalized and vicious rural women in the 1921 plot; Patsy Flynn, an old IRA hanger-on busily causing disaster in the new Troubles; the chaplain of Judith's disbanded convent; and Cormac, the teenage son of Grainne and an IRA recruit in the making. The structure resembles an action thriller, were it not for the moral seriousness and demanding intelligence of the writing.

All of these elements give strong evidence for the high valuation of this novel among O'Faolain's works. There is, however, another reason for its popularity among critics of Irish literature; its subject fits more readily than her other novels into an Irish studies tradition: her stereoscopic rendering of the Irish Troubles in 1922 and in 1979 published at the height of the recent war in Northern Ireland when it was spilling over into the Republic. Unique among her novels and most of her short stories, *No Country for Young Men* limits itself to Ireland and Irish politics and to the ways these have been complicated and distorted by the misguided interference of Irish American patriots eagerly supporting the nationalist dream with support for violent actions. Moreover, the characters and events in this novel represent – with O'Faolain's characteristic ambition for the big subject – the most elevated of twentieth-century Irish figures, a fictionalized Éamon de Valera-like character and his dynastic family through three generations of (male) nationalist heroes.

One of the original elements of the novel is the way in which these characters and events are filtered through the harsh lens of the eyes of the women of the family, giving prominence to the experience of women in these wars. Grainne, a protagonist in the 1979 sections, reflects on women's situation in Ireland where the "laws ... had not changed, nor people's attitudes underneath. Not for women" (O'Faolain 1980:101). Indeed, an angry Grainne, reflecting on Irish men's attitudes to women, goes so far as to suggest that Irish men, educated by clerics, eventually took on their mentors' attitudes: "Monastic tradition described women as a bag of shit and it followed that sexual release into such a receptacle was a topic about as fit for sober discussion as a bowel movement" (155).

We find this kind of attitude towards Irish men fairly constant among her female characters from her earliest published fiction. For example, in "A Pot of Soothing Herbs," a sexually eager 21-year-old Irish virgin, burdened with a Catholic convent school sex education, asks, "Can they – men – really not control themselves? I don't mean Irish men, because they don't seem to have any needs at all. Or they're queer" (O'Faolain 1978:56). The savage indignation that drives these satirical passages reveals the approach to cultural history that is found in all of O'Faolain's fiction. Intent on demystifying destructive myths and uncovering the occluded history in each of the cultures she treats, O'Faolain creates characters, situations, and language that challenge the canons of received tradition. The main characters are usually women, but can also be subaltern men, as in her first novel, *Godded and Codded* (1970), and her most recent novel in English, *The Judas Cloth* (1992). (Her 1999 novel, *Ercoli e il guardiano notturno*, has not been published in English translation so does not form part of this discussion, but it, too, shares the personal/political structure of her other novels.)

The following discussion will sketch a chronological map of the most important of O'Faolain's works in English, and we find again and again the thematic concerns that figure in this pre-eminent novel, *No Country for Young Men*: the effects of major cultural patterns and upheavals on the lives of those without public power; the strain and ruptures these create in personal relations; the need for subaltern characters to navigate challenging moral dilemmas; and the futility of violence in creating justice. As in all her work, the cast of characters in *No Country* stretches across class, gender, age, and geographic divisions, showing how peripheral or socially unimportant characters and events can act with the force of destiny in the lives of strangers. In this novel, for example, we find represented the thinking, speech, and actions of the dominant men in the society; those of the subordinate men who either opt out (usually through alcohol) or choose to cling to the coattails of the powerful; and those of a variety of women, usually not publicly dominant in O'Faolain's fiction, sometimes trying to survive through resistance or subversion but, more likely, through cynical, watchful acquiescence in an inescapable status quo. Her genius is that she can create the voices and motivations that make all of these different folk sound real and their lives, to echo Trevor, "about something."

Among the several studies of *No Country for Young Men*, Ann Owen Weekes' discussions are especially fine. The first appears in *Éire-Ireland* and the second, a reprise of the first, forms a chapter of her ground-breaking book, *Irish Women Writers: An Uncharted Tradition*. Both explore the ways in which O'Faolain has used the myths of Finn, Grainne, Diarmuid, and Oisín, layering these into the history of the Irish Free State and the Republic of Ireland. Weekes' studies emphasize how thoroughly grounded O'Faolain is in the mythic lore and history of her native land. But, as Weekes points out, O'Faolain's use of these materials is resolutely demythologizing. This, she explained in an interview with Weekes, is the result of watching her writer parents, Seán O'Faoláin and Eileen Gould, react "romantically and enthusiastically to the birth of the fledgling Irish state" only to become as disillusioned later with the Republic as with the older empire it replaced (see CHAPTER 38, CHANGING TIMES), "ma[king] romanticism impossible" for their daughter (Weekes 1990:175). Instead, as we shall see in the following discussion, all of O'Faolain's work has "an acid intelligence that strips away layers of tradition, affection, and affectation, exposing an often grotesque core" (Weekes 1990:175). We see a particularly fierce example of this in her only short story dealing with the Troubles, a title story of the collection *Daughters of Passion*, where the hunger-striking, jailed IRA "heroine" is treated as a foolish terrorist guilty of a misguided murder not even dignified by a belief in the nationalist cause while the real reasons for her behavior, an abusive childhood in an Irish Catholic orphanage and the strange, intense relationships among the orphans, never figure in the public explanation, nor are they foregrounded in the disconcerting story (O'Faolain 1982).

O'Faolain's earliest published book is a collection of short stories, *We Might See Sights!*, which appeared in 1968, just at the beginning of the second wave of twentieth-century feminism. While these stories do not focus as intently on gender violence as many of her later works do, she was already educating herself in the history of this ubiquitous, pan-historical form of social injustice. This we see in a book of non-fiction writings she and her husband, the Italian American scholar Lauro Martines, collected and published in 1973. In this collection, *Not in God's Image: Women in History from the Greeks to the Victorians*, they use the writings of men (and women where possible in the early modern period and the nineteenth century) to explore attitudes towards women through 2,000 years of European literary history. Their purpose is to present "a close-up picture of the lives of ordinary women from different social classes," excepting only the few royal women whose lives were so exceptional that they gave little sense of the reality of ordinary lives (O'Faolain and Martines 1973:xiii). This collection, we are told, differs from other books on women being published at that time, presumably feminist treatises, in that it is not polemical. Instead it attempts a faithful transcription of voices from the past, "allowing them to explain behaviour which might at first strike a modern reader as cruel, arbitrary or perhaps abject" (xiv). This claim of neutrality is a little disingenuous, given that the book's title is borrowed from St Augustine, also quoted in the book's opening epigraph, in which he states that the "woman herself alone is not the image of God" while "man alone is the image of God"; this with an epigraph from St John Chrysostom: "women taught once and ruined all" (xiii). But in the same spirit of demystification referred to above, O'Faolain and Martines do not, through their selection of quotations, merely pillory men's treatment of and attitudes about women; they also include selections that point to the ways in which women have been trained to accept their position, willing handmaidens to male supremacy, "female Don Quixote[s] ... [who] have lost touch with the actualities around them, liv[ing] in a formally-organized fantasy-world" (xviii). As we shall see, this quixotic state of mind is one she explores in depth in a novel set in sixth-century Gaul, *Women in the Wall* (1975).

As *Not in God's Image* indicates, O'Faolain was certainly in the vanguard of second-wave feminist thinking, and an early published voice in one of the most significant political movements of recent history. Even in 2006 she still described herself as a "feminist writer" (Cooney 2006:116). This longstanding concern finds its most forthright, least nuanced expression in an early short story, "Man in the Cellar," in the collection of the same title (1974). In this hilarious remake of Poe's "The Cask of Amontillado," an abused wife manages to shackle her violent and spoiled (by his mother and by his patriarchal culture) Italian husband in their basement. When, after some weeks, she relents and frees him, she is badly beaten but manages to escape to her native England where she later divorces him, another story of a woman's survival in a sexist world, although one in which the woman is an accomplice in the husband's violence. Even as she keeps him locked in the basement, furiously writing about his crimes, she still wants him: "I love *him*. Himself. ... Possessively. Tenderly. With lust" (O'Faolain 1974:29). The story vacillates between humor and earnestness; the latter lessens the story's achievement but it does lay out one of O'Faolain's abiding concerns: "Being a female doesn't make me different. 'Feminine' strategies are responses to an objective situation: lack of power. There is no 'natural' love of subservience in women" (48).

Despite the exception of "Man in the Cellar," her very early short stories are not so much feminist in tone as they are explorations of the coming of age of inexperienced Irish girls, sometimes in foreign situations that make adventure or experimentation possible. These girls might use men as much as they are used by them. Although O'Faolain's realistic treatment of social contexts show how men have much closer connections to actual power, and may be all too eager to prey on ingénues, O'Faolain is also unflinching in her depiction of the way girls and women might also use boys and men. A particularly revealing example of this occurs in one of her earliest stories, "First Conjugation," where an Irish university student in an Italian class first falls in love with her glamorous female Italian teacher, then falls in lust with her teacher's

Italian husband, who pursues her behind his wife's back. When the young woman follows up on his advances and calculatedly tracks him to his home during his wife's absence, she blames him for the tryst when they are discovered by the wife, and sticks to her lie even when it breaks up the Italians' marriage, the last straw for the wife who has suffered many such betrayals by the faithless husband. The young Irish woman here suffers only passing guilt, and that is quickly assuaged by the thought that the wife "would be well rid of him" (O'Faolain 1978:31). When she sees the abandoned and ruined husband a few months later, she says "I cannot remember if I spared him a passing regret" (31), as she busily sets out to seduce a local Irish boy "who had become muscular, tanned and worldly during a summer in the south of France" (31). The young woman has agency here; she sees clearly the folly and venality of the man whose advances she may have welcomed or even initiated, recognizes her own complicity, and determinedly seeks survival on her own terms.

The ease of escape from a compromising sexual misadventure found in this story is not repeated in any of O'Faolain's novels, with the exception of *The Irish Signorina* (1984), O'Faolain's least successful novel, in which a young Irish woman, Anne Ryan, visits the estate of an aristocratic Tuscan family where her mother had served as an au pair a generation earlier. Although Anne discovers in the course of this richly allusive novel that the heir of this family – with the Dantean name of Guido Cavalcanti, medieval poet of love – is actually her father, the novel ends with her actually contemplating marrying him. This personal audacity is set against a background of a more widespread social recklessness, the violent insurrection of the Italian Brigate Rosse which forms the novel's political background and is an important part of the protagonist's Italian adventures.

To be sure, O'Faolain's first novel, published two years after "First Conjugation," *Godded and Codded* (1970), resembles that earlier story in creating an adventurous foreign-language student embarking on a sexual relationship, but its outcome is decidedly different and more complex. In this novel, the young protagonist Sally Tyndal goes to the Sorbonne in the late 1950s to do a graduate degree, as did O'Faolain herself (as well as studying at the University of Rome). Sally has been armed with parental advice; her father, successful in the bacon business, tells her that the "society of the opposite sex is at all times a danger to a young girl. The nuns told you that, I hope" (O'Faolain 1970:168); but he is too late: unbeknown to her parents, Sally has already become pregnant in the first months of her stay in Paris. Her mother gave more pragmatic, albeit bitter, advice: be "independent of the Male" even though "society is made by and for them. They use you up to the hilt, without having to know they're doing it" (11). Sally knows this to be true ("she reads novels"), but then, "you had to have one, didn't you?" (12). And it had taken no time at all for Sally to fall in love with an Algerian medical student named Mesli, who is eagerly striving to join in what the novel treats as the romance of the Algerian war against colonial France. Mesli is inflamed by such texts as an 1840 French report exhorting the French colonizers to hunt the "natives" like "wild beasts," driving them from the "neighbourhood of inhabited places ... farther and farther towards the desert" (96). Sally is sympathetic up to a point, particularly when she experiences the intense racism of the French against her lover and other Algerians, but Mesli's political passions remind her too much of the kind of talk she grew up hearing – what she calls "Cromwell," code for all the Irish revolutionary rhetoric her generation found too "crusted over with reverence" to be real (48). Against the backdrop of the Algerian war, as experienced by and through the Arab students in France longing for the brotherhood of revolutionary action, Sally has to find her own story; it won't be in Algeria, where she fears another prison for women not unlike the one she has fled in Ireland, nor will it be in academia, as her doctoral dissertation never even gets to the point of a chosen topic, much less to completion.

In his review of this novel in *London Magazine* at the time of its publication, Alan Ross praised it as "an immensely stylish and richly allusive performance"; this allowed him to forgive what he called its unoriginal treatment "of the wayward affair between a sexy Irish student from the bogs [Dublin] and a wily[?], Arab revolutionary" with "its fairly routine plot about sexual awakening" (Ross 1970:109–10). Ross has, to my mind, completely missed the importance of the novel in which personal stories, Sally's, Mesli's and Fintan's (an Irish artist who *is* from "the bogs") are imbricated in important political action. The canvas of Paris as a place of possibility offers these young people access to different kinds of lives and to important life knowledge. Sally's "sexual awakening" is a misnomer; sexual activity here is a given, whereas the *consequences* of liberated sex in that time form an important part of the struggle Sally faces as she breaks the contract her parents expect of her: marrying the "solid son of one of her father's friends" in order to "start the cycle again for the honour and glory of the R.C. Republic" (181). When Mesli joins the revolution, choosing the brotherhood over Sally, she has difficult decisions to make about her unwanted pregnancy; her choice finally is to seek an illegal and highly dangerous abortion through the help of one of Mesli's medical student friends. To someone familiar with Irish literature in this period or indeed in any period, O'Faolain's treatment of this subject is remarkable. In what is perhaps a uniquely frank treatment of the subject in literature, every aspect of this abortion is represented – physical and emotional – after Sally decides that she will not marry Mesli although he offers this possibility in a half-hearted fashion as he embarks on a career as a guerrilla fighter. This, she knows, would be the "end for her, not for *him* who had male doings awaiting him." She refuses to be "Dido, Medea, Ariadne, her own mother, left on a dull domestic shore, reduced to animality" (204). Sally wants to be a partner in his struggle; she has read about the sub-proletariat of discriminated-against Algerians and feels that in the "balance of the truly wretched of the earth, this guaranteed genuine stuff of history" her own claim to suffering was "ridiculous" (207). Personal, yes, but not ridiculous. In the late 1950s, a decade before the liberalization of abortion law in England and France and over two decades before Ireland copperfastened the impossibility of abortion in the Republic in the Eighth Amendment to the Irish Constitution in 1983, Sally's predicament is disastrous. Marriage and a move to Algeria to live with Mesli's unwilling family is out of the question: "illegitimate," impoverished single parenthood in

Ireland or in France would severely damage her future. Sally's awakening is not to sex as such but to the meaning of transgressive sex in an Irish woman's life. The end of the novel leaves her no longer pregnant after a nearly lethal abortion, but she is in the position of having to make other cruel and compromising decisions as a way of surviving. Although she is newly penniless, having lost her scholarship and parental support, she is young, clever, beautiful, and not unwilling to be a little ruthless in seeking survival; with such advantages, she manages to contrive a means of living. The terms are not her own but they will do for the time being. To quote the protagonist of "Man in the Cellar," "'Feminine' strategies are responses to an objective situation: lack of power" (O'Faolain 1974:48). This novel, like all O'Faolain's novels, has an unfinished, indeterminate, ending. While her work fits roughly within the tradition of realism, such endings and dislocations of narrative carry her beyond realism into the postmodern. And yet she insists in a 1998 essay about Irish fiction that "for writers realism can be the perfect instrument for dealing with a reality so corrupted by myth" (O'Faolain 1998:10). She then adds an important hint for reading her own form of realism – that "myths themselves can be turned to account often by turning them around" (10). In other words, there exist other options for women than virgin, whore, or downtrodden mother. Her fiction explores what these might look like in various times and places.

Godded and Codded was about to be released in England and Ireland by Faber & Faber when it was pulled due to a threatened libel suit. One of the characters "allegedly resembled" someone O'Faolain knew, and the woman sued (Cooney 2006:114). Rather than risk the solicitor's fees, O'Faolain withdrew the book (although a copy exists in the Special Collections of the University of Victoria), publishing it a year later under the title *Three Lovers* in 1971 in the United States where the libel laws protect the writer more comfortably. A lesson learned, she decided to play it safe by avoiding contemporary topics for a while, using the material she had amassed researching *Not in God's Image* to publish a story in 1974 and a novel in 1975 about a fascinating period of early European history (Cooney 2006:115). Her subjects in these works were actual historical characters caught in the horrendous violence of internecine and cross-border wars in sixth-century Merovingian Gaul. They include Queen (later abbess, mystic, and, finally, saint) Radegunda; her violent, but, in O'Faolain's handling, not entirely unsympathetic ex-husband King Clotair and his allies and enemies; Agnes, saved as a girl by Radegunda and later a member, then the abbess, of Radegunda's convent; and a poet-priest and hagiographer, Fortunatus, who becomes the lover of Agnes in O'Faolain's reading of his "playful and passionate" (O'Faolain 1985:11) published letters to the nun. As for the veracity of the latter relationship, O'Faolain wickedly comments in her Introductory Note, "Recent evidence tends to show that flesh subdued by monastic vows can and does requicken" (11).

The events of the time offer a vast canvas of riveting events and bigger-than-life people; O'Faolain's achievement here is to marshal all these into a narrative frame in which the scope and intensity of the action and the foreignness of the religious belief system are made convincing despite the differences in thinking across more than a millennium. The wall of the title refers, on one level, to an actual stone wall that imprisons a young anchoress in a tiny cell in the convent's cloister. This young woman, Ingunda, one of O'Faolain's fictional creations, is the illegitimate daughter of Agnes and Fortunatus. In AD 586, while still a girl, she insists on immuring herself behind the wall, taking a vow of silence that hides her motives. After two years isolated within the cell with food passed through a grill and her feet slipping in her own excrement she goes completely mad. When another war breaks out, brigands violate the sanctuary of the convent, which should have been impregnable according to the religious orthodoxies of the time. This violation has been instigated by a runaway young nun with a grudge against Abbess Agnes, seeking her own advantage in urging the soldiers to penetrate the convent's vulnerable defenses. The convent walls, battlements in fact, had previously kept the nuns within them safe from the exterior violence, but finally the tangled jealousies, betrayals, and aspirations among some of the women within the walls and the cupidity and violence of forces outside them bring the convent to the brink of destruction. As the soldiers pierce through the slit in her wall, young Ingunda cries out and is killed, shouting out that her task within her prison has been to "pay the demons for my mother's sins" (321). Witnessing her death, her mother, Abbess Agnes, steps into the cell where she in her turn assumes the penitential imprisonment.

The narratives of Agnes and Fortunatus form one nucleus of the novel, and they were so important to O'Faolain that she had already published a version of their story in her 1974 *Man in the Cellar* collection. Its title, "This Is My Body," repeats the sacred words of transubstantiation in the Catholic Mass; they are applied here sacrilegiously to the bodies of the lovers who make "a sort of communion out of [their] love" (O'Faolain 1974:63) (in *Women in the Wall*, this chapter is only one strand of the tale). Equally important is Radegunda's story, whose mysticism makes her one of those "female Don Quixotes ... [who] have lost touch with the actualities around them, liv[ing] in a formally-organized fantasy-world" (O'Faolain and Martines 1973:xviii). The novel opens with the descent into madness of Ingunda, the anchoress – a challenge to a modern reader to whom such forms of spirituality seem merely masochistic. But then the novel immediately moves back half a century to Radegunda at age 11 witnessing the massacre in AD 531 of what remains of her royal Thuringian family, and her capture by King Clotair, who eventually makes her one of his six wives. In the process she is Christianized and, much to her distress, quickened into sexual pleasure by her husband. For these moments of sexual *jouissance* she punishes herself savagely, with flagellation, hair shirts, and other mortifications of the body. In time, she convinces Clotair to let her leave with her "morning-gift" (24), allowing her enough resources to found a convent so that she can join with "a greater Spouse" (24). This subjugation of the body to achieve spiritual communion with God becomes her life mission, but she fails in her own eyes because despite her demanding self-discipline she can never "leave the senses ... she did lose herself in ecstasy, did achieve trances which burned, thrilled, even made her swoon with delight but afterwards, she was humiliated at the precision with which she was able to detect the sensual element involved" (200). But even as Radegunda seeks sainthood through these spiritual methods she also develops a dangerous and hubristic temporal mission under the misguided belief that a convent would never be broached by exterior violence; she decides to help Gaul be "united under one king anointed by the Holy Church" (287) and in this mode she makes the decision to sequester within her convent's walls the besieged prince of this future kingdom whose claims she supports. Rebellion from within the convent among self-important and resentful royal postulants, and revolution from without through the agency of anarchic nobles, bring the convent to the brink of destruction. It is "saved" by the local bishop who, after the death of Radegunda and the immuring of Agnes, appoints as abbess the monstrous young nun who had fomented the rebellion. As an anointed member of the church hierarchy, the bishop controls the female convent but knows nothing of its inhabitants' inner lives. The final, cruel irony of the novel occurs in its last sentence: "Some years later, [Bishop] Maroveus, being old and full of days, died and was succeeded as bishop by the poet, Fortunatus" (326). As always, no narrative voice directs the reader's reaction other than the skillful placement of detail. This novel abounds with evil actions, corrupt and weak characters, and good but ineffectual ones, but the author never makes these human actors mere caricatures. The evil of the violence may be condemned as we see the effects on characters' lives but the behavior of the characters within those charged and difficult times receives complex and human treatment.

Although Julia O'Faolain is not an observant Catholic, she was raised in the Catholic Irish Republic and was educated in a Catholic convent school. Like her father Seán O'Faoláin, she finds the long hegemony of the Catholic hierarchy and its institutionalized morality unacceptable. Although she notes in 1998 that the "powers" of "Catholicism, nationalism and indeed the family are in retreat," she argues that their disappearance leaves a "void" "into which rush anarchy, consumerism and yob-rule" (O'Faolain 1998:8). She goes on to state that a "bulwark has collapsed, and this is disconcerting in Ireland, where Catholics, relying on the Church for their ethics, failed to develop a secular code of conduct based on some kind of civic ideal" (9). There is no turning back, she says, although in what I call her three "Catholic" novels she shows fundamentalist factions seeking to do just that. O'Faolain may have no formula for an ideal ethic of the future, but she spends a great deal of her writing energy exploring how institutional Catholicism affects the lives of ordinary people, and finally the hierarchy of the church itself. Her interest in the politics of the Catholic Church runs deep, and three of her novels, spanning much of her writing career, deal with this subject: *Women in the Wall* (1975); *The Obedient Wife* (1982); and finally, her most recent novel written in English, *The Judas Cloth* (1992). It is to the latter two of these novels that we turn in conclusion.

In each book the characters are faced with difficult choices in times of immense change in which the certainties of their lives, grounded in inherited religious belief, are undermined. The two novels work especially well together if one considers their historical frameworks, with *The Obedient Wife* exploring the after-effects among Catholics of the Second Vatican Council (1962–65) and *The Judas Cloth* actually sketching out in fascinating and enormous detail what O'Faolain treats as the corrupt machinations of the First Vatican Council (1869–70) presided over by Pope Pius IX. In this nineteenth-century Council the deeply problematic doctrine of papal infallibility was decreed, and the doctrine of the "Immaculate Conception" of Mary, Mother of Jesus, first decreed in 1854, reaffirmed, in part because of the supposed support given by the Blessed Virgin Mary herself in an apparition at Lourdes, France, to a 14-year-old girl. Needless to say, there is much grist here for the unbeliever who will think these are not innocent developments. Perhaps this unsympathetic historical focus is the reason why these novels have received less praise that they deserve. And yet when one considers that Catholics (in their many cultural forms) are among the largest religious groups in the world, numbering over a billion, the subject can hardly be considered parochial.

The Obedient Wife is set in 1979 after the Second Vatican Council when the winds of change were blowing mightily through the lives of the Catholic laity and of priests and nuns. This date marks the time the Vatican denied the Swiss reform theologian and priest Hans Küng the right to teach Catholic theology because he challenged, among other orthodoxies, the doctrine of infallibility decreed at Vatican I. The event of his firing forms a crisis in the novel for the progressive Catholics who hoped for church reform. And while this American Catholic crisis is the dominant context of the novel, O'Faolain puts an atheist, "a pagan" (O'Faolain 1983:100), at its center: an Italian woman, Carla Verdi. Carla, along with her 13-year-old son, Maurizio, is marooned in Los Angeles – "cracked California" (9) – where O'Faolain herself lived with her son and husband. Carla's Italian husband has gone home to Italy some months earlier, ostensibly to conduct business but also to conduct a love-affair. He urges his wife to have sexual dalliances so that she can become more like him, taking advantage of "one of the world's playgrounds" to learn "the erotic" (35), perhaps in preparation for divorce, both ideas extremely distasteful to Carla, who believes in maintaining the old customs of Italian family life. But then, if one is an obedient wife and a husband's rule no longer honors such customs, what is a woman to do? Although she has earned an excellent law degree in Italy, it is useless "outside the purview of the Napoleonic Code" and in her conservative way she decides it would be "psychologically rash" to "forsak[e] one system for another" (10), that comically used verb, "forsake" at the beginning of the novel adumbrating the rest of her story. She struggles against her husband Marco's orders, but has a brief romance with a Catholic priest who falls in love with her and wants to marry her. In the end, she decides to stay with her husband. One of the important elements of this character is that while she plays the perfect Italian housewife it is not religious scruple that keeps her in line. Carla was raised by a socialist, atheist father whose own anarchist father kept his anti-clerical issues of *L'Assiette au Beurre* (1901–12) in the family library within "a stone's throw of the Vatican" (152). Trained into disbelief (it is no surprise that O'Faolain dedicates this novel to her father), she lives thoroughly in the present, expecting no heavenly reward. As she explains to her ex-lover, Father Leo, "I like keeping things together – we have to do that, you know, those of us who believe only in the temporal world. ... That's *our* morality" (229–30).

O'Faolain deploys several complicated plots in this novel, including a delightful one in which Carla's son Maurizio contrives to convince his parents to adopt an abused child who lives in the neighborhood. But the intellectual energy – which is substantial – goes into satirizing 1980s Catholicism and, in particular, the conservative Catholic thinking that pushes the church squarely back into the nineteenth century of Pope Pius IX. For this purpose she creates a particularly egregious character, a transplanted Londoner named Terry Steele who runs a Catholic talk-show on California radio whose fare includes such things as the promotion of the Right to Life Movement and the necessity of corporal punishment for children. With the plot device of the radio show, she can create a variety of voices spouting doctrinal certainties. So, for example, a Father Feeney explains the doctrine of the Immaculate Conception in which the Virgin Mary "had been virginal not only before and after but *in the very act* of giving birth to Jesus Christ," something "people of modernist tendency [who] want to sin without feeling guilt" try to discredit (143). Terry feeds this priest lines about "back-sliding Catholics," building a conversational crescendo until "there you have it," "Sex, apathy, pride. One thing leads to another. Where will it end? Phone in and give us your thinking on this" – whereupon, his voice cuts into an ad (143).

Terry Steele's wife Sybil, an overburdened mother of five and a friend of Carla's, at first in love with Leo herself, backslides into her own form of wifely obedience by the end of the novel. Early in the novel, however, she declares herself "crucified by [papal] encyclicals" (26), specifically *Humanae Vitae* promulgated *ex cathedra* by Pope Paul VI in 1968, forbidding not just abortion but also all "artificial methods" of contraception. By the end of the novel Sybil has returned to the family/church fold and she and her husband will together create a new radio series "funded by religious organizations," promoting the old idea of the superiority of the "normal married couple" (219). In its way, although seemingly so different from the free-thinking Carla's arrangements, the results are the same, the restoration of obedience to authorities and established traditions, religious or cultural. Infallibility triumphant.

But this is not O'Faolain's last, despairing, word on the subject. In *The Judas Cloth*, she devotes some 600 pages to exploring the myth-making that went into the doctrines of infallibility and the Immaculate Conception, skillfully entwining vicious Vatican politics with those of monarchist France in the period of Napoleon III, along with the events of the Risorgimento movement, the Garibaldi-led unification of Italy. But mostly she takes her readers inside the Vatican with a cast of historical and fictional characters vast enough to require a preliminary list of principal characters as well as a glossary. At the center is a boy of illegitimate birth, Nicola Santi, who grows into manhood during the novel, a character whose protectors are so powerful he is allowed to become a priest, then a bishop, despite his illegitimacy. The mystery of his birth (as it happens, his father is Pope Pius IX, and his mother, latterly, a saintly nun) is one of the fascinating threads O'Faolain weaves through the narrative. But this story of Nicola Santi, engaging in its way, is in fact a narrative device allowing O'Faolain to penetrate into the private lives and political intrigues of the church hierarchy in the last days of its temporal reign. We find here a historical novel of immense learning; it is so densely written and labyrinthine in its intrigues that one critic describes it as a "generally difficult slog" (Callaghan 1996:957). And yet the novel offers many rewards to the careful reader. We see on display here O'Faolain's superb gifts of characterization and of intelligent, brilliant dialogue, while the serious-ness of her moral concerns and the scope of the historical drama are as engaging here as anywhere in her fiction. She makes liberal use of epistolary narratives, weaving together myriad voices and political opinions. She has fun cooking the small fry: "O.R. to Earl of C. Private and secret. The Irish bishops are a hopeless set of humbugs! Cunning and deceitful as Neapolitans, they all declare themselves delighted with the stringency of the peace preservation law for Ireland and the suppression of pestilent newspapers ... But who can tell whether they are sincere?" (O'Faolain 1992:506). But the Irish Church and churchmen are mere tangents; her main target is nothing less than the Pope, the Curia and the whole Vatican world. Her long-standing feminist concerns about women's experience figure here in a subordinated but poignant way in the lives of Maria Gatti, Nicola's lover in his youth, and his mother Sister Paola, but the focus here is the world of men: soldiers, politicians, businessmen, aristocrats, students, but mostly the world of Italian seminarians and clergy gathered from around the world for the Vatican Council.

In her introductory note to the novel, O'Faolain explains that her subject, the time and the figure of Pius IX, is important because during this era, the church "was pushed ever further towards polarisation" (O'Faolain 1992:vi), a situation which persists to this day. So in her creation of Nicola Santi she tries "to imagine what is was like to be a moderate dependant of [Pius IX]" (vi), putting Nicola at the confusing center as he swings to and fro, always seeking moral certainties, "clarity, a trial and a summing-up" (556) but wanting, too, to be open, rational and generous. In the end, his attempts to be moderate in an immoderate time lead him to realize that the clerical garb is a "Judas cloth" and he discards it and its privileges with furious disappointment. O'Faolain captures with great sensitivity Nicola's experience of vulnerability in an unsafe and shifting world. In its way, the following passage speaks volumes about a commonly shared motivation, not for the doctrine of papal infallibility, but for people's willing-ness to accept it; "a foundling without a true family name, he had hated knowing that he was a false word made flesh and yearned for facts to be unshakeable. No doubt many of the Pope's subjects had since come to feel the same way" (452). There is real pity here for the human need for stability, even as there is a refusal to indulge it.

So, in this work as in all her earlier fiction, we see an author relentlessly demy-thologizing social, religious, and personal myths that may comfort but also mislead. She is not alone among Irish writers in this exercise. But she is unique in the scope of her historical explorations and her ability to create intricate, detailed tapestries that capture, through the lives of her characters, the spirit of times and places in great turmoil. To quote again her self-description, she is drawn again and again to "certain moral dilemmas and situations [in which] I see hesitant characters destroying them-selves and the morally certain ... destroying others" (Cooney 2006:114). She is far too intelligent a writer to pretend to solve the dilemmas, but she is masterful at laying bare their elements which could enlighten if we attended.

REFERENCES AND FURTHER READING

Burleigh, D. (1985). "Dead and Gone: The Fiction of Jennifer Johnston and Julia O'Faolain." In M. Sekine (Ed.). *Irish Writers and Society at Large* (pp. 1–15). Gerrards Cross: Colin Smythe.

Callaghan, M.R. (1996). "Julia O'Faolain." In R. Hogan (Ed.). *Dictionary of Irish Literature: Revised and Expanded Edition, M–Z*. Westport, CT: Greenwood Press.

Cooney, M. (2006). "An Interview with Julia O'Faolain." *Nua: Studies in Contemporary Irish Writing*, 5.1 (Fall), 111–20.

Fitzgerald-Hoyt, M. (1990). "The Influence of Italy in the Writings of William Trevor and Julia O'Faolain." *Notes on Modern Irish Literature*, 2, 61–67.

Hargreaves, T. (1988). "Women's Consciousness and Identity in Four Irish Women Novelists." In M. Kenneally (Ed.). *Cultural Contexts and Literary Idioms in Contemporary Irish Literature* (pp. 290–305). Gerrards Cross: Colin Smythe.

Maloy, K. (1997). "Decolonizing the Mind: Memory (and) Loss in Julia O'Faolain's *No Country for Young Men*." *Colby Quarterly*, 33, 236–44.

Moore, T.R. (1991). "Triangles and Entrapment: Julia O'Faolain's *No Country for Young Men*." *Colby Quarterly*, 27, 9–16.

O'Connor, T. (1996). "History, Gender, and the Postcolonial Condition: Julia O'Faolain's Comic Rewriting of *Finnegans Wake*." In T. O'Connor (Ed.). *The Comic Tradition in Irish Women Writers* (pp. 124–48). Gainesville: University Press of Florida.

O'Faolain, J. (1968). *We Might See Sights! and Other Stories*. London: Faber & Faber.

O'Faolain, J. (1970). *Godded and Codded*. London: Faber & Faber. Published in the USA as *Three Lovers*. New York: Coward, McCann & Geoghegan, 1971.

O'Faolain, J. (1974). *Man in the Cellar*. London: Faber and Faber.

O'Faolain, J. (1978). *Melancholy Baby, and Other Stories*. Dublin: Poolbeg Press.

O'Faolain, J. (1980). *No Country for Young Men*. Middlesex: Penguin.

O'Faolain, J. (1982). *Daughters of Passion*. London: Faber & Faber.

O'Faolain, J. (1983). *The Obedient Wife* (1982). Middlesex: Penguin.

O'Faolain, J. (1984). *The Irish Signorina*. New York: Viking.

O'Faolain, J. (1985). *Women in the Wall* (1975). London: Virago.

O'Faolain, J. (1992). *The Judas Cloth*. London: Sinclair-Stevenson.

O'Faolain, J. (1998). "The Furies of Irish Fiction." *Graph*, 3.1 (Spring), 6–11.

O'Faolain, J. (1999). *Ercoli e il guardiano notturno*. Rome: Editori Riuniti.

O'Faolain, J. and L. Martines. (Eds). (1973). *Not in God's Image: Women in History from the Greeks to the Victorians*. London: Temple Smith.

Pelan, R. (2005). *Two Irelands: Literary Feminisms North and South*. Syracuse: Syracuse University Press.

Rooks-Hughes, L. (1996). "The Family and the Female Body in the Novels of Edna O'Brien and Julia O'Faolain." *Canadian Journal of Irish Studies*, 22.2 (December), 83–97.

Ross, A. (1970). "Carry on Codding." *London Magazine*, 10.8 (November), 109–10.

St Peter, C. (1994). "Reconstituting the Irish Nationalist Family Romance: Julia O'Faolain's *No Country for Young Men*." In M. Duperray (Ed.). *Historicité et métafiction dans le roman contemporain les Iles Britanniques* (pp. 151–66). Aix-en-Provence: Université de Provence.

St Peter, C. (2000). *Changing Ireland: Strategies in Contemporary Women's Fiction*. London: Macmillan.

Trevor, W. (1980). "Review of *No Country for Young Men*." *Hibernia*, 44.23 (June 5), 25.

Van Dale, L.B. (1991). "Woman Across Time: Sister Judith Remembers." *Colby Quarterly*, 27, 17–26.

Weekes, A.O. (1986). "Diarmuid and Gráinne Again: Julia O'Faolain's *No Country for Young Men*." *Éire-Ireland*, 21, 89–102.

Weekes, A.O. (1990). *Irish Women Writers: An Uncharted Tradition*. Lexington: University Press of Kentucky.

45

Holding a Mirror Up to a Society in Evolution: John McGahern

Eamon Maher

John McGahern attained a significant reputation in Irish and international literary circles before his death in March 2006. His work has a particular resonance for Irish readers, many of whom experience the slightly eerie sensation that he is in some way telling their story, recounting their lives, laying bare their innermost secrets. This may go some way towards explaining the strong reaction to his earlier novels, the second of which, *The Dark*, was banned in 1965 amid a storm of controversy. This novel had not only described the masturbatory activities of its adolescent main character, but also went so far as to depict inappropriate sexual behavior by a priest towards an adolescent male cousin and sexual abuse by a father of his son. It was a heady cocktail in 1960s Ireland and led, not surprisingly, to McGahern losing his teaching position in Belgrove National School, Clontarf.

In addition to writing what he referred to humorously as "a dirty book," McGahern had also brought aggravation on himself by getting married in a registry office in London to a Finnish divorcee whom he met during a sabbatical from teaching made possible by the McAuley Fellowship that he was awarded the previous year. The "McGahern Affair" caused quite a stir at the time, with many public figures getting involved. In the end, the intervention of the then archbishop of Dublin, John Charles McQuaid, was decisive in ensuring McGahern's removal from his post, the Catholic Church having responsibility for the management of the vast majority of primary schools in Ireland at the time. The controversy surrounding McGahern's sacking faded in due course, as often happens. Samuel Beckett was prepared to add his weight to any further protests being planned on McGahern's behalf, but the author declined, not wishing to draw any more attention to the episode (Ní Anluain 2000:144–45).

Naturally, McGahern was affected by what had happened, so much so that he was unable to write for a protracted period afterwards. He emigrated to England, but

A Companion to Irish Literature, edited by Julia M. Wright
© 2010 Blackwell Publishing Ltd

returned to Ireland after a few years and eventually settled back in his native Leitrim. People who knew him in Aughawillan, Mohill, Ballinamore, Cootehall, Carrick-on-Shannon, and the surrounding area viewed him simply as a member of their community, a man whom they met at marts selling his livestock or in the local shops or pubs. While many realized he was a highly regarded literary figure, this did not in any way alter their opinion of him. For those who read his novels and short stories, and most particularly *Memoir*, the place-names, characters, and landscape would have been familiar, perhaps dangerously so. In his canvass of Leitrim-Roscommon, he immortalized a people with a distinctive culture and jealously preserved rituals. From the harsh realism of the early novels, he attained a control and mastery of his material in *Amongst Women* (1990), his best novel in many people's estimation, and a serenity and gentleness not palpable in the earlier work in his final fictional offering, *That They May Face the Rising Sun* (2002).

The last few decades of his career thus saw his reputation soar: *Amongst Women* won *The Irish Times*/Aer Lingus Irish Fiction Prize, the *Sunday Independent*/Irish Life Arts Award, and the Bank of Ireland Hughes and Hughes Award. It was also shortlisted for the Booker Prize and was made into a highly successful TV drama. From 1990 until his regrettably premature death in 2006, McGahern regularly appeared on radio and television programs and was spoken of by no less an authority than Declan Kiberd as "the foremost prose writer in English now in Ireland" (Kiberd and Maher 2002:86). His death on March 30, 2006, generated a string of tributes which illustrated the esteem and affection in which he was held. The editorial of *The Irish Times* (April 1, 2006) described him as "a writer with a keen sense of the national psyche" and went on to remark, "The ordinary and commonplace, which became central themes in his work, were transformed by the sureness of his imagination and his forensic attention to language." By sculpting away at his words, by trying to get the exact image and rhythm, McGahern managed eventually to make the ordinary scene extraordinary, to transform the local experience into a universal one.

Fintan O'Toole summed up his achievements succinctly: "He [McGahern] changed Ireland, not by arguing about it, but by describing it" (O'Toole 2006:2). For Eileen Battersby, his main quality was an ability to listen, feel, and suffer with his characters: "Most importantly, it was he [McGahern] who encouraged a reluctant country which has never enjoyed looking at itself to shed the old sentimentalities and complacencies and admit the hypocrisies" (Battersby 2006). The Nobel laureate, Seamus Heaney, a long-time friend, wrote, "McGahern not only did good work himself, he established high standards, standards of artistic excellence and personal integrity that worked silently and strongly within the entire literary community" ("The King is Dead" 2006).

I mention these tributes to give readers a flavor of the standing McGahern enjoyed within the literary establishment at the time of his death. For many years he has been held in high regard in France, where *The Barracks* featured on their *agrégation* course (a type of taught Ph.D.) and where his books sold very well in translation. It took him longer to get a real foothold in the US, but his last novel (published under the title *By the Lake* in its American edition) and *Memoir* (*All Will be Well: A Memoir*) successfully broke into that lucrative market. One monograph, David Malcolm's *Understanding John McGahern* (2007), has appeared since his death, but we can expect quite a few more in the coming years as the complexity of his depiction of a particular time and place in Ireland's evolution – a complexity that can be masked by a deceptively simple, accessible style – begins to be fully appreciated. Kiberd hinted as much when saying that his grave in Aughawillan "has become a place of pilgrimage," adding, "Since his passing, his already immense reputation has further soared" (Kiberd 2008:20–21).

McGahern belongs to a group of fiction writers who emerged in the decade 1955–65 that includes Aidan Higgins, Brian Moore, Edna O'Brien, and William Trevor. Their immediate predecessors, of whom Frank O'Connor and Seán O'Faoláin were the most notable, had been involved in the struggle for Irish independence and felt a responsibility to assume a prominent role in public life through their writing. The earlier group, represented by James Joyce, Samuel Beckett, and Flann O'Brien, employed daring literary devices designed to revolutionize form and belonged more to the international modernist movement than to any Irish literary movement per se. McGahern and his generation were likewise not unduly bothered with the question of defining their Irishness. So they moved away from the ideals of O'Connor and O'Faoláin – for whom the writer (even in fiction) had a duty to pronounce on issues of a national nature – in order to plunge the depths of personal experience. Maurice Harmon points out that, whereas Irish fiction in the 1930s and 1940s was concerned "with the struggle between society and the individual," since the 1950s "The emphasis is not so much on the nature of the environment, as on the private graph of feeling within the individual person" (Harmon 1975/76:55–56). We will see that McGahern was particularly adept at charting that "private graph of feeling" within his characters, most of whom struggle to find a fulfilling role for themselves in society and are more concerned with their personal relationships within the confines of family than with society at large.

While his books are situated in a clearly identifiable narrow area of Leitrim-Roscommon and whereas he is perceived as a discernibly "Irish" writer, McGahern nevertheless invariably quoted international writers when it came to citing influences. Yes, there were the Irish reference points such as Joyce, Beckett, Tomás Ó Crohan, Patrick Kavanagh, Ernie O'Malley, Kate O'Brien, and Michael MacLaverty, but interspersed with these names was a host of internationally renowned figures such as Proust, Flaubert, Camus, Thomas Hardy, Tolstoy, Chekhov, Alisdair MacLeod, and John Williams, all of whom displayed qualities that he was seeking to emulate in his own work. Writing of Joyce's *Dubliners*, McGahern quoted at length from Flaubert's correspondence with George Sand. Flaubert sought to detach himself from his material, as is captured in his immortal phrase, "The author is like God in nature, present everywhere but nowhere visible." McGahern compared Flaubert's desire to write a novel that would be held together by style alone to Joyce's "scrupulous meanness":

Joyce does not judge. His characters [in *Dubliners*] live within the human constraints in space and time and within their own city. The quality of the language is more important than any system of ethics or aesthetics. Material and form are inseparable. So happy is the union of subject and object that they never become statements of any kind, but in their richness and truth are representations of particular lives – and all of life. (McGahern 1991a:36)

What appeals to McGahern particularly in *Dubliners* is that it is written in a style that "never draws attention to itself" (McGahern 1991a:36), something that could equally be said of his own best prose. Similarly, the idea of material and form being inseparable, of the author declining to judge or pronounce on his characters' actions, qualities exemplified by Joyce and Flaubert, were also elements that McGahern would try to emulate in his own writing.

In "The Solitary Reader," he described how certain books act like mirrors that reflect something dangerously close to our own life and the society in which we live. These are the books that stay with us, long after we have read them: "The quality of the writing becomes more important than the quality of the material out of which the pattern or story is shaped" (McGahern 1991b:21). It was the "quality of the writing" that attracted McGahern in a special way to the Blasket writer Tomás Ó Crohan's memorable autobiography, *An tOileánach* (*The Islandman*). Here was a man struggling to capture the essential ingredients of living on an Atlantic island off the south-west coast of Ireland at the beginning of the twentieth century. Life was precarious for the few inhabitants left on the island and Ó Crohan knew that it was imperative to commit to paper the essence of this civilization before it became extinct. McGahern admired the "simple, heroic poetry" of Ó Crohan's account and, in words that offer a good summary of his own work, commented, "so persistent is the form of seeing and thinking that it seems always to find its right expression: unwittingly, through the island frame, we have been introduced into a complete representation of existence" (McGahern 2005:10).

The first publication is an important landmark in any writer's career. McGahern burst on the literary scene with *The Barracks* in 1963. The way in which the young writer manages to get into the mind of the main character, Elizabeth Reegan, a middle-aged woman who is diagnosed with terminal cancer, is his crowning achievement in this novel. The choice of subject was a clever one, as it allowed some distance between the author and his material. Kate O'Brien, reviewing the book, heaped praise on McGahern: "it is difficult to find words exact enough to express my admiration of this subtle, close-woven, tender, true, poetic work" (O'Brien 1963:59). Elizabeth's tedious, humdrum existence as the second wife of a widowed police sergeant and stepmother to his children is memorably captured. During her rare free moments, she thinks back to her time as a nurse in London during the Blitz and her affair with Dr Halliday, a disturbed and highly strung man whose dark depression led him eventually to commit suicide. On one occasion, he asked, "What's all this living and dying about, anyway, Elizabeth? That's what I'd like to be told" (McGahern 1963:85).

In some ways, McGahern's work is an attempt to unravel some of the mysteries associated with "all this living and dying." The difference between Elizabeth and Halliday is that she has a strong inner life that sustains her in her time of need. She also has a genuine commitment to prayer, especially the Rosary: "It had grown into her life, she'd come to love its words, its rhythm, its repetition, its confident chanting, its eternal mysteries" (McGahern 1963:220). Elizabeth's religion is based on personal prayer and reflection more than on any attachment to the institutional Church, which she finds oppressive and dogmatic.

Life in the police barracks is no bed of roses. Apart from the cooking and cleaning, looking after her husband's children from a first marriage, she is also forced to deal with her husband's professional displeasure at having to take orders from the young Superintendent Quirke, whom he despises. Elizabeth is left very much on her own as she struggles to survive a mastectomy and the subsequent fatal recurrence of the cancer. An intelligent, resourceful woman, she chooses to make the best she can out of her life:

> She was Elizabeth Reegan: a woman in her forties: sitting in a chair with a book from the council library that she hadn't opened: watching certain things like the sewing-machine and the vase of daffodils and a circle still white with frost under the shade of the sycamore tree between the house and the river: alive in this barrack kitchen … with a little time to herself before she'd have to get another meal ready: with a life on her hands that was losing the last vestiges of its purpose and meaning: with hard cysts within her breast she feared were cancer. (McGahern 1963:49)

The tragedy of Elizabeth's life becomes apparent with her sudden awareness of the beauty of the material world that she is soon to leave behind: "It was so beautiful when she let the blinds up first thing that, 'Jesus Christ,' softly was all she was able to articulate as she looked out and up the river to the woods across the lake" (170). It could be argued that the language employed in *The Barracks* falls short of the polished prose of the later work. There is a jarring awkwardness in certain expressions as well as in the punctuation. Such minor deficiencies are forgivable in a first novel, especially when considered in conjunction with the masterful empathy with Elizabeth's plight.

With the second novel, *The Dark*, the setting is once more the oppressive rural Ireland of the 1940s and 1950s. This time the main character is an adolescent striving to grow to independence and manhood. While it could be described as a *Bildungsroman*, there is none of the uplifting liberation that characterizes the experience of Stephen Dedalus in Joyce's *A Portrait of the Artist as a Young Man*. In fact, after winning a university scholarship on the strength of his Leaving Certificate results, Mahoney ends up in Galway with all the possibilities for independence and sexual liberation that this move opens up. However, he chooses to leave college and opts for the permanent position he is offered with the Electricity Supply Board.

Mahoney's lack of confidence has to be seen in the light of the psychological and sexual abuse he endures from his father, a widowed farmer who struggles to raise a young family on his own. Beatings are commonplace and often unprovoked. The opening scene of *The Dark* is distressing. The boy has been heard uttering a curse under his breath and is forced to strip and bend over a chair while his father brings the leather down, not on his exposed backside, but on the armrest beside his head. The horror of the simulated beating is as bad as, if not worse than, the real thing and, in terror, his urine flows all over the chair. Bad as this torture is, the sexual abuse is worse. Sharing a bed with his father exposes the boy to the "dirty rags of intimacy," as the father strokes his son's stomach and genitalia, causing both to reach orgasm. (A very similar abuse perpetrated on McGahern by his father is described in *Memoir*.) Guilt and a sense of worthlessness are exacerbated by regular bouts of masturbation, which result in the boy feeling unworthy of fulfilling the promise to his mother that he would one day become a priest.

The idea of the priesthood offering an escape from the grip of his father and the hardship of life on the farm has to be balanced against the natural desires of the flesh. A trip to stay with his cousin Gerald, a priest, marks the end of any vocation. Father Gerald visits his room during the night on the pretext of discussing his future. He climbs into bed alongside him and begins to explore in an intrusive way the boy's sexual fantasies. At a certain stage, Mahoney recognizes that his cousin's behavior is inappropriate: "What right had he to come and lie with you in bed, his body hot against yours, his arm around your shoulders. Almost as the cursed nights when your father used stroke your thighs" (McGahern 1965:74).

Given the issues broached in *The Dark*, it was inevitable that the novel would fall foul of the Censorship Board at the time. McGahern was opening up all sorts of vistas that Irish society was not prepared to face up to. The abusive and violent father, the priest who seems poised in his turn to embark on a course of abuse if the opportunity arises, the sordid Mr. Ryan – a respected parishioner of Father Gerald's – and his lurid behavior towards Mahoney's sister Joan while she is working in his shop, the guilt-ridden and sexually repressed Catholics who cannot find healthy outlets for their natural desires: it is a far from positive picture of rural Ireland that McGahern paints in this novel.

In terms of artistic evolution, the shifting point of view is probably *The Dark*'s most distinctive feature. From the traditional third-person-singular narration, McGahern switches towards the end of the novel to the first- and second-person-singular in an attempt, I would argue, to convey the uncertainty and insecurity of a young man who is unable to embrace change. He gets his father to come to Galway in order to discuss his future. After meeting with one of the deans of residence in the university, they decide that the best thing for everyone is for him to accept the permanent post and pension in the Electricity Supply Board. Some critics found the accommodation reached between father and son, after all the enmity and abuse that have characterized their relationship, unjustified. By adopting a different point of view, however, McGahern does succeed in making the reader see that the emotionally scarred young man prefers the familiar to the unknown. So his feeling of elation after making the decision transports him momentarily from his usual morbid thoughts and allows him to address himself in the following manner:

You were walking through the rain of Galway with your father and you could laugh
purely, without bitterness, for the first time, and it was a kind of happiness, at its heart
the terror of an unclear recognition of the reality that set you free, touching you with
as much foreboding as the sodden leaves falling in this day, or any cliche. (188)

The first stage of McGahern's career can be thus seen to be uneven. The jerky style
betrays a lack of mastery that will only come with years of experience and experimentation. *The Dark* announced that such a process was in train, but it is only in the next
two novels, *The Leavetaking* (1974, revised in 1984) and *The Pornographer* (1979), that
he really began to adopt a style and approach which would eventually yield positive
results.

The Leavetaking is remarkable for the fact that McGahern, in light of some infelici-
ties of style that he noticed when reading through the novel's French translation by
Alain Delahaye, decided to rewrite it ten years after it was first published. The second
version, while better, is nevertheless still problematic. The main obstacle lies in the
close identification between events in real life (the death of McGahern's mother and
his dismissal from his teaching post in Belgrove) and those related in the novel. To
McGahern's credit, he did acknowledge this in his preface to the second edition: "I
had been too close to the 'Idea,' and the work lacked that distance, that inner formality or calm, that all writing, no matter what it is attempting, must possess" (McGahern
1984). The problem is not resolved in the second edition either and for the very reason
he outlines in the preface – he remained "too close to the 'Idea'." That is not to say
that the novel is poor – it contains some poignant, moving passages, particularly in
part I where the narrator and main character, a teacher, reflects on his mother's illness
and subsequent death – but simply that it draws too heavily on autobiography.

It can be argued that McGahern incorporated a lot of his own experiences into all
his fiction and that there are characters in his short stories and novels who are closely
modeled on people he knew in real life. But there is no other McGahern novel where
fact and fiction become so blurred as in *The Leavetaking*. When *Memoir* appeared in
2005, certain passages were transposed word for word from the novel. The close reader
of McGahern is left wondering where reality ends and fiction begins. The devout
mother, a national schoolteacher married to a Garda sergeant, and who dies of cancer,
closely resembles Susan McGahern. The repeated entreaty by the sick woman to her
eldest child that he become a priest echoes the type of exchange McGahern regularly
had with his own mother. The mastectomy that precedes the last dose of cancer, the
advice given by the doctors that it is inadvisable for her to conceive any more children,
the circumstances surrounding the last pregnancy when the husband returns home
from the barracks in a nearby village and, in the throes of passion, fatally impregnates
her, the birth of the sickly child, a son, the return of the cancer, the removal of the
children to the barracks where their father is stationed before the mother's death – all
of these events are uncomfortably close to actual events in the McGahern household.
The tension between father and eldest son, the jealousy of the former in relation to
the close bond between mother and son, his attempts to pull them apart – these too

have their basis in fact. There is a literary process in train also, however, a process that seeks to impose a certain order on events. The young schoolteacher in the novel is aware of the role of memory and imagination in the circle that is life: "Two worlds: the world of the schoolroom in this day, the world of memory becoming imagination: but this last day in the classroom will one day be nothing but a memory before its total obliteration, the completed circle" (McGahern 1984:35). The second Part of *The Leavetaking*, recounting the dismissal of the main character from his teaching position, mainly on account of his irregular marriage in a registry office to an American divorcee, lacks the intensity of the opening half. The first lines reveal that the promise to his mother has not been forgotten:

> "One day I'd say Mass for her."
>   I felt I had betrayed her in that upstairs room. Through the sacrifice of the Mass I would atone for the betrayal, but that in its turn became the sacrifice of the dream of another woman, became the death in life, the beginning only in the end. (85)

The other woman to whom he refers, Isobel, is an unconvincing portrayal. She lacks depth and the ability to touch the reader in any meaningful way. It is clear that she does not compare favorably with the deceased mother, but then again it is doubtful that any woman could. Much of the action in the latter half of the novel is situated in London, and McGahern does not seem comfortable in this setting. There is a struggle evident throughout the narrative as the author seeks to find the rhythm and style that suit him. In places he succeeds in matching content and form and there are hints of the transcending power of love in the closing pages, something one does not encounter too often in McGahern:

> The odour of our lovemaking rises, redolent of slime and fish, and our very breathing seems an echo of the rise and fall of the sea as we drift to sleep: and I would pray for the boat of our sleep to reach its mooring, and see that morning lengthen to an evening of calm weather that comes through night and sleep again to morning after morning, until we meet in first death. (170–71)

These concluding lines offer the type of hope that is not evident in any of McGahern's previous novels – *The Pornographer* was published after the first edition of *The Leavetaking* appeared. It brings together many elements – the gulls the teacher observes in the opening passage as he does yard duty, memory, imagination, and death. Terence Killeen asserts that the very possibility of a hopeful future for the couple shows how far we have moved from the world of *The Barracks* and *The Dark* (Killeen 1991:73). It is certainly hinted that memory and art can bring healing to those in the throes of pain. *The Pornographer*, to which we turn now, presents an existential perspective, and in this it represents another important phase in McGahern's literary development.

     The choice of subject matter and the manner in which McGahern inserted examples of real pornography into his text show how he was prepared to attempt something new. He stated in an interview that "*The Pornographer* was a deliberate attempt to see could sex be written about. The reason that the main character is so uninteresting is that this obsession with sexuality is enervating" (Maher 2003:148). The main character remains nameless throughout, and he is not nearly as "uninteresting" as McGahern states. Sex is the central theme of the novel. The pornographer, inflamed by the sexual antics of the Colonel and Mavis, the key figures of his pornographic writing, regularly prowls the dance halls of Dublin in search of female "prey." It is in one of these places that he meets with a bank official, Josephine, with whom he embarks on an ill-judged affair. She becomes pregnant because of her unwillingness to allow him use a condom – "It turns the whole thing into a kind of farce," in her words (McGahern 1979:56) – and he informs her that while he is willing to support her in any way he can he will not marry her. She moves to London to have the baby; he visits her before and after the birth, but sticks to his decision to cut all links between them.

Running parallel to this doomed relationship is the more positive one he embarks on with a nurse, Brady, whom he encounters when visiting his terminally ill aunt in hospital. Brady represents a source of positive love that distinguishes her from the other sexual encounters, driven by pure lust, which the pornographer has known to date:

> This body [Brady's] was the shelter of the self. Like all walls and shelters it would age and break and let the enemy in. But holding it now was like holding glory, and having held it once was to hold it – no matter how broken and conquered – in glory still, and with the more terrible tenderness. (177)

With this woman, he feels liberated from the prison of his body and he reaches out for something mysterious, almost mystical. His decision at the end of the novel to return to live on the farm left to him by his parents in the west of Ireland with the nurse, if she will have him, is predicated on the fact that he senses that it is in this environment that he has the best chance of achieving happiness. When he is in the presence of his aunt or unmarried uncle, he is a different person. After this novel, McGahern's fiction does not stray again from the country, which will be the setting for his final two novels. Returning to Dublin with his boss Maloney, the pornographer tries unsuccessfully to explain his decision. Maloney has had his fill of the repressive Ireland that shaped his youth and inspired his decision to deal in pornography: "Ireland wanking is Ireland free. Not only wanking but free. Not only free but wanking as well" (25). The pornographer achieves a type of catharsis as he sees the path he will follow stretching out in front of him, holding out the promise of happiness and fulfillment: "What I wanted to say was that I had a fierce need to pray, for myself, Maloney, my uncle, the girl, the whole shoot. The prayers could not be answered, but prayers that cannot be answered need to be more completely said, being their own beginning as well as end" (252). *The Pornographer* allowed McGahern to come to grips with certain issues that are to the forefront of his early and middle fiction: religion, family, sex, life and death. It contains some gems of insight: the rituals associated with visiting his aunt in hospital are classic, as is his description of his uncle's self-sufficiency. Maloney is amazed to see him back at work in his sawmill the day after his sister's funeral and tells his friend that he is someone who has found the key to contentment: "There's one man who knows he's going everywhere by staying put" (250). It also presents a sophisticated philosophical life-view:

> The womb and the grave ... the christening party becomes the funeral, the shudder that makes us flesh becomes the shudder that makes us meat. They say that it is the religious instinct that makes us seek the relationships and laws in things. And in between there is time and work, as passing time, and killing time, and lessening time that'd lessen anyway. (30)

This type of dark philosophy is at the core of many of McGahern's short-story collections. The best of the stories in *Nightlines* (1970), *Getting Through* (1978) and *High Ground* (1985) were brought together, with some revisions, in *The Collected Stories* (1992), which also contains the classic "A Country Funeral." Then *Creatures of the Earth: New and Selected Stories* appeared posthumously in 2006. The short-story genre suited McGahern's penchant for concision and reshaping. The stories he wrote are concerned mainly with fraught domestic relationships, especially between fathers and sons, the end of innocence, the difficulties associated with male–female interactions, the harshness of life for the emigrant Irish laborers in London, the pull of the country. Those that stand out in particular are "Wheels," "Korea," "Peaches," "My Love, My Umbrella," "The Wine Breath," "High Ground" and "Gold Watch." Each of them in its own way provides a snapshot of existence, which is in keeping with McGahern's view of the short story as "a small explosion" which requires the reader fill in the blanks in order to figure out what takes place after the story ends: "And it generally makes one point and one point only, and has a very strict rhythm, and every word counts in it" (Louvel et al. 1995:28).

McGahern was superb in his depiction of the rituals surrounding death. "The Country Funeral" is exemplary in this regard. In it, we witness how three brothers, John, Philly, and Fonsie Ryan, undergo a change in their relationship as they travel west from Dublin to attend the funeral of their maternal uncle, Peter. Their mother, a widow, used to take them to her unmarried brother's farm every summer, mainly as a cost-saving measure. Now, as they prepare to get into the car and begin their journey, she warns them, "Everything you do down there will be watched and gone over. I'll be following poor Peter in my mind until you rest him with Father and Mother in Killeelan [cemetery]" (McGahern 2006:373–74).

McGahern knew the significance of a funeral in rural Ireland. It was not simply a question of putting a corpse in a coffin and burying it. No, certain customs had to be observed: food and drink bought for the wake; a detailed discussion and appraisal of the man's life; the funeral Mass and the laying to rest of the body. Philly is struck by the warmth of his uncle's neighbors and feels a strong attraction for the area around Gloria Bog, where Peter lived. At the end of the story, he decides he will buy the farm from his mother and go to live there eventually. Fonsie, confined to a wheelchair, does not share Philly's enthusiasm for the area or its people. Yet, as he watches the funeral cortège making the tortuous ascent towards Killeelan, he cannot help finding "the coffin and the small band of toiling mourners unbearably moving" (399).

In his short stories McGahern develops much of the material and themes that mark his two final novels. *Amongst Women* emerged after a long period of gestation and rewriting. The result can be gauged from the tight style, where everything is condensed to the bare essentials. The novel is, in the words of John Cronin, "a stylistically seamless work" (Cronin 1992:173). I do not think this quality would have been possible had the emotion and antipathy McGahern felt for his father come to the fore. There can be no doubt that the character Michael Moran and Frank McGahern share a number of traits: they are both self-absorbed, dissatisfied, domineering, unpredictable, mean-spirited, delusional individuals whose happiest moments are spent during the struggle for Irish independence. After the glow and excitement of their time as guerrilla leaders, life falls short of their expectations. Moran regularly questions if the type of society that has emerged as a result of men like him putting their lives on the line was worth the effort: "Some of our own johnnies in the top jobs instead of a few Englishmen. ... What was it all for? The whole thing was a cod" (McGahern 1990:5).

Most upsetting for the widower is his realization that he is no longer in control. His eldest child, Luke, whom he reputedly drove away as a result of a particularly violent beating, operates outside of his orbit in London and shows no desire to return to the fold. Time and again Moran refers remorsefully to his absent son in a way that reveals he finds it difficult to accept that he counts for nothing in Luke's eyes. His second wife, Rose, makes the mistake early on in their marriage of defending Luke, which earns her a harsh rebuke: "Did you ever listen carefully to yourself, Rose? If you listened a bit more carefully to yourself I think you might talk a lot less" (54). It is the women in Moran's life who remain central in maintaining the illusion of "Daddy," a wonderful, heroic man who exists only in their imagination. They dismiss his violent outbursts as they would the tantrums of a child and persevere in preserving an image that is tinged with romance: "No matter how far in talk the sisters ventured, they kept returning, as if to a magnet, to what Daddy would like or dislike, approve of, or disapprove of" (131). Their loyalty makes them emotionally dependent but is not rewarded by any tenderness or sensitivity on the part of their father. For example, when Sheila gains a university scholarship and announces that she would like to study medicine, she is subtly encouraged to choose a profession more in keeping with her social standing and academic ability: "Sheila could not have desired a worse profession. It was the priest and doctor and not the guerrilla fighters who had emerged as the bigwigs in the country Moran had fought for. For his own daughter to lay claim to such a position was an intolerable affront" (88). It is clear from this that Moran's repeated declaration that he loves all his children equally does not stack up when considered in the light of how he repeatedly puts obstacles in the way of their stated ambitions. He has long dreamed of working the land with his two sons, but in time that dream is crushed by Luke's self-imposed exile and Michael's move to join his brother in London. Moran's tragedy is that he is so busily absorbed in getting control of his family and farm that he fails to appreciate the comforting presence of both until it is too late. He spends his old age alone with Rose in Great Meadow, a man of no special importance anywhere other than in the eyes of his wife and daughters. He realizes a moment of catharsis shortly before his death when he "sees" for the first time the splendor that surrounds him: "To die was never to look on all this again. It would live in others' eyes but not in his. He had never realized when in the midst of confident life what an amazing glory he was part of" (179). Like Elizabeth Reegan in *The Barracks* (and perhaps McGahern himself after the diagnosis of his own cancer), Moran has an intuition of the beauty of everyday life just as he is on the point of dying. If we do not exactly feel sympathy for his plight, we can at least understand it. In some ways, he is the product of a harsh upbringing and his training as an assassin. He is nowhere so competent as when taking aim and bringing others to the ground.

After eleven years without any significant publication, McGahern's last novel, *That They May Face the Rising Sun*, appeared in 2002. It is a gentle celebration of life in a community living around a lake in a setting that bears more than a passing resemblance to McGahern's dwelling in Aughawillan, County Leitrim. Its tone is completely different to the preceding novels, which may well be due to the fact that it was inspired by the happy memories of the time spent with his mother in this part of the world. The lake and its surroundings resemble a rural idyll, and even if there are certain characters who have a rough edge (the handyman Patrick Ryan for example), or who are obsessed with sex and exploitative of women (the womanizer John Quinn), they do not detract from the general atmosphere of joy and commemoration. Unpalatable things happen to people: for example the farm-boy Bill Evans, the product of a life spent in care, is sent to work for people who treat him abominably; the unfortunate Johnny falls head over heels in love with a woman whom he follows to England, only to be ditched and forced to live the rest of his life in exile. But rather than being a source of pain and critical analysis, these are accepted as the fruit of a society in evolution.

Joe and Kate Ruttledge form the focal point of this close-knit community, their house being a meeting place for the fun-loving, gossip-driven neighbor Jamesie (Johnny's brother), Joe's uncle, memorably known as "the Shah," as well as the aforementioned Patrick Ryan and Bill Evans. Joe has brought his wife from London to live on the remote farm, a move that was easier for him because he originally came from the area and understood its people and appreciated its calm landscape. After a time, Kate feels as comfortable in her new abode as she could feel anywhere. The novel moves seamlessly through the seasons, with the various rituals like saving the hay, going to the mart, and celebrating Christmas and Easter. People call at the Ruttledges' house and playfully poke fun at each other, give news of the inhabitants around the lake or of their families. Certain events occur more than once, such as Johnny's return home for his summer holidays. Every year he is collected from the train by his brother and forced to consume several drinks before returning to the meal Jamesie's wife,

Mary, has prepared for them. During his stay he does the rounds of the neighbors' houses, declaring everything to be "alphabetical," his word for perfect.

There is no real plot in this novel, no exciting events to hold our interest and attention. It is bound together, in the Flaubertian sense, by style alone – by the atmosphere generated through this style. We feel as though we are living alongside the characters, rather than reading a novel as such. The fact that the majority of the community are middle-aged or old means that death is a daily consideration. One of the most telling descriptions is when Johnny dies during one of his summer visits. In the absence of Patrick Ryan, Ruttledge is asked to lay the body out. The ritual assumes a metaphysical resonance: "The rectum absorbed almost all of the cotton wool. The act was as intimate and warm as the act of sex. The innate sacredness of each single life stood out more starkly in death than in the whole of natural life" (McGahern 2002:273). When reflecting on the experience with Kate, Ruttledge explains, "It made death and the fear of death more natural" (279). The strong pagan element present in the lakeside community is evident in the way they choose to bury Johnny. Patrick Ryan outlines why they do this, in words that explain the title of the book: "He sleeps with his head to the west ... So that when he wakes he may face the rising sun. ...We look to the resurrection of the dead" (282). There is an obvious fusion of the pagan and the Christian here, with the adoration of the sun being counterbalanced by the belief in the Resurrection. Their closeness to nature binds the community together. Kiberd observes that "nature is far stronger than any human, and stronger even than art" (Kiberd 2008:26). The lake, trees, animals, and foliage will survive long after the inhabitants have passed away. In some ways, this appreciation of nature is what gives *That They May Face the Rising Sun* its tone of pastoral elegy. He laments being wrenched from the contemplation of such rare beauty:

> The night and the lake had not the bright metallic beauty of the night Johnny had died: the shapes of the great tree were softer and brooded even deeper in their mysteries. The water was silent, except for the chattering of the wildfowl, the night air sweet with the scent of the ripening meadows, thyme and clover and meadowsweet, wild woodbine high in the whitethorns mixed with the scent of wild mint crawling along the gravel on the edge of the water. (296)

When I read this passage for the first time, I was convinced that McGahern would not write any more novels after this one. The commemorative, nostalgic tone is that of a man who is keenly aware of the transience of life and appreciative of its beauty. McGahern had also moved into the autobiographical mode which, instead of looking backwards, concentrated on his present life spent beside the lake in the company of his wife Madeline, and his family and friends. It did not surprise me therefore when I discovered that *Memoir* was en route and, on reading it, that it contained no real revelations that had not already been shared with readers of the fiction.

Now that he has departed this world, certain issues like the abuse he endured at the hands of his father might be dealt with in a more open manner. His wounded, weather-beaten face had a kindliness and vulnerability about it, a hint that behind the social mask there lurked a story, at once sinister and beautiful, that demanded to be told. If *Memoir* reveals anything, it is that writing was therapy for McGahern. He could only understand something by writing about it. Thus we encounter a number of the same characters, settings, and situations in the different novels and stories, which in essence form one major painting. What emerges over the four decades of his work is the control of emotion through style, the refinement of presentation, the perfection of rhythm and tone.

McGahern's appeal extends beyond boundaries and cultures because of the powerful images and moving human situations he sketches. He shows us the circular nature of life, so well evoked in the final lines of the short story "Wheels": "all the vivid sections of the wheel we watched so slowly turn, impatient for the rich whole that never came but that all the preparations promised" (McGahern 2006:12). "The rich whole" for McGahern, if not possible during his lifetime, was certainly realized in a corpus of work that captures in an admirable manner much of what is essential in the human condition.

REFERENCES AND FURTHER READING

Battersby, E. (2006). "A Simple Farewell, a Silent Prayer that He May Face the Rising Sun." *The Irish Times*, 3 April, 5.

Brannigan, J. (Ed.). (2005). *John McGahern*. Special issue of the *Irish University Review*, 35.1 (Spring/Summer).

Carlson, J. (1990). "John McGahern" (interview). In J. Carlson (Ed.). *Banned in Ireland: Censorship and the Irish Writer* (pp. 53–68). London: Routledge.

Cronin, J. (1992). "John McGahern's *Amongst Women*: Retrenchment and Renewal." *Irish University Review*, 22.1 (Spring/Summer), 168–76.

Harmon, M. (1975/76). "Generations Apart: 1925–1975." In M. Harmon and P. Rafroidi (Eds). *The Irish Novel in Our Time* (pp. 49–65). Lille: Publications de l'Université de Lille 3.

Kiberd, D. (2008). "Forms of Life." *The John McGahern Yearbook*, 1, 20–29.

Kiberd, D. and E. Maher. (2002). "John McGahern: Writer, Stylist, Seeker of a Lost World" (interview). *Doctrine and Life*, 52.2, 82–97.

Killeen, T. (1991). "Versions of Exile: A Reading of *The Leavetaking*." *Canadian Journal of Irish Studies*, 20, 69–78.

"The King is Dead." (2006). *The Irish Times* (March 31), 17.

Louvel, L., G. Ménégaldo, and C. Verley. (1995). "John McGahern – 17 November 1993" (interview). *La Licorne*, 32, 19–31.

Maher, E. (2003). *John McGahern: From the Local to the Universal*. Dublin: Liffey Press.

Malcolm, D. (2007). *Understanding John McGahern*. Columbia: University of South Carolina Press.

McGahern, J. (1963). *The Barracks*. London: Faber & Faber.

McGahern, J. (1965). *The Dark*. London: Faber & Faber.

McGahern, J. (1970). *Nightlines*. London: Faber & Faber.

McGahern, J. (1978). *Getting Through*. London: Faber & Faber.

McGahern, J. (1979). *The Pornographer*. London: Faber & Faber.

McGahern, J. (1984). *The Leavetaking* (1974). Rev. edn. London: Faber & Faber.

McGahern, J. (1985). *High Ground*. London: Faber & Faber.

McGahern, J. (1987). *The Rockingham Shoot*. BBC/Channel 4 co-production.

McGahern, J. (1990). *Amongst Women*. London: Faber & Faber.

McGahern, J. (1991a). "Dubliners." *Canadian Journal of Irish Studies*, 17.1, 12.

McGahern, J. (1991b). "The Solitary Reader." *Canadian Journal of Irish Studies*, 17.1, 19–23.

McGahern, J. (1991c). *The Power of Darkness*. London: Faber & Faber.

McGahern, J. (1992). *The Collected Stories*. London: Faber & Faber.

McGahern, J. (2002). *That They May Face the Rising Sun*. London: Faber & Faber.

McGahern, J. (2005). *Memoir*. London: Faber & Faber.

McGahern, J. (2006). *Creatures of the Earth: New and Selected Stories*. London: Faber & Faber.

Ní Anluain, C. (Ed.). (2000). "John McGahern." In *Reading the Future: Irish Writers in Conversation with Mike Murphy* (pp. 137–55). Dublin: Lilliput Press.

O'Brien, K. (1963). Rev. edn. of *The Barracks*. *Irish University Review*, 3.4, 59–60.

O'Toole, F. (2006). "Picking the Lock of Family Secrets." *The Irish Times Weekend Review* (April 1), 1–2.

Sampson, D. (1993). *Outstaring Nature's Eye: The Fiction of John McGahern*. Washington: Catholic University Press.

Whyte, J. (2002). *History, Myth and Ritual in the Fictions of John McGahern: Strategies of Transcendence*. Lewiston, NY: Edwin Mellen Press.

Part Ten

Contemporary Literature:
Print, Stage, and Screen

46

Brian Friel: From Nationalism to Post-Nationalism

F.C. McGrath

Brian Friel has established himself as one of Ireland's pre-eminent playwrights. He unquestionably belongs in a pantheon of Irish dramatists that includes Wilde, Shaw, Synge, O'Casey, Behan, and Beckett. His oeuvre includes more than thirty plays and adaptations, as well as more than thirty short stories. His plays have dominated the Irish theater scene since the 1960s. Joe Dowling, who has been artistic director of the Abbey Theatre and directed Friel plays, says that Friel "is the one who has most consistently over the last twenty-five years reflected the changes in Ireland" (Friel 1999b:140). I would extend that range of influence to include the past forty to forty-five years.

More than twenty academic books, in addition to scores of articles, have been devoted exclusively to Friel's work. By far the most important secondary reading for his plays are the two collections of his own essays, interviews, and diaries (Friel 1999b; Delaney 2000). These collections overlap to some extent, but they give us access to the thinking of a writer who generally has been extremely reluctant to talk or write about his own work. The collections of essays on Friel (Peacock 1993; Kerwin 1997; Roche 1999, 2006; Harp and Evans 2002; Morse et al. 2006) suffer from the typical limitations of that genre – weak organizing principles and uneven quality of the essays. Roche (2006) is an exception to the former limitation; it is organized chrono-logically and according to several topics particularly relevant to Friel's work. Despite being somewhat dated, Peacock's collection is still very useful. Kerwin's volume also is notable for its inclusion of important early essays by Richard Kearney on Friel's language plays and by Declan Kiberd on *Faith Healer*. Given Friel's emphasis on language – for example, about *Translations* Friel says "the play has to do with language and only language. And if it becomes overwhelmed by that political element, it is lost" (Friel 1999b:75) – it is surprising how both sympathetic and hostile readers

A Companion to Irish Literature, edited by Julia M. Wright
© 2010 Blackwell Publishing Ltd

have often misunderstood or misinterpreted his work, either because they focus on political or social issues without taking into account Friel's complex views about the interrelations of language, politics, and culture or because they focus on purely formal aesthetic concerns to the neglect of others. Even most of the books on Friel tend to ignore his central focus on the role of language in the construction of personal, social, cultural, and political realities. Although she has not written a book on Friel, Edna Longley should be mentioned here as one of the playwright's most severe critics, and her essay "Poetry and Politics in Northern Ireland" (Longley 1986) is representative of her anti-nationalist, revisionist position.

Friel's work exists in the context of Ireland's effort to redefine itself after decades of post-Independence cultural and economic isolation dominated by nationalism and its own particular brand of Catholicism, decades often referred to as the "age of de Valera." Contenders in shaping that identity including traditional forms of nationalism, republicanism, and Unionism, as well as more contemporary influences of a renovated, updated nationalism, feminism, historical revisionism, and consumer capitalism. Starting from a desire to renovate traditional nationalism, Friel acknowledged the hybrid legacy of Ireland's long colonization, particularly the legacy of language, and appropriated it as uniquely Irish. In the process the trajectory of his writing career has mirrored Ireland's evolution from a nationalist to a post-nationalist state.

Stages of Postcolonial Development

Most formerly colonized countries typically progress through a number of developmental stages, including (1) colonial subjection; (2) nationalist resistance; (3) liberation; (4) post-liberation nationalism; (5) hybridity; and (6) polycentrism. Progress through these stages is not linear or uniform; stages may overlap and different parts of a population may inhabit different stages. Ireland has been subjected to varying degrees of British domination, accompanied by varying degrees of collaboration, acquiescence, and resistance, since the late Middle Ages. At the end of the eighteenth century organized resistance based on nationalist principles began to emerge with the United Irishmen Uprising of 1798, which was followed by other nationalist resistances until liberation was achieved in 1922 after the treaty that ended the Anglo-Irish War. The period of post-liberation nationalism lasted in the Irish Free State, which later became the Republic of Ireland, from 1922 until the 1960s. This "age of de Valera" was characterized by economic and cultural isolation, and a narrow nationalism defined in terms of the frugal independence of a rural, Gaelic, Catholic culture.

Once a nationalist state begins to mature and feel more politically and culturally secure as an equal among other nations, it begins to recognize and accept itself as a hybrid of its native and colonial past. It accepts its colonial history and its implications but still retains its own identity by appropriating and redefining that colonial inheritance and making it uniquely its own. The master-narratives of both the native nationalism and the former colonial power are rewritten from the margins between the two cultures. At this point in a nation's history its structures and values are still determined to an extent by the response to the experience of being colonized and marginalized, but the exclusivity and defensiveness of previous stages of nationalism begin to moderate and the voices of non-nationalist minorities begin to be heard from the margins of the hegemonic nationalist culture.

In the final stage of postcolonial development the various definitions of center and periphery break down and identity is determined less in relation to a single hegemonic culture than by relations among a variety of centers at different levels. Even regions within a state may define themselves in terms of their relations with other states or other regions. Ideally these relations involve full recognition of and respect for difference and diversity, what in the Irish context has been called parity of esteem. For example, John Hume (Derry native, founder of the Social Democratic and Labour Party in Northern Ireland, Member of the European Parliament, and co-winner of the 1998 Nobel Peace Prize) sees the Derry region of Northern Ireland forming its identity today in relation to Northern Ireland, the Republic of Ireland, other countries and regions within the United Kingdom and the European Union, and the Irish diaspora. According to Hume,

> a polycentric rather than an imperial vision is driving Europe forward. Associated with the development of multiple centres is the creation of multiple layers of identities. Simultaneously or successively, we can be Europeans, British, Irish, Northern Irish, Derrymen or Derrywomen – whatever we choose. In this new world, there are no incompatibilities between identities, there is no superiority of one identity over another, we can be free to invent ourselves. Ultimately, identity will simply become a matter of comfort and convenience, not a sign of tribal loyalty. This is the world we must seek and perhaps, invent. (Hume 1996:154–55)

Hume was a Member of the European Parliament, and his model for polycentrism derives from his vision of a "Europe of the Regions" (Hume 1996:153), which he sees as the ultimate accomplishment of the regional development policies of the European Union.

While the six stages suggest a general evolutionary development in relation to colonialism, at any given point in Irish history articulations of more than one stage of development can be found. I realize that historians and cultural critics will disagree over the details of this schema, for example over whether Ireland was colonized in the first place or whether nationalism led to liberation or other forms of colonization. However, I make no ontological claims for it but offer it for heuristic purposes only. In any case, under this schema by 1960 the Republic of Ireland had passed through the first four stages. When Sean Lemass succeeded Éamon de Valera as taoiseach in 1959, Ireland abandoned its economic and cultural isolationism and began to search for a new identity based on new values that would sustain it in a post-nationalist world. A number of things drove this search. The opening up of the economy to mostly American multinational corporations brought with it the culture of consumer capitalism. Ireland's entry into the European Union in 1973 brought closer ties with

Europe and eventually huge investments in the Irish economy. The Irish women's movement of the 1970s and 1980s, culminating in the election of Mary Robinson as President of Ireland in 1990, combined with the introduction of European Union social policies to liberalize Irish social practices. Since the 1990s, a series of scandals has rocked the Catholic Church in Ireland and helped to speed up the process of secularization and the concomitant diminution of the Church's influence in Ireland.

At the same time that nationalism was beginning to fade in the Republic – its last robust public outburst was the fiftieth anniversary of the 1916 uprising in 1966 – in Northern Ireland the civil rights movement of 1968 inaugurated three decades of violence that reignited nationalist sentiment among the Catholic population of the North and some Protestant sympathizers. The violence also ignited British nationalism among the Unionist population of the North. Because of the partition of Ireland and because of the uniquely different histories of north and south since 1922, nationalism in the north of Ireland developed along a different trajectory and has been out of phase with nationalism in the south. From 1921 until 1972 Northern Ireland was governed by "a Protestant parliament for a Protestant people" and Catholics were disenfranchised and relegated to second-class citizenship. The resistance begun in 1968 first opposed the inequities of Stormont rule and then fought direct British rule after the Stormont parliament was prorogued in 1972. Even though many of the civil rights movement's goals were achieved within a few years, nationalist resistance continued until the signing of the Belfast Agreement in 1998. That agreement set up a power-sharing government in which Catholics had an equal voice with Protestants. The Belfast Agreement ended most of the violence in the North, but it was not fully implemented until 2007. Northern Ireland arguably is passing through a stage of liberation, but in addition to being eighty-five years behind the Republic, northern nationalists also have a split identity by virtue of identifying with the post-liberation culture of the south as well as their own situation.

Friel's writing career spanned these critical decades in Irish history from the late 1950s to the first years of the twenty-first century, and part of his importance as an Irish writer derives from his engagement with issues that dominated those decades in both Northern Ireland and the Republic. Friel had been brought up with staunch Irish nationalist values, but like John Hume he recognized the necessity of modifying and updating traditional Irish nationalism, whether of the constitutional or the physical force traditions, in order to make it viable for contemporary Ireland. That nationalism in the North and in the Republic were out of phase with each other made the process of modifying it more complicated for Friel, who came from the North but in many ways identified with the Republic.

Most of Friel's published plays focus on the last three stages of Ireland's postcolonial development and helped to invent the new Ireland Hume called for. Many of his plays critique the narrow traditional nationalism and its supporting myths that characterized the first post-liberation stage. Friel also critiques post-1960s Ireland, particularly its bourgeois materialism, political corruption, and social and cultural decay that resulted from modernization; and he critiques the American source for much of that vulgar materialism. Friel's decade-long involvement with Field Day, energized by the history and troubles of Northern Ireland, concentrated his attention on recognizing the hybridity of Irish culture and the necessity for redefining Irish nationalism in terms of that hybridity. After Friel left Field Day his plays tended to focus on more personal concerns and on translations and adaptations of European writers, including Chekhov, Turgenev, and Ibsen. In this final, polycentric, phase Friel seems to be less concerned with exploring Irish identity in terms of public/historical issues (with the notable exception of *The Home Place* [2005]) than with more personal issues and with establishing his own relationship with writers from other times and other places.

Friel's Nationalism

In a recent study of Friel, Scott Boltwood, following the practice of David Lloyd and others influenced by *Subaltern Studies*, minimizes the significance of the playwright's nationalism. However, this distorts his contribution to Irish culture. Coming from a traditional Catholic nationalist background in Northern Ireland, Friel often felt "the frustration and the resentment of a Catholic in the North of Ireland" (Delaney 2000:49). Prior to the civil rights movement in Northern Ireland he had joined the Nationalist Party, but found that venture moribund and futile (Friel 1999b:110–11). The civil rights movement in the North, however, rekindled nationalism for many Catholics, and for Friel restored its vitality and dignity (1999b:28). While Friel's Catholicism faded somewhat over the years, his nationalism did not (Friel 1999b:26). When he visits Dublin, Friel says, he has "a twinge of emotion when I pass the Post Office, because I admire the men of 1916" (1999b:31). Although he was born and worked as a teacher in Northern Ireland, and had dual citizenship in the United Kingdom and the Republic of Ireland, he chose to live in the Republic rather than under what he termed the "absurd" and "iniquitous" Stormont government (1999b:28). Although Friel has serious reservations about both the Republic and Northern Ireland, he nevertheless considers Ireland as a whole as his cultural home and he has never accepted the border either "intellectually or emotionally" (1999b:28). In this sense, at least, that is, culturally, Friel is a thirty-two-county republican. He also shares the republican position on the British presence in Ireland. Talking about his play *Translations* (1980), he says it is "concerned with the English presence here. No matter how benign they may think it has been, finally the presence of any foreigner in your land is malign" (1999b:80). He adds, "There will be no solution until the British leave this island" (1999b:87).

Despite its intensity, Friel's lifelong nationalism has never been uncritical, and it evolved over the course of his career. Much of his work is devoted to questioning what it means to be Irish. Friel notes,

> The generation of Irish writers immediately before mine never allowed this burden to weigh them down. They learned to speak Irish, took their genetic purity for granted,

and soldiered on. For us today the situation is more complex. We are more concerned with defining our Irishness than with pursuing it. (1999b:45)

This lack of confidence in old certainties undoubtedly had a good deal to do with growing up Catholic in Northern Ireland, but modernization and globalization in the Republic also eroded the old certainties of nationalism. This led Friel and other writers to the questions, "Who are we?" and "How do we articulate who we are?":

> But when we try to identify ourselves, it means you've got to produce documents, you've got to produce sounds, you've got to produce images that are going to make you distinctive in some way. If there's a sense of decline about how the country is, it's because we can't readily produce these identification marks. (Delaney 2000:189)

Friel's own writing has produced a number of documents that have contributed to a new identity for the Irish in a post-nationalist world. Friel's questioning of nationalism led him to reject the traditional nationalism he inherited, and with his involvement in Field Day he tried to forge a new conception of nationalism that was more ecumenical and open to others than traditional nationalism. After he parted ways with Field Day, Friel pursued more personal forms of identity, and in a number of plays, especially his translations and adaptations, he sought to see himself in relation to European figures and writers.

Friel's Critique of Nationalism

Friel's critique of traditional Irish nationalism manifests itself in a number of plays, but *The Gentle Island* (1971) and *The Communication Cord* (1982) deal most directly with Friel's rejection of traditional nationalism. These plays question the idealism and myths upon which the Republic of Ireland was founded, including the republican ideals of 1916 and the de Valerean myth of frugal, Catholic, Gaelic, rural Ireland as the foundation of the state. Friel attacked the rural idyll especially savagely in *The Gentle Island*, a bleak naturalistic tragedy that depicts a depopulating island off Ireland's west coast as seething with violence, anger, and visceral sexuality. In contrast to the peasant society of Inishkeen, the relationship of a visiting gay couple from Dublin is characterized as caring and civilized. Like Patrick Kavanagh's *The Great Hunger*, *The Gentle Island* depicts peasant life in the west of Ireland as barren, infertile ground for human compassion, love, and sexuality.

The Communication Cord is a hilarious farce at the expense of traditional Irish nationalism. The set translates the interior of a traditional thatched peasant cottage into a slightly too perfect modern "reproduction, an artefact of today making obeisance to a home of yesterday" (Friel 1983:11). This artefact has its psychological counterpart in the pietistic attitudes of the traditional nationalism the cottage represents. In the play these attitudes are held mainly by the older generation, represented by Jack's father, who restored the cottage, and Senator Donovan. According to the discourse of traditional nationalism, as rendered sardonically by Jack, "Everybody's grandmother was reared in a house like this. ... This is where we all come from. This is our first cathedral. This shaped all our souls. This determined our first pieties" (15). For Senator Donovan the cottage is "the touchstone," "the apotheosis," "the absolute verity" (31), "the true centre" (43). At one point Donovan, who was born in a thatched cottage himself, describes milking the family cow at the milking post inside the cottage as "a little scene that's somehow central to my psyche" (55). In the process of demonstrating how the cow was chained to the post, he chains himself literally to his memory when the rusty clasp on the chain refuses to open. Despite the broad farcical humor of the play, the implications of Senator Donovan's literal attachment to the set are clear: traditional nationalism is an anachronistic reproduction that chains the Irish unproductively to their past. But even those who do not share the Senator's enthusiasm for his peasant past cannot escape its destructive effects in the present. Like the Yeatsian symbol that it is, the cottage itself seems to have a will and a power of its own. The play concludes with the house, appropriately and symbolically, collapsing on the younger generation of characters, who have little sympathy with the nationalism of their elders. Again the suggestion is clear: both chaining oneself to the past and antipathy to that past are equally risky approaches to one's heritage.

Friel's Critique of the Republic of Ireland

Friel's critique of nationalism spills over into his critique of the Irish Republic. According to Friel, in Ireland "a man's relationship with his country ... is always very tenuous and very strained" (Delaney 2000:92). And while he remains loyal to the Republic, it is the kind of loyalty one has to an elderly parent who has begun to decline (Friel 1999b:112). To say that Friel identified with the Republic does not mean that he endorsed it. Despite this identification, or perhaps because of it, he has been a severe critic of its social, cultural, and political ills. Most of his stories and plays are set in the Republic, particularly rural Donegal, where a number of his plays are set in the fictional town of Ballybeg.

All his early published plays critique the Republic in one way or another, particularly its importation of crass American materialism and the myths that sustained the post-liberation nationalist phase of the de Valera years. In *Philadelphia Here I Come!* (1964), the protagonist Gar is torn between the stultifying atmosphere of his Ballybeg home and the opportunity offered by his vulgar Irish American aunt, which includes his own air-conditioned room in their ground-floor apartment, with color TV and private bath and access to an air-conditioned car, all underpinned with "fifteen thousand bucks in Federal Bonds" (Friel 1986:59, 65). In *The Loves of Cass McGuire* (1966) Cass returns from more than fifty years of living in lower Manhattan's Bowery to an upwardly mobile brother whose upper-middle-class lifestyle cannot tolerate the brash, vulgar Bowery manners of his returning émigré sister. Both of these plays and three plays that follow – *Lovers* (1967), *Crystal and Fox* (1968), and *The Gentle Island* – depict an Ireland in which love and other emotional attachments have no nourishment in a repressive and claustrophobic society.

The Mundy Scheme (1969), which in its own way is as savage as *The Gentle Ireland*, attacks the corrupt materialism of Irish political culture and its American inspiration. In this political satire a Texas millionaire persuades a corrupt Irish government to turn the west of Ireland into a burial ground for space-starved industrial states. Crass American commercialism and rampant political corruption clash with the idealism and myths upon which the Republic of Ireland was founded. In a 1972 interview Friel said that *The Mundy Scheme* expressed his fears that "Ireland is becoming a shabby imitation of a third-rate American state. ... We are no longer even West Britons; we are East Americans" (Friel 1999b:49). When Americans appear in Friel's plays they are always negative in some way – Gar's vulgar aunt, Cass's Bowery manners, or emotionless, clueless academics like Dodds in *The Freedom of the City* (1973), Tom Hoffnung in *Aristocrats* (1979), or David Knight in *Give Me Your Answer, Do* (1997).

America, of course, is not the sole source of Ireland's ills. As *Lovers*, *Crystal and Fox*, and *The Gentle Island* suggest, it is also decaying from within. This internal decline is also the focus of *Volunteers* (1975) and *Aristocrats*. In *Volunteers*, under a seemingly frivolous surface of comedy and make-believe, IRA prisoners metaphorically depict a postcolonial psyche that has replicated many of the structures of the colonial situation in which the Irish, in the stories and narratives they tell about themselves, continue to perpetuate the victim mentality of colonial times. In understated Chekhovian fashion *Aristocrats* portrays the futile aspirations of socially decaying provincial gentry. *Aristocrats* plays a variation on the Irish Big House narrative, only its inhabitants are not Ascendancy Protestants but Castle Catholics, that is, a family that has served whatever power structure was in place, including the British prior to 1922. Friel focuses, however, not on the assimilation of the English and Irish, which became the focus of his subsequent Field Day plays, but on the assimilation of a privileged landed class by a rising Irish bourgeoisie. As each generation of O'Donnell males has descended in status in the legal profession, the current O'Donnell children have married beneath their class. The genetic decline mirrors that of Yeats' *Purgatory*, but without Yeats' nostalgia for the aristocratic tradition. The social decline in *Aristocrats* depicts the disintegration of a class that is as much a liberation as it is a loss. But a liberation into what? *Aristocrats* is not optimistic about the possibilities offered the O'Donnell children by the postcolonial, bourgeois Republic. Like the invalid father O'Donnell, *Aristocrats* depicts Ireland as "the old parent who is now beginning to ramble" (Friel 1999b:112).

Friel's Critique of Northern Ireland

Irish politics and history have had an intimate and sometimes troubled relationship with Irish writing. Every Irish writer has had to arrive at some accommodation with history and politics. For years Friel avoided writing about the situation in Northern Ireland. Except for the appearance of sectarianism in *The Blind Mice* (1963), Friel's stories and plays prior to 1973 gave little indication that their writer was from Northern Ireland. His most eloquent exploration of the writer's dilemma vis-à-vis history and politics is his early play *The Enemy Within* (1962). In this play sixth-century St Columba struggles to free himself from the political and military entanglements of family and tribe so that he may pursue his religious vocation unhindered. Torn between his God and his *patria* (as Joyce dubbed the combined temptation of family and country), Columba, like Joyce, refuses the call of Cathleen ni Houlihan to sacrifice his soul for his country. Columba's dilemma is a thinly veiled metaphor for the situation Northern Irish writers often found themselves in. About the hero of *The Enemy Within*, Friel says,

> Columba left the country because it was politically too hot for him, for one reason. And the second reason and equally strong one was that his family were driving him up the walls, literally. But I didn't have and I don't have any great interest in the historical play as such. The theme at that time when I was writing seemed to me to be relevant to my own attitude at the time and to my feeling about the country at the time. (Delaney 2000:91)

Politics and history were everyday events for residents of the North. Friel says that "The demands of the tribe in this part of Ireland are enormous," and he is very articulate about the kinds of problems this presents for an artist, which he defines as a difficult and challenging conflict between the public self, which requires "effort" and "engagement," and the artistic self, which requires "privacy," "secrecy," and "introversion" (Friel 1999b:124). Friel obviously had internalized the tensions of living in the North, and in the figure of Columba he resolves, intellectually at least, to resist the lure of politics in his art. But when he wrote *The Enemy Within* the latest round of the Troubles had not yet begun in Northern Ireland, and the rhetorical and emotional register of the play, as opposed to the thematic register, turns out to be a better indicator of Friel's future direction. Friel casts the internal struggle of Columba between his allegiance to his family and his allegiance to his spiritual vocation as a contrast between competing discourses, between a nationalist rhetoric of nostalgia and a biblical rhetoric of spiritual aspiration. While in the end spirit triumphs somewhat conventionally over worldliness, unfortunately for the play's conclusion and its thematic thrust, the discourse of spiritual aspiration lacks the energy and emotional power of the nationalist discourses of kinship and nostalgia for the land. Even though Columba is the most sympathetic portrait of a priest in Friel's published canon, Friel's more powerful identification with the nationalist tradition rather than with the Maynooth tradition he once rejected seems to govern the dramatic balance here. We understand in the end why Columba rejects the nostalgic appeal of home and family, but because of the rhetorical imbalance we are not made to feel the passion of the struggle.

Friel's position on the relation of art and politics in *The Enemy Within* was soon to be challenged. After the civil rights movement began in Northern Ireland in 1968 and the violence intensified, it became even more difficult for northern writers to eschew the public work in favor of a private world of imagination. Friel initially refused to have his art drawn into the increasingly turbulent politics of the North. He defended his position on the grounds of lacking objectivity to northern politics and the political situation itself lacking in dramatic conflict because it was not "a conflict of equals" (Friel 1999b:48). All this changed, however, with Bloody Sunday in January 1972 and the subsequent Widgery Report, an official inquiry into the shootings that whitewashed the killing by British troops of thirteen unarmed protesters marching against internment. Friel had been working on a play about poverty in the eighteenth century, but after his experience of Bloody Sunday (he had been one of the marchers) and the Widgery Report, the play about poverty turned into *The Freedom of the City* (1973), which became Friel's first major attempt to deal with the Troubles in Northern Ireland. The play, set in Derry at the Guildhall and the nearby city walls, makes no attempt to reproduce the events of Bloody Sunday but it quite deliberately evokes them. The character of the Judge, for instance, employs language from the Widgery Report, shootings which absolved the military of all blame. Despite Friel's anger and nationalist sympathies, the play, with considerable critical acumen, demonstrates how the prevailing public discourses on all sides conspire to snuff out the lives of three protesters. These public discourses fall into at least three ideological categories – those that assume allegiance to the British government, those that sympathize with the Irish victims, and those that purport to be disinterested and objective. Contrary to those who see *The Freedom of the City* as nationalist propaganda, Friel is as hard on the Irish sympathizers – the clergy, the press, Irish politicians, and the sentiment on the Derry streets represented by the Balladeer – as he is on the Judge and the other British sympathizers. This more balanced view of the play does not deny Friel's genuine sympathy for his three victims or for the Catholic cause in the North. It does claim, however, that Friel's tough-minded sympathy is not blind to the distortions of discourse on either side nor to how the distortions on both sides contributed to the tragedy.

With respect to Northern Ireland, *The Freedom of the City* marked a transition in Friel's oeuvre from a colonial to a postcolonial consciousness. While some of the earlier plays did deal with postcolonial symptoms of the Republic of Ireland, the general invisibility in Friel's early work of the border between Northern Ireland and the Republic indicates that as a British subject of Northern Ireland Friel had not yet openly acknowledged his colonized status. As a writer his nationalist identification with the Republic enabled him to repress his colonized status in the North. Friel's heightened linguistic awareness in *The Freedom of the City*, however, signals the emergence of his recognition of colonization into the full light of consciousness. Frantz Fanon points out that once the colonized call their colonial situation into question, they begin the process of decolonization, and "all decolonization is successful" (Fanon 1963:37). As the civil rights movement in Northern Ireland made northern nationalists realize that they shared a condition with the oppressed world-wide, so *The Freedom of the City* marks the beginning of decolonization for Friel as a northern nationalist writer.

Some critics would argue that the troubles of Northern Ireland are reflected in most of Friel's plays even though they ostensibly deal with the Republic or pre-partition Ireland. Certainly there is some truth to this claim. St Columba's dilemma in *The Enemy Within*, the IRA in *Volunteers*, the origins of the characters in *Faith Healer* (1979), all invoke the situation in the North in one way or another. All of Friel's Field Day plays, however, because of their Field Day context and rhetoric, deal more explicitly with the North. Field Day placed Friel and his work at the center of Irish cultural debate seeking to redefine Ireland and Irishness in the wake of the Republic's new openness after 1960 and the troubles in the North after 1968. Competing with traditional nationalists, Unionists, historical revisionists, feminists, and proponents of consumer capitalism and globalization, Friel and Field Day tried to define a renovated nationalism that would be more open and accommodating to other cultural constituencies than traditional nationalism had been. This new ecumenical nationalism would also be more accepting of its British heritage, a consequence of its centuries of colonization. Both *Translations* (1980) and *Making History* (1988) explore the hybrid identity of the Irish and argue for accepting the British heritage, including the English language, but at the same time making that British heritage their own.

Friel says that "*Translations* was about how this country found a certain shape" (Friel 1999b:102). The play, set in 1833, focuses on two key events in Irish cultural history: first, a new system of national schools replaced the indigenous, illegal hedge schools established during the years of the Penal Laws, and second, the creation of a standardized map of Ireland. Both of these projects involved language. Hedge schools often taught in Gaelic and taught the Irish perspective on history, while the new national schools would teach in English with materials written in English, including an English version of Irish history. The new maps would anglicize all the Irish place-names. The form of the play, with all of the Gaelic speakers actually speaking in English but understood to be speaking Gaelic, creates the perfect linguistic metaphor for the transformation of a Gaelic culture into an anglicized culture. Friel actually denied permission for bilingual performances of the play because it would violate the metaphorical logic of the linguistic convention (Delaney 2000:162). This literal and metaphorical anglicization reinforces the play's thematic significance – acceptance of the English heritage and at the same time its transformation into something uniquely Irish, or, in other words, accepting the hybrid identity of Irish culture but without either nostalgia for the old Gaelic traditions or continued submission to British cultural imperialism. At one point in the play Hugh, the hedge schoolmaster, points to the book in which Irish place-names are being anglicized and says, "We must learn those new names. ... We must learn where we live. We must learn to make them our own. We must make them our new home" (Friel 1986:444). Hugh reinforces this theme of Irish hybridity in another comment, saying, "it is not the literal past, the 'facts' of history, that shape us, but images of the past embodied in language. ... we must never cease renewing those images; because once we do, we fossilize" (445). With its metaphorical stage convention of representing Irish in English, *Translations* itself renews an image of Irish history at the point when the old Gaelic culture was being translated, as Friel translates it, into another language.

Making History also asserts the hybridity of Irish history and culture. Friel modeled his protagonist on Seán O'Faoláin's revisionist biography *The Great O'Neill*, in which Hugh O'Neill is portrayed less as the last of the great Irish chieftains than as a profoundly ambivalent man torn between the Irish culture of his birth and the English culture where he was fostered and educated. For O'Faoláin, O'Neill was not the mythic hero of Gaelic Ireland but Ireland's first European Renaissance man. Friel's play shows how the Gaelic hero was created in the hagiography of Archbishop Lombard over the objections of an O'Neill torn between loyalty to his fellow chieftains and to the colonial English culture that he married into. Although *Making History* is deeply flawed dramatically, like *Translations* it still makes a strong intellectual case for the hybridity of Irish culture. Friel's O'Neill, like O'Faoláin's, looks toward Europe as well as England. In a sense, Friel and O'Faoláin saw O'Neill as some of the the Field Day writers saw Joyce – as someone who europeanized Irish culture and hibernicized European culture.

Personal and Polycentric

During the decade in which Friel was actively involved with Field Day his playwriting production was cut in half and he was often torn between his dedication to the public project of Field Day and his desire to write plays that had more personal significance to him. Even in the early days of Field Day, Friel felt torn. In a 1983 RTE documentary on Field Day, he notes,

> I'm caught in a situation where I'm trying to protect myself and protect my work on one level and at the same time trying to keep this enterprise of Field Day vibrant. I don't know whether I'll be able to do these two things; maybe one will have to go. (Delaney 2000:190–91)

A decade later he followed the example of his Columba in *The Enemy Within* and let Field Day go after a falling out with co-founder Stephen Rea over not giving *Dancing at Lughnasa* (1990) to Field Day.

Once Friel ceased his regular involvement with Field Day in the early 1990s, the pace of his production picked up again. From 1990 to 2008 he wrote six original plays and seven adaptations. Not only did the pace of his production increase, but Friel's focus also shifted somewhat after he left Field Day. Except for *The Home Place*, which would have made a good Field Day play, all the plays of this period derive from Friel's more personal concerns as opposed to the more public, historical or political, concerns of the Field Day period and earlier. *Dancing at Lughnasa*, drawn from the life of Friel's maiden aunts, "is about the necessity for paganism," according to Friel, while *Wonderful Tennessee* (1993) is about the "necessity for mystery" (Friel 1999b:148), and *Give Me Your Answer, Do!* (1997), a play about a writer trying to decide whether or not to sell his manuscripts to an American university, is about the "necessary uncertainty" in life (Friel 1997:79–80). *Molly Sweeney* (1994), a play about blindness, was written when Friel was having trouble with his own eyesight. These plays are not limited to personal concerns, however: *Dancing at Lughnasa* also probes issues of 1930s social, spiritual, and economic life in Ireland; both *Wonderful Tennessee* and *Give Me Your Answer, Do!* critique the bourgeois consumerism and materialism of the contemporary Irish Republic; and *Molly Sweeney* uses the restoration of sight to a young woman to explore epistemological issues about perception and the structure of our perceptual apparatus. Friel, however, used those personal concerns, as opposed to events from Irish history and culture, as the seeds for developing the plays.

One of the most prominent of the personal themes in Friel's later plays is how to express the ineffable. Friel had used many different techniques to achieve a poetry of the theater that he could not achieve with words alone, although it often involved or was built out of words. Examples would include the narrators in *Lovers, Living Quarters* (1977) and *Dancing at Lughnasa*; the two Gars in *Philadelphia Here I Come!*; scenes of fantasy and illusion in *The Loves of Cass McGuire, Lovers, Aristocrats, Wonderful Tennessee*, and *Afterplay* (2002); the dead acting along with the living in *Living Quarters, The Freedom of the City*, and *Performances* (2003); a collapsing stage set in *The Communication Cord*; the staging of public discourses in *The Freedom of the City*; monologues in *Faith Healer* and *Molly Sweeney*; and Gaelic speakers rendered in English in *Translations*. But Friel also strove for theatrical effects that went beyond words. Two techniques he used to accomplish this were music and dance. About the use of music in *Philadelphia Here I Come!* and *Dancing at Lughnasa*, Friel says,

> at that specific point in both plays when the *céilí* music is used, words offer neither an adequate means of expression nor a valve for emotional release. Because at that specific point emotion has staggered into inarticulacy beyond the boundaries of language. And that is what music can provide in the theatre: another way of talking, a language without words. And because it is wordless it can hit straight and unmediated into the vein of deep emotion. (Friel 1999b:177)

Dance achieves similar effects beyond language. At the end of *Dancing at Lughnasa*, Friel's narrator Michael remembers his mother and sisters dancing "as if language had surrendered to movement – as if this ritual, this wordless ceremony was now the way to speak, to whisper private and sacred things, to be in touch with some otherness. … Dancing as if language no longer existed because words were no longer necessary" (Friel 1999a:107–08).

In addition to the more personal themes, Friel's post-Field Day period also looked more toward Europe, particularly eastern Europe. With the exception of *The London Vertigo* (1992), all his translations/adaptations are from Turgenev, Chekhov, and Ibsen.

Even one of his original plays employs an east European protagonist – the Czech composer Leoš Janáček in *Performances*. Consequently of his thirteen post-Field Day plays seven look toward Europe. Friel had long felt that discussions of Irish drama were much too "insular" and ignored the "global context" (Friel 1999b:48, 50). He admired John Hume because he saw him as a new type of Irish politician – "a committed European with vision" (Delaney 2000:225). He also hoped that his own work, though focused on Ireland, would be relevant to other parts of the world, a hope that was realized when *Translations* was performed in other countries where two languages and cultures come together (Friel 1999b:82). This European orientation contrasts with the early orientation toward the United States that characterized his short stories and half of his stage plays of the 1960s.

The play that perhaps most epitomizes Friel's polycentric outlook during his post-Field Day period is *Performances*. In this play the protagonist Leoš Janáček argues posthumously with Anezka, a Czech graduate student who is writing her thesis on Janáček's second string quartet, also known as "Intimate Letters," a reference to the passionate correspondence he carried on with a much younger married woman Kamila Stösslová. Anezka, who believes in a firm "connection between the private life and the public work" (Friel 2003:21), says,

> I will try to show that when you wrote this quartet – *"Intimate Letters"* – you call it that yourself when you were head-over-heels in love with her – my thesis will demonstrate that the Second String Quartet is a textbook example of a great passion inspiring a great work of art and it will prove that work of art to be the triumphant apotheosis of your entire creative life. (22)

Friel's Janáček just as firmly resists linking his life with his work. Echoing Yeats, he says, "I never considered the life all that important. I gave myself to the perfection of the work" (37). He insists that Kamila Stösslová was "a woman of resolute ... ordinariness," "a slave to small-town tyrannies," practically illiterate, and totally incapable of comprehending the "labyrinth of interweaving melodies" in his quartet (25, 28). What he poured into his letters were his dreams for his music and over time Kamila became identified with those dreams. Like Joyce's Stephen Dedalus, Janáček wished "to meet in the real world the unsubstantial image which his soul so constantly beheld" (Joyce 1993:67). Kamila became "the music in the head made real, become carnal"; but the closest Janáček came to the dreams in his head was not the real woman but his music. Consequently the Kamila he wrote to was a muse of his own invention representing "what was the very best in himself" (Friel 2003:34). He advises Anezka that she would "learn so much more by just listening to the music" (30–31), which plays throughout the performance. Anezka, aghast at Janáček's narcissism and misogyny, abruptly departs.

Despite his objections to Anezka's insistence that "a full appreciation of the quartet isn't possible unless *all* the circumstances of its composition are considered" (21–22; Friel's emphasis) and that knowing the love letters "enriches our intimacy with the work" (37), in the end Janáček agrees that "both readings can coexist. ... Even be seen to illuminate one another." "But finally," he asserts, "the work's the thing. That must be insisted on. Everything has got to be ancillary to the work" (38). The play ends with Janáček leafing through Anezka's copy of his letters to Kamila, but then leaning back and closing his eyes as he listens to the final movements of his quartet. This wordless gesture repeats the same gesture in *Dancing at Lughnasa* when Michael describes his mother's "dance without music" with his father: "with her head thrown back, her eyes closed, her mouth slightly open. ... No singing, no melody, no words" (Friel 1999a:65, 66). This effort to achieve "a language without words" that could express the inexpressible is the goal of Friel's personal artistic journey and, given the trajectory of that journey, it is entirely appropriate that near the end of his career Friel has a Czech musician sum up his convictions about the limits of language: Janáček says,

> Thank God my first language was music. And a much more demanding language it is, too. ... Because we reach into that amorphous world of feeling and sing what we hear in the language of feeling itself; a unique vocabulary of sounds created by feeling itself. ... The people who huckster in words merely report on feeling. We *speak* feeling. (Friel 2003:31; Friel's emphasis)

Fundamentally *Performances* dramatizes Friel's argument with himself about the competing claims of life and art. Forty-one years on, it rewrites the argument of *The Enemy Within*, only this time the primary theme also has the strongest rhetorical arguments, and the Catholic, nationalist, priest-politician Columba has been replaced by an east European musician, an indication of the distance Friel has traveled from his early nationalist days to the polycentric world of his later work.

REFERENCES AND FURTHER READING

Andrews, E. (1995). *The Art of Brian Friel: Neither Reality Nor Dreams.* New York: St Martin's Press.

Boltwood, S. (2007). *Brian Friel, Ireland, and the North.* Cambridge: Cambridge University Press.

Coult, T. (2003). *About Friel: The Playwright and the Work.* London: Faber & Faber.

Dantanus, U. (1988). *Brian Friel: A Study.* London: Faber & Faber.

Delaney, P. (Ed.). (2000). *Brian Friel in Conversation.* Ann Arbor: University of Michigan Press.

Fanon, F. (1963). *The Wretched of the Earth.* C. Farrington (Trans.). New York: Grove.

Friel, B. (1983). *The Communication Cord.* London: Faber & Faber.

Friel, B. (1986). *Selected Plays: Brian Friel.* Washington, DC: Catholic University of America Press. Republished as *Brian Friel: Plays One.* London: Faber & Faber, 1996.

Friel, B. (1997). *Give Me Your Answer, Do!* Oldcastle: Gallery Press.

Friel, B. (1999a). *Brian Friel: Plays Two.* London: Faber & Faber.

Friel, B. (1999b). *Brian Friel: Essays, Diaries, Interviews: 1964–1999.* C. Murray (Ed.). London: Faber & Faber.

Friel, B. (2003). *Performances.* Oldcastle: Gallery Press.

Harp, R. and R.C. Evans. (2002). *A Companion to Brian Friel.* West Cornwall, Conn.: Locust Hill Press.

Hume, J. (1996). *A New Ireland: Politics, Peace, and Reconciliation*. Boulder: Roberts Rinehart.

Joyce, J. (1993). *A Portrait of the Artist as a Young Man*. New York: Penguin.

Kerwin, W. (Ed.). (1997). *Brian Friel: A Casebook*. New York: Garland Press.

Longley, E. (1986). *Poetry in the Wars*. Newcastle upon Tyne: Bloodaxe.

McGrath, F.C. (1999). *Brian Friel's (Post)Colonial Drama: Language, Illusion, and Politics*. Syracuse: Syracuse University Press.

Morse, D.E., C. Bertha, and M. Kurdi (Eds). (2006). *Brian Friel's Dramatic Artistry: "The Work Has Value."* Dublin: Carysfort Press.

O'Brien, G. (1989). *Brian Friel*. Dublin: Gill & Macmillan.

O'Donnell, D. (1981). "Friel and a Tale of Three Sisters." *Sunday Press* (30 August), n.p.

O'Faoláin, S. (1970). *The Great O'Neill: A Biography of Hugh O'Neill, Earl of Tyrone, 1550–1616*. Dublin: Mercier Press.

Peacock, A. (Ed.). (1993). *The Achievement of Brian Friel*. Gerrards Cross: Colin Smythe.

Pine, R. (1999). *The Diviner: The Art of Brian Friel*. Dublin: University College Dublin Press.

Roche, A. (Ed.). (1999). Special issue on Brian Friel. *Irish University Review*, 29.1.

Roche, A. (Ed.). (2006). *The Cambridge Companion to Brian Friel*. Cambridge: Cambridge University Press.

47

Telling the Truth Slant: The Poetry of Seamus Heaney

Eugene O'Brien

In an interview with Dennis O'Driscoll, Seamus Heaney is asked the telling question, "What has poetry taught you?" Heaney answers that it has taught him that "there's such a thing as truth and it can be told – slant" (O'Driscoll 2008:467). Heaney's *The Redress of Poetry* develops a visual image of the complicated truth of poetry in his structure called the quincunx. In a specifically Irish context, he sets out the parameters in a five-point structure which would grant the plurality of what he terms an Irishness that "would not prejudice the rights of others' Britishness" (Heaney 1995a:198). This is a "diamond shape" of five towers with the central one being the tower of prior Irelandness, the round tower of insular dwelling (199). The other four points are representative of Kilcolman Castle, Edmund Spenser's "tower of English conquest"; Yeats' Ballylee, where the "Norman tower" was a deliberate symbol of his attempt to "restore the spiritual values and magical world-view that Spenser's armies and language had destroyed" (199); Joyce's Martello tower; and Carrickfergus Castle, associated with Louis MacNeice, where William of Orange once landed in Ireland (199). For Heaney it is the interaction of these towers into a "field of force" (Heaney 1980:56) that symbolizes the value of poetry, which has to be "a working model of inclusive consciousness. It should not simplify" (Heaney 1995a:8). Telling the truth slant, or seeing the world from a different perspective, as well as valuing that difference, is at the core of Heaney's aesthetic imperative, and he has invoked Osip Mandelstam to criticize "the purveyors of ready-made meaning" (Heaney 1988:91).

His first four volumes – *Death of a Naturalist, Door into the Dark, Wintering Out,* and *North* – are all preoccupied with working through issues of inheritance and tradition. Thus in "Digging," he emblematically compares pen and gun in one of the most famous similes in contemporary writing: "Between my finger and my thumb / The squat pen rests; snug as a gun" (Heaney 1966:13). These lines have been taken as an

A Companion to Irish Literature, edited by Julia M. Wright
© 2010 Blackwell Publishing Ltd

artistic credo in which Heaney stresses a type of writing through which he will under-
take an exploration of his personal past, and this a poem where a generational reflection
is set out: "the old man could handle a spade. / Just like his old man" (13). The
"I" is located relationally within and against his family and tradition. Having
connected all three generations, the poem, in the penultimate and final stanzas, deconstructs this continuity by looking awry at the posited connections as "the curt cuts
of an edge / Through living roots awaken in my head." The break with tradition is
healed by a slanted version of the Heaney tradition of digging: "Between my finger
and my thumb / The squat pen rests. / I'll dig with it" (14). One could see this as
the first of the bog poems – a series of poems, wherein the soft mossy ground of parts
of Ireland is seen as a metaphor of a Jungian psychic memory, which are to be found
in the opening sections of *Wintering Out* and *North* (Parker 1993 is excellent on the
connections between Heaney's life and work).

As he began writing, the Troubles in Northern Ireland began to claim lives, and
the situation also claimed Heaney's attention and caused him a deal of stress in terms
of demanding some sort of poetic response. Given Heaney's increasing sense of identification with his own community – the movement from "I" to "we" – in "Bogland,"
"We have no prairies / To slice a big sun at evening" (Heaney 1969:55), the notion
of racial or psychic memory that he touched on in this poem was further reinforced
when he read P.V. Glob's *The Bog People*, which gave him the Yeatsian example of
writing in a public crisis by "making your own imagery and your own terrain take
the colour of it, take the impressions of it" (Randall 1979:13). This is precisely what
Heaney does in his bog poems – he tells a truth about the Troubles in a slanted way.
Glob argues in his book that a number of the Iron Age figures found buried in the
bogs, including "the Tollund Man, whose head is now preserved near Aarhus in
the museum at Silkeburg, were ritual sacrifices to the Mother Goddess" (Heaney
1980:57). For Heaney, this notion of these people as bridegrooms to the goddess, as
sacrifices which would ensure fertility in the spring, was symbolic of an "archetypal
pattern," and he tells of how the photographs in the book fused with photographs of
contemporary atrocities in his mind. He writes about the Tollund Man in the future
and conditional tenses – "Some day I will go to Aarhus. ... I will stand a long time.
... I could risk blasphemy. ... I will feel" (Heaney 1972:47–49) – as he has not, as
yet, actually seen him; however, the descriptions are all in the past tense, and told
as if they are being recalled from memory. That the speaker of the poem has never
actually seen the Tollund Man has already been made clear: the use of the future tense
means that any actual encounter has not, as yet, taken place: hence "I will go. ... I
will stand." However, the verbs representing the "I" of the poem in the second and
third sections are not all in the future tense. Some are in the conditional tense ("I
could risk"; "Should come to me"), while the final stanza returns to the future: "Out
there in Jutland / In the old man-killing parishes / I will feel lost, / Unhappy and at
home" (Heaney 1972:48). What we might call the tribalization of his personal
"digging" and "bog land" motifs achieves a climax in the bog poems of *North*;
however, it is important that such poems be placed in context. To see Heaney as

someone almost intoxicated by the violence and carving out a role as the voice of his tribe is to adopt an over-simplistic approach, at the levels of both biography and poetics. The reality is far more complex. This is one mode of Irishness that is developed in his quincunx – a real mode and a true mode but only one of many.

This reading is underscored by the next bog poem, "Punishment," a poem for which Heaney has been severely criticized for seeming to justify the nationalist community's attempts at punishing young Catholic girls who dated British soldiers. Once again, the past–present dialectic is the structural and thematic kernel of the poem, as the speaker empathically feels "the wind / on her naked front," a reference to the Windeby girl, who was punished for adultery in Iron Age Germany by being bound, tied to a "weighing stone," and drowned. Heaney realizes that while he affects horror at the death of the "Little adulteress," he has been aware of similar punishments of young Catholic women who were seen as having relations with British soldiers, and in the closing stanza he explains the reasons for his inaction: "who would connive / in civilized outrage / yet understand the exact / and tribal, intimate revenge" (Heaney 1975:38). Here, Heaney appears to be voicing the atavisms of his tribe. At a rational and intellectual level, Heaney, as an educated man, would express "civilized outrage" at such barbaric treatment of people in the twentieth century; however, at a communal and visceral level, he does understand why "his" community feels the need to act in such a manner. The Provisional IRA, the people carrying out such a "punishment," see themselves as the defenders of the Catholic community, and any action that would give aid or comfort to the enemy is deemed as being in need of "punishment." It is part of the strength of these poems that, in them, Heaney allows that visceral aspect of his nationalist, Catholic identity to speak out. The same voicing of this element of Irishness is to be found in "Kinship," where he foregrounds that initial image of unearthing the past, the spade, seeing it in completely symbolic terms: "I found a turf-spade / hidden under bracken, / laid flat, and overgrown / with a green fog" (Heaney 1975:42). Heaney tells us of his visceral attraction to this sense of his tradition, noting how he "grew" out of this sense of the past as sacred, comparing himself in simile to a "weeping willow" which was inclined to "the appetites of gravity" (43), and this leads to the final section of the poem where he defines himself as part of a tribal identity, making his grove on an old crannog (an altar of stones) in honor of "Our mother ground," and asking Tacitus to "report us fairly," as he goes on to describe how "we slaughter / for the common good" and "shave the heads" of the notorious (45). These lines, a classic example of "memory incubating the spilled blood" (Heaney 1975:20), would seem to copperfasten the view of Heaney as the voice of his tribe; however, as in the previous poems, there is a more complicated perspective at work. In section IV of the poem, having described the "appetites of gravity," he tells how "I grew out of all this," a phrase which is highly ambiguous as it can mean that he traces his roots back to this visceral sense of territorial loyalty, or, significantly, that he has outgrown this past sense of loyalty. Indeed, he noted that after *North* he wanted "a door into the light" (Randall 1979:20) (for an interesting account of the postcolonial aspect of Heaney's writing see Andrews 1998).

Writing about the deaths of real, contemporary people in *Field Work* allowed Heaney to discuss how death can affect the individual who has been exposed to it. Without the communal security blanket of tribal bonding, such violent deaths have a chilling effect on the individual. "The Strand at Lough Beg" refers to Colum McCartney, "a second cousin" of Heaney's who was "shot arbitrarily" as he was "coming home from a football match in Dublin" (Randall 1979:21). At the end of the poem, Heaney imagines himself washing the dead body with "handfuls of dew," and dabbing it "clean with moss" before plaiting "Green scapulars to wear over your shroud" with rushes that grow near Lough Beg (Heaney 1979:18). Another elegy, "Casualty," describes a fisherman, Louis O'Neill, who used to come to Heaney's father-in-law's public house in County Tyrone:

> He was blown to bits
> Out drinking in a curfew
> Others obeyed, three nights
> After they shot dead
> The thirteen men in Derry.

> (22)

In *Field Work* there is also a change in the type of stanzaic structure and rhythm that is used. There is a more self-conscious sense of the structure of the line and of experimentation with different poetic forms in this book, with the "Glanmore Sonnets" standing out as a set piece which places Heaney firmly within the English and European poetic traditions by his use of this most poetic of constructions.

Poetry as a form of communication between self and other is enunciated in the opening line: "Vowels ploughed into other: opened ground" (Heaney 1979:33). Seeing Glanmore as a "hedge-school" (34), Heaney finds time to write about himself and his rural surroundings. It was the similarity between Glanmore and Mossbawn that allowed him to write about the place in which he was living. Here, it is on personal and marital growth that he can concentrate, going on to implicitly compare himself and Marie, his wife, to "Dorothy and William" Wordsworth (35), and to discuss the etymological associations of "boortree" and "elderberry" (37). This poem heralds a preoccupation with language in all of its variety, a preoccupation that registers the difference between this and his "first place," Mossbawn (Heaney 1980:18).

Like Wordsworth, his reaction to nature is mediated through language, and indeed, the very fact that William and Dorothy, while brother and sister, are mentioned as a literary couple implies that this response to nature will be literary in tenor and in tone, seeing a cuckoo and corncrake, for example, at twilight as "crepuscular and iambic" (Heaney 1979:35). Indeed, he places himself and Marie in the context of other literary couples in the final sonnet: "Lorenzo and Jessica in a cold climate / Diarmuid and Grainne waiting to be found" (42). These couples, one Shakespearean from *The Merchant of Venice*, and the other Irish from the *fiannaíocht* cycle of tales, serve to foreground the literary nature of their rural idyll. This taking on of literary exemplars will be furthered in his next collection (see Parker 1993 for a discussion of the role of Glanmore in Heaney's writing).

In *Station Island*, his questioning of the role of art in a political situation, of the role of the aesthetic with respect to the political, is being teased out all the time, and the consistent references to Dante underscore this questioning process. Whereas in *North* he used his art to utter the concerns of his tribe, in this collection, he attempts to transform that consciousness through a focus on his own growth. This is the driving force behind the central sequence of the book, the poems that comprise "Station Island" itself.

St Patrick's Purgatory is an island in Lough Derg, County Donegal, which has been a site of Roman Catholic pilgrimage since medieval times. Heaney's pilgrimage has some measure of parallel with the *Divine Comedy* of Dante in that Heaney will explore a spectral underworld, where spirits will visit him, as opposed to Dante's poem, in which he and Virgil visit the souls of the dead. Heaney has made the point that Dante's *Purgatorio* has been an immense influence on his work, specifically in terms of the nature of the relationship between poetry and politics. The mode of pilgrimage allowed Dante to use the journey metaphor to catalogue changes and developments in himself; for Heaney, this would prove to be a potent symbolic avenue through which he could explore the "typical strains which the consciousness labours under in this country ... to be faithful to the collective historical experience and to be true to the recognitions of the emerging self" (Heaney 1985:18–19). In a way, this is the fruit of that growth he spoke of in "Kinship" – "I grew out of all this." In his doorway into the dark, he probed the givens of history and the past; in his doorway into the light, he can choose and crate the spectral figures of a personal aesthetic history.

He is thus able to create the ghosts to act as mirror-images or refractions of aspects of his own personality. His first ghost, Simon Sweeney, exemplifies this qualified assent to the demands of pilgrimage. He is "an old Sabbath-breaker," who adjures Heaney to "stay clear of all processions" (Heaney 1984:61, 63). The second ghost is William Carleton, who wrote "The Lough Derg Pilgrim" in 1828 (see CHAPTER 25, RECONCILIATION AND EMANCIPATION: THE BANIMS AND CARLETON). Heaney, in section I, has Carleton call himself a "traitor" (he converted to Protestantism) and give the advice that "it is a road you travel on your own" (65), terms which illustrate the guilt associated with leaving a communal religious identity. Carleton's advice to the poet is to "remember everything and keep your head" (66). Patrick Kavanagh, a poet who exerted a strong early influence on Heaney, and who also wrote about Lough Derg, appears in section V. His comment is similarly scathing – "Forty-two years on / and you've got no farther" (73) – and all three figures voice Heaney's frustration that parts of his psyche have not yet outgrown the societal and religious givens of his culture.

Perhaps the most important aspect of this sequence is that it allows Heaney to speak through the personalities of others: through these encounters with different ghosts he is able to give voice to doubts and uncertainties using these personalities as sounding boards to enunciate different perspectives. This accusation is made directly in section VIII by the shade of Colum McCartney, Heaney's cousin and the subject of "The Strand at Lough Beg" in *Field Work*. He reminds Heaney that he was "with poets when you got the word," and stayed with them while his "own flesh and blood" was brought to Bellaghy (Heaney 1984:82). He goes on to accuse Heaney of having "whitewashed ugliness," adding, "You confused evasion with artistic tact / The Protestant who shot me through the head / I accuse directly, but indirectly, you" (83). The third voice from the political world is that of hunger striker Francis Hughes, and the poem opens with a gesture towards the bog imagery of the earlier books: "My brain dried like spread turf," as the IRA man recalls his career "a hit-man on the brink, emptied and deadly" (84). Here is the voice of militant nationalism: the response to the killing of Colum McCartney. And there is an aspect of Heaney that feels that he should have, at times, adopted a more militant stance: "I hate how quick I was to know my place" (85). Once again, the forces of the quincunx are in motion and the complexity of issues of language and identity is foregrounded.

This interplay of the religious, literary and sexual voices from his past achieves a dawning of perspective, a realization that his reaction to his culture and to the historical situation of that culture must be individual: he is not, nor can he be, the savior of his tribe. In "Station Island," Joyce is similarly dismissive of Heaney's "peasant pilgrimage," urging him to focus on his own personal growth, as opposed to that "subject people stuff" which he calls "a cod's game" (Heaney 1984:93). In the closing poem of the sequence, he has Joyce encourage this process of refutation: "Your obligation / is not discharged by any common rite. / What you must do must be done on your own" (92–93). In some ways this is a continuation of the debate that was explored in "Exposure," where Heaney wondered about his audience, or in "Glanmore Sonnets," where he wondered about his "apology for poetry." Now, in terms of the relationship between the individual and his community, he has come to a decisive point: the Ireland of the mind to which he will turn will be an imaginative one, predicated on present and future, and will be written about on his own terms:

> Keep at a tangent.
> When they make the circle wide, it's time to swim
> out on your own and fill the element
> with signatures on your own frequency.
>
> (93–94)

There is a surety of purpose and a strong sense of self-confidence to be found in the lyric "I" of all of these middle books, and it is best captured by two epigraphs in *The Haw Lantern*. The epigraph to the book itself demonstrates the transforming power of language: "The riverbed, dried-up, half-full of leaves. / Us, listening to a river in the trees" (Heaney 1987:vii). This image is more complex than it seems on first reading: does he mean the sound of wind in the trees is like a river, or does he mean that the rustling of the leaves in the riverbed is like a river in the trees, or does he mean both at the same time? In a book where presence and absence interact in a dialectical fashion, this epigraph sets the tone, as it develops the ghostly images of the "Station Island" sequence.

Here, the notion of the "I" that we saw being unfolded or unwound in the last books is further developed as different aspects of his individuality are afforded "second thoughts" in a series of broadly political poems, four of them connected by anaphoric titles: "From the Frontier of Writing," "From the Republic of Conscience," "From the Land of the Unspoken," and "From the Canton of Expectation," with two more, "The Mud Vision" and "Parable Island," completing the sequence. In all of these poems, the reader is unsure whether Heaney is writing from within these places or has just come from them. This deliberate level of ambiguity is part of the ethical strength of these poems, as he attempts to write in a broadly political way without returning to the obliquities of *North*. In "Parable Island," a poem about language, tradition, and the different beliefs of a country, he could be referring to Northern Ireland "an occupied nation" whose "only border is an inland one" (Heaney 1987:10) or, then again, he might not, as there are no referential connections to make this certain. So the "mountain of the shifting names" called, variously "Cape Basalt," the "Sun's Headstone," and the "Orphan's Tit" may parallel the shifting names of "Ulster," "Northern Ireland," the "North," the "Province," or again, it may not. The difference between this pragmatic plurality of names and the optative desire that "(some day)" the "ore of truth" will be mined from a place underneath this mountain where "all the names converge" (Heaney 1987:10), is the difference between the early and the middle Heaney. Unlike the anguished figure in "Exposure," he can now comment on the "subversives and collaborators" who are always vying with each other "for the right to 'set the island story' straight" (11). These terms, analogous to the earlier "internee" and "informer," are viewed far more dispassionately, indicating his sense of distance from both positions (Hart 1992 is informative on this part of Heaney's career).

In "From the Frontier of Writing," he again eschews the use of the "I" in a manner which makes it very different from an analogous poem in *Field Work* entitled "The Toome Road." In both poems there is an encounter with the British army, but in "The Toome Road" there is a palpable antagonism towards the "armoured cars," an antagonism flagged by the clear use of possessive pronouns: "How long were they approaching down my roads / As if they owned them?" (Heaney 1979:15). In this poem however, there is no "I"; instead there is the colloquial "you" which ambiguously refers to both speaker and listener, and the idea of absence, as opposed to the aggrieved presence of "The Toome Road," is stressed from the outset: "The tightness and nilness around that space" (Heaney 1987:6).

In a very real sense, space has much to do with the sequence "Clearances," in memory of his mother, who died in 1984. Here, in a silent communion, paralleling the more formal, religious ceremony, while "the others were away at mass"; he recalls himself and his mother silently peeling the potatoes: "I was all hers. ... Never closer the rest of our lives" (Heaney 1987:27). It is in sonnet 7 that her death is described in terms of its effect on those in the room with her: "That space we stood around had been emptied / Into us to keep, it penetrated / Clearances that suddenly stood open" (31). Here, in his mother's death, the notion of space and absence as sources and as necessary aspects of identity is made clear. In the closing sonnet he refers to the "decked chestnut tree" which was cut down in Mossbawn, a tree which was his "coeval," planted by his aunt at his birth and associated with him. This image of rootedness would not have been out of place in the earlier books, but here it is an image transformed, as he talks of walking "round and round a space / Utterly empty, utterly a source," and goes on to explain how presence had become absence, but an absence transformed: its "heft and hush become a bright nowhere ... Silent, beyond silence listened for" (32).

In "The Settle Bed," this new-found sense of freedom is applied to both his early family home and then, in that dialectical fashion which has been very much a *modus operandi* of *Seeing Things*, to his broader political and religious homeland. The bed, made of "seasoned deal," is full of echoes of "the long bedtime / anthems of Ulster" with its connotations of "Protestant, Catholic, the Bible, the beads," as he attempts to locate himself in the broader context of his heritage (Heaney 1991:28). The bed stands for the weight and bulk of tradition and history "unshiftably planked / In the long ago" (28). The notion of an "inheritance" being "willable forward" can be seen to permeate contemporary Irish social and political life on both sides of the border. Interestingly, he compares this imagined barrage of settle beds to "some nonsensical vengeance come on the people" (29), a comment which ironically revisits his earlier notions of understanding the "exact and / tribal, intimate revenge," and of seeming to validate the idea of "slaughter / for the common good" (Heaney 1975:38, 45). But this poem turns on the "door into the light" of the middle books, and of this he suggests that "Whatever is given / Can always be reimagined, however four-square, / Plank-thick, hull-stupid and out of its time / It happens to be" (Heaney 1991:29). It is this reimagining of the past that is the key to this poem, and by extension, to this book. The purpose of writing, it would seem, for Heaney, is now to enable and ratify this process of transformation, of "pure change." This is clear from the "Glanmore Revisited" sequence, where the introspection and questioning of the "Glanmore Sonnets" of *Field Work* is replaced by a new calmness and surety of his poetic vocation, "an old / Rightness half-imagined or foretold" (Heaney 1991:31). No longer self-conscious about his "apology for poetry" (Heaney 1979: 41), he can now speak of Glanmore as "the same *locus amoenus*" and can tell that he is able to "swim in Homer" (Heaney 1991:32, 36). Whereas before he was questioning the role of the poet in terms of his or her cultural affiliations and givens, now he is increasingly aware of the "book of changes" that writing allows him to create: "Who ever saw / The limit in the given anyhow?" (Heaney 1991:46). The inheritances of the past can be changed, reimagined, redrawn in order to become more of a source than a hindrance, a source of the marvelous as well as of the malign: "Me waiting until I was nearly fifty / To credit marvels" (50). In part II of *Seeing Things*, the "Squarings" sequence cumulates into a long poem of 576 lines in four equal parts. This sequence, itself the culmination of a generic tendency that reaches back to "A Lough Neagh Sequence" in *Door into the Dark*, is part of a continuing experiment with form, an effort that attempts to find a form that will combine the fluid and the phantomatic, an experiment which will be continued in his prose. This form consists of "forty-eight twelve-liners, each of the poems arranged in four unrhymed tercets in freely handled iambic pentameter" (Andrews 1998:156), which can be seen as a looser version of Dante's *terza rima*. The sequence is full of those moments of attention to process and movement which can defamiliarize the quotidian so fully that it becomes the stuff of vision and change. In the opening section, "Lightenings," he speaks of "Shifting brilliancies" (Heaney 1991:55), of "Test-outs and pull-backs, re-envisagings" (57), of the "music of the arbitrary" (59), of Thomas Hardy's imagining "himself a ghost" and of how he "circulated with that new perspective" (61). He poses the question, redolent of so much of this book, of whether one could "reconcile / What was diaphanous there with what was massive?" (64). The second section, "Settings," is equally full of such defamiliarizing visions of the ordinary, expressed in terms of process: "I stood in the door, unseen and blazed upon" (71). In "Crossings," the third section, this theme of process and dialectic is further developed, as "Everything flows" (85), and moments of clarity are found wherein a "pitch" is reached beyond "our usual hold upon ourselves" (86). He talks of a "music of binding and of loosing" (87), and exemplifies this through speaking of "a meaning made of trees. / Or not exactly trees" (89), while in the final section he invokes poems by "the sage Han Shan," who is able to write about a place "Cold Mountain," and refer, at the same time to "a place that can also mean / A state of mind. Or different states of mind / At different times" (97). Here we see the results of the "Lightenings," "Settings," and "Crossings" that have led to this final section, "Squarings," of the sequence as a whole. The given, set notion of place and tradition, a notion heavily interlinked with language, naming, and what he later terms "cold memory-weights / To load me, hand and foot, in the scale of things" (100), is now placed in a fluid relationship which both "lightens" and allows for "crossings" in an architectonic structure which has room for the traditional notion of place, and at the same time for transformative notions of that place – they are another incarnation of the quincunx (O'Donoghue 1994 is valuable on Heaney's language).

In *The Spirit Level*, we see a desire for balance as well as for a sense of spiritual equanimity. The notion of process and of reaching towards distant shores is again the subject of "A Sofa in the Forties," a poem which treats material that is also the kernel of his Nobel Prize Lecture *Crediting Poetry*. Here he speaks of a family sofa which, through childish imagination, was transformed: "for this was a train," and thence something that could achieve "Flotation" (Heaney 1996:7). The sofa becomes a paradigm of his own work, and of the Irish cultural psyche as it is "Potentially heaven-bound" but "earthbound for sure" (8). A further imaginative transformation took place on that sofa "under the wireless shelf," as it was here that Heaney first heard voices from beyond, from further, different shores, be they the "*Yippee-i-ay*" of the "Riders of the Range" or the news, read by "the absolute speaker." This voice, probably the clipped English of a BBC newsreader, is significant as between "him and us" a "great gulf was fixed where pronunciation / Reigned tyrannically" (8). However, this gulf provided the opportunity for yet another "crossing," as, brought in by the "aerial wire," this "sway of language and its furtherings" allowed him to enter "history and ignorance" (8) and be "transported" (9).

In "The Flight Path," the interrogation of the role of art, specifically his own art, in the face of violence becomes explicit in an interchange that is central to both the poem and the book. It is a poem that mimics a *Bildungsroman* of the poet's life, describing his development and physical journeys to "Manhattan," "California," and again, the stressed importance of his sojourn in Glanmore: "So to Glanmore. Glanmore. Glanmore. Glanmore. / At bay, at one, at work, at risk and sure" (Heaney 1996:23). "Jet-setting" has become so familiar that the "jumbo" jet reminds him of "a school bus," an image which describes the learning curve which he is undergoing.

In section 4 of this poem, that debate which has simmered through the body of his work, becomes overt. On a "May morning, nineteen-seventy-nine" he is confronted by "this one I'd last met in a dream." He describes the dream where he had been asked by this school friend, presumably a member of the Provisional IRA, to "drive a van," presumably loaded with explosives, "to the next customs post / At Pettigo" (24), and then leave it and get driven home "in a Ford" (25). Now, in a railway carriage, their encounter is more real, and it encapsulates the antinomy that we have been tracing in his work between the political and the aesthetic: "'When, for fuck's sake, are you going to write / Something for us?' 'If I do write something, / Whatever it is, I'll be writing for myself'" (25). Heaney has told Denis O'Driscoll that this was Danny Morrison, a Sinn Féin activist (O'Driscoll 2008:257–58). This notion of the gradual prioritization of the developing self as against a self that is pre-defined by the givens of community has been at the core of Heaney's development. That it should find such direct expression here would seem to indicate that it is still an ongoing preoccupation.

Electric Light is a book which revisits many of Heaney's old topics and themes but in a manner which complicates and deepens the psychic material and which considerably enhances the Heaney canon. Given the early use of place-names in his poetry, and given the specific use of "Toome" in *Wintering Out*, the opening poem, "At Toombridge" is almost a *recherche du temps perdu*, as he revisits the earlier poem where the sound of the word conjured up images of the Irish past "loam, flints, musketballs," and saw him imaginatively immersed in "bogwater and tributaries, / and elvers tail my hair" (Heaney 1972:26). In the new poem, the river is seen as the "continuous / Present" while the past is no longer mythological but quantifiable. He refers to where "the checkpoint used to be" and to the "rebel boy" who was hanged in 1798, but goes on to stress the new importance of "negative ions in the open air" which are "poetry to me." This is an important point as it is the negative and the present that will be the inspiration of this book, as opposed to the "slime and silver of the fattened eel" which were inspirations "before" (Heaney 2001:3). He is taking his inheritance and making it "willable forward."

This concentration on the present and the future, at the expense of the past, extrapolates from a thematic movement in the later books, as he focuses on the "music of what might happen." It becomes a recurrent topos throughout the book, as he speaks about the "everything flows and steady go of the world" (4), or the "erotics of the future" (5) or "a span of pure attention" (54). The book embraces the ordinary, endowing it with a significance of memory and hindsight. Thus, he can speak of the courting days of himself and his wife Marie, in a poem entitled "Red, White and Blue," a title which immediately raises expectations of a political subtext, suggesting the colors of the British Union Jack. Instead he eschews the political in favor of the personal, referring to three different-colored pieces of clothing worn by his wife, Marie, at different stages of their life together: a "much-snapped scarlet coat" (28); a "cut-off top" in the labor ward, of "White calico" (29), and a "blue denim skirt / And denim jacket" (30). This favoring of the personal over the political is another sign of his progression, as it is his personal and familial past which is now important, as opposed to the old flags and banners.

The final section of this poem recalls a young Heaney and Marie, hitchhiking in the Republic of Ireland, meeting a *"veh"* British couple who were admiring the "gate-lodge and the avenue / At Castlebellingham," and this memory stirs a memory of Marie in "a Fair Isle tank-top and blue denim skirt," calling her a "Botticelli dressed down for the sixties" (Heaney 2001:30). This image, a syncretism of Irish and classical, is a synecdoche of the main thrust of this book and, I would suggest, of his oeuvre as a whole – the fusion and interaction of Irish and continental European culture. Oddly enough, this European dimension, flagged by an unusually large amount of literary and linguistic allusion, brings Heaney full circle in terms of his own poetic development. He saw the *Collected Poems* as the "first 'grown up' books" he owned (Heaney 1989:17) but, rather than being an inspiration, the book represented Heaney's sense of "distance" from the mystery of literature (1989:18). The early Heaney was stylistically and culturally far removed from Eliot and yet, in *Electric Light*, the polyglot allusiveness of *The Waste Land* hovers over Heaney's writing. Indeed, there is a sly homage to *The Waste Land* in "Vitruviana," where Eliot's lines from "The Fire Sermon," "On Margate Sands / I can connect / Nothing with nothing" (Eliot 1974:300–02), find an allusive analogue in Heaney's "On Sandymount strand I can connect / Some bits and pieces" (Heaney 2001:53). Indeed, one could go so far as to say that it is this construction of a series of intercultural and interlinguistic connections that is the underlying imperative of this book. It is worth examining the number of foreign words, phrases, literary allusions, and generally cosmopolitan references that are to be found studded throughout the poems. A casual glance through *Electric Light* reveals references to Asclepius (7), Epidaurus (8), Hygeia (9), Virgil (11), Grendel (18), El Greco (22), Lycidas, and Moeris (31), as well as a pantheon of modern English, American, and European writers – Friel, Dante, Auden, Wilfred Owen, Ted Hughes, Czesław Miłosz, Joseph Brodsky, Zbigniew Herbert, George MacKay Brown ... the list goes on. Linguistically, we see snatches of Latin: *poeta doctus* (7); *miraculum* (8); *carmen, ordo, nascitur, saeculum, gens* (11); *Pacatum orbem* (12); *rigor vitae* (14); *in medias res* (24); Macedonian: *Nema problema* (19); German: *ja* (23); French: *de haut en bas* (23); Italian: *Godi, fanciullo mio; stato soave* (26); and Irish: *cailleach; Slieve na mBard,*

Knock Filiocht, Ben Duan (43). It is as if the gradual allusiveness that we have traced
through his other books has suddenly burst forth in all its glory. To borrow from the
metaphor of the book's title, it is as if a switch had been turned on by a *poeta doctus*
(Vendler 1998 makes some interesting points on the development of Heaney's style
through his books).

However, in keeping with the structural matrix which we have been tracing,
intersecting with this cosmopolitan range of names and places there are a number of
local names and places which take their place in this constellation: Toombridge, the
Bann, Lough Neagh, Butler's Bridge, St Columb's College, Ballynahinch Lake, Dr
Kerlin, John Dologhan, Bob Cushley, Ned Kane, Owen Kelly, and Gerry O'Neill, as
well as those remembered in elegies. What the book achieves is the placement of these
different cultures in the same structure, so that each can maintain its integrity while,
in the manner of the quincunx, also create the conditions for change. This is clear
from much of "The Real Names," but specifically in the lines, "'Frankie McMahon,
you're Bassanio. / Irwin, Launcelot Gobbo. Bredin, Portia'. / That was the cast, or
some of it" (48). Here, we see the transformation wrought by the literary as imagination allows for such changes: "The smell of the new book. The peep ahead / At words
not quite beyond you" (46).

Perhaps the key thematic element of this book is the fusion of this cosmopolitan
and polyglossic range of reference and allusion with the remembered experience of a
poet from his own personal past into a structure that is adequate to contemporary
Ireland. Thus, in "Out of the Bag," the family doctor who delivered all of the Heaney
children, Dr Kerlin, is described in terms of how he appeared to the young Heaney.
Given the traditional Irish reticence about matters sexual and gynecological, the
fiction was maintained that "All of us came in Doctor Kerlin's bag," and the accurate
adjectival description of the doctor's ministering has all the hallmarks of Heaney's
earlier style. However, in describing the doctor's eyes, Heaney uses the adjective
"hyperborean," and this word is the hinge, or in Derridean terms, *brisure*, upon which
that fusion of Ireland and classical Europe is achieved. The term refers to a member
of a race of people who, in Greek mythology, lived in a land of sunshine and plenty
beyond the north wind, worshiping Apollo, and this connection is furthered in the
second section where poetry and medicine are also connected: "A site of incubation,
where 'incubation' / Was technical and ritual, meaning sleep / When epiphany
occurred and you met the god" (Heaney 2001:8). It is such epiphanies that allow the
oneiric connection in this poem between Dr Kerlin, Asclepius, and Hygeia, his daughter; between Bellaghy, Epidaurus, and Lourdes; between medicine, sleep, and poetry;
between dream and reality: "The room I came from and the rest of us all came from
/ Stays pure reality where I stand alone" (9). All are aspects of his field of force, his
constellation, and all are granted their place and their transformative potential.

This process is furthered in *District and Circle*, where the ghosts of the two great
modern and modernist poetic avatars, Yeats and Eliot, haunt the book while, at a
more personal level, his aunt, Mary Heaney, and his father also figure as spectral presences. The epigraph is for Ann Saddlemyer, the owner of the cottage at Glanmore in

County Wicklow where *North* and *Field Work* were written. It makes the explicit connection between Saddlemyer, as an enabling presence in Heaney's work, and Augusta Gregory who similarly provided a roof and a locus of composition for W.B. Yeats:

> Call her Augusta
> Because we arrived in August, and
> from now on
> This month's baled hay and
> blackberries and combines
> Will spell Augusta's bounty.

> (Heaney 2006:v)

That Heaney should see comparisons with Yeats is a clear sign of a sense of his own place in the contemporary literary scene – the old shade of Incertus (the uncertain one) that appeared in his earlier poetry is now replaced with a sureness of self that resounds through these poems. This is to be seen in the framing device of the book, which begins in Glanmore and ends with a poem about "The Blackbird of Glanmore." It was in Glanmore that Heaney said that he felt he began as a poet to find his proper voice. One thinks of "Exposure" in *North*, where he speaks with a sureness of tone about his "responsible *tristia*" and about the "once-in-a-lifetime portent" and his liminal status as an "inner-émigré" (Heaney 1975:73). In *Field Work*, his next book, Glanmore was very much the locus of the poetry and of the poet's mind, and the "Glanmore Sonnets" are at the core of that book. Now, he sees himself from the perspective of the blackbird: "I've a bird's eye view of myself / A shadow on raked gravel / In front of my house of life" (Heaney 2006:77). The cottage in Glanmore has been a house of poetic life for Heaney and in this sense the title of this book is polysemic: it refers to the district of a poet's mind, the correlation between Glanmore and his own poetic first place, Mossbawn, which was also a house of life, and there is a circular connection to his return to Glanmore in the framing poems of the book.

In *District and Circle* a number of themes cohere. Heaney's fondness for the sonnet form is clear as throughout the book sonnets appear on different subjects, almost creating a chain. There are also a number of poems (and this is in keeping with a trend initiated in *Electric Light*) in which names appear: names of the living and the dead; of the famous and those known to the poet in his personal life. In this book we have evocations of Mick Joyce, Bobby Breen, George Seferis, Eoghan Rua Ó Suilleabháin, Barney Devlin, Robert Donnelly, T.S. Eliot, Tommy Evans, Harry Boyle, Edward Thomas, Philomena McNicholl, Czesław Miłosz, Barrie Cooke, Toraiwa, Niall Fitzduff, Pablo Neruda, Sarah, Mary, Dorothy Wordsworth, and W.H. Auden. What these names evoke is the individuality and personhood that has become such an ethical strand in Heaney.

In the central sequence of the book, "The Tollund Man in Springtime," past metaphors are revisited in the light of this evocation of the individual life as being of pure value in itself. In this sequence, the original mythopoeic and emblematic figure of the Tollund Man, seen as a symbol of the power of the past to return with frightening force into the politics of the present, is evoked again. It was the role of the man as sacrificial victim for his community that was the focus of the poems in Heaney's earlier books, but in this sequence it is on the individual man, as on the individual names already listed, that the focus now lies; on the concrete experience of the imagined individual as individual: "Coming and going, neither god nor ghost, / Not at odds or at one, but simply lost" (Heaney 2006:54). Again, in contrast to the other poems, where mythic discourse was the norm, in these poems it is the sense of life in the revived and imagined consciousness that is the crucial point, and it is expressed in a beautiful phrase: "then once I felt the air / I was like turned turf in the breath of God" (55).

In the fourth poem of the section, the opening lines enunciate this sense of the power and the ethical weight of the individual:

> "The soul exceeds its circumstances."
> Yes.
> History not to be granted the last
> word
> Or the first claim.
>
> (57)

In this book, the individual voice rings true and as such it is a culmination of the ethical project which Heaney's work has been tracing from the early books, namely stressing the value of each individual in themselves, as opposed to their place in the tribe or social structure. The power of poetry as a restorative force in human affairs is embodied in the Tollund Man's method of healing himself by telling his wrists to be "like silver birches"; his "old uncallused hands" to be like "young sward" and the spade cut to heal: "and got restored / by telling myself this" (57). It is this power of language to heal the wounds of the actual that is the core of his work, and of this volume.

Heaney is a poet who is seldom seen as a love poet, but in the final lines of "The Aerodrome" he gives a definition of love which is both accurate and beautiful in its complexity:

> If self is a location, so is love:
> Bearings taken, markings, cardinal
> points,
> Options, obstinacies, dug heels
> and distance,
> Here and there and now and then,
> a stance.
>
> (Heaney 2006:11)

This stance, which imbricates a complicated and interstitial response to the ethics, politics, and aesthetics of being human, is what makes the voice of Seamus Heaney a resonant one for our age.

References and Further Reading

Andrews, E. (1988). *The Poetry of Seamus Heaney: "All the Realms of Whisper."* London: Macmillan.

Andrews, E. (Ed.). (1998). *The Poetry of Seamus Heaney.* Icon Critical Guides. Cambridge: Icon Books.

Corcoran, N. (1998). *Seamus Heaney (1986).* London: Faber & Faber.

Curtis, T. (Ed.). (2001). *The Art of Seamus Heaney (1982).* 4th rev. edn. Dublin: Wolfhound Press.

Eliot, T.S. (1974). *Collected Poems, 1909–1962.* London: Faber & Faber.

Hart, H. (1992). *Seamus Heaney: Poet of Contrary Progressions.* New York: Syracuse University Press.

Heaney, S. (1966). *Death of a Naturalist.* London: Faber & Faber.

Heaney, S. (1969). *Door into the Dark.* London: Faber & Faber.

Heaney, S. (1972). *Wintering Out.* London: Faber & Faber.

Heaney, S. (1975). *North.* London: Faber & Faber.

Heaney, S. (1979). *Field Work.* London: Faber & Faber.

Heaney, S. (1980). *Preoccupations: Selected Prose 1968–1978.* London: Faber & Faber.

Heaney, S. (1984). *Station Island.* London: Faber & Faber.

Heaney, S. (1985). "Envies and Identifications: Dante and the Modern Poet." *Irish University Review*, 15 (Spring), 5–19.

Heaney, S. (1987). *The Haw Lantern.* London: Faber & Faber.

Heaney, S. (1988). *The Government of the Tongue: The 1986 T.S. Eliot Memorial Lectures and Other Critical Writings.* London: Faber & Faber.

Heaney, S. (1989). "Learning from Eliot." *Agenda: Seamus Heaney Fiftieth Birthday Issue*, 27, 17–31.

Heaney, S. (1990). *The Cure at Troy.* London: Faber & Faber.

Heaney, S. (1991). *Seeing Things.* London: Faber & Faber.

Heaney, S. (1995a). *The Redress of Poetry: Oxford Lectures.* London: Faber & Faber.

Heaney, S. (1995b). *Crediting Poetry.* Oldcastle, Ireland: Gallery Press.

Heaney, S. (1996). *The Spirit Level.* London: Faber & Faber.

Heaney, S. (1999). *Beowulf.* London: Faber & Faber.

Heaney, S. (2001). *Electric Light.* London: Faber & Faber.

Heaney, S. (2002). *Finders Keepers.* London: Faber & Faber.

Heaney, S. (2004). *The Burial at Thebes: Sophocles' Antigone.* London: Faber & Faber.

Heaney, S. (2006). *District and Circle.* London: Faber & Faber.

Molino, M. (1994). *Questioning Tradition, Language and Myth: The Poetry of Seamus Heaney.* Washington: Catholic University Press.

Morrison, B. (1982). *Seamus Heaney.* London: Methuen.

O'Brien, E. (2003). *Seamus Heaney and the Place of Writing.* Gainesville: University Press of Florida.

O'Brien, E. (2004). *Seamus Heaney Searches for Answers.* London: Pluto Press.

O'Brien, E. (2005). *Seamus Heaney: Creating Irelands of the Mind. Studies on Contemporary Ireland Series.* 2nd edn. Dublin: Liffey Press.

O'Donoghue, B. (1994). *Seamus Heaney and the Language of Poetry.* Hemel Hempstead: Harvester Wheatsheaf.

O'Driscoll, D. (2008) *Stepping Stones: Interviews with Seamus Heaney.* London: Faber & Faber.

Parker, M. (1993). *Seamus Heaney: "The Making of a Poet."* Dublin: Gill & Macmillan.

Randall, J. (1979). "An Interview with Seamus Heaney." *Ploughshares*, 5.3, 7–22.

Vendler, H. (1998). *Seamus Heaney.* London: HarperCollins.

48

Belfast Poets: Michael Longley, Derek Mahon, and Medbh McGuckian

Richard Rankin Russell

Michael Longley, Derek Mahon, and Medbh McGuckian are the best-known poets (along with Ciaran Carson) to emerge from Belfast in the second half of the twentieth century. The reputation of each has been eclipsed by that of Seamus Heaney (see CHAPTER 47, TELLING THE TRUTH SLANT), who grew up in rural County Derry, but Longley's poetry has recently been the subject of significant critical attention by Fran Brearton, Peter McDonald, and the present author, among others, while the first monograph on Derek Mahon (by Hugh Haughton) appeared from Oxford in 2007, and a steady stream of articles on McGuckian continues to be published. Although each poet grew up in Belfast, each has spent significant time outside the city: Longley, beginning in the 1970s, at the naturalist David Cabot's home in the townland of Carrigskeewaun in County Mayo; Mahon, in Paris, London, Dublin, and Kinsale, Ireland, where he now resides; and McGuckian, in Ballycastle, on the Northern Irish coast. Longley (b. July 27, 1939) and Mahon (b. Nov. 23, 1941) began serious poetry writing during their time together at Trinity College Dublin in the late 1950s, where their mentor was the late Alec Reid. After graduating, both returned to Belfast, where Longley was part of Philip Hobsbaum's renowned Belfast Group of creative writers, including Heaney, while Mahon was not. Despite writing very different poetry, Heaney, Longley, and Mahon were often grouped together in the critical and public imagination in the 1960s and, indeed, each published his first volume in that decade.

Longley's first major poem, "Epithalamion," which begins his first volume, *No Continuing City* (1969), suggests his split cultural and literary heritage by consciously echoing the Anglo-Irish poet Edmund Spenser's poem of the same name. For instance, Spenser's poem has 365 long lines (five or more metrical feet) to signify the passing of a year, while Longley's has thirteen stanzas, each rhyming ababb, for a total of 65

A Companion to Irish Literature, edited by Julia M. Wright
© 2010 Blackwell Publishing Ltd

lines, echoing Spenser's numerological and rhyme scheme. "Epithalamion" also establishes Longley's classical credentials (such marriage poems were often written by Greek and Latin poets, such as the Roman Catullus), highlights his marked interest in form, and displays his penchant for love poetry. The epigraph to *No Continuing City* is from Hebrews 13:14: "For here we have no continuing city ... [but we seek one to come]," and this first poem accords with this theme of earthly things passing away, as time itself does with the dawning of the new day, beginning in the transition between stanzas 7 and 8. "Epithalamion" shows another influence as well – that of John Milton's long, periodic sentence in such works as *Paradise Lost* – and the poem consists of only three sentences: the first in the first stanza, the second in stanzas 2 through 7, and the third in stanzas 8 through 13. But within the same volume, Longley reveals an opposing inclination – for the miniature – in poems such as "Nausicaa," "Narcissus," "Persephone," "Gathering Mushrooms," "Man Friday," and "Rip Van Winkle" – each of which is composed of only a few series of couplets. This dialectic between poems composed of long, enjambed sentences and those made up of couplets obtains throughout Longley's career and demonstrates his suppleness with lineation. While "Epithalamion" attempts to be, like Spenser's fictional bride and his poem itself, a timeless artistic monument to the passing day that it celebrates in thirteen ababb-rhyming stanzas, Longley's later poetry often registers its own ephemerality and thus links its own fragility with the fleeting lives of its subjects such as the moths, one of which dies, that are drawn to the lighted window of the couple.

Such a view of poetry's own mortality probably developed gradually as the conflict in Northern Ireland wore on into the 1970s, 1980s, and mid-1990s. While Longley and Mahon had established their poetic voice and formed many of their artistic attitudes long before the beginning of the so-called "Troubles," each has responded thoughtfully to sectarianism in his poetry – Longley by emphasizing the continuity between the fragility of the natural and human worlds, Mahon by adapting an insider/outsider position. Because McGuckian (b. Aug. 12, 1950) has lived most of her adult life during the Troubles and because her interiorized feminine aesthetic has been wrongly thought not to deal with politics, the contours of her complex engagement with the Troubles are harder to ascertain, but nonetheless significant. But the profound, varying types of poems written by all three of poets mark them as far more than simply "Belfast poets" or "Troubles poets," but as poets of the highest order who consistently engage imaginatively all the troubles of this world that beset us and the joys that delight us. Longley's poems on the Troubles remain some of the very best to emerge from that conflict. Poems such as "Wounds," "Wreaths," "The Ice-Cream Man," and "Ceasefire" have garnered widespread acclaim for their portrayal of the ephemerality of human life. And his poems about the flora and fauna of the western Irish counties suggest his general concern with the fleeting and our responsibility to preserve it. Longley's famous poem "Wounds," from *An Exploded View* (1972), recognizes the contribution of Ulster Protestants to the battle of the Somme in World War I, but also acknowledges contemporary victims of political violence in the province by concluding the poem with an imagined re-creation of a Protestant bus-conductor murdered by the IRA before he could give evidence against them for their hijacking and burning of his bus. The poem begins in World War I, focusing on the service of the Ulster Division and his father at the Somme:

> First, the Ulster Division at the Somme
> Going over the top with "Fuck the Pope!"
> "No Surrender!": a boy about to die,
> Screaming "Give 'em one for the Shankill!"

(Longley 2007:62)

The first section ends with a glimpse of Longley's father's death: "He said ... 'I am dying for King and Country, slowly.' / I touched his hand, his thin head I touched" (62). In the second section of the poem, Longley mourns the death of "Three teenage soldiers, bellies full of / Bullets and Irish beer" (62) and places them beside his father in a grave, suggesting their kinship across religion and time through their service to abstract ideals. These lads are the three Scottish teenage British army soldiers killed by the IRA on March 9, 1971, connecting them in the poet's mind to his father who fought in the London Scottish Regiment during World War I.

Longley's portrayal of their bewilderment while in service shows his recognition of the often confusing and inhumane nature of war. He also laments their squandered youth, imaged by the "heavy guns [which] put out / The night-light in a nursery for ever" (62). Longley goes on to link the "service" rendered by his father and the British soldiers with that of the bus-conductor, since he throws the "bus-conductor's uniform" into the grave as well. In its imaginative re-creations of violence and its aftermath, Longley's elegy accords with Fran Brearton's reading of it and his elegies generally in that they "reveal not only the short-term, tangible damage caused by violence, but also the long-term effects not immediately, or possibly ever, readily apparent" (Brearton 2000:258).

After a twelve-year period in which he published no full volumes of poetry, Longley released *Gorse Fires* in 1991. The volume's concluding poem, "The Butchers," directly concerns Odysseus' return home after his journey, but also obliquely critiques the horrific murders of Catholics by the Shankill Butchers, as they came to be called, in Belfast in the mid-1970s, and violence undertaken for the sake of vengeance. The poem's continuity flows from Longley's seamless stitching together of the events at the end of book 22 and those from the opening of book 24 of *The Odyssey*, in which Hermes takes the shades of the suitors down into the underworld. Longley's penchant for the long poetic sentence may well originate in his great fondness for the poetry of Louis MacNeice, a favorite exemplar, who often employed the sentence (Longley has edited two selections of MacNeice's poetry), and in his love of Milton's periodic sentences in *Paradise Lost*.

In "The Butchers," he uses the long sentence as a formal strategy to incorporate a series of correspondences and complexities between the atrocities at the conclusion of the *Odyssey* and those in 1970s Northern Ireland, suggesting in the sweeping and continuous qualities of the line the connection between vengeful violence in the past and present. For example, the dragging of Melanthios' body and the cutting off of his "nose and ears and cock and balls" links Odysseus and his men's vengeful killing to that conducted by the Shankill Butchers, who would often assassinate Catholics after IRA attacks on the security forces or other people. Furthermore, Longley connects both the violence sometimes associated with the Royal Ulster Constabulary and the extremist Protestant clergyman Ian Paisley with Hermes, who is described as waving "the supernatural baton" in a manner "Like a clergyman" (Longley 2007:194) as he leads the suitors to the underworld. Yet the poem also implicitly condemns all vengeance in the past and present.

In 1995 Longley published *The Ghost Orchid*, which contains his best-known poem about the Troubles, "Ceasefire." This Shakespearean sonnet, originally published in the *Irish Times*, imagines the joint weeping of the Greek Achilles and the Trojan king Priam during the Trojan War, but its contemporary title and date of composition a few days before the 1994 IRA ceasefire suggest possible opening steps toward reconciliation in Northern Ireland. And Priam's last words recommend a posture in which he humbles himself in order to offer forgiveness to Achilles: "I get down on my knees and do what must be done / And kiss Achilles' hand, the killer of my son" (Longley 2007:225).

Longley's focus on the ritual undertaken by this unrelated, yet linked, father and son suggests his belief that ceremony deflates hatred and violence, a position that accords with that of W.B. Yeats in "A Prayer for My Daughter." Although Yeats may have been wishing a sort of naive innocence for his daughter in that poem, Longley clearly wishes a tough-minded innocence for Achilles and Priam, a state in which the disturbing particular violence of the immediate past can be recognized and forgiven (but not forgotten) through the ceremony they enact and through the ceremonial form of this broken Shakespearean sonnet. As I have noted elsewhere, "The public life that the poem acquired suggests that its specific image of forgiveness resonated for a number of individuals in the province" (Russell 2003:233).

If Longley's elegies for the dead of the Trojan War, World War I, victims of the Holocaust, and the recent Troubles in Northern Ireland seek to inscribe individual lives on our consciousness, so too, do his lovely poems about the flora and fauna of his adopted townland of Carrigskeewaun in County Mayo. While Longley has spent much time at the naturalist David Cabot's house in Mayo, he has also enjoyed exploring the Burren area of County Clare. This karst limestone area has very little soil or trees, but bursts into bloom for a brief period every year. Its profusion and variety of flowers and their almost magical annual appearance are fitting for a poet who is so attuned to both the quotidian and the spiritual. Longley has claimed that "Naming anything well is a poetic act" (Longley 1996:115), and "The Ice-cream Man," which appeared in *Gorse Fires* (1991), enacts that theory by opening with a catalog of ice cream flavors, closing with a catalog of flowers from the Burren, and pivoting on another flower image: the carnations Longley's daughter placed outside the man's shop. As I have suggested elsewhere, "The sheer variety and profusion of the wild flowers both offers a glimpse of a natural repository that the urban ice cream man vaguely and unconsciously mimicked in his celebratory recitation of flavors ... *and* acts as a beautifully intricate metaphorical wreath of flowers with which Longley adorns the man's memory" (Russell 2003:236). Counting and cataloging the plants, creatures, and human beings of rural Mayo and Clare along with those from urban Belfast, naming them and celebrating their loves with tender care and affection, has enabled Longley to incorporate these denizens into a timeless community of plant, animal, and human life, a fragile ecosystem in which one death sends shock waves through the entire population. He is not only one of the world's greatest living love poets, as "Epithalamion," "The Linen Industry," "The Scissors Ceremony," "The Pattern," and many other poems attest, and not only Ireland's best living nature poet, but a poet for our global world of deracination, moving as easily through the trenches of World War I, Japanese temples, and the war zones of Belfast and Nazi Germany as he does through gorse in western Ireland.

But for all his explorations of different places, Longley is securely rooted in comparison to his brilliant countryman, Derek Mahon, perhaps the most critically neglected contemporary Irish poet and easily one of its most subtle and talented. Mahon's poetry has long had a few defenders, such as the critics Terence Brown and Edna Longley (and of course Longley and Heaney) and more lately Hugh Haughton, Elmer Kennedy-Andrews, and Peter McDonald, but he has yet to attract the critical attention he fully deserves, partly because of his refusal to promote himself and his work through interviews and public appearances.

Mahon, like Longley, was educated at the Royal Belfast Academical Institution and then at Trinity College Dublin, where he studied French, this last an early sign of his cosmopolitanism and penchant for travel. But he has returned to Northern Ireland and especially to the Irish Republic, living in the province after having left for London in 1970, for example, from 1977 to 1979; he lived in Kinsale during the late 1980s, in Dublin, from the early 1990s to 2003, and again in Kinsale, from 2003 to the present. In an article for *Magill* published in 1979 that he entitled "The Coleraine Triangle," Mahon surveys the literal and social landscape of the north coast of Northern Ireland, focusing on the towns of Coleraine, Portstewart, and Portrush. He concludes the essay with an imagined threnody for this place, which is itself an apt description of the condition to which many of his poems aspire: "I imagine a hypothetical future in which everyone has departed. ... There is no sign of life. Nothing happens here, and maybe nothing ever happened" (Mahon 1996:219). The last sentence partially echoes the last line of Philip Larkin's "I Remember, I Remember" (itself a deflation of the much-loved poem "Adlestrop" by Edward Thomas): "Nothing, like something, happens anywhere" (Larkin 1989:82). The usual literary precedent invoked with Mahon is Beckett, not Larkin, but Larkin's poem, with its air of uncertainty, procession of negative statements, and general refusal to ascribe special importance to a particular place, uncannily anticipates a significant strand of Mahon's poetry and his attitude toward place.

Unlike Heaney, whose early poetry was marked by its evocative descriptions of his family farm in rural County Derry, Mahon's upbringing in 1950s Protestant-dominated Belfast may have served to untether him from affinities with particular places. Citing Mahon's 1970 essay, "Poetry in Northern Ireland," Brown has convincingly argued that Mahon's dislocation stems from his position as a Protestant in Northern Ireland, observing that Mahon, along with poets such as James Simmons and Longley, are "ironic heirs of a threadbare colonialism," and "have as their inheritance" a "fragmentation" common to northern Protestants (Brown 2003:134).

Despite this interest in deracination and disconnection, Mahon's connection to both Longley and Belfast is evident from his poem "Spring in Belfast" in *Collected Poems* (originally titled "The Spring Vacation" and dedicated to Longley in his 1968 volume, *Night-Crossing*). The speaker vows at the end of the first stanza, "Once more, as before, I remember not to forget" (Mahon 1999:13), and the poem concludes with one of Mahon's best-known stanzas, which strives to articulate an epistemology of local geography:

> One part of my mind must learn to know its place.
> The things that happen in the kitchen houses
> And echoing back streets of this desperate city
> Should engage more than my casual interest,
> Exact more interest than my casual pity.

(Mahon 1999:13)

Notice that only "One part of my mind must learn to know its place"; the other part or parts of the speaker's mind presumably may wander freely in other places. And even that determined first line of this last stanza is undercut by the "Should" that begins the penultimate line, leading us to ask, "It should, but will it?" The chiasmus of "casual, "interest," "Exact," "interest," and "casual" of the last two lines semantically summarizes Mahon's typical strange admixture of specificity and complacent disinterest. Despite using "Exact" as a verb here, its placement as the crux of the chiasmus suggests Mahon often sets an exact locale against a backdrop of seeming casualness or insouciance.

With the exception of poems such as "Spring in Belfast," Mahon generally avoided engaging with the province's recent violent history in his first two volumes, *Night-Crossing* and *Lives* (1972), but he began engaging with that history explicitly in *The Snow Party* (1975). Mahon's "A Disused Shed in Co. Wexford," which was first published in 1973 and collected in *The Snow Party*, has become the most anthologized contemporary Irish poem. Michael Longley includes it as one of three Mahon poems in his selection *20th-Century Irish Poems*, published by Faber in 2002. The poem engages deeply with Ireland's Troubles from the 1920s and more recently, but also with atrocities and disasters ranging from the Holocaust all the way back to Pompeii. Continuing Mahon's penchant for portraying life in out-of-the-way corners, the poem depicts "A thousand mushrooms" that "crowd to a keyhole" in a disused shed "Deep in the grounds of a burnt-out hotel" in County Wexford. The first stanza resoundingly begins, "Even now there are places where a thought might grow –" and proceeds to contemplate such places, including "Peruvian mines," "Indian compounds," "Lime crevices behind rippling rain-barrels, / Dog corners for bone burials," and finally "a disused shed in Co. Wexford, / Deep in the grounds of a burnt-out hotel" (Mahon 1999:89). Hotels recur throughout Mahon's poetry as way-stations for lives in transit. But this hotel, recalling as it does the burned-out Big Houses of the Anglo-Irish torched by the Irish Republican Army in the 1920s, and its residents, the stalwart mushrooms, are resolutely anchored, albeit largely forgotten. The mushrooms are described as "waiting for us in a foetor / Of vegetable sweat since civil war days," over fifty years before the poem was written. Their anxiety combined with their faithfulness in waiting for the "expropriated mycologist" to return recalls that of Beckett's tramps in *Waiting for Godot*. But Vladimir and Estragon inhabit a no-place, while these supplicant mushrooms live in a particular outbuilding on the grounds of a certain hotel in a particular Irish county. But their needs, like those of Beckett's characters, are universal: they want to be noticed and have their story told. The poem concludes with the speaker realizing,

> They are begging us, you see, in their wordless way,
> To do something, to speak on their behalf
> Or at least not to close the door again.
> Lost people of Treblinka and Pompeii!

                                                                    (90)

Such pleading of these "Magi, moonmen, / Powdery prisoners of the old regime," as they are described in the penultimate stanza, awakens all our empathy. Yet Mahon suggests our response to victims must be carefully measured and could even prove destructive. If the presumed tourists, with their "flash-bulb firing-squad" and "light meter" seriously entertain the wordless fungi's request "at least not to close the door again," the blinding light of the outside world may well kill them, just as it is implied their bright flash bulbs are currently doing. Do the mushrooms really know what they are asking when they exclaim in the last stanza, "Save us, save us," and then ask, "Let the god not abandon us / Who have come so far in darkness and in pain" (90)? The mushrooms have previously fed off darkness and pain, but what will nourish them if they are "saved"? The poem argues that surely we must tell the stories of atrocities wherever they may occur, but that in so doing, we run the terrible risk of doing further violence to the victims unless we are appropriately reverential and subtle and shade them from the pain of exposure.

The future in which nothing happens that Mahon imagines at the end of his essay cited above, "The Coleraine Triangle," and in a cluster of other poems, is juxtaposed against another strand of his poetry focused on the future bright with potential, a place and time of fecundity epitomized on the cover of his *Poems 1962–1978*, which reproduces Botticelli's pen-and-ink drawing, *Abundance*. Botticelli's female figure is all curves and billowing dress and holds the hand of a boy clutching grapes, who is followed by two other children, all of them signifying natural fertility. In one of Mahon's earliest poems, "In Carrowdore Churchyard," dedicated to the then recently deceased Northern Irish poet Louis MacNeice, he concludes by juxtaposing the present grim reality of the harsh winter and the killing season the province is experiencing in the Troubles with the hope of spring and peace in the future. For example, he mentions the wintry hills around the churchyard, which "are hard / As Nails, yet soft and feminine in their turn / When fingers open and the hedges burn" (Mahon 1979:17). The poem concludes with a startling picture of MacNeice, "from the ague / Of the blind poet and the bombed-out town" bringing "The all-clear to the empty holes of spring / Rinsing the choked mud, keeping the colours new" (17).

In one of the new poems included at the end of Mahon's *Poems 1962–1978* his remarkable verse letter to Desmond O'Grady, "The Sea in Winter," written while Mahon was Writer in Residence at the University of Ulster at Coleraine from Autumn 1977 to 1979, the text vacillates between a striking optimism and a more grim realism. For example, re-employing the contrasting imagery associated with winter and spring that he had used in "In Carrowdore Churchyard," he suggests in the eighth stanza (changed to the seventh stanza in Mahon 1999:116) that both Mahon and O'Grady have faith in poetry's generative powers:

> faith that the trivia doodled here
> will bear their fruit sometime, somewhere;
> that the long winter months may bring
> gifts to the goddess in the spring.
>
> (Mahon 1979:111)

Yet by stanza 15 the poet admits, "And all the time I have my doubts / About this verse-making" (112). But in stanza 17, Mahon hopes that "One day, / Perhaps, the words will find their mark / And leave a brief glow on the dark" (113). Stanza 20 references Botticelli's "strangely neglected / Drawings for *The Divine Comedy*" and concludes with the poet proleptically offering us his own drawings of the future: "I trace / The future in a colour-scheme, / Colours we scarcely dare to dream" (114). These lines recall the hopeful concluding line of "In Carrowdore Churchyard," with Louis MacNeice "Rinsing the choked mud, keeping the colours new." Stanza 21 gives perhaps the most positive picture of the future in Mahon's oeuvre to that point, with images of the Dying Gaul reviving, a "girl among the trees" who walks, stones that speak, a rainbow that ends, wine being passed "among the friends," the lost being found, and estranged lovers "at peace beneath the covers" (114).

These colorful, projected visions of peace and abundance, however, are just that – projections – and the poem concludes on an altogether more somber note, with the last stanza opening by stating, "Meanwhile the given life goes on / There is nothing new under the sun." Even "if the dawn / That wakes us now should also find us / Cured of our ancient colour-blindness," the poet realistically concludes by remarking, "I who know nothing go to teach / While a new day crawls up the beach" (114). The reference to "colour-blindness" is ambiguous, perhaps connoting the sectarian divisions of Northern Irish life. Mahon's final beach scene in his last stanza may also transmute the hopeful central line of Larkin's "To the Sea" about the continuities of summer that the English poet found on a trip to the beach with his elderly mother: "Still going on, all of it, still going on!" (Larkin 1989:173). Mahon's line, "Meanwhile the given life goes on" instead accepts the prosaic, quotidian life he was living on the north coast of Northern Ireland at a time of great personal crisis and contrasts it against the imagined, bright future he limned in earlier stanzas.

Mahon heavily revised "The Sea in Winter" for its publication in his 1999 *Collected Poems*, excising ten full stanzas, which results in a twelve-stanza poem achieved at the cost "of autobiographical directness," as Hugh Haughton points out (Haughton 2007:139). Mahon is known for making extensive changes to his poetry: Haughton argues that, beginning with the revisions found in *Poems 1962–1978*, "All of Mahon's later collections show the same predilection for retitling, cutting, and revising poems, and from this point a lot of his work exists in multiple textual reincarnations" (Haughton 2007:126). Removed from the 1979 edition of "The Sea in Winter" are many of the stanzas cited above where the poet speculates on the function of poetry (except for the stanza about the "trivia doodled here") and added is a completely new stanza about history. The poet vows in this new stanza, "But let me never forget the weird / facticity of this strange seaboard," going on to remind himself not to "ever again contemptuously / refuse its plight" (Mahon 1999:117). He will no longer do these things because "history / ignores those who ignore it, not / the ignorant whom it begot" (117). Thus the poet chides himself on the edge of the new millennium for having ignored specifically the history of Northern Ireland and relegating himself to the wings, as it were, as he realizes that the "ignorant" of the province (presumably those who practice sectarianism) were at least actors in its history while he was largely an audience member in exile for years.

Peter McDonald has argued that while "Derek Mahon's poetry might seem at first to have effected its escape from the pressures of history with singular grace and efficiency," the poems nonetheless "come from a clearly recognizable point and persona – one form in which the poet succeeds notably being the verse-letter – and exercise a technical accomplishment and descriptive fidelity which are themselves parts of an altogether more social enterprise" (McDonald 1997:87). Formally, therefore, Mahon's poetry complicates the often distanced geographies of its content with an intimacy derived from the personal verse letters he writes, such as "The Sea in Winter." Other verse letters include "Beyond Howth Head," Mahon's first such poem (collected in *Lives*), *The Yaddo Letter* (1991), *The Hudson Letter* (1996), and "Resistance Days" from Mahon's 2005 volume, *Harbour Lights*.

The new stanza's focus on facing up to history that was added to "The Sea in Winter" on the cusp of the millennium accords with Mahon's musings on history during the same period throughout one of his most remarkable volumes, *The Yellow Book*, published in 1998. Consisting of twenty-one meditations, this volume's title recalls both the medieval Irish *Yellow Book of Lecan* (1391) with its version of the Irish epic *Táin Bó Cúailnge* ("The Cattle Raid of Cooley") along with the yellow book that exerts such a fascination on Oscar Wilde's Dorian Gray (almost certainly Huysman's

A Rebours, or *Against Nature*) and the Aubrey Beardsley-edited quarterly *The Yellow Book* of the 1890s. Heavily sprinkled with allusions to past and present writers and cultures, from Stevie Smith and her *Novel on Yellow Paper* to Philip Larkin's "High Windows," to French Decadent culture and "the plain Protestant fatalism of home" in Northern Ireland (Mahon 1999:261), the volume shows the amazing range and depth of Mahon's poetry and his newly rejoined struggle with the pressure of history as a muscular iambic pentameter runs throughout, contradicting his adopted Decadent pose of enervation.

The new millennium has brought two outstanding new Mahon volumes, *Harbour Lights* and *Life on Earth*. *Harbour Lights* won the *Irish Times* Poetry Now Award and *Life on Earth* was one of Read Ireland's eight poetry volumes chosen for its "Best Books for 2008." The concluding poem in *Harbour Lights*, "The Seaside Cemetery," features a Mahon still drawn to lonely places (it was inspired by the Mont St Clair cemetery in Paul Valéry's native village of Sète in south-west France). Long a lover of seashores for their panoramic perspectives, Mahon wonders about his own future demise, picturing himself as "sniff[ing] already my own future smoke," but "bursting with new power" (Mahon 2005:72). As the poem concludes, the poet orders himself to revive:

> No, no; get up; go on to the next phase –
> body, shake off this meditative pose
> and, chest, inhale the first flap of the air.
> A palpable new freshness off the sea,
> an ozone rush, restores my soul to me
> And draws me down to the reviving shore.
>
> (75)

As the poet attempts to begin writing poetry, his notebook pages are blown into the sea; bidding farewell to them, he enthusiastically exclaims, "fly off then, my sun-dazzled pages / and break, waves, break up with ecstatic surges / this shifting surface where the spinnaker flocks!" (75). Embracing change in a landscape composed of blue and gold colors, the poet surrenders to nature's power and finds life in its abounding flux. As his own history advances, Mahon continues writing supremely rendered poems for our time and the future.

Although she has become known for her feminist poetics, McGuckian is quick to point out the influence of Heaney and Yeats, along with Michael Longley, upon her. She has written a fascinating pamphlet study on Heaney entitled *Horsepower, Pass By! A Study of the Car in the Poetry of Seamus Heaney* (1999). Moreover, she was taught at Queen's University in Belfast by Heaney and has spoken often of him warmly. She feels strongly linked to Yeats through Heaney, having noted once, "if he hadn't been there, Heaney wouldn't be, and if Heaney hadn't been there, I wouldn't be. I feel that there is a continuum between Yeats and me through Heaney" (quoted in Gray 1993:167). In 2003 McGuckian contributed an essay entitled "Michael Longley as a Metaphysical" to the special issue of the *Colby Quarterly* on Longley's work, and she has often spoken warmly of him. In turn, Longley has written approvingly of her poetry and uses lines from McGuckian's poem "Glove-silver," published in *The Face of the Earth* (2002) – "the sparks of his father curved / into the west of the lake" – as the epigraph to his 2004 volume *Snow Water*.

McGuckian's values are drawn from her Catholic upbringing, a faith that lingers in her perception of herself as a conduit through which a higher power writes. She has told interviewers of her frustrated desire to be a Catholic priest and related to Cecile Gray in conversation, "when I write a poem ... I feel that I am not even writing the poem. I sometimes feel that ... some creative force is writing the poems through me" (Gray 1993:168). Her poetry itself, characterized by its profusion of images and medley of colors, undoubtedly flows from her immersion in Irish Catholicism. In an essay based upon her diaries kept from 1970 to 1973, entitled "Women Are Trousers," McGuckian's musings about her attendance at Mass in an entry from March 1970 offer a glimpse of how her poetic imagination was fired by her early Catholic devotion, especially in her emphasis on colors: "I lit a candle in St. Mary's. Some sort of God was behind the colour of the flowers that embraced me. The sun kept being born and dying in grey winds" (McGuckian 2000:162).

Despite her great interest in spirituality derived from her childhood Catholicism, which was often authoritarian, McGuckian's poetry engages with the question of authority in striking ways, as both Clair Wills and Danielle Sered have argued. Wills holds that McGuckian "constructs a mode of operation in which the achievement of authority in an Irish or European poetic tradition depends precisely on the poetry's semantic impenetrability and resistance to paraphrase" (Wills 1993:158). And Sered points out that "the sheer grammatical difficulty of McGuckian's poetry, evident in everything from sudden shifts in subject and tense to the abundance of ellipses and sub-clauses, is compounded by a crafted disruption of the speaking voice and the authority it promises to secure" (Sered 2002:273). An early poem such as "Smoke," from *The Flower Master and Other Poems* (1982), demonstrates McGuckian's grammatical difficulty and also how such difficulty reinforces her particular content. Both lines 2 and 7 feature comma splices that suggest, respectively, the fire's uncontrolled nature in stanza 1 and the speaker's lack of control in stanza 2. She wonders "what controls it, can the wind hold / that snake of orange motion to the hills" in lines 2 and 3. She finds herself out of control as well, "unable even / to contain, myself, I run" (McGuckian 1997:13; unless otherwise noted, all quotations of McGuckian's verse cite this edition). McGuckian's refusal to use semicolons connecting each set of independent clauses here brilliantly underscores the shared volatility of fire and speaker as the lines run on past the slight pause of the commas.

Another aspect of McGuckian's relationship to authority concerns her preoccupation with centos, from the Latin for "patchwork" – groups of lines she borrows from past poets and inserts, largely without identification, into her poems. Shane Murphy points out that, for example, that her cryptic poem "Frost in Beaconsfield," from *On Ballycastle Beach*, "borrows heavily from the letters collected in *Robert Frost and John Bartlett: The Record of a Friendship*," enabling her to use these "embedded quotations" to recall not only Frost's anxious letter to Bartlett that conveys the poet's need for praise of his first volume, *A Boy's Will*, but also McGuckian's "questioning about her own poetry" (Murphy 2003:199).

McGuckian shares with Longley an intense interest in the local that, if focused properly, opens onto new prospects of the mind. Longley's praise of McGuckian's poetry suggests just how such particularity can offer expansiveness:

> McGuckian is a perfect example of how a true poet can mine for gold in the back yard. Her subject matter tends to be domestic, but her treatment of it is so intense, concentrated and versatile, that somehow she manages to imply the whole world which extends beyond. (n.d.)

In her repeated descriptions of the interior of rooms and houses, McGuckian, along with the Irish poet Eavan Boland (see CHAPTER 50, EAVAN BOLAND'S MUSE MOTHERS), must surely be seen as one of the supreme chroniclers of women's domestic lives in the last third of the twentieth century.

As if to signal this interest, the cover of McGuckian's *Selected Poems* features a lovely illustration entitled *Sleeper* by the artist Martin Gale, which depicts a woman indolently sprawled in sleep, surrounded by folds of sheets that are variously blue, grey, and white. Both the voluptuousness of the image, paradoxically heightened by the woman's pajamas, and her loneliness become major concerns of McGuckian's poetry. For example, the lonely niece of "Aunts," which was collected in *The Flower Master and Other Poems*, hungrily watches her aunts "shading in their lips / from sugar pink to coral, from mulberry to rose" and feels left out of their conspiracies to get boys and their planned dances, even the private dance she catches them in when "Once out of the blue / I caught them dancing on the bed" (18). Even the grown speaker who has a lover in "The Hollywood Bed," from the same volume as "Aunts," feels displaced by her lover, noticing how "the headboard is disturbed / by your uncomfortable slew" and realizes that she would fill his outline were he gone (19).

Repeatedly, McGuckian invents striking similes and images that strain the bounds of the language and challenge the capacity of our imagination. In "The Sitting," originally published in *Venus and the Rain* (1984), for example, the speaker describes "the coppery head" of her half-sister whom she is painting as "bright as a net of lemons" (33). In the title poem of *On Ballycastle Beach* (1988), a poem dedicated to the poet's father, she describes his hand as "dark as a cedar lane by nature" (50). In "Candles at Three Thirty," from *Captain Lavender* (1994), the dwindling year "glitters as it withers / like an orange stuck with cloves / or Christmas clouds" (76). Such verbal delights spill out of almost any McGuckian poem and demonstrate Wills' contention that the difficulty of paraphrasing the poems enables them to establish their considerable authority. For if we must constantly quote the poetry rather than paraphrase it, the poet retains control over her original language and our own critical language becomes merely mimetic.

Often thought to be apolitical, McGuckian's poetry, especially beginning with *Captain Lavender*, which was published in 1994, the year of both the Provisional IRA and the Combined Loyalist Command ceasefires, deeply engages with history and politics, including those of her troubled province. Of course, the verbal singularity of all her poetry stands as an alternative to the repetitions that passed for political discourse so often in the province's past. "The Albert Chain," from *Captain Lavender*, opens with a powerful simile directly likening a fruit hanging on a dead stem to a terrorist: "Like an accomplished terrorist, the fruit hangs / from the end of a dead stem, under a tree / riddled with holes like a sieve" (88). These lines imply that terrorists eventually kill that which nourishes them. Later in the same stanza, the speaker spies a "wild cat" that has been "half-stripped of its skin," along with "a squirrel stoned to death" (88). Employing these animal images suggests that terrorism is not natural, and artificially violates the natural and human world. The speaker announces in stanza 2, "I am going back into war, like a house / I knew when I was young," and indeed the whole poem seems to announce a deliberate turning toward examining conflict by incorporating war as a sort of domestic subject. "The War Degree," also from *Captain Lavender* and the concluding poem of *Selected Poems*, uses the language of hope – "when the treaty moves all tongues" – yet also recalls "a wartime, heart-stained autumn" that "drove fierce half-bricks into the hedges" (92). The unifying possibilities of "the treaty" are undercut by the following stanza's bellicose images, just as those latter lines themselves show how nature has been violated by unnatural violence.

Shelmalier (1998), McGuckian's sixth volume, has five parts, united by a focus on the United Irishmen's failed Uprising in 1798 (see CHAPTER 16, UNITED IRISH POETRY AND SONGS). In her "Author's Note," McGuckian recalls having conducted research on the 1798 Uprising and then finding "what I had written in the form of epitaph and commemoration or address for the present-day disturbances in the North fitted like an egg into its shell that previous whirlwind moment when, unbelievably, hope and history did in fact rhyme" (McGuckian 1998:13). The concluding phrase about hope and history rhyming is a nearly verbatim citation of one of the memorable lines from Heaney's 1990 Field Day play, *The Cure at Troy*, his version of Sophocles' *Philoctetes*. Heaney's play looked forward hopefully but cautiously to a thaw in sectarian relations as the 1990s began, while McGuckian's poems, appearing in 1998 – both the bicentenary year of the Uprising led by the United Irishmen who supported Catholic civil rights and the year in which the landmark Good Friday Agreement was signed that articulated a power-sharing agreement between Catholics and Protestants in the province – celebrate the ecumenical spirit of the Uprising and the agreement. Shelmalier is "both a placename for a barony in Wexford and a battalion of seabird hunters" and the volume signals McGuckian's "being suddenly able to welcome into consciousness figures of an integrity I had never learned to be proud of" (McGuckian 1998:13), presumably the radical Protestants who initiated the 1798 Uprising. Despite its profusion of martial images, the volume implies that the egg of hope "laid" 200 years before by the United Irishmen has finally hatched into a hope for a future of peace in the province. If, as Sered has argued, citing lines about a flaming "you" from "The Porcelain Bell" in *Captain Lavender*, McGuckian seeks to resuscitate herself and reinscribe her authority through a process of verbal self-annihilation (Sered 2002:284), then, in *Shelmalier*, she implicitly aligns that earlier self-reclamation project with the hope that political rapprochement in Northern Ireland is springing from the ashes of the contemporary Troubles. That hope is expressed supremely in "The Society of the Bomb," in which an unnamed woman (perhaps a symbol of Ireland itself) wakes from sleep "to people / like half-making love or the wider now, exceptionally sunlit spring" (McGuckian 1998:109). "The wider now, exceptionally sunlit spring" implicitly contrasts the narrow past of the province's recent history in which sectarianism flourished.

McGuckian has written a flurry of six volumes since 1998, as many as she had published from 1982 through 1998. In this later phase of her career, she seems to increasingly open herself to visitations of the marvelous, much as Heaney has done in his later poetry beginning with *Field Work* (1979) and especially in *Station Island* (1984) and *Seeing Things* (1991). For example, *The Book of the Angel* (2004) draws on the *Liber Angeli*, a document in Latin about St Patrick's dialogue with an angel in which he is granted the ecclesiastical seat of Armagh. Angels are also invoked in poems such as "Catherine's Blue" and "Ironer with Backlight," from the 2007 volume, *The Currach Requires No Harbours*, and in, for example, "The Inferno Machine," "Shot Angel," and "The Sin Eater," from her 2008 volume, *My Love Has Fared Inland*.

But the poems about the conflict in Northern Ireland and its aftermath of an uneasy peace also continue to feature in this later work. The title poem of *Drawing Ballerinas* (2001), for example, is dedicated to "Ann Frances Owens, schoolfellow and neighbour, who lost her life in the Abercorn Café explosion, 1972." McGuckian's concluding note also explains her curious title: "The painter, Matisse, when asked how he managed to survive the war artistically, replied that he spent the worst years 'drawing ballerinas'" (McGuckian 2001:15). This touch of the whimsical and airy in the midst of war is characteristic of later McGuckian. In "The Miniver," also from *Drawing Ballerinas*, she describes "This brittle peace, a palmsbreadth in length," as "always morning," and suggests it "gives the ever-narrower interior a feeling of being outside" (McGuckian 2001:50) in lines reminiscent of the sunlit "wider now" of spring in "The Society of the Bomb." In their continuing dialectic between the explosive history of the province and ethereal spiritual concerns, McGuckian's poems after 1998 suggest how religion can be both disabling and enabling, constraining and freeing.

McGuckian lost her place of retreat at Ballycastle on the Northern Irish coast, Marconi's Cottage, shortly before her most recent volume, *My Love Has Fared Inland* (2008), was published. She celebrated this dwelling, her home away from Belfast, in the title poem of *Marconi's Cottage*:

> I open my arms
> to your castle-thick walls, I must learn
> to use your wildness when I lock and unlock
> your door weaker than kisses.

> (73)

Despite the "castle-thick walls" of the cottage, she admits its fragility in the fourth line of this stanza about its door. In "The Muse of Electricity," from *My Love Has Fared Inland*, she meditates upon the cottage as a place of refuge and inspiration as she watches light traveling across the interior. The cottage has been a place of both change and constancy as McGuckian restored it over a period of time. Now, viewing it sitting empty, she spies in "the bright, unoccupied room," the winter elements having descended on its contents: "A table is laid / with a bowl of ice; / there is snow on the furniture" (McGuckian 2008:55). This crystalline natural light of winter seems lasting, whereas the addition to the back of the cottage, "with its pirated electricity, its piped Mozart" (55) is unnatural, yet is probably the place where the poet was inspired by the muse of electricity, as the sixth stanza suggests:

> Continual repair, gradual
> piercing of the dark, until finally
> a light shone
> shiny as wine from just one window
> of this strangely unfinished house:
> as if an ordinary person
> has been lost in it.
>
> (56)

With the electricity in the addition to the cottage now off, the speaker feels lost in another way, dislocated from her home away from home. The poem concludes with an image of the speaker sitting "on a cliff / looking out over the bay" (57). McGuckian seems ready to expand her literal and metaphorical horizons even as she mourns her cottage and the inspired work she has done there over the years. For a poet dedicated to charting the vagaries of the domestic life, the poem becomes an elegiac farewell to a particular home even as she looks confidently forward to her own future and the promising future of Northern Ireland.

REFERENCES AND FURTHER READING

Brearton, F. (2000). *The Great War in Irish Poetry: W.B. Yeats to Michael Longley*. Oxford: Oxford University Press.

Brown, T. (2003). "Mahon and Longley: Place and Placelessness." In M. Campbell (Ed.). *The Cambridge Companion to Contemporary Irish Poetry* (pp. 133–48). Cambridge: Cambridge University Press.

Gray, C. (1993). "Medbh McGuckian: Imagery Wrought to its Uttermost." In D. Fleming (Ed.). *Learning the Trade: Essays on W.B. Yeats*

and Contemporary Poetry (pp. 165–77). West Cornwall, CT: Locust Hill Press.

Haughton, H. (2007). *Derek Mahon*. Oxford: Oxford University Press.

Larkin, P. (1989). *Collected Poems*. A. Thwaite (Ed.). New York: Noonday.

Longley, M. (1996). "A Tongue at Play." In T. Curtis (Ed.). *How Poets Work* (pp. 111–21). Bridgend: Seren.

Longley, M. (2007). *Collected Poems*. Winston-Salem, NC: Wake Forest University Press.

Longley, M. (n.d.) "Medbh McGuckian's Poetry." The Michael Longley Collection. Box 25, folder 23. Special Collections Department, Robert W. Woodruff Library, Emory University.

Mahon, D. (1979). *Poems 1962–1978*. Oxford: Oxford University Press.

Mahon, D. (1996). *Journalism: Selected Prose 1970–1995*. Loughcrew, Ireland: Gallery Press.

Mahon, D. (1999). *Collected Poems*. Loughcrew, Ireland: Gallery Press.

Mahon, D. (2005). *Harbour Lights*. Loughcrew, Ireland: Gallery Press.

Mahon, D. (2008). *Life on Earth*. Loughcrew, Ireland: Gallery Press.

McDonald, P. (1997). *Mistaken Identities: Poetry and Northern Ireland*. Oxford: Oxford University Press.

McGuckian, M. (1997). *Selected Poems 1978–1994*. Winston-Salem, NC: Wake Forest University Press.

McGuckian, M. (1998). *Shelmalier*. Loughcrew, Ireland: Gallery Press.

McGuckian, M. (2000). "Women Are Trousers." In Kathryn Kirkpatrick (Ed.). *Border Crossings: Irish Women Writers and National Identities* (pp.157–89). Tuscaloosa: University of Alabama Press.

McGuckian, M. (2001). *Drawing Ballerinas*. Loughcrew, Ireland: Gallery Press.

McGuckian, M. (2002). *The Face of the Earth*. Loughcrew, Ireland: Gallery Press.

McGuckian, M. (2003). *Had I a Thousand Lives*. Loughcrew, Ireland: Gallery Press.

McGuckian, M. (2004). *The Book of the Angel*. Winston-Salem, NC: Wake Forest University Press.

McGuckian, M. (2007). *The Currach Requires No Harbours*. Winston-Salem, NC: Wake Forest University Press.

McGuckian, M. (2008). *My Love Has Fared Inland*. Loughcrew, Ireland: Gallery Press.

Murphy, S. (2003). "Sonnets, Centos, and Long Lines: Muldoon, Paulin, McGuckian, and Carson." In M. Campbell (Ed.). *The Cambridge Companion to Contemporary Irish Poetry* (pp. 189–208). Cambridge: Cambridge University Press.

Russell, R.R. (2003). "Inscribing Cultural Corridors: Michael Longley's Poetic Contribution to Reconciliation in Northern Ireland." *Colby Quarterly*, special issue on Michael Longley, 39.3, 221–40.

Sered, D. (2002). "'By Escaping and [Leaving] a Mark': Authority and the Writing Subject of the Poetry of Medbh McGuckian." *Irish University Review*, 32.2, 273–85.

Wills, C. (1993). *Improprieties: Politics and Sexuality in Northern Irish Poetry*. Oxford: Oxford University Press.

49

Eiléan Ní Chuilleanáin's Work of Witness

Guinn Batten

I

"The hidden" dominates the major critical studies of Eiléan Ní Chuilleanáin's poetry, and has indeed motivated those interpretive strategies that have proved most persuasive. It serves, first, to define her work's most evident characteristic (her poems are obscure, secretive, mysterious); second, to define a central and longstanding trope in her poetry and prose (she is attracted to the cloister, the enclosure, the recessive place or space, that which is locked or locked up or otherwise kept private); and third, to define her strategy for representing – for at once revealing and concealing, exposing, and preserving – what inspires her commitment to feminist and republican traditions that value self-governance.

Ní Chuilleanáin's contributions to those political traditions have been secondary for critics preoccupied with what we might call a "rhetoric" of "absence." As several essays by Irene Gilsenan Nordin suggest, as do similar investigations by Borbalo Farago, Catriona Clutterbuck, Lucy Collins, Helen Emmit, Jeff Holdridge, and Patricia Coughlan, rhetoric has proved compatible with poststructuralist theology, feminist and ecological ethics, and language theory. Central to these studies of Ní Chuilleanáin has been a presumption that "spirit," silence, and secrecy express the "feminine" in this poet's oeuvre. Yet Ní Chuilleanáin, in an interview with Nordin and, earlier, with one of her first and best-known critics Patricia Haberstroh, claims not to be interested in "the spiritual" per se as a phenomenon, including as a locus of "authenticity" or "truth," but rather in how "spirit" is situated in historical and community contexts, such as church ritual and the liturgical calendar. Women in Ní Chuilleanáin's poems serve important roles not only as spiritual but also as historical witnesses of what she calls, in "The Copious Dark," the spectacle of "grand procession":

A Companion to Irish Literature, edited by Julia M. Wright
© 2010 Blackwell Publishing Ltd

The blighted
Shuttered doors in the wall are too many to scan –
As many as the horses in the royal stable, as the lighted
Candles in the grand procession? Who can explain
Why the wasps are asleep in the dark in their numbered holes
And the lights shine all night in the hospital corridors?

(Ní Chuilleanáin 2009)

Within the packed cells and corridors of contemporary social formations, the witnesses in her poems remind us that peaceful coexistence with the neighbor on the other side of a papery partition depends as much on the shuttering as on the opening of doors.

Just as fragile, as Dillon Johnston has observed (Johnston 1989), is the border between the living and the dead in traditions of Irish writing, an observation he updates to suggest that crossings of that border enter into etymological, and historical, contact with sensual spectacle (Johnston 1997). Partitions in Ní Chuilleanáin's poetry are part of a longer history, Johnston notes, that of Baroque art and the wars fought over hidden images and public access to truth in the Reformation and Counter-Reformation (Johnston 1997, 2007). Ní Chuilleanáin's value of "secrets" in religious and other communities revises, he argues, the Baroque philosophy of Leibniz. "In touch with each other," Johnston observes of "monads" in her poems, they are nevertheless "locked, partitioned, or private, or otherwise not sharing the same space" (Johnston 2007:58). Another word for such proximity might be Eamon Grennan's in his insightful study of Ní Chuilleanáin – "parable" (Grennan 1999).

Such parallel existences accommodate Ní Chuilleanáin's insistence on individual autonomy, on the necessity that one should risk imprisonment to make real that autonomy, and, most important of all, on the reality of beauty as an expressive freedom within confinement. In Ní Chuilleanáin's understanding of communities, individuals may exist apart from one another precisely because, within the constraints of the cell, they are at once unique, separate, and independent, even as they are capable, even in prison, of creating changes, affecting other lives through testimony. Ní Chuilleanáin's ethics, aesthetics, and politics of "stricture" as the basis for witness do not require us to unlock such cells. Languages, and cultures, should "keep their sharp edges, their strangeness to one another," she suggests. "I want the alien to go on keeping its distance. ... Even if it is one's own people's past, even if it is a past that has been formally handed to one in trust, as to a member of a diminishing group, it must not become too domestically familiar" (Ní Chuilleanáin 1995a:572–73). The editor of the prison journals of Joseph Campbell, handed to her "in trust" by her mother, Ní Chuilleanáin suggests that the best arbiters of literary art are those who must decide which written texts they will carry with them into prison (Ní Chuilleanáin 2002b).

What women have seen, in prisons and in hospitals, leads to judgment: the "eye of a woman" in the poem "Doubling" "screens" as it "sieves and scores division" (Ní Chuilleanáin 1996:74). What women have said (or found ways rhetorically to make present *without* saying) as a consequence sheds light, Ní Chuilleanáin suggests here as elsewhere, on what theory calls "the gaze," whether in the surveilled prison or sexual predation. It also, however, illuminates, as in "The Copious Dark," the anguish of the nightwatch in the hospital corridor, a topic that appears with special frequency in *The Brazen Serpent*. The difference between these sites of enclosure is the difference, this poet suggests, between sleeping – "the wasps in their dark numbered holes" – and waking.

Awakening to that difference is the measure of an ethical, and political, imagination that is alert to what Ní Chuilleanáin calls in an interview the "unspeakable," what is passed over in silence, the literal translation of the rhetorical device *praeteritio*. Yet language is never more than a failed "attempt to cope with ... the suffering of, for instance, the famine, massacres, or political suffering" (Nordin 2003:76). That very word "cope" suggests, however, to the long-time reader of Ní Chuilleanáin a term (albeit one from a different root) that she often relates to *praeteritio* in Renaissance rhetoric, a term which remains here unstated, perhaps as a deliberate *praeteritio*: the "copious," or the excessive, with which one must, in emergency, cope. There are always, Ní Chuilleanáin says as she continues her response to this question on suffering and Kristevan language, "possible other ways of saying things," including "in other languages" (Nordin 2003:76). For Ní Chuilleanáin, while "copious" language may manifest a maternal fecundity it is also, at the same time, expressive of abjection, the simultaneity or coincidence of feminine nurture and famine, of "private" but also *political* grounds for suffering, and for relief.

We witness these grounds in the example of "a perfect *praeteritio*" Ní Chuilleanáin offers in answering yet another interviewer's question concerning "absent presences" in her work, an example taken from events leading up to the Good Friday Agreement:

> I heard a fine conversation between John Hume and a Unionist spokesman the other day in which Hume said, "It is time to forget the past and move forward," and the Unionist made some grouse. And Hume said, "We could not mention, of course who shot Constable X." ... His definition of forgetting the past was an Irish one. (Ray 1996:73)

If we follow this definition – "the past is there ... in the present" (Ray 1996:73) – we might say that the hidden is Ní Chuilleanáin's insistent present, and she makes it live by realizing the copious, alternative ways of an event's being seen and said by those who were present at (or at least aware of) something sufficiently dangerous either to seek to make it disappear, or to deliver its message, or (through *praeteritio*) to do both at once. What was witnessed almost – but not quite – goes, or more accurately goes *on*, refusing to go away, *because* it remains unspoken in the ongoing task of testimony that links, in effect, the *praeteritio* and the copious in the coexistence of many presences, which are by no means visible simultaneously, or to all equally, in the present. That, she observes, is "the reality" – what she goes on to call "the real thing" (Ray 1996:63, 65).

Chosen carefully, the right words allow one to live next to or beside whatever is too close, to walk "beside," as Ní Chuilleanáin notes in sly revision of Stephen Dedalus in "Sites of Ambush" "not on," Sandymount Strand (Ní Chuilleanáin 1991a:19). As Ní Chuilleanáin writes in "Gloss/*Clós*/Glas," whatever it is that the scholar seeks as "the price of his release" "must be as close / As the word *clós* to its meaning in a Scots courtyard ... As close as the grain in the polished wood, as the finger / Bitten by the string" (Ní Chuilleanáin 2002a:40). Words may bring literally close to hand the deceased, as these lines remind us, for summoned in those words "string" and "finger" is the life's work of Ní Chuilleanáin's sister, a concert violinist whose death the poet mourns also in the poem whose title glosses *praeteritio*, "Passing Over in Silence." For Ní Chuilleanáin, to witness suffering already implies sufferance, the ability to "suffer" the too proximate presence of the deceased, as of the abject or even the abhorred. The neighbor about or to whom one speaks, even in a shared tongue or family history, is also the foreigner or stranger whose death does not stop the work of witness, or the copious possibilities, for better and for worse in communities of survivors, of making the silenced string do work for the living. The persistence of closeness beyond death may never allow the full closure promised at the end of the work of witness. In "Following," in another book opened by the scholar, "her heart's blood is shelved / Between the gatherings / That go to make a book" (Ní Chuilleanáin 1995b:32).

This suggests just how perceptive is Ní Chuilleanáin's writing about secrets, politics, and sexuality concerning the psychodynamics not only of trauma and catastrophe, which includes the "singularity theory" that has followed from Maurice Blanchot's writing, but also, in more openly political theory, of what has been promoted as "the Neighbor" in the work of Slavoj Žižek and of the "state of emergency" in that of Giorgio Agamben. Yet the insights offered by Ní Chuilleanáin's poems into these and other intersubjective complexities of power in modern states that were founded on republican ideals have not been sufficiently recognized. For example, she reminds us in "Borderlands of Irish Poetry" that the very notion of separate "regions" of Irish poetry (that is, the presumption that one writes from "south" or "north" of a border) denies that the border established by "an Act of British parliament," transforms an "event in history" into an ongoing trauma that seems transhistorical and "natural" (Ní Chuilleanáin 1992:25). "We instantly find ourselves in a double life," she writes, "cut in two by a line of bars": the Irish writer is barred or confined, in effect, by a "historical event" regardless of which side of the border she lives on. As a consequence, those who are visibly interned by the British government, and are witnessed as such by northern poets and an international press for which "Irish politics" are defined by such crises, "signal," Ní Chuilleanáin continues, "under a changing light that makes it hard to see which group is locked in, which at large" (Ní Chuilleanáin 1992:25). How, in this situation, does one discern the difference between darkness and light, between political sleep (or dream) and alert wakefulness? The image of "urban paranoia" with which she closes the essay (citing the poet Derry O'Sullivan) offers a series of "distorted strangers" behind the spyhole in a front door called, in honor of a well-known witness, a "Judas" (Ní Chuilleanáin 1992:38, 39).

Because the witness may betray and thus destroy what he has seen, may do harm as well as good as he or she plays a part in a larger historical narrative that must, she suggests, offer some personal agency, Ní Chuilleanáin employs rhetorical strategies that educate her readers in political discernment. For example, she may slyly impede her reader from arriving too quickly, and therefore without a deeper, affective relationship to, the politics not simply of visible histories but, more abstractly, of the phenomenon of the visible – the dynamics of seeing and being seen, as in the "Judas" – that her poems explore. This helps to explain Ní Chuilleanáin's ambivalent fascination with light, but also her refusal to mystify darkness. She is suspicious of claims that "truth" and "historical knowledge" are synonymous, but nevertheless insists on the multiple lives of the historical detail, even when she acknowledges that she distorts them to tell a more truthful story. Her poems may deliberately withhold closure, as Peter Sirr has noted, yet she believes that poems, including her own, may be seen – like the children's stories her mother wrote – as a whole, as a complete or completable aesthetic experience that may lead to personal liberation. The self is not less insistent on its autonomy in her poetry and, in her prose, demands an effacement that is deliberate and is not in every case deployed to express "femaleness." The truths her writings offer are no less urgent because they are made apparent through a rhetoric of florid concealment that requires of the reader, as of the writer, a continuous and active unfolding in the only history where the work of witness is done, and change is possible: the present.

II

"Somebody changes sex in 'Site of Ambush'," Ní Chuilleanáin comments, "I think myself emerging from the shadow of the expected masculine forms" (Williams 1997:43). Her longest, and most overtly political, poem, "Site of Ambush," was published in 1975, the same year as Seamus Heaney's *North*. Yet while the Heaney volume was read by critics as an authentication of place, and through it of violence, "Site of Ambush" "attracted respectful bafflement," as John Kerrigan recalls in the most significant reading to date of Ní Chuilleanáin's Irish and political contexts (Kerrigan 1998:87). Her poetry, compared with certain well-known poems from Northern Ireland, he notes, is characterized by a "scepticism about verse which frames the poet against an authenticating place," even as she herself acknowledges her deep roots in a Cork landscape and heritage (Kerrigan 1998:86). Kerrigan situates this politically ambitious early work by Ní Chuilleanáin within a tradition of Cork poetry that is both pre-modern and republican in its clandestine tendencies. He believes Ní Chuilleanáin reproduces this tradition by hiding or "withholding" "topicality," to "disperse" across geological time the "significance of the event" that is the poem's historical and political basis: an IRA attack at Kilmichael in November 1920 that was one of the major events (some historians call it the turning point) in the Irish War for Independence (86, 87). "There's something about that country," Kerrigan cites Ní Chuilleanáin as having said, "which has never been violated completely" (85). As Thomas McCarthy, a Munster poet with a republican family history, has noted, "it is not possible to read ["Site of Ambush"] and remain unconnected to a revolutionary history and a territory raked by guerrilla warfare. ... a universal place of cruelty and insurrection. ... Ní Chuilleanáin's instincts are fed from the broad myth-kitty of revolutionary Cork" (McCarthy 2007:235–36). Kerrigan concludes that in the sequence she "uses indeterminate settings, mythical voyages and legends to make the burden of history metaphysical," including the burden of family history (Kerrigan 1998:87).

The land itself in this poem imitates a filtering, sedimenting memory, engaged in the work of accepting "death" by effacing (literally) the individual death, notably in the second section "Narration." This work of natural process, extended through geological time, is in itself an agent (perhaps echoing the agency of "Autumn" in John Keats' ode) as it conducts – in a landscape made palpably silent as if still shocked by the intrusion of human violence – the work of mourning. The dead "rust" and "soften," becoming as they dissolve "light between long weeds," "separated for good" in "water too thick and deep to see" (Ní Chuilleanáin 1991a:15). Through verb tense Ní Chuilleanáin situates this work in the cheerful present, as though the past were simply a bad dream ("the lorry now is soft as last night's dream," "A watch vibrates alone in the filtering light; / Flitters of hair wave at the sun" [15]). The reader, with the poet, inhabits that place in an act of eye-witness, literally at ground zero, that nevertheless makes us feel also that we are absent or apart from it and, after the fact, awakening from historical nightmare to an enlightened present.

Yet it is precisely the "softening" work of natural time that, on re-reading, provokes the deepest sorrow here: the edges that distinguish individuals and things from one another, keeping them proximate but distant, dissolve into anonymity and oblivion. We begin to celebrate the pained resistance of the single, "upright femur" that refuses to lie down in darkness with the dead because it refuses to cease to suffer (Ní Chuilleanáin 1991a:16). With its resistance we "ache," we "can feel the tough roots close / Gently over bone"; "Only the flesh such strict / Embraces knows" (16). Those lines alone might lead us to question just how "metaphysical" the "burden of history" actually becomes in this poem, particularly its family history: the fatal illness of the poet's father whose "reminiscences" of republican military campaigns in part inspired it. (A recent poem "On Lacking the Killer Instincts" returns to that topic [Ní Chuilleanáin 2007].)

Alert to what natural process may not heal, we return to the prosopopoeia that opens the first section, significantly called "Reflection": what was swallowed, through an act of violence, into the reflecting surface of historical "perspective," is the insistent return of a still unappeased host, "republicanism." Its presence, just beneath the reflective surface of the ordinary present, has indeed made it difficult to create a "patient republic / Of the spider and the fly" where life might be peaceful because "natural" in the Irish Republic (1991a:21). When the speaker proclaims to "reflection," "You will devour them all," "The houses, flowers, the salt and ships," she is addressing, and acknowledging the power of, the republican ghosts reflected in this watery partition between the past and the present that turns historical witness into the immortality of myth (14). How can the poet revive, for her own purposes, the republican dream, now softening and decaying beneath the surface, in a present that seems suspended in cold pastoral, the patient but also mortifying delay of that dream's resurrection? Time, in the section titled "Narration," occurs as a crisis at a crossroads, an ambush that takes place in the "synchronised" time of "heartbeats" of "enemy commanders" (15). That crisis ends – ostensibly – with the erection of memorials at the end of plowshares (literally with an "upright" "spade" "swapped," the poet noted in a recent e-mail conversation, "by the emigrating rural labourer for the navvy's shovel on the English building-site"), the "upright" masculine "minute hand" of excavation converted into the moment's monument, "time at a stand" (16). That standstill arrests violence, but without the work of reanimation; beyond "reflection" alone, it also arrests the republic's growth.

That growth resumes in the visionary, even apocalyptic, time of the poem's climax. In contrast to that crossroad of crisis, followed by the stasis of memorial crosses, revival happens in the final stanza, where life resumes as feminine, the "criss-crossed" "symmetrical breasts of [the] hills" (Ní Chuilleanáin 1991a:21). A deaf boy, who dies seeking water from a well when the ambush begins, is resurrected as a girl who "came back from the well," restored to the process of living, who in turn saves, literally, the day (21). Through an act of emotional and physical transformation, she reclaims the significance of that historical crossroads neither naturally nor gradually but in the performatives of lines that conclude with the "strict embrace" of an event too important to surrender to historical oblivion: "When the child comes back / Soaked from her drowning / Lay fast hold of her / And do not let go" (20). Metamorphosis ensues, with "A muscular snake / Spidery crawling / Becoming a bird / Then an empty space … Shivering naked / The child exhausted / Comes back from her sleep" (20–21). A boy who was deaf is now a girl who is awake, because something has changed. But what? An interviewer has asked Ní Chuilleanáin, "Are you yourself the shape-changer here? Are you the holder and the held? The instructor and the performer?" (Williams 1997:42). Ní Chuilleanáin replies affirmatively for, as she states, it is she who assumes her sex in this act of historical witness, metamorphosis, and reclamation, her "strict embrace" of historical memory.

Those words from "Site of Ambush" – "strict" and "embrace" – are in turn revived, in somewhat different context, in the poem published three decades later, "Gloss/*Clós*/ Glas." The femur in "Site of Ambush" continues to refuse to lie down, and the sympathetic flesh that in "Site of Ambush" offered the only vehicle through which one may witness, or "know," "such strict / Embraces" (Ní Chuilleanáin 1991a:16) is now felt, in the later poem, as "close to the bone," a fingerbone "bitten" by the string's closeness (Ní Chuilleanáin 2002a:40). (See also "Autun": "no music but the skeleton tune / the bones make humming" [Ní Chuilleanáin 2002a:36]). The "repeated note" of the "hairs" on the violin that – recalling those of the dead that "flitter" in the stream in "Site of Ambush" – are "bent," proximate but distant, restore the two words from "Site of Ambush": "Two words / Closer to the bone than the words I was so proud of, / *Embrace* and *strict* to describe the twining of bone and flesh" (Ní Chuilleanáin 2002a:40).

III

The girl in "Site of Ambush" who, returned from the well, is embraced, "held fast," by the speaker suggests a myth, common in fairy tales but also in Edmund Spenser, for which Ní Chuilleanáin has acknowledged a special fondness: the quest in which a girl disguised as a boy can return, once her task is achieved, unmasked as herself because she has restored the life of the beloved, and therefore her own. The girl sent on such a quest, like Spenser's Britomart, must save the object that came to her in a vision in order to possess it, but the task in tales of journeys to wells may simply be set for inexplicable reasons by a formidable female as in Ní Chuilleanáin's poem "The Water Journey." So where might we locate the historical "realism" we typically associate with the political poem for this writer who admits that she "clings" to the mysteries of "romance almost as tightly as to history"?

The literary and political traditions embraced by Ní Chuilleanáin, from the myths of prehistory to the romance tales her own mother wrote, have always, Ní Chuilleanáin frequently reminds us, included women not only as witnesses but also as prophets (a category in which Ní Chuilleanáin includes Oscar Wilde's mother, Speranza, who offers, she notes, her own feminist version of the well journey). "Witches, viragos, martyrs, hermits – I do admit their humanity and their femininity; I do not think they have dissolved their women's bodies because they may be eight feet tall or dressed in knightly armour" (Ní Chuilleanáin 1995a:574). (What better form of concealment than armor, one might ask?) These traditions that Ní Chuilleanáin brings into the present include women who, as writers and as fictional characters, shaped for their own purposes of sexual independence the courtly love poetry of *Dánta Grá* (see CHAPTER 3, THE RECEPTION AND ASSIMILATION OF CONTINENTAL LITERATURE); Eibhlín Dubh Ní Chonaill's transformation of the female keening formula "from an instrument of communal acceptance of the inevitable, to an assertion of personal freedom"; and Maria Edgeworth's insistence that domesticity breeds secrets that keep women confined to their homes and to a troubled past (Ní Chuilleanáin 1985a:119).

Such women have energetically exploited the very resource that troubles Eavan Boland in her essay "Writing the Political Poem in Ireland" – the hiding of the speaker behind "the powers of language he or she can generate" (Boland 1995:487). Yet the alternative, to be suspicious of power without stealing, with Promethean courage, from the powerful the language of intimidation, not only reinforces the locks of victimization but also, Ní Chuilleanáin insists, promotes speaking and writing that can only be dull because it insists on the authority of what it already knows: the view of the Crucifixion, or the superstructure, from the perspective of the base, whether what is exalted is the washing of Jesus' feet or the scrubbing of a floor (Ní Chuilleanáin

1995a:579). Ní Chuilleanáin, in an essay published simultaneously with that just cited by Boland, argues that the work of witness for the woman writer in the Renaissance – and by implication today – "survives," and offers strategies for survival, in the *"Lives and Diaries"* of "the oddest women, geniuses or martyrs or lunatics or women with power" (Ní Chuilleanáin 1995a:574). "It is the ability of the Renaissance reader to be carried and mastered by rhetoric that staggers me," Ní Chuilleanáin notes later in this essay, "as language is shown with teeth and using them" (579).

Only an insistence on the power, and not simply the authenticity or the availability to the dispossessed of an alternative language of "care" – the insistence, she notes, of "the Renaissance humanists and their successors … that language is not like any other medium; its prime feature, even for the artist, is its meaning, its power to persuade and change, its relation to truth and right" – can offer full resources, Ní Chuilleanáin believes, to the poet whose community suffers (Ní Chuilleanáin 1995a:577). The visible forms of power under which it suffers may, in extremity, include the individual's bodily exposure to public view in the act of capital punishment, "the routine display of segments of the bodies of the Queen's enemies" that was daily witnessed by the early modern Irish "in the population centres of their own country" (572). Without a powerful language, the witness, Ní Chuilleanáin continues, does not have the capacity to "flash out into articulate and it would seem poetic speech in defiance of the rhetoric of power surrounding her" (572). There is a difference, this example leads us to see, between "seeing" as simple "recognition" of what one is looking at, or looking for, and seeing with the "flash" that throws into sharp relief the horror one Renaissance *cailleach* observed in Spenser's time, the old woman to whom Ní Chuilleanáin refers as having been granted "poetic speech" through her fury. What this hag figure witnessed, the drawing and quartering of the Irish political martyr for whom she once cared, Ní Chuilleanáin reminds us, gave her words the power to reach us through those of a poet, Spenser, who did not know her language (Ní Chuilleanáin 1995a:572).

In her own writing process, Ní Chuilleanáin has said in an interview, language extends, and refracts, a precipitating ethics: it contributes to the structuring of the "moral or political position" from which her poems "almost always start," gathering "back again into mythology" that initial, contingent position because "at a certain point language takes over" (Nordin 2003:77). That, she concludes, "does expose the whole business of the nature of language," and, by implication, what, and whom, poetic language changes: the poet herself and, through her use of a common language, others (Nordin 2003:77). Ní Chuilleanáin's understanding of the role of language in ethical and political agency is, as we can see by these examples, enriched but also complicated by her sophisticated relationship, as a professor of early modern literature at Trinity College Dublin, to rhetoric and to non-English languages. As a longtime resident of an island divided by a still recent border, as a frequent traveler across many such politically divisive borders in Europe, and as a professor of a few centuries in literary history when such borders stimulated cultural expression even as they provoked wars, she repeatedly tells us that proximity may promote, rather than erode or eradicate, barriers between individuals, and between communities, even as it enables exchange and, therefore, change.

These barriers include those of sexual difference and religious affiliation that, separately and in combination, beyond Ireland but also within its borders, produce particular challenges for the work of witnessing (the plural is important) Irish histories, including the troubled histories of the Magdalene institutions that have figured prominently in Ní Chuilleanáin's poems. On the one hand Ní Chuilleanáin justly insists – in poems but also in such essays as her introduction and contribution her edited *Irish Women: Image and Achievement* – that women are not simply *seen*: they are not incapable of reacting to the realities that impinge on their so-called "hidden lives," making them subject to an intrusive male and perspectival gaze as in her poems "Daniel Grose" or "Man Watching a Woman." Women are themselves fully able to *see* what she calls in "The Real Thing," but not without qualification, "the real thing, the one free foot kicking / Under the white sheet of history" (Ní Chuilleanáin 1995b:16). Such seeing sometimes sees also the necessity of the sheet. If, as Ní Chuilleanáin has suggested in relation to this poem, women's bodies and the relics of saints are both subject to – and hidden by the rules and regulations of – the church, and if both are sustained by prurience and perhaps, indeed, fetishism, then the task of the witness is not simply to expose. Disenchantment does not in itself redress injustice, and indeed can lead to a reforming zealot's pleasure in spurning the image, in the very refusal of visual satisfaction.

If "woman" is not only to be capable of *seeing* but also to be capable of *saying* what she has seen, and through that persuade others to change the present, then image and myth may be needed as well as truth, and language as well as dialectics, as Ní Chuilleanáin notes in an essay on the Renaissance humanists Erasmus and Sir Thomas More (1988). Yet even Mary Magdalene, who figures largely in Ní Chuilleanáin's poems and scholarly work, if she is to have access to the power of rhetoric, must herself be subject, no less than male speakers or writers, to the constraints of language. While often the women, old and young, in Ní Chuilleanáin's poems seem to have access to histories that have secret authority *because* they have been ignored, nevertheless they do not possess, merely by virtue of gender, greater access to an "immediate" (and therefore "real") "thing" through a relationship to it that bypasses, because enhanced by "bodily" intuition or "feeling," a mediating linguistic structure.

Mary Magdalene, Ní Chuilleanáin notes in an interview, is on the one hand "the patron saint of preachers" (Nordin 2003:79). On the other, "there is all this extraordinary bodily imagery about it, which is probably not Mary Magdalene at all – the hair and the weeping and all that." Rather than reconcile these images Ní Chuilleanáin celebrates their multiple possible trajectories as they continue to live in local stories of the saint. There are several women who contribute to the ideal image, "Mary Magdalene," she observes as a historian, and, at the same time, there are multiple narratives associated with those lives. As she continues, "I like the story [of the saint] because I like Medieval narrative, the way it goes on, and on, and on, it says 'and then, and then, and then, and then'" (79). The story's, or stories', absence of closure does not diminish, she insists, the existence of "Mary Magdalene" as "an important symbol as the woman speaking, as the woman surviving, and I have to say, because of the long hair, there is quite a strong identification" (79). Ní Chuilleanáin's acknowledged identification with a feminine part-object does not preclude, we should note, an identification with its *relationship* to "speech," but neither does it make "hair" synonymous with speech (79).

If that hair becomes a fetish for subsequent believers, and Ní Chuilleanáin humorously counts herself among the fetishists, she also suggests, in "St Mary Magdalene Preaching at Marseilles," that having become "at the end of her life ... all hair" this patron saint of preachers possesses also another residue of bodily process: "a voice / Breaking loose from the loose red hair, / The secret shroud of her skin" (Ní Chuilleanáin 1991b:33). It is how these now discrete entities, in effect, leave the home, or tomb, of the self, abandoning its "secret shroud," that they perform and fulfill her life-giving mission. "She wanders," we are told, in the strange city's "shaded squares," where the threat, but also perhaps the excitement, of the unknown raises "hairs on the back of her wrists" (33). Fully alive to what she may yet take pleasure in witnessing, even at the end of her life, she makes witty analogies (boys skimming prostrate on carts are "like breathless fish"), takes visual pleasure in the "shining traps" for light that "clear" waters provide, until she recognizes in what she is witnessing an objective correlative for that damp hair that – through a single, unanticipated act of compassion for a foot-sore Jesus – led her own feet to carry his teachings (through, make no mistake, *her* words and *her* encounters) on a mission of conversion to the masses that is mimicked, in a remarkable conceit for the suddenness but also the naturalness of mass change: "Not a hook or a comma of ice / Holding them, the water-weeds / Lying collapsed like hair / At the turn of the tide; / They wait for the right time, then / Flip all together their thousands of sepia feet" (33).

Alert to the correspondences in the living world to what she had witnessed all those years ago with her own body, Mary Magdalene in this stunning poem demonstrates that autonomy and courage are required of the woman who witnesses if she is to convert those who did not see with their own eyes the damaged body, or its emergence, beyond the sealed darkness of the tomb, into full presence, restored in a world beyond touch – but not beyond *vision*. Closeness may not bring grief's closure, but faith in (and to) its truth in fact allows, here as in strikingly similar lines in "Gloss/*Clós*/Glas," a female presence to emerge precisely when there is no longer a gendered pronoun to possess, or to convey, what was witnessed. "Like weeds in water" the rags of language in the later poem are revived, as in the earlier, in an act of plural change: weeds "turn with the tide" (Ní Chuilleanáin 2002a:40). Not the female preacher but, in this case, a male scholar, rejuvenated by his own journey to the well of words, arrives at the end of his mission: he "reaches the language that has no word for *his*, / No word for *hers*, and is brought up sudden / Like a boy in a story faced with a small locked door. / Who is that he can hear panting on the other side? / The steam of her breath is turning the locked lock green" (40). "*Glas*" is the Irish word for "green."

Ní Chuilleanáin's poems inspire, and reward, attentiveness to the miraculous dimension of abject life that may be passed over in silence in more than one language. Such lives are close, or proximate, to perceived reality but they set askew, rather than confirm, what seems otherwise to be common or shared experience. As in the linguistic phenomenon called "doubling," in which verbal elision impedes understanding, the *praeteritio* provokes discrimination, and proliferates diction, precisely because it withholds what is needed to hear or see meaning directly, even as it evokes what is unseen: "I see I cannot see ... is it he / Or she, native, invader?" (Ní Chuilleanáin 1996). That eye may become itself an object of fascination, or even obsession, as in the poem "From an Apparition," which opens "Where did I see her, through / Which break in the cloud, the woman / In profile, a great eye like a scared horse?" (Ní Chuilleanáin 2002a:23). There could hardly be a more perfect image of the very way in which "images" of "woman" are created by cultures, but this feminine apparition possesses agency: she is engaged in simultaneous, but different, acts with her two hands. One is performing music, but silently, "the fingers landing precisely as if / They stopped notes on a lute," while "it seemed / That her other hand protected something fragile" (23). A wild creature ("she half sprang to her feet"), she is also a prisoner, "a captive warding off," blocking from within the view of the speaker beyond the window with "a long swathe of silk" (23). Like the silk that is spun by another woman in "Vierge Ouvrante" who is subjected to a gaze that, even in compassion, violates (Ní Chuilleanáin 1995b:36–37), this woman's use of textile is textual, and it is *performative*, and it closes the eye of the witness by closing the "screen that sieves and scores division" ("Doubling"), her "silk text building against the glass" until "the pane darkened / And closed like a big fringed eyelid into sleep" (23). As in the "sheet" that closes our view to the "real thing" in the earlier poem, "sleep" in this later poem closes a feminine interior to an intrusive gaze. What began as a single image has, through that image's own movement, multiplied into copious redundancy (one eye staring at another) and indeed called into question the very status – and originary *place* – of the organ of witness and the question that its gaze first engendered: "where?" (23).

The apparition may be not *what* was seen – "through / Which break in the cloud" (23) – but precisely the evanescence of that movement of "breaking," of clouds seeming to unveil a hidden truth or meaning when, in fact, they are simply (with all of the affective meaning that the verb entails) *breaking*. What happens between *seeing* and *saying* is, as Ní Chuilleanáin observes in another poem, the observer's capacity to "know how things begin to happen" but that knowledge does not tell us in advance that, or when, or even with what results the happening ends: indeed what happens may end at the very moment of happening. Unlike the well that is opened by the "sharp-eyed girl" in a poem titled "The Apparition" – its miracle becoming the ordinary commerce of "every Friday at noon the same; / The trains were full of people in the evenings / Going north with gallons of sour water" (Ní Chuilleanáin 1991:49) – the present may be copious, but in Ní Chuilleanáin's poems it may be for that reason fleeting (Ní Chuilleanáin 1991:51).

What happens without our acknowledgment (if not necessarily without unconscious experience) may be, as in the darkening sun that leads to miracle in "The Apparition" or the "reflection" in "Site of Ambush" that swallows both sun and moon a source of power, but it may also be politically a dead end. Her own work is, as Ní Chuilleanáin characterizes it, "oblique and obscure, and ... very unlikely to make people vote for divorce, or the Good Friday Agreement" (Nordin 2003:77). Obliquity, obscurity: Good Friday, which in an interview Ní Chuilleanáin pointedly associates with a dialectic of light and darkness – "too much light killing the image" – she says she particularly values as a day when winter's darkness seems alleviated by the shared "communal expression" of a funeral, the ritual passing through darkness to resurrection by torchlight, as she once witnessed in Italy (Ray 1996:64). That remembered intimacy, which was shattered by the untimely glare of a photographer's flash, is closely linked for Ní Chuilleanáin with "the question of the unthinkable, and the things which cannot be said" (Ray 1996:64), which include whatever happens to the woman in "Vierge Ouvrante" (a title that at the same time gestures, perhaps not entirely with irony, to the promise of the Virgin's opened womb) and also the horrors of a public execution, such as the *cailleach* witnessed, when the state exercises its power to declare as criminal, and to open the bodies of, those who challenge its authority.

Those communities whose dissenting religious practices, when visible, incur the wrath of power must take particular care in speaking, learning to relate to one another through strategies of *not* speaking. But to fail to speak may in itself create suffering, notably (as Ní Chuilleanáin reminds us) in states, as in families, where the past is prematurely dismissed. Faithful witness, she has said, requires that the writer put feeling into words, even if that includes anger, or shame. "I found that I wrote a number of poems about family secrets, the idea that I am constantly being asked to tell this story and I do not necessarily want to tell it" (Haberstroh 1994:67). Yet if we do not witness what she calls the "truly shocking" images, the "unspeakable" among which she includes the sickroom but also the Crucifixion, for "they're real," she insists, "they are the real thing" (Haberstroh 1994:65), then how can we understand when we are in the presence of "joy, music, mystery, freedom?" (Ní Chuilleanáin 1995a:575).

While it is anger towards her mother that, the poet has said, in part inspires "The Witness," and dissatisfaction with her maternal grandmother's lack of feeling as a witness that also inspires that poem (see the interviews with Nordin and Haberstroh), "joy" is the strong and positive emotion Ní Chuilleanáin proclaims to characterize what her mother's family, and her mother in particular, gave to her. Joy, with "mystery" and "freedom," she localizes in a picture of Botticelli's *Primavera* (that hung, she wryly notes, where one might have expected "an icon of the Sacred Heart" in an Irish Catholic family). Such presents (so to speak) from her personal history enabled this poet, as her mother lay dying in a well-lit hospital room, to remember when they together witnessed a moment – the Assumption of the mother of Jesus through a sun-struck image within, or rather *on*, a cathedral cupola in Parma. In this poem Ní Chuilleanáin and her mother, flooded by the light admitted into darkness by the ceiling's opening, stepped "Back, as the painter longed to / While his arm swept in the large strokes. / We saw the work entire" (Ní Chuilleanáin 1995b:10).

The poem, "Fireman's Lift," continues, "This is what love sees, that angle: / The crick in the branch loaded with fruit" (1995b:10). Johnston has associated this work of seeing with that of mourning, a necessary separation or distance from the dead that paradoxically enables love to live in the present, an art in which the poem instructs the reader:

> To step back from this poem, as the poet longs to – to paraphrase "Fireman's Lift" – we may see the work entire, recognizing that it raises ultimate questions, such as "where do the dead reside?" ... Through the medium of art, we can perceive that they exist separate from, and coterminous with, ourselves, as if in an architectural space inaccessible to us, but perceptible through art. (Johnston 2007:57)

"Copiousness" is a feminine "crick" rather than a patrilineal branch in the family tree, a maternal source of generation that is a side narrative to that of temptation, the Tree of Knowledge, and of original sin in Genesis. Like the "torn end of the serpent" in "The Real Thing," which "Tilts the lace edge of the veil," this Tree of Life revives the daughter, herself the fruit of that particular crick. She, herself, she wryly suggests, might be experiencing a crick in her neck through such sustained, upward seeing: "testing those muscles in the neck," the image is "just out of our reach," witnessing from a child's admiring perspective the "full-grown, sexual body." Once again that body can be seen whole, and seen *as* whole, as what "belongs to the parent, exists on a heroic scale, exercising the neck muscles" (Ní Chuilleanáin 1995a:577, 575). Glimpsing such fruit beneath garments disheveled by the exigencies of the sickroom, the speaker sees it as beautiful.

This is perhaps how Mary Magdalene herself saw, as the "visionary" Ní Chuilleanáin admires, the unspeakable as beautiful. That this poet would herself be able to witness in life's final mystery both "joy" and "freedom" does not surprise Ní Chuilleanáin's longtime readers. For she prepared us with a declarative, insistent in its use of the first person plural and of four spondees, that concludes an earlier poem likewise haunted by what is left by a mother who, like Mary Magdalene, prefers travel (and words) to staying silent and in one place: "We live here now" (Ní Chuilleanáin 1991b:24).

References and Further Reading

Batten, G. (2003). "Boland, McGuckian, Ní Chuilleanáin, and the Body of the Nation." In M. Campbell (Ed.). *The Cambridge Companion to Contemporary Irish Poetry* (pp. 169–88). Cambridge: Cambridge University Press.

Batten, G. (2007). "'The World Not Dead After All': Eiléan Ní Chuilleanáin's Work of Revival." *Irish University Review*, 37.1, 1–21.

Boland, E. (1995). "Writing the Political Poem in Ireland." *The Southern Review*, 31.3, 485–98.

Clutterbuck, C. (2007). "Good Faith in Religion and Art: The Later Poetry of Eileán Ní Chuilleanáin." *Irish University Review*, 37.1, 131–56.

Collins, L. (2003). "'Why didn't they ask the others?' Resisting Disclosure in the Poetry of Eileán Ní Chuilleanáin." In M. Böss and E. Maher (Eds). *Engaging Modernity: Readings of Irish Politics, Culture, and Literature at the Turn of the Century* (pp. 169–81). Dublin: Veritas.

Coughlan, P. (2007). "'No lasting fruit at all': Containing, Recognition, and Relinquishing in *The Girl who Married the Reindeer.*" *Irish University Review*, 37.1, 157–77.

Emmit, H. (2000). "'The One Free Foot Kicking under the White Sheet of History': Eileán Ní Chuilleanáin's Uncanny Landscapes." *Women's Studies*, 29, 477–94.

Grennan, E. (1999). *Facing the Music: Irish Poetry in the Twentieth Century*. Omaha: Creighton University Press.

Haberstroh, P.B. (1994). "An Interview with Eileán Ní Chuilleanáin." *Canadian Journal of Irish Studies*, 20.2, 63–74.

Haberstroh, P.B. (1996). *Women Creating Women: Contemporary Irish Women Poets*. Syracuse: Syracuse University Press.

Holdridge, J. (2007). "'A Snake Pouring over the Ground': Nature and the Sacred in Eileán Ní Chuilleanáin." *Irish University Review*, 37, 115–30.

Johnston, D. (1989). "Next to Nothing: Uses of the Otherworld in Modern Irish Literature." In J. Brophy and E. Grennan (Eds). *New Irish Writing* (pp. 121–40). Boston: Twayne.

Johnston, D. (1997). "'Our bodies' eyes and writing hands': Secrecy and Sensuality in Ní Chuilleanáin's Baroque Art." In A. Bradley and M. Valiulis (Eds). *Gender and Sexuality in Modern Ireland* (pp. 187–211). Amherst: University of Massachusetts Press.

Johnston, D. (2007). "'Hundred-pocketed time': Ní Chuilleanáin's Baroque Spaces." *Irish University Review*, 37.1, 53–67.

Kerrigan, J. (1998). "Hidden Ireland: Eileán Ní Chuilleanáin and Munster Poetry." *Critical Quarterly*, 40.4, 76–100.

McCarthy, T. (2007). "'We could be in any city': Eileán Ní Chuilleanáin and Cork." *Irish University Review*, 37.1, 230–43.

Ní Chuilleanáin, E. (1984). "Time, Place and the Congregation in Donne's Sermons." In J. Scattergood (Ed.). *Literature and Learning in Medieval and Renaissance England: Essays Presented to Fitzroy Pyle* (pp. 197–216). Blackrock: Irish Academic Press.

Ní Chuilleanáin, E. (1985a). "Introduction." In E. Ní Chuilleanáin (Ed.). *Irish Women: Image and Achievement* (pp. 1–11). Dublin: Arlen House.

Ní Chuilleanáin, E. (1985b). "Women as Writers: Dánta Grá to Maria Edgeworth." In E. Ní Chuilleanáin (Ed.). *Irish Women: Image and Achievement* (pp. 111–26). Dublin: Arlen House.

Ní Chuilleanáin, E. (1988). "The Debate between Thomas More and William Tyndale, 1528–33: Ideas on Literature and Religion." *Journal of Ecclesiastical History*, 39.3, 382–411.

Ní Chuilleanáin, E. (1991a). *The Second Voyage* (1977). Rev. edn. Winston-Salem: Wake Forest University Press.

Ní Chuilleanáin, E. (1991b). *The Magdalene Sermon and Earlier Poems*. Winston-Salem: Wake Forest University Press.

Ní Chuilleanáin, E. (1992). "Borderlands of Irish Poetry." In E. Andrews (Ed.). *Contemporary Irish Poetry: A Collection of Critical Essays* (pp. 25–40). Basingstoke: Macmillan.

Ní Chuilleanáin, E. (1995a). "Acts and Monuments of an Unelected Nation: The *Cailleach* Writes about the Renaissance." *The Southern Review*, 31, 570–80.

Ní Chuilleanáin, E. (1995b). *The Brazen Serpent*. Winston-Salem: Wake Forest University Press.

Ní Chuilleanáin, E. (1996). "Doubling." *Eire-Ireland*, 31.1–2, 74.

Ní Chuilleanáin, E. (2001). "Introduction." In E. Ní Chuilleanáin (Ed.). *"As I was Among the Captives": Joseph Campbell's Prison Diary, 1922–1923* (pp. 1–15). Cork: Cork University Press.

Ní Chuilleanáin, E. (2002a). *The Girl Who Married the Reindeer*. Winston-Salem: Wake Forest University Press.

Ní Chuilleanáin, E. (2002b). "Who Needs Critics?" *Cyphers*, 53, 53–4.

Ní Chuilleanáin, E. (2003). "Speranza, an Ancestor for a Woman Poet in 2000." In E. Ní Chuilleanáin (Ed.). *The Wilde Legacy* (pp. 17–34). Dublin: Four Courts.

Ní Chuilleanáin, E. (2006). "Daddies and Telephones: The Wild and the Tame in

Children's Literature." In M.S. Thompson and C. Keenan (Eds). *Treasure Islands: Studies in Children's Literature* (pp. 187–99). Dublin: Four Courts.

Ní Chuilleanáin, E. (2007). "On Lacking the Killer Instinct." In A. Fowler (Ed.). *The March Hare Anthology* (pp. 206–07). St John's: Breakwater Books.

Ní Chuilleanáin, E. (2009). "The Copious Dark." *Poetry Ireland Review*, 97, 14.

Nordin, I.G. (2003). "The Weight of Words: An Interview with Eileán Ní Chuilleanáin." *Canadian Journal of Irish Studies*, 28.2–29.1, 75–83.

Nordin, I.G. (2007). "'Like a Shadow in Water': Phenomenology and Poetics in the Work of Eileán Ní Chuilleanáin." *Irish University Review*, 37.1, 98–114.

Nordin, I.G. (2009). *Reading Eilean Ni Chuilleanain, a Contemporary Irish Poet: The Element of the Spiritual*. Lewiston, NY: Mellen.

Ray, K. (1996). "Interview with Eileán Ní Chuilleanáin." *Eire-Ireland*, 31.1–2, 62–73.

Sirr, P. (1995). "'How things begin to happen': Notes on Eileán Ní Chuilleanáin and Medbh McGuckian." *The Southern Review*, 31.3, 450–67.

Williams, L. (1997). "'The stone recalls its quarry': An Interview with Eileán Ní Chuilleanáin." In S. Shaw Sailer (Ed.). *Representing Ireland: Gender, Class, Nationality* (pp. 29–44). Gainesville: University Press of Florida.

50

Eavan Boland's Muse Mothers

Heather Clark

Eavan Boland's poetry and prose have, for several decades, been propelled by a desire to untangle the complex relationship between woman, history, and the Irish nation. In Boland's work, Ireland's fractured political body finds its analogy in a pair of quarreling lovers; dark interior spaces symbolize the shadowy place of women in Irish history; classical female heroines illuminate contemporary feminist struggles; and images of rape are linked to women's political silence. Boland's treatment of these themes has always been bold and assured, even, at times, polemical. She has struggled to confront an insular Irish male poetic tradition that often portrayed women as passive objects – be it Mother Ireland or Cathleen ni Houlihan – who represented both the purity and suffering of colonial Ireland. These male poets, says Boland, made little room for ordinary women as active subjects: Irish poetry, she famously wrote, was one "in which you could have a political murder, but not a baby" (Boland 1995a:204). Boland has sought to revise this tradition, and make room for those women whose voices have been silenced over time – women who died of fever in a maternity ward, prostitutes who worked at the British garrisons, young emigrants bound for a life of domestic service in Boston and New York, and finally, the postwar suburban mother who stands in her garden at dusk and calls her daughter home. These are the figures, Boland insists, who have always existed "outside history," and whose absence she seeks to atone for and redress.

Guinn Batten has called Boland "probably Ireland's most influential feminist" (Batten 2003:169), while Peggy O'Brien has written that she is "the one Irish, female poet with an international, particularly American, reputation" (O'Brien 1999:xvi). Albert Gelpi has called her "the first great woman poet in the history of Irish poetry" (Gelpi 1999:210). Few dispute that Boland's work, in its admirable confrontation with an outmoded political and historical paradigm, has been a major force in opening

A Companion to Irish Literature, edited by Julia M. Wright
© 2010 Blackwell Publishing Ltd

up the parameters of Irish poetry. But her work has, at times, stirred controversy. Yeats famously said, "We make out of the quarrel with others, rhetoric, but of the quarrel with ourselves, poetry" (Yeats 2000:285). Boland's critics suggest that she has engaged too exclusively in a quarrel with others rather than a quarrel with the self – that her poetry too often resembles rhetoric. Catriona Clutterbuck argues that Boland criticism has been "particularly outspoken" and "negative" (Clutterbuck 1999:276), a condition that Jody Allen Randolph reads in light of "an intellectual refusal to allow women in Ireland to come to the center of Irish poetry and take up their proper roles in redefining it" (Allen Randolph 1999b:207). Clutterbuck notes that Irish critics in particular tend to read her poems "as being, first and foremost, disguised political tracts," and points out that what rankles these critics is an "underlying suspicion that a Boland industry prompting mimetic criticism is flourishing: that is, that the poet's own carefully planted commentary on her poetic practice may be surfacing as other critics' 'autonomously' developed critical insight on the poems themselves" (see Clutterbuck 1999:276, 277, and *passim* for a summary of Boland's critical standing in this period). Edna Longley, for example, has said that Boland "has been too easily allowed to set the terms of her own reception" (Longley 1995:764).

Yet Boland's poetry has been too easily dismissed, just as it has been too easily praised. While some of her poetry is indeed polemical, her best work is as lyrically satisfying as that of her Irish contemporaries. These poems often center on motherhood, a subject Boland has almost single-handedly restored to twentieth-century poetry (with help from Sylvia Plath). While these poems celebrate the joys of mothering, they also chart the widening distance between mother and child as the child grows. They are, on the surface, the least overtly political poems in her oeuvre, yet, as Andrew Auge has noted, they present a powerful revision of traditional female iconography in the Irish poem; Auge has also discussed Boland's tropes of motherhood in light of Kristeva's understanding of the mother as a "split subject" (Auge 2004:122). Boland's tropes of motherhood serve as a Trojan horse of sorts: while appearing to conform to familiar depictions of the feminine domestic, these poems in fact work to destabilize female nationalist imagery. This is because, as Boland writes, "Political poetry operates in the corridor between rhetoric and reality. It is an ineffective presence there if the poet provides the rhetoric while the reality remains outside the poem. How to draw the reality into the poem, and therefore into a subversive relation with the rhetoric, is the crucial question" (1995b:497–98). In poems such as "Night Feed," "Partings," "Endings," "Fruit on a Straight-Sided Tray," "The Pomegranate," "The Blossom," "Daughter," "Mother Ireland," and "The Making of an Irish Goddess," Boland successfully composes such a "subversive reality" when she creates an alternative to the image of a possessive Mother Ireland who demands loyalty and sacrifice from her sons and daughters. As Batten puts it, "The maternal body and the united motherland underwrite a masculine fantasy that gives the male body/spirit 'unity' through its narcissistic mirroring" (Batten 2003:171). Auge too has written about the pull of the motherland on the Irish psyche: "it militated against the dislocating effects of colonialism by projecting an attachment to the native soil that is as integral and primal as the individual's umbilical connection to her mother" (Auge 2004:123). In Boland's hand, this trope of Mother Ireland becomes modernized and stripped of its atavistic power; while the poems are still elegiac, she conceives a new type of *aisling* figure, one who grants autonomy rather than demands subservience. In doing so, Boland suggests that the fledgling Irish nation need not focus on its painful history; instead, she sets up a post-nationalist paradigm where Mother Ireland might release, rather than subjugate, her children. This essay will examine the political ramifications of Boland's poems of motherhood in the context of her wider efforts to resituate women as both active participants and regular inhabitants of Irish poetry.

Boland's frequent references to Sylvia Plath and Adrienne Rich have led critics to view her as someone who, lacking female poetic models in Ireland, turned to America. Boland has not discouraged the connection; after Plath's death, she wrote, "From now on I would write, at least partly, in the shadow of that act: unsettled and loyal" (Boland 1995a:113). As for Rich, Boland called *Diving into the Wreck* "a cornerstone volume" (quoted in Gelpi 1999:210). However she has cautioned critics – perhaps in a moment that displays some anxiety of influence – against reading too much into such an inheritance. In her introduction to Rich's *Selected Poems*, she underscored the extent to which her feminism differed from Rich's; the poems, she wrote, "describe a struggle and record a moment that was not my struggle and would never be my moment. Nor my country, nor my companionship. Nor even my aesthetic" (Boland 1996:i). Boland is right to point out that her feminism needs to be understood in an Irish, postcolonial context. As Batten notes, Boland and her contemporary Eiléan Ní Chuilleanáin are indebted "less to twentieth-century Anglo-American feminist traditions ... than to the subject matters of the most influential Irish poet of that century, W.B. Yeats" (Batten 2003:173). Boland has also written extensively about her debt to Patrick Kavanagh: "Poets like Kavanagh were intended to exemplify the oppressions of Irish history by being oppressed. Kavanagh resisted. He rejected a public role in favour of a private vision. It was a costly and valuable resistance – exemplary to poets like myself who have come later, and with different purposes, into that tradition" (Boland 1995b:496) (see CHAPTER 39, "IRELAND IS SMALL ENOUGH"). Neil Corcoran has read Boland's tributes to Plath and Kavanagh as "a clear indication of the double heritage which Boland aims to hand on" (Corcoran 1997:118). It is worth emphasizing that this double heritage is as Irish as it is feminist; American critics, in particular, have often focused on the latter at the expense of the former.

Boland herself has expressed ambivalence about her status as a feminist writer. While she has written extensively about her perceived marginalization at the hands of the Irish male poetic tradition and community, which she has called "chauvinist" (Boland 1995a:244), she has also rejected the idea that women writers ought to dismiss writing by men as irrelevant and inherently sexist. In 1994 she told Allen Randolph, "I couldn't be a feminist poet. Simply because the poem is a place of experience and not a place of conviction" (Allen Randolph 1993:125). As she wrote in *Object Lessons*, her memoir of coming of age in Ireland as a woman poet, "Separatist thinking is a persuasive and dangerous influence on any woman poet writing today. It tempts her to disregard the whole poetic past as patriarchal betrayal. It pleads with her to discard the complexities of true feeling for the relative simplicity of anger. It promises to ease her technical problems with the solvent of polemic" (Boland 1995a:244–45). Importantly, Boland laments what she sees as the tendency of separatist feminists to "cast aside preexisting literary traditions" (243). Despite her anger towards the male poetic tradition as a whole, she has not abandoned formal poetic structures to the extent that separatist feminists might wish. Unlike her Northern Irish peer Medbh McGuckian, whose impressionistic and surrealist verse is much closer to Hélène Cixous' ideal of *écriture féminine*, Boland's verse has remained "traditional," even "patriarchal," in its engagement with form. Longley has noted that Boland's poem "The Journey," for instance, fails "to upset male or Irish norms in any aesthetically radical way" (Longley 1995:765).

Boland's feminism resides not so much in the form of her work – though, like Plath, her verse has become looser over time – but in her interrogation of the relationship between woman and nation in Ireland. While this was not the presiding preoccupation of her first two collections, *New Territory* (1967) and *The War Horse* (1975) – both formally ambitious, like Plath's early work – these volumes contain hints of what was to come. "From the Painting *Back from Market* by Chardin" in *New Territory*, for example, was the first of many poems that would explore the psyche of the silent female model rather than the male artist. Boland presents Chardin as someone who "has fixed / Her limbs in colour, and her heart in line" (Boland 2008:17; all quotations from Boland's verse cite this edition), suggesting that his version of the woman is stagnant, even domineering. Boland continues, "I think of what great art removes: / Hazard and death, the future and the past, / This woman's secret history and her loves – " (17). Here the phrase "great art" is deployed ironically; Boland suggests it is the preserve of male artists who have ignored women's "secret histories" in favor of a simplified, romanticized version of the feminine. The relationship between Chardin and the woman back from market will become emblematic of Boland's later attempt to restore active subjecthood to women in the Irish poem.

While *The War Horse* is preoccupied with poems that address the Troubles in Northern Ireland, poems such as "Suburban Woman" and "Ode to Suburbia" look forward to Boland's later work in exploring ordinary, suburban woman's experience: "The dial of a washing machine, the expression in a child's face. ... I wanted them to enter my poems. I wanted the poems they entered to be Irish poems" (Boland 1995b:492). Yet these early "suburban" poems are full of military imagery and tropes of violence which speak obliquely to anxiety over the political situation in the North. Boland has written that this was the point at which she nearly became a "public" poet. After writing "The War Horse," in which the intrusion of a traveler's horse into the speaker's garden provides the occasion for a meditation on violence in Ulster, she felt a great sense of pleasure:

The poem had drawn me easily into the charm and strength of a public stance. ... To write in that cursive and approved script can seem, for the unwary poet, a blessed lifting of the solitude and skepticism of the poet's life. ... The poem takes on a glamour of meaning against a background of public interest. (Boland 1995b:488)

Yet it was at this point that she began to feel there were dangers in such a project:

In my poem, the horse, the hills behind it – these were private emblems that almost immediately took on a communal reference against a background of communal suffering. In a time of violence, it would be all too easy to write another poem, and another. To make a construct where the difficult "I" of perception became the easier "we" of a subtle claim. Where an unearned power would be allowed by a public engagement.

In such a poem, the poet would be the subject. The object might be a horse, a distance, a human suffering. It would hardly matter. The public authorization would give such sanction to the poet that the object would not just be silent; it would be silenced. The subject would be all-powerful. (488–89)

For Boland, then, this was the turning point. She redirected her energies away from writing "public" poems that addressed the suffering of those in Northern Ireland and instead began writing poems that addressed the suffering of women. She began to feel strongly that an individual's private vision must become a part of the political poem in Ireland, and intended "to challenge the assumption, which is without intellectual rigour, that public poetry ... is necessarily political poetry. The two may overlap, but they are not the same" (498).

Nearly all of the poems in 1980's *In Her Own Image* struck a new note, both thematically and stylistically, in their concentration on feminist themes and imagery of the female body. Boland called it a book of "anti-lyrics" which she hoped would counter Irish culture's "complicated silences about a woman's body" (Allen Randolph 1999a:298). Yet as she began to find her voice and struggled to revise conceptions of Irish womanhood in the national imaginary, critics began to question her ideological position. Carol Rumens, Anne Stevenson, and Dennis O'Driscoll were dismayed by the overtly political tone of *In Her Own Image*; Stevenson went so far as to suggest that Boland was working "to the detriment of her talent" (quoted in O'Donnell 2007:167). Reviewing *The Journey* (1980), Catherine Byron wrote, "Beneath the make-up and the dimity, behind all those sketched-in apparent portraits, is – Eavan Boland, with a pen in her hand and a mirror before her" (1987/88:50). Denis Donoghue also took issue with Boland's focus on the self in his review of *In a Time of Violence*: "She tends to see herself in a dramatic and representative light, such that her censoriousness is to be understood as exemplary, her moods as universally significant" (Donoghue 1994:26). Others have claimed that Boland's representation of women is essentialist (see, for instance, Martin 1993; Meaney 1993). Perhaps the most influential critiques of Boland's work came from Clair Wills and Longley, who suggest that Boland is too loyal to the idea of the nation even as she questions the nation's treatment of women. Wills criticized Boland for writing a nationalist poetry that desires "a restoration of the culture to itself," a restoration which like all restorations opposes itself to modernity, losing itself in a nostalgic celebration of a pure, organic and mono-cultural society. ... Her argument could be summed up as a version of "No taxation without representation"; Boland is, in effect, a suffragette. She seeks not to challenge the basis of the poet's authority, but to widen the political constituency, adding women to the electoral rolls. (Wills 1991:256–57)

For Longley, too, it was not necessarily Boland's feminism that rankled, but her refusal to question nationalism:

> Although Boland criticizes male poets for having made woman a silent object in their visionary odes ... she insists: "in all this I did not blame nationalism." Because she does not blame Nationalism, her alternative Muse turns out to be the twin sister of Dark Rosaleen. ... By not questioning the nation, Boland recycles the literary cliché from which she desires to escape. (Longley 1994:188)

Elsewhere Longley has written, "It may not be enough for poets to renegotiate the contract between 'the feminine and the national' (Boland's phrase), since there are problems with the national, too" (Longley 1998:526). Other critics, however, have supported Boland's efforts: Jody Allen Randolph, Catriona Clutterbuck, Guinn Batten, Anne Fogarty, Marilyn Reizbaum, Peggy O'Brien, Albert Gelpi, and others have all championed Boland's work. As Declan Kiberd writes, "In seeking to free her own voice as a woman, Boland expanded and enriched the definitions of a nation" (Kiberd 1995:608). Kiberd has argued with Longley's criticism of Boland, noting that "Longley does not manage to define any ground other than the nation from which a poet might conduct such an enquiry. Boland, for her part, adopts the view that myths are best dismantled from within" (607).

For Boland, the most insidious myth in need of dismantling was that of Mother Ireland – variously known through her other incarnations as Cathleen ni Houlihan, the Sean Bhean Bhocht, the Poor Old Woman, Hibernia, or Dark Rosaleen. All are *aisling* figures, part of a tradition in which a woman representing the Irish nation appears to a young man in a dream vision and exhorts him to overthrow the colonial oppressors. Whether she is an old hag who will turn into a queen or a young maiden who persuades through her beauty, this avatar demands that her sons sacrifice their lives in exchange for her eventual liberation. While Boland does not question the concept of nationalism to the extent that Longley or Wills would like, there are moments in her work in which she presents an alternative to this particular nationalist paradigm. In her poems of motherhood, she describes a different kind of relationship between mother and child – not one in which the mother refuses to liberate her progeny, but one in which she willingly grants them autonomy. There is a lesson in these poems – not of national liberation, but of personal liberation from the national myth.

Originally part of the collective folk memory, the icons of Dark Rosaleen and Cathleen ni Houlihan were popularized by James Clarence Mangan and W.B. Yeats.

Mangan published his poem "Dark Rosaleen" in the Young Ireland newspaper *The Nation* in 1846; the poem was based on a rough translation of "Róisín Dubh" (The Black Rose) by Samuel Ferguson (who based his translation, in turn, on the version in James Hardiman's *Irish Minstrelsy*, which he had reviewed for the *Dublin University Magazine* in 1834 [Storey 1988:11]) (see CHAPTER 26, DAVIS, MANGAN, FERGUSON: IRISH POETRY 1831–1849). In Mangan's translation, Dark Rosaleen becomes an *aisling* figure, while the symbol of the black rose, stained with the blood of Ireland's martyrs, would eventually become a powerful nationalist motif. Cathleen ni Houlihan was introduced into Irish folk culture at the end of the eighteenth century through a ballad entitled "Shan Von Vocht" (in Irish, *an sean-bhean bhocht*, "the poor old woman") celebrating the ill-fated rebellion at Killala, County Mayo, in 1798. In the ballad, the old woman rallies the men to arms against the British; the Irishmen "swear that they'll be true / To the Shan Von Vocht." The figure of Cathleen ni Houlihan originally derived from a love ballad but eventually merged with the figure of the Shan Von Vocht to become a personification of Ireland in her political bondage. The old woman is transformed into a beautiful young girl once she has secured the loyalty of her countrymen.

The symbol of Cathleen was appropriated most powerfully by Yeats in his 1902 play *Cathleen Ni Houlihan*, which played to packed houses at the Abbey Theatre in Dublin (Maud Gonne played the role of Cathleen). In the play, an old woman visits the cottage of a peasant family in Killala on the day of the French landing, and implores the young man of the house, Michael Gillane, to leave his fiancée and fight for Ireland: "If anyone must give me help," she says, "he must give me himself, he must give me all" (Yeats 1967:228). Cathleen convinces Michael to abandon his fiancée for Ireland's cause and, when he leaves to fight, Cathleen becomes a beautiful young woman. The play is a blatant call for blood sacrifice. But if Yeats helped to popularize the icon of Cathleen, he also helped to undermine her. In "Man and the Echo," he wondered "Did that play of mine send out / Certain men the English shot?" (Yeats 1983:345). As Gregory Castle notes, by the time James Joyce published *A Portrait of the Artist as a Young Man* in 1916, the symbol of Cathleen ni Houlihan had become "both a powerful emblem of the aspirations of cultural nationalism and an obvious target of parody" (Castle 2009:200). Joyce bitterly satirized Cathleen ni Houlihan in the "Telemachus" chapter of *Ulysses*, in which an old milkwoman who knows no Irish becomes emblematic, in Stephen Dedalus' mind, of the "crazy queen, old and jealous" who wants him for "odd jobs" (Joyce 1990:20): "Silk of the kine and poor old woman, names given her in old times. A wandering crone ... To serve her or to upbraid, whether he could not tell: but scorned to beg her favour" (Joyce 1990:14). Louis MacNeice, writing a little over twenty years later, also scorned the figure of Cathleen. In section XVI of *Autumn Journal*, he wrote,

> Kathaleen ni Houlihan! Why
>   Must a country, like a ship or a car, be always female,
> Mother or sweetheart? A woman passing by,

> We did but see her passing.
> Passing like a patch of sun on the rainy hill
>   And yet we love her for ever and hate our neighbor
> And each one in his will
>   Binds his heirs to continuance of hatred.
>
>   (MacNeice 1979:132)

Still later, Paul Muldoon's "Aisling," written during the republican hunger strikes in Northern Ireland in the early 1980s, presents the *aisling* as "Anorexia" while, in "Gathering Mushrooms," Muldoon implies that the *aisling* figure's plea for the speaker to "Come back to us" – that is, to join the republican struggle – is an invitation to death (Muldoon 2001:127, 106). Nuala Ní Dhomhnaill's "Cathleen" is likewise dark and satirical: "Old Gummy Granny" has an

>   uncanny
>   knack of hearing only what confirms
>   her own sense of herself, her honey-nubile form
>   and the red rose, proud rose or canker
>   tucked behind her ear, in the head-band of her blinkers.
>
>   (Ní Dhomhnaill 1999:171)

Boland, then, is certainly not the first Irish writer to subvert the trope of Cathleen, but she is the first to show how constricting that figure has been for women in Ireland, particularly women poets:

> What female figure was there to identify with? There were no women in those back streets. None, at least who were not lowly auxiliaries of the action. The heroine, as such, was utterly passive. She was Ireland or Hibernia. She was stamped, as a rubbed-away mark, on silver or gold; a compromised regal figure on a throne. ... She was invoked, addressed, remembered, loved, regretted. And, most important, died for. She was a mother or a virgin. Her hair was swept back or tied, like the prow of a ship. Her flesh was wood or ink or marble. And she had no speaking part. (Boland 1995a:66)

Boland's first real efforts to dismantle the myth of Mother Ireland as an emblem of Irish womanhood have often been dated to her poem "Mise Eire," a subversive revision of Patrick Pearse's "I am Ireland." In that poem, the speaker tells us

>   I won't go back to it –
>
>   my nation displaced
>   into old dactyls,
>   oaths made
>   by the animal tallows
>   of the candle.
>
>   (128)

The speaker will no longer sanctify "the songs / that bandage up the history, / the words / that make a rhythm of the crime" (128). But Boland slyly undermines her vow in the penultimate stanza, where three words are in fact dactyls ("immigrant," "guttural" and "homesickness"). Boland describes an emigrant woman

> mingling the immigrant
> guttural with the vowels
> of homesickness who neither
> knows nor cares that
>
> a new language
> is a kind of scar
> and heals after a while
> into a passable imitation
> of what went before.
>
> (129)

Thus the poem, often read as triumphant renunciation, may actually end on a note of despair. The women in the poem, a prostitute and an emigrant – emblematic of women on the margins of Irish history – have no choice but to go back to the romanticized version of their a nation because there is no viable alternative. The "new language" which will displace "the old dactyls" still does not exist.

Boland herself seeks to create this "new language." She seeks a "muse mother" – an ordinary mother from the suburbs – who will replace not just the avatar of Cathleen ni Houlihan, but also the traditional female muse of poetry. In "Tirade for the Mimic Muse," Boland personifies both Mother Ireland and the "Mimic Muse" and suggests that they are collaborators who have conspired to keep women outside history and poetry:

> How you fled
> The kitchen screw and the rack of labour
> The wash thumbed and the dish cracked
> The scream of beaten women,
> The crime of babies battered,
> The hubbub and the shriek of daily grief
> That seeks asylum behind suburb walls –
> A world you could have sheltered in your skirts –
> And well I know and how I see it now,
> The way you latched your belt and itched your hem
> And shook it off like dirt.
>
> (72)

Boland will challenge and hopefully even displace this muse by writing poetry that does not ignore the reality of ordinary women's experience: "I will wake you from your sluttish sleep. / I will show you reflections, terrors" (72).

Throughout her work, Boland has kept her promise to reveal the "terrors" of female experience typically ignored by male poets: in "In His Own Image," she writes of domestic violence; in "Anorexic," of a woman who starves herself; in "Mastectomy," of male surgeons' callousness; in "The Journey," of women who have lost their babies to disease; in "The Making of an Irish Goddess," of Famine women who ate their own children; in "Mise Eire," of prostitutes who serviced British soldiers; in "Tree of Life," of infants who died soon after birth. The new muse behind these poems, as Boland imagines her in "The Muse Mother," is a suburban mother, wiping her child's face clean in the rain. She is not an erotic figure, but rather a nurturer, a protector. Boland yearns for this muse mother to

> ... teach me
> a new language:
>
> to be a sibyl
> able to sing the past
> in pure syllables,
> limning hymns sung
> to belly wheat or woman –
>
> able to speak at last
> my mother tongue.
>
> (103)

In fact, this new muse mother looks very much like Boland herself. Just as Stephen Dedalus yearns to become his own father in *Portrait of the Artist*, Boland, it would appear, desires to become her own mother. As she told Allen Randolph in 1999, "There was only one poetry world in Ireland and I seemed to be putting myself at odds with it. ... the idea of the poet it offered was not mine. I couldn't use this inherited authority and pretend it was mine. I had to make it for myself" (Allen Randolph 1999a:297). Indeed, in the later poem, "Is It Still the Same?," Boland writes that the "young woman who climbs the stairs" to write poems will now inhabit a "different" tradition: "This time, when she looks up, I will be there" (305). Boland situates herself as the "muse mother" to the next generation of female poets.

Boland's project of revising the traditional, sexualized muse goes hand in hand with her desire to reclaim and revise the image of the *aisling* in Irish poetry. Her efforts in this vein may have begun well before "Mise Eire." Indeed, her attempts to introduce what she has called a "subversive reality" into the political poem started with the early "Child of Our Time," an elegy for a child who died in the Dublin car bombings of 1974. The poem mourns the child but also questions the commitment to violent nationalism that led to his death. Here it is clear that Boland does in fact "blame nationalism":

> We who should have known how to instruct
> With rhymes for your waking, rhythms for your sleep,
> Names for the animals you took to bed,

Tales to distract, legends to protect,
Later an idiom for you to keep
And living, learn, must learn from you, dead,

To make our broken images rebuild
Themselves around your limbs, your broken
Image, find for your sake whose life our idle
Talk has cost, a new language. Child
Of our time, our times have robbed your cradle.

                                                                                (41)

Although the bombing was perpetrated by loyalist paramilitaries, Boland assumes a
collective guilt: "we" are at fault rather than "they." "Idle talk" – nationalist and loyalist
rhetoric – has cost the child his life; Boland vows to find "a new language" with which
to "rebuild" the divided community. While the poem's formal unity – each stanza has
three rhymes – provides a sense of completion and fulfillment, Boland never suggests
that the elegy itself represents the "new language" she seeks. Thus the poem is an
example of what Wills has called "a turn away from conventional elegy and towards
alternative modes of remembrance, which can take account of absence and articulate
a sense of loss without offering the poem as substitute or consolation for that loss"
(Wills 1998:599). While the lost child is an innocent victim of the Troubles, Mother
Ireland is still to blame; she is the old sow who eats her farrow.

Mother Ireland may also play this role in "In Her Own Image," which appeared
in Boland's collection of the same title. In that poem, a mother strangles her infant
daughter, whom she then buries in the garden. "Let her wear amethyst thumbprints,
/ a family heirloom, / a sort of burial necklace" (73), Boland writes. Allen Randolph
has noted that the poem enacts "a ritual of family violence; the death is revealed to
be an act of self-hatred by a woman who has confused her own body with that of her
female child" (Allen Randolph 1991:51). While Allen Randolph's analysis is perceptive, she does not read the poem – or indeed any of the poems in *In Her Own Image*
– in a specifically Irish context. Given Boland's desire to draw attention to the destructive elements of the Mother Ireland allegory, it may be that the "ritual of family
violence" invokes the cult of martyrdom inspired by devotion to the national "mother";
if this is the case, the "self-hatred" that leads the speaker to murder her child has
larger political ramifications. Also, the mother's use of the word "bed" instead of
"bury" ("I will bed her") suggests her kinship to the erotic *aisling*; here, the seductive
maiden and the wronged mother merge into one figure, whose identity is "unfixed
and unstable" (Allen Randolph 1991:51). The poem's speaker calls her dead baby "the
one perfection / among compromises," a line that recalls Sylvia Plath's "Edge," in
which the Medea figure and her dead children lie "perfected" (Plath 1981:272). Here,
however, Boland recasts Mother Ireland as Medea.

Jacqueline Belanger has argued that Boland's "Anorexic," from *In Her Own Image*,
also alludes to Cathleen ni Houlihan in the speaker's determination to become "angular
and holy / past pain" (76):

Flesh is heretic.
My body is a witch.
I am burning it.

Yes I am torching
her curves and paps and wiles.
They scorch in my self denials.

(75)

Belanger suggests that Boland is

using the anorexic speaker of her poem to undermine the notion of redemption through
female suffering which underlies many of the representations of Ireland as woman. ...
Boland is questioning whether what is in reality disempowering mutilation can really
be equated with an heroic and spiritualised idea of self-sacrifice – a question which
becomes even more important in terms of the overtly political uses of starvation in
hunger strikes. (Belanger 2000:246–47)

However, she sees Boland's use of these tropes as problematic, arguing that her poems,
"while expanding the parameters of female experience admitted into the 'canon' of
Irish poetry, do not ultimately take apart the limits of these parameters which insist
on woman, and woman's bodies, as being read metaphorically" (Belanger 2000:249).
By reading the poem in an Irish context, unlike other feminist critics who often read
the poems as examples of *écriture féminine* (see Allen Randolph 1991), Belanger echoes
the critiques of Longley and Wills. Like these critics, Belanger argues that Boland's
work emphasizes ideas she seeks to undermine. I would add that, in *In Her Own Image*,
Boland similarly undermines her determination to write in a "new language," for she
relies too heavily on the style and themes of Plath. The short lines, the enjambment,
the repetition, the exclamation points, the imagery of fevers, witches, burning, rebirth,
male surgeons mutilating the female body, striptease artists, and so forth, are all
derivative. But by grafting Plath's voice onto Irish themes, Boland was able to move
closer to the more original voice that would appear in her next, seminal collection,
Night Feed.

Night Feed offers a more successful revision of the *aisling* genre. "Night Feed,"
"Partings," "Endings," "Fruit on a Straight-Sided Tray," and "In the Garden" all
celebrate the union between mother and child even as they acknowledge the painful,
inevitable separation that must occur in order for the child to become autonomous.
While these poems are set squarely in the domestic sphere of house and garden, they
possess a political subtext. "Night Feed," perhaps Boland's single best poem, tenderly
depicts the bond between a mother and her nursing child in the small hours of
morning, but ends by invoking the "long fall from grace" (93) that both begin as the
sun rises. In "Partings," too, "light finds us / with the other loves / dawn sunders /
to define" (96). The new day brings with it a reminder not of promise and possibility,
but of looming separation; it is only at night, in the nursery, that the mother feels
"we are one more and / inseparable again" (96). In both poems, the mother registers

her awareness of what is to come without bitterness; she understands she will not be able to protect and shelter her child forever, and will have to give her up to the workaday world symbolized by the intrusion of dawn.

Similarly, in "Fruit on a Straight-Sided Tray," Boland transforms a still-life into another meditation on the increasing distance between mother and child. The painter's "true subject" is not the pieces of fruit themselves, Boland writes, but "the space between them": "the pleasure of these ovals / is seen to be an assembly of possibilities; / a deliberate collection of cross purposes." This is "the study of absences":

> This is the geometry of the visible, physical tryst
> between substances, disguising for awhile the equation
> that kills: you are my child and between us are
>
> spaces. Distances. Growing to infinities.
>
> (98)

While the mother expresses acute pain at the prospect of her child's increasing independence, she also knows that the absences in the painting stand for "possibilities" and "cross purposes." Although the distances between mother and child will grow to infinity, those distances (or "absences") are what allow for possibility and plurality. The sense of possibility "disguises" the sorrow the mother will feel when the child no longer needs her. The fact that Boland finds "an assembly of possibilities" while contemplating "the study of absences" suggests that the child's inevitable leavetaking *must* happen, no matter how bereft it leaves the mother.

Boland revisits this theme again in "The Blossom," in which a mother, "lost in grief," wonders, "How much longer / will I see girlhood in my daughter?" (262). The mother imagines the daughter's response to her sadness:

> *imagine if I stayed here,*
> *even for the sake of your love,*
> *what would happen to the summer?*
> *To the fruit?*

The mother then imagines the daughter – the metaphorical "blossom" of the poem's title – touching her in an act of departure, absolution, and fulfillment. She

> holds out a dawn-soaked hand to me,
> whose fingers I counted at birth
> years ago.
>
> And touches mine for the last time.
>
> And falls to earth.
>
> (263)

In these poems, the mother's grief is abstract; she is not literally grieving the death of her child but the birth of an autonomous adult. If we read these poems as politically subversive – as examples of work where "rhetoric meets reality" – then we might understand them as inverted pietàs that reject not only the symbolism of Cathleen ni Houlihan but also the imperial branding of the colony as a child in need of protection. In both scenarios, the "child" is dependent on the "mother," whether the mother stands for the colonizer or the colonized. As Auge writes, Boland is "acutely aware of how the former colony's counter-representations can themselves manifest dangerous totalizing tendencies" (Auge 2004:132). Boland reverses this power dynamic so it is the mother who releases the child, however reluctantly, and grants her independence. She even manages to make a subversive gesture through her invocation of the blossom, which recalls the *aisling* figure in Yeats' "The Song of Wandering Aengus," the "glimmering girl" with "apple blossom in her hair" (60) whom Yeats associated with Maud Gonne (see also "The Arrow"). In Boland's poems, the blossoms represent the ephemeral in a different way. As she writes in "Ceres Looks at the Morning,"

> Apple trees
> appear, one by one. Light is pouring
> into the promise of fruit.
>   Beautiful morning
> look at me as a daughter would
> look: with that love and that curiosity –
> as to what she came from.
> And what she will become.
>
>   (264–65)

The apple blossoms do not inspire the viewer to follow the waning vision in the hopes of capturing it, as in Yeats' poem, but to step back and behold "the promise of fruit" (265).

Boland's mother–daughter poems – such as "Daughter," "The Pomegranate," "Ceres Looks at the Morning," and "The Making of an Irish Goddess" – frequently allude to the myth of Ceres and Proserpine (the Roman counterparts to Persephone and Demeter). While there are various versions of the myth, the best-known states that Pluto abducted Ceres' daughter Proserpine while she was picking flowers. He then brought her to the Underworld, as Ceres, goddess of the harvest, searched for her. During this time, the earth grew so barren that Jupiter (Zeus) decreed that Proserpine could return to earth. Before she left, however, Pluto persuaded her to eat six pomegranate seeds. This act ensured that she could not leave the Underworld forever, since pomegranate was the fruit of the dead. Thus, she was allowed to remain with her mother Ceres for six months of the year, and with Pluto for the other six. The myth helped to explain the changing of the seasons: during the winter, Proserpine stayed in the Underworld as Ceres mourned her absence and refused to make things grow. In the spring and summer, however, when Ceres was reunited with Proserpine, the earth bloomed.

In "Daughter," Boland alludes to the loss of Proserpine as the speaker recalls a memory in which her daughter runs toward her but "will not look at me" (264). In the final section of that poem, titled "The Bargain," the mother intimates that in order for her daughter to flourish, she must let her go:

> The garden creaks with rain.
> The gutters run with noisy water.
> The earth shows its age and makes a promise
> only myth can keep. *Summer. Daughter.*
>
> (264)

In "The Pomegranate," too, Boland invokes Ceres and Proserpine as the speaker watches her teenage daughter sleeping beside a plate of uncut fruit. She remembers the pomegranate, and how the story could have ended differently if only Proserpine had not eaten it. But the mother decides not to warn her child about the complexities of her impending womanhood: "If I defer the grief I will diminish the gift" (216). The gift is autonomy. In Boland's "The Making of an Irish Goddess," Ceres again serves as a model, but she is ultimately an "insufficient" one (Thurston 1999:242). As Michael Thurston notes, "the Irish goddess is fashioned from events that have unfolded over time in Ireland, and from the famine most of all" (Thurston 1999:242). The speaker in Boland's poem seeks to record "an accurate inscription / of that agony":

> the failed harvests,
> the fields rotting to the horizon,
> the children devoured by their mothers
> whose souls, they would have said,
> went straight to hell,
> followed by their own.
>
> (179)

This shocking image acknowledges the horrific realities that the new Irish goddess must embody, but also suggests what she must *not* become: the sow that eats her farrow, the Black Rose made dark from the blood of martyrs. Notably, the poem ends with the speaker gazing on her daughter, "her back turned to me" (179). The image has political as well as personal resonance: the new Ireland must allow its children to face outward.

In "Mother Ireland" Boland finally liberates Cathleen herself. The symbol who was once only seen now begins to see; she learns her name, rises up, and tells her own story. "It was different / from the story told about me," she says (261). When the fields realize she has left them, they murmur, "*Come back to us*" (262). But Mother Ireland has decided she will not "go back to it" (128), as Boland wrote in "Mise Eire." Yet she does not renounce or condemn her nation; she simply whispers, "*Trust me*" – a clever inversion of the mother–child relationship we have seen thus far in Boland's work. In this case, it is the "mother" who yearns for independence from the "child."

Boland suggests that once the nation lets go of atavism, of loyalty to Dark Rosaleen, it might finally come of age.

The sundering that takes place in these mother–daughter poems is painful but necessary in order for the mother to grant her child "the gift" of autonomy. As Auge writes, "To convert rupture into aperture requires sacrifice, an act of renunciation that opens the space for difference to blossom forth" (Auge 2004:127). Indeed, the sundering creates a rend between mother and child that leads toward dispersal rather than cohesion. But dispersal here is like Joyce's idea of parallax: it represents the beginnings of multiplicity, the ability to view a home, a mother, or a nation from different perspectives. If we read these poems in an Irish as well as feminist context, we might ask whether Boland, in her revision of the Cathleen symbol and in her predetermined role as Ireland's "muse mother," seeks to offer a new paradigm for a post-national modernity – one that can best be defined as "an assembly of possibilities" (97).

References and Further Reading

Allen Randolph, J. (1991). "Ecriture Feminine and the Authorship of Self in Eavan Boland's *In Her Own Image*." *Colby Quarterly*, 28.1, 48–59.

Allen Randolph, J. (1993). "An Interview with Eavan Boland." *Irish University Review*, special issue on Eavan Boland, 23.1, 117–30.

Allen Randolph, J. (1999a). "A Backward Look: An Interview with Eavan Boland." *Colby Quarterly*, 35.4, 292–304.

Allen Randolph, J. (1999b). "Introduction." *Colby Quarterly*, 35.4, 205–09.

Auge, A. (2004). "Fracture and Wound: Eavan Boland's Poetry of Nationality." *New Hibernia Review*, 8.2, 121–41.

Batten, G. (2003). "Boland, McGuckian, Ní Chuilleanáin and the Body of the Nation." In M. Campbell (Ed.). *Cambridge Companion to Contemporary Irish Poetry* (pp. 169–88). Cambridge: Cambridge University Press.

Belanger, J. (2000). "'The Laws of Metaphor': Reading Eavan Boland's 'Anorexic' in an Irish Context." *Colby Quarterly*, 36.3, 242–51.

Boland, E. (1995a). *Object Lessons: The Life of the Woman and the Poet in Our Time*. New York: W.W. Norton.

Boland, E. (1995b). "Writing the Political Poem in Ireland." *The Southern Review*, 31.3, 485–98.

Boland, E. (1996). "Introduction." *Adrienne Rich: Selected Poems*. Knockeven, Ireland: Salmon Press.

Boland, E. (2008). *New Collected Poems*. New York: W.W. Norton.

Byron, C. (1987/88). "Bandaged but Unhealed." Review of Eavan Boland, *The Journey and Other Poems*. *Poetry Review*, 77.4, 50.

Castle, G. (2009). *Modernism and the Celtic Revival*. Cambridge: Cambridge University Press.

Clutterbuck, C. (1999). "Irish Critical Responses to Self-Representation in Eavan Boland, 1987–1995." *Colby Quarterly*, 35.4, 275–87.

Corcoran, N. (1997). *After Joyce and Yeats: Reading Modern Irish Literature*. Oxford: Oxford University Press.

Donoghue, D. (1994). "The Delirium of the Brave." Review of Eavan Boland, *In a Time of Violence*. *New York Review of Books*, 41.10, 26.

Gelpi, A. (1999). "'Hazard and Death': The Poetry of Eavan Boland." *Colby Quarterly*, 35.4, 210–28.

Heaney, S. (1998). *Opened Ground*. London: Faber & Faber.

Joyce, J. (1990). *Ulysses*. New York: Vintage.

Kiberd, D. (1995). *Inventing Ireland: The Literature of the Modern Nation*. London: Vintage.

Longley, E. (1994). *The Living Stream: Literature and Revisionism in Ireland*. Newcastle upon Tyne: Bloodaxe.

Longley, E. (1995). "Irish Bards and American Audiences." *The Southern Review*, 31.3, 757–71.

Longley, E. (1998). "An ABC of Reading Contemporary Irish Poetry." *Princeton University Library Chronicle*, 59.3, 517–46.

MacNeice, L. (1979). *Collected Poems*. E.R. Dodds (Ed.). London: Faber & Faber.

Martin, A. (1993). "Quest and Vision: *The Journey*." *Irish University Review*, 23.1, 231–41.

Meaney, G. (1993). "Myth, History and the Politics of Subjectivity: Eavan Boland and Irish Women's Writing." *Women: A Cultural Review*, 4.2, 136–53.

Muldoon, P. (2001). *Poems 1968–1998*. New York: Farrar, Straus & Giroux.

Ní Dhomhnaill, N. (1999). "Cathleen." In P. O'Brien (Ed.). *The Wake Forest Book of Irish Women's Poetry 1967–2000* (pp. 170–71). Winston-Salem: Wake Forest University Press.

O'Brien, P. (Ed.). (1999). "Introduction." *The Wake Forest Book of Irish Women's Poetry 1967–2000* (pp. xv–xxxii). Winston-Salem: Wake Forest University Press.

O'Donnell, M. (2007). "From *In Her Own Image*: An Assertion that Myths are Made by Men, by the Poet in Transition." In J. Allen Randolph (Ed.). *Eavan Boland: A Critical Companion* (pp. 167–68). New York: W.W. Norton.

Plath, S. (1981). *Collected Poems*. T. Hughes (Ed.). London: Faber & Faber.

Storey, M. (Ed.). (1988). *Poetry and Ireland Since 1800: A Source Book*. London: Routledge.

Thurston, M. (1999). "'A Deliberate Collection of Cross Purposes': Eavan Boland's Poetic Sequences." *Colby Quarterly*, 35.4, 229–51.

Wills, C. (1991). "Contemporary Irish Women Poets: The Privatization of Myth." In H.D. Jump (Ed.). *Diverse Voices: Essays on Twentieth Century Women Writers in English* (pp. 248–72). Hemel Hempstead: Harvester Wheatsheaf.

Wills, C. (1998). "Modes of Redress: The Elegy in Recent Irish Poetry." *Princeton University Library Chronicle*, 59.3, 594–620.

Yeats, W.B. (1967). *Eleven Plays of William Butler Yeats*. A.N. Jeffares (Ed.). New York: Scribner.

Yeats, W.B. (1983). *Collected Poems of William Butler Yeats*. R.J. Finneran (Ed.). New York: Scribner.

Yeats, W.B. (2000). "Per Amica Silentia Lunae." 1918. In J. Pethica (Ed.). *Yeats's Poetry, Drama, and Prose* (pp. 285–87). New York: W.W. Norton.

51
John Banville's Dualistic Universe

Elke D'hoker

While John Banville may not be the most widely read or best-selling novelist in Ireland today, he is, surely, the author who can boast the greatest critical attention. Since Rüdiger Imhof's pioneering critical introduction of 1989, Banville's work has been studied in nine monographs and more than a hundred articles, and the interest shows no sign of abating – quite the contrary. This is not to say that Banville is only a "writer's writer," as reviewers of his early work sometimes called him. His novels deal with a wide variety of topics – from astronomy and computer science over spying and notorious crimes to art and the theater – often borrowed from Europe's past or recent history. The amount of criticism is, rather, an indication of the sheer density of his work, which offers critics a mine of ideas, a rich network of intertextual references, and a rewarding sense of unity. In an early interview, Banville stated that "each book ... follows on more or less from its predecessor" (Imhof 1981:9) and, over the past four decades, he has honored this principle, giving shape to an impressive and coherent oeuvre that commands a central place in contemporary Irish literature.

The sense of unity of Banville's novelistic oeuvre is, in part, consciously constructed through a network of recurring characters, scenes, or metaphors. Yet it is also the result of Banville's strikingly similar male protagonists and of the single set of fears and dreams that seems to guide them. In fact, Banville's thirteen novels offer as many variations on a single story: the story of how an isolated, divided self tries to deal with a strange, indifferent world. The human condition this story illuminates is that of modernity and the world-view which inspires it is fundamentally dualistic: it tells of a large gap between subject and object, mind and matter, self and world. In the absence of God, Banville's protagonists feel called upon to overcome this gap and to restore the sense of harmony, unity, and truth which has been lost. Guided by elusive glimpses of such harmony in nature or in women, they rely on intellect and the

A Companion to Irish Literature, edited by Julia M. Wright
© 2010 Blackwell Publishing Ltd

imagination to construct brilliant theories, beautiful artworks, or masterful narratives which carry the promise of wholeness and meaning, order and truth. These grand ambitions and fond hopes are, however, constantly offset by doubts and despair, by the knowledge that unity cannot be recovered, order cannot be found, and truth does not exist. This, then, is the opposition which infuses all of Banville's novels: the tension between a romantic quest for wholeness and an ironic awareness that such harmony does not exist; between a fundamental awareness of the gap between self and world and a defiant attempt to overcome this gap; between a postmodern understanding of self-division and multiplicity and a profound yearning for a single, true self.

Critics have tried to define this recurring conflict in Banville's fiction in different ways. It has been read as a conflict between romantic hope and postmodern despair (Imhof 1997), as a tension between modernist and postmodernist tendencies (McMinn 2000), as the result of the dual Irish legacy of James Joyce and Samuel Beckett (Hand 2002; Powell 2005), or as the evidence of a fundamental spiritual vision in a skeptical world (McNamee 2008). Yet whatever label one chooses, it is clear that the modern, dualistic world-view and the attendant alternation of hope and despair are absolutely fundamental to Banville's fictional universe, from the stories of lost harmony in *Long Lankin* to Max Morden's quest for his past and his self in *The Sea*. This dualistic world-view determines Banville's plots and shapes his characters in a variety of ways and it even determines his creation of an authorial alter ego (Benjamin Black) for his recent detective novels, *Christine Falls* (2006), *The Silver Swan* (2007), and *The Lemur* (2008). In what follows, therefore, I propose to trace the different instantiations and metaphors of splitting, division, and dualism in Banville's oeuvre as well as the quests and ruses – whether heroic or pathetic, ambitious or comic, imaginative or stunted – which his protagonists devise to overcome these splits. I will focus on Banville's novels, as they form the major part of his literary output. His autobiographical travel book (*Prague Pictures*, 2003), his adaptations of Kleist's plays (*The Broken Jug*, 1994; *God's Gift*, 2000; *Love in the Wars*, 2005), his screenplays for television (*Reflections*, 1983; *Seachange*, 1994), and his three volumes of crime fiction will not be considered. Banville's extensive work as an essayist and reviewer, mainly for *Hibernia*, *The Irish Times*, and *The New York Times Book Review*, will only be mentioned in so far as it sheds light on his novels.

Long Lankin (1970) stands out from the rest of Banville's oeuvre in that it is his first and only collection of short stories. In an interesting article which traces the book's genesis, Kersti Tarien reveals that the stories go back to the mid-1960s, when the young Banville was following the strategy of every aspiring writer: writing stories for publication in literary magazines (Tarien 2001). Only later did Banville think of gathering the stories in a book publication organized around a central theme: that of a relationship between two people disturbed, and possibly destroyed, by a third character, an interloper figure. Several earlier stories were adapted to bring out this theme and a novella, "The Possessed," was added which told the story from the point of view of the outsider or interloper figure himself. Although this novella was later omitted from the revised edition of *Long Lankin* (1984), its narrator can be seen as the prefiguration of the prototypical Banville protagonist. Ben White is an aspiring writer who tries to free himself from an incestuous closeness with his sister and from the jaded pretensions of the middle-class party he crashes. After a symbolic ritual of guilt and atonement, Ben White wonders what he will do with his newly found freedom:

> I think I might write a book. I could tell a story about the stars and what it's like all alone up there. He looked into the sky, but there were no stars, and he smiled at her and said – I mustn't feel sorry for myself. And anyway there are all kinds of things I could do. Join a circus maybe. (Banville 1970:188)

Ben White, the quintessential lonely outsider, thus slyly announces the topics of Banville's subsequent novels: the astronomical concerns of *Doctor Copernicus* and *Kepler* and the world of the circus in *Birchwood*. First, however, Ben White will himself appear as the protagonist-narrator of Banville's first novel, *Nightspawn* (1971).

Looking back on *Nightspawn* ten years after its publication, Banville called it "a betrayal of the reader's faith in the writer's good faith," of "the novelist's guild and its secret signs and stratagems" (Imhof 1981:6). Betrayal is certainly a central preoccupation of this novel, with its improbable plot involving politics, love, and writing in Greece. Yet the novel's stance towards literary tradition could perhaps more accurately be described as another act of exorcising. In *Nightspawn*, Banville frees himself from the plots and myths of realism, from the novelistic dissection of character, and from the influence of Joyce, so strong still in the stories of *Long Lankin*. He does so through irony and parody, through subversion and postmodern play, thus luring the reader on a quest for meaning which is constantly undermined. All this makes *Nightspawn* Banville's most explicitly postmodern novel, the self-conscious statement of an ambitious young novelist, determined to make his mark on the international literary scene. At the same time, however, the novel is also pervaded by a sense of loss, as if the disappearance of truth, beauty, and meaning in the modern world is less a cause for postmodern rejoicing and play than for yearning and loneliness.

With the sardonic iconoclasm of *Nightspawn*, Banville appears to have cleared a space in which to carve out his own literary voice. He does so with *Birchwood* (1973), a pseudo-historical novel involving – in jumbled chronology – an Irish Big House in decline, a traveling circus, and several dark family secrets. At the end of the novel its narrator, Gabriel Godkin, returns to his ancestral house, claiming his inheritance. He announces, "I shall stay here, alone, and live a life different from any the house has ever known. Yes" (Banville 1973:174). As so much else in this metapoetic novel, this can be read as an artistic credo of the author who decides to return to Ireland and to realism, but on his own terms (Murphy 2006). Certainly, Banville will continue to use such postmodern strategies as intertextuality, mirroring, and metafiction in his fiction, but the postmodern stance of the novels after *Nightspawn* and *Birchwood* will increasingly be muted by a mode of realism – a peculiar blend of a Jamesian focus on consciousness and an Irish predilection for storytelling.

In other ways too, *Birchwood* sets out the shape and parameters of Banville's fictional universe. The novel is framed by two references to modern philosophers, which, taken together, determine Banville's dualistic world-view. "I am, therefore I think. That seems inescapable": Gabriel opens his narrative with this inverted dictum of Descartes, the architect of the dualistic universe and the father of modern skepticism (Banville 1973:11). And he ends his story with Wittgenstein's romantic invocation of a mysterious truth which is beyond language and knowledge, and can only be experienced: "I find the world always odd, but odder still is the fact that I find it so, for what are the eternal verities by which I measure these temporal aberrations? Anyway, some secrets are not to be disclosed under the pain of who knows what retribution, and whereof I cannot speak, thereof I must be silent" (Banville 1973:175). Between ironic skepticism and romantic yearning, Banville's stories will unfold, guided by the lonely protagonist who tries – and always fails – to make sense of the "oddness" of the world, other people, his life.

After *Birchwood*, Banville embarked upon what is commonly known as the science tetralogy: a series of four books which would chart the development of modern science. The first two novels, *Doctor Copernicus* (1976) and *Kepler* (1981), follow this project quite literally as they trace the life and achievement of the two greatest astronomers of the modern age. *The Newton Letter* (1982), however, only deals tangentially with that great scientist, and *Mefisto* (1986) is really no longer the book about Heisenberg or Einstein which Banville originally envisaged. All four books are, however, centrally concerned with the scientific attempt to find an order and meaning underlying the apparent chaos of the world. They are all after "the deepest thing: the kernel, the essence, the true" (Banville 1976:79). In his description of the life and work of his scientists, Banville emphasizes their creativity. Their scientific quest is put on a par with the artistic quest. For Banville, these quests are alike in their dreams of harmony, beauty, and truth and in their use of the creative imagination to mediate between self and world. This analogy between the creative and the scientific project is further highlighted through the extended intertextual references to modernist artists in all four books. Thus, *Doctor Copernicus* and *Kepler* contain many references to Wallace Stevens' *Notes Towards a Supreme Fiction* and Rilke's *Duino Elegies*, respectively; *The Newton Letter* is partly modeled on Hugo von Hofmannsthal's *Ein Brief*, and the plot of *Mefisto* is heavily indebted to Goethe's *Faust*. Because the first three of these literary texts are explicitly metapoetic as they chart the difficult attempt of the modernist artist to express the world, they interestingly reflect on Banville's own poetics and his affinity with the modernist project (D'hoker 2004a).

Despite differences in setting, plot, and characters, the four novels of the science tetralogy also chart a highly similar line of development, one which is fundamentally defined by Banville's modern world-view. After a prelapsarian experience of harmony, the protagonists embark on a quest for order or truth by which they hope to close the gap between mind and matter or self and world. Although they are rewarded by glimpses of harmony or visions of truth, their quest inevitably ends in failure as they realize that the truth does not exist or, if it exists, that it cannot be expressed in words.

At the end of the novels, however, this despair is again replaced by hope, or by a new attempt to find the truth in another way: through an acceptance or acknowledgment of commonplace reality, which the scientists, in their hubris, have sought to transcend. As Copernicus learns on his deathbed, "we *are* the truth. The world, and ourselves, this is the truth. There is no other, or, if there is, it is of use to us only as an ideal, that brings us a little comfort, a little consolation, now and then" (Banville 1976:239). All the scientist – and the artist – has to do, therefore, is to "dispos[e] the commonplace, the names, in a beautiful and orderly pattern that would show by its very beauty and order, the action in our poor world of the otherworldly truths" (Banville 1976:240). This artistic ideal echoes Wallace Stevens' supreme fiction and Rilke's artistic project of interiorization, both of which Banville has explicitly linked to his own artistic project: "Together the Stevens and the Rilke quotations create a synthesis which is the very core of art. It is out of the tension between the desire to take things into ourselves by saying them, by praising them to the Angel, and the impossibility finally of ever making the world our own, that poetry springs" (Banville 1981b:16). It is again the tension between trying and failing, between skepticism and Romanticism, which is so typical for Banville's fiction.

The mysterious truth of the commonplace, which has to be shown rather than expressed, is evoked in the science tetralogy through epiphanies which frequently erupt in the midst of the usual clamor and chaos of the world (D'hoker 2000). Gabriel Godkin refers to these epiphanies as "rare moments when a little light breaks forth, and something is not explained, not forgiven, but merely illuminated" (Banville 1973:33) and Kepler is led to exclaim after precisely such a moment: "How innocent, how inanely lovely, the surface of the world. The mystery of simple things assailed him" (Banville 1981a:61). Even Gabriel Swan in *Mefisto* records such epiphanies: "Things shook and shimmered minutely, in a phosphorescent glow. Details would detach themselves from their blurred background as if a lens had been focused on them suddenly, and press forward eagerly, with mute insistence, urging on me some large, mysterious significance" (Banville 1986:77). If Banville's scientist-heroes are only allowed occasional glimpses of this mystery, other characters are presented as more fundamentally in touch with the mysterious significance of life. These people are typically children or childlike characters, such as Kepler's brother Heinrich, "a forty-year-old-child, eager and unlovely," yet possessed of a peculiar kind of innocence (Banville 1981a:94). Versions of these half-savage, half-innocent characters recur throughout Banville's fiction: the child Michael in *The Newton Letter*, whose "ancient gaze, out of a putto's pale eyes, was unnerving" (Banville 1982:10), the deaf mute Sophie in *Mefisto*, Freddie Montgomery's retarded son in *Book of Evidence* and *Ghosts*, Maskell's brother in *The Untouchable*, the uncanny Myles in *The Sea*. Frequently, these characters are mute or silent. They present an enigma to Banville's narrators, who believe they might embody a more primitive form of being, one that is more in touch with the essential mystery of the world.

Because of the dense philosophical patterning of *Doctor Copernicus* and *Kepler* especially, these novels have lent themselves to a variety of interpretations. First received within the context of postmodernism as historiographic metafictions (Hutcheon 1985), versions of a Nietzschean epistemology (Jackson 1997), or intricate formalistic designs (Imhof 1997), subsequent critics drew attention to the novels' debt to contemporary chaos theory (Berensmeyer 2000), to poststructuralism (Lunden 1999), and to Stanley Cavell's theory of skepticism (D'hoker 2004b). Whatever theoretical perspective one chooses, however, it may be clear that these are extremely rich and ingeniously crafted novels, which have allowed Banville to leave his mark on the international literary scene. And even though Banville returned to an Irish setting and Irish themes with *The Newton Letter*, *Mefisto*, and subsequent novels, his intertextual frame of reference remains decidedly European. Banville himself has expounded his intertextual practice as follows:

> we're part of a tradition, a European tradition; why not acknowledge it? And then, books are to a large extent made out of other books. Why not acknowledge that too? Also, I find that the incorporation of references to other works, and even quotations from those works, gives the text a peculiar and interesting resonance, which is registered even when the reader does not realize that something is being quoted. (Imhof 1981:13)

Although the nature of Banville's literary background – Irish versus international – has led to some critical controversy in the past (Berensmeyer 2000; Hand 2002), it is fair to say that his work is firmly rooted in both traditions. While the majority of his novels are set in Ireland, their intertextual framework is that of the Western literary tradition as a whole, and the themes he addresses deal with universal human fears and concerns.

Apart from a return to Ireland and the Big House, *The Newton Letter* also constitutes a return to the first-person narrative mode, which has become one of the defining features of Banville's fictional oeuvre. Banville's male I-narrators, from Ben White to Max Morden, strongly mark the stories that they tell. They clearly constitute the center of the novels, and their thoughts, memories, and perceptions are at least as important as the stories they tell. Each character's voice, which quite literally shapes his narrative, is typically that of a cultured, arrogant yet self-doubting, modern man who contemplates his position in an indifferent universe. Banville's protagonists are all solipsistic narrators – one could even call them compulsive monologists – who are constrained within the confines of the self. In spite of the grand quests they frequently embark upon, they are far more interested in the workings of their own minds than in events in the world outside. All in all, their narratives leave little room for the voices of others: dialogue is rare and other characters are presented through the gaze and voice of the narrator. In this way, the narrative situation dramatizes the dualistic split of Banville's fictional universe as the narrator's position as solipsistic observer reinforces his separation from the world and other people. The narrator finds himself out of place in an odd, indifferent world and different from other people, whom he fails to understand. To a certain extent, Banville's narrators thus echo the Romantic paradigm of the outsider, which has been quite central to Irish literature.

Yet, his protagonists are not rebellious heroes who proudly defy church, state, and society. They are, rather, anti-heroes who frequently note that they do not fit into this world and are both jealous and contemptuous of those who do.

In a review of *Birchwood*, Martin Amis predicted that Banville would "get nowhere with this kind of hero, the opinionated sensualist forever spellbound by the difference between himself and everybody else" (quoted in Harper 2003). Yet Banville's work has clearly proved him wrong. Indeed, one of the main preoccupations of the narrator of *The Newton Letter* – a historian, writing a biography of Newton – is to "gaze" and "wonder" at other people with a "remote prurience" (Banville 1982:12). Those people are the inhabitants of an Irish Big House, whose lodge he has rented in an attempt to finish his magnum opus. And even though he professes to be haunted by their "enigma," he quite confidently proceeds to discover the "truth" behind appearances. He constructs a grand interpretation based on speculation and stereotype which, in the manner of the science tetralogy, proves to be all wrong. Somewhat chastened, he admits, "I dreamed up a horrid drama and failed to see the commonplace tragedy that was playing itself out in real life" (Banville 1982:79). This failure has many parallels in this short but densely crafted novel: in the existential crisis Newton experienced when a fire destroyed his papers, in the linguistic crisis Hofmannsthal describes in *Ein Brief*, and in the historian's own failure to complete his biography. Nevertheless, the ending of his fictional letter is again hopeful: "in the end of course I shall take up the book and finish it: such a renunciation is not of this world" (Banville 1982:81). His closing words, with their mixture of hope and despair, echo those of Gabriel Godkin in *Birchwood* and prefigure those of Gabriel Swan in *Mefisto* who announces,

> I have begun to work again, tentatively, I have gone back to the very start, to the simplest things. Simple, I like that. It will be different this time, I think it will be different. I won't do as I used to, in the old days. No. In future, I will leave things, I will try to leave things, to chance. (Banville 1986:234)

As the reference to chance – the first and the last word of *Mefisto* – indicates, the emphasis has shifted from truth to order and from chaos to chance in this last novel of the science tetralogy. Yet if the terms of the quest have been changed, its essence has remained largely the same. Gabriel Swan is a child prodigy who uses his mathematical gift to search for "order ... symmetry and completeness" (Banville 1986:19). Like his namesake in *Birchwood*, he locates the origins of his quest in the loss of his twin brother at birth: "I had something always beside me. It was not a presence, but a momentous absence. ... Emptiness weighed on me. ... Sometimes this sense of being burdened, of being imposed upon, gave way to a vague and seemingly objectless yearning" (17–18). The lost twin thus becomes a metaphor for the sense of division or lost wholeness with which Banville's protagonists struggle. The motif of the twin first appears in *Birchwood*, both in the form of the imaginary twin sister Gabriel searches for and in the form of his real and slightly evil twin brother Michael who pursues him. Both forms will recur in Banville's fiction with a remarkable insistency. On the one hand, there are the actual twins, from Ada and Ida in *Birchwood* to Chloe and Myles in *The Sea*, who seem to symbolize both duality and a horribly fascinating kind of unity. As the narrator of *The Sea* puts it,

> I had never encountered twins before, in the flesh, and was fascinated and at the same time slightly repelled ... there must be between them an awful depth of intimacy. How would it be? Like having one mind and two bodies? If so it was almost disgusting to think of. (Banville 2005:80)

On the other hand, Gabriel Godkin's twin brother Michael recurs as a slightly sinister alter ego to the protagonist in most of Banville's novels. He can be recognized in Copernicus' brother Andreas, his complete opposite yet eventual alter ego, and in Felix, the Italian soldier whom Kepler envies for his raucous liveliness. In *Mefisto* the sinister alter ego of Gabriel Swan is also called Felix, and a highly similar red-haired Felix will later return in *Ghosts*, *Athena*, and *Eclipse*. The Faustian intertext of *Mefisto* highlights the Mephistophelian characteristics of Felix. He is a worldly, knowing, scheming tempter; both the double of and complement to the idealistic, dreamy Gabriel. Felix possesses what Gabriel lacks: an intimate knowledge of people's weaknesses and a shrewd awareness of human mortality. In a sense, therefore, Gabriel and Felix – and the other twin figures – dramatize again the modern split of mind and matter in Banville's dualistic universe.

The science tetralogy was followed by another set of novels, which critics initially dubbed the "art trilogy": *The Book of Evidence* (1989), *Ghosts* (1993), and *Athena* (1995). In 2001, however, Picador published a compilation of these three novels with the same protagonist under the title *Frames Trilogy*. While both titles bring out the central role of paintings in these novels, the latter title also draws attention to Banville's continued preoccupation with "framing" reality – in scientific theories, artworks, or narratives – as a way of bridging the gap between subject and object, self and world. In this second set of books, however, it is no longer the world but its people which form the center of attention. Questions about the power and the limits of the imagination in representing the world thus acquire a moral dimension in this trilogy, centered as it is on the brutal murder committed by its narrator-protagonist.

We first meet Freddie Montgomery in *The Book of Evidence*. He is in prison awaiting trial, and writes a testimony addressed to judge and jury, not, he argues, "to excuse my actions, only to explain them" (Banville 1989:11). Still, many readers have remarked on Banville's remarkable feat of procuring sympathy for his narrator, whose narrative seems to perfect the urbane, witty, and solipsistic voices of many previous narrators. Freddie relates how money problems drove him from the southern island where he lived with his wife and his retarded son, back to his mother in Dublin. Because she sold the paintings he regarded as his inheritance, he visits the Big House of the family friend and art dealer who bought them from her. There, he is struck by a seventeenth-century Dutch portrait of a lady, called "Portrait of a Woman with

Gloves." In his attempt to steal the portrait, he is interrupted by the maid, whom he drags to his car and bludgeons to death with a hammer.

In the course of his narrative Freddie comes up with several explanations for his crime: it was fate; it was the evil double inside him; it was pure chance. Yet the one he settles upon eventually is a "failure of the imagination," the fact that "I never imagined her vividly enough, that I never made her be there sufficiently, that I did not make her live. ... I killed her because I could kill her, and I could kill her because for me she was not alive" (Banville 1989:215). Freddie thus opposes his imaginative sympathy for the woman in the portrait – he "successfully" imagines a life for her – to his failure to really imagine the life and reality of the maid. The imagination, which was introduced in the science tetralogy as the creative capacity behind the scientists' heroic but doomed attempts to find the truth, is thus hailed as the force necessary to mediate, or even bridge, the gap between self and others. Even though this presentation of the sympathetic imagination as an important moral force is a familiar one in moral philosophy, several critics have pointed out that there are factors in Freddie's narrative which undermine this reading of the events (D'hoker 2002; Müller 2004). First, there is the question whether Freddie's imaginative reconstruction of the woman in the portrait was really all that successful. Did he not also frame the woman in a fiction of his own making, a fiction, moreover, which ultimately heralded her death, as the last thoughts he gives to her are "now I know how to die. ... She feels numbed, hollowed, a walking shell" (Banville 1989:108). As Anja Müller has argued, Freddie does not really bring her to life, but "rather kills [her] too, by inventing a story in which the imaginary female sitter is drained of her individuality through being portrayed" (Müller 2004:192). Second, Freddie's claim that he did not sufficiently *see* the maid is contradicted by the very vivid impression he has of her in the moments before he kills her:

> I was filled with a kind of wonder. I had never felt another's presence so immediately and with such raw force. I saw her now, really saw her, for the first time, her mousy hair and bad skin, that bruised look around her eyes. She was quite ordinary, and yet, somehow, I don't know – somehow radiant. (Banville 1989:113)

What Freddie seems to experience in this moment is the reality of the maid: her actual otherness and threatening proximity which can no longer be held at arm's length, can no longer be controlled through an aestheticizing representation in stereotypes or frames. That the reality of the woman's bodily presence – both different from and similar to his own – is indeed experienced as threatening to Freddie, can further be considered in the light of the representation of women in Banville's fiction as a whole.

From Banville's earliest novels onwards, the occurrence of pairs of female figures can be noted: Ida and Ada or Martha and Beatrice in *Birchwood*, the whore and the green girl in *Doctor Copernicus*, Barbara and Regina in *Kepler*, Ottilie and Charlotte in *The Newton Letter*, Adele and Sophie in *Mefisto*, Daphne and Anna or the maid and the

painted woman in *The Book of Evidence*. These pairs usually have contrasting characteristics which replicate the whore-virgin or bitch-maiden stereotypes so pervasive in
Western literature (Frehner 2000). The "whores" are physical creatures, whose insistent materiality is both fascinating and threatening to Banville's cold heroes. The
"virgins," on the other hand, are wholly spiritualized: they have an air of composure,
stillness, and self-containment which the narrators typically associate with art, as in
the description of Kepler's stepdaughter, Regina:

> She was like a marvellous and enigmatic work of art, which he was content to stand and
> contemplate with a dreamy smile, careless of the artist's intentions. To try to tell her
> what he felt would be as superfluous as talking to a picture. Her inwardness, which had
> intrigued Kepler when she was a child, had evolved into a kind of quietly splendid
> equilibrium. She resembled her mother not at all. She was tall and very fair, with a
> strong narrow face. (Banville 1981a:100)

While this kind of splitting of the female figure in opposed pairs – as mind and body,
good and bad – is a form of stereotyping with a long tradition in art and literature,
it is also another instantiation of Banville's dualistic universe. Banville's intellectual
heroes usually have an uneasy relation with the real and the physical. To the scientists,
matters of body and sexuality are expressive of the chaos of the world which should
be superseded in beautiful theories. To Freddie Montgomery, the body is something
which has to be contained and sublimated through art. Moreover, women's bodies are
especially threatening as they symbolize the mortality which Banville's protagonists
seek to deny or transcend. The representation of women in dualistic pairs is therefore
another form of containing them, of emphasizing their otherness and negating any
shared humanity.

This realization of woman as the quintessential other is further emphasized in the
trilogy through the metaphor of the gaze. Freddie is forever looking at women, thus
fixing them in the position of object and frequently framing them in images borrowed
from art and literature. Thus he remarks how his mother "had the florid look of one
of Lautrec's ruined doxies," he imagines that the tinker girls who steal his hat had "a
Fagin waiting for them," and he introduces his wife in terms of an eighteenth-century
mythical painting: "I see her, my lady of the laurels, reclining in a sun-dazed glade,
a little vexed, looking away with a small frown" (Banville 1989:23, 166, 7). The trope
of the male gaze is further intensified in *Ghosts* and *Athena* as Freddie sets out on his
mission to make up for his crime by imagining a girl into existence. In both novels,
this attempt is both cast in an artistic light – Freddie as a latter-day Pygmalion – and
makes use of paintings. In *Ghosts* Freddie finds inspiration in the paintings of Watteau
(called Vaublin in the novel); in *Athena* he is inspired by pictorial representations of
classical myths, in particular "The Birth of Athena." In spite of these similarities,
however, the atmosphere of both novels is remarkably different.

Ghosts could be described as the fictional re-creation of the dreamlike space conjured
up in the paintings of Watteau. Most of the action takes place in a dilapidated

mansion on a semi-deserted island, which Freddie has retired to after his release from prison. Yet there is very little action in the novel, beyond what happens in the narrator's head. The novel contains many references to Beckett's *Trilogy*, in particular *Malone Dies*, in which the narrator also tries to bring a world into being. In both novels, for instance, the narrative situation can be called inconsistent in narratological terms, since the first-person narrator also confidently records, or rather imagines, the thoughts and feelings of other people (D'hoker 2006). As in Beckett's *Trilogy* moreover, the narrator's imaginative creation of others is intimately connected to his own search for an authentic identity: "I was determined at least to try and make myself into a – what do you call it? – monomorph, a monad. And then to start again, empty" (Banville 1993:26). Freddie believes that with the redemption of his crime and the restitution of a life will come wholeness and "pure being" for himself as well. At the end of *Ghosts*, however, he has to admit defeat in "this birthing business" and he comments: "I am told I should treasure life, but give me the world of art anytime" (Banville 1993:239).

In *Athena*, nevertheless, Freddie is ready for a second attempt at restitution. Only partially disguised by the hopeful-sounding pseudonym of "Morrow," he returns to a city on the mainland, presumably Dublin, where he becomes a pawn in the hands of a criminal gang of thieves and art dealers, under the colorful leadership of "The Da." As with Freddie's murder of the maid in *The Book of Evidence*, here too the events are partially inspired by actual events: the spectacular theft of eleven paintings from Russborough House in County Wicklow. While Freddie's authentication of these paintings forms one part of the plot, the real focus of the novel is his sexual, and increasingly violent, relationship with the mysterious A., whose shadowy presence haunts the pages of Freddie's memoir. A. is the girl on whom Freddie fixes his avid gaze and feverish imagination. Yet at the end of the novel it remains an open question whether he has finally succeeded in his creative mission. Patricia Coughlan (2006) has argued that the novel's real redemption comes not from Freddie's representation of A., but from his kindness to his aging Aunt Corky, whom he takes into his apartment to care for.

With the colorful figures of Aunt Corky and The Da, Freddie's quest for authenticity is also cast in a new light. For unlike Freddie, who is haunted by his division and lack of presence, they have made a virtue out of inauthenticity. While The Da's outlandish disguises successfully keep him out of reach of the police, Aunt Corky has over the years constructed a wholly fictional identity for herself. Freddie muses admiringly, "I am still not sure which one of Aunt Corky's many versions of her gaudy life was true, if any of them was. ... She lied with such simplicity and sincere conviction that really it was not lying at all but a sort of continuing reinvention of the self" (Banville 1995:22). That the cultivation of the mask may indeed be another way to deal with a divided self is further explored in *The Untouchable* (1997). Yet while *Athena* realizes this option in a comic way through the many grotesques inhabiting Freddie's narrative, in Banville's next novel the interaction of self and mask is viewed in a somewhat more tragic light.

For the protagonist of *The Untouchable*, Victor Maskell, Banville drew on the English art critic and soviet spy, Anthony Blunt. Blunt had for years been a respectable member of the English establishment: director of the Courtauld Institute of Art, Keeper of the King's Pictures and a personal friend of the queen. All this made his public exposure a one of the Cambridge Spies in the late 1970s of course all the more shocking. In *The Untouchable*, Banville takes over most elements of Maskell's life and spying activities, yet he adds additional layers of deceit so as to highlight the novel's central themes of masking and betrayal. He gives Maskell an Anglo-Irish past, complete with Protestant upbringing and Gaelic roots, and he makes him not just a homosexual, like Blunt, but one who is married with children. In *The Untouchable*, Maskell delves back into his past, retracing the many conscious and unconscious choices which have made him what he is. Although he prides himself on his superb acting talent – his claim, "I am a great actor, that is the secret of my success" (Banville 1997:7), echoes Freddie's, "What an actor the world has lost in me" (Banville 1989:179) – he describes his intention with this narrative as follows: "I shall strip away layer after layer of grime – the toffee-coloured varnish and caked soot left by a lifetime of dissembling – until I come to the very thing itself and know it for what it is. My soul. My self" (Banville 1997:7). Even though he immediately laughs away this grand ambition as impossible, his narrative is again suspended between the Romantic yearning for an authentic self and the ironic awareness that such a self does not exist. Maskell explains his taking on of other masks, other identities – as English gentleman and Russian spy, art critic and communist, homosexual, husband, and father – as attempts to cover up his lack of wholeness and identity. Yet, his memoir forces him to acknowledge that these masks have only aggravated the lack they sought to remedy (D'hoker 2004a). All that is left, in the end, is his narrative itself, which imposes an arbitrary coherence and unity on his disparate experiences and manifold identities.

Both *Eclipse* (2000) and *Shroud* (2002) continue this quest for identity and its attendant metaphors of acting, masking, and mirroring (Schwall 2006). With its references to Beckett (Duffy 2003) and its predominantly lyrical quality, *Eclipse* also echoes *Ghosts* and anticipates *The Sea* – novels which are marked by the relative absence of plot and the lack of reference to "real" events. Alex Cleave, the narrator of *Eclipse*, is a famous, aging actor who returns to the isolation of his childhood home after experiencing a crisis of identity on the stage. Like Maskell, he hopes that this return to the past will somehow provide him with a more stable identity. And if Maskell's name refers to masks as somehow more convincing and real than the self they serve to hide, Cleave's name reveals the typical, "cloven" or divided state of Banville's protagonists, a division of which he hopes his narrative of return will cure him:

> Free then of all encumbrance, all distraction, I might be able at last to confront myself without shock or shrinking. For is this not what I am after, the pure conjunction, the union of self with sundered self? I am weary of division, of being always torn. I shut my eyes and in a sort of rapture see myself stepping backward slowly into the cloven

shell, and the two halves of it, still moist with glair, closing round me. (Banville 2000a:70)

Equally divided are the women who occupy Cleave's imagination: his big, imposing wife Lydia and the slender, waif-like Lily. An even more insistent if absent presence in the book is Cleave's daughter Cass. A literary critic who is conducting some – to her father – mysterious research abroad, she is only present in memories and odd phone calls. At the end of her novel, her death makes her into another of the elusive ghosts haunting Cleave's memoir.

Cass Cleave also provides the link to the companion novel to *Eclipse*, *Shroud*. This novel is narrated by Axel Vander, a clear alter ego of Alex Cleave. Banville has loosely based this character on the figure of Paul de Man, the Yale critic who was discovered to have published some anti-semitic journalistic pieces in Belgium during World War II. Yet Banville again adds to his protagonist's duplicity by making "Axel Vander" an assumed identity only. In *Shroud* it is Cass Cleave who has discovered Axel's "real" identity, which brings the aging scholar to Turin to confront her. Axel's excessively immoral, selfish, and misogynistic behavior raises with renewed urgency the question of the (un)reliability of Banville's solipsistic narrators. To what extent are they indeed unreliable, removed from, or at odds with the implied author, to be exposed by the reader? While the obvious flaws and moral failings of these compulsive monologists could be cited in favor of their unreliability, their extreme self-consciousness as narrators and the fact that the same narrator returns in different guises throughout Banville's fiction contradict this interpretation again. In an interview with the *Irish Times* after the publication of *Eclipse*, Banville recognized the fact that his narrators are "all the same voice" and he argued that "even though [Alex Cleave] behaves dreadfully to his wife, for instance," he did not "find it hard to identify with him, because he's what we all are when we don't turn the mask on" (Banville 2000b). Yet this universal aspiration cannot fail to be qualified by the exclusively masculine perspective of novels such as *Book of Evidence*, *Eclipse*, and, especially, *Shroud*. Banville's narrative voice is intensely male and his female characters are filtered through the male gaze only. This is paradoxically confirmed by the passages in *Shroud* which are narrated in the third person and ostensibly give Cass's take on the events. As Imhof (2004) has pointed out, however, there are several indications in the novel that they are after all only a construction of Axel Vander, another version of Freddie Montgomery's failed attempts to create a girl. Moreover, the image of Cass Cleave revealed in these passages does little to allay suspicion. In spite of her schizophrenic condition, she is presented as another of Banville's frail, self-contained, and spiritual female figures from whom any physical presence or erotic desire seems oddly absent.

In comparison with the angry voice of Axel Vander, who often fumes with rage at the world, other people, and himself, the narrative of Max Morden, the protagonist of *The Sea*, is remarkably resigned. Although Morden shares many characteristics with other narrators (including an indulgence in alcohol, which has become steadily more noticeable since *The Book of Evidence*), he is one of the most likeable of Banville's cold heroes. On a – by now familiar – quest for past and self after the death of his wife, the dilettante art critic Max Morden revisits the seaside town where he spent his childhood holidays. His memories obsessively return to a particular summer when, on the brink of adolescence, he first experienced love, desire – and death. Death looms large in this novel: from the name of doctor De'Ath who treated his wife's cancer to his own sinister surname, and from the death by drowning of his summer friends, the twins Chloe and Myles, to the prospect of Max's own death which a drunken fall brings perilously close. At the same time, it can be said that Max reaches a greater acceptance of difference, otherness, and mortality than any of Banville's protagonists. His wife Anna and daughter Clare, for instance, are amongst the most fully realized female figures in Banville's fiction, and the novel closes with a feeling of oneness with the sea, that great metaphor for the world's strangeness and indifference in several of Banville's novels (McMinn 2006). It is perhaps not surprising therefore, that it is precisely *The Sea* which finally procured the Booker Prize for Banville. It is both a just reward for a poised, lyrical, and moving novel and a fitting recognition of Banville's status as one of the major novelists writing in English today.

References and Further Reading

Banville, J. (1970). *Long Lankin*. London: Secker & Warburg.

Banville, J. (1971). *Nightspawn*. London: Secker & Warburg.

Banville, J. (1973). *Birchwood*. London: Secker & Warburg.

Banville, J. (1976). *Doctor Copernicus*. London: Secker & Warburg.

Banville, J. (1981a). *Kepler*. London: Secker & Warburg.

Banville, J. (1981b). "A Talk." *Irish University Review*, 11.1, 13–17.

Banville, J. (1982). *The Newton Letter*. London: Secker & Warburg.

Banville, J. (1986). *Mefisto*. London: Secker & Warburg.

Banville, J. (1989). *The Book of Evidence*. London: Secker & Warburg.

Banville, J. (1993). *Ghosts*. London: Secker & Warburg.

Banville, J. (1995). *Athena*. London: Secker & Warburg.

Banville, J. (1997). *The Untouchable*. London: Picador.

Banville, J. (2000a). *Eclipse*. London: Picador.

Banville, J. (2000b). "A World Without People." *The Irish Times*, September 28.

Banville, J. (2002). *Shroud*. London: Picador.

Banville, J. (2005). *The Sea*. London: Picador.

Berensmeyer, I. (2000). *John Banville: Fictions of Order*. Heidelberg: Winter.

Coughlan, P. (2006). "Banville, the Feminine, and the Scenes of Eros." *Irish University Review*, 36.1, 81–101.

D'hoker, E. (2000). "Books of Revelation: Epiphany in John Banville's Science Tetralogy and *Birchwood*." *Irish University Review*, 30.1, 32–50.

D'hoker, E. (2002). "Portrait of the Other as a Woman with Gloves: Ethical Perspectives in John Banville's *The Book of Evidence*." *Critique*, 44.1, 23–37.

D'hoker, E. (2004a). *Visions of Alterity: Representation in the Works of John Banville*. Amsterdam: Rodopi.

D'hoker, E. (2004b). "'What then would life be but despair?': Romanticism and Scepticism in John Banville's *Doctor Copernicus*." *Contemporary Literature*, 45.1, 49–78.

D'hoker, E. (2006). "Self-Consciousness, Solipsism and Storytelling: John Banville's Debt to Samuel Beckett." *Irish University Review*, 30.1, 68–80.

Duffy, B. (2003). "Banville's Other Ghost: Samuel Beckett's Presence in John Banville's *Eclipse*." *Études Irlandaises*, 28.1, 85–106.

Frehner, R. (2000). "The Dark One and the Fair: John Banville's Historians of the Imagination and their Gender Stereotypes." *BELLS*, 11, 51–64.

Hand, D. (2002). *John Banville: Exploring Fictions*. Dublin: Liffey.

Harper, G. (2003). "John Banville." In M. Mosely (Ed.). *British and Irish Novelists since 1960* (pp. 30–38). Detroit: Gale.

Hutcheon, L. (1985). *Narcissistic Narrative: The Metafictional Paradox*. New York: Methuen.

Imhof, R. (1981). "An Interview with John Banville." *Irish University Review*, 11.1, 5–12.

Imhof, R. (1997). *John Banville: A Critical Introduction* (1989). Rev. edn. Dublin: Wolfhound.

Imhof, R. (2004). "'The Problematics of Authenticity': John Banville's *Shroud*." *ABEI Journal*, 6, 105–27.

Izarra, L. (1998). *Mirrors and Holographic Labyrinths. The Process of a New Aesthetic Synthesis in John Banville's Work*. Bethesda: International Scholars Publications.

Jackson, T. (1997). "Science, Art, and the Shipwreck of Knowledge: The Novels of John Banville." *Contemporary Literature*, 38.3, 510–33.

Lunden, B. (1999). *Re-educating the Reader: Fictional Critiques of Poststructuralism in Banville's* Doctor Copernicus, *Coetzee's* Foe, *and Byatt's* Possession. Göteburg: Acta Universitatis Gothoburgensis.

McMinn, J. (1999). *The Supreme Fictions of John Banville*. Manchester: Manchester University Press.

McMinn, J. (2000). "Versions of Banville: Versions of Modernism." In L. Harte and M. Parker (Eds). *Contemporary Irish Fiction: Themes, Tropes, Theories* (pp. 79–99). London: St Martin's.

McMinn, J. (2006). "'Ah! This plethora of metaphors! I am like everything except myself': The Art of Analogy in Banville's Fiction." *Irish University Review*, 30.1, 134–50.

McNamee, B. (2008). *The Quest for God in the Novels of John Banville 1973–2005: A Postmodern Spirituality*. Lewiston: Edwin Mellen.

Müller, A. (2004). "'You have been framed': The Function of Ekphrasis for the Representation of Women in John Banville's Trilogy." *Studies in the Novel*, 36.2, 185–205.

Murphy, N. (2006). "From *Long Lankin* to *Birchwood*: The Genesis of John Banville's Architectural Space." *Irish University Review*, 36.1, 9–24

Powell, K. Tarien (2005). "'Not a son but a survivor': Beckett … Joyce … Banville." *Yearbook of English Studies*, 35, 199–215.

Schwall, H. (2006). "'Mirror on Mirror Mirrored Is All the Show': Aspects of the Uncanny in Banville's Work with a Focus on *Eclipse*." *Irish University Review*, 30.1, 116–33.

Tarien, K. (2001). "Trying to Catch Long Lankin by his Arm: The Evolution of John Banville's *Long Lankin*." *Irish University Review*, 31.2, 386–403.

52

Between History and Fantasy:
The Irish Films of Neil Jordan

Brian McIlroy

Neil Jordan is Ireland's best-known filmmaker, having produced to date fifteen feature films. It is less known that he began creatively as a writer of fiction. As my title suggests, this essay will explore the particular world that Jordan has created for audiences and readers alike. It is one that is supported by – but bends – normative conceptions of history, often of an Irish hue. Equally, his work depends on the fantastical, whether understood in the context of the Anglo-Irish gothic tradition or in the context of the fantasy horror thriller. Embedded within both strains is his interest in the connections among violence, love, and transgression. On occasion, these streams meet in sections and sequences in his fiction and film, and this overlap is what often accounts for a "Neil Jordan work." In this essay, I concentrate on Jordan's specifically Irish feature films, of which there are currently seven. At time of writing, he is working on another film, a tale of an Irish fisherman who catches in his net a woman whom he believes to be a mermaid. The real made surreal while remaining emotionally authentic is a distinctive quality of this award-winning writer-director.

Jordan and Irish History

Of Jordan's seven Irish films, four (*Angel* [1982], *High Spirits* [1988], *The Miracle* [1991], and *The Crying Game* [1992]) are, on the surface, contemporary stories of the 1980s and early 1990s, yet the immediate and long-term past dominate their narratives. *Michael Collins* (1996), *The Butcher Boy* (1997), and *Breakfast on Pluto* (2005) are period pieces covering, respectively, the War of Independence and Civil War, the repressive late 1950s and early 1960s, and the late 1960s to mid-1970s. In the year that Neil Jordan was shooting *Michael Collins*, historian Robert Rosenstone (1995a,

A Companion to Irish Literature, edited by Julia M. Wright
© 2010 Blackwell Publishing Ltd

1995b) published two books on the problematic but stimulating relationship between film and history. Rosenstone's contribution to the debate on "historical film" is to make it clear that films cannot be held captive to books, since the former are primarily visual and oral documents. Films have their own rules and codes of representation, and any criticism must take these into account. Little is to be gained by too closely comparing a film to received written history, yet it seems equally limiting to isolate history from film representations and to view them as separate activities. What Rosenstone valorizes instead is a film that revisions our conception of history. In his writings, he shows us that films can do important historical work, providing insight into both the past and the current figuration of that past.

Rosenstone's strengths are in the area of American history and film, having acted as a historical adviser for Warren Beatty's *Reds* (1981). He believes that costume dramas, a category to which *Michael Collins*, *The Butcher Boy*, and *Breakfast on Pluto* arguably belong, are less important than independent and experimental films, which interact forcefully, and self-reflexively, with notions of historical truth. For Rosenstone, films do present a historical truth, one reading of the past that must be assessed alongside, not against, accounts using other media. That truth may alter, omit, invent, condense, and exaggerate more than professional historians would prefer, but films are nonetheless thinking and historical works. To be sure, historians do not fabricate evidence, but they must place emphasis to make an argument, and it is over these emphases that historians and filmmakers debate.

As I have mentioned above, Rosenstone would not place great historical store by Jordan's films, yet as Guy Westwell (1997) has suggested, strong reasons exist to believe that the conventional historical film can provide us with "progressive models" to revision history. *Michael Collins* is one such progressive model, a film that explicitly looks backward but implicitly looks to the present and future. Before one can argue this position to its fullest extent, one must first measure *Michael Collins* against the Hollywood model of classical cinema. David Bordwell (1986), informed by Russian formalist writings, has written at length on the specific characteristics of this kind of cinema that we now take for granted to the point of near-blindness to its operations.

As Bordwell outlines it, Hollywood cinema is both structurally and stylistically recognizable. We expect three acts or sections: an established scene, a violation or disturbance of that scene, and an eventual reassertion of order. We expect causal links; time compression; a plot and subplot; a deadline to be met; a likable, psychologically defined individual as the main interest; secondary characters who are one-dimensional; characters defined by their objectives; and presentation over description. Stylistically, we expect establishing shots; shot/reverse-shot formations; matching cuts; background music; locations chosen to suit the psychology of the characters or the dynamics of the action; a camera viewpoint with an omnipotent or privileged perspective; and smooth or invisible editing. More generally, we expect a heterosexual romance; meaning to be communicated through content not structure; clarity of lighting, sound, and framing; a happy ending or definitive closure; and anemic politics. From an economic and marketing perspective, Hollywood cinema is also recognizable. For a mainstream studio budgeted feature, over $20 million is normal; big-name stars are required, and supporting roles are also often played by well-known actors and actresses.

Jordan's $30 million film accords with most of the above, but with some major and minor departures that are worthy of comment. One could not argue that the politics of the film are in any way anemic; if anything, the film is about politics. Within the confines of this classical Hollywood film, it is difficult to deal effectively with historical and biographical material when action and dramatic pacing must be constantly sought out. Yet it is to Jordan's credit that he is both true to the historical record in places – Michael Collins did, for example, have a romantic relationship with Kitty Kiernan, and Harry Boland and he did seek her affections – and yet also finds space in places to grapple with controversial historical interpretation: the role, for example, of Éamon de Valera in Collins' death. This, then, is no ordinary biographical film, or "biopic" as the genre is known. It looks only at the 1916–22 period, with the guerrilla leader turned politician Collins as its center. In this respect, Jordan interestingly departs from the usual Hollywood approach, which would have looked to early childhood events to explain subsequent actions – for example, the murder of Frankie McGuire's father in Alan Pakula's *The Devil's Own* (1997) is recounted visually to "explain" the son's IRA membership and violence, thereby personalizing the politics to its detriment. By eschewing this approach, Jordan forces us to deal with the politics head on. In fact, the weakness of the heterosexual romance, in terms of extended screen time, also helps to direct the audience's attention to the political issues involved. Another departure from the Hollywood norm is the cut near the end of the film to actual 1920s black and white footage of Michael Collins' funeral cortège, attended by hundreds of thousands of Irish people. This aesthetic decision adds weight and gravitas to the authenticity of the historical record that Jordan is seeking to explore. Finally, the way in which the assassinations are choreographed alerts us to the makeshift, awkward nature of murder. The style used for the killings is circumspect, not in a Sam Peckinpah or Quentin Tarantino mode of representation, where blood and gore are either aestheticized or parodied, but much more in the vein of Martin Scorsese's *Mean Streets* (1973) in which the act of shooting people is shown to be painful and frequently haphazard. Even so, the cross-cutting technique utilized between the assassinations of the English secret service agents and Collins and Kiernan in the Gresham Hotel is a fairly standard device, employed in films such as Francis Ford Coppola's *The Godfather* (1972). *Mean Streets* may also be an influence on Jordan in terms of the representation of the uneasy relationship between Roman Catholicism and violence.

In looking backward to the War of Independence and the Civil War, Jordan's film approximates the ideals of a "national imaginary," a D.W. Griffith *Birth of a Nation* (1915), minus the race issue. This ambition helps to explain the Irish Film Censor's unusual comment on the film as a "landmark" in Irish cinema, and the parade of political figures to the film's opening in Ireland. Since the two main political parties of the Republic of Ireland, Fine Gael and Fianna Fáil, have their origins in the actions and beliefs of Michael Collins and Éamon de Valera respectively, it is not surprising that the film would elicit questions about the state's progress and development from its turbulent beginnings.

What Jordan illustrates is the barbarity of this struggle for nationhood, even if the necessity for it is unquestioned. The escalation of the violence from killing Irishmen who work for the British administration, to killing English secret service agents, to the killing of former comrades is presented as a seductive drug motivated by the prospect of control and power. This interpretation works best in any analysis of Jordan's de Valera (Alan Rickman) who seems to be the arch manipulator, with a greater, though deceitful, strategic sense than that possessed by Collins. De Valera sent Collins to negotiate the peace treaty knowing that hardline republicans would not be able to accept any compromise. In that sense, de Valera gave himself options, and he chose civil war rather than exert his undoubted abilities of persuasion to seek accommodation. Although Jordan implies that de Valera was "in the mix" with the plans to ambush Collins, a problematic interpretation to many historians, it is not the most provocative aspect of the film, nor is it a new accusation.

If the film serves to release the ambivalence felt in the Republic of Ireland about its violent genesis, it most likely succeeds. It effectively speaks to the notion that the new state grew out of violence to be, for the most part, a peaceful country. The film then carries this transformative notion as a metaphor for the then current situation in Northern Ireland. It is a problematic carry forward because the differences are as confusing as the similarities. The reason for Collins to attend the peace talks in London was ostensibly because he could by force of personality convince both British and Irish people of the seriousness of the issues at stake, and he could best deliver the hardliners. In much the same way, Provisional Sinn Féin and the IRA in Northern Ireland needed Gerry Adams and Martin McGuinness to attend peace talks to find a way to disengage from a very long war that could not be won militarily. But, as with Collins' experience, negotiations carry risks once a compromise is reached. Feared splits within the IRA membership over the prospect of a compromise have turned out to be reality, as evidenced by the 2009 murders of two British soldiers, and a Northern Irish policeman by the breakaway group the Continuity IRA. The rhetoric of Jordan's film is utilized in part to explain to a wide audience in Ireland, Britain, and the United States of America that the men and women of violence, as represented politically by Adams and McGuinness, will need to be accepted into negotiations and, further, *helped*, to accede to what became the Good Friday Agreement.

On a more specific level, the film reverberates with northern issues – the casting of Liam Neeson as Michael Collins is fascinating. Neeson is from Ballymena in Northern Ireland, a town represented by the ultra-Unionist Ian Paisley. Neeson is thus a Roman Catholic who grew up within a very Protestant culture. This casting decision, although many years in the works, does link the minority Catholic population of the North with a form of liberation from Britain. On the other side of the coin we have Ned Broy, played by Stephen Rea, an Ulster Protestant who is on record as having no sympathies for the Unionist position. It seems no accident that Rea plays the role of a government employee who is persuaded by the republican arguments of Michael Collins, since it appears that Rea has taken that political route in his own life. This subtext literally explodes on one occasion – when a Belfast police detective (Ian McElhinney) arrives in Dublin to bring some "Belfast efficiency" to the southern Irish police force, and is immediately blown up in his car. This scene has been much commented upon. The anachronistic use of car bombs (a feature of the IRA's 1970s campaign, not of that of Collins' volunteers during the War of Independence) is cited first, leading to the comment that it is a not-so-subtle veiled attack on Protestantism and Unionism. Even the use of an armored car at the Croke Park massacre, another historical "mistake," is suggestive of the army and police vehicles that traversed Northern Ireland in the 1970s and 1980s. Furthermore, the black and white newsreel footage of the introduction of the Black and Tans, who are billed as having fought at the battle of the Somme in 1916, is another potent northern metaphor. These unruly figures are akin to the violent "B" Specials (part-time policemen) who were active in Northern Ireland in the 1920s and late 1960s suppressing nationalist aspirations and civil rights for Catholics. The petrol bombing of the Black and Tans at one point in the film brings this connection strongly to the surface, as an action commonplace at the beginning of the recent Troubles; in addition, the reference to the Somme is significant, since it is the Ulster Protestant and Unionist sacrificial event of note in 1916, as distinct from the Easter Rising.

Moreover, the specter of the North hovers ominously during the catalog of assassinations in the film, conjuring up the many hundreds of English soldiers and Northern Irish police who have been killed in the more recent conflict. The often hyperventilating young volunteers who do the killing put a human face on dark deeds, a choice that can be contrasted with the cold efficiency of murders in classic gangster films and contrasted even with contemporary accounts of the Ulster crisis, such as Alan Clarke's *Elephant* (1989). Jordan also raises the controversial connection between the Roman Catholic Church and the armed struggle. One of the assassins prays in church before he kills his fellow Irishman, even uttering a blessing to the condemned man before he shoots. Another policemen is shot leaving a church, and one is very conscious of the religious icon atop the hill from where the anti-treaty forces ambush and kill Collins. The Protestant Unionist perception that the Roman Catholic Church is too often ambivalent in its attitudes to the IRA insurgency is, in a sense, confirmed by the film.

The concentration on Collins forces Jordan to omit a great deal. One can only do so much in two hours of screen time. From a southern perspective, the War of Independence is fought for the most part as a Dublin-centered affair, ignoring the many rural "flying columns" (mobile guerrilla units) that typified the era, as found portrayed in one of the first indigenous Irish features, Tom Cooper's *The Dawn* (1936). Jordan is also pressed to convey the social and collective nature of Sinn Féin's spectacular victory in the elections of 1918. The omission of the treaty negotiations in London, undramatic as they would be visually, prevents the viewer from seeing Collins the politician in action, leaving us only with a few speeches in town squares and in the Dáil (the Irish parliament). The absence of these negotiations allows Jordan to bypass the embarrassing affair Collins supposedly had in London with Hazel Lavery and to omit the arguments about accommodating partition and on what terms. From a northern perspective, the omission of the negotiations extends to the general structuring absence in the film of the Unionist case. Why one million Irish people did not want a united, republican Ireland remains unasked and unanswered. If Gerry Adams is a modern Michael Collins, then perhaps it is a politically moral act for Jordan not to have to include Collins' famous line that he had signed his death warrant when he appended his name to the treaty with the British.

What historical, social, and cultural work does Jordan's film ultimately do? For the Republic of Ireland, it lays to rest the violent past; it puts Collins and de Valera together as two separate roads that Ireland could have chosen between but for the ambush and death of Michael Collins in 1922. For Jordan to use the comment of de Valera's, reportedly uttered at the fiftieth anniversary of the 1916 Rising, that Collins would prove to be the most important figure in twentieth-century Irish history at the expense of the "Long fellow," is to suggest that even de Valera, who had enormous influence throughout the Republic of Ireland from the 1920s to the 1970s, was conscious of the major contribution of a man who changed from a guerrilla fighter to a man of treaty and compromise. It was, after all, a path de Valera followed in the late 1920s. More narrowly, de Valera's comment, and the film generally, help to bind Fine Gael, Fianna Fáil, and Sinn Féin as equal elements of the political mosaic of the Republic of Ireland. If a bias exists in the film, it is toward the Dublin-centered Free Staters, who formed Fine Gael, and whose party now represents a mainly urban and educated bourgeoisie, not unlike Jordan himself. This educated elite have accepted that the Unionists of the North must consent peacefully to any future united Ireland, and if they do not, they should not be forced into one. As Jordan has said, albeit uneasily, "There are many ways of being Irish, and I suppose that Protestant Unionist is one of them" (Carr 1996).

Despite Jordan's often conflicting commentary on this matter in interviews, the film is a warning to Provisional Sinn Féin, the IRA, and nationalist and republican voters. Violence and assassination may be good enough to get to the conference table, but they do not provide the political courage to honor a compromise. To the Unionist population, however, Jordan's film reaffirms the anti-imperialist myth: that republicans need deal only with Britain and not with the Ulster Protestant and the Unionist voter, who are judged as weak and "deluded lackeys" (Nairn 1981:231). For the Unionist audience of Northern Ireland, then, Jordan's *Michael Collins* crosses the border and visualizes them out of history.

A cynic might argue that Éamon de Valera's rise to prominence only led to the repressive culture depicted in Jordan's *The Butcher Boy* (1997). A co-scripted work with the novelist Pat McCabe, the film delves much deeper within the Irish neurosis, the recent past of 1962 Ireland, a time similar to Jordan's own upbringing. As a youth, Jordan was fed a staple of religious films (see Jordan 1992:36), and one can certainly argue that *The Butcher Boy* is a keenly religious but anti-Catholic film. The fragmented town life of Francie Brady (Eamonn Owens) is beset with internal and external pressures. We are not so much watching an extended metaphor of Francie as an abused child of Irish history, as one critic has suggested (McLoone 2000:213–23), but rather an exploration of the inadequacy of traditional Ireland and its institutions, particularly the Roman Catholic Church, and its failure to nurture its young, to confess to its own sickness, to acknowledge that its various forms of denial have created and perpetuated mental illness. It is now commonplace to observe that, from the late 1950s onwards, Ireland began a slow and painful process of internationalization, of opening out to the world, inviting foreign investment and industries. Initially, however, this modernization was tied to the urban centers, particularly Dublin. It is no accident that Francie's trip to Dublin from his Monaghan town sees him attend the illicit – a science fiction horror movie about alien invasion (a typical American displaced manifestation about the fear of Russian invasion during the Cold War). Also, he purchases here a model of an Irish country family, depicting a happy colleen sewing outside her cottage; it is ironic that he must travel to modern Dublin to find a distillation of an idealized rural Ireland. He buys this gift for his mother Annie (Aisling O'Sullivan), unaware that she has killed herself, possibly pushed over the edge by the fact that Francie had temporarily run away from home. To arrive at his mother's funeral cortège with this imaginary happy family tucked under his arm reveals the lie of de Valera's desire for an Ireland of "comely maidens," whereas the reality of many is mental illness, domestic violence, depression, and suicide. Jordan complicates this apparent urban/rural division by analyzing the small town, a place neither completely rural nor completely urban; it is always a place of becoming, beckoning sometimes to the urbane future, and sometimes to the unsophisticated, natural past. It is also a border county, close to that other "British" Ireland of Northern Ireland.

The urbane future is full of shocks and horrors of a different kind than the rural stagnant past. At first, it seems to be liberating. The arrival of television, on which Francie and Joe (Alan Boyle) can sneak peeks of their favorite *Lone Ranger* series as well as the series entitled *The Fugitive* (actually broadcast 1963–67), ushers in a fantasy world as much as the comic books they steal from Phillip Nugent (Andrew Fullerton). One of the facts of early 1960s comic books in Ireland and the UK is that the Americans produced many of them in color, whereas the homegrown product was invariably in black and white. No doubt this helps to explain why Jordan accompanies the film's opening credits with drawings of these attractive American comic-book heroes. The myth of the American West as frontier is not so far removed from the small town in rural Ireland, though it is interesting that the boys can identify with Sitting Bull and Geronimo as much as with the Lone Ranger. Are they noble savages or delusional Robin Hood figures? But this American influence intrudes in a very real way via radio reports of the Cuban missile crisis and the possibility of nuclear anni-hilation. This news feeds into Francie's imaginings, and his depressing reality. He moves into the world of "What if?," projecting a nuclear strike in his home town which would create devastation and the emergence of mutants with pig and bug heads; in some respects, to Francie, this would explain perfectly the reality of his current existence, his family laid waste by the metaphorical bomb of small town and Church expectations. Doctors and priests logically, therefore, take on alien heads, and he senses he is living in a world of grotesquery, assisted by the fact that he acquires a job in a slaughterhouse. It is as if he is one of the few survivors in the world of that other classic 1950s movie, Don Siegel's *Invasion of the Body Snatchers* (1956).

If America connotes agency, freedom, and risk, Ireland is replete with feelings of repression, failure, limitation, and dullness. Its horrors are too visceral. Francie must seek the miraculous for his active mind to survive, and he achieves this by having visions of the Virgin Mary, played in a coy manner by singer Sinead O'Connor (a controversial casting decision in itself, given her famous ripping up of the Pope's picture on television, and her allegations of child abuse when she was a young girl, the authenticity of which has been challenged by her own family). The cycle of illness – Francie's father also seems to have been through a reform school run by a Catholic order – appears to be tied to Francie's self-loathing and desire to see himself above what he calls the "Bogmen" with their "bony arses" with whom he has to consort. These people are the peasants synonymous with the rural Ireland that de Valera embraced, and which Francie (and Neil Jordan) seem to think of as an unimaginative and limited form of Irish identity.

Strangely, though, while we understand that Francie sees rural Ireland as a nightmare experience, which is perhaps why he sees the Virgin Mary in the middle of a peat bog, a substance fully representative of Ireland's traditional economy, it is odd on the surface that all his hatred should focus on the Nugents, who have returned from England with "airs." This jealousy revolves around wealth – Phillip Nugent can afford American comic books and has a television at home, good clothes, and so on. This wealth and middle-class aspiration steals away his friend Joe, despite their blood-brother partnership. England also figures largely in the failure of his musician father (Stephen Rea), for Francie's Unclo Alo (Ian Hart), like many Irish, traveled, worked, and eventually settled in London to make their way in the world. To go to England for work was not exactly an Irish dream, but a practical necessity, often undermining the self-esteem of those who stayed behind (and, it should be said, the emigrants themselves often received a frosty reception in England). In this way, Francie's father sees himself as a failure, a feeling picked up by his son all too clearly. The latter's gross murder of Mrs Nugent (Fiona Shaw), his daubing of the walls in her blood, and his attempt at a fiery suicide are his response to an Irish society that is sick beyond redemption, and which has made him sick. In an odd and disturbing way, a boy influenced by American action heroes murders a woman influenced by British culture. The triple colonization of Britain, America, and de Valera's rural and small town imaginary – a nation of small shopkeepers, as some commentators opined – literally explodes the Irish family depicted.

Jordan's third period piece, *Breakfast on Pluto*, is the most hopeful, an unusual affirmation that despite the horrendous obstacles – personal, political, and historical – Irish individuals can find the courage to seek happiness. Patrick "Kitten" Braden

(Cillian Murphy) is the illegitimate son of Father Bernard (Liam Neeson) and his housekeeper. Abandoned by his mother, he is brought up unhappily in an ordinary foster family with no masculine presence in the house. Effeminate, with a penchant for wearing women's clothing, he is a natural rebel. In book-like chapter sections, we follow Kitten's movements through significant moments in contemporary Irish history. He watches his Down syndrome friend die in a random car bomb explosion, witnesses the racism of British troops at a checkpoint while crossing into Northern Ireland, and experiences the rampant homophobia of IRA gunmen, who decide he is not even worth a bullet. Kitten travels to London, meeting a menagerie of exploitative individuals and, while he seems to be having fun dancing with an off-duty British soldier, he happens to be in the night-club that was blown up by the IRA cell that includes one of his childhood friends. Grabbed by the police, who figure that since he is Irish he must be guilty, he is interrogated and tortured in a scene not dissimilar to Gerry Conlon's ordeal in Jim Sheridan's *In the Name of the Father* (1993). Kitten volunteers a confession, but it is so ridiculous that he is released, and even one of his former torturers finds him safe, secure work in a legal peep-show operation. Here, in a scene obviously "lifted" from Wim Wenders' *Paris, Texas* (1984), Father Bernard reveals his true parentage and the London address of his mother.

Kitten visits his mother, pretending to be a telephone company market researcher. He faints at first sight of her, although he recovers to quietly depart, and, later, reconnects strongly with his father. The Oedipal triangle is set up, but nothing tragic occurs, even though his mother remains unaware of who he is. At the end of the film, Father Bernard and Kitten are burned out of their Irish home, presumably by those threatened by non-traditional lifestyles. A more positive life is envisioned in England. Ireland, certainly that of the 1970s, in Jordan's eyes, still fails the liberal and imaginative test. Its conventional history is a curse.

Jordan and Fantasy

One of the truisms of English imperial power – and one that is often misunderstood – is that it successfully ruled and colonized Ireland just as much by manufacturing consent and negotiation as by the threat of force and Protestant settlement. It was this fact that drove Irish nationalists and republicans in the late nineteenth century and early twentieth century to look for a Gaelic Revival to differentiate the Irish from the English and to force the "West Brits" (Irish people steeped and comfortable in British culture – represented, for example, by Gabriel Conroy in James Joyce's short story, "The Dead") to make a stark choice.

Part of this political program purposely put a lot of value on the Irish peasant experience and folklore, for it was these people who had suffered the most during the Famine and British rule generally. In the imaginings of W.B. Yeats and Patrick Pearse, Celtic mythology became a source of strength and mystery, a counterbalance to the conservative Roman Catholic Church, and this pagan power suggested a necessary founding myth of the putative Irish nation. In this context, the recourse to the supernatural, including leprechauns, faeries, banshees, faith healing, somnambulism, and plain old miracles is more readily appreciated. The ignorant Irish peasant lout of English caricature is reframed as an idiot savant with a magical channel to a natural and supernatural reservoir of knowledge and spirituality.

But this is only one camera position from which to "treat" Ireland, and through which Robert Stevenson's *Darby O'Gill and the Little People* (1959), for example, is informed. Neil Jordan leans more favorably towards the influences of Bram Stoker and Oscar Wilde, which present a camera position from a minority urban sensibility forced to consider a majority rural perspective. We are now in the world of the much-written-about Anglo-Irish gothic, a mode inextricably tied to the Anglo-Irish settler culture and the colonial experience generally. In this paradigm, with theoretical help from Frantz Fanon and Homi Bhabha, it is assumed the Protestant populace's awareness of its insecurity produces a monstrous tension that reveals itself in supernatural and highly emotional writing. Indeed, Alison Milbank argues that Bram Stoker's *Dracula* (1897) was perceived by his peers as an attempted "mediating between Catholic and Protestant conceptions of Christianity" (Milbank 1998:12), though others simply argue that the vampire in his castle stands in for the rapacious British and Protestant colonizer and settler emanating out from Dublin Castle and other de facto garrisons with the express purpose of feasting on the native Irish. Seamus Deane (1997) – perhaps too cleverly – sees a direct (yet perversely inverted) link between Stoker's 1890s Dracula, who travels by sea in a coffin during the day, and the so-called "coffin-ships" which poor Irish Famine emigrants had to endure to reach North America. Both were living dead, and both would come back to haunt.

What Milbank and other writers on the gothic, such as W.J. McCormack (1993), have ventured is that the Act of Union in 1801 that dissolved the Dublin parliament left the Irish Protestant elite directionless. Specifically, it created a duality – apparent supporters of the colonial system but also victims of it, since the center of local power had shifted from Dublin to London. Julian Moynahan (1995) also points out that Charles Maturin and Joseph Sheridan Le Fanu, two of the great Irish gothic writers, emerged from Dublin-based Huguenot heritage, not the landed gentry of the (Protestant and Anglican) Big House (see PART FIVE, THE RISE OF GOTHIC). They had, in other words, in their family history faint echoes of Catholic persecution in France. So, one can see the Irish gothic as Protestant unease within Ireland, penned by almost reluctant and guilty intellectuals speaking for and about a native Irish who were still struggling in the 1800s to articulate a sense of self-worth in political terms. One can also see the various mechanisms of literary gothic as an acceptance of the irrational not just in religious terms but also in the areas of personal activity and feeling. Vampirism, for example, attracts and repels in equal measure, whether it be read or viewed in Stoker's *Dracula*, Murnau's *Nosferatu* (1922), or Jordan's *Interview with the Vampire* (1993).

Jordan and the Gothic

Yet, the interesting question here is why Neil Jordan, an Irish Catholic-educated writer, should find the so-called Protestant gothic of particular force. Recent Irish gothic theorists, such as Richard Haslam (2007), have explored the sub-category of an Irish Catholic gothic, and would rather see the gothic as a mode available to all, without the political and religious overtones of a tradition. Arguably the Dublin-centered Jordan shares with such urbane sophisticates as Maturin and Le Fanu an equal sense of fear and wonder about the wild Irish countryside and its inhabitants. More directly, he prefers the exploration and release of the supernatural because it allows ready discussion of race, gender, and nationality issues. Of course, it further allows the sensational treatment and examination of sexuality, matters most difficult to address in a culture that has often tried to deny the reality of such desires. This restrictive atmosphere is best revealed by the continual (though mostly narrow) debates over abortion, effectively still illegal in Ireland. In March 2002 a referendum was held in the Republic of Ireland to decide whether a 1992 Supreme Court ruling that a woman could have an abortion if she were deemed suicidal should be struck down. The vote was 51% to 49% in favor of the Supreme Court ruling. The urban vote was largely liberal; the rural vote was largely conservative. Every year, it is esti-mated that 7,000 young women travel from Ireland to England for abortion services. In Northern Ireland, abortions can occur for "medical reasons," but by refusing to transfer the 1967 "liberalization Act" of England and Wales (which effectively decriminalized homosexuality and abortion) to Northern Ireland the current Northern Ireland Assembly aligned itself with the policy of the Republic of Ireland.

Beyond the political and social climate, Jordan is clearly influenced by many artistic strains – the linking of violence and Catholicism in Martin Scorsese's gangster films, such as *Mean Streets*, mentioned above, or the whimsical nature of many European art films of the 1960s, such as Antonioni's *Blow-Up* (1966) – but mostly he seems com-fortable within Hollywood's general melodramatic tendencies, where sentiment and emotion are encouraged. Witness the passions in *The End of the Affair* (1998), which depends on the supernatural – a religious miracle – to play a major part in how the main characters experience the meaning of their existences. Look at the exotic titles of Jordan's fictional works – *Night in Tunisia* (1979), *The Dream of the Beast* (1983), *Sunrise with Sea Monster* (1994), and the ghostly *Shade* (2004). He uses the term "Miracle" for his 1991 film to describe a boy discovering emotionally and sexually his long-lost mother, not to mention the ambiguous term "Angel," the title of his first feature film (aka *Danny Boy* [1982]). His work with Angela Carter on *The Company of Wolves* (1984) and with Anne Rice on *Interview with the Vampire* opens his gothicism out in plain view.

Even when Jordan turns to a rather unsuccessful attempt at Hollywood comedy in *High Spirits* (1988), we see his recycling of all the themes discussed above: the mon-strous, incestuous familial bonds, the presence of the past as a determining power, and the outbreak of general madness and mayhem. In *High Spirits*, Castle Plunkett is in dire straights and Peter Plunkett (Peter O'Toole) chances upon the idea of marketing his Irish castle as one full of ghosts and ghouls. While his American tourists are unimpressed with the staff's best ghostly efforts to scare them, the guests do suffer and enjoy the awakening of the dead Plunketts. Much of the humor rests on the conceit of living people loving most of all those people who are dead.

This raising of the dead forces a revaluation of contemporary relationships and sexuality. Sharon (Beverley D'Angelo) has been sent over by her father Jem Brogan, the Irish American who will retain the rights to the castle if the Plunketts cannot make their loan payments. He wishes to transfer it to California, brick by brick, to create a kind of theme park. Peter Plunkett delivers a vicious assault on Jem Brogan's family by suggesting that one of his ancestors hoarded food during the Famine. Ironically, Peter Plunkett's decision to market Irish heritage (a haunted castle) as a tourist destination is not qualitatively different from Jem Brogan's intentions. One of the niceties of Jordan's script is that Sharon Brogan ultimately falls in love with a male ancestor, Martin Brogan (Liam Neeson), thereby suggesting not just a necrophiliac romance but also an incestuous one. With Jack's (Steve Guttenberg) marriage to the once dead Mary Plunkett (Daryl Hannah), who magically lives as Sharon dies, the productive link between Ireland and America is solidly made. Of course, this strategic move in the scripting taps into the fantasy of many Irish Americans fascinated with their heritage and the romantic notion of returning to claim a special touchstone to the past. Additionally, Jordan's interest in making this into a sex comedy reveals itself in his fervent satire of the Catholic priesthood and its strictures against fornication and sexual thoughts in general. The American Brother Tony (Peter Gallagher) sees this trip as a retreat to finally decide his path within the Church. He is fully tempted by Miranda (Jennifer Tilly), and he succumbs to his general happiness. A most compelling image is this white-collared novitiate surrounded by ghostly nun habits while steam rises from his groin, almost as punishment for desiring Miranda. Such images, along with jokes about Martin Brogan's body odor and natural functions, mean that Irish hang-ups about sex and the body could hardly be made more obvious or critiqued more clearly.

Despite the general attempt at humor – and this film did not succeed well critically or commercially – there is a difficulty with the reliance upon the past as a form of modernization for the castle. At one level, the real family ghosts appear, in what is probably the best scene in the film, appalled at the failure of the Plunketts and the staff to create believable ghosts and save the castle; at another level, Jordan seems to be suggesting, much in keeping with notions of the gothic, that harmony is restored when past and present are reunited. This explains the rather touching scene between father (Ray McAnally) and son, a conversation about feelings that probably could only occur because one of the participants is dead. So, in this film, the strange happenings in the middle of the night, so common to gothic and melodramatic works, turns out to be restorative and life-affirming. The gothic horror frees his characters to be themselves.

The gothic license, as defined by transgression of norms, is expressed further with the addressing of lesbianism in *Mona Lisa* (1986), homosexuality and bisexuality in *The Crying Game*, and the feminized male in many of his works, although some observers may regard this interest as an unfortunate form of erotic and sexual tourism. As Jordan himself admitted in updating the story "Guests of the Nation" by Frank O'Connor to the script of *The Crying Game*, he felt what was missing was the erotic thread, one sure to be controversial and destabilizing.

The horror genre film proper is another more accepted way to explore these boundaries, and it has often allowed deep anxieties and fears to be articulated – fear of technology runs riot in James Whale's *Frankenstein* (1931) and Fritz Lang's *Metropolis* (1926), and fear of the female body runs throughout Brian De Palma's *Carrie* (1976), normally considered a displaced discourse on the taboo of menstruation. To steal the title from Barry Grant's 1996 book, it is the "dread of difference" that drives the narrative and compels us to watch. But Jordan's films are not horrific in the cheap, sensational way seen in many horror movies – his characters are too well formed to allow the plot to rattle along at a tremendous, unthinking speed. If there is a problem with a film like *In Dreams* (1999), it is because Jordan takes all the necessary plot points of a horror/thriller, and then refuses to up the tempo, attracting the criticism that his timing and talent do not fit the conventional melodramatic horror or thriller film. The film did poorly at the box office – on a $30 million budget, it recouped only $11.3 million in North America, in contrast to the $50 million budget for *Interview with the Vampire* which recouped over $100 million in the USA alone, and $221 million worldwide. Jordan argued that he was attempting to make a serious horror movie with a psychological exploration, rooted in childhood fairy tales – in this case *Snow White*. Earlier, his *The Company of Wolves* (1984) had explored werewolves and a variation of *Little Red Riding Hood*.

One might say that his success with *The Crying Game* was fortuitous, coming at a point in North American cultural discourse where these very issues of gender identity were being debated: Judith Butler's *Gender Trouble* was published two years before the film appeared, for example. His success with *Interview with the Vampire* relied to a great extent on the star billing of Tom Cruise and Brad Pitt, and the pre-sold property of Anne Rice, but it allowed him to delve into the *Company of Wolves* territory that he shared with the writer Angela Carter in the mid-1980s. The point about both these films, somewhat similar to *High Spirits*, is their confidence in alternative realities and yet, equally, the confidence that these realities are neither utopias nor fully dystopias. The vampires of *Interview with the Vampire* live forever, liminal characters that haunt our imaginations. They are appealing hybrids.

Despite the personal, commercial, and cultural imperatives to seek out the gothic, Jordan's work is a kind of Wildean sublime, an exalted state that induces awe and terror, a negative pleasure. The gothic attracts Jordan's interest for it is a literary (and filmic) form that appeals to the visual, to excess, to fragmentation, to the refusal to serve a particular ideology. It is an artist's weapon against conformity. In the surplus value that gothic seems to provoke, one can see the impossibility of certitude for a bourgeois subject and an aspiring bourgeois society. The horror that Jordan's gothic brings to Irish society is one predicated upon an inner knowledge that the healthy imagination cannot express itself in a suffocating, institutionalized culture.

REFERENCES AND FURTHER READING

Bordwell, D. (1986). "Classical Hollywood Cinema: Narrational Principles and Procedures." In P. Rosen (Ed.). *Narrative, Apparatus, Ideology: A Film Theory Reader* (pp. 17–34). New York: Columbia University Press.

Butler, J. (1990). *Gender Trouble: Feminism and the Subversion of Identity*. New York: Routledge.

Carr, J. (1996) "Fighting Irish." *Vancouver Sun*, October 24.

Coogan, T.P. (1996). *Michael Collins: The Man Who Made Ireland*. Boulder, CO: Roberts, Rinehart.

Deane, S. (1997). *Strange Country: Modernity and Nationhood in Irish Writing since 1790*. Oxford: Clarendon Press.

Grant, B.K. (1996). *The Dread of Difference: Gender and the Horror Film*. Austin: University of Texas Press.

Haslam, R. (2007). "Irish Gothic: A Rhetorical Hermeneutics Approach." *The Irish Journal of Gothic and Horror Studies*, 2 (March), online.

Hopper, K. (2008) "Undoing the Fanaticism of Meaning: Neil Jordan's *Angel*." In D. Farquharson and S. Farrell (Eds). *Shadows of the Gunmen: Violence and Culture in Modern Ireland* (pp. 119–41). Cork: Cork University Press.

Jordan, N. (1992). "Neil Jordan's Guilty Pleasures." *Film Comment*, 28.6 (November–December), 36.

Jordan, N. (1996). *Michael Collins: Screenplay and Film Diary*. London: Vintage.

Jordan, N. (1997). *The Collected Fiction of Neil Jordan*. London: Vintage.

Jordan, N. (2004). *Shade*. London: John Murray.

McCormack, W.J. (1993). *Dissolute Characters: Irish Literary History through Balzac, Sheridan, Le Fanu and Bowen*. Manchester: Manchester University Press.

McIlroy, B. (2001). *Shooting to Kill: Filmmaking and the "Troubles" in Northern Ireland*. Richmond, BC: Steveston Press.

McLoone, M. (2000). *Irish Film: The Emergence of a Contemporary Cinema*. London: British Film Institute.

Milbank, A. (1998). "'Powers Old and New': Stoker's Alliances with Anglo-Irish Gothic." In W. Hughes and A. Smith (Eds). *Bram Stoker: History, Psychoanalysis and the Gothic* (pp. 12–28). New York: St Martin's Press.

Moynahan, J. (1995). *Anglo-Irish: The Literary Imagination in a Hyphenated Culture*. Princeton: Princeton University Press.

Nairn, T. (1981). *The Break-Up of Britain: Crisis and Neo-Nationalism*. London: Verso.

O'Rawe, D. (2003). "At Home with Horror: Neil Jordan's Gothic Variations." *Irish Studies Review*, 11.2, 189–98.

Pramaggiore, M. (2008). *Neil Jordan*. Chicago: University of Illinois Press.

Rockett, E. and K. Rockett. (2003). *Neil Jordan: Exploring Boundaries*. Dublin: Liffey Press.

Rosenstone, R.A. (1995a). *Visions of the Past: The Challenge of Film to our Idea of History*. Cambridge, MA: Harvard University Press.

Rosenstone, R.A. (Ed.). (1995b). *Revisioning History: Film and the Construction of a New Past*. Princeton: Princeton University Press.

Westwell, G. (1997). Review of Rosenstone's *Visions of the Past* and *Revisioning History*. *Screen*, 38, 99–105.

Zucker, C. (2008). *The Cinema of Neil Jordan: Dark Carnival*. London: Wallflower Press.

53

"Keeping That Wound Green": The Poetry of Paul Muldoon

David Wheatley

Life and Background

Paul Muldoon is among the foremost living poets in English. From his precocious beginnings as a teenager, his work over forty years in poetry, drama, libretto, and criticism has won him every accolade short of the Nobel Prize. No Irish poet since Yeats has possessed his capacity for verbal surprise and pyrotechnics. He has served as the Oxford Professor of Poetry and combines an academic chair at Princeton with the post of poetry editor at the *New Yorker*. He has been the subject of numerous monographs and critical studies, and as a focus of critical esteem is matched only by a select group of other living poets, a list that would include John Ashbery, Seamus Heaney, Geoffrey Hill, Les Murray, Derek Walcott, and Jorie Graham. He writes out of a profound engagement with his Irish background and Irish tradition, but in a style that has reshaped the contemporary and postmodern lyric in Ireland, Britain, North America, and beyond.

Muldoon was born in Portadown, County Armagh, on June 20, 1951. His father Patrick was a farmer and laborer educated to primary school level only, while his mother Bridget (née Regan) trained as a teacher and moved the family to the north Armagh village of Collegelands, following a posting at the local primary school. Like Heaney, Muldoon was a beneficiary of the 1947 Education Act and its widening of access to third-level education, but even before studying at Queen's University, Belfast, his poetic talent was apparent. In a much-repeated story, the teenage Muldoon sent Seamus Heaney, then a lecturer at Queen's, a sheaf of juvenilia, asking Heaney to tell him what was wrong with them; "I can't," came the reply. His first collection, *New Weather*, appeared in 1973 while he was still an undergraduate. A printer's error meant the book was printed entirely in italics, leaning impatiently into the future.

A Companion to Irish Literature, edited by Julia M. Wright
© 2010 Blackwell Publishing Ltd

Critics were not slow to reward its promise, and subsequent collections – *Mules* (1977), *Why Brownlee Left* (1980), and *Quoof* (1983) – followed in quick succession. Throughout these years Muldoon worked as a radio producer for the BBC in Belfast, but after a transitional period during which he held fellowships at the universities of Cambridge and East Anglia he moved to the United States in 1987. This was the year of his fifth collection, *Meeting the British*, and of his marriage to American writer Jean Hanff Korelitz. His immersion in all things American is reflected in *Madoc* (1990), while *The Annals of Chile* (1994), with its twin elegies for the artist Mary Farl Powers ("Incantata") and the poet's mother ("Yarrow"), exposed Muldoon to ever dizzier heights of critical adulation. His *Poems 1968–1998*, incorporating his next book *Hay*, was a defining poetry book of its time, and has been followed by *Moy Sand and Gravel* (2002) and *Horse Latitudes* (2006). The Clarendon lectures delivered by Muldoon in 1998 became *To Ireland, I* (2000), and a term as Oxford Professor of Poetry (1999–2004) produced the lectures collected as *The End of the Poem* (2006). Of his side projects, Muldoon's collaborations with composer Daron Eric Hagen have been particularly important, resulting in the libretti *Shining Brow* (1993), *Bandanna* (1999), and *Vera of Las Vegas* (2001). Muldoon's musical interests have also found an outlet in the garage rock group Rackett, whose lyrics he writes. A selection of these can be found in *General Admission* (2006). He has also written for children.

Early Work

Muldoon's poetic corpus begins with a fall from grace. "The Electric Orchard," the first poem in *New Weather*, tells the story of a tribe mysteriously endowed with the power to conduct electricity. In their curiosity to explore their surroundings the electric people suffer repeated injuries, until finally legislation is passed to stop them climbing electricity poles. They achieve safety at the cost of disenchantment: "None could describe / Electrocution, falling, the age of innocence" (Muldoon 2001:4). The childhood landscapes evoked throughout Muldoon's early work often seem idyllic, but are seldom without a specter of menace and loss of innocence. Muldoon had published a pamphlet with Ulsterman Editions in 1971 called *Knowing My Place*, a title that hints at both class consciousness and the Irish *dinnseanchas* tradition of topographical lore (the very young Muldoon wrote poetry in Irish, and he has continued to translate from that language). While an earlier Northern Irish poet, John Hewitt, had attempted to foster a spirit of Ulster regionalism, Muldoon operated from the outset on a more sophisticated level, moving with ease between his native mid-Ulster and the wider world. Poems such as "Clonfeacle," "Macha," and "Dancers at the Moy" exploit a rich local mythopoeia, but never without a hint of skepticism or outright leg-pulling. "Dancers at the Moy" describes an abundance of horses brought to the village of Moy to be sold to some visiting Greeks about to go to war. When peace is declared the horses run wild, but are finally absorbed into topographical lore:

> The local people gathered
> Up the white skeletons.
> Horses buried for years
> Under the foundations
> Give their earthen floors
> The ease of trampolines.
>
> (Muldoon 2001:11)

New Weather is among the most precocious debuts in contemporary poetry, but is not without faults. Muldoon's scansion does not always run true, for one thing. The influence of Robert Frost is everywhere on show (Frost has remained a career-long lodestar), layering Muldoon's stories of rural life with self-conscious pastoral sophistication, but sometimes contorting a poem, as in "Cuckoo Corn," into a tone of excessive knowingness.

Muldoon's interest in Native America is reflected in "The Indians on Alcatraz," which commemorates the occupation of Alcatraz Island between 1969 and 1971 by Native American protestors, and "The Year of the Sloes, for Ishi," *New Weather*'s closing long poem. Ishi was the last surviving member of the Yahi Indians of northern California, and had lived in hiding with a remnant of his tribe for almost half a century before entering white society in 1911. In Muldoon's poem, he is emblematic of the non-communication between native and settler cultures. He is also ideally placed to act as a vehicle for uncomfortable truths requiring oblique expression: Muldoon has described this poem as "a direct response to Bloody Sunday, 1972, a fact that may not be immediately apparent to many readers" (quoted in Wills 1998:38). A stanza in *New Weather* cancelled from *Poems 1968–1988* captures eerily the spectacle of aestheticized death:

> In the Moon
> Of the Trees Popping, two snails
> Glittered over a dead Indian.
> I realised that if his brothers
> Could be persuaded to lie still,
> One beside the other
> Right across the Great Plains,
> Then perhaps something of this original
> Beauty would be retained.
>
> (Muldoon 1973:56)

Throughout his writings on Native American culture Muldoon has stayed alert to the risk of appropriation and exoticism. He pointedly rejects racial purity in favor of confusion and mongrelization ("My grand-father hailed from New York State. / My grand-mother was part Cree. / This must be some new strain in my pedigree," as he writes in "Immram" [2001:94]). Ireland's link to Native America, after all, is fraught with colonial ironies: the Choctaw nation sent famine relief to the starving Irish in

1847, but the Irish were far from blameless in the destruction of Native America, as *Madoc* reminds us. On the lexical level alone, however, Muldoon enriches his English with Native American vocabulary to a level unmatched by any other major contemporary poet. If this is a tribute to Muldoon's cultural omnivorousness, it is also a reflection of his profoundly questioning sense of Irish identity, and of Ireland and Irish poetry's engagement with other world cultures.

As befits the editor of the *Faber Book of Beasts*, Muldoon has always written well about animals. The title poem of his second collection, *Mules*, was prompted by news footage of mules being parachuted into combat by the US army during the Korean War. If that seems an odd juxtaposition, the mule itself is a hybrid beast, a juxtaposition of one thing and another. *Mules* abounds in other hybrids, including a merman, centaurs, and a bearded woman. In an essay on Andrew Marvell, Christopher Ricks draws attention to the metaphysical quality of Muldoon's imagination and that of other Northern Irish poets, coining the phrase "self-infolded simile" (Ricks 1984:56) for their Marvellian habit of turning lines self-reflectively back on themselves ("Seeing the birds in winter / Drinking the images of themselves" [Muldoon 2001:25]). The fact that, like Marvell, Muldoon is writing in a period of religiously inspired civil unrest adds extra suggestiveness to his use of this trope, and in "The Boundary Commission" (from *Why Brownlee Left*) he pursues the condition of dividedness to comic extremes, describing a village whose main street is bisected by the border and a pedestrian caught in a rainstorm "wonder[ing] which side, if any, he should be on" (Muldoon 2001:80).

The careful phrasing here renders convincingly the tight-lipped quality of Northern Irish social intercourse, as summarized in the Seamus Heaney title "Whatever You Say Say Nothing." Muldoon's attunement to tribal shibboleths informs one of his most remarkable early poems on the Troubles, "Anseo," also from *Why Brownlee Left*. "Anseo" makes a striking contrast with poems on the Troubles by southern Irish writers such as Paul Durcan. While Durcan feels free to condemn the men of violence openly and unequivocally, the speaker of "Anseo" is aware of the neighborly dimension to the conflict (the "neighbourly murder" of Heaney's "Funeral Rites"), where victims and perpetrators alike may come from his immediate community. Its title means "here" in Irish, an answer to the teacher's roll-call rarely provided by the delinquent Joseph Mary Plunkett Ward. Ward's reaction to the punishment meted out to him is one of masochistic over-identification, as he carves his initials into the hazelwand with which the teacher beats him. Later, the speaker meets him as an adult: Ward is "fighting for Ireland, / Making things happen," and describes how he reads the roll to his volunteers each morning, who "would call back *Anseo* / And raise their hands / As their names occurred" (Muldoon 2001:84). Muldoon heavily implies a causal link between Plunkett's paramilitary activity and the abuse he suffered as a child. Is this to trivialize his political commitment? Or, if not, to suggest that Anglo-Irish relations follow an abusive parent–child model (though Plunkett's teacher is Irish, not English)? (In his own attempt at political Freudianism, Heaney had earlier suggested husband–wife relations as a paradigm for the Troubles in "Act of Union.")

"Those to whom evil is done / Do evil in return," as Auden put it in "September 1, 1939" (Auden 1977:245).

A shorter poem, "Mink," touches on the exotic story of Robert Nairac, an under-cover British army officer killed by the IRA in 1977. Nairac, an old Ampleforthian, recklessly attempted to pass for a local republican sympathizer around Armagh while simultaneously, it is alleged, colluding with loyalist paramilitaries. His tale is the stuff of trashy thrillers, but exemplifies the nightmarish confusion of Muldoon's Troubles, where it becomes increasingly difficult to tell who is really who any more, who is fighting for what, and why. Another example of this on a much larger scale is "Immram," the long poem that closes *Why Brownlee Left*. "Immram" means "journey," and among the early Irish voyage poems behind "Immram" is the *Immram Curaig Máele Dúin*, which inspired a version by Tennyson (described by Muldoon as "dread-ful" [quoted in Kendall 1996:83]). The original story, which ghosts Muldoon's, applies a Christian gloss of forgiveness to a picaresque tale of violence and revenge. While the Irish context is important, the poem splices it onto a Los Angeles setting and the febrile atmosphere of a Raymond Chandler thriller. Muldoon is a mere twelve years Seamus Heaney's junior, but a striking difference between the two is the central-ity to Muldoon's work, and near-total absence from Heaney's, of popular culture, in the form of rock music, film noir, and other bric-a-brac; and "Immram" shows how much more there is to this than modish zeitgeist-chasing.

At the heart of the poem is a search for the father, who has disappeared while traf-ficking drugs, leaving behind a suicidal wife. As in any Old Irish journey poem or Chandler novel there are monsters to be faced down before we can get close to the truth. Just as Muldoon slams all manner of different influences and registers together, there is an element of brilliant slapstick to the poem's violence too, as when the pro-tagonist sidesteps two heavies "So they came up against one another / In a moment of intense heat and light, / Like a couple of turtles on their wedding-night" (Muldoon 2001:96). The poem "Good Friday, 1971. Driving Westward" from *New Weather* associates a westward trip with intimations of mortality (as in Joyce's "The Dead"), and the declaration that "It seemed that I would forever be driving west" (Muldoon 2001:96) confirms the edge-of-the-world feel that hovers over the poem. Muldoon's Los Angeles is a city of immigrants and transients, in search of origins that are proving elusive or were perhaps never there in the first place, as when a local Irish American policeman explains his father's theory that "the American Irish / Were really the thir-teenth tribe, / The Israelites of Europe" (Muldoon 2001:99). When the protagonist is finally admitted into the presence of the drug lord he finds a deranged Howard Hughes figure who offers forgiveness before demanding a dish of "Baskin-Robbins banana-nut ice-cream" (Muldoon 2001:102). As with the "Mr and Mrs Alfred Tennyson" who appear in the following stanza, he is a Hitchcockesque MacGuffin, a possibly empty signifier whose purpose it has been to drive the plot forward, trailing mystery as he goes. What he cannot do, however, is provide us with any resolution. Mystery is all.

If there is no resolution in many of these poems it is frequently because their characters fail to read the evidence in front of their eyes. In "Promises, Promises,"

Walter Raleigh returns to the colony of Roanoke, Virginia, where he grapples with the disappearance of its white settlers. Amid a scene of carnage he finds but cannot interpret "one fair strand in her braid, / The blue in an Indian girl's dead eye" (Muldoon 2001:86). Their interbreeding with the local tribes has reduced the settler presence to a ghostly trace, just as the ghost of an old affair begins to stir in the poem's speaker, stretched out under the lean-to of his tobacco shed in North Carolina. "The More a Man Has the More a Man Wants" returns to these Native American obsessions at much greater length, in what is surely the masterpiece of Muldoon's early period. Muldoon is one of the great modern sonneteers, and in this poem uses its forty-nine sonnets as stanzas, with no less variety and momentum than the ottava rima stanzas of Byron's *Don Juan*. This time round it is America that comes to Ulster: the poem begins with the arrival in Belfast of the shady Gallogly (whose name conflates "gallowglass," a mercenary, the Oglala Sioux tribe and Óglaigh na hÉireann, the Irish form of Irish Republican Army), where he embarks on a criminal spree that involves the murder of a Ulster Defence Regiment corporal before a flashback to the US, where he has raped and murdered a woman. He is being stalked throughout by Mangas Jones, a character driven by an ancestral memory of the Ulster contribution to the massacre of the Native Americans. Drugs feature again, giving the poem a hallucinatory quality, and provide the opportunity for a sly intertext with Heaney's "Punishment" when we encounter a woman who has been tarred and feathered for drug use. As in Heaney's poem, the woman is stripped of her identity by tribal violence, but the female figures who flit through this poem, in their very mysteriousness, are granted an oneiric freedom not always available to the brutally silenced female figures of *North* (Gallogly's murder victim Alice A, for instance, mutates into Lewis Carroll's Alice in Wonderland).

The poem ends with Mangas Jones and Gallogly both dying in a booby trap. The dying Mangas Jones echoes Thoreau's last words (*"Moose ... Indian"* [Muldoon 2001:146]), but the piece of quartz he is inexplicably clutching in death represents one final link to Muldoon's beloved Robert Frost. The poem ends with the commentary of two watching old codgers, laced with humorous solecisms that, one last time in this tragicomedy of errors, get everything all wrong. The severed hand recalls the bloody Red Hand of Ulster:

> "Next of all wus the han'." "Be Japers."
> "The sodgers cordonned-off the area
> wi' what-ye-may-call-it tape."
> "Lunimous." "They foun' this hairy
> han' wi' a drowneded man's grip
> on a lunimous stone no bigger than a ...'"
>
> "Huh."

> (Muldoon 2001:147)

In Frost's poem too ("For Once, Then, Something") the quartz is an object of mystery ("Truth? A pebble of quartz? For once, then, something" [Frost 1995:208]), and the secrets of Jones' ethnicity, loyalty, and motivation all finally elude us. Once again we have been chasing Muldoonian MacGuffins.

Given Muldoon's interest in Bob Dylan (*Oh Mercy* features in "Sleeve Notes" and Dylan's receipt of an honorary degree from Princeton in 1970 is commemorated by a poem in *Horse Latitudes*), it is hardly an exaggeration to compare his early volumes to Dylan's 1960s albums, with their rapid evolution from folksy beginnings to the defining and most imitated style of the day (Irish and British poetry in the 1970s, 1980s, and 1990s is littered with Muldoon epigones). To read these books in sequence is to witness a remarkable exfoliation of talent, scarcely able to keep pace with itself – its "footfalls," to use a metaphor from Muldoon himself, "already pre-empted by their echoes" (Muldoon 2001:198).

The Violence of Interpretation

Muldoon's slipperiness as a poet has been as maddening as it is seductive to his critics. The question of how best, ethically and aesthetically, to meet the challenge of the Troubles is a profound one, with the poet liable to charges of escapism if he fails to depict their visceral horror and to charges of voyeurism is he does. Muldoon's work could hardly be more violent, but the question of where he stands in the midst of it all has always been more problematic. If he sets out deliberately to befuddle the reader he at least disarms simplistic responses to his poetry, but is the sowing of readerly confusion a virtue in itself? A number of vintage Muldoon poems from *Quoof* illustrate this central dilemma in how we approach his work. In "A Trifle," for instance, a bomb scare causes a woman to evacuate a building with a lunch-time trifle on a plate:

> I had been trying to get past
> a woman who held, at arm's length, a tray,
> and on the tray the remains of her dessert –
>
> a plate of blue-pink trifle
> or jelly sponge,
> with a dollop of whipped cream on top.
>
> (Muldoon 2001:121)

Offering a political reading, Sean O'Brien accuses his fellow critic Tim Kendall of "missing much of the point" when Kendall sees in this incident only the persistence of everyday life far from the scruples and ruminations on violence we find in the poetry of Heaney (Kendall 1996:91–92; O'Brien 1998:171). O'Brien by contrast sees the trifle's blue-pink trifle and dollop of white cream as a metaphorized Union Jack, reminding us in mammary form of the "tit of imperial subsidy" that props up the Northern Irish economy and behind it the greater evils of British colonialism. We may worry that this is an excessive and po-faced reading, but how far along this road of (over-)interpretation can we claim to have been led by Muldoon himself? If the author of teasing poems such as "A Trifle," "Why Brownlee Left," or "Ireland" was from Southern rather than Northern Ireland, would his work find itself hostage to obligatory political (over-)readings? Hardly. Yet, conscious as Muldoon must be of his politics' subtexts, his attitude towards the reader who would have him spell them out is for the most part like that of Samuel Beckett towards his first biographer, Deirdre Bair: he will "neither help nor hinder."

Neil Corcoran's 2000 conversation with Muldoon is all the more welcome, therefore, for coaxing this usually noncommittal poet into a public position on this question, specifically in reference to "A Trifle." "Somewhere between that word 'her' and 'dessert'," Muldoon comments, "the poem resides" (Corcoran 2006:172), showing a full awareness of the fine line he traces between reticence and explicitness (the woman's potential "remains," had the bomb gone off, rather than just the "remains of her dessert"), evasion and commitment. But O'Brien's reading appears to go too far for him:

> I'm not so persuaded by the extent to which one can pursue such a reading. You know? That's not to say – and these ... of course, the colours are politicised – but I don't find that as fruitful an avenue as just the simple, fairly direct, one-dimensional, in a sense, reading of it. (Corcoran 2006:172)

Another possibility again is that O'Brien's reading is all too accurate, and that Muldoon is attempting to put his interlocutor off the scent. But even if this were the case, there remains a world of difference between a Muldoon poem with a vaguely nationalist whiff to it and O'Brien's far blunter cultural politics.

"The Frog" is another poem that both embodies and tropes Muldoon's authorial knowingness. The frog population of Ireland, it tells us, descends from a pair "left to stand / overnight in a pond / in the gardens of Trinity College." Having spun his inconsequential anecdote, Muldoon comments,

> There is, surely, in this story
> a moral. A moral for our times.
> What if I put him to my head
> and squeezed it out of him,
> like the juice of freshly squeezed limes,
> or a lemon sorbet?
>
> (Muldoon 2001:120)

Toads, if not frogs, are endowed by legend with jewels within their skulls, and here Muldoon offers us the poem as goose with a golden egg, to use another animal comparison. Do we do violence to the poem in coaxing it to yield up its secrets? Despite its warnings of animal slaughter, Muldoon's poem is not denying that its story does indeed conceal "A moral for our times," which it still refuses to surrender.

One last example is "Aisling." The poem may be a tease, again, but it is also one of Muldoon's most forceful political statements. Whereas Heaney's *North* (1975) had been widely seen (by Edna Longley and Ciaran Carson, among others) as applying a gloss of mythic respectability to the ugliness of sectarian violence, "Aisling" is a daringly anti-republican poem, raffishly insulting the ideology that sustained the hunger strikes of 1981 in which ten republican prisoners died. Its name is a common Irish girl's name but also a genre of patriotic Irish-language poetry in which Ireland appears to the bard as a woman and commands him to defend her honor. During a visit to Belfast's Royal Victoria Hospital to have himself checked for a sexually transmitted disease, the poem's speaker sees "the latest hunger-striker / to have called off his fast" attached to "a saline / Drip" (Muldoon 2001:126–27). Though sexually promiscuous and irresponsible, the speaker receives an all-clear from his doctor, whereas the purist republican has come down with a possibly fatal STD transmitted by his congress with Mother Ireland. Ireland is indeed, in Stephen Dedalus' words, "the old sow that eats her farrow" (Joyce 1960:203). At this high level of poetic sophistication Muldoon's dandy persona and the demands of political commitment on the battlefield of the Troubles may not be so incompatible after all.

Middle Period

As sure as in the Irish earthquake it describes in one poem, the ground of Muldoon's style shifts in *Meeting the British* (1987). Perhaps the remark in "Cherish the Ladies," from *Quoof*, that it was the "last poem about [his] father" (Muldoon 2001:117) marked the moment at which Muldoon's self-referentiality ascended to the meta-level, but *Meeting the British* is full of knowing, self-enfolding touches, whose suaveness cannot quite mask an underlying anxiety over the volume's new direction. "Bechbretha" is that strange one-off in the Muldoon canon, a poem apparently written under the influence of Tom Paulin, who was then making a strong showing (*Fivemiletown*, Paulin's single strongest volume, had appeared in 1987). The volume's last poem, too, "7, Middagh Street," lacks the swagger of inevitability that pervaded "Immram" and "The More a Man Has," and when read alongside them, for Kendall, is simply "a failure" (Kendall 1996:123). In its defense, few contemporary poems could expect to do well in such a comparison, so it is only critical justice to acknowledge that "7, Middagh Street" is not without considerable merits. It is written as a series of monologues by a remarkable group of artists gathered for a Thanksgiving dinner in New York in 1940, including W.H. Auden, Salvador Dali, and Louis MacNeice. Auden had recently written his great elegy "In Memory of W.B. Yeats" with its much-quoted insistence that "poetry makes nothing happen" and, having fled wartime Britain for the US (MacNeice, though also present at the dinner, was about to move in the opposite direction), he had urgent grounds for pondering the tangled knot of poetry and politics.

When Muldoon edited the *Faber Book of Contemporary Irish Poetry* in 1986 he declined to write a preface, but the extract from a radio conversation between Louis MacNeice and F.R. Higgins he used in its place was patently a vicarious statement on the question of a writer's responsibilities, to his art, his tribe, and history. Auden's thoughts on Yeats in "7, Middagh Street," equally patently, continue Muldoon's theorizing on the subject. The Yeats lines remembered by Auden are from "The Man and the Echo," in reference to Yeats' youthful play *Cathleen ni Houlihan*:

> As for his crass, rhetorical
>
> posturing, "Did that play of mine
> send out certain men (*certain* men?)
>
> the English shot...?"
> the answer is "Certainly not."
>
> If Yeats had saved his pencil-lead
> would certain men have stayed in bed?
>
> (Muldoon 2001:178)

Once again Muldoon defends obliquity, denying a simple cause-and-effect relationship between art and politics. His next volume, *Madoc*, would be both his most oblique to date and, coincidentally, a devastating portrait of the failure of artists when given the chance to exercise actual, as opposed to imaginative, power. This portrait occurs in the long title poem, a vast Rubicon of a work across which many admirers of the early Muldoon had (and still have) the greatest difficulty crossing. Despite being set in frontier America in the late eighteenth century, the poem is being scanned from the retina of a prisoner in the futuristic city of "Unitel." Its eighteenth-century narrative tells the story of S.T. Coleridge and Robert Southey's scheme for a "Pantisocratic" community on the banks of the Susquehanna river in Pennsylvania, a scheme which, needless to say, never came off. In yet another narrative framing device, each of the poem's more than two hundred sections carries as its title, or operatic "surtitle," the name of a philosopher from Thales to Hawking; the book is thus, among much else, a potted history of Western thought. A more fanciful reading of the poem would be as a coded account of Muldoon's and Heaney's adventures in American academe, though on this reading, if Muldoon is Coleridge, then Heaney, rather unflatteringly, is Southey. (Muldoon's work has from its beginnings conducted close and not uncritical conversations with Heaney, another of which can be found in the short poem "The Eel" preceding the long title sequence.)

Southey did in fact write a poem called *Madoc*, about a Welsh prince who traveled to America in the twelfth century and whose followers were believed to have interbred with Native Americans. The Pantisocratic idyll established by Muldoon's Coleridge and Southey is of short duration, as their scout Cinnamond abducts Coleridge's wife Sara and, when punished by Southey, burns the compound down, rapes Southey's wife, and kills Coleridge's son. Southey becomes a tyrant, swapping universal brotherhood for a recognizably Ulster siege mentality (there is an Ulster on the Susquehanna) in the renamed settlement of Southeyopolis. Coleridge meanwhile embarks on an odyssey in search of his wife, turning up evidence of the Welsh Indians as he goes into the strangest (sexual) situations.

The story of the Welsh Indians remains, by scholarly consensus, a myth, but Muldoon's grasp of Native American history is full of sensitive nuance. Despite his lifelong passion for Robert Frost, Muldoon has steered an opposite course from Frost's blithe belief, in "The Gift Outright," in pioneer America as a *terra nullius* ("The land was ours before we were the land's" [Frost 1995:316]). While the various prose letters by Southey interpolated in the text are fictional, the stirring letter from the Seneca leader Red Jacket ("Go, then, and teach the whites. … Make them less disposed to cheat Indians" [Muldoon 2001:246]) is genuine. The prisoner from whose retina the story is being scanned is a descendant of Southey named South, showing what the Enlightenment ideals of Pantisocratism have come to in practice: an abiding cycle of exploitation and violence. "Madoc" is a heroic folly, a *tour de force* comparable in its virtues and vices to Ed Dorn's *Gunslinger* (which also features a talking horse). This is not to claim the post-*Madoc* Muldoon as a born-again American poet, though his work is increasingly rooted in American English, but to note his embrace of an increasingly maximalist aesthetic, unabashed by the prospect of incomprehension on the grand scale, risks perfectly (or imperfectly) embodied by a more recent poem such as "Sillyhow Stride" from *Horse Latitudes*.

As critics have followed the trajectory of Muldoon's career it has become tempting, too tempting perhaps, to see his later work as a decadent falling away from the freshness and innocence of his beginnings. It is worth insisting, then, that his 1994 volume *The Annals of Chile*, which is full of his by now signature tics and self-referentiality, is perhaps his single best volume, not just for its technical brilliance but also for its deep and moving humanity. Among its best poems is "Milkweed and Monarch," an elegy for Muldoon's parents and a villanelle, though one that breaks the rules of that form at a crucial moment. The rhyme words from the second lines of the poem's first seven tercets (the poem is six lines longer than a standard villanelle) are "tarragon," "stricken," "Oregon," "gherkin," "darken," "reckon" and "hurricane," typical Muldoon polyrhymes, but not so stretched that the reader will fail to notice how the poem's third-last line gets the rhyme word wrong: "He'd mistaken his mother's name, 'Regan', for Anger" (Muldoon 2001:330). The rhyme should be "Regan," his mother's maiden name, though its anagram, "Anger," conveniently rhymes (at a Muldoon pinch) with the surrounding end-words "samovar," "father," and "other" (330). The allusion to *King Lear* reminds us of another misrecognition, when Shakespeare's tragic hero fails to recognize the malice of his daughters Regan and Goneril, but here the speaker's repressed anger at his mother is allowed to irrupt into the poem, and with such force that it throws the rhyme-scheme out of sequence. A common but apparently mistaken derivation of the word "sincere" is from the Latin *sine cera*, "without wax," referring to the practice whereby classical sculptors would cover flaws in their work with wax. "Milkweed and Monarch" not only does not cover but also foregrounds its flaw, the better to dramatize the fierce intensity of mother and son's relationship.

The real masterpiece of *The Annals of Chile*, however, is "Yarrow." Muldoon has always been a virtuoso rhymer, but with "Yarrow" he brings rhyme to new levels of sophistication and control. Rhyme is an aural technique, but one aspect at least of the rhymes in "Yarrow" defies the attention span of even the most attentive ear. The poem's architectonics are truly Byzantine: "Yarrow" comprises twelve "exploded" sestinas, or more correctly stumps of sestinas of six, nine, and twelve lines, with a total of ninety rhyme words. If the opening poem is taken as a composite unit, it rhymes (in its entirety) with sixteen other poems spread through the sequence. Another aspect of this patterning is that the first poem mirror-rhymes the last, the second does the same with the second last, and so on all the way to the center (see Kendall 1996:228): the poem thus forms an enormous Rorschach pattern, folding in on itself. The Rorschach comparison is particularly apt for a poem whose *raison d'être* is to summon buried and forgotten memories and associations, a project that also chimes with the idea of rhymes calling to one another inaudibly across hundreds of intervening lines. For all the poem's efforts at anamnestic reintegration, the temptation to see the past as irretrievably scattered and lost is also strong. The poem opens,

> Little by little it dawned on us that the row
> of kale would shortly be overwhelmed by these pink
> and cream blooms, that all of us
>
> would be overwhelmed, that even if my da
> were to lose an arm
> or a leg to the fly-wheel
>
> of a combine and be laid out on a tarp
> in a pool of blood and oil
> and my ma were to make one of her increasingly rare
>
> appeals to some higher power, some *Deo*
> this or that, all would be swept away by the stream
> that fanned across the land.
>
> (Muldoon 2001:346–47)

Even in the space of twelve lines, Muldoon recapitulates much of what makes his mature style so compelling. There is the slow-unfurling Muldoon syntax, with its tentative approach ("Little by little") and repeated subclauses ("that all of us," "that even if"), the latter a typical example of Muldoonian anaphora; the accumulated resonances across half a dozen previous volumes of the poet's family history and parental agon; the resonances, too, of previous Muldoon poems and those of a central influence such as Robert Frost ("Cuckoo Corn," from *New Weather*, with its evocation of an agricultural accident, and "Out, Out"); the variable lines, pulsing between three to eight stresses; and the brilliant interplay between the individual poem and the larger structure and narrative behind it.

The female figure of "S – " represents republican intransigence and an ever-present voice of rebuke to the narrator for his lack of political conviction. As in "Anseo," with its hints of overlap between masochistic pathology and extremist politics, there is something damaged about "S – ," as evidenced by her sexual vulnerability, though a devout republican reader might read the "S – " character as evidence of a morbid and unexamined misogyny on Muldoon's part instead. This would be unfair. To his detractors, such as John Carey and Helen Vendler, Muldoon has always been a postmodern trickster lacking emotional depth, but earlier in *The Annals of Chile*, in "Incantata," Muldoon shows himself to be a poet capable of great tenderness and empathy with his female subjects. Conversely, the portraits of "S – " and his mother in "Yarrow" round out his depictions of women with robust and honest portraits of emotional blight and waste too. *The Annals of Chile* is a work of fully inclusive emotional maturity. The closing envoi of "Yarrow" gathers the poem's themes (and wandering rhyme words) into a terza rima statement of loss that remains a high point in Muldoon's work, though a sobering one, descending to a watery grave on "a trireme, laden with ravensara, / that was lost with all hands between Ireland and Montevideo" (Muldoon 2001:392).

Recent Work

It is too soon to speak of late Muldoon just yet, but if *The Annals of Chile* is among his strongest books, the comparative weakness of *Hay* raises questions about middle-period Muldoon and (since repetition is such a dominant theme of that volume) self-repetition or even self-parody. To take one obvious point of comparison: like all of his other volumes, *Hay* ends with a long poem, but where "The More a Man Has the More a Man Wants" addresses itself to the chaos and tragedy of the Troubles, "The Bangle, Slight Return," with its shenanigans in an expensive French restaurant, cannot help seeming self-indulgent and overcooked in comparison. As Tim Hancock comments, the defenses of endless verbal riffing (noodling, one might say, given the setting) by the Virgil character "turn him into something of a bore, and when exemplary toccatas are 'lost in the groundswell of muzak' … we should recognize the indiscriminacy of poetic association, its apparent inability to distinguish the truly inspired from the humdrum" (Hancock 2006:97). To Justin Quinn the poem's atmosphere is "stifling … clotted with self-parody" (Quinn 2008:184). But while *Hay*, like its two successors *Moy Sand and Gravel* and *Horse Latitudes*, contains its share of poetic fatty tissue (and even a poem called "Paunch"), it is imperative not to lose sight of the continuing evolution it represents, and its share of excellent poems too.

Doubling and repetition feature in "Lag," a poem about the conjoined twins Chang and Eng, while "Symposium" welds odds and ends of proverbs into new Muldoon hybrids ("You can lead a horse to water but you can't make it hold / its nose to the grindstone and hunt with the hounds" [Muldoon 2001:409]). The self is doubled up in "Between Takes" ("I was standing in for myself, my own stunt double" [Muldoon 2001:410]), a poem that also rhymes words with themselves (including "double" and "double"). The sum effect is to undermine rather than shore up our sense of the unitary self. The fifty lines of "They That Wash on Thursday" all end on the word or syllable "hand" (or "hands"), over-insisting on its singularity to the point where it begins to swim before our eyes. Identity disperses into multiplicity, yet not all Muldoon's efforts are centrifugal. The matter of Ireland remains stubbornly at the core of his imagination. There was always something ghostly about Muldoon's evocations of Ireland and his family background, even when he was still living there, and this has only intensified since his move to the US. Muldoon has elegized his parents to the point of obsessiveness but, of his many reconstructions of his father's life, "First Epistle to Timothy" must count as one of the most remarkable. As a young man, Muldoon senior would look for work at hiring fairs, and Muldoon's poem imbues rural Ireland in the 1920s with a Hardyesque poignancy, with the added menace of omnipresent sectarianism.

1998 was the year of the Belfast Agreement, as reflected in a number of poems in *Moy Sand and Gravel*, on the decommissioning process that dragged out the Troubles' endgame. The volume opens with "Hard Drive," which works a Proustian spell on the poetry of place-names:

> With a toe in the water
> and a nose for trouble
> and an eye to the future
> I would drive through Derryfubble
>
> and Dunnamanagh and Ballynascreen,
> keeping that wound green.

(Muldoon 2002:3)

The past is not a site of reassurance, where everything obediently keeps its place, but a source of danger and wounding, and elsewhere in the book he offers a version of Montale's "L'anguilla" ("Eugenio Montale: *The Eel*"), a poem in which the journey home leads inevitably to death. As an index of Muldoon's sharply rising lifestyle curve since his move to the States, a concordance of his vocabulary would be a highly revealing document (not least, as Hancock's essay on his restaurant poems shows, where images of food and drink are concerned [Hancock 2006]). It would be easy for Muldoon to keep the primal Irish scene of "Hard Drive" fenced off from his professorial adventures in New Jersey but, in "Unapproved Road" (Muldoon 2002:4–7), he riskily mixes the Hardyesque pastoral of "Third Epistle to Timothy" with a much more American-inflected vocabulary. The poem also uses a frequent recent trope of Muldoon, dating back to "Errata" in *Hay* (Muldoon 2001:445–46), in which words are played off against near-synonyms. "Unapproved Road" ends with a description of how "the bourne fades into the boreen" (an Irish laneway): Muldoon is insisting, once again, on the interconnectedness of the outward journey and the home place lurking behind it. The home place too, in its way, is refreshed and reconstituted by these explorations. Another consideration again is the Jewish heritage of his wife and children, which Muldoon pleats into his poetry's previously Irish DNA of home and family in the long last poem, "At the Sign of the Black Horse, September 1999."

Muldoon's most recent full collection is *Horse Latitudes* (2006), published to a mixed reception. For Jim McCue, the book was a disappointment: "Repeatedly, the book's erudition is for show, and wordplay stands in for meaning instead of standing up for it" (McCue 2006:28). Among the aspects of this wordplay that may have antagonized McCue is Muldoon's increased use of nonsense fillers, the "dum de dum" and "hey nonny no" constructions that first broke out in *Madoc*, and which threaten to swamp some of the poems in *Horse Latitudes* altogether. The book features several examples of hypertrophy and failure of poetic economy: the sequence "The Old Country" is an over-extended conceit that might have succeeded on a much smaller canvas. The title sequence is a series of nineteen poems on battles, all of which begin with the letter B, but symbolically missing Baghdad, though the invasion of Iraq is everywhere hinted at.

Repeated references to horses in warfare bring us circling back, too, to *Mules*. As always with Muldoon, everything reminds him "of something else, then something else again" (Muldoon 2001:173). This now extends to the prose persona he has cultivated in the last decade, in *To Ireland, I* and *The End of the Poem*. Muldoon as critic might be compared to an internet search engine and, after a certain amount of prestidigitation (Muldoon's prose is essentially a conjuring act), the reader starts to wonder when he is going to start sifting the endless allusions he amasses and tell us which matter and which do not – doing the work of a critic, in other words. There can be a coercive flippancy about Muldoon's capacity to insert himself "like an ampersand" (Muldoon 1994:16) between violently yoked-together subjects, and one from which the reader might easily turn in exasperation. Misgivings such as these in no way discredit the many excellencies of Muldoon's prose but, as Geoffrey Hill wrote of John Crowe Ransom, "It is not only the 'bad artists' who are cruelly judged. The good are too" (Hill 1984:137). It is also important to grasp the distinctiveness of the genre Muldoon is practicing, which lies somewhere mistily between criticism, poetics, free association, and prose poetry. His constant evocation of the *féth fiadha* or fairy mist in *To Ireland, I* is more than an excuse for self-indulgence: it serves to remind of the specter of death and dispersal from which he seeks to retrieve the past with his self-parodic desire to "only connect." In this sense it is of a piece with the overriding commitment in his work, from at least *The Annals of Chile* on, to the elegiac mode. *Horse Latitudes* is dedicated to a sister who died of cancer, as Muldoon's mother did too, and one of its most moving poems forswears slipperiness in its title to assert, boldly and baldly, "It Is What It Is." It ends on the note of abiding heartbreak that this most talented and moving of contemporary poets has made so much his own:

> Her voice at the gridiron coming and going
> as if snatched by a sea wind.
> My mother. Shipping out for good. For good this time.
> The game. The plaything spread on the rug.
> The fifty years I've spent trying to put it together.
>
> (Muldoon 2006a:49)

It may not be in Muldoon's interest to solve this puzzle any time soon. It may even be that this most all-knowing poet's doubts, hesitations, and confusions before the larger human questions of love and loss are what conspire to keep his "wound green" and the prospect of the volumes still to come so beguiling.

References and Further Reading

Auden, W.H.. (1977). *The English Auden: Poems, Essays and Dramatic Writings, 1927–1939*. E. Mendelson (Ed.). London: Faber & Faber.

Buxton, R. (2004). *Robert Frost and Northern Irish Poetry*. Oxford: Oxford University Press.

Corcoran, N. (2006). "Paul Muldoon in Conversation with Neil Corcoran." In E. Kennedy-Andrews (Ed.). *Paul Muldoon: Poetry, Prose, Drama: A Collection of Critical Essays* (pp. 165–87). Gerrards Cross: Colin Smythe.

Frost, Robert (1995). *Collected Poems, Prose, and Plays*. R. Poirier and M. Richardson (Eds). New York: Library of America.

Hancock, T. (2006). "Dining Out with Paul Muldoon: Poetic and Personal Relations in the Restaurant Poems." In E. Kennedy-Andrews (Ed.). *Paul Muldoon: Poetry, Prose, Drama: A Collection of Critical Essays* (pp. 85–99). Gerrards Cross: Colin Smythe.

Hill, G. (1984). *The Lords of Limit: Essays on Literature and Ideas*. London: André Deutsch.

Holdridge, J. (2008). *The Poetry of Paul Muldoon*. Dublin: Liffey Press.

Joyce, J. (1960). *A Portrait of the Artist as a Young Man*. London: Penguin.

Kendall, T. (1996). *Paul Muldoon*. Bridgend: Seren.

Kendall, T. and P. McDonald (Eds). (2004). *Paul Muldoon: Critical Essays*. Liverpool: Liverpool University Press.

Kennedy-Andrews, E. (Ed.). (2006). *Paul Muldoon: Poetry, Prose, Drama: A Collection of Critical Essays*. Gerrards Cross: Colin Smythe.

McCue, J. (2006). "MacNeice Knew When to Stop." Review of *Horse Latitudes*. *The Independent on Sunday (ABC)*, November 5, 28.

Muldoon, P. (1973). *New Weather*. London: Faber & Faber.

Muldoon, P. (Ed.). (1986). *The Faber Book of Contemporary Irish Poetry*. London: Faber & Faber.

Muldoon, P. (1994). *The Prince of the Quotidian*. Oldcastle: Gallery Press.

Muldoon, P. (1998). "Getting Round: Notes Toward an Ars Poetica." *Essays in Criticism*, 48.2, April, 107–28.

Muldoon, P. (2000). *To Ireland, I*. Oxford: Oxford University Press.

Muldoon, P. (2001). *Poems 1968–1998*. London: Faber & Faber.

Muldoon, P. (2002). *Moy Sand and Gravel*. London: Faber & Faber.

Muldoon, P. (2006a). *Horse Latitudes*. London: Faber & Faber.

Muldoon, P. (2006b). *The End of the Poems: Oxford Lectures on Poetry*. London: Faber & Faber.

O'Brien, S. (1998). *The Deregulated Muse: Essays on Contemporary British & Irish Poetry*. Newcastle upon Tyne: Bloodaxe.

Quinn, J. (2008). *The Cambridge Introduction to Modern Irish Poetry, 1800–2000*. Cambridge: Cambridge University Press.

Ricks, C. (1984). "Andrew Marvell: 'Its Own Resemblance'." In *The Force of Poetry* (pp. 34–59). Oxford: Clarendon Press.

Wills, C. (1998). *Reading Paul Muldoon*. Newcastle upon Tyne: Bloodaxe.

54

Nuala Ní Dhomhnaill and the "Continuously Contemporary"

Frank Sewell

I bhfaite na súl imíonn trí chéad
milliún bliain thar bráid, gan buíochas d'Einstein.

In the blink of an eye, three hundred
million years go by, no thanks to Einstein.

(Ní Dhomhnaill 1991:127)

Three quotations have influenced the writing of this essay on the poetry of Nuala Ní Dhomhnaill. The first is David Wheatley's description of Ní Dhomhnaill as "the one-woman embodiment of Irish-language poetry" in the anglocentric eyes of certain prominent critics and anthologists (Wheatley 2003:252). Wheatley's warning reminds readers (if necessary) that Ní Dhomhnaill's work represents just *one* important oeuvre among those, for example, of more recent poets (including Biddy Jenkinson and Gearóid Mac Lochlainn) and of her near-contemporaries from the 1970s *INNTI* generation. The latter includes Liam Ó Muirthile, Gabriel Rosenstock, and Michael Davitt who, at University College Cork in March 1970, founded *INNTI* as a dynamic and ground-breaking Irish-language poetry broadsheet and, more generally, as a Beat-inspired counter-cultural movement characterized by youthful vigor, modernity and internationalism. The second quotation is Ní Dhomhnaill's recent description of Turkish poet Orhan Veli's poetry of the 1930s (and after) as "continuously contemporary" (Ní Dhomhnaill 2005:195). For Ní Dhomhnaill, poetry need not even be so recent for it to be "continuously contemporary"; it could be as old as Sappho or some of the oral folk tales that, in her view, enliven or shed light on present-day life which would otherwise be duller without them. The third guiding quotation is Ní Dhomhnaill's observation,

A Companion to Irish Literature, edited by Julia M. Wright
© 2010 Blackwell Publishing Ltd

I am painfully aware of the lack of tolerance of cultural diversity often found in Ireland. I understand the contest of a threatened minority language attempting to resist the colonial pressure to assimilate. We all make our peace with the language in a different fashion, and it would seem that I have a "vocation to the missions." I allow translations, indeed encourage them, so long as the books that result have a dual-language format. There are still problems: most of the translated poems, for example, are taken out of context, and the architectonics of the original publications therefore mislaid. (Ní Dhomhnaill 2005:200)

The reference above to "architectonics" suggests that it would be worthwhile to choose one representative but less-discussed collection of Ní Dhomhnaill's poems, and to examine not only its characteristic themes and tropes but also its own individual architectonics. Naturally, these architectonics will not be known to readers without Irish, who encounter Ní Dhomhnaill's poems in various editions of "selected" poems where comparatively less attention is given to structure (as in *Selected Poems / Rogha Dánta* or *Pharaoh's Daughter*), or where the collection is a thematically linked series of poems (as in *The Fifty-Minute Mermaid*).

Ní Dhomhnaill's publishing history shows, unsurprisingly, that she first produces a collection of poems in Irish before subsequent bilingual "selections" are published. Each original Irish-language book is constructed in a consecutive series of linked sections, and begins with a foreword comprising an excerpt from a folkloric tale which points towards a dominant theme in the collection as a whole. The poet's first collection, *An Dealg Droighin*, begins thus with the tale of a "brother" (representing the male or masculine in society or the psyche) who hangs his "sister" on a tree and cuts off her arms, leaving her helpless (Ní Dhomhnaill 1981:3; unless otherwise noted, all references to her poetry cite this edition; where published translations from her various bilingual collections are available, sources appear in square brackets; otherwise, translations are mine). He asks if "that" (the pain and hurt) goes through her heart. The sister replies that it does but adds remarkably (in a show of faith that makes one suspect that Christian monks at some point doctored these *béaloideas* [oral tales]) that "Christ suffered more and we paid him scant attention, even though it was for us." She also, however, curses her brother: "May a blackthorn spine enter your foot and stay there until my two dear white hands remove it" (3).

Her initial Christian forbearance is rewarded with a visitation from Christ's mother, Mary, who rescues and restores the girl, reuniting her with her arms and sending her on home. Returning, she finds a tree already sprouting from her brother's foot through the roof of the house, regrets her curse, and finally *heals* her psychotic brother by removing the thorn with a pin from her shawl. The tale is vivid and mystifying, especially at first, and not least because it insists on its own veracity: "agus an tuairt a dhéin an crann nuair a thit sé cualathas ar fuaid na dúthaí é" ("and the thud the tree made when it fell was heard all throughout the district"; 4). However, rather than lop the story down with a single, reductive interpretation, the essay that follows will offer one possible gloss. Gradually, the tale's relation to the "contemporary" and to Ní Dhomhnaill's work as a whole should become clear.

Early Poems

Ní Dhomhnaill's first collection, *An Dealg Droighin*, is divided into three sections, dating in chronological order from 1968 to 1980: "early poems" (written when the poet, born in 1952, was between 16 and 20 years old); "poems on emigration"; and poems on the poet's "return to Ireland." The very first poem of the first section is noteworthy and prescient because, as its title "Sabhaircíní i Samhain" ("Primroses in Autumn" – or even "November") suggests, it concentrates on a surprising survival. Late autumn should spell death or oblivion for primroses but, in this poem, they are discovered in the garden of the teenage poet's school. Transplanted into this, her first prize-winning poem, the primroses stand as a living visual symbol of past vitality ("gártha úra an naíonán nua-bheirthe" ["the fresh cries of the new-born child"]) and pride ("níor chás dhuit rí a chur chun boird ann" ["it was an apt place to cater for a king"]) that has somehow managed to live on into the present.

What is significant in this piece of, admittedly, juvenilia is that the past is *not* represented as something negative and nightmarish, casting its *shadow* on the present, but as a lively, colorful element that actually brightens a present that would be more dull ("fuíollach is dríodar is lathach / an Fhómhair thiar" ["the refuse, dregs, and slime / of late Autumn"]) without this "ruainne beag an Earraigh" ("remnant of the Spring"). In this poem, vital elements of the past typically call Ní Dhomhnaill's imagination to life with (to paraphrase T.S. Eliot) fragments to shore against our present ruins. In other words, past and present overlap productively in her work; it is not a matter of exclusive, binary opposites but of creative amalgamation. This is shown not least in the poem's focus on both the Irish past *and* present-day reality in a work which stylistically (through its use of free verse, reportage, and, to an extent, confessionalism) also bears clear signs of influence from American poets of the period, particularly John Berryman, who is named in a later poem in the collection (86 [1988a:146]) and whose "Dream Song 171" is also translated here. Berryman, arguably, was also an influence on Ní Dhomhnaill's still "early" poems of four years later, 1972, in which she employs a persona – not a contemporary "Henry" à la Berryman but, in Ní Dhomhnaill's terms, a "continuously contemporary" Celtic goddess, Mór.

Mór is one of the many personae-narrators or speakers in Ní Dhomhnaill's poetry. While these are not always female, they are often powerful figures such as warriors, goddesses, and queens – in short, reminders of a time in Ireland when women had more say and sway. Mór, whose name can be translated as "great one," was a daughter of the sun. The estranged wife of Donncha Dí, she was also a fertility goddess whose memory, living on in place-names and stories, still dominates the west Kerry landscape. Interestingly, her name and power are first adopted by Ní Dhomhnaill in "Dúil" ("Desire"), a ground- and taboo-breaking poem that gives open verbal expression to female sexual desire. The speaker of the poem views a man's body as a mouthwatering "hamper" of "fresh fruits" before she finally, and semi-ironically, swoons:

oop-la!
barrathuisle,
Mór ar lár.

Oop-la!
She stumbles.
Mór is down.

                                                    (15 [1988a:31])

At this point, the poem notably shifts from first to third person. Is Mór simply brought in at the end as a fig-leaf or mask for modesty's sake? That is not the whole story. This poem was written in 1972, early days for the women's movement, especially in Ireland. Thus it was brave of Ní Dhomhnaill to tackle such material, and delightfully mischievous of her to use a figure not only drawn from Irish tradition but also one who, as a force of nature, brings to the drier contemporary soil some of the revolutionary color and vitality of those "primroses" that appeared in an earlier autumn. This is entirely in keeping with Ní Dhomhnaill's aesthetic: Mór is "continuously contemporary," as relevant today as in her own time. Indeed, the reason why Mór's power and authority (even if it is the power to be unruly) are called upon by Ní Dhomhnaill in this poem is to help enable her as a female poet to radically replace the usual "male gaze" of poetic (and cinematic) tradition with a *female* gaze for a change. This goes some way towards leveling a previous imbalance between male and female, with the suggestion that if both were "down" at the same level, it might ("oop-la") be more fun for both.

Three other Mór poems follow in a sequence. They are less celebratory but show Mór in a variety of moods: broody, capable of destruction *or* enjoyment in "Mór Goraí" ("Mór Hatching" or brooding); a wildly sexual life-force turning into a destructive or negative female archetype in "Teist Dhonncha Dí ar Mhór" ("Donncha Dí's Testimony"); and boxed in and depressed in "Mór Cráite" ("Mór Anguished"), the final, bathetic poem that ends the series. These brief highlights from the "early poems" provide a foretaste of the poet's subsequent oeuvre and concerns, including nature; the "continuously contemporary"; male–female relations (including the sexual); the dualities of human potential (for example, for creativity and/or destruction); and depression – all dramatically imaged through symbols drawn from the natural world, and through personae adapted from folklore.

Notably, the poems themselves bear evidence of stylistic influence from contemporary models in English (as noted, mainly American poets such as Berryman), and other Irish poets (including, especially, those of the *INNTI* group, who also were influenced by American and French practitioners of *vers libre*). Typically, however, these contemporary influences coincide with far more ancient sources: Ní Dhomhnaill quotes on the back cover of *An Dealg Droighin* another Irish writer, Helen Waddell, the great translator of classical poetry who, in *Mediaeval Latin Lyrics*, bore "pagan" poetry full of sensuality across to the comparatively and repressively prim shores of Ireland in the 1930s and after. Ní Dhomhnaill seems to have responded, from a modern female perspective, to the intense celebrations of nature, and to the ancient *carpe diem* philosophy of, for example, "Copa Surisca" ("Dancing Girl of Syria"; Waddell 1929:2–5). Such themes and tropes surface in later Ní Dhomhnaill poems such as "Táimid Damanta, a Dhearfëaracha" (1984; "We are Damned, my Sisters").

Poems on Emigration

Section two of *An Dealg Droighin*, entitled "Dánta ar imirce" ("Poems on Emigration"), contains a signature poem by Ní Dhomhnaill: the underestimated and rarely discussed "Turas Oíche" ("Night Journey"). The poem refers to a Japanese sea-diver who gathers shellfish, scallops, clams and, in any *one* dive, a *single* oyster which may have "cloch luachmhar i lár a bhrollaigh" ("a precious stone inside"; 52). He only picks one of these at a time in order to "protect the environment." However, he still picks one, no doubt for his own upkeep, and he views it as a great pity that his mother died "gan oisrí a bhlaiseadh" ("without ever having tasted oysters"; 52). Typically, Ní Dhomhnaill allows the soft "s" sounds in this phrase to make the shellfish appear all the more mouth-watering and tempting. But what is this poem getting at? At first, it seems like an odd little poem, uncharacteristic of Ní Dhomhnaill with its "foreign" character and unspecified setting. However, the poem's oddness and open-endedness make it linger in the memory (not unlike the details of a folk tale), and the seasoned Ní Dhomhnaill reader is tempted to wonder if this image of a sea-diver (a threshold-crosser, a transgressor into another realm, who returns with a possible "pearl," a valu-able "find") represents an image of the artist herself, mining the sea-bed of language and imagination for gems that can be turned into poems.

Ní Dhomhnaill draws mainly from Irish, but sometimes also from international, folklore, for example for phrases and images that she can creatively combine (or jux-tapose) with the contemporary contexts of her poems. Her use of folklore, it is worth stressing, is not driven merely or mainly by a cultural nationalist agenda (as is sus-pected of Yeats by some reductionist commentators); rather, she is aesthetically enabled by such cross-channeling to find "the words to say it" (Marie Cardinal, quoted in Stallybrass and White 1986:181), words and images to convey the things that *contemporary* experience or observation prompt her to say. Thus, for example, in "Máthair" ("Mother"), the folkloric phrase "Féile Uí Bhriain / is a dhá shúil ina dhiaidh" ("O'Brien's feast [or bounty] / as he watches after [or begrudges] every bestowal"; 28 [1988a:40]) is used to convey a sense of resentful giving from a modern, overly controlling mother to a would-be liberated daughter. Readers unfamiliar with the folkloric source can work out the gist of the reference from the context, and be verbally enriched or enticed by the allusion, while other readers, familiar perhaps with the source-tale, can appreciate more knowingly this example of postmodern *bricolage* and feminist free play with tradition.

Pithy phrases and powerful images drawn from *béaloideas* provide poets such as Ní Dhomhnaill (and, earlier, Yeats) with rich material that can sometimes help them to bridge the gulf "between imagination and creative ability" as they step "through the purgatory of art" (49). Successful artistic redeployment of, for example, folkloric material in unexpected, often contemporary, contexts may sometimes produce for the poet (in the first instance and, latterly, for readers) a linguistic or imagistic lightning bolt, a "fire-bolt from the heavens / that strikes us to the board" or fixes us to the spot (38–39).

Sometimes, contrastingly, Ní Dhomhnaill produces whole poems (not just single phrases or images) consisting of folk-tale scenarios that try to cast a spell of wonder over readers. This occurs, for example, in "Na Sceana Feola" ("The Meat Knives"):

> *Is tusa an bhanphrionsa*
> *a éalaíonn amach as tigh a hathar*
> *i lár an fhéasta.*
> *Tugann tú leat*
> *na sceana feola éabharláimhe*
> *mar uirlis chosanta, b'fhéidir,*
> *ar do aistear.*
>
> You are the princess
> who escapes from her father's house
> in the middle of the feast.
> You take with you
> the ivory-handled meat knives
> for protection, perhaps,
> on your journey.
>
> (56 [1988a:46])

This is a deliberately intriguing poem: why the "perhaps" in line 6? The "princess" goes to see her lover with her two ladies-in-waiting who wait outside (one of whom narrates the tale). They all have to return before the king, who will need the knives to carve the meat at his feast, notices they are missing. The three ladies return in haste but the narrator realizes that the knives are left behind and wonders, finally, whether she should return to find them, again, "perhaps." The reader is left wondering: does the narrator know where the knives are? Is that why she may or may not go back? Do the "ivory-handled knives" currently protrude from the meaty flesh of the princess's lover, perhaps? All this is left open in a frustratingly puzzling fashion or, alternatively, in a really teasing, whodunit fashion where steps and clues can be retraced in a more active and engaged reading. Such Ní Dhomhnaill poems, including the later much-anthologized and twice-translated "Geasa" (Ní Dhomhnaill 1984; "Taboos" [1988a]; "The Bond" [1990]), are comparable to the kind of ancient oral tale that inspires this poet, and which she has described as "a gift from the subconscious that cannot be rationally explained. But it can be pondered, worried over, wondered at, told over and over again, and because of its deeply symbolic significance it never loses anything in the telling" (Ní Dhomhnaill 2005:86).

Ní Dhomhnaill's delving into tradition, her occasional stepping back in time or into the shoes of past personae such as Mór, lead to the inevitable conclusion that she is a transgressive artist. She steps across bounds and over limits, daringly challenging taboos, including "customs men" (Ní Dhomhnaill 1990:146), along the way. Moreover, she does so by simply *being* a female poet in a tradition that she has described as "sexist and masculinist to the core" (quoted in Dorgan 1996:114); by writing frankly and funnily about sex (and other bodily functions); by questioning attitudes towards gender and sexuality among various religions and societies; and by assailing rationalist, empiricist, scientific Western mindsets with the subconscious, inexplicable, and even supernatural.

She is best known perhaps for her love poetry, for poems such as "Dúil," discussed above, which inverts male tradition and asserts the female right to gaze back at the male, objectifying the latter not to denigrate but to place male and female on the one, equal, mutually satisfying level. Some other early love poems such as "Malairt" ("Metamorphosis") are less effective because they are, naturally, at that early point in the poet's career, youthful, romantic, and rather abstract:

> Da mba thú an ghrian shoilseach
> do bheinnse i m'scamall
> is do leáfeá le teas mé
> idir neamh agus talamh.

(32)

> If you were the shining sun
> I would be a cloud
> and you would melt me with your heat
> between heaven and earth.

The love poems get stronger in quality and originality, however, when (as Seamus Heaney observed of Patrick Kavanagh) ethereality and imagination become more "earthed in the actual" (Heaney 1980:119). In "Réalt Reatha" ("Shooting Star") below, Ní Dhomhnaill effectively combines abstract imagination and personal feeling with concrete imagery drawn from her west Kerry landscape and own early experience. Thus when the lovers finally kiss,

> pléascfaidh amach sa ghalacsaí
> réalt nua ...
> ag tarraingt orainn aird
> na bpáistí gona mbuataisí
> ag tóirseáil insan gclaí
> is nuair a scinnfimid anuas sa díog
> déanfar orainn guí.

(33)

> a new star
> will explode in the galaxy ...

> drawing the attention
> of children in their water-boots
> lamping [birds] in the hedgerows;
> and when we skim down into the ditch,
> they'll pray for us.

Gradually, her love poetry becomes increasingly transgressive and original. In "Typewriter," for example, the speaker fantasizes about being the eponymous "typewriter" under the fingers of an otherwise work-distracted lover:

> *Táim sásta bheidh i m'stangadh*
> *is cromadh síos ar chruncaí …*
> *is mo cheann …*
> *ag iompó ó thaobh go taobh*
> *le clingeadh an chloigín.*
> *Do bheinn i m'chlóscríbhneoir*
> *ach do mhéaranna inniúla*
> *a bheith ag raideadh ar mo dhroim.*

(34)

> I'm happy to get down
> on my hunkers and stay still …
> my head …
> turning from side to side
> at the ding of the bell.
> I'd be a typewriter
> as long as your deft fingers
> were tip-tapping on my back.

The comedy of this poem possibly disguises its daringly open (for the time) expression of female desire and longing.

The latter is made audible, almost tangible on the tongue, in "Leaba Shíoda" ("Labysheedy – The Silken Bed") with its soft "l" sounds and rustling, silky "s" sounds which won over the critic Seán Ó Tuama, and set a difficult challenge for any would-be translator:

> *Is bheadh do bheola taise*
> *ar mhilseacht shiúcra*
> *tráthnóna is sinn ag spaisteoireacht*
> *cois abhann*
> *is na gaotha meala*
> *ag séideadh thar an Sionna*
> *is na fiúisí ag beannú duit*
> *ceann ar cheann.*

> And your damp lips
> would be as sweet as sugar
> at evening and we walking
> by the riverside
> with honeyed breezes
> blowing over the Shannon
> and the fuchsias bowing down to you
> one by one.
>
> (36 [1988a:155])

The last line above in the Irish plays on the ambiguous phrase "ceann ar cheann" which may mean "one by one" but can also mean, literally, head by head or, in this case, flower-head, each bowed in adoration. The transgression in this poem lies in its completely natural, sensual celebration of sexuality and the body. This is part of a deliberate attempt by Ní Dhomhnaill to counteract an imbalance that she perceives in Irish individuals and society:

> without wishing to exonerate established Christianity from an unmistakably patriarchal bias it may be that the death-dealing propensities of our head-hunting Celtic forebears had a role to play in perverting the basically moderately life-enhancing qualities of the message of Christ into the particularly virulent life-denying force that has come to be Irish Catholicism. (Ní Dhomhnaill 2005:85)

Noting that the head was the "central icon of the Celts," Ní Dhomhnaill goes on to conclude that "our [Irish] ancestors were severely cut off from what the French feminist literary theorists call the 'language of the body'." Her entire oeuvre, with its celebrations of nature and focus on the body, can be seen as one artist's struggle to counterbalance such limiting binary oppositions and damaging exclusivity. One should note, however, that the potentially violent and abusive psychoses to which these latter give rise are not unique to Catholicism (see Mahon 1975:13) or even to Celts.

It is also worth reminding oneself, if necessary, that Ní Dhomhnaill's poems are often dramatizations and/or are written in the voice of various named and sometimes unnamed female personae. Furthermore, although some poems are (partly) autobiographical, even those are not exclusively so. Recently, for example, Ní Dhomhnaill has commented that her two companion poems, "Máthair" ("Mother") and "Athair" ("Father"), which are both often read in autobiographical terms, actually combine to describe

> the two sides of the same shilling, *the Irish family* where the father was mostly absent – an absentee father – and the mother was correspondingly too caught up in her children, living vicariously through them, for she could not go out to work because of the marriage ban [against married women working]. (Ní Dhomhnaill 2005:199)

Also, just as the title "Máthair" means "a mother" or "mother-figure," and not necessarily or exclusively "my" (or the poet's own) mother, many of Ní Dhomhnaill's love poems are left deliberately and similarly open in terms of who the lovers may be and even, in some cases or readings, what gender they might be. The poem "Litir" ("A Letter"), for example, mentions "beirt bhan nocht ar na braillíní" ("two naked women on the sheets"; 38) which allows for some speculation that this poem and, potentially, some others could refer to gay or lesbian love as readily as they may refer to hetero-sexual love. Whatever the case may be, the reader comes away with a strong sense of the all-round humanity of the characters in these poems, that they have feelings and *bodies* as much as thoughts and *heads*. Moreover, without becoming preachy or didactic, the poems show that (if we didn't know it already) love and its physical expression are not exclusive to (or exclusively the right of) any one group in society.

Certain love poems do specify that they refer to characters and personae in long-standing, even marital relationships: for example, "Póg" ("Kiss") is spoken in the voice of a woman (with her own "man," possibly "husband"), who is kissed by another man whose wife is "waiting at the door for him" (45 [1988a:38]). Transgressions, it seems, exist not only in the poetry of a feminist or rebel poet such as Ní Dhomhnaill but (it is implied) out there in real, hypocritical society at large where this "other man" wants his own wife at home and another married woman on the side. "Póg" is, therefore, one of a group of poems (see also "Do m'Fhear Chéile" ["For my Husband" – a clearly autobiographical poem]) that refers to the pressures that long-term relationships can come under but also survive: the other man's kiss, we are told, has "no effect" ("níor bhraitheas faic"), whereas when the speaker actively recalls her husband's kiss,

> *critheann mo chromáin*
> *is imíonn*
> *a bhfuil eatarthu*
> *ina lacht.*
>
> I shake, and all
> that lies
> between my hips
> liquefies
> to milk.
>
> (45 [1988a:38])

Here, in "Póg," the female speaker takes possession and ownership of her own body after the "turn" or *volto* in this sixteen-line sonnet. In stanza 1, the woman's body had literally been invaded by the stranger, the other man suddenly putting his tongue into her mouth, causing her to verbally dismiss his advance in enforced conversation. In the self-contained second stanza (above), it is the female "I" who acts freely, recall-ing and responding to the man of *her* choice.

In such poems, Ní Dhomhnaill represents male–female relations that are "continu-ously contemporary" or significant, regardless of whether they refer directly to a modern woman *such as* (but not necessarily) herself, to a friend with her toy-boy/play-boy lover (57), or to numerous ancient accounts, including those of parthenogenesis which repeatedly recur in her poetry, and which date back centuries to the foundations of various world myths, legends, and religions. Hailing from a nation where, after the Famine of 1845–52, "economic imperative dictated vigorous sexual restraint" and where "sex became taboo" as the "Catholic Church fixated on sex as sin" (McGarry 2009), Ní Dhomhnaill is particularly fascinated by tales of parthenogenesis. Such tales center on those moments when a human being (for example, Mary in Christian theology) is said to have been impregnated by a deity – an occurrence usually bleached (by modern religions) of its sexual connotations. Ní Dhomhnaill is not alone as an artist in returning to such moments, for example, in "Scéala" ("Annunciations") and in two poems in section 2 of *An Dealg Droighin*: "Aingeal an Tiarna" ("The Angel of the Lord") and "An Cuairteoir" ("The Visitor"). Both, significantly, are written in the first person, from the point of view of the (usually passive or silent) female recipient of the visit from the "angel of the lord." In "An Cuairteoir," the visitation is described in the light of an aggressively erotic encounter:

> Is fáisceann tú gan trua an dé deiridh asam
> is ní fhanann puth anála im' scámhóg.
> … ní fiú mé go dtiocfá faoi mo choinne
> ná scaoilfeá tharam an chailís seo, a Chríost?
>
> (58)

> and you squeeze out my last gasp
> and the last puffs in my lungs collapse.
> … Domine non sum dignus –
> Christ! Let this chalice pass!

Contrastingly, in "Aingeal an Tiarna," an erotic encounter is described in the light of a spiritual or religious release. Either way, Ní Dhomhnaill is concocting an explosive mixture of sex and religion, a pairing that did not usually meet openly in recent centuries in Irish society, including in the 1970s when these poems were written.

Such Ní Dhomhnaill poems in part remind us that while religion (in this case, Christianity) has relied on or used women, it has also often tended to render women as silent or passive vessels, downplaying, denying, or distrusting women's role and power. Such denial or distrust of the female (or even simply of the "other"), moreover, is not unique (Ní Dhomhnaill acknowledges) to Christianity in Ireland but sometimes extends to other religions and countries, including Islam and Turkey. While male keepers of the seal or religious fundamentalists in "I nGort Lus na Gréine" ("In the Sunflower Field") may be unaccommodating or unappreciative towards the "other," especially the female, Ní Dhomhnaill's poems repeatedly illustrate that nature itself is multi-dimensional and inclusive. It is no surprise, therefore, that she echoes William Blake in insisting that the speckled tiger lily is just as much a reality or gift of nature as the lamb-white lily of St Joseph: see "Athchuairt ar Valparaiso" ("Valparaiso Revisited"). In feminist terms, Ní Dhomhnaill is once again opposing binary opposites (the "either/or" of exclusivist, imbalanced, allegedly "male" mindsets) with the more healthily inclusive "both/and" alternative of feminist ideology.

Furthermore, Ní Dhomhnaill's inclusiveness, in some of her most transgressive poems, extends to accept not only the corporeal and animal aspects of human nature, but even what might be termed the "grotesque." There are two taboo-breaking poems, for example, that refer to breaking wind: "An Braim" ("The Fart") and "Dinnéar na Nollag" ("Christmas Dinner"). In the former, the poet dares to wonder

> *an féidir nach bhfuil sa domhan ar fad*
> *sa séipéal is sna tithe geala néata*
> *atá fillte mar phléataí ar ghúna Domhnaigh, –*
> *nach bhfuil ansiúd ar fad (dá mhéid iad)*
> *ach braim ollmhór amháin as bundún Dé?*
>
> (60)

> is it possible that the whole world,
> the chapel and the nice neat houses
> folded like pleats on a Sunday dress –
> that they (for all they are worth) are nothing
> but one enormous fart from the arse of God?

With that irreverent, darkly comic, anarchic thought, section 2 of *An Dealg Droighin* ends. But, notably, this is not crudeness for its own sake. Rather, such comically deflating frankness and forthrightness about the body as in "Dinnéar na Nollag" is partly what links Ní Dhomhnaill to Irish comic tradition, as Mary O'Connor notes:

> she [Ní Dhomhnaill] has a satirical eye and a keen sense of the absurd, and her mockery of people in high places and co-opting of the grotesque and the fantastic into her comic vision, all expressed in the most lively and playful of glorious sound and vernacular argot, mark her as heir and transmitter of the earliest (oral) comic tradition. (O'Connor 1996:153)

On Return to Ireland

"Venio ex Oriente," the first poem of section 3 of *An Dealg Droighin* dramatizes the poet's (or her representative persona's) return from abroad, a sojourn that has enriched her with Arabian scents and secrets from the bazaars, all of which combine with her own original "musk" and "taste." She embodies the enrichment that can come from crossing cultures and shores – a positive image of human potential to contain and combine disparate elements. The fact that this power derives partly from possessing "secrets" and spices which "ná gealfaidh do láimhín bán" ("would not make bright your small white hand") explains why they have to be kept "faoi cheilt" ("hidden"; 65), and suggests that such genuine pluralism, such hybridity, such mixing and matching, is likely to be opposed by monocultural purists, "Gestapo voices" of whatever singular hue or persuasion (see, for example, "Guthanna" ["Voices"] and "An Mhaighdean Mhara" ["The Mermaid"], where allusions to fascism also indicate the influence of Sylvia Plath on Ní Dhomhnaill [MacMonagle 1995:144–45]).

Similarly, in the very next poem, "Dán Beag an Earraigh Bhig" ("A Short Poem of Early Spring"), Ní Dhomhnaill acknowledges that some narrow versions or interpretations of modernity, some monocular proponents of the philosophy of "progress," lead us all towards a single scientific, fixed outlook that would delimit nature and "set" the seasons. However, all this occurs, the poet attests, despite the evident unruliness of nature itself (personified here by the Celtic goddess Bríd):

> *ní thagann aon ní slán*
> *ó ionsaí glas an nuafháis*
> *is ón raidhse geall le do-thuigthe*
> *atá tugtha léi ag Bríde.*

(66)

> nothing is safe
> from the green advance of new growth
> and the almost mind-blowing profusion
> given forth by Bríd.

Ní Dhomhnaill could have ended this poem with one of her favorite quotations from Shakespeare: "There are more things in heaven and earth, Horatio, / Than are dreamt of in your philosophy" (Shakespeare 1989: 1.5.166–67). Bríd is clearly invoked as one such "thing": a powerful precursor and feminine life-force heedless of regulations from Europe in Greenwich or any other Mean Time.

Other strong, independent, female characters and exemplars are celebrated in poems such as "In Memoriam Elly Ní Dhomhnaill: 1884–1963" (1990:27) and "Freagra na Mná Ceiltí" ("The Celtic Women's Reply") – the former poem referring to a recent foremother and the latter referring to more ancient foremothers whose significance is "continuously contemporary" according to this poet's aesthetic and cultural outlook. Ní Dhomhnaill's relative Elly is celebrated for her courage and independence in facing down the parish priest, a powerful figure in mid-twentieth-century Ireland. Similarly, it was no mean feat for her (as a woman) to obtain a degree in 1904, even if afterwards no appropriate job or husband was available to her (or deemed worthy by her). Ní Dhomhnaill describes Elly as "spiorad uaibhreach / nár chall di luí / le fear a diongbhála" ("that proud spirit / who had no call to lie / with a man her match"; 70), and accounts for her uncompromising nature by alluding finally to the violence and injustice of Irish history, including that visited upon her own ancestors who "were herded into Macha na Bó." The poet goes on to entertain the possibility that some of her own independent and rebellious nature can be traced back to this foremother figure. Clearly, here and elsewhere, Ní Dhomhnaill suggests that genetics play a huge role in identity formation, whether or not this is recognized by others. For example, she detects in some of the otherwise inexplicable hostility (among some Irish people) to the Irish language a cross-generational post-traumatic stress disorder that dates back to the Famine and the British empire's policy of suppressing indigenous languages.

One way out of post-Famine and postcolonial shadows, according to Ní Dhomhnaill, can be to reach further back to the positive examples set by previous female goddesses and warriors such as Bríd and Mór, and to listen back to "na Mná Ceiltí," who boast that they "lie out in the open" with the "bravest in action" whereas Roman wives "mate undercover with weaklings and traitors." In stanza 2, the poet's voice enters the poem as narrator to conclude regretfully that the modern descendants of these ancient Celts are now "rómhór faoi chúing / ag nósanna Rómhánacha" ("too hidebound / by Roman notions"; 74).

Importantly, however, for all her daring and challenging celebrations of female freedom, of positively independent mother archetypes, Ní Dhomhnaill does not fail to acknowledge that there are also negative mother archetypes, and that (female) transgression or taboo-breaking often leaves the individual woman or artist under emotional or psychological strain. We have already seen one negative mother archetype in "Máthair" but a more monstrous and frightening version appears in the poem "Cliseadh Misnigh" ("A Loss of Courage"):

> *Táim ar mo theicheadh uait,*
> *a bhean na ndrochfhiacal.*
> *Raghainn isteach i bpoll miongáin*
> *ach gan éisteacht leis an glaoch gutháin*
> *a chuirfidh tú.*
>
> (67)

> I am fleeing from you,
> woman-of-the-bad-teeth.
> I'd crawl into a periwinkle
> not to hear your phone call.

This is an early manifestation or incarnation of numerous female monsters (external and internal) that haunt Ní Dhomhnaill's poetry. Their nay-saying negativity and destructiveness (together with patriarchy) is what necessitates, for psychic balance, recourse to more positive mythic and historical female archetypes.

One of Ní Dhomhnaill's contributions to Irish poetry, therefore, is to explore female experience some of which was previously suffered in silence and absent from literature. For example, in "Breith Anabaí Thar Lear" ("Miscarriage Abroad"), the traumatized mother/speaker states that

> *ní raghad*
> *ag féachaint linbh*
> *nuabheirthe mo dhlúcharad*
> *ar eagla mo shúil mhillteach*
> *do luí air le formad.*

I will not go to see
my best friend's new born child
because of the jealousy
that stares from my evil eye.

(73 [1988a:50])

Pain has hurt the speaker into becoming, potentially, a hurtful being – a possibility of deep concern to this poet. Sometimes the trauma experienced by the female speakers in Ní Dhomhnaill's poems derives from having to cross artificial borders and bounds, to break limits often set by patriarchal society. Note, for example, the extreme predicament of "The Mermaid" in Ní Dhomhnaill's "An Mhaighdean Mhara":

Ní gan pian
a thangas aníos
ar thalamh ...
do mhalairtíos snámh
ar luail cos. ...

D'imís
is thógais leat mo cháipín draíochta.
Níl sé chomh furast orm teacht air,
is a bhí sa scéal
i measc cearachaillí an díona.

Not without pain
did I come up
to earth ...
and swapped swimming
for treading foot. ...

You left
and took with you my magic caul.
It's not so easy to find
among the rafters
as it was in the story.

(81; my translation [see also 1988a])

Several comments from the poet about this poem (Somerville-Arjat and Wilson 1990:154–55) have led some readers to interpret it solely in the context of Irish-language issues in Ireland, as referring, perhaps, to Ní Dhomhnaill's own situation as a minority-language writer surrounded and outnumbered by a majority of anglophone monoglots in contemporary Ireland. However, the poem itself is left teasingly open in terms of its possible meaning, significance or relevance, and it could well be said to image the all-too-human predicament of any go-between who has crossed geographical or psychic borders, or embarked on a new life and ended up feeling lost along the way. Meanwhile, the poem suggests that (to paraphrase David Bowie) the alien or "other" is still to be loved because of, not despite, her otherness:

> *Má tá eireaball éisc féin orm*
> *nílim gan dathúlacht éigin*
> *... tá loinnir óm' ghainní*
> *ná chífeá riamh ag mná mhíntíre.*
>
> (81)

> Even if I have a fish's tail,
> I'm not without a certain beauty.
> ... there's a shimmer from my scales
> you won't see on land-women.

Why can the mermaid (and her currently overly controlling lover) not have the best of both worlds? That, according to Ní Dhomhnaill's aesthetic, would require acceptance of duality, even equality, between realms such as sea and land, science and nature, female and male. Currently, one element (the male, represented by the "tú"/"you" of the poem) has limited the other's (the mermaid's) freedom to move and be, appropriating her "cáipín draíochta" ("magic caul") with, in the final image, devastating consequences for all: "Theip an taoide orainn chomh maith / is tá francach ag cogaint na gréine" ("The tide has gone out on us, too, / and there's a rat gnawing at the sun"; 82). Typical of Ní Dhomhnaill's work, this poem seems on the surface to refer to the destruction caused by an imbalance in relations between one male and one female, but by implication it could refer to similar imbalance and destruction in the individual psyche (which is made up of male and female elements), in any given society, between societies, or in the world at large where an "inner conversion [towards harmony and balance] must be made in face of the imminent destruction of this planet" (Ní Dhomhnaill 2005:198). What once might have sounded hippy-ish and naive from this poet, whose teens coincided with the late 1960s, increasingly seems prescient if not Cassandra-like in these war-torn, globally warmed, late 2000s.

Some of the pain that is memorably imaged in Ní Dhomhnaill's poems also seems to derive from her experience of being an artist – someone who necessarily journeys (a common motif) between realms (whether physical or psychological) for "pearls" of art (52) but, in doing so, risks drowning or being led under the waves by, for example, "fear an chaipín deirg" ("the red-capped man") of "An Bóithrín Caol" (94; "The Narrow Path" [1990:61]), a folkloric personification of a dangerous spirit, an all-too-male obstacle to full individuation or, in this case, female progress. Sometimes, therefore, human help is acknowledged as necessary to stay on one's feet, as in "Ualach an Uaignis" ("This Lonely Load"):

> *ná téir i bhfolach*
> *laistiar de cheo na bhfocal.*
> *Táimid caillte sa cheo chéanna*
> *sa bhfaill os cionn an locha*
> *tabhair do láimh dom*
> *is treoraigh mé ón bpoll.*

> don't go and hide
> behind a fog of words.
> We're lost in the same fog
> on the cliff over the loch.
> Give me your hand
> and lead me from the abyss.

(83 [1990:55])

Without such temporary help from the "other," the contrasting element, it seems that the speaker in this poem, as in many Ní Dhomhnaill poems, can become "lost" even to herself – a state usefully imaged by the poet's invocation of the "changeling" from Celtic folklore, combined and updated with the plural "I" or multiple self of modern psychology: "ní mé féin a bheidh ann / nuair a bheidh muid béal ar bhéal" ("it won't be me that's there / when we are mouth to mouth"; 83). All too often, however, the speaker (whether she's a go-between, pilgrim spirit, or artist) does not encounter a welcoming hand from the other side, dimension, or gender, but a "ceobhrán lem mhúchadh gan faoiseamh" ("relentless choking fog"; 89) or even a let-down from her own "sisters" – as in "Féachaint Romham Siar" ("Looking Behind Me"): "Scread máthar / boirbe mná rialta ar ghuthán, / is bím ag féachaint síos sa duibheagán" ("A mother's scream, / the sharpness of a nun on the phone / and I'm looking down into the abyss"; 84). Elsewhere she receives or perceives the blind eye of indifference cast by male spiritual leaders who pay more attention to patriarchal ritual than to the feminine in themselves, in society and in, possibly, God – as in the poem "I nGort Lus na Gréine" ("In the Sunflower Field"):

> *Is a fhearra bhféasóg lán*
> *a ghoireann Allah,*
> *cúig n-uaire sa lá*
> *ní raghaidh sibh saor*
> *de bharr bhur bpéine,*
>
> *mar is ag leanbh na gceannaithe bán*
> *a bhfuil a béal gealgháiriteach lán*
> *atá rún diamhair*
> *lus na gréine.*

(77)

> And you full-bearded men
> who call Allah
> five times a day,
> you will not go without blame
> for all your effort,
>
> because it's the fair girl-child,
> whose laughing mouth is full,
> who possesses the deep secret
> of the sunflower.

Lost in mists of hostility or indifference, her human worth under-appreciated, the pilgrim spirit or, especially female, artist may end up feeling that she personally and the feminine in general are cut down or reduced, skinned alive in "siopa an fhion-nadóra" ("the furrier's shop"), and forced into aggressive defense, as in "Sionnach" ("The Fox"): "Bainim snap / as láimh mo chothaithe" ("I bite / at the hand that feeds me"; 86 [1988a:147]). Just such a bite is taken out of the hand of a priest who advises the poet to "change [her] theme" or tune in "Athrú Téama" (85), suggesting an unfeasible form of birth control or predetermination over the unpredictable incarnations of poetry. The poet snaps back that the priest would know better "[dá m]bíodh ciall aige / nó leanbh" (if he had "some sense / or a child").

However, from this collection and on, Ní Dhomhnaill does not only "snap" back at interfering nay-sayers or "Gestapo voices," but sings, celebrates, and even sounds some hopeful notes of potential reconciliation. For example, there are two traditional "occasional" poems of welcome in the final section of *An Dealg Droighin*: "Fáilte Bhéal na Sionna don Iasc" ("The Shannon Estuary Welcoming the Fish") and "Fáilte an Ghalláin Roimh Titim na hOíche" ("The Standing Stone Welcoming Nightfall"). Both are marvelous examples of Ní Dhomhnaill's imagination and verbal dexterity in writing in persona and using allegory. The former poem (88 [1988a:158]) is a sensuous celebration of mutually dependent (male and female) elements in nature, and also one of the sexiest poems of marital love that you are likely to encounter:

> *Bia ar fad*
> *Is ea an t-iasc seo ...*
> *Fiche punt teann*
> *Dírithe*
> *Ar a nead sa chaonach néata.*

> This fish
> is nothing but meat ...
> twenty pounds of muscle tautened,
> aimed
> at its nest in the mossy place.

Such harmony between the sexes, Ní Dhomhnaill suggests in other poems, was more common before certain puritanical versions of Christianity took hold. In her view, an Eve-blaming, woman-fearing and -hating doctrine of the Fall replaced a more balanced attitude towards nature and sexuality with, very often, a mind-scarring denigration of the feminine, to the detriment of all:

> *Ach anois*
> *tá an greim bainte*
> *an t-úll ite*
> *an chnuimh ginte ...*
> *is táimid luite*
> *sa dorchadas síoraí*
> *mar a bhfuil gol is gárthaíl*
> *is díoscán fiacal*
> *go heireaball timpeall.*

> But now
> the bite has been bitten,
> the apple eaten,
> the maggot begotten ...
> and we lie
> in eternal darkness
> in a vale of tears and yells
> and gnashing of teeth
> to tail.

Above in "Na Súile Uaine" (90; my translation; see also "The Green Eyes" [1988a:148]), Ní Dhomhnaill concentrates on the snake as the apple-biter, rather than repeating the traditional focus on Eve. Also, although "nathar" ("snake") is a masculine noun in Irish which explains the use of the masculine "sé" ("he" or "it") throughout the poem, the creature is best thought of (and "sé" translated) as an "it," representing here the appetite, desire, or over-reaching aspect of all of us, male and female. Ní Dhomhnaill has an anarchic streak in her that makes her more sympathetic to, or understanding of, the "snake" in this poem than the prescriptive, "life-denying" forces that would turn Eve into a scapegoat, Eden into a vale of tears, and this world into a living hell.

Significantly, however, this first collection does not end on a note of conflict or with a violent war-cry against patriarchy, religious or otherwise. It concludes with a fragile but optimistic note and offering, putting a whole new positive twist on Eve and even the snake itself. The poem "Manach" ("Monk"; 96 [1988a:56]) has as its speaker an unnamed female who represents what Ní Dhomhnaill has called the "deep feminine" (Ní Dhomhnaill 2005:85) across time and the ages, and present in both the psyche and society at large. Here, that female persona tries to tempt the male mindset (characterized by binary opposites and exclusion or unhealthy purgation) to move towards a more inclusive and, actually, loving way of thinking, being, and behaving. Addressing a holy, but isolated, hermit or male saint, the speaker in the poem "Temptation" explains that

> ... *ní chun do chráite*
> *a éirím gach lá,*
> *ach chun do bháite*
> *faoi leáspairtí grá ...*
> *faoi deara dhom triall riamh ort*
> *a apstail, a mhanaigh.*

> ... it's not to torment you
> every day I rise –
> but to drown you
> in love's delights ...
> That's the only reason I haunt you:
> my monk, my apostle, my priest.

In such poems, the "deep feminine," the buried or suppressed female side of the story, gets its chance to be heard, not to shout down or cast out the male or masculine element but to balance it: as above, the "she" gets to have her her say, and what it represents is a "rising up from powerlessness" much more than any one-sided seizing of power that would only institute a new imbalance (O'Connor 1996:163).

Finally, with balance in mind, it is worth remembering that Ní Dhomhnaill's poems are as valuable for their music, imagery, linguistic free play, and, often, humor, as they are for their feminist insights. They are written in Irish, which she likes to think of as "yeast" that gives rise to Irish culture in general (Ní Dhomhnaill 1988b:117). To contemporary Irish poetry in particular, Ní Dhomhnaill and her fellow *INNTI* poets and heirs have contributed not just yeast but a great deal of the overall taste, flavor, and variety.

References and Further Reading

Campbell, M. (Ed.). (2003). *The Cambridge Companion to Contemporary Irish Poetry*. Cambridge: Cambridge University Press.

de Paor, P. (1997). *Tionscnamh Filíochta Nuala Ní Dhomhnaill*. Dublin: An Clóchomhar.

Dorgan, T. (Ed.). (1996). *Irish Poetry since Kavanagh*. Blackrock: Four Courts.

Heaney, S. (1980). *Preoccupations: Selected Prose 1968–1978*. London: Faber & Faber.

MacMonagle, N. (Ed.). (1995). *Lifelines: Letters from Famous People about their Favourite Poem*. 2nd edn. Dublin: Town House and Country House.

Mahon, D. (1975). *The Snow Party*. London: Oxford University Press.

McGarry, P. (2009). "Roots of a Warped View of Sexuality." *Irish Times Weekend Review*, Saturday, June 20, 4.

Ní Dhomhnaill, N. (1981). *An Dealg Droighin*. [The Spine of Blackthorn]. Dublin: Mercier Press.

Ní Dhomhnaill, N. (1984). *Féar Suaithinseach* [Amazing Grass]. Maynooth: An Sagart.

Ní Dhomhnaill, N. (1988a). *Selected Poems / Rogha Dánta*. Dublin: Raven Arts Press.

Ní Dhomhnaill, N. (1988b). "The English for Irish." *Irish Review*, 4, 116–18.

Ní Dhomhnaill, N. (1990). *Pharaoh's Daughter*. Oldcastle: Gallery Press.

Ní Dhomhnaill, N. (1991). *Feis*. Maynooth: An Sagart.

Ní Dhomhnaill, N. (1992). *The Astrakhan Cloak*. Oldcastle: Gallery Press.

Ní Dhomhnaill, N. (1998). *Cead Aighnis*. [Leave, or Permission, to Speak]. An Daingean: An Sagart.

Ní Dhomhnaill, N. (1999). *The Water Horse*. Oldcastle: Gallery Press.

Ní Dhomhnaill, N. (2005). *Selected Essays*. Dublin: New Island.

Ní Dhomhnaill, N. (2007). *The Fifty-Minute Mermaid*. Oldcastle: Gallery Press.

O'Connor, T. (Ed.). (1996). *The Comic Tradition in Irish Women Writers*. Gainesville: University Press of Florida.

Ó Fiannachta, P. (Ed.). (1986). *Léachtaí Cholm Cille XVII: An Nuafhilíocht*. Maynooth: An Sagart.

Sewell, F. (2000). *Modern Irish Poetry*. Oxford: Oxford University Press.

Shakespeare, W. (1989). *The Illustrated Stratford Shakespeare*. London: Chancellor Press.

Somerville-Arjat, G. and R.E. Wilson (Eds). (1990). *Sleeping with Monsters: Conversations with Scottish and Irish Women Poets*. Edinburgh: Polygon.

Stallybrass, P. and A. White. (1986). *The Politics and Poetics of Transgression*. London: Methuen.

Waddell, H. (1929). *Mediaeval Latin Lyrics*. London: Constable.

Warner, M. (1994). *Managing Monsters: Six Myths of Our Time*. London: Vintage.

Wheatley, D. (2003). "Irish Poetry into the Twenty-First Century." In M. Campbell (Ed.). *The Cambridge Companion to Irish Poetry* (pp. 250–67). Cambridge: Cambridge University Press.

55

The Anxiety of Influence and the Fiction of Roddy Doyle

Danine Farquharson

In the course of an extremely successful writing career, Roddy Doyle has become a pre-eminent contemporary Irish writer: his work is widely reviewed and increasingly the subject of sustained scholarly attention; he is a much-sought-after interview guest, book prize judge, and literary festival attendee; and his ideas and opinions are reproduced in media around the world. Roddy Doyle is a mercurial writer. He is never content to remain within one mode of narrative, and yet his fiction revisits many characters and locations – the Rabbittes, Spencers, and Smarts occur in more than one novel or short story and always exist in an imagined Dublin. As a writer Doyle never sits still but often returns to characters and situations: he wants to write of a changing Irish world and he wants things to stay the same. The wonderfully and frustratingly paradoxical element of all of Doyle's fictional work, however, is that while it is possible to offer general comments, exceptions exist to foil any overarching argument about theme or narrative style. Thus it is no exaggeration to write that Doyle is one of the leading contemporary writers, Irish or no. However, that Doyle's fictional career owes a great debt to Irish literary forefathers, James Joyce and Sean O'Casey in particular, suggests an anxiety of influence at work in all his fiction.

Clearly an active and adventurous writer, Roddy Doyle's career thus far has brought him international recognition and fame. Since 1987 he has published seven novels, and the first three (*The Commitments*, *The Snapper*, and *The Van*, later collected as *The Barrytown Trilogy*) have been made into films. The fourth novel, *Paddy Clarke Ha Ha Ha*, won the Man Booker Prize in 1993. Following that achievement, he published *The Woman Who Walked into Doors* in 1996 with a sequel, *Paula Spencer*, in 2006. Then came *A Star Called Henry* (1999) and its sequel *Oh, Play That Thing* in 2004. He has also written a memoir about his parents, *Rory and Ita* (2002), several books for children, theater plays, *Family* for BBC TV, an original screenplay – *When Brendan*

A Companion to Irish Literature, edited by Julia M. Wright
© 2010 Blackwell Publishing Ltd

Met Trudy (2000, directed by Keiron J. Walsh) – and most recently a collection of short stories, *The Deportees and Other Stories* (2007). While the focus of this discussion will be his fictional works and the influences that inform them, there is much to be said about his texts for children, the stage, and the screen. He is a writer loath to remain in one narrative style for very long and his literary creations are ripe for study.

In Doyle's first novel, *The Commitments*, protagonist Jimmy Rabbitte Jr. accepts or rejects potential band members based solely on their answer to his question "Who're your influences?" Jimmy knows that the way musicians claim allegiance to musical forebears will tell him something vital about their suitability and, more importantly, will tell him something essential about not only their musical tastes but also about themselves. Twenty years later, Jimmy reappears in the fictional world of Roddy Doyle in "The Deportees," the title story in a collection of short fiction published in 2007. The plot of "The Deportees" is the same as that of *The Commitments*: Jimmy is trying to build a band from a motley crew of musicians, but the Dublin setting has changed drastically in those two decades, even if Jimmy's attempt to ascertain the musical influences of potential band members is unswerving. As a collection, *The Deportees* has an obvious political and social agenda of exposing racism and raising awareness of Dublin's quickly increasing immigrant population. In the foreword Doyle writes, "I went to bed in one country and woke up in a different one" (Doyle 2007:xi). What is more interesting than the bland consciousness-raising is how *The Deportees* relates to Doyle's previous fictional worlds in terms of style, content, and literary influences. Obviously, Doyle's own work is an influence, as witnessed in the continuation of the story of Jimmy Rabbitte. He writes that in the collection there is a "sequel, sort of, to *The Commitments*" (2007:xiii). This coy reference – mocking the critics who note his penchant for returning to previous characters or books – indicates both a mature writer as well as a writer still uneasy with the question of influences. The discussion that follows will summarize the major critical analyses of Doyle's fiction, highlighting key elements of his narrative style that persist, and then present two of his works (*A Star Called Henry* and *The Deportees and Other Stories*) as texts deeply embedded in a fraught and fascinating relationship to other texts and other writers. Despite Doyle's refusal to acknowledge it, the anxiety of influence in his fiction has helped produce wildly popular and significant Irish writing.

Doyle's Dublin Voices

Taken as a whole, responses to Roddy Doyle's fiction comment on his deft construction of dialogue – often labeled as brilliantly funny and gritty in its realism – his mastery of comedy and satire, his wry use of popular culture (particularly American), his focus on family and community dynamics, and his consistent imagining and reimagining of Dublin as a geographical place and a psychological space. That he is undeniably a writer of Dublin lives is likely the first and foremost reason that comparisons to Joyce and O'Casey abound in the critical commentary (Hall 1999; Costello 2001; White 2001; Phelan 2004). That commentary is housed in two major book-length studies, a great number of book reviews, and an equal number of interviews with Doyle has resulted in some surprising critical consensus.

Two books offer significant commentary on Doyle's fiction: Dermot McCarthy's *Raining on the Parade* and Caramine White's *Reading Roddy Doyle*. McCarthy's major achievement is reading Doyle's work up to 2003 as giving voice to those who were once the mostly ignored inhabitants of Dublin and modern Ireland. McCarthy also focuses on Doyle's characters as individuals struggling with a quickly and quixotically changing world. McCarthy sees Doyle's contribution to modern Irish writing as threefold: it is profound and significant in its satire, it is new and provocative in its focus on class, and it is worthy of attention because of its rejection of indulgent nationalist ideologies. Perceptive in his location of Doyle's fiction in a changing socio-political Irish world, McCarthy argues that Doyle makes "a positive contribution to a new imagining of 'Ireland'" and that Doyle confidently engages with post-modern ideas and styles (McCarthy 2003:231). White's book focuses more on Doyle's writing style (in his first five novels) – in particular his use of dialogue and narrative voice. White offers one of the best commentaries on the character of Sharon in *The Snapper*, an often neglected novel and a glossed-over character in the briefer studies of Doyle's fiction. Her major observation is that there is a pattern in Doyle's fiction of "confronting graver and more serious social problems" as he grows as a writer (White 2001:145).

Others have devoted time to studying Doyle's fiction with compelling verdicts on his importance. As Gerry Smyth writes, "His work has crystallized with great insight and force many of the significant themes and debates of contemporary Irish culture" (Smyth 1997:66). Further, "it is important to acknowledge that Doyle is the only contemporary Irish writer tackling the subject of the social and cultural impact of the Celtic Tiger on Ireland in a committed manner" (Burke 2009). Doyle's novels are significant and worthy of critical assessment, even if some reviewers are less than kind. White offers an excellent overview of the mixed reactions to Doyle's fiction, noting that his use of comedy and satire sometimes prevents his work from being taken seriously (White 2001:4–11). Two common themes emerge from all this attention to dominate the discussion of Doyle's fiction: his Dublin setting and his mastery of speech, either in dialogue or in narrative voice.

Reviews of almost all of his books, including the one devoted to his parents, *Rory and Ita*, fall into some kind of Dublin categorization: Aisling Foster's "Culchie and Dub" and Anthony Lane's "Dubliners" are but two examples of reviews that immediately label Doyle as a Dublin writer. Doyle readily admits this geographical element of his work. In an interview about the film *When Brendan Met Trudy*, he says, "I had to make a big effort to get Dublin the way it is now. It's changed so much in the last decade, and I wanted to get that" (Gerrard 2001). Smyth's work on Doyle examines the Dublin-ness of his fiction at great length. He writes that from the first pages of

The Van it is obvious that "Doyle was engaging seriously with the complexities of the new urban order" (Smyth 2000:23). Notable for Smyth is Jimmy Rabbitte Sr.'s "exclusion from both house and street. In the earlier novels of the trilogy, the suburb of Barrytown functions as a knowable community. … [T]here is also a sense of a larger urban milieu which the characters cannot (fully) know" (2000:23–24). Even the studies of films made from Doyle's work cannot avoid dealing with the Dublin locale. For example, Michael Cronin notes the importance of place more than once in his *Ireland Into Film: The Barrytown Trilogy*.

The Dublin of Doyle is specific: it is working-class and male-dominated. If his major concern is "the exploration between individuals and the collectives in which they find themselves, especially that collective known as the family" (Smyth 1997:66), then that family is quite obviously the paterfamilias. Smyth's observation that "the sense of frustration and impotence is caught in the image of two middle-aged, working-class men (Jimmy Sr and his friend Bimbo)" (Smyth 2000:24) could be applied to many Doyle characters. And yet for many readers the Dublin of Doyle becomes increasingly universal as well. As Cronin argues, Doyle's early novels and films of them "constitute a body of work that not only gives voice to the particular preoccupations of the recent Irish past but remain startlingly contemporary in the manner in which it articulates the specific relationship between Irish locality and global futures" (Cronin 2006:1). There is a tug between the past and the present in much of Doyle's fiction – a desire to capture a past Ireland but at the same time write the new and emerging Ireland. Temporal issues aside, Doyle's Dublin remains the home of frustrated fathers, rebellious sons, troubled parents, and their struggling children. The exception to Doyle's imaginings of Dublin is *Oh, Play That Thing*. The sequel to *A Star Called Henry*, the novel may still follow the crazy life of Henry Smart but this time he is in America. Continuing to mix history and fiction, Doyle has Henry spend much of his time in the company of Louis Armstrong. Their relationship allows Doyle to pursue his interest in American music, first witnessed in *The Commitments*, and anticipates the deep concern over racism that dominates *The Deportees*.

The majority of Doyle's protagonists are male, but there is a significant exception in Paula Spencer. First appearing in the BBC TV series *Family*, Paula is the first-person narrator of *The Woman Who Walked into Doors* and she returns as the main character in the sequel *Paula Spencer*. Paula is predictably a Dubliner and a working-class character, but what is surprisingly new about these texts is Paula's voice: Doyle wrote the story of an alcoholic, abused wife in her own words in *The Woman Who Walked into Doors*, to much critical acclaim (Adair 2006; Binchy 2006). One critic argued that it was "the added fact that Paula Spencer finds her voice self-consciously through the act of writing that makes this Doyle's most fully realised work to date" (Hand 1996:14). *Paula Spencer*, which shifts the narrative voice from first person to third person, is but one example of the fact that "Doyle is interested in stretching himself as a writer both formally and conceptually, as well as testing the limits of novelistic discourse generally" (Smyth 1997:84).

Indeed, Doyle's mastery of voice is the most commented-on stylistic aspect of his writing. From the lightning-paced dialogue of *The Commitments* to the poignant inner workings of Paula's mind, Doyle has proven himself brilliantly capable of creating and sustaining many different voices. Paddy Clarke is arguably the most recognized of such voices. With an imagination fired by "American television shows and British football teams" (Smyth 1997:79), Paddy is a 10-year-old boy in 1960s Ireland trying to negotiate life in the midst of his parents' break-up. Set once again in Dublin, "the novel's boldest feature is its infantile style of narrative. ... Paddy's account may be inefficient, incoherent and chronologically incapable, but there is never a glimpse of the author at his shoulder, directing operations or forcing him to dwell on portentous moments" (Imlah 1993). Beyond the setting and the narrative voice, there is another element in *Paddy Clarke Ha Ha Ha* that echoes other Doyle fiction: the relationship between a father and a son is central. Paddy might have an interesting relationship with his mother, but the heartbreaking words near the end of the novel that mark Paddy's movement past childhood are all about his father:

> – Paddy Clarke –
> Paddy Clarke –
> Has no da.
> Ha ha ha!
> I didn't listen to them. They were only kids. (Doyle 1993b:281)

Paddy Clark "both hates and loves his father" (Smyth 1997:80) and that familial dynamic is one that not only recurs in other novels, such as *A Star Called Henry*, but also characterizes Doyle's literary relationship to other writers.

In his consideration of Irish literary renaissance writers, Declan Kiberd claims that Joyce, O'Casey, and Yeats deal with some kind of father–son relationship, but most notably the spectacle of the emasculated son taking the place of a "weak and ineffectual father" (Kiberd 1995:381). Further, the texts of the Irish Revival are full of the revolts of artistic sons against fathers, disenchantments "with the Irish male as father" and responses to a social order that is crumbling amid such widespread change that a "reversal of the relations between fathers and sons" is inevitable (1995:382). Doyle, some sixty years later, is also writing of a crumbling social order in much of his fiction, and many of his fathers struggle with their loss of power. In *The Snapper*, Jimmy Sr. must "review his assumptions regarding his role as father" when his daughter Sharon gets pregnant, and *The Van* is an "exploration of Jimmy Sr's fragile identity, and especially his masculinity" (Smyth 1997:72–74). All of Henry Smart's actions in *A Star Called Henry* can be read as reactions to and rejections of his father, Henry Sr. That there are so many junior and senior characters – Jimmy, Henry, the two Larrys in "Guess Who's Coming for the Dinner" – is not simply titular realism, but also a clear indication that fathers and sons are a major part of the Dublin make-up in Doyle's fictional worlds. All this is by way of suggesting that Doyle himself suffers from an anxiety of paternal influence that plays itself out in both his fiction and his public voice.

Who Are Your Influences?

The question of literary influences on Doyle's fictional worlds is present from the earliest responses to his work. White, in particular, traces Joycean moments and argues for clear connections between Stephen Dedalus and Paddy Clarke (White 2001:100–03). In noting the presence of Joyce and O'Casey, Smyth refers to an "uncertainty of influence" (Smyth 1997:66) in Doyle, but also mentions the importance of Charles Dickens and American culture. Even Cronin's discussion of the *Barrytown Trilogy* films notes Joyce and O'Casey as crucial elements of Doyle's fictional history (Cronin 2006:2). Doyle has added fuel to the influence fire by constantly commenting on the lack of said influences: in Smyth's interview with Doyle, Smyth asks "Are there any traditions – literary, cultural, social – that you are conscious of writing within or against?" and Doyle's response is "No" (Smyth 1997:98). Such clear rejection is followed by a long discussion of how critics are always looking for traditions after the fact, and Doyle rejects completely such analyses. Smyth believes that Doyle's hesitation to commit to inheriting anything from literary forefathers reflects the changing nature of Dublin itself. I contend that Doyle is objecting too much and that there are undeniable Joycean elements in his work. Further, Doyle owes a great literary debt to O'Casey even though he rarely mentions that influence. Finally, Doyle's most recent fiction sees him enter a self-referential phase whereby he notes and plays with his own influence. There is no doubt that Doyle's fictional career is a vibrant and lively response to a changing world, but his work is also troubled by a relationship to other Irish writers and texts.

The Case of Henry Smart

A Star Called Henry and its sequel, *Oh, Play That Thing*, are O'Casey-style autobiographies. In the same way that O'Casey satirizes and toys with the narrative voice of memoir and autobiography (see Kenneally 1987), the narrator Henry Smart is by turns self-aware and self-deluded. Just as O'Casey narrates his own birth so too does Henry Smart spend much time in the opening pages of *A Star Called Henry* narrating his entrance into the world:

> Melody pushed and I –
> Me –
> Henry Smart the Second or Third came charging into the world on a river of water and blood that washed the news off the papers. (Doyle 1999:21)

The beautifully hesitating self-coming-into-being that is narrator and subject Henry Smart Jr. marks a change from Doyle's masterful Dublin voices toward a playful postmodern dance of identity.

Doyle's *A Star Called Henry* is about a young man, Henry Smart, who is first caught up in the revolutionary violence of 1916 and is then sucked back into the subversive guerrilla war with England in 1919. This novel is another departure for Doyle: it is his first novel of Irish historical content, tackling the major events of the Easter Rising and the War of Independence. He merges real men with fictional characters as Pearse, Connolly, and Collins all cross paths with the narrator Henry Smart in a wonderful and ambitious historiographic metafiction. Henry narrates himself into historical events of 1916, and to do so he must write against conventional wisdom and established histories. Indeed, Doyle interrogates the way that history is told, the way that memories are recorded, and the way that identities are constructed – an ambitious project for him at this stage of his career, and one that is largely successful. Through this story, Doyle tackles the behemoth of Irish nationalism, and he does not hold back in his critique. The prevailing critical opinion about Doyle's representation of historical events in *A Star Called Henry* is that he subverts the "official" history and popular mythologies, and by doing so he challenges the "hegemonic nationalist version of the birth of the modern nation" of Ireland (McCarthy 2003:196). José Lanters writes that the novel "presents events through a late twentieth-century lens that highlights politically correct issues such as class, gender, and ethnicity" (Lanters 2002:248). If identity is a changeable narrative, then so too is history.

McCarthy argues that *A Star Called Henry* is a novel that should be read in a broader context that takes into consideration three recent movements: the new cultural nationalism that emerged in Ireland during the mid- to late 1990s; the ongoing debate over historical revisionism; and the more recent discursive-ideological controversy over the application of postcolonial theory to Irish politics, society, and culture (McCarthy 2003:191). He goes on to argue that the novel is knee-deep in a struggle between the state and its ideologues: "Doyle has written a historical fiction that enters into a negative dialectic with both official history and elite nationalist historiography" (2003:223). He claims that Doyle does all this to seamlessly construct a textual fabric of history and fiction, invention and research, that challenges both the history of 1916 and the genre of the historic novel itself. I agree that Doyle exposes the official histories and myths of the Irish nation to be fragile and inadequate. However, McCarthy argues that the "most important revisionist feature of the novel is its construction of a *social* and *economic* rather than nationalist-political context for the 1916 Rising" (2003:205; italics in original). The social-economic context is undeniably vital in *A Star Called Henry*, but it is also a novel about how the relationship between fathers and sons affects identity.

The young Henry embarks on a perilous life journey without realizing the extent to which he is only following in his father's footsteps. And with classic Doyle humor, those footsteps are as uneven and irregular as Henry Sr.'s one-legged gait. His father's mostly absent presence in Henry's life is a ghost that haunts the developing man, and Henry clings to his father's wooden leg as not only a reminder of the mythology surrounding his father's larger-than-life persona but also as a diviner of violence and a token reminder of his heritage. Henry is obsessed with his father – "Who was he and where did he come from?" (Doyle 1999:9) – but he also hates him in a predictably Freudian way: "I moved and hit the shore with my forehead and tried to kill my father's face and his hands and his voice" (61). But Henry Jr. is no more able to kill the father than Stephan Dedalus, and Doyle has Henry adopt his father's leg as his "birth certificate." If there are Joycean echoes in *Paddy Clarke Ha Ha Ha*, then such echoes recur here. In the case of Henry Jr., like Hamlet and Stephen Dedalus, the father's ghost is a motivating factor in the young man's self-invention. How could Doyle reject these connections and his own ghostly presences in his writing life?

The case of O'Casey is a place to start. Doyle regularly mentions and speaks about his relationship to O'Casey. In an interview with Stephen Costello, Doyle said, "I loved reading and enjoyed doing a third year paper on Sean O'Casey, comparing the politics of his autobiography to the politics of *The Plough and the Stars*" (Costello 2001:88). Doyle had earlier, in 1999, granted O'Casey the status of influence on the use of the dash to signify characters talking in *The Commitments*: "I do it because I saw it used in O'Casey in his autobiography, and I liked this" (Sbrockey 1999:543). In speaking about *A Star Called Henry*, Doyle easily admits that the looters he depicts during the Easter Rising are "the exact same people" as O'Casey's characters in *The Plough and the Stars* (Taylor 1999). None of these interviews shows Doyle experiencing any anxiety over his writerly admiration for and tutelage under O'Casey. But on the acknowledgments page for *A Star Called Henry* there is no mention of O'Casey or *The Plough and the Stars* at all. This omission is peculiar.

Doyle is not generally reluctant to acknowledge his influences, just O'Casey and Joyce. The notes at the end of *A Star Called Henry* include a list of books that Doyle testifies inform his work: an authorial gesture to be expected in a novel steeped in Irish history and populated with historical figures. Interestingly, among the long list of books is Joyce's *Dubliners* and *Ulysses*, and I will return to Joyce's influence later. The list is not organized by author or title or publication date. It is an apparently random list of books, perhaps even as they appeared at some point on the author's shelves. Joyce is the eighteenth of twenty-four writers mentioned. O'Casey is not mentioned and yet Kevin C. Kearns' *Dublin Tenement Life: An Oral History* is the first in the list. There are at least three possible reasons for Doyle's neglecting to cite O'Casey as an influence in this instance. The first is simply that he forgot: O'Casey's plays and politics are so much a part of Doyle's literary consciousness that it is difficult to separate the two. The second possible reason, related to the first, is that there is no anxiety about the relationship. Doyle is perfectly happy to see connections with O'Casey and maybe even thinks them obvious. The third reason is more cynical: perhaps O'Casey had too much influence on Doyle's novel. As reviewer Paul Dillon notes, "Despite the claims of the publisher's blurb, politically there is nothing worthwhile in *A Star Called Henry* that wasn't said a long time ago, for example in Sean O'Casey's controversial autobiographies" (Dillon and O'Brien 2000). It is possible that Doyle avoids mentioning O'Casey because the novel owes too much to him.

A fourth and even more cynical reason suggests itself. There is no cultural currency to be gained in the game of influences when it comes to O'Casey. Unlike James Joyce

– the man, the writer, the cultural icon, the cultural industry – the mere mention of O'Casey does not provoke the media attention that saying something about Joyce does. Doyle can avoid mentioning O'Casey in those acknowledgments because he has already noted the man's influence and the omission will not provoke that much commentary. O'Casey simply does not carry the same cultural clout as Joyce. In 2004, as Bloomsday events around the globe were getting press and media coverage, Doyle made inflammatory comments to a New York audience: Joyce needed a good editor, *Ulysses* doesn't deserve the reverence it gets, to read *The Wake* is to squander time better spent elsewhere. None of these jabs at Joyce is original or new or even that surprising. What is far more interesting is the timing of Doyle's comments so close to the looming Bloomsday celebrations. Doyle's offensive produced articles in the *Guardian*, letters to the editor of the *Irish Times*, and newspapers from Toronto to Sydney to Rio picked up the story. Bloggers give a whole new life to the increasingly sensationalized battle over Joyce. The pro-Doyle or anti-Doyle, pro-Joyce or anti-Joyce debates threatened to overtake the Bloomsday events themselves. The Doyle/Joyce affair became something people had to have an opinion on. Even David Norris piped up, calling Doyle "foolish" and hinting that he was only a "moderate talent" (quoted in Beplate 2005:3). It got personal. Doyle's immersion in this kind of controversy is not accidental.

There is, therefore, much cultural currency to be traded when speaking about Joyce. Long before the short-lived but intense media frenzy around Doyle and the 2004 Bloomsday celebrations, Doyle had trouble with Joyce. He often spoke of the burden of being a contemporary Irish novelist and having to address the question of Joyce's influence. In a 2001 interview with White, Doyle admitted that he thinks Joyce wrote "to show off his brain" "particularly in the later Joyce" (White 2001:162). He goes on to challenge the idea that there are any Joycean moments in *Paddy Clarke Ha Ha Ha*. And there is discernible anger in his comment that *Finnegans Wake* is "a complete waste of time" and that "it's a great pity, because Joyce spent so much time writing that shite that he could have spent writing real books" (White 2001:167). If O'Casey is a kindly grandfather whose birthday you often forget, then Joyce is that annoying and scandalous uncle you cannot escape and your family simply will not stop talking about. As with his way of dealing with O'Casey, there are at least three reasons why Doyle reacts to Joyce and the Joyce industry in such an aggressive away.

First, and most strongly connected to one of Harold Bloom's categories of anxiety of influence, the reason may be a desire for *kenosis* or the breaking away from an earlier influence, a defense mechanism against repetition compulsion (Bloom 1973). Doyle has said, "if you're writing about Dublin in any shape or form, the Joyce comparisons are always there. Some critic will always say he's on your shoulder" (Phelan 2004). Doyle's defense against such critics is that the critic is lazy: "I find comparisons to Joyce are a bit lazy. … I don't see it. … He was never on my shoulder" (Lippman 1996). Doyle thus rejects Joyce as a literary father. But if Joyce is not at Doyle's back then the critics and the cultural industry of Joyce certainly are. "The problem is," Doyle says, "it's like a gun is put to your head – Do you like Joyce? – It has to be yes or no" (Lippman 1996). Just as Doyle argues that everyone needs an opinion about Joyce, Doyle's attack on Joyce produced another situation where opinion was demanded. The question of influence has shifted. No longer is Doyle railing against literary comparisons between himself and Joyce, it has become the idea of Joyce being ever present – a transcendental signifier of taste – that Doyle rebels against. Or, maybe, Doyle is pushing the Joyce question to the side to include room for the Doyle question.

A second reason for Doyle's aggression against "Joyce" is not related to the literature at all but to the legacy. As Justin Beplate adroitly noted in the *Times Literary Supplement*, the real target of Doyle's broadside was not Joyce, but a literary culture in which indebtedness to him is simply assumed. The Roddy Doyle affair, however brief and overblown, demonstrates the persistence of such tensions in Joyce's legacy. Beyond the familiar "anxiety of influence" chorus of self-appointed Joyce authorities, the incident betrays lingering and deep-seated cultural sensitivities over Joyce's appropriation by "foreign" interests – an international Joyce industry that routinely exploits his name as part of Dublin's heritage and tourism industry. Doyle has some support in his attack on the Joyce industry. John Sutherland wrote in the *Guardian*, "Doyle is, I think, in one sense right. Joyce has become a cult and too much intellectual and cultural energy is expended on him." And thus a third reason for Doyle's engagement of these issues arises. Sutherland astutely notes that, in a globalized culture industry, "room is at a premium." So Doyle's outrageous gestures are a way of elbowing Joyce aside and carving open some prized space for discussion of Doyle's works. In 2004 the Bloomsday celebrations and the Joyce debate coincided with the release of Doyle's sequel to *A Star Called Henry*. *Oh Play That Thing* was getting lukewarm reviews at best and comparatively short shrift in the literary press. The magician's sleight of hand – Doyle's criticism of Bloomsday and Joyce – could be covering up or distracting from the lackluster reception of Doyle's novel.

The Unacknowledged Dinner Guest

Questions of influence are a tricky political and cultural game, particularly in an increasingly international and globally economic literary world. The globalization of literature is relevant to Doyle's relationships with Joyce and O'Casey chiefly because all three writers are considered "Dublin" authors. The *Barrytown Trilogy* clearly places Doyle's early novels as portraits of a city: a particular part of Dublin in a particular time. Dublin has been known for a very long time as a literary city. But Doyle is experiencing anxiety over the loss of "his" Dublin. And that anxiety takes an interesting turn in his creation of a series of short stories published as *The Deportees*.

Doyle is no longer gesturing toward (or away from) Joyce or O'Casey but obviously referring to both American culture and his own work. The first story in *The Deportees*, "Guess Who's Coming to the Dinner," is clearly inspired by Stanley Kramer's Academy Award-winning 1967 film starring Sidney Poitier, Katharine Hepburn, and Spencer

Tracy, *Guess Who's Coming to Dinner*. Even though Doyle neglects to mention the film in his foreword, the short story tackles issues of race and ethnic prejudice in twenty-first-century Ireland with Doyle's usual comic flair as a father must survive dinner when his daughter brings home Ben, a Nigerian asylum-seeker. Doyle has said repeatedly that part of Irish identity is going where the work is: to be an "economic migrant," and so Irish people living in Ireland must be accommodating and understanding of immigration into Ireland. Scholars such as Maureen Reddy have thoroughly analyzed Doyle's writing for *Metro Éireann* (the multicultural paper that published the first version of "Guess Who's Coming"). The story has seen various incarnations in print and on stage, but here I am interested in addressing the nature of the multi-ethnic Ireland that Doyle advocates when the base text for these stories and plays is an American film made at the time of the civil rights movement of the 1960s.

In Kramer's film, two white parents entertain their daughter's guest, a black man, for dinner. The interracial couple are engaged to be married and are visiting her parents to seek their blessing. In Doyle's short story, this isn't quite the case. In the film, the black man's parents (who are not adapted into Doyle's version) round out the drawing-room comedy structure whereby different combinations of an ensemble cast are allowed brief but revealing conversations. In Doyle's short story, there is more hubbub and chaos of a family dinner with three daughters. In fact, the dinner only concludes the film, while it is the central scene in the short story. Both film and short story are obviously about the racial tensions that exist among apparently open-minded people. There is one significant difference between the two texts, and that has to do with class. In the film Hepburn and Tracy play incredibly wealthy San Francisco parents to a rather precious daughter. In the short story, the Linnane family is decidedly working-class, the mainstay of so many Doyle fictional worlds. In the economic setting of the household, which comes to represent the culture of the time, Doyle evacuates the elitism of the Hollywood film, and film stars, and sets his story in more familiar territory.

The cultural context of both texts is very important. Kramer's 1967 film is classical Hollywood, as much for its cinematic techniques as for its pairing of Tracy, in his last film, with Hepburn. *Guess Who's Coming to Dinner* opened to wide release not long after the 1967 Supreme Court case of *Loving v. Virginia*, which ruled that restrictions on interracial marriage were unconstitutional. In *Hollywood Fantasies of Miscegenation*, Susan Courtney writes that while the court decision "boldly indicts the 'White Supremacy' of anti-miscegenation laws," the landmark case "remains silent on the histories of institutional oppression and exploitation they sanctioned" (Courtney 2005:261). Beyond the context of the US legal system, the crucially important shift in American racial politics occurring in the mid- to late 1960s is also cultural currency for the film. Donald Bogle notes that the period of the film is one of turbulence over the failings of interracial civil rights strategies, and *Guess Who's Coming to Dinner* is right in the middle of the clash between old and new means of understanding and protesting racism in the US. Bogle writes, "In 1960, Negroes were quietly asking for their rights. By 1969, blacks were demanding them. The decade moved from the traditional goal of cultural and academic assimilation to one of almost absolute separatism and the evolution of a black cultural aesthetic and black militancy" (Bogle 2001:195).

So if *Guess Who's Coming to Dinner* played center stage in such a shift, then so too was Sidney Poitier's career right in the middle of this turbulence. Poitier made a career of playing thoughtful, graceful, decent, strong but dependable characters. His screen persona embodies intelligence, integrity, honor, kindness, good looks, and, in the context of the rise of black militancy, passivity. In *Guess Who's Coming to Dinner* Poitier is more than merely nice and decent: he is "sexually neutral" (Bogle 2001:182) – the only expression of physical love between him and Joanna is one kiss, and even that is seen through a cab-driver's rear-view mirror as if several layers of reflectors are necessary to show the interracial action. Doyle's story (set during a time in Ireland that was witnessing unprecedented immigration into the country by Africans and Europeans) maintains this sexual neutrality of his black character, but introduces a humorous note. Larry thinks his daughter and Ben want to marry, but finds out that he has jumped to the wrong conclusion, to good comic effect.

When Larry meets Ben in "Guess Who's Coming to the Dinner," the narrator indicates that "He'd been expecting someone like Eddie Murphy, without the grin and the shine. But that type of look. But this was more like meeting Sidney Poitier" (Doyle 2007:11). It is as though Larry knows the 1967 film and absorbs its plot to such an extent that he thinks Ben and Stephanie will get married because that is what happens on screen. Regardless of this plot shift away from that of the film, the story remains consistent with the racial politics of 1967 America. Remarkably, neither black protagonist is threatening physically or sexually. They are both intelligent, daunting in their presence, and fully able to engage the male patriarch in social, moral, and political discussion. Thus, both Ben and John are what another critic of the film calls "the ebony saint. Neither Uncle Tom nor militant, he remains nonviolent despite enormous provocation, and like ebony itself he remains cool. He is obviously superior in skills and ability. Nevertheless, the ebony saint recognizes that society imposes limitations on him and he implicitly accepts those that are not blatantly racist. He poses no threat to established social or sexual mores" (Leab 1975:163). Not only has Doyle adapted the basic plot of Kramer's film, but he has also neutralized the potentially volatile politics in the same manner as the movie.

There appears to be a very simple mode of adaptation going on here. Doyle has transplanted the plot and the characterization of 1967 American Hollywood to working-class 2007 Dublin. However, more than just character and plot are in translation here. Nominally an ironic comedy about mildly racial attitudes toward new Irish immigration, the short story is far more preoccupied with delineating a relationship between the two men: white father, black young man. Yet again, Doyle returns to fathers and sons or son-like characters. This relationship remains central to Doyle's fictional worlds. The interracial friendship will not threaten the power of the white man in his home or his community. Thus, the film and the short story both betray "subtle and ambiguous responses to the realities of the political moment" (Levine 2001:382). Poitier's character and the film only serve to resolve white men's problems. The same betrayals are at work in Doyle's story. In an interview, Doyle said that "the idea [is] to bring people from different cultures together. It's a challenge. … it's a very deliberately light and funny story that shows what happens, or the potential – what can happen. It was deliberately done to see the funny possibilities, the human possibilities" (Drewett 2003:346–47). Doyle still asserts that increased migration to Ireland is "a great opportunity. … The Irish did it, and do it all the time, so why not here? What's the threat? Do we need to be white? No! Do we need to be Catholic? Jesus Christ, no! What is it that we are trying to protect? I don't see it. All I can see is enlargement" (Drewett 2003:347).

Reddy has already done great work teasing out the implications of this ideal of "enlargement" as expressed in Doyle's stories published in *Metro Éireann*, the multi-cultural paper where this story first appeared. She notes that "discussions of race get displaced onto discussions of Irishness/not-Irishness, with the racial dimension that determines this discourse neatly hidden" (Reddy 2005:376). And while Doyle's stories are a "sustained intervention" into this discourse, with their "heavily ironic and delib-erately distanced" structure, they are still "placed within a particular context for readers who are really recent immigrants and Irish nationals sympathetic to the idea of multiculturalism" (2005:376–77). Thus, according to Reddy, "the story is reassur-ing: African immigrants do not want to marry your daughters; they just want to work and live in peace in Ireland. In this story, racism is entirely personal, not systemic or social, not intimately intertwined with all the basic conditions of daily life. … Doyle surely knows on some level that this view of racism is fantastical and grossly over-simplified" (2005:381). This view also misses the entire cultural and political matrix of the host text for the story wherein interracial civil rights movements were failing, black militancy was gaining momentum, and the need to assuage white men's fears was paramount.

What is striking is that the 1960s version of racial accommodation that sets the stage for the Irish version sees so very little revision, so little translation. It is as if Doyle's story says 1960s America is the way for Ireland to go in the twenty-first century. Neither of the stories "encourage[s] change in that audience but instead [they] offer reinforcement of already-established views" (Reddy 2005:383). While Doyle is tackling new issues and new characters in *The Deportees*, the fiction remains tied to an Ireland of the past and a Doyle universe of earlier texts. Yet in classic Doyle mercurial form there is a hint of something else going on. The opening story in the collection returns to that Doyle universe.

Return of the Rabbittes

In the title story of *The Deportees*, Doyle comes full circle to the origins of his writing career, sort of. "The Deportees" brings back Jimmy Rabbitte Jr. – this time he is a father and he is going through a mid-life crisis not unlike Jimmy Sr.'s in *The Van*. Cobbling together a group of immigrant Irish musicians based largely on their response to his question of whether or not they like The Cranberries, Jimmy moves through a fraught adventure in live music that is a near-replica of *The Commitments*. Some things have certainly remained the same: the Dublin locale, the quick-paced dialogue, Jimmy's love of American soul music; even Mickah Wallace makes an appearance. Other things have changed: the band is made up of immigrants from all over the world, the fear of deportation is constant, and the politics of the novel are obvious. Doyle is playing a lovely game with this quaintly flawed short story. He knows that influences matter (in another story a character travels to America to research the influence of the Harlem Renaissance on Irish literature), but questions to what end. A genealogy might be constructed to draw a Doyle literary family tree, and tracking of images or styles may be substantiated with close critical readings, but none of that activity, just like Jimmy's interview questions, guarantees a pay-off of truth or success.

REFERENCES AND FURTHER READING

Adair, T. (2006). "Poor Paula Finds Crumbs of Comfort but Still Walks into Walls." Review of *Paula Spencer*. *Scotland on Sunday*, August 26.

Beplate, J. (2005). "No Mistakes: Are Joyce's Failings Merely Failures of Discovery?" *Times Literary Supplement*, 5326 (April 29), 3–4.

Binchy, M. (2006). "Coming Clean in New Ireland." Review of *Paula Spencer*. *The Times*, September 2.

Bloom, H. (1973). *The Anxiety of Influence: A Theory of Poetry*. Oxford: Oxford University Press.

Bogle, D. (2001). *Toms, Coons, Mulatores, Mammies, and Bucks: An Interpretive History of Blacks in American Films*. New York: Continuum.

Burke, M. (2009). "Writing a Different Country." Review of *The Deportees*. *Irish Literary Supplement* (Spring), 14.

Costello, S.J. (2001). "Roddy Doyle: Writer." In *The Irish Soul: In Dialogue* (pp. 85–99). Dublin: Liffey Press.

Courtney, S. (2005). *Hollywood Fantasies of Miscegenation*. Princeton: Princeton University Press.

Cronin, M. (2006). *Ireland into Film: The Barrytown Trilogy*. Cork: Cork University Press.

Dillon, P. and M. O'Brien (2000). "*A Star Called Henry*: Two Differing Reviews." http://www.geocities.com/finghin2000/syucd/articles/star.html.

Doyle, R. (1988a). *The Commitments*. London: Heinemann.

Doyle, R. (1988b). *The Snapper*. London: Heinemann.

Doyle, R. (1991). *The Van*. London: Heinemann.

Doyle, R. (1993a). "An Interview." *New York Times*, December 20.

Doyle, R. (1993b). *Paddy Clark Ha Ha Ha*. London: Secker & Warburg.

Doyle, R. (1994). *Family*. BBC Television.

Doyle, R. (1996). *The Woman Who Walked into Doors*. London: Jonathan Cape.

Doyle, R. (1999). *A Star Called Henry*. London: Jonathan Cape.

Doyle, R. (2002). *Rory and Ita*. London: Jonathan Cape.

Doyle, R. (2004). *Oh, Play That Thing*. London: Jonathan Cape.

Doyle, R. (2006). *Paula Spencer*. London: Jonathan Cape.

Doyle, R. (2007). *The Deportees and Other Stories!* London: Jonathan Cape.

Drewett, J. (2003). "An Interview with Roddy Doyle." *Irish Studies Review*, 11.3, 337–49.

Foster, A. (2002). "Culchie and Dub." Review of *Rory and Ita*. *Times Literary Supplement*, 5204 (December 27), 27, 23.

Gerrard, N. (2001). "What Keeps Roddy Rooted." *Observer*, Sunday, April 15.

Hall, B. (1999). "Don't Cry for Me Mother Ireland." Review of *A Star Called Henry*. *Village Voice*, September 1–7.

Hand, D. (1996). Review of *The Woman Who Walked into Doors*. *Irish Literary Supplement*, (Fall).

Imlah, M. (1993). "A Boy's Own Adventure: *Paddy Clarke Ha Ha Ha*." *Independent*, June 13.

Kenneally, M. (1987). *Portraying the Self: Sean O'Casey and the Art of Autobiography*. Irish Literary Studies 26. Gerrards Cross: Colin Smythe.

Kiberd, D. (1995). *Inventing Ireland*. Cambridge, MA: Harvard University Press.

Lane, A. (1994). "Dubliners." Review of *Paddy Clarke Ha Ha Ha*. *The New Yorker*, January 24, 91–94.

Lanters, J. (2002). "Demythicizing/Remythicizing the Rising: Roddy Doyle's *A Star Called Henry*." *Hungarian Journal of English and American Studies*, 8.1, 245–58.

Leab, D.J. (1975). *From Sambo to Superspade: The Black Experience in Motion Pictures*. Boston: Houghton Mifflin.

Levine, A. (2001). "Sidney Poitier's Civil Rights: Rewriting the Mystique of White Womanhood in *Guess Who's Coming to Dinner* and *In the Heat of the Night*." *American Literature*, 73.2, 365–86.

Lippman, L. (1996). Interview with Roddy Doyle. *Baltimore Sun*, May 21.

McCarthy, D. (2003). *Roddy Doyle: Raining on the Parade*. Dublin: Liffey Press.

Phelan, S. (2004). "Something in the Eire: Interview with Roddy Doyle." *Sunday Herald*, September 12.

Piroux, L. (1998). "'I'm Black an' I'm Proud': Reinventing Irishness in Roddy Doyle's *The Commitments*." *College Literature*, 25.2, 45–57.

Reddy, M.T. (2005). "Reading and Writing Race in Ireland: Roddy Doyle and *Metro Éireann*." *Irish University Review*, 35.2, 374–88.

Sbrockey, K. (1999). "Something of a Hero: An Interview with Roddy Doyle." *Literary Review*, 42.4, 537–52.

Smyth, G. (1997). *The Novel and the Nation: Studies in the New Irish Fiction*. London: Pluto Press.

Smyth, G. (2000). "The Right to the City: Representations of Dublin in Contemporary Irish Fiction." In L. Harte and M. Parker (Eds). *Contemporary Irish Fiction: Themes, Tropes, Theories* (pp. 13–34). London: Macmillan.

Sutherland, J. (2004). "Ireland's Shakespeare." *Guardian*, February 10.

Taylor, C. (1999). "Bad Blood: The Salon Interview with Roddy Doyle." *Salon*, 7, (September), www.salon.com.

Wagner, E. (2008). "White Irish Need Not Apply." Review of *The Deportees and Other Stories*. *New York Times*, January 20.

White, C. (2001). *Reading Roddy Doyle*. Syracuse: Syracuse University Press.

56

The Reclamation of "Injurious Terms" in Emma Donoghue's Fiction

Jennifer M. Jeffers

Born in 1969 in Dublin, Emma Donoghue has an astonishingly long list of publications in several genres. Although her genres to date include radio drama, a screenplay and literary history, Donoghue is probably best known as a lesbian novelist and short fiction writer. For instance, she has won the Stonewall Book Award for *Hood* (1997) and the Ferro-Grumley Award for Lesbian Fiction with *Slammerkin* (2000). Virtually all of Donoghue's work involves either creating a sustainable lesbian identity in contemporary Ireland or the reclamation of women in history whose stories were lost or misrepresented. As we know, the problem in attempting to recover a minority identity (women, racial or ethnic minorities, gays and lesbians) is that the minority identity is always already named or branded by the hegemonic society in which the minority exists. Donoghue's early fiction and her more recent historical fiction are examples of her attempt to establish a place for lesbian identity. It is my contention that *Stir-fry* (1995), *Hood* (1996), and *Life Mask* (2004) establish a lesbian identity by turning the heteronormative derogatory terms given to lesbians back on themselves in order to dismantle the power of the disparaging terms and labels given to lesbians. In all periods people are called or "hailed" by the institutions in power; to be "hailed" is, according to Louis Althusser, to be interpellated by the hegemonic powers that be:

> I shall then suggest that ideology "acts" or "functions" in such a way that it "recruits" subjects among the individuals (it recruits them all), or "transforms" the individuals into subjects (it transforms them all) by that very precise operation which I have called *interpellation* or hailing, and which can be imagined along the lines of the most commonplace everyday police (or other) hailing: "Hey, you there!" (Althusser 1971:174)

A Companion to Irish Literature, edited by Julia M. Wright
© 2010 Blackwell Publishing Ltd

Since everyone is interpellated by the state and society, it seems pointless to try to chafe against authority. However, in *Bodies that Matter*, Judith Butler adopts Althusser's idea of interpellation in order to show that, however authoritarian or brutal the one who hails you – the policeman who calls "Hey you!" in order to bring you into the state's ideology – there is still a possibility that the terms for recognition might be perverted or "queered" by the one who is called (Butler 1993:121). The question Butler asks in terms of inverting the heteronormative is how the injured subject can infiltrate the power system, thereby perverting the "everyday police" of the state: "If one comes into discursive life through being called or hailed in injurious terms, how might one occupy the interpellation by which one is already occupied to direct the possibilities of resignification against the aims of violation?" (Butler 1993:123). Of course, the answer to Butler's question is that one must repeat the terms and through this repetition produce a difference that repositions the "injurious terms"; queer theory, and by extension queer history, would take ownership of the offending names and defuse them.

This strategy echoes medieval historian Carolyn Dinshaw's theoretical approach in *Getting Medieval: Sexualities and Communities, Pre- and Postmodern*:

> Appropriation, misrecognition, disidentification: these terms that queer theory has highlighted all point to the alterity within mimesis itself, the never-perfect aspect of identification. And they suggest the desires that propel such engagements, the affects that drive relationality even across time. … Pleasure can be taken in the assertion of historical difference as well as in the assertion of similarity, and any such pleasure should not be opposed to "truth." (Dinshaw 1999:35)

In this way, one can change the meaning of a term or retell a narrative so that it takes back the disparaging meaning given by those in power and those with authority to record events. Dinshaw suggests that narratives open up the possibility of difference and that all narratives are suspect. In *Life Mask*, for instance, Donoghue positions her narrative so that the historical lives and events she recounts present an oscillating view of history – not just a reductive oppositional view. Her texts not only allow those traditionally not accorded a history to have a story, but also imply that standard heteronormative history has distorted the truth.

At first glance, Donoghue's early fiction does not seem to have much in common with her late fiction. The early novels represent lesbian experience in contemporary Ireland, while much of her later work centers on eighteenth-century historical events. Yet in both the early fiction and the late historical fiction Donoghue attempts to make a place for those who are hailed by injurious terms – to give them a voice and an identity. Donoghue's first novel, *Stir-fry* (1995), is a lesbian "coming out" novel published soon after Ireland decriminalized same-sex relations (for a discussion of *Stir-fry* and *Hood* as novels that queer the *Bildungsroman*, see Jeffers 2002). In June 1993 the Irish Senate passed a bill into law "abolishing all previous laws criminalizing homosexual acts between men, and replacing them with a new gender-neutral law with common age of consent with heterosexuals and no special privacy restrictions"

(O'Carroll and Collins 1995:13). The coming out novel in the Irish context in the mid-1990s is therefore a fairly cutting edge endeavor.

Barely out of university herself, Donoghue presents Maria, a 17-year-old University College Dublin student from the west of Ireland. Maria's big-city adventure begins when she rents a room from two older women who, unbeknown to her, are lesbian lovers. As Maria experiences life at university away from home, she further separates herself from her previous sense of heterosexual identity. In both *Stir-fry* and her next novel, *Hood*, Donoghue portrays contemporary lesbian life in Ireland as bifurcated: at home and to your family you are in the closet; in the city among friends you are out of the closet. In a 2000 interview Donoghue emphasizes the duplicity of lesbian and gay life in Ireland:

> And in Ireland there's a general ethos of sort of making do with what you've got, as it were. I would say one particular aspect of the Irish lesbian and gay world rather than that world in any other country is that vast numbers are still in the closet. It's not as bad as it used to be, but still most people live with the closet in some form or another. I know a lot of people who are very out and proud when they're in Dublin, but back home down the country not a word to the family, and it might be the same about jobs, so there's a lot of living in worlds. It's not that they're entirely in the closet, it's that there are things they speak about with their friends and there are things they speak about with their parents and that's two different kinds of conversation, so there's a real ethos of accommodation and working around conflict rather than facing it head on. (Bensyl 2000:76)

Donoghue's fictional portrayal of lesbian life in the 1990s focuses on issues of coming out and remapping the terrain of Irish identity that repels the injurious terms by which lesbians are "hailed." In *Stir-fry*, Maria is preoccupied with appearing to be "normal"; when she feels she is slipping from the perceived norm, she always thinks of the image of "Nelly the Nutter" from her home town: the only woman she knew who was not a wife and mother except for a few teachers and "the young ones heading for the Univ. ... Nelly the Nutter, who sat on the steps of the Town Hall, scratching her ankles" (Donoghue 1995:27). In this, Maria links lunacy with her still latent lesbian feelings.

The voice of (heterosexual) reason, Maria's friend Yvonne attempts to get Maria to move out of the apartment she shares with the lesbian couple, Jael and Ruth. Believing that her friend has been swindled into a bad, if not dangerous, situation, Yvonne advises Maria that Jael and Ruth "got a month's rent out of you on false pretenses" (80). Maria denies Jael's and Ruth's culpability, and explains that "They probably assumed I knew" (80). But Yvonne knows that the standard in Irish culture and society is heterosexual dominance, and counters, "That's outrageous. I mean, it's not the first thing that's going to spring into your head when you go househunting, is it? I mean, you don't say to yourself, oh yes, must check where my flatmates are lesbian lovers, just in case!" (80). Maria, who is attracted to Ruth, defends her remaining with Jael and Ruth:

"I appreciate your looking after me, I really do. Now, will you kindly lay off? I've been busy with my job; four evenings this week. I haven't had time to think whether I'll be moving out or not."

"What's to keep you there?"

"For one thing, I like them."

"I know you do. Maria, you're a very friendly person." Yvonne hugged her knees in exasperation. "But they're hardly your sort. I mean, don't you find them a bit, you know?"

"A bit what?"

She squirmed slightly. "Butch and ranty." (80–81)

The stereotype of the "butch" lesbian is one of overt masculinity and aggression. "Ranty" in the context of the quote mostly likely describes a lesbian activist who rants (and raves) about gender injustice and sexual repression. Each term is used in an "injurious" manner; Yvonne upholds the heteronormative perspective which uses these terms only in a derogatory sense.

According to Marilyn R. Farwell, the butch–femme couple is often presented as "parody of sex-gender alignment" (Farwell 1996:99). Sue-Ellen Case theorizes that the butch-femme lesbian couple work together: "The femme ... foregrounds her masquerade by playing to a butch, another woman in a role; likewise, the butch exhibits her penis to a woman who is playing the role of compensatory castration" (Case 1989:290). Both *Stir-fry* and *Hood* present a butch–femme couple that, by the end of each novel, has been transformed into a lesbian couple that does not exist along the butch–femme spectrum. In this way, Donoghue is copying the butch–femme stereotype to move lesbian relationships completely off the masculine–feminine heterosexual standard. For example, in *Hood* the lesbian couple of Pen O'Grady, the narrator of the text, and her lover, Cara Wall, have been together since they were teenagers. The narrator, Pen, reflects on the thirteen years with Cara who, at the beginning of the novel, has died in a car accident. Several aspects of Ruth's and Jael's personalities surface in the characters of Pen and Cara. Ruth and Pen are the femme partners in the relationship; they are the monogamous, suffering partners. Jael and Cara are the butch partners who actively pursue liaisons with other women. Donoghue parodies the stereotypical butch–femme couple to present what is familiar to many readers only to imperceptibly destroy this stereotype by the end of each novel. In this way, Donoghue presents alternative identities to "women who love women" to get beyond the offensive "butch and ranty" label.

In *Hood*, Donoghue shows that language and labels in contemporary Ireland circulate throughout all levels of society. Bumper stickers, badges, T-shirts, a Right to Choose banner, and pamphlets often declare that derogatory labels repeated in postmodern spaces take back the injurious term by which, in this novel, the lesbian is interpellated. A lucid example of how the display of postmodern language can be turned from disparaging to empowering appears when Pen goes to a bookstore café for lunch:

Out of the corner of my eye I have spotted her badge and am going light pink. It's not even one of those joined women symbols or a discreet labrys. It's a yellow badge with "BY THE WAY, I'M A DYKE" emblazoned across it.

In order to dissociate myself from this lunatic I take a vast mouthful of pastry crust. She leans over and says, "That's quite a waistcoat." (Donoghue 1996:92)

A seemingly insignificant label turns out to be a strong surprise attack on heterosexuality; the badge disassembles even Pen's ability to react. The statement "BY THE WAY I'M A DYKE" reappropriates the injurious terms by which this woman and others are "hailed" very much along Butler's line of parody and repetition with difference.

However, Donoghue's undermining of the social and cultural stereotypes of the lesbian couple in her early novels is only the beginning of her attempts to make a lesbian space that is of the lesbian's own making. The desire to find a unique lesbian identity and space leads Donoghue toward historical subjects. How did women who love women function in a heterosexual society in the past? Traditional history suggests that there were no such liaisons, but Donoghue's texts work tirelessly to create a very different picture. Donoghue's interest in historical figures, especially women who engaged in same-sex desire, is first found in *We Are Michael Field* (1998). In her introduction, she describes her discovery of the archival materials that first led her to become so intensely interested in two women writers, Katherine Bradley and Edith Cooper, who took the pseudonym Michael Field: "When I realized that approximately thirty volumes of unpublished journals and letters lay in the British Library, I was daunted, but could hardly stay away. These papers turned out to hold the key to most of the mysteries about Michael Field" (Donoghue 1998:8). This text bears no pretense of a "plot" or the elaborate period detail that Donoghue develops later with her historical fiction *Slammerkin* (2000), *Life Mask* (2004), and *The Sealed Letter* (2008). In *We Are Michael Field*, Donoghue relishes the chance to "set the record straight" insofar as Bradley and Cooper are concerned. Donoghue claims that the aunt and niece are still misconstrued by contemporary readers:

Even today, some critics assume the Michaels were far too innocent to have sex. But though most of their contemporaries took for granted what their friend Logan Pearsall Smith mockingly called their "unsullied chastity," it is clear from their diaries that Katherine and Edith were lovers in a highly sexual sense for several decades. Other more hostile misinterpretations continue to flourish: that Edith was a timid femme follower; that Katherine was a talentless butch parasite; that the aunt loved more than the niece, and ruined the niece's life by preventing her from marrying a man. (Donoghue 1998:8)

In this passage Donoghue points to the "hostile misinterpretations" of the writers as centering around their image as a lesbian couple. Posterity cannot think outside the normative category of masculine–feminine, and thus makes Katherine "a talentless butch parasite" on the Edith who, at least, was adhering to her feminine stereotype of the day, "a timid femme follower."

Needless to say, the move from the depiction of lesbians in a contemporary world to a historical era with different ideas of identity involves complex issues of representation. First, we are confronted with the difficulty of formulating categories and labels for individuals that we would now call "homosexual," or those who engaged in same-sex desire. Yet "homosexual" is often used as derogatory term; for instance, Leo Bersani makes plain in *Homos*: "No one wants to be called a homosexual" (Bersani 1995:1). Even "same-sex desire" is problematic in defining historical identities: "I hold that the most seemingly objective and clinical of these terms, *same-sex desire*, potentially imports the greatest danger of anachronism to the extent that it may pretend to be a term somehow removed from history (have any actual people ever described themselves using this term?)" (Jones 2007:7). Another alternative is to use the ubiquitous term "gay" which, too, is anachronistic: "Gay history, based on this 'real' category of homosexual, may in fact be a necessary for gay community, for it may serve not only as community resource but as proof of the community's conceptual justification, proof of its capacity to cohere at all" (Dinshaw 1999:29–30). With the idea of a solidified "gay" community emerges the next issue in the problem of representation of gays and lesbians in history: is a separatist gay and lesbian identity preferable to one that assimilates everyone into a larger picture of history?

Undoubtedly, Donoghue and others writers of gay and lesbian history are attempting to recover the stories and identities squelched by official history. Yet does the recovery divide gay subculture from heterosexual hegemonic culture? I would argue that this problem inevitably surfaces in a reconstruction of a society in terms of known sexual categories and practices. The attempt to represent the epistemology and cultural sensibility of a historical period is an issue that Donoghue deals with in her latest historical novels. Certainly with *Life Mask* Donoghue begins with heterosexual hegemonic culture, and, in *Slammerkin*, goes to great length to describe minute details of the eighteenth-century London "beau monde" in terms of attire, manners, speech, milieu, and attitudes. This assiduously researched novel presents the "beau monde" of Lord Derby and his peers from 1787 to 1797. Over 600 pages long, it begins with the introduction of Lord Derby's long, celibate courtship of the period's comedic actress Eliza Farren. While this relationship commences *Life Mask*, the focus of the novel is actually Anne Damer, who under the novel's "Dramatis Personae" is presented as "The Honourable Mrs Anne Seymour Conway Damer, widow of the Honourable John Damer, half-sister of the Duchess of Richmond, daughter of Field Marshal Conway and Lady Ailesbury, cousin of Walpole. Sculptor, honorary exhibitor at the Royal Academy, sometime Foxite campaigner" (Donoghue 2004:610). This description is rather anodyne given the fact that it is an accusation that Anne Damer is a "Sapphist" or a "Tommy" that is the nucleus of the novel. It takes Donoghue hundreds of pages to verify that Anne Damer has even kissed a woman (in Italy after her husband's suicide); it would therefore seem that Donoghue's strategy to resignify the injurious terms by which one is hailed is to bury those terms in the heterosexual hegemonic culture of the past.

Eibhear Walshe argues that writers such as Emma Donoghue and Colm Tóibín reach into the past to "avoid the reductively utopian contemporary lesbian or gay coming-out novel. They deploy a fictionalization of the past as a strategy for register-ing liminality within the present" (Walshe 2008:141). Walshe does not account for why Donoghue and Tóibín shun Irish historical figures – for English historical figures in Donoghue's work, and for American writer, Henry James, in London, in Tóibín's. Could it be that it is easier or more easily distanced to write about non-Irish people? Is it less problematic to write about another country's "gay past" rather than your own? Or, perhaps the colonization of Ireland by Britain overshadows all other types of dissident stories other than those relating to on the ongoing struggle with Britain. Walshe claims that Tóibín's *The Master* and Donoghue's *Life Mask* "dramatise media and societal homophobia at times of public tension and disorder and the historical parallel is used to highlight contemporary political and cultural disorder, charting the link between this wider disorder and the internalized fears and self-policing of the gay protagonist" (Walshe 2008:142). If one is attempting to "highlight contemporary political and cultural disorder," then why go to the past – someone else's past – to expose the present day, not present-day Ireland, but instead present-day Western politics and culture? In "Lesbian Encounters, 1745–1997," Donoghue claims that she has been "delighted to discover" that there is a recorded lesbian tradi-tion in Ireland: "At least two dozen Irish writers, from the late eighteenth century to the late twentieth century, have touched on lesbian themes in their works" (Donoghue 2002:1090). Yet, Donoghue's "two dozen examples" include George Moore, Pádraig Standun, Edna O'Brien, and Maeve Binchy; given these examples, there is indeed a dearth of evidence of a lesbian tradition in Ireland.

Liana Borghi posits that "there can be little doubt about the value of Donoghue's and Lisa Moore's reconstruction of a British "sapphic" literary canon of the seven-teenth and eighteenth centuries, which has shown yet again the importance of under-standing changes in concepts of sexual identity in distant as well as recent history" (Borghi 2000:156). While she may show changes in understanding sexual identity, Donoghue, I contend, uses the genre of historical fiction not only to rewrite or overwrite the accepted heteronormative historical past, but also to show, perhaps indirectly, that the boundaries between lesbian and straight (or gay and straight) are difficult to decipher. The labyrinthine nature of *Life Mask* and its sheer bulk suggest that Donoghue wishes us to plunge into the late eighteenth century to begin to see and feel like those of that period; our total submersion in London in the late eighteenth century is pursued in order for us to understand that people living then, especially women, were also hailed by injurious terms. In fact, Anne Damer is nearly "ruined" by accusations that appeared in the scandal sheets. Damer likens herself to the character Clarissa Harlowe in Samuel Richardson's *Clarissa* (1748), who is "ruined" (raped) by the libertine Lovelace. After the second major publication of some lines of verse suggesting that Eliza Farren and Damer are lesbian lovers and Eliza banishes Damer from her life, Damer falls into a mental and physical fugue: "What was wrong with her was not something that Fordyce could cure with his powders, liniments or bleedings. The maids put trays outside her door at intervals, she could smell the sickening trail. *Did Clarissa eat*, she wanted to ask the doctor? Did any woman ever eat after she'd been ruined" (Donoghue 2004:462). Instead of thinking of herself as lesbian who has been "outed," she thinks of herself a victim of rape. According to Robert Padgug, straight and gay identities are a modern phenomenon:

> "Homosexual" and "heterosexual" *behavior* may be universal; Homosexual and hetero-sexual *identity* and *consciousness* are modern realities. These identities are not inherent in the individual. In order to be gay, for example, more than individual inclinations (however we might conceive of those) or homosexual activity is required; entire ranges of social attitudes and the construction of particular cultures, subcultures, and social relations are first necessary. To "commit" a homosexual act is one thing; to *be* a homo-sexual is something entirely different. (Padgug 1989:60)

The injurious terms used to "hail" Damer and Eliza are so esoteric and "dirty" that Eliza does not even initially understand what the accusations mean. Mrs Piozzi (perhaps better known as Mrs Henry Thrale, writer and friend of Samuel Johnson) is all too eager to enlighten Eliza about the meaning of the rumors started by the scandal sheet. Although there is not any historical reason for Mrs Piozzi's hatred of Damer, the implication is that Piozzi is jealous of Damer's status as sculptor and member of the "beau monde." Cornering Eliza in a cab, Piozzi quizzes Eliza about her relation-ship with Damer and her understanding of the "epigram going the rounds":

> "Your innocence appals me, my 'dear'," said the older woman. ... "Don't you know what sort of times we're living in? There's an unnatural, fantastical vice spreading across Europe, from Italy to France and now to our own shores. ... Haven't you ever heard of those monsters who haunt their own sex?"
>
> "Ah," said Eliza, on surer ground. "You mean sodomites. Why are you telling me this?"
>
> "Because you may be in danger," hissed Mrs. Piozzi.
>
> "From a sodomite?" ...
>
> "I'm speaking of man-hating *females*. Monsters in the guise of women. They go by a Greek name, *Sapphists*, after the criminal passions of Sappho, don't you know." ...
>
> "I thought she was a poet."
>
> "That and worse," said Mrs Piozzi darkly. "They're known as Tommies too."
> (Donoghue 2004:208–09)

This exchange is one of the most overt *naming* passages in the novel. Donoghue uses strong injurious terms: *monsters*, *Sapphists*, and *Tommies*. Part of the historical backdrop is the unrest in France, alluded to by Mrs Piozzi here; throughout the novel, there are references to Marie Antoinette having female lovers and suggestions that the Dauphine's private court was wanton and lewd. The Englishwoman (who was actually Welsh-born) Mrs Piozzi knows that all the vile Tommy monster lesbians must be foreign.

Donoghue uses this period of history not only for the events in France which created fear and unrest in England, but also for the fact that the era saw the rise of the popular press, pamphleteers, and, of course, the scandal sheets. The "epigram" that Mrs Piozzi shows Eliza is supposed "proof" of Damer's lesbianism:

> *Her little stock of private fame*
> *Will fall a wreck to public clamour,*
> *If Farren leagues with one whose name*
> *Comes near-aye, very dear – to DAMN HER.*
>
> (Donoghue 2004:210)

Eliza Farren is being hailed by injurious terms and she has no recourse, primarily because during this period she was a well-loved and very public actress in London. However, things calm down for Eliza and Damer, and their friendship resumes for a number of years before the slander begins to circulate again. The slander is revived while Eliza is on stage: "two men" "roar ... Tommies! Tommies!" (453). Damer is in the audience and witnesses Eliza's humiliation and, at the same moment that Eliza is fleeing the stage, Damer "registered that some of the troublemakers were facing into the auditorium ... One of them was pointing. Could he possibly be pointing at Anne? His arm jerked like a gun. Below her, above her, the hissing of snakes. 'Filthy Sapphists!' " (453). Eliza, prompted by Lord Derby (an old friend of Damer's), decides to end all association with Damer. From a historical perspective, this long unraveling of the relationship between Eliza Farren and Anne Damer may be accurate; yet, from a fictional point of view, the labyrinthine prose that leads to the second series of accusations might be too cumbersome. Although most of the novel is devoted to Farren and Damer's relationship, the curious aspect is that Eliza Farren and Anne Damer were never lovers (in Donoghue's version, in any case).

Although the two women were apparently never sexually involved, archives and public records of various sorts would have recorded Eliza Farren's relationship with Anne Damer. Donoghue uses the highly public nature of this relationship simply as a precursor for *the* lesbian relationship in the novel. Eliza Farren goes on to marry Lord Derby and bear him four children. The fact that their lives, especially in the 1780s, are intertwined with Damer's as well as those of Horace Walpole, Richard Brinsley Sheridan, and Charles James Fox, is all historical background for a very political and sexually complex society. Donoghue revels in the multifarious heterosexual alliances many members of the "beau monde" participated in during this period. Donoghue is almost vociferous when she presents even second-string players in her historical intrigue as the "sometime lover" of "Prinny" or the "sometime lover of many including Devonshire and Richmond" (Donoghue 2004:610–11). Even Georgiana Spencer Cavendish, duchess of Devonshire, one of Damer's oldest friends, maintains a curious relationship with Lady Bess Foster in addition to having many extramarital affairs. The point of this listing is that heterosexual liaisons abounded in this period – even married women going off to Europe to have their lover's child, only to return to the husband after a respectable period of time – but Sapphists were deemed unnatural and monstrous.

Despite being publicly hailed as monstrous, Anne Damer initiates and consummates the novel's only lesbian relationship with Mary Berry, benefactress of Walpole, at the seaside town of Bognor – conveniently distant from the eyes of London's "beau monde." 550 pages into the novel the reader's fortitude pays off with the event that has been hovering throughout. Up to this point, the novel might have been called the "public trials and tribulations of a suspected Sapphist." Even Anne Damer does not know her own sexual inclination. Having only kissed an Italian girl after her husband's suicide, Damer had become celibate. Eliza Farren's involvement with Damer was in fact platonic. Donoghue therefore has two primary reasons for lingering on the Eliza Farren and Anne Damer "scandal." First, Donoghue shows that anyone can be hailed by "injurious terms" and that one's ability to "answer" or even know what one is being called does not matter to the institutions or those in power. When Damer begins her sexual relationship with Mary Berry, Berry believes that Damer has had other lesbian sexual encounters:

> "You thought me an accomplished Sapphist, in fact." Anne threw the word into the darkness.
> Mary twitched at that. "I suppose I must have done." (Donoghue 2004:569)

Although Damer and Berry still find it awkward to *name* their sexual desire, with this passage Damer takes back the injurious term of Sapphist.

The novel's focus on Damer's realization that she has always been sexually attracted to women, without knowing what to do with her desire or how to act, brings us to Donoghue's second concern in the novel: lesbian desire has always been present and does not have to function as a subculture or exist as a separatist part of history. Damer's relationship with Berry, which lasts until Damer's death, is presented as an afterthought because Donoghue is most interested reclaiming Damer's entire life-story in the context of her era and society. In this way, Donoghue not only repeats with a difference the injurious terms of Sapphist and Tommy, but also repeats with a difference the "official history" of this period. As Dinshaw puts it, "appropriation, misrecognition, disidentification: these terms that queer theory has highlighted all point to the alterity within mimesis itself" and Donoghue's mimetic narrative of eighteenth-century London forces us to recontextualize and rethink not only that period, but potentially all periods of history (Dinshaw 1999:35). The injurious terms "butch," "dyke," and "Sapphist" used to interpellate lesbians are reclaimed in Donoghue's fiction. The reclamation does more than turn around the meaning of the injurious term; the repetition with a difference also calls into question all forms of interpellation, from the eighteenth century with *Life Mask* to contemporary Ireland with *Stir-fry* and *Hood*.

REFERENCES AND FURTHER READING

Althusser, L. (1971). *Lenin and Philosophy and Other Essays*. B. Brewster (Trans.) New York: Monthly Review.

Bensyl, S. (2000). "Swings and Roundabouts: An Interview with Emma Donoghue." *Irish Studies Review*, 8.1, 73–81.

Bersani, L. (1995). *Homos*. Cambridge, MA: Harvard University Press.

Borghi, L. (2000). "Lesbian Literary Studies." In T. Sandfort, J. Schuyf, J.W. Duyvendak, and J. Weeks (Eds). *Lesbian and Gay Studies: An Introductory, Interdisciplinary Approach* (pp. 154–60). London: Sage.

Butler, J. (1993). *Bodies that Matter*. New York: Routledge.

Case, S. (1989). "Toward a Butch-Femme Aesthetic." In L. Hart (Ed.). *Making a Spectacle: Feminist Essays on Contemporary Women's Theatre* (pp. 282–99). Ann Arbor: University of Michigan Press.

Dinshaw, C. (1999). *Getting Medieval: Sexualities and Communities, Pre- and Postmodern*. Durham: Duke University Press.

Donoghue, E. (1995). *Stir-fry*. London: Penguin.

Donoghue, E. (1996). *Hood*. London: Penguin.

Donoghue, E. (1998). *We Are Michael Field*. Bath: Absolute Press.

Donoghue, E. (2002). "Lesbian Encounters, 1745–1997." In A. Bourke, et al. (Eds). *The Field Day Anthology of Irish Writing, vol. IV: Irish Women's Writing and Traditions* (pp. 1090–1140). New York: New York University Press.

Donoghue, E. (2004). *Life Mask*. London: Virago.

Farwell, M.R. (1996). *Heterosexual Plots and Lesbian Narrative*. New York: New York University Press.

Jeffers, J.M. (2002). *The Irish Novel at the End of the Twentieth Century: Gender, Bodies, and Power*. New York: Palgrave Macmillan.

Jones, N.W. (2007). *Gay and Lesbian Historical Fiction: Sexual Mystery and Post-Secular Narrative*. New York: Palgrave Macmillan.

O'Carroll, I. and E. Collins (Eds). (1995). *Lesbian and Gay Visions of Ireland: Towards the Twenty-First Century*. London: Cassell.

Padgug, R. (1989). "Sexual Matters: Rethinking Sexuality in History." In M. Duberman, M. Vicinus, and G. Chauncey Jr. (Eds). *Hidden from History: Reclaiming the Gay and Lesbian Past* (pp. 54–66). New York: Meridian.

Walshe, E. (2008). "'A Different Story to Tell': The Historical Novel in Contemporary Irish Lesbian and Gay Writing." In B. Foragó and M. Sullivan (Eds). *Facing the Other: Interdisciplinary Studies on Race, Gender and Social Justice in Ireland* (pp. 137–39). Newcastle: Cambridge Scholars Press.

57

Martin McDonagh and the Ethics of Irish Storytelling

Patrick Lonergan

It was the first day of February in 1996, and Galway's new civic theater was about to open its doors for the first time. Druid Theatre, a highly respected local company, had been selected to produce the first play in the new venue. Much to everyone's surprise, its artistic director Garry Hynes had decided to present a new work from an entirely unknown playwright: a young man called Martin McDonagh, born to Irish parents in London in 1970. His play, audiences were told, was called *The Beauty Queen of Leenane*.

As they gathered outside the new theater, the Galway audience seemed excited, but perhaps they were also a little perplexed by what seemed a surprisingly old-fashioned title. Galway city, like the rest of Ireland, had only recently begun to experience a series of transformations that seemed to signal an abrupt rupture from the past. The old authorities of Irish life – church, state, and family – were being severely undermined by ongoing revelations of corruption, cover-up, and the systematic abuse of the vulnerable. But there were signs of positive change too. In November 1995 – only three months before the play opened – the Irish people had signaled their society's growing liberalization when they narrowly voted in favor of the introduction of divorce; homosexuality had been decriminalized in 1994; and, at the beginning of the 1990s, Mary Robinson had become the first woman to be elected president of the Republic of Ireland. Unemployment was falling rapidly, as was the rate of emigration. And although the IRA had broken the ceasefire it had declared in 1994, there were encouraging signs at that time that peace in Northern Ireland might yet be attainable. Ireland, in short, was beginning the slow process of replacing an obsession with the past with a sense of hope for the future.

So the title of Druid's new play seemed curiously at odds with the feeling in the air: that Ireland was looking forward rather than backwards: becoming cosmopolitan,

A Companion to Irish Literature, edited by Julia M. Wright
© 2010 Blackwell Publishing Ltd

prosperous, and, in every sense, at peace with itself. Leenane, the audience knew, is a small and relatively isolated village in the north of County Galway; to be crowned the "beauty queen" of such a tiny community would be an achievement so trivial as to be almost meaningless. The name of McDonagh's play thus seemed to call to mind an Ireland that was parochial, old-fashioned, and full of an exaggerated sense of its own importance. In other words, the title called to mind the Ireland that the audience thought they were leaving behind forever.

As they filed into their seats, some of those theater-goers might have taken a moment to look at the stage – and would immediately have seen a set that also presented an image of Ireland that seemed outmoded. Like hundreds of Irish plays before it, *Beauty Queen* takes place in a kitchen in a rural cottage. The usual paraphernalia was exactly where one would expect to find it. On the wall, there was a crucifix; beside it, there was a framed photograph of Robert and John F. Kennedy. Of course, the furniture was shabby: there was a small television perched in the corner, a bare table center-stage, and at stage left a long black range (a kind of stove), with a stack of peat turf and a seemingly innocuous black poker beside it. And of course, there was water running down the windows at the back of the set, signifying rainfall. So before the action had even begun, the audience felt securely located in the world of the play, which seemed indistinguishable from so many of the Irish plays that had come before.

What most members of that audience did not realize was that Hynes had deliberately chosen to open the new theater with *The Beauty Queen of Leenane*, not because it was old-fashioned but, on the contrary, because she knew that its apparent familiarity would lull viewers into a false sense of security. Indeed, two weeks before opening night, Hynes had outlined her plans in a press interview. She knew her audience would arrive at the theater "expecting a particular kind of play" – that is, a work similar to Druid's signature productions of plays by J.M. Synge and Tom Murphy. "For the first few moments," stated Hynes, "the audience will feel *oh lovely, this is a Druid play, we know where we are*. And then. ..." Hynes left unspoken her ideas about what would happen next, but it was clear that she too wished to signal a radical break from Ireland's past – and that she intended to use *The Beauty Queen of Leenane* to mark that rupture (Woodworth 1996:10).

Hynes' strategy proved remarkably effective. As the play opened, the audience was presented with a scene that seemed instantly to recall Tom Murphy's *Bailegangaire*, the classic Irish play first produced by Druid in 1985. Both plays are set in a rural Irish cottage, and both focus on a hostile but interdependent relationship between two women of different generations: a woman called Mary and her grandmother Mommo in *Bailegangaire*, and a mother and daughter called Mag and Maureen in *Beauty Queen*. Hynes further emphasized the resemblance between the two plays by casting Marie Mullen, who had played Mary in *Bailegangaire*, in the role of Maureen.

In the first moments of *Beauty Queen*, mother and daughter bicker about a variety of subjects, some more trivial than others: how to make Complan and porridge, the ongoing problems associated with emigration from Ireland, and the differences between the Irish and English languages. The Galway audience laughed along with these jokes, and everyone seemed comfortable during the play's first moments. It was only at the end of that first scene that they began to realize that something was slightly unusual about this play. Mag refers in passing to a news report about a "fella [who] up and murdered the poor oul woman in Dublin and he didn't even know her" (McDonagh 1999:6). That vision – of an Ireland in which random murders take place – seemed to clash with the normally idyllic stage presentation of the country that the audience was accustomed to. But most of the people there probably did not notice Mag's rather threatening qualification: the killer's actions are particularly strange to her, she says, because he "didn't even know" his victim – hinting, that is, that violence towards those whom we *do* know is far easier to comprehend.

As the second scene began, the audience was again faced with a surprisingly familiar image: "Mag is sitting at the table, staring at her reflection in a hand-mirror" (7). The Galway audience would almost certainly have seen that image before: in the second act of Synge's *The Playboy of the Western World* (1907), the second act of Murphy's *A Whistle in the Dark* (1961), the opening scene of Brian Friel's *Dancing at Lughnasa* (1990), and elsewhere. McDonagh, like other Irish playwrights, seemed to be using the metaphor of the mirror to think about the relationship between identity and representation in Ireland. So, as Hynes predicted, the audience was once again made to feel comfortable through the presentation of an apparently familiar image.

But as the action progressed the audience slowly began to realize that this was definitely not a typical Irish play. Many of its themes and techniques had been seen before, but there was a bleakness in the author's outlook, a cruelty in his humor, and a jarring blend of traditional Irish culture, on the one hand, and global pop culture on the other that would have unnerved many that evening. By the time the play had moved into its shockingly violent and hopeless final two scenes – when the poker shown in the opening moments becomes a murder weapon – the audience would largely have abandoned their expectations, and would instead have become entirely immersed in the action. And, as *Beauty Queen* concluded, they must have been aware that they had seen something that was simultaneously over-familiar and alienating: a play that was full of codes and signals that seemed to promise conventional meanings, but which instead had led them down several interpretive blind alleys. It was clear already that some of the people present were excited by this experience, while others were deeply irritated. And what was also obvious on that evening, the first time that an audience had seen a Martin McDonagh play, was that something significant had occurred.

Within the short period that has passed since that night, Martin McDonagh has, with astonishing speed, become one of the most successful playwrights on the planet. *Beauty Queen* was joined in 1997 by *A Skull in Connemara* and *The Lonesome West* to become *The Leenane Trilogy*. *The Cripple of Inishmaan* appeared in the same year, and in 2001 a second "Aran Islands" play called *The Lieutenant of Inishmore* was produced. In 2003 McDonagh's first non-Irish work, *The Pillowman*, premiered in London to enormous acclaim. Those six plays have now been produced in countless countries, translated into countless languages, and seen by countless audiences – everywhere. In

2006 McDonagh won his first Oscar, for the short film *Six Shooter*, which he wrote and directed. Three years later, he was nominated for a second Academy Award for *In Bruges*, a feature film starring Colin Farrell, Brendan Gleeson, and Ralph Fiennes, which McDonagh again wrote and directed. Put simply: in February 1996 McDonagh was an unknown playwright, hoping for a good response from a curious Galway audience; in February 2009 he was a disappointed nominee at the Oscars in Los Angeles, who had just announced that his seventh play, *A Behanding in Spokane*, would open on Broadway in early 2010. The rapidity of that transformation – from being a nobody in Galway to a star in Hollywood and New York – is unprecedented in the history of Irish literature.

Yet within the same period McDonagh also became one of the most controversial dramatists in the world. Theater practitioners and journalists, for instance, have attacked him for what they see as his arrogance: McDonagh, states Penelope Dening, has an "undoubted ability to get up the nose of the theatrical establishment," both in Britain and Ireland (Dening 1997). There are many instances of his having provoked such irritation. Aleks Sierz, for one, complained about McDonagh's comparison of himself to the young Orson Welles, and criticized his attack on older playwrights for being "so ugly" and "really badly dressed" (Sierz 2001:205). And McDonagh was roundly attacked for the public pronouncements attributed to him in press interviews. Theater, he was quoted as saying, was the least stimulating of the art forms; he was interested in writing only because he wanted to avoid getting a real job; and he suggested that he learned how to write not by studying the techniques of the great writers but by watching soap opera. He was also accused of being dismissive of the work of his fellow playwrights: for example, Richard Eyre claims that when McDonagh was asked what he thought of *Skylight*, a new play by David Hare, he replied, "Well I didn't write it, so it's crap" (Eyre 2003:364). It does not matter that such remarks are often taken out of context or exaggerated – and many of them have been completely inaccurately reported. They have nevertheless had an enormous impact on the construction of McDonagh's public persona (this is discussed in more detail in Lonergan 2009:101–27).

Academic critics have also been generally hostile towards McDonagh – both the man and his work. For many, he is exploiting anti-Irish stereotypes for financial gain, "selling out" to the English, in Mary Luckhurst's memorable expression (2004). Victor Merriman suggests that McDonagh is to Irish drama what Jerry Springer is to American television: a showman who is exploiting "white trash" for the amusement of a smug, complacent, and "voyeuristic" middle-class audience (Merriman 2004:254). His defenders have argued that, in fact, McDonagh is exploiting and undermining international audiences' awareness of Irish stereotypes, for dramatic as well as political purposes. That argument is supported to a certain extent by the textual evidence, as I discuss below in relation to *The Cripple of Inishmaan*, but it does tend to lose some of its credibility when we are faced with the realization that many audiences and producers do seem to take McDonagh's presentation of Ireland as a literal representation of realities in the country (see Lonergan 2004).

What is notable, therefore, is that the reception of McDonagh's career has revolved – perhaps even stagnated – around critics' confusion between authorial intention and audience response. Is a play any better or worse if its author is arrogant – or if he is presented as such by journalists who actually know very little about theater? Is McDonagh to blame if audiences throughout the world have sometimes misunderstood his treatment of Irishness? If he makes money because of such misunderstandings, should he refuse to cash his royalty cheques – and why are academic critics so resentful of his financial success? And what is the relationship between his often tactless public pronouncements and his plays' apparent ambiguity? These are the questions that now dominate discussion of McDonagh's work.

In fact, the clash between authorial intention and audience response has been an important feature of McDonagh's work from the beginning. His second produced play, *The Cripple of Inishmaan*, made these themes explicit when it opened in London in January 1997. Set in 1934 on Inishmaan (a tiny island off the coast of Galway, and one of the three Aran Islands), the play dramatizes the response of the islanders to the filming by Robert Flaherty of the documentary *Man of Aran* on the nearby Inishmore. His documentary claims to represent authentically the lives of the islanders, yet throughout the play they repeatedly challenge its claims to represent the truth about their lives.

McDonagh's plot follows closely the "rags to riches" storyline so beloved of early Hollywood producers and their audiences. Billy Claven, a young man who is isolated from his fellow islanders due to his disability, his sensitivity, and his intelligence, dreams of escaping to Hollywood – not just to affirm a sense of his own value, but also to escape the tedium of his life at home. He is unexpectedly successful in his attempts to travel to America, but is not hired as an actor; he returns to Inishmaan claiming to have realized the true value of the people he left behind before winning the love of the woman who had ignored and mistreated him before his departure. That, on the surface, is how the story appears.

What is notable about *The Cripple*, however, is that McDonagh takes pains to challenge our assumptions about truth, fiction, and literary convention. Storytelling, he suggests, is not just a form of escapism but also a necessary method of coping with life. To make this case, he dedicates a great deal of attention to undermining the credibility of those media that claim to be able to represent the truth, asserting instead the value of play and invention. For instance, the audience is reminded at an early stage not to believe everything they read in the newspapers. "There's a fella here, riz to power in Germany, has an awful funny moustache on him," states Inishmaan's local gossip Johnnypateenmike, reading from the latest edition of the paper. "Ah he seems a nice enough fella, despite his moustache. Good luck to him" (McDonagh 2008:373). Clearly if Johnypateenmike can form the impression that Hitler is a "nice enough" person, the source of his information must be misleading in some crucial respects.

Likewise, the defining narratives of Irish history are subjected to a skeptical scrutiny throughout the play. Michael Collins – one of the leaders of the Irish war against England from 1919 to 1921 and the chief negotiator of the treaty that partitioned Ireland – is referred to only as "one of the fat ones" in the annals of Irish history (387).

Given that Collins was assassinated in 1922 (only twelve years before the action is set), this is an astonishingly dismissive description. And Anglo-Irish relations in general are reimagined as a cruel game between Billy's love interest Helen and her brother Bartley, whom she teaches to play "England versus Ireland":

> *Helen*:   Stand here and close your eyes. You'll be Ireland. ... I'll be England.
> *Helen picks up three eggs from the counter and breaks the first against Bartley's forehead. Bartley opens his eyes as the yolk runs down him, and stares at her sadly. Helen breaks the second egg on his forehead.*
> *Bartley*:   That wasn't a nice thing at all to ...
> *Helen*:   I was giving you a lesson about Irish history.
>
> (378–79)

McDonagh's intention here is to force audiences to consider how the narrative of Ireland being oppressed by England is deployed simply to excuse bad behavior, whether the apathy of Bartley or the sadism of Helen.

McDonagh also pokes fun at Hollywood's presentation of Ireland. This is most evident in Billy's "death" in the play's seventh scene. The action is set in an American motel, and features the ailing Billy's consideration of how much he misses his parents (who died when he was an infant), and the islanders he left behind. As this scene comes to a conclusion, Billy appears to die – an event intend to have a major impact on the audience's sympathies. Yet we learn soon afterwards that what we had taken for a tragic moment, in which Billy achieves self-awareness before his death, was actually a rehearsal for a screen-test – and, to make matters worse, Billy was not just acting, but acting so badly that he did not get the part for which he was auditioning. "It wasn't an awful big thing at all to turn down Hollywood," he tells Bartley upon his return, laughing at the "the arse-faced lines they had me reading for them," which he describes as a "rake of shite" (401). But later he admits that his performance was very poor: the producer's attitude was that it would be "better to get a normal fella that can act crippled than a crippled fella who can't fecking act at all" (404). So the audience is being reminded of the dangers of accepting as reality what was in fact a poorly performed rehearsal of a clichéd and sentimental script.

McDonagh also seems determined to attack the notion that Ireland is a friendly place that the rest of the world is keen to visit. There is a recurring joke in the play about how Ireland "mustn't be such a bad place" if German or French tourists – or sharks – want to visit the country. This belief in Ireland's international reputation, McDonagh suggests, serves as a form of self-deception, a distraction from the realities of the islanders' life and the responsibilities they must face. This is probably best illustrated in a scene in which Johnnypateenmike speculates about whether Billy is ill, but is distracted momentarily by an article in the newspaper. "They all want to come to Ireland, sure. Germans, Dentists, everybody," he tells his mother, before offering the following explanation for the country's international popularity: "In Ireland the people are more friendly. ... Everyone knows that. Sure isn't it what we're famed for?" (He pauses for a moment before resuming his deliberations on Billy's health.) "I'd bet money on cancer," he muses (373). McDonagh thus juxtaposes the illusion that Ireland is a friendly place against the reality that Johnypateenmike sees Billy's possible illness as a story that he can spread around the island for financial gain.

Only one character in the play shows himself to be committed to the truth: the island's doctor. In a rare moment of empathy during the play, Billy calls for an end to malicious gossiping in his community, citing the example of Jim Finnegan's daughter, who has a reputation for being promiscuous. "It's only pure gossip that Jim Finnegan's daughter is a slut," he protests. "No," says the doctor. "Jim Finnegan's daughter is a slut. ... Just take me word" (406). Soon afterwards, the doctor refuses to allow Billy to exaggerate the positive qualities of his parents.

> *Billy*:   I've heard me mammy was a beautiful woman.
> *Doctor*:   No, no, she was awful ugly.
> *Billy*:   Was she?
> *Doctor*:   Oh, she'd scare a pig. But, ah, she seemed a pleasant enough woman, despite her looks, although the breath on her, well, it would knock you.
> *Billy*:   They say it was that Dad punched Mammy while she was heavy with me was why I turned out the way I did.
> *Doctor*:   Disease caused you to turn out the way you did, Billy. Not punching at all. Don't go romanticising it.
>
> (407)

This is an important exchange. We have seen throughout the play a skepticism about storytellers who claim to be telling the truth, from Flaherty's making of a "documentary" to Johnypateenmike's frequently inaccurate news reports. Yet it is notable that the doctor's commitment to the truth seems one of the most cruel acts committed during the play: he denies Billy the chance to believe something positive about his parents, and denies him also the opportunity to "romanticize" his disability.

McDonagh also draws intriguing parallels between filmmakers' mediation of reality and the stories that are told by Johnypateenmike. That character, like Flaherty, tells stories for economic gain and although he is despised by his fellow islanders for his manipulations of reality, his stories are revealed as necessary – precisely because the truth of the islanders' lives is so unbearable. It is Johnypateenmike, after all, who tells a story about Billy's parents that Billy is prepared to live with – and it does not matter if that tale is (or appears to be) untrue. Likewise, although Billy is probably the most admirable character in the play, he lies constantly – about his illness, his reasons for leaving Ireland, and his reasons for returning home. The play thus has a double function: it attacks Hollywood for misrepresenting reality, but then celebrates the role of the artist-storyteller in providing solace from that reality.

Issues of interpretation and authority also dominate McDonagh's next two plays, *A Skull in Connemara* and *The Lonesome West*, both of which premiered in the summer of 1997, again in Galway's Town Hall Theatre. The first of those plays is a kind of whodunit, in which a police officer seeks evidence to support his belief that one of the villagers in Leenane, Mick Dowd, killed his wife. Significantly, however, McDonagh shows that, when the policeman cannot find that evidence, he simply invents it. *Skull* is often regarded as the weakest of McDonagh's plays (it has in any case been produced less frequently than the others). Yet, more than any of his other works, it celebrates the value of indeterminacy, leaving unanswered the question of whether Mick is responsible for the murder of which he is accused. Interestingly, McDonagh also showed an awareness of his own increasingly negative reputation by giving one of the play's supporting characters the Irish version of his own name, Mairtin O'Hanlon, who is by far the most loutish and idiotic of all of McDonagh's creations.

The Lonesome West has been characterized as an Irish response to Sam Shepard's 1980 *True West*. The resemblances between the two plays are strong. All of McDonagh's plays focus on familial relations: the six plays he premiered between 1996 and 2003 all feature troubled relationships between siblings (Ray and Pato in *Beauty Queen*, Mairtin and Tom in *Skull*, Helen and Bartley in *Cripple*, Mairead and Davey in *Lieutenant*, and Katurian and Michal in *The Pillowman*). But this theme is at the center of *The Lonesome West* which, like Shepard's play, explores a deeply hostile yet strangely interdependent relationship between two brothers, called Coleman and Valene in McDonagh's play.

A significant feature of the play is its treatment of Irish Catholicism. Leenane is shown to a town in which "God has no jurisdiction" (McDonagh 1999:134); its local priest Father Welsh commits suicide, signaling the increased impotence and irrelevance of the Catholic Church as an institution in modern Ireland. Religion is shown to be both literally and figuratively in meltdown in the country: the play's abiding image is of a collection of religious statuettes being placed in an oven, where they are boiled down into molten plastic. Ireland, McDonagh shows, may think of itself as a land of saints and scholars: priests may continue to occupy a prominent position in Irish communities, and religious language and allusions may still dominate Irish speech and the Irish imagination – yet Christian behavior is nowhere to be found in the *Leenane Trilogy*. This treatment of the status of religion in Ireland is the most profound, and the most challenging, expression of the difference between appearance and reality in McDonagh's plays.

The work that makes most clear the difference between the "real" Ireland and McDonagh's imagined community is *The Lieutenant of Inishmore* (2001), a black farce about a crazed terrorist called Mad Padraic, who returns to Inishmore (one of the other Aran Islands) when he learns that his pet cat is unwell. It will be entirely obvious to anyone who has visited the real Inishmore that there are very few accurate references to the local geography in McDonagh's play – to the island's prehistoric forts, to its stone walls and steep cliffs, to its rugged and windswept landscape. And of course no one in the play speaks Irish, which remains the first language of most of the real Aran Islanders.

Probably the best example of McDonagh's indifference to geographical accuracy can be found in the chronology evident through the stage directions. Padraic arrives on Inishmore at night, meeting a young woman called Mairead by "moonlight" (McDonagh 2009:32). We do not know at what time of night this scene happens, but it does occur before the play's comic duo Donny and Davey go to sleep at five in the morning, or "early blue dawn" (36). Padraic does not arrive at his father's house until seven hours later, at "twelve noon" according to the stage directions (38). Given that the entire island of Inishmore is only nine miles in length, it seems strange that it takes Padraic at least ten hours to travel to his father's house from the island's harbor. McDonagh has his protagonist arrive home at this time because high noon is traditionally the moment for a showdown in Westerns: that is, style rather than accuracy is his priority.

McDonagh has given an interesting explanation for this indifference to geographical authenticity. In an interview with Dening, he claimed that the decision to locate *Lieutenant* on the Aran Islands arose because "for plot purposes, [he] needed 'a place in Ireland that would take a long time to get to from Belfast'. Inishmore fitted the bill" (2001). His initial impulse was to write about the Troubles in Northern Ireland but, remembering that there were three Aran Islands, McDonagh then considered composing a trilogy. After he had completed *Lieutenant*, he turned to *The Cripple of Inishmaan* and the (as yet) unproduced *Banshees of Inisheer*. The implication here is that, for McDonagh, plot rather than setting is of primary importance: he does not seek to provide an authentic representation of any of the places that he portrays, but instead chooses locations that are appropriate to the stories that he wishes to tell.

There are perhaps some problems with this apparent indifference to how the material in these plays corresponds to the real world. This is particularly notable in relation to the treatment in *The Lieutenant of Inishmore* of real victims of the IRA and INLA, who are alluded to in the play, sometimes for humorous purposes. For instance, Padraic refers to attacking "chip-shops" (2009:13), a possible reference to the 1993 bombing by the IRA of a chip shop on the Shankill Road which led to the death of nine civilians. He also mentions shooting builders (44), which again is a reference to a real IRA atrocity in which eight Protestant builders were murdered in 1992 because they were working on a military base. There are also references to Airey Neave (29), murdered by the INLA in 1979; to the Guildford Four (33); to Richard Heakin, an off-duty British soldier who was murdered by the IRA in Belgium in 1988 (55, 77); to Nicholas Spanos and Stephen Melrose, two Australian tourists killed by the IRA in the Netherlands in 1990 when they were mistaken for off-duty British soldiers (55, 77); and to Jonathan Ball (aged 3) and Timothy Parry (aged 12), killed when the IRA bombed Warrington in 1993 (57, 77). In total, twenty-three innocent victims of Irish terrorists are alluded to during *The Lieutenant*; there is also a joke about the thirteen people killed in Derry by the British army during Bloody Sunday (28).

It is difficult to know how to react to McDonagh's inclusion of this information. Is he laughing at the expense of people who were killed by the IRA, thereby intensifying the pain of their loved ones? Some critics believe so – an accusation that is not helped much by the fact that the play specifically refers to thirty-six real victims of the Troubles, but deals with the perpetrators of that violence only in very general terms: there are no jokes about the leaders of the IRA or its political wing Sinn Féin. It is significant that, unlike people in Ireland and England, the vast majority of McDonagh's international audiences will not get these jokes or know that they refer to real people. In this respect, the clash between authorial intention and audience response takes on interesting dimensions: it seems as though McDonagh is laughing at the expense of the dead, and getting away with it because most of his audience do not understand the joke.

This is important because that link between intention and response had ensured that, by the time *The Lieutenant* appeared, McDonagh's reputation in Ireland had deteriorated severely. When four of McDonagh's plays appeared simultaneously in Ireland in the summer of 1997 it seemed that he was setting out to challenge some of the major authorities of Irish society during a period when the country was struggling to come to terms with revelations about political corruption, clerical child abuse, and institutional incompetence. *The Cripple of Inishmaan* attacked Ireland's presentation of itself to the world as a friendly country at a time when *Riverdance* and similar cultural exports were rebranding the nation for global consumption. *The Beauty Queen of Leenane* exploded the myth of the happy Irish family only months after the legalization of divorce. *A Skull in Connemara* suggested that the country was lawless and amoral, presenting an entirely inept police officer at a time when the Irish police seemed to be losing their grip on organized crime, especially after the assassination of the journalist Veronica Guerin. And *The Lonesome West* presented the Catholic Church as being in a state of dire crisis at a time when the first revelations of clerical child abuse were emerging.

However, as his plays became more famous outside Ireland, McDonagh's reputation changed within the country itself. Many journalists and academics began to express the fear that international audiences might think that McDonagh's version of Ireland was authentic: that he might be reinforcing negative stereotypes about the Irish as stupid, drunken, lazy, provincial, inarticulate, prone to acts of mindless violence, and impoverished – intellectually as well as financially. To an extent, those fears seemed somewhat justified when early British reviews of the plays appeared. For instance, Michael Billington of the *Guardian* told his readers that McDonagh's aim in the *Leenane Trilogy* was not to challenge Irish stereotypes but to suggest bluntly that "*the reality* [about Ireland] is murder, self-slaughter, spite, ignorance and familial hatred" (Billington 1997:26; emphasis added). Similarly, in 1999, one of the earliest regional US stagings of *Beauty Queen* took place in Virginia, where the production's director declared outright that the play is "a true representation of Ireland, particularly in the north." Irish critics were horrified at the suggestion that international audiences might mistake McDonagh's work as presenting the "reality" or a "true representation" of their country. But rather than criticizing the people who had misunderstood McDonagh's plays, Irish critics instead often attacked the writer himself.

The Pillowman, premiered at London's Royal National Theatre in 2003, has often been characterized as McDonagh's response to that criticism. It has been suggested by a number of critics that, because *The Pillowman* was the sixth McDonagh play to be produced, it can be seen as a reaction to the reception of the previous five. As is so often the case with McDonagh's plays, this approach is logical but inaccurate.

In "A Mind in Connemara," a lengthy 2006 interview with Fintan O'Toole, McDonagh claims to have written *The Pillowman* in 1994, at the same time as the other five plays he has had produced, along with *The Banshees of Inisheer*. While there is a need for caution about accepting the accuracy of views attributed to McDonagh in press interviews, we do know that *The Pillowman* was actually the third of his plays to be performed publicly, in a rehearsed reading in Galway in April 1997. So it is inaccurate to see that play as responding to events that occurred once McDonagh became famous; rather, the appearance of the play so early in his career can be seen as evidence that McDonagh was preoccupied from the start with the themes that dominated his reception afterwards.

The basic storyline of the play was present in 1997. A writer in a totalitarian state is interrogated by two police officers, who are investigating a series of murders that appear to follow the plot of several of the writer's short stories. The problem for the writer is that only one other person knows those stories: his intellectually disabled brother, who just happens to be under interrogation in the next room. By the time *The Pillowman* was fully produced six years later, McDonagh had increased the length of the play, but its essential questions remained. Can stories change the way that people think? Is a writer responsible when people misinterpret his or her stories? And what, if any, are the responsibilities of writers to themselves, their audiences, and their societies?

In response, the play's protagonist Katurian outlines three artistic principles that, to many, seem to represent McDonagh's own views. They are that the first (or the only) duty of a storyteller is to tell a story (McDonagh 2003:7), that "if you've got a political what-do-you-call-it, go write a fucking essay" (7), and that readers can "draw [their] own conclusions" (11) because "I'm not trying to say anything at all! That's my whole fucking thing!" (16). So it is important to note that, long before McDonagh was famous, and long before he was attacked for the way in which people interpreted his plays, he was already thinking about issues of misinterpretation, authorial responsibility, and the link between the two.

What is often neglected in discussions about *The Pillowman* is that, although Katurian's artistic principles may seem similar to McDonagh's, he does not in fact live up to his own precepts. Indeed, there are several ways in which McDonagh suggests that Katurian may not be an especially talented writer – and that he may be overwhelmingly lacking in self-awareness. For instance, the play is sometimes presented as a statement about an author's right to freedom of speech, yet Katurian offers to burn his own stories more than once, saying that if there is a political element in any of them he wants his interrogators to "show me where the bastard is. I'll take it straight out. Fucking burn it. You know?" (8). And, in Katurian's autobiographical story "The Writer and the Writer's Brother," the protagonist reads his brother's story, describing it as "the sweetest, gentlest thing he'd ever come across. … So he burnt the story" (34). Interestingly, McDonagh actually shows Katurian burning the tale onstage. So while Katurian is very interested in protecting his own reputation, he is perfectly happy to destroy the work of others, especially if it is better than his own.

There are other reasons to be cautious about accepting the veracity of Katurian's statements. We might think that Katurian is willing to give up his own life to protect his art, though it should be noted that he decides to confess to the various murders in the play only after he has realized that his own execution is unavoidable. And, perhaps more admirably, he is motivated by many duties beyond simply telling a story. He kills his parents because of their mistreatment of his brother, for example, and then kills his brother to save him from a crueler execution by the police.

This helps us to understand better Katurian's rejection of the idea that fiction reveals something of its author. "I kind of hate any writing that's even vaguely auto-biographical," he states. "I think people who only write about what they know only write about what they know because they're too fucking stupid to make anything up" (76). He concedes, however, that his tale "The Writer and the Writer's Brother" is "the only story of mine that isn't really fiction" (76). Yet in fact almost every story told in the play reveals something about the storyteller and how he sees himself: most of them are dramatizations of the abuse suffered by Katurian and Michal at the hands of their parents, and most of them also dramatize the desire for revenge against such parents. For example, the story of the "Little Apple Men" features a child who, like Katurian, tries to revenge herself on an abusive parent, not realizing that this act of vengeance will ultimately lead to her own death. In "The Tale of the Town on the River," a child offers help to an adult, who promptly chops off the child's toes. It emerges that the adult is the Pied Piper, come to Hamlin to steal the townspeople's children away. By disabling his victim, he ensures that the child will not be able to follow the other children from the town to their demise. This story exemplifies a philosophy that has dominated Katurian and Michal's life: that suffering can indirectly benefit its victim. To the extent that it attempts to make sense of both men's upbringing, "The Tale of the Town on the River" is therefore autobiographical.

Also important is the fact that Katurian is a writer who is generally very inarticulate. "I'm not one of these ... you know?" he tells his interrogators at an early stage in the play (3). His stories do not have a political "what-do-you call-it" (7), he concedes, but at least one of them is "something-esque. What kind of 'esque' is it? I can't remember" (18). In contrast, the police display an obsession with precision, in relation not only to language, but also to issues of representation and role-playing. They refuse to believe that stories can only have a surface meaning, and both men see themselves as operating in a symbolic capacity. Ariel, for instance, asserts that as a policeman he "stands for something" (78), while Tupolski insists that Katurian's stories are "saying to me, on the surface I am saying this, but underneath the surface I am saying this other thing" (5). Where Katurian denies that his stories can be political, Tupolski is convinced that politics operates in the same way that stories do:

> We like executing writers. Dimwits we can execute any day. And we do. But you execute a writer, it sends out a signal, y'know? (*Pause*) I don't know what signal it sends out,

that's not really my area, but it sends out a signal. (*Pause*). No, I've got it. I know what signal it sends out. It sends out the signal "DON'T ... GO ... AROUND ... KILLING ... LITTLE ... FUCKING ... KIDS." (30)

The two policemen constantly show an awareness that they are playing a role. "Oh, I almost forgot to mention," says Tupolski. "I'm the good cop, he's the bad cop" (12). "Me and Ariel," he continues, "we have this funny thing, we always say 'This reminds me' when the thing hasn't really reminded us of the thing we're saying it reminds us of at all. It's really funny" (14). Ariel admits to using "fake blood" for dramatic effect (29), and encourages Michal to pretend he is being tortured: "he said I did it really good," says Michal, beaming with the pleasure of an actor who has received a positive review (38). It is hardly surprising, then, that Katurian will conclude that the investigation is "just like storytelling" (39).

Perhaps most significantly, there is a strong Christian element in the stories, and indeed in the play itself – a suggestion that pain and suffering, and the representation of both through art, can achieve or inspire positive ends, even if those ends are not instantly discernible. This theme is evident in many ways, from the little boy whose life is saved when he is maimed by the Pied Piper, to another story about a little boy who welcomes being tortured because he believes that he will like the stories his brother will write about these terrible events, to the "Little Jesus" who is crucified onstage. The conclusion of the play is therefore very different from Katurian's stories, in that it is sentimental and unfashionably upbeat – it has a happy ending, of sorts.

What emerges from the play, then, is the suggestion that, while authorship and the debate over meaning are important, the only part of a work that is genuinely worth talking about for McDonagh is how it is interpreted. *The Pillowman* rejects the notion that an author is responsible for how others receive his work, and indeed rejects the notion that we can blame others for our own choices. We cannot blame authors for what they write, our parents for our "problem childhoods," or McDonagh for our insecurities about how Irishness is seen abroad. So *The Pillowman* can be seen as offering a way of thinking about McDonagh's work in its entirety. It illustrates his belief that what matters is not the views of the author, but the actions of the audience. His challenge to audiences is – and always has been – to see ourselves as active in the interpretation and analysis of what we see: not to receive a play passively, but instead to see ourselves as actors too, as creators of meaning, and as people who have responsibilities as a result.

What was obvious in 2003 with *The Pillowman* could also be discerned in Galway on that opening night in February 1996: the issues of interpretation and authorial responsibility have been central to McDonagh's sensibility from the beginning. *The Beauty Queen* was not trying to communicate a message from the author to the audience, but instead to reveal to that audience the strangeness of their own presuppositions and assumptions. This placed the responsibility for the creation of the play's meaning upon those who were watching it: we were forced, that is, to examine afresh our own sense of how the Irish stage scene is constituted, and to question the values that are assumed by that presentation. In using this strategy, McDonagh revealed his own goals as a playwright. Like the proverbial tree that falls in a forest when no one is present to hear it, McDonagh's plays seem to declare that they are meaningful only when they are performed before an audience: he is not trying to communicate with the viewers of his work, but to inflict an experience upon them – an experience that will at least partially be determined by the needs, interests, and assumptions of the individual audience members themselves. An author certainly has intentions in creating a play, McDonagh concedes – but he appears to be denying that there is a direct causal link between his own intentions, the performance of his plays, and the responses of audiences to his work. Instead, his plays in their entirety can be understood as stating the necessity in everyday life for storytelling – and as considering the ethical dimensions of the interpretive acts that inevitably arise when audiences encounter such stories.

REFERENCES AND FURTHER READING

Billington, M. (1997). "Excessive Talent for Plundering Irish Past." *Guardian*, August 10, 26.

Chambers, L. and E. Jordan (Eds). (2006). *A World of Savage Stories: The Theatre of Martin McDonagh*. Dublin: Carysfort Press.

Dening, P. (1997). "The Wordsmith of Camberwell." *Irish Times*, July 8, A6.

Dening, P. (2001). "The Scribe of Kilburn." *Irish Times*, April 18, 12.

Eyre, R. (2003). *National Service: Diary of a Decade*. London: Bloomsbury.

Grene, N. (1999). *The Politics of Irish Drama*. Cambridge: Cambridge University Press.

Hoggard, L. (2002). "Playboy of the West End World." *Independent*, June 15.

Huber, W. (2005). "From Leenane to Kamenice: The De-Hibernicising of Martin McDonagh?" In C. Houswitsch (Ed.). *Literary Views on Post-Wall Europe: Essays in Honour of Uwe Boker* (pp. 283–94). Trier: WVT.

Lonergan, P. (2004). " 'The laughter will come of itself. The tears are inevitable': Martin McDonagh, Globalization, and Irish Theatre Criticism." *Modern Drama*, 47.4, 636–58.

Lonergan, P. (2009). *Theatre and Globalization: Irish Drama in the Celtic Tiger Era*. Basingstoke: Palgrave.

Luckhurst, M. (2004). "Martin McDonagh's *Lieutenant of Inishmore*: Selling (-Out) to the

English." *Contemporary Theatre Review*, 14.4, 34–41.

Maguire, T. (2006). *Making Theatre in Northern Ireland: Through and Beyond the Troubles*. Exeter: University of Exeter Press.

McDonagh, M. (1999). *Plays 1*. London: Methuen.

McDonagh, M. (2003). *The Pillowman*. London: Faber & Faber.

McDonagh, M. (2008). *The Cripple of Inishmaan*. In P. Lonergan (Ed). *The Methuen Drama Anthology of Irish Plays* (pp. 331–421). London: Methuen.

McDonagh, M. (2009). *The Lieutenant of Inishmore*. Student edn. P. Lonergan (Ed.). London: Methuen.

Merriman, V. (2004). "Staging Contemporary Ireland: Heartsickness and Hopes Deferred." In S. Richards (Ed.). *The Cambridge Companion to Twentieth-Century Irish Drama* (pp. 244–57). Cambridge: Cambridge University Press.

Morash, C. (2001). *A History of Irish Theatre*. Cambridge: Cambridge University Press.

O'Toole, F. (1997). "Nowhere Man." *Irish Times*, April 26, Weekend section, 1–2.

O'Toole, F. (2006). "A Mind in Connemara: The Savage World of Martin McDonagh." *New Yorker*, March 6, 40–47.

Pilkington, L. (2001). *Theatre and the State in Twentieth-Century Ireland*. London: Routledge.

Rees, C. (2006). "How to Stage Globalisation? Martin McDonagh: An Irishman on TV." *Contemporary Theatre Review*, 16.1, 114–22.

Richards, S. (2003). "'The Outpouring of a Morbid, Unhealthy Mind': The Critical Condition of Synge and McDonagh." *Irish University Review*, 33.1, 201–14.

Richards, S. (2004). *The Cambridge Companion to Modern Irish Drama*. Cambridge: Cambridge University Press.

Roche, A. (2009). *Contemporary Irish Drama*. Basingstoke: Palgrave.

Russell, R.R. (Ed) (2007). *Martin McDonagh: A Casebook*. London: Routledge.

Sierz, A. (2001). *In-Yer-Face Theatre: British Drama Today*. London: Faber & Faber.

Woodworth, P. (1996). "Druid – Celebrating in the Present Tense." *The Irish Times*, January 24, 10.

Index

This is primarily an index of names of authors (literary and scholarly), with some attention to selected legislation, events, groups, historical figures, artists, and recurring literary concepts and characters. While some religious and group categories are included, the most common (e.g., Catholicism, Protestantism) are not, being too ubiquitous to be useful. Works without definitively attributed authors are indexed by title. Some variant forms of names and terms are provided parenthetically. Saints are listed under their first names.